CLASSICAL MYTHOLOGY
The Myths of Ancient
Greece and Ancient Italy

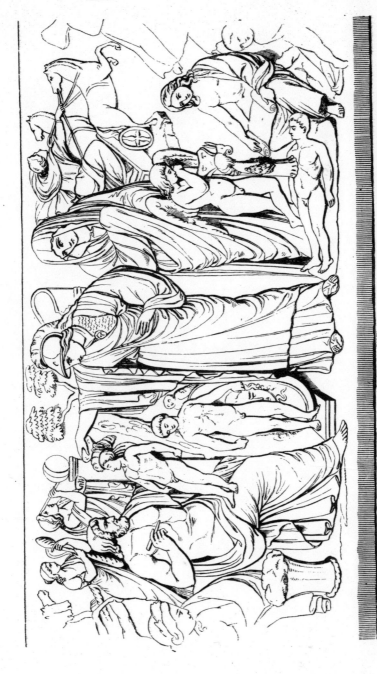

Creation, vivification and death of Man. From the Pamfili Sarcophagus of the Capitoline Museum. 2.—3. Cent. after Christ.

CLASSICAL MYTHOLOGY
The Myths of Ancient Greece and Ancient Italy

By

THOMAS KEIGHTLEY

Revised
and Edited by

L. SCHMITZ, PhD. LL.D.

ARES PUBLISHERS INC.
CHICAGO   MCMLXXVI

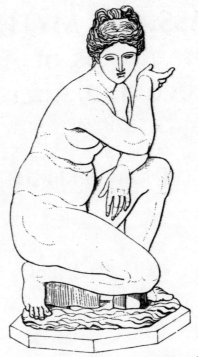

Crouching Venus.   After Dædalus of
at Athens.   Sicyon. Vatican.

Unchanged Reprint of the Edition:
London 1902
ARES PUBLISHERS INC.
612 N. Michigan Avenue
Chicago, Illinois 60611
Printed in the United States of America
International Standard Book Number:
0-89005-177-1

EDITOR'S PREFACE.

THE third edition of Mr. Keightley's 'Mythology of Ancient Greece and Italy' appeared in 1854, and he then expressed a doubt as to whether he should live long enough to witness the demand for a fourth. His life was indeed prolonged until the 4th of November, 1872, but owing to loss of sight during his latter years, he was unable to do much towards the further improvement of his work. Still, however, he made a few alterations and corrections in his own copy, which have been incorporated in the present edition. In 1857 there appeared at Göttingen the first volume of Welcker's great work 'Griechische Götterlehre,' and Mr. Keightley had the satisfaction of finding in its Preface, p. ix., the confirmation of a report which had already reached him before, that that eminent scholar and mythologist had spoken in terms of high praise of his manual of mythology; for Welcker there says, "It has gratified me much to observe that many germs scattered by me long since together with Buttmann and K. O. Müller have thriven remarkably well in Mr. Keightley's well-known and excellent manual, the only work of the kind in England, where hitherto little inclination has been shown for these studies."

After praise from such a quarter, it is needless for me to add anything about the value of the book either to the student of ancient literature or to the educated among the general public. One remark only I may be allowed to make. In an addition on p. 12. made by Mr. Keightley for a fourth edition, he expresses in strong terms his disapproval of the views of those modern mythologists who endeavour to throw

light upon the Mythology of Greece by comparing it with that
of ancient India. He even goes so far as to class them among
the *Mystics*. I feel certain that Mr. Keightley, if he had been
able to follow the researches of recent Oriental, and especially
of Sanscrit scholars, would have greatly modified his opinions;
for even as it is he occasionally turns to Indian mythes in
order to find analogies or explanations of those of Hellas. It
is a universally acknowledged fact that the various branches
of the great Aryan race, when they began their migration in
different directions, took with them their language, and that
the languages of Aryan origin, although greatly modified and
altered during the long period that has elapsed since their
separation, still bear unmistakable marks of their original
identity. Can it have been otherwise with their religion?
Certain as it is that they continued to speak the same language,
equally certain is it that their form of worship and their religious ideas remained essentially the same as before. Whatever
changes time and circumstances may have wrought, the funda-
mental conceptions about the gods and their relation to man
and the world must have remained essentially the same in all
the branches of the Aryan race. In the course of time the
mythes brought from their original homes were altered, and
their true meaning was forgotten and even changed into something that may appear to us absurd; but just as in the case of
language, their real significance may often still be ascertained
by tracing them to their origin, or by comparing them with
their primitive forms presented to us in the sacred books of
India. Therefore to deny all connection and affinity among
the mythes of the Aryan races appears to me as unreasonable as
it would be to deny the affinity of their languages. The recog-
nition of this original identity is not based upon the mere
similarity of names; and still less, as Mr. Keightley seems to
believe, on the vain assertions of learned pundits trying to
impose upon credulous Europeans, as did the priests of ancient
Egypt, who tried to prove to the Greeks that the Greek religion
and civilisation were derived from the land of the Nile; it is
founded upon the solid foundation of philological and historical
investigation.

However, Mr. Keightley's main object in writing his work was to explain the mythology of Greece, as far as possible, by and through itself, and to give to the student a clear and distinct idea of the manner in which the Greeks themselves viewed their religion and its traditions, so as to enable him to understand and appreciate the numerous allusions to mythical subjects occurring in the poets and other writers; and that object the author has attained in a manner that leaves little to be desired.

The present edition, with the above-mentioned exceptions, is not much more than a reprint of the third. A few manifest errors I have corrected, and throughout the work I have introduced the correct spelling of Greek names, in regard to which Mr. Keightley was not very consistent.

In the preface to his last edition Mr. Keightley bewailed the decline of classical learning. His gloomy forebodings are fortunately not realised. The universities and public schools, though less exclusively than before, are still the great cultivators of classical learning, and as long as this continues to be the case there is no reason for despair. May the present work continue to contribute its share, as it has done before, towards a right understanding and appreciation of the noble works of the ancient Greeks.

L. Schmitz.

London, *August*, 1877.

. In order to facilitate reference, care has been taken to make the pages of this edition correspond, as nearly as possible, with those of the third edition.

Metope from the Parthenon. British Museum.

Metope from the Parthenon. British Museum.

CONTENTS.

MYTHOLOGY OF GREECE.

PART I.—THE GODS.

—◆◇◆—

Bœotian Coin.   Coin from Delphi.

MYTHOLOGY OF ITALY.

Amazon. Possibly after Polycletus.
Berlin.

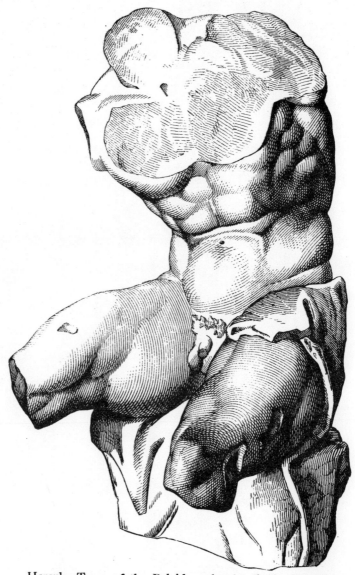

Hercules-Torso of the Belvidere, by Apollonius of Athens.
1. Cent. after Christ.

The younger Centaur of the Capitol, by Aristeas and Papias of Aphrodisias, in Asia Minor. Time of Hadrian.

Sarcophagus from Vulci.

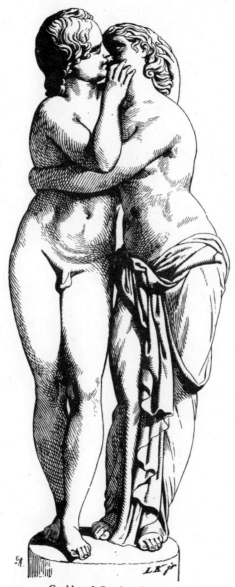

Cupid and Psyche. Capitol.
Abt. A. D. 100—150.

Isis. Capitol. 2. Cent. after Christ.

THE
MYTHOLOGY
OF
ANCIENT GREECE AND ITALY.

MYTHOLOGY OF GREECE.
PART I.—THE GODS.

CHAPTER I.

INTRODUCTION.

Of Mythology in general.

MYTHOLOGY is the science which treats of the *mythes*,[1] or various popular traditions and legendary tales, current among a people as objects of general belief.

These mythes are usually the fabulous adventures of the imaginary beings whom the people worship; the exploits of the ancient heroes, real or imaginary, of the nation; the traditions of its early migrations, wars, and revolutions; the marvellous tales of distant lands brought home by mariners and travellers; and the moral or physical allegories of its sages and instructors.

The legends which compose a nation's mythology may be divided into two classes. The first will contain the true or fabulous EVENTS which are believed to have occurred either among the people itself, as its own adventures, and those of its princes and heroes, and which may therefore be called *domestic*; or those of ancient or distant nations, handed down by tradition or brought home by voyagers, and these we may entitle *foreign*. The second class will consist of DOCTRINES or articles of popular belief, and will comprise the earliest attempts of man to account for the various phænomena of the heavens and the earth, and moral instructions conveyed in the mythic form. These are all however, in the popular mode of viewing them, as much events as

---

[1] Μῦθοι. The word μῦθος is in Homer equivalent to λόγος. In the time of Pindar it had acquired the signification in which it is here employed.

the former, as they were propounded by their inventors in the
nistoric or narrative form.

The wonderful is usually a component part of mythology. The
deities of the popular creed are very frequent actors in its legends,
which differ from ordinary tales and fables in this circumstance,
and in that of their having been at one time matters of actual
belief.

Mythology may therefore be regarded as the depository of the
early religion of the people. It also stands at the head of their
history, for the early history of every people, with whom it is of
domestic origin, is mythic, its first personages and actions are
chiefly imaginary.[1]   It is only gradually that the mist clears
away, and real men and deeds similar to those of later times begin
to appear; and the mythic period is frequently of long duration,
the stream of history having to run a considerable way, before it
can completely work off the marvellous and the incredible.

Origin of Mythology.

It is an interesting but by no means an easy task to trace out
and explain the various causes and occasions that have given
origin to the different legends which form the mythology of a
people, such as the Greeks, for example, with whom it is rich and
complicated. We regard the following as the most probable mode
of accounting for their existence.

Polytheism, or the belief in a number of beings of a nature
superior to man, and who can be of benefit or injury to him, seems
congenial to the human mind. It is always the religion of unen-
lightened tribes, and even in lettered and polished nations it still
retains its hold upon the minds of the weak and the ignorant.[2]
An appearance so general can only be the result of some law
of the mind; and those who have directed their attention to
the language and ideas of man, in different stages of culture,
will probably concede that there is a law which impels the
human mind to ascribe the attribute of intelligence to the efficient
cause of natural phænomena, particularly those which are of rare
occurrence. The less the mind is expanded by culture, the more

[1] We therefore, as may be seen, include under the title of mythology the
Mythe and the *Sage* of the Germans. By the former is meant some moral
or physical truth habited in a garb of fiction, and whose truth therefore is
what is termed subjective, not objective. The latter, which we may render
tradition or *tale*, in its original sense, has for its basis some real or objective
truth, but so enveloped in and penetrated by fiction that it can rarely be
ascertained with certainty. In the following pages, if our theory be well-
founded, the genuine *Sage* will not often appear.

[2] The belief in fairies and similar beings, for example, among the common
people in various countries. See my *Fairy Mythology*, passim.

powerful is the operation of this law; and while the philosopher ascribes all effects to *one* great intelligent cause, and usually views not so much Him as the secondary unintelligent causes which He employs—the simpler children of nature, who cannot rise to so just and elevated a conception, see *multitude* where he contemplates *unity*, and numerous intelligent causes actively engaged in producing the effects which he refers to one single mind. Either then the true idea of One God has been resolved by the vulgar into that of a plurality; or the numerous deities of the people have been by the philosopher reduced to one, possessed of the combined powers of all; or both hypotheses are true : man commencing with the knowledge of one God, gradually became a polytheist; and philosophy, slowly retracing the steps of error, returned to the truth which had been lost.

It is utterly impossible to fix historically the date of the rise of polytheism among any people. Supposing, for the sake of hypothesis, a race to have been from some unassignable cause in a state of total or partial ignorance of the Deity, their belief in many gods may have thus commenced. They saw around them various changes brought about by human agency, and hence they knew the power of intelligence to produce effects. When they beheld other and greater effects, independent of and beyond human power, they felt themselves, from the principle we have already stated, invincibly impelled to ascribe their production to some unseen being, similar, but superior to man. Thus when the thunder rolled and the lightning flamed along the sky, the terrified mortal regarded them as sent forth by a god who ruled the heavens; when the waves rose in mountains and lashed the shore or tossed the bark, the commotion was referred to a god of the sea; the regular courses, the rising and the setting of the sun and moon, appeared to him plainly to indicate the presiding care of peculiar deities; the rivers which flowed continuously, which swelled and sank, must be under the control of intelligences; and trees at regular seasons put forth and shed their foliage beneath the care of unseen deities.[1] In this manner all the parts of external nature would have become animated; and the thoughts of courage, wisdom, and love which involuntarily rise in the soul of man, and the ready eloquence which at times flows from his lips, being referable to no known cause, would be attributed to the unseen working of superior beings.[2]

Man is incapable of conceiving pure spirit, and he knows no form so perfect or so beautiful as his own, and none so well

[1] Comp. Völcker, *Myth. der Jap.* 253, 254. The Jews and Mohammedans assign the offices to angels, as ministers of the Supreme Being.
[2] See Hom. *Il.* i 55. with Wolf's note. *Od.* v. 427: see also *Il.* ix. 459.

adapted to be the vehicle of mind.[1] He naturally, therefore, fell into the habit of assigning a human form to his gods; but a human form divested of weakness and imperfection, and raised to his highest ideal of beauty, strength and power, yet still varying according to the character and occupation of the deity on whom it was bestowed. Thus the Grecian votary viewed manly strength and vigour as the leading attributes of the god who presided over war and inspired daring thoughts; while in the god of archery and music beauty and strength appeared united, and dignity and majesty of mien and countenance distinguished the father of gods and men and ruler of heaven.

These deities, so like to man in form, were held to exceed him far in power and knowledge, but to be, like him, under the influence of passion and appetite. They had their favourites and enemies among mankind, were gratified by prayers and offerings, and severely punished slight, neglect, or insult. They dwelt in celestial houses, but similar in form to those of man; and, like man, they stood in daily need of food and repose. Chariots drawn by horses or other animals of celestial breed conveyed them over earth, sea, and air; their clothing and arms were usually of the form of those of mortals, but of superior workmanship and materials.[2] The gods were not, strictly speaking, eternal: they were born, according to most systems of mythology; and some, at least, assigned a period to their duration.

In the eyes of their worshippers these gods had each his distinct personal existence and sphere of action. The Greek, for example, fully believed that Hélios, the Hindú that Surya, guided the course of the sun each day. When, therefore, we shall in future speak of gods of the sea, the sun, the moon, we would not be understood to mean *personifications* properly speaking of these objects: for in truth, a personification of the sea or sun is not a very intelligible expression. We mean in general by these gods, deities presiding over and directing them, but totally distinct from them; *regents* of them, in the sense in which the archangel Uriel is by Milton called the regent of the sun.[3] Personification properly accords only with qualities and attributes; and we shall in our progress meet with a class of deities, such as Mischief, Strife, Prayers, which are strictly speaking such.

---

[1] Comp. Aristotle, *Pol.* i. 3.

[2] See the minute description of Héra dressing herself in Homer, *Il.* xiv 170 *seq.*

[3] "Mithras, Sun. . . . certainly different from Ormuzd, and from the sun itself, but its Genius, who appears with it and is invoked at sunrise and sunset." Bohlen, *Das alte Indien,* i. 258.

When a people had thus formed for themselves a system of gods so like to man, and yet ruling over the world, it was natural that a body of mythes, or legends of their adventures, and of their dealings with mankind, should gradually arise; and as they passed from hand to hand, receive various embellishments and additions, till what was at first but a mere dry assertion or conjecture became a marvellous or an agreeable tale. It is the opinion of one of the ablest mythologists of the present day, that there is a certain stage in the culture of a people in which the mythic is the natural mode of representation, to which men are led by a kind of necessity, and in which they act almost unconsciously. He gives as an instance the pestilence in the commencement of the Ilias. Allowing, he says, the carrying away captive of the daughter of Chrysés and the pestilence itself to be actual and real facts, all those who heard of them, and who had at the same time a firm belief in the avenging power of Apolló, whose priest Chrysés was, would pronounce, with as full conviction as if it had been something which they had seen and experienced themselves, that it was the god who had sent the pestilence on the prayer of his priest.[1]

This theory we regard as being perfectly well-founded and applicable to all countries and all peoples, and as a convincing proof of its author's deep insight into the true nature of mythology. We may add, that when the name or an epithet of a god or a hero had become obscure in consequence of the loss of its true etymology the mind was led to conjecture what *might* have been its origin, and whatever presented itself with the greatest air of probability was esteemed to be the truth. It was the same with the names of places; some act or adventure of a god or hero suggested by the place's name was regarded as the occasion of it. Finally, when the adventures of one hero were found to coincide in general with those of another the coincidence was supposed to be still more perfect, and the parallelism was completed by invention, regarded however as a discovery of the truth; for in nearly all these cases, as we have just observed, the mind acted almost unconsciously.

The sources, or the occasions of the production, of mythes may, we think, be arranged under the following heads, which fall into two classes, namely, of *things* and of *names*.

1. The sages of remote antiquity appear to have had a peculiar fondness for enveloping moral and physical truths in the garb of symbol, mythe, and allegory; and the legends which they thus

---

[1] Müller, *Proleg.* 78, 111, 112, and elsewhere.

devised form no inconsiderable portion of the various bodies of mythology.

2. As a second source may perhaps be added the pride of family and the flattery of poets, which would seek to cast lustre on the origin of some noble house by placing a deity at the head of its pedigree, or to veil the transgression of one of its daughters by feigning that a god had penetrated the recesses of her chamber, or met her in the wood or at the fountain. Legends of this kind are to be placed among the latest. Indeed we very much doubt if this be a real original source of mythes,[1] and we place it here only because it has been generally so regarded.

3. A great number of legends in all countries are indebted for their origin to the extreme desire which men have to assign a cause for the various phænomena of the natural world. The Scandinavian mythology is full of instances, and the subsequent pages will present them in abundance. We cannot, however, refrain from giving in this place the following instance, as it combines the ancient and modern legendary explanations of the same natural appearance.

It is well known that most of the rivers of the Peloponnése have their sources in lakes situated in the high valley-plains of Arkadia, which are so completely shut in by mountains that the streams leave them by subterranean passages, called by the ancient Arkadians Zerethra (ζέρεθρα, i.e. βέρεθρα,[2]) and by the moderns Katavóthra. The plain of the district of Pheneos had two of these passages piercing the surrounding mountains, one of which gives origin to the river Ladón. On the rocky faces of two of the hills, which advance into the plain, at a height of about fifty feet, runs a line, below which the colour of the rocks is lighter than it is above. The natural, though probably incorrect, inference is that the waters stood one time at that height. The ancient Arkadians said that Apolló, incensed at Héraklés' having carried off the tripod from Delphi and brought it to Pheneos, inundated the valley, and that the hero formed the chasms by which the waters ran off.[3] Others said that Hadés carried off the daughter of Démétér through one of these chasms under Mount Kylléné.[4] The moderns account for the origin of the chasm by the following legend. Two devils once possessed the lake: they dwelt on opposite sides of it, and were continually quarrelling: a

---

[1] The earliest allusions to this practice we have met with are in Euripides: see Bac. 26 seq.; Ión, 1523 seq.   [2] See Strab. viii. 8, 4. p. 389.
[3] Paus. viii. 14, 2.   Plut. De Sera Numinis Vindicta, 12.   Catull. lxviii. 109
[4] Conon. Narrat. 15.   It is not quite certain, however, that it is of these chasms he speaks.

furious contest at length took place between them on the top of Mount Saktá, whose base was washed by the lake. The devil who lived on the west side adopted the ingenious expedient of pelting his adversary with balls of ox-fat, which sticking to his body and there taking fire, annoyed him beyond measure. To free himself from this inconvenience, the worsted fiend plunged into the lake and dashed through the side of the mountain Saktá, thus forming the passage through which the waters flowed off and left the plain dry.[1]

To this head may be referred the practice of the Greeks to assign the origin of animals and plants to transformations effected by the power of the gods, a practice of which we shall have to record numerous instances.[2] Even in the Mohammedan East examples of this procedure (which was probably learned from the Greeks) are to be found. Thus the origin of the rose is ascribed to the Prophet;[3] the tulip is said to have sprung from the blood of the unhappy Ferhád, the lover of the fair Sheereen;[4] and from the haft of the axe with which he slew himself arose the first pomegranate-tree.[5] When, as the Sháh-námeh tells, Siyáwush, the beautiful and the brave, was slain by treachery, there sprang from his blood a flower named Siyáwush-blood, which bears his name impressed on its petals. In China the prophet Buddha Dharma cut off his eyelids because sleep hindered his devotions, and from the place where he threw them grew the sleep-repelling tea-plant.[6] Many changes in the natural world have also been effected by the Saints, according to the popular creed in most parts of Europe.

4. The desire to account for the phænomena of the moral world has also led to the invention of legends. Thus the laws of Manú explain the difference of castes in India, by saying that the Brahmins, that is the priests, were produced from the mouth of Brahmah; the warriors from his arms; the traders from his thighs; the Sudras, or lowest class, from his feet. The poor Laplanders account for the difference between themselves and their more fortunate southern neighbours by the following

---

[1] Leake's *Travels in the Morea*, iii. 148.

[2] We meet with instances of this practice even in Homer: see *Od.* xix. 518. It would seem to have been originally almost peculiar to Grecian mythology, and in the majority of cases, as we may observe, the mythic person is merely a personification of the name of the plant or animal.

[3] See Ouseley, *Persian Miscellanies*, p. 145. Lane, *Thousand and One Nights*, i. 221. *Fairy Mythology*, init.

[4] Malcolm, *Sketches of Persia*, ii. 98.

[5] See Von Hammer, *Shirin*, II. vii. 69.

[6] Kaempfer, *Amœn. Exot.* p. 608, *ap.* Bohlen, *Alt. Ind.* i. 327. *Téh* in Chinese is eyebrow; the Greeks assigned a similar origin to the cabbage-plant: see Schol. *Aristoph. Eq.* 536.

legend. The Swede and the Laplander, they say, were brothers in the beginning, but when there came on a storm the former was terrified, and sought shelter under a board, which God caused to become a house, but the latter remained without; whence ever since the Swede dwells in a house, while the Laplander lives in the open air.[1]

5. Many legends have arisen from the necessity of giving some account of the invention of arts and implements, and of assigning a cause for traditionary ceremonies and observances, the memory of whose true origin had been lost. The festival of the Hyakinthia at Sparta, for example, originally it would seem celebrated in honour of Démétér,[2] was probably indebted for its name to the flower Hyakinthos; and the legend of the boy beloved by Apolló was a later fiction. The Fasti of Ovid will present instances of the application of this principle, and in the following pages we shall have occasion to notice it.

The second class of legends will come under the three following heads.

6. The epithets of gods, when their true origin was unknown or had been lost, were usually explained by some legend. Of this practice also we shall meet with instances as we proceed; for the present we will content ourselves with a single example.

In the island of Samos stood a temple dedicated to the Gaping Dionýsos, of whose origin the following legend was related. A Samian named Elpis, having made a voyage to Africa, saw, as he was one day on the sea-shore, a huge lion approaching him with his mouth wide open. In his terror he uttered a prayer to Dionýsos and fled to a tree, up which he climbed. The lion came and laid himself at the foot of the tree with his mouth still open, as if he required compassion, and Elpis saw that a bone was stuck fast in his teeth which prevented him from eating; he took pity on him, and came down and relieved him. As long as the ship stayed on the coast the grateful lion brought each day a portion of the produce of his hunting, and Elpis on his return to Samos built a temple to the Gaping Dionýsos.[3]

7. Casual resemblance of sound in words, and foreign, obsolete or ambiguous terms, were another abundant source of legends. In Greek λᾶας is a *stone*, and λαὸς a *people*; hence the legend of Deukalión and Pyrrha restoring the human race by flinging stones behind them.[4] There was a place at Rome called *Argiletum*; this word, which is said to signify a place abounding in

[1] Geijer, *Svea Rikes Häfdar*, i. 417   [2] Müller, *Dor*. i. 373.
[3] Plin. *Nat. Hist*. viii. 16, 56
[4] Pind. *Ol*. ix. 45. (68.) see also , Schol. Apollon. i. 7, 2.

potter's earth (*argilla*),[1] may be divided into two words (*Argi letum*), signifying *death of Argus;* and hence arose a legend noticed by Vergil.[2] A part of the province of Seestán in Persia is named Neem-róz, i.e. *half-day;* and the popular tradition is, that it was once covered by a lake, which was drained by the Jinn (i.e. Genii) in *half a day.*[3] But, as the writer from whom we have taken this legend justly observes, Neem-róz is also *midday;* a term which, in several languages, denotes the *south;* and this district lies due south of Balkh, the first seat of Persian dominion. To return home, there is a point of land between Hastings and Pevensey, on the coast of Sussex, called Bulverhithe;[4] that is, plainly, Bulver-landing-place, such being the meaning of the old word *hithe.* But as this term has gone out of use, the honest fishermen thereabouts will gravely tell you, that when William the Conqueror, after landing in Pevensey-bay, was advancing to Hastings, on coming to this place he took a *bull's hide* and cut it into thongs, which he tied together, resolving to halt and give battle at the spot where the line he made of them should terminate. These instances may suffice to show the generality of this principle.

In Grecian mythology names are sometimes capable of more than one derivation, and hence we shall find legends of the same mythic personages of different kinds, owing to these different derivations; Pégasos is an example. This we shall term *secondary derivation.*

8. Finally, metaphoric language understood literally may have given occasion to legends. Thus cause and effect, and other relations, are in various languages, particularly the Oriental, expressed by terms of kindred. The Hebrews termed sparks, *sons of the burning coal;* one who is to die, a *son of death.* The Arabs call a traveller, a *son of the way;* a warrior, a *son of battle;* springs, *daughters of the earth;* mist, *daughter of the sea;* tears, *daughters of the eye;* and dreams, *daughters of night:* an ass is with them the *father of hanging ears.*[5] A similar mode of expression prevailed among the Greeks. Pindar[6] calls the showers of rain *children* of the cloud; Æschylos terms smoke the *brother* of fire,[7] and dust the *brother* of mud;[8] and Hippónax[9] said that the fig-tree was

---

[1] Varro, *De L. L.* v. 157. ed. Müll.: see my Ovid's *Fasti,* Excurs. I.
[2] *Æn.* viii. 345. Servius *in loc.*
[3] Malcolm's *Hist. of Persia,* i. 41. 8vo edit.
[4] Now covered by St. Leonard's.
[5] This phraseology is still employed in the south of Europe. Sancho Panza is in Don Quixote called *the father of proverbs* (*padre de los refranes*); Ariosto (*Orl. Fur.* iv. 3) terms Brunello *di finzioni padre.*   [6] *Ol.* x. 3.
[7] *Seven against Thebes,* 484.   [8] *Agam.* 494.   [9] *Athen.* iii. 78.

the *sister* of the vine. A person born on the bank of a lake or river may have been called its son;[1] one coming by sea have been styled a *son of the sea*; and when the metaphor came to be understood literally, persons thus spoken of may have been looked upon as children of the river- or sea-god, and legends have been devised accordingly.[2] A *branch* or *shoot of Arés* (ὄζος Ἄρηος) is the Homeric appellation of a warrior, and in Latin a lucky fellow was styled a *son of Fortune*.[3] Our English king Richard I. was called Lion-heart (*Cœur de Lion*), on account of his valour and intrepidity; and this title gave occasion to a legend, alluded to by Shakspeare,[4] of his combat with a lion, and pulling out his heart. The rich melodious language of poets and orators has been often compared by the Greeks and others to the delicious food of the bees; hence it was fabled that bees settled on the infant lips of Pindar and Plató, of Lucan and St. Ambrose.

Theories about the Origin of Mythology.

The theory already given appears to us to be the one which most simply and satisfactorily explains the origin of by far the greater portion of, if not all, the legends of mythology; but, both in ancient and modern times, theories of a more restricted kind have been advanced, and supported with much ingenuity and learning. The ancient systems we shall notice when treating of the progress of Grecian mythology; in this place we will enumerate those which have been most prevalent in modern times. These may, we think, be divided into three classes: the Historic, the Philosophic, and the Theologic.

1. THE HISTORIC: according to which *all* the mythic persons were once real human beings, and the legends are merely the actions of these persons poetically embellished. The chief maintainers of this hypothesis are G. J. Voss,[5] Bochart,[6] and Bryant,[7] who see in the Grecian mythes the true history of the personages of Sacred Scripture; Rudbeck,[8] who regards them as being drawn from the history of the North of Europe; the Abbé Banier,[9] who maintains that Grecian mythology is Egyptian and Grecian history in a poetic dress. Banier's countrymen, Larcher, Clavier, Raoul-Rochette, and others have of late years supported this

---

[1] *Il.* ii. 865. (Heyne *in loc.*): see also *Il.* xvi. 174.

[2] "Hic Messapus per mare ad Italiam venit; unde Neptuni dictus est filius." Serv. *on Æn.* vii. 691: see Paus. iv. 2, 2.

[3] Hor. *Sat.* ii. 6. 49. It is in a somewhat different sense that the Œdipus of Sophoklés (*Œd. Tyr.* 1080) calls himself a son of Fortune.

[4] *King John*, Act ii. scene i.   [5] *De Origine et Prog essu Idololatriæ.*

[6] *Canaan and Phaleg.*   [7] *Analysis of Heathen Mythology.*

[8] *Atlantica.*   [9] *Mythologie et Fables expliquées par l'Histoire.*

theory, and it has been maintained by Hug[1] and Böttiger[2] in Germany. The newest and most plausible is the Indian theory commenced by Sir William Jones, and most fully developed by Mr. Pococke in his 'India in Greece.' According to this theory, Egypt, Palestine, Greece, and even the British Isles, were colonised from the banks of the Ganges and Indus, the Himalaya mountains, Tibet, Cashmeer, Afghánistán, the banks of the Oxus, &c. The moving cause was the religious wars of India, and the colonists were the defeated and expelled Búddhists. Every name therefore in Grecian mythology and geography is taken from that of some people, person or place in those countries. Thus Attica is connected with Attock on the Indus; Bœotia with the Behút; the Ionians, the Scots, and the Irish had a common origin in the mountains of Afghánistán. We need not say that great ingenuity is exerted in making these approximations; but as the proofs, exclusive of similarity of sound, are very trifling, we will only observe that, beside its affinity to the Western languages, such is the copiousness of the Sanscrit, and so boundless is the number of names of persons and places in those extensive regions, that a very moderate portion of etymologic skill suffices to effect combinations similar to those which we have noticed. But surely this is a slender foundation for so gigantic an edifice!

II. THE PHILOSOPHIC: which supposes mythology to be merely the poetic envelope of some one, single branch of human science. The illustrious Bacon[3] exercised his ingenuity in deriving ethical and political doctrines from some of the Hellenic mythes. Their concealed wisdom is *Physics* and *Ethics,* according to Boccaccio[4] and Natalis Comes;[5] *Chemistry* according to Tollius[6] and others. Finally, Dupuis[7] and some other ingenious writers, chiefly French, look to *Astronomy* for the solution of the enigmatic legends of antiquity.

III. THE THEOLOGIC: which assigns mythology a higher rank; regarding it as the theology of polytheistic religions, and seeking to reduce it to harmony with the original monotheism of mankind. G. J. Voss endeavours to show that the fables of heathenism were only a distortion of the revelations made to man by the true God; and, at the present day, Creuzer, Görres and others,[8]

---

[1] *Untersuchungen über die Mythen,* &c.
[2] See *Amalthea,* i. 12.   *Ideen zur Kunst-Mythologie,* ii. 7.
[3] *De Sapientia Veterum.*   [4] *Genealogia Deorum Gentilium.*
[5] *Mythologiæ, sive Explicationis Fabularum, Libri X.*
[6] *Fortuita Critica.*   [7] *Origine de tous les Cultes.*
[8] Lobeck terms these writers *synchytic* mythologists, " who think that the religions of all nations, old and new, were the same from the beginning, and deduce the most recent fables from the springs of the primigenial doctrine."
—*Aglaoph.* p. 1268.

assigning a common source to the systems of India, Egypt, Greece and other countries, and regarding the East as the original birth-place of mythology, employ themselves in tracing the imagined channels of communication; and as they esteem every legend, cere-mony, usage, vessel and implement to have been symbolic, they seek to discover what truth, moral, religious or philosophic, lies hid be-neath its cover. These men are justly denominated *Mystics*.[1] Their whole science is founded on accidental resemblances of names and practices, their ideas are conveyed in a highly coloured figurative style, and a certain vague magnificence appears to envelope their conceptions,—all calculated to impose on the ignorant and the unwary.[2] It is against this system that we are most anxious to warn and guard our readers. In our eyes it is disgusting from its indelicacy as well as its absurdity; it approaches the confines of impiety, and at times seems even to pass them. The study and adoption of it can hardly fail to injure the intellectual powers, and to produce an indifference toward true religion. The latest, purest and most rational form of this theory is what is termed compara-tive mythology, advocated by Professor Max Müller, the Rev. Mr. Cox and some men of learning in Germany. But it will not stand the test of sane, sober criticism. In fact, if the theory of these men be true, the necessity for Christianity becomes a question.[3]

Of these three classes the last alone is peculiar to modern times; the two former theories were, as we shall presently see, familiar to the ancients. We must also observe, that all are true to a certain extent. Some mythes are historic, some physical, some moral, some theologic; but no single one of these theories will suffice to account for the whole body of the mythology of any people. Some of them, too, apply more to one system than to another: the Scandinavian mythology, for example, is of a more thoroughly physical character than the Grecian: the Indian is more metaphysical than either the Grecian or the Scandinavian.

The mythologies which offer the widest fields for inquiry are those of ancient Greece, of India, and of Scandinavia. To these, though far more scanty, may be added that of ancient Egypt. Italy has left no mythology, properly speaking, though for the sake

---

[1] "Mysticism is an irregular mixture and confusion of feelings and ideas," says Hermann, *Ueber das Wesen*, &c. p. 26. The secret of mysticism and of obscurity in general, and at times of what is called profundity, is the lavish use of metaphor and ellipsis.

[2] It is remarkable enough that the German mystic mythologists have eithe: embraced Popery or shown a strong tendency toward it.

[3] We would advise those who have studied the writings of Creuzer, Görre, Schelling, Sickler, and other writers of this school, to read as a sure antido. the *Antisymbolik* of Voss, and the *Aglaophamus* of Lobeck. Comp. son. remarks in my Preface. Fn

of uniformity we so denominate the account of its deities and religion given in the present work. The Persian cycle, which is preserved in the Sháh-námeh of Ferdúsee, is purely heroic; and the Keltic tribes of Ireland and the Scottish Highlands had also a small heroic cycle, of which Cuchullin, Fingal, Gaul, Oscar, and other personages whose names are familiar to the readers of the pseudo-Ossian, are the heroes.[1]

It is chiefly to the explanation of the rich and elegant mythology of Greece that modern inquirers have applied themselves; and by the labours of Voss,[2] Buttmann, Müller, Völcker, Welckei and other writers, whose names will appear in the following pages, it has in our opinion been reduced to its true principles, and brought within the sphere of useful and necessary knowledge. The scholars of the North, especially the learned Finn Magnusen, have exerted themselves, and not without success, in developing the true nature and character of the venerable mythology of their forefathers, chiefly on the physical theory.[3] For the mythology of India philosophy has as yet done but little; it has been the sport of the wildest mysticism, and has led to the degradation of those of other countries. The Asiatic Researches, and the works of Polier, Ward and some others, with the various translations that have been made from the Sanscrit, present a large mass of materials to the inquirer. Jablonski and Zoega have laboured diligently in the field of Egyptian mythology, and to their labours are now to be added those of Champollion, Lepsius, Bunsen, Prichard and others.

Rules for the Interpretation of Mythes.

The following rules should be attended to in mythologic inquiries.

1. To consider the mythology of each people separately and independently, and not to suppose any connection between it and any other till both have been examined minutely and carefully,

---

[1] In the author's *Tales and Popular Fictions*, chap. iv., will be found some account of the Sháh-námeh, and one of its most interesting narratives. The reader will also meet in the same place with some remarks on Ossian.

[2] We shall frequently find ourselves under the necessity of differing in opinion with this estimable critic, but we most heartily concur in the following just panegyric on him: " Dum hæc studia vigebunt, dum patrius sermo coletur, dum recto veroque suum constabit pretium.

Semper honos nomenque viri laudesque manebunt."
Lobeck, *Aglaoph.* 1295.

[3] "Nearly the whole of the Northern mythology revolves around the incessant conflict between Light and Darkness, the warmth of Heaven and the cold of the Deep; which has given origin to an almost endless number of mythes and comparisons."—Magnusen, *Den Aeldre Edda*, i. 151.

and so many points of resemblance have presented themselves as to leave no doubt of the original identity of the systems.[1]   It is to the neglect of this rule that we owe so much of the absurdity to be found in the works of many mythologists, and nothing has tended more to the bringing of the science of mythology into neglect and contempt.   The ancient Greeks were led from ignorance to give credit to the cunning priesthood of Egypt, and to believe that they had received their religion from that country ; and it is but too well known how, in our own days, Sir William Jones and his followers have been deceived by their own imaginations, and the impostures of artful pundits, in their efforts to connect the religions of Greece and India.

2. In like manner the mythes themselves should be considered separately, and detached from the system in which they are placed; for the single mythes existed long before the system, and were the product of other minds than those which afterwards set them in connection, not unfrequently without fully understanding them.[2]

3. We should pay particular attention to the *genealogies* which we meet with in mythology, as they frequently form the key to the meaning of a mythe, or even of a whole cycle.[3]   Great caution however should be used in the application of this rule, or it may lead us into error and absurdity if carried beyond its legitimate bounds.

4. The same or even greater caution is required in the application of *etymology* to this subject.[4]   If applied judiciously it will give most valuable results, and prove, in fact, to be the master-key of mythology; if under no guidance but that of caprice and fancy, it will become the parent of all sorts of monsters and *lusus naturæ*.

5. Finally, though we should never pronounce a mythe which we have not examined to be absolutely devoid of signification, we should not too confidently assert that every mythe *must* have an important meaning, for certainly some have been but the creation of capricious fancy.[5]   On these occasions it would be well to bear in

---

[1] Comp. Völcker, *Myth. der Jap.* pp. vi. vii.

[2] Comp. Buttmann, *Mytholog.* i. 155, 157.   Müller, *Proleg.* 218, 219. *Orchom.* 142.   Hermann, *Ueber das Wesen,* &c. 71, 125, 132.

[3] Comp. Völcker, *Myth. der Jap.* passim.   Müller, *Proleg.* 274 *seq.*

[4] Comp. Müller, *Proleg.* 232.

[5] Völcker asserts positively that there is no mythe without a meaning. *Myth. der Jap.* 50.   This may be true, but the meaning is often a trifling one. As examples of this kind of mythe, we may give the conversion of the clowns into frogs by Létó, of the boy into a lizard by Démétér, and the account of the birth of Oríon, all mere sports of fancy.

mind the following words of Johnson :[1] "The original of ancient customs is commonly unknown, for the practice often continues after the cause has ceased; and concerning superstitious ceremonies, it is vain to conjecture, for what reason did not dictate reason cannot explain." We use the words *bear in mind,* for if adopted as a principle it will only serve to damp ardour and check inquiry. The rule should be,—this mythe most probably has an important meaning, but it is possible it may have only a trifling one.

As, in the following pages, we shall frequently have occasion to apply the principles of etymology, we will here add something further on that important subject.

At the time when most of the mythes and mythic names of Hellas were formed, its language was in an earlier state than that in which we find it even in the Homeric poems. It is further a fact, well-known to philologists, that the earlier the condition of a language is, the longer are its words and the more numerous its formative syllables. Such, then, we will assume to have been what we will call the mythic language of Hellas; and keeping this principle in view, we shall be able to obtain a good sense for names which are nearly devoid of meaning as long as we suppose the final syllables to be original portions of the words.

Thus we find in the later language the final syllables ευς, μος, δης, της, τηρ, τος, των, τωρ, &c., used as formative, and active in sense. Supposing, then, these to have been originally longer, a letter, usually a liquid or σ, being prefixed, we at once arrive at the elucidation of many mythic names otherwise nearly inexplicable. Such are Tydeus, Odysseus, Nestór. There seem also to have been other formative syllables which went almost totally out of use, such as λος, λιων, νιων, οψ, ωψ, πος and probably κυς and τυς (as in Phorkys and Diktys), and others. An ancient feminine termination was ω (as in Kalypsó, Échó), active, and answering to the participles in ουσα and ασα; another similar to this, and also active, was ως,[2] while those in πεια, πη and in στη, στις, corresponded with the masculines in πος and στης, στηρ, στωρ. In some cases there seems to have been a double termination, as in Pénelopeia.[3]

[1] *Rasselas*, chap. 48. See Niebuhr, *Hist. of Rome*, i. 480. Lobeck, *Aglaoph.* 172 seq. Buttmann, *Mytholog.* ii. 294, 295. Welcker, *Tril.* 249.

[2] There are only three with this termination, 'Ηὼς, Δώς (*Giver*, a name of Démétér), and Αἰδὼς, i.e. *Shamer*, what excites the sense of shame (αἰδὼς sc. ὑμῖν γίνοιτο. *Il.* v. 787).

[3] Πήνη, ΠΗΝΗΛΟΣ, Πηνελόπεια. On this principle we may perhaps explain the enigmatic names Œdipus and Melampus: οἰδέω, ΟΙΔΙΠΟΣ; Οἰδιπόδης, Οἰδίπους; μέλας, ΜΕΛΑΜΠΟΣ, ΜΕΛΑΜΠΟΔΗΣ, Μελάμπους. In this way βασιλεὺς may come from ΒΑΩ, βάζω, or from ΒΑΩ, βαίνω.

We may finally add, contrary to the assertion of many eminent critics, that the quantity of the vowels is not to be regarded in etymology, as those which are long in one language or dialect are often short in another, and *vice versâ*.[1] It need hardly be observed that an accurate knowledge of the commutability of consonants is essential to the etymologist.

CHAPTER II.

GRECIAN MYTHOLOGY.

Its Origin.

THE remote antiquities of Greece are involved in such total obscurity, that nothing certain can be adduced respecting the origin of the people or their mythology. Reasoning from analogy and existing monuments, some men of learning venture to maintain, that the first inhabitants of that country were under the direction of a sacerdotal caste, resembling those of India and Egypt; but that various circumstances concurred to prevent their attaining to the same power as in these countries. In the Homeric poems, however, by far the earliest portion of Grecian literature, we find no traces of sacerdotal dominion; and in the subsequent part of our work we shall bring forward some objections against this hypothesis.[2]

It is certainly not improbable that these ancient priests, if such there were, may have had their religion arranged systematically, and have represented the various appearances and revolutions of nature under the guise of the loves, the wars, and other actions of these deities, to whom they ascribed a human form and human passions. But the Grecian mythology, as we find it in the works of the ancients, offers no appearance of a regular concerted system. It is rather a loose collection of various images and fables, many of which are significant of the same objects.

The ancient inhabitants of Greece were divided into a great variety of little communities, dwelling separately, parted in general by mountains and other natural barriers. As they were naturally endowed with a lively imagination, there gradually grew up in each of these little states a body of tales and legends. These tales of gods and heroes were communicated by wandering minstrels and travellers from one part of the country to another.

---

[1] Thus the Latin diphthong *au* becomes *ŏ* in Italian and French; as *aurum*, *ŏro*, *ŏr ; glōria* is *glŏria*, It., while *tĭmeo* is *tĕmo*, It.

[2] Comp. Müller, *Proleg.* 249 *seq.* ; *Min. Pol.* ?.

Phœnician mariners probably introduced stories of the wonders of the East and of the West, which in those remote ages they alone visited; and these stories, it is likely, were detailed with the usual allowance of travellers' licence. Poets, a race indigenous in the favoured clime of Hellas, caught up the tales, and narrated them with all the embellishments a lively fancy could bestow; and thus at a period long anterior to that at which her history commences, Greece actually abounded in a rich and luxuriant system of legendary lore. This is proved by the poems of Homer and Hésiod, which, exclusive of the ancient legends they contain, make frequent allusion to others; some of which are related by subsequent writers, and many are altogther fallen into oblivion.

These poems also bear evident testimony to the long preceding existence of a race of poets,—a fact indeed sufficiently evinced by the high degree of perfection in the poetic art which they themselves exhibit. Modern mythologists have therefore been naturally led to the supposition of there having been in ancient Greece *æedic* schools, in which the verses of preceding bards were taught, and the art of making similar verses was acquired.[1] One of the ablest of our late inquirers[2] is of opinion that the original seat of these schools was Pieria, at the northern foot of Mount Olympos. He has been led to this supposition by Heyne's remark, that Homer always calls the Muses *Olympian*, which remark he extends by observing that the Homeric gods in general are the Olympian, and no others. In this however we can only see that, as we shall presently show, Olympos was in the time of Homer held to be the seat of the gods. It does not appear to us that any one spot can be regarded as the birth-place of the Grecian religion and mythology; they were, like the language and manners of the people, a portion of their being; and the knowledge of the origin of the one is as far beyond our attainment as that of the other.[3]

The Greeks, like most of the ancient nations, were little inclined to regard as mere capricious fiction any of the legends of the different portions of their own race or those of foreign countries. Whatever tales they learned, they interwove into their own system; taking care, however, to avoid contradiction as far as was possible. When, therefore, they found in them any foreign deities possessing the same attributes as some of their own, they at once

---

[1] Wolf, it is well known, held this opinion. The Schools of the Prophets among the Hebrews were evidently of the same nature.

[2] Völcker, *Myth. der Jap.* p. 5 *seq.*: see also Böttiger, *Idcen zur Kunst-Myth.* ii. 50. Müller, *Proleg.* 219.

[3] From what has been said in my Introduction, it is clear that the first elemer. of the Hellenic religion must have come with the people from the East.—kᴅ

inferred them to be the same under different names; but where the legends would not accord, the deities themselves were regarded as being different, even when they were in reality perhaps the same.[1]

Beside the original deities of the Hellénic race, we meet in Grecian mythology with many gods and mythic personages who are indebted for their origin to epithets of those higher divinities. An epithet, when thus separated from its subject, became sometimes another deity of the same kind, or even a hostile power; at other times a child or a companion of the original deity. Such apparently were Pan, Phaethón, Hekaté, Medusa, Kallistó, and others, which will meet us on our progress.

On taking a comprehensive view of the whole of the mythology of ancient Greece, and carefully considering all the tales of gods and heroes which it contains, the conviction almost necessarily arises that these beings are nothing more than the personifications of natural and moral powers and objects, and that the various mythes are merely the vehicles of physical and ethical truths. Grecian mythology is in fact like that of most other countries, philosophy or religion clothed in the garb of poetry, and hence it may often receive illustration from the poetry of other times and other regions. The reader therefore will not be surprised to meet with passages from modern and even Oriental poets adduced in illustration of it in the following pages.

Historic View of Grecian Mythology.[2]

The poets of ancient Hellas having taken possession of the popular legends, adorned, amplified, added to them, and sought to reduce the whole to a somewhat harmonious system.[3] They however either studiously abstained from departing from the popular faith, or were themselves too much affected by all that environed them to dream of anything which might shock the opinions of their auditors. Accordingly we may be certain that the mythes contained in Homer and Hésiod accord with the current creed of their day, and are a faithful picture of the mode of thinking prevalent in those distant ages.

As knowledge of the earth, of nature, her laws and powers, advanced, the false views of them contained in the venerable mythes of antiquity became apparent. The educated sometimes sought to reconcile tradition and truth; but the vulgar still held fast to the legends hallowed by antiquity and sanctioned by govern-

---

[1] See Buttmann, *Mythol.* i. 24. Welcker, *Tril.* 95.
[2] See Heyne, *ad Apollod.* p. 911 *seq.*   [3] See Müller, *Proleg.* 212.

ments.[1] A prudent silence therefore became the safest course for those who exceeded their contemporaries in knowledge.

The philosphers of Greece early arrived at the knowledge of one only God, the original cause and support of all. Anaxagoras is said to have been the first who openly taught this truth; and he was in consequence charged with atheism, and narrowly escaped the punishment of death. Philosophers took warning, and truth was no longer brought into public view. But such is the nature and connection of things, so profuse the resemblances which the world presents to view, such is the analogy which runs between the operations of mind and those of matter, that several of the mythes afforded the philosophers an opportunity of holding them forth as the husks in which important moral or physical truths were enveloped; in which in reality many such truths had been studiously enveloped by ancient priests and sages.[2]

After an intercourse had been opened with Asia and Egypt, mysteries came greatly into vogue in Greece. In these it is thought,[3] but perhaps not with sufficient evidence, that the priests who directed them used, for the credit of the popular religion whose reputation they were solicitous to maintain, to endeavour to show its accordance with the truths established by the philosophers, by representing them as being involved in the ancient mythes, which they modified by the aid of fiction and forgery so as to suit their purposes.

About this time, also, the system of *theocrasy* (θεοκρασία), or mixing up, as we may call it, of the gods together, began to be employed.[4] It was thus that the wine-god Dionýsos was made one with the sun-god Hélios, and this last again, as some think, with the archer-god Phœbos-Apolló. As we proceed we shall have frequent occasion to notice this principle.

While in the schools of the philosophers, and the temples devoted to the mysteries, the ancient legends were acquiring a new and recondite sense, another class of men, the artists, had laid hold of them. The gods of their forefathers were now presented under a new guise to the Greeks, who, as they gazed on the picture or the statue, saw the metaphors of the poets turned to sense, and wings, for example, adorning those deities and mythic

---

[1] See Buttmann, *Mythol.* i. 45. Müller, *Proleg.* 171. In Lucian'(*De Luctu*, 2.) may be seen a convincing proof of how firmly the vulgar, even in his time, clung to the old notions.   [2] See Müller, *Proleg.* 66, 99. Welcker, *Tril.* 89.

[3] This is the theory of Voss. We share the doubts of Lobeck (*Aglaoph.* 1295) respecting its soundness. The Exégetæ, or *ciceroni*, at the various temples were more probably the persons who gave explanations of this kind to strangers.   [4] See Lobeck, *Aglaoph.* 78, 79, 614, 615. Müller, *Proleg.* 91.

personages to whom the poet had in figurative style applied the expression *winged* to denote extraordinary swiftness.[1]

The poets soon began to regard the ancient legends as mere *materials*. The belief in their truth having in a great measure vanished, the poets, especially the later dramatists, thought themselves at liberty to treat them in whatever manner they deemed best calculated to produce the meditated effect on the feelings of their audience.[2] They added, abstracted, united, separated, at their pleasure; ideas imported from Egypt were mixed up with the old tales of gods and heroes; and the *fable* to be represented on the stage often varied so much from that handed down by tradition, that, as is more especially the case with Euripidés, the poet appears at times to have found it necessary to inform his audience in a long prologue of what they were about to witness.

Such was the state of the ancient mythology of Greece in her days of greatest intellectual culture. Few of the mythes remained unaltered. Priests, philosophers, and poets combined to vary, change, and modify them. The imagination of these various classes produced new mythes, and the local tales of foreign lands were incorporated into the Grecian mythic cycle.

When the Ptolemies, those munificent patrons of learning, had assembled around them at Alexandria the scholars and the men of genius of Greece, the science of antiquity was, by the aid of the extensive royal library, assiduously cultivated; and the ancient mythology soon became a favourite subject of learned investigation. Some worked up the mythes into poems; others arranged them in prose narratives; several occupied themselves in the search after their recondite meaning.

At this time what is named *Pragmatism,* or the effort to reduce the mythes to history, began greatly to prevail.[3] It is not improbable that this took its rise from the Egyptian priests, who, as we may see in Hérodotos, represented their gods as having dwelt and reigned on earth.[4] Hekatæos of Milétos, one of the

---

[1] See Voss, *Myth. Br.* passim. "The language of the Hindús had an influence not to be mistaken on the form and representation of the mythes, inasmuch as it described poetically by significant epithets the metaphysical beings of which they told; as *many-* or *long-armed* (Maháváhús) for powerful; *thousand-eyed* (Sahasradric) for omniscient: or strove to express in the name itself the nature of the god, as Vishnús (*the penetrator*); Agnis (*the rapid, the mover*), the firegod, etc. These the plastic art gladly adopted and sought to render still more clear by additional symbols."—Bohlen, *Das alte Indien,* i. 180.

[2] See Müller, *Proleg.* 89 seq., 209. *Orchom.* 269. *Dor.* i. 59. Welcker, *Tril.* 462, 469. "Quam fecunda tragicorum ingenia in fabulis variandis, per tot exempla edocti, fuisse putabimus!"—Heyne *ad Apollodor.* p. 859. Id. *ib.* 920.

[3] Comp. Müller, *Proleg.* 97 seq. Lobeck, *Aglaoph.* 987 seq. Buttmann, i. 197.

[4] Hérod. ii. 144

earliest Grecian historians, would seem to have laboured to give a rational form to the old legends;[1] and we may observe in the explanation given by Hérodotos, after the Egyptian priests, of the legend of the soothsaying pigeon of Dódóna, and in other places of that historian, a similar desire.[2] This mode of rationalizing was carried to a much greater extent by Ephoros: but the work which may be regarded as having contributed by far the most to give it vogue, was the Sacred History ('Ιερὴ 'Αναγραφή) of Euhémeros, which was so celebrated in antiquity that we will here stop to give a brief account of it.[3]

Euhémeros said, in this work, that having had occasion to make a voyage in the Eastern ocean, after several days' sail he came to three islands, one of which was named Panchaia. The inhabitants of this happy isle were distinguished for their piety, and the isle itself for its fertility and beauty, in the description of which the writer exerted all the powers of his imagination. At a distance of several miles from the chief town, he says, lay a sacred grove, composed of trees of every kind, tall cypresses, laurels, myrtles, palms, and every species of fruit-tree, amidst which ran rivulets of the purest water. A spring within the sacred district poured forth water in such abundance as to form a navigable river, named the Water of the Sun,[4] which meandered along, fructifying the whole region, and shaded over by luxuriant groves, in which during the days of summer dwelt numbers of men, while birds of the richest plumage and most melodious throats built their nests in the branches, and delighted the hearer with their song. Verdant meads, adorned with various flowers, climbing vines, and trees hanging with delicious fruits, everywhere met the view in this paradise. The inhabitants of the island were divided into priests, warriors, and cultivators. All things were in common except the house and garden of each. The duty of the priests was to sing the praises of the gods, and to act as judges and magistrates: a double share of everything fell to them. The task of the military class was to defend the island against the incursions

---

[1] Hekatæos began his work in these words: " I write as it appears to me to be true ; for the narratives of the Hellénes are very various and ridiculous, as it seems to me." He said that Kerberos was a serpent that lay at Tænaron.

[2] Hérod. ii. 54–57.

[3] The chief remains of this work are to be found in the fifth book of Diodóros (42 seq.) and in the fragment of the sixth book preserved by Eusebios in his Evangelic Preparation. There are fragments remaining of the Latin translation of Ennius; and the work is frequently referred to by Sextus Empiricus and the Fathers of the Church.

[4] This name is borrowed from the Fount of the Sun (κρήνη Ηλίου) at the temple of Ammón. Hérod. iv. 181.

of pirates, to which it was exposed. The garments of all were of the finest and whitest wool, and they wore rich ornaments of gold. The priests were distinguished by their raiment of pure white linen, and their bonnets of gold tissue.

The priests derived their lineage from Kréte, whence they had been brought by Zeus after he had succeeded his predecessors Uranos and Kronos in the empire of the world. In the midst of the grove already described, and at a distance of sixty stadia from the chief town, stood an ancient and magnificent temple sacred to Triphylian Zeus, erected by the god himself while he was yet among men; and on a golden pillar in the temple the deeds of Uranos, Zeus, Artemis, and Apolló had been inscribed by Hermés in Panchæic letters, which the voyager says were the same with the sacred characters of the Egyptian priests. Zeus had, according to this monument, been the most potent of monarchs : the chief seat of his dominion had been Kréte, where he died and was buried, after having made five progresses through the world, all whose kings feared and obeyed him.

The object of Euhémeros in inventing this Utopia, which by the way many navigators sought after but no one ever found, was evidently to give a blow to the popular religion, and even to make it ridiculous; for though he seems to have treated some of the higher gods, as Zeus for example, with a degree of respect, he was less particular with the inferior ones and with the heroes. Thus of Aphrodité he says, that she was the first who reduced gallantry to an art, and made a trade of it, that she might not appear to be more wanton than other women.[1] Kadmos, he tells us, was cook to a king of Sidón, and he ran away with Harmonia, a female flute-player.[2]

The work of Euhémeros was vehemently attacked by all who retained a veneration for the old religion, and the writer himself was stigmatised as an atheist:[3] but it exerted a great influence over the subsequent historians, as we may perceive in the case of Diodóros of Sicily. It was translated into Latin by Ennius, of whose work some fragments remain;[4] and the Æneïs of Vergil alone will suffice to show the degree in which it affected the old Italian mythology.[5] Finally, the Fathers of the Church employed it to advantage in their conflicts with the supporters of the ancient religion.

[1] Ennius, *ap. Lactant. Div. Inst.* i. 17.   [2] Athénæus, xiv. 658.
[3] See Kallimachos, Fr. (Bentl.) 86. Plut. *de Is. et Os.* 23. Lobeck, 138.
[4] "Infidelity was introduced by the Calabrian Greek Ennius, and became naturalised as morals declined."—Niebuhr, *Hist. of Rome,* i. 137.
[5] See *Æn.* vii. 47 *seq.*, 177 *seq.* ; viii. 355 *seq*

While Euhémeros thus fixed on an imaginary island in the Eastern ocean as the original abode of the deities adored in Greece, others, among whom Dionysios of Samos or Mytiléné was the most celebrated, chose the Western coast of Africa for the same purpose.[1] For this they seemed to have Homéric authority; as the poet calls O'keanos, whose abode was placed in the West, the origin of the gods.[2] According to these writers the coast of Ocean on this side, fertile as Panchaia itself, was inhabited by a people named Atlanteians, distinguished for their piety and their hospitality to strangers. The first king who ruled over them was named Uranos. He collected into towns the people, who had previously dwelt dispersedly, and taught them agriculture, and thus reformed their manners. He gradually reduced under his sway the greater part of the world. By study of the heavens, and thus learning to foretell the celestial phænomena, he obtained the reputation of being of a nature superior to man ; and when he died, his people gave him divine honours, and named the heavens after him.

By several wives Uranos was the father of forty-five children, eighteen of whom, the offspring of Titaia or Earth, were named Titans. The most distinguished of their daughters were Basileia and Rhea, also named Pandóra. The former, who was the eldest, aided her mother to rear her brothers and sisters, whence she was called the Great Mother. She succeeded her father in his dominion ; and after some time she married Hyperíon, one of her brothers, to whom she bore two children, endowed with marvellous sense and beauty, named Hélios and Seléné. But the other Titans now grew jealous, and they murdered Hyperíon, and flung Hélios into the river E'ridanos, where he was drowned. At the tidings Seléné, who loved her brother beyond measure, cast herself from the roof of the palace and perished. Basileia lost her senses through grief, and went roaming in madness through the country with dishevelled locks, beating drums and cymbals. She disappeared at length in a storm of rain, thunder, and lightning. The people raised altars to her as a goddess, and they named the sun and moon after her hapless children.

The Titans then divided the realm of their father among themselves. The coast of Ocean fell to Atlas, who named the people and the highest mountain of the country after himself. Like his father he was addicted to astronomy; he first taught the doctrine of the sphere, whence he was said to support the heavens. Kronos, the most impious and ambitious of the Titans, ruled over Libya, Sicily, and Italy. He espoused his sister Rhea, who bore a son

---

[1] Diodor. iii. 56 seq.

[2] Ὠκεανόν τε, θεῶν γένεσιν καὶ μητέρα Τηθύν.—Il. xiv. 201.

named Zeus, in all things the opposite of his grim sire; whence the people, delighted with his virtues, named him Father, and finally placed him on the throne. Kronos, aided by the other Titans, sought to recover his dominion; but the new monarch defeated him, and then ruled, the lord of the whole world and the benefactor of mankind. After his death he was deified by his grateful subjects.

We will not pursue any further these dreams of the mythographer, for the tasteless system never seems to have gained general credit. We therefore proceed to relate the further course of the Grecian mythology.

As we have already observed, the allegoric system of interpretation prevailed at the same time with the historic. This mode of exposition had begun to appear even before the Persian war; it was employed by the sophists, and occasionally by Sókratés and Plató; but its greatest cultivators were the philosophers of the Stóic sect. It was chiefly physical truths that they deduced from the ancient mythes, and they generally regarded the gods in the light of personifications of the powers of nature. There were some, however, such as Anaxagoras and Antisthenés, who discovered moral ideas under the envelope of the mythe.

When the Romans became acquainted with Grecian literature, they identified the gods of Greece with such of their own deities as had a resemblance to them. Thus Hermés became Mercurius, Aphrodíté Venus, and the mythes of the former were by the poets, and perhaps in the popular creed, applied to the latter. As in Greece, some believed, some disbelieved in the popular deities, and the former sought the solution of the mythes in the schools of philosophy or the temples of the mysteries. The valuable work of Cicero, On the Nature of the Gods, shows in an agreeable manner the ideas entertained on this subject by the most accomplished Romans of his time.

After the conflict had commenced between Heathenism and Christianity, the allegorising principle was applied to the former with still greater assiduity than heretofore. The New Platonists endeavoured by its aid, in union with Oriental mysticism, to show, that the ancient religion contained all that was required to satisfy the utmost needs of the human soul. The Fathers of the Church laid hold on the weapons thus presented to them, to defend the new and attack the old religion. By the aid of the principles of Euhémeros they robbed the gods of Greece of their divinity; by that of the allegorising principle of the Stóics they extracted truth from the legends of Greek theology, and discovered mystery in the simplest narratives and precepts of the Hebrew Scriptures.

Unfortunately in this process many of the mythes and practices of Heathenism became incorporated with the pure religion of the Gospel,[1] and Christianity also had soon a mythology of its own to display. On the final overthrow of Heathenism its mythology slept along with its history and literature the sleep of the dark ages ; but at the revival of learning it was eagerly laid hold on by poets and artists,[2] and it attracted the attention of antiquaries and philosophers. The various theories by which it was sought to reduce it to system, which we have already enumerated, were then revived or devised; and mythology forms at present an important branch of learning and philosophy.

Of late years the mythology of Greece has in the hands of men of genius and learning, especially in Germany, resumed the simple and elegant attire which it wore in the days of Homer and Hésiod, and in which the following pages will attempt to present it to the reader.

Literature of the Grecian Mythology.

A brief view of the literature of the Grecian mythology, or of the works whence our knowledge of it has been derived, seems a necessary supplement to the preceding sketch of its history.

The Ilias and the Odyssey, as the two great heroic poems which are regarded as the works of Homer are named, are the earliest occidental literary compositions now extant; yielding, however, in antiquity, to some parts of the Hebrew Scriptures and to the sacred books and epics of India. Their origin is enveloped in the deepest obscurity, and the questions whether they are the production of one or of many minds, whether they were originally written, or were orally transmitted for centuries, have for some years engaged the pens of critics. It seems to be now generally agreed that the two poems are the productions of different minds, and that in both there are interpolations, some of which are of no small magnitude, but that notwithstanding they may be regarded as faithful pictures of the manners and opinions of the Achæans or Greeks of the early ages.[3] Beside the Ilias and the Odyssey, the ancients possessed some other narrative poems, which were ascribed, but falsely, to the same author. All these poems, however, have long since perished.

The age of Hésiod is equally uncertain with that of Homer. Three only of the poems ascribed to him have come down to us, viz. the didactic poem named Works and Days, the Theogony, and

---

[1] Thus the popular idea of Hell is much more like the Tartaros of Plató and Vergil than the Gehenna of the New Testament.

[2] The earliest modern work on this subject is Boccaccio's *Genealogia Deorum*, written in the fourteenth century.

[3] Our own theory respecting the poems will be found in the Appendix.

the Shield of Héraklés. Hésiod was also said to be the author of a poem in four books named the Catalogues, or Eœæ,[1] which related the histories of the heroines or distinguished women of the mythic ages; but of this also a few fragments have been preserved. The same is the case with the poems named the Melampodia, the Ægimios, and the Wedding of Kéyx, likewise ascribed to this ancient bard.

Homer and Hésiod were succeeded by a crowd of poets, who sang all the events of the mythic ages. The chief of these were Stasínos of Kypros, Arktínos of Milétos, Leschés of Lesbos, Kynæthos of Chios, Eumélos of Corinth, Agias of Trœzén, and Eugammón of Kyréné. Their poems were the Kypria, the Æthiopis, the Little Ilias, the Iliupersis or Taking of Ilion, the Nostæ or Returns of the Chiefs, the Télegonia, or Death of Odysseus, &c. There were also Hérakleiæ, or poems on the subject of Héraklés, by Peisander, Panyasis, and other poets, a Théséis on the adventures of Théseus, poems on the wars of Thébes,[2] a Titano-machia, an Amazonia, a Danaïs, a Phorónis, &c.

In the reign of Ptolemy Philadelphus, king of Egypt, the critic Zenodotos of Ephesos united several of these poems with the Ilias and Odyssey into one whole, commencing with the marriage of Heaven and Earth, and ending with the death of Odysseus. This was named the Epic Cycle, and it continued to be read during some centuries of the Christian æra.[3] Of this, however, the Homéric portion alone has come down to us: for our knowledge of the events contained in the remainder of the Cycle we are chiefly indebted to the works of the later poets Quintus Smyrnæus, Kolu-thos, and Tryphiodóros, and to the various scholiasts or commen-tators and compilers.

The lyric succeeded the epic poets. Mythic legends were neces-sarily their principal materials, as their verses were mostly dedi-cated to the worship of the gods, or the praise of victors in the public games, or were sung at banquets or in funeral processions. These too have disappeared, excepting a portion of those of Pindar. It is much to be lamented, in a mythologic view, that so little remains of Stésichoros of Himera.

The tragedians followed: they took their subjects from the epic poems, and their remaining works preserve much mythic lore.

---

[1] 'Hoίαι from the words ἤ οἵη or such as, with which each narrative began. See the commencement of the Shield.

[2] The Thébaïs was ascribed to Homer. In the opinion of Pausanias (ix. 9, 5.) it was next in merit to the Ilias and Odyssey. There was another Thébaïs by Antimachos, but written at a much later period.

[3] By far the best account of the Epic Cycle, its authors and contents, will be found in Welcker's excellent work, Der epische Cyclus (Bonn, 1853).

After the epic poetry had ceased, and writing, by means of the Egyptian papyrus, was become more common in Greece, a set of writers arose who related in succinct prose narratives, arranged in historic order, the various mythic legends which formed the Epic Cycle, the Eœæ, and other poems of the same nature. The principal of these writers were Pherekýdés, Akusiláos, and Hellaníkos; of *their* works also only fragments remain.

The historians, Hérodotos, Thukydidés and their followers, occasionally took notice of the mythic legends. Ephoros and Theopompos were those who devoted most attention to them, as their fragments still remaining show.

The sophists and philosophers employed the mythic form as the vehicle of their peculiar systems and ideas. Such was Prodikos' beautiful fiction of the Choice of Héraklés, and Protagoras' story of Prométheus and his brother.[1]

We are now arrived at the Alexandrian period. In this the mythes were treated in two different ways. Lykophrón, Euphorión, Apollónios, Kallimachos, and the remainder of the Pleias, as they were named, formed poems from them; while Apollodóros, following Pherekýdés, and adding the fictions of the tragedians, framed a continuous narrative of which an epitome alone has come down to us; and Kratés, Aristarchos, and the other editors of the ancient poets gave the legends a place in their commentaries.

The latin poets of the Augustan age drew largely on the Alexandrian writers, after whom chiefly they related in their verses the mythic tales of Greece, in general pure and unaltered, as appears from the Metamorphoses of Ovid, of whose legends the Greek originals can, with few exceptions, be pointed out.[2]

The summaries of Parthenius, Antoninus Liberalis and others contain numerous mythic legends, as also do the Scholia, or notes on the classic writers of Greece, especially those on Homer, Pindar, Apollónios, and Theokritos; those of Tzetzés on Hésiod and Lykophrón, and the tedious commentary of Eustathius on Homer. The notes of Servius on Vergil are also very valuable in this respect as likewise are the collections which go under the name of Julius Hyginus and the Violet-bed[3] of the empress Eudokia. It would be tedious to particularise all the other sources of information, for in fact there is hardly a classic writer in either language who does not relate or refer to some of the mythic legends of Greece; even the Fathers of the Church contribute to augment

---

[1] Plato, *Protagoras*, p. 320.
[2] As we proceed we shall be careful to do so whenever they can be discovered.
[3] 'Ιωνιά or *Violarium*. It forms the first volume of Villoison's *Anecdota Græca*.

our knowledge of the mythic tales of the religion against which their literary artillery was directed.

There is one author of a peculiar character, and whose work is of the most interesting nature, we mean Pausanias, who travelled in Greece in the second century of the Christian æra, and gathered on the spot the legends of the temples and the traditions of the people. He has thus preserved a number of mythic narratives unnoticed by preceding writers, which had probably been transmitted from father to son from the most remote times.

If to the sources already enumerated we add the long poem of Nonnos on the adventures of Dionýsos, we shall have given the principal authorities for the contents of the following pages. We have been thus succinct on the present occasion, as it is our intention to notice the literature of each of the mythic cycles in its proper place.[1]

Chapter III.

MYTHIC VIEWS OF THE WORLD AND ITS ORIGIN.

Mythic Cosmology.

For the due understanding of the mythology of a people, a knowledge of their cosmology, or views of the world, its nature, extent, and divisions, is absolutely requisite. Without it we shall be for ever falling into error; and by applying to the productions of the remote and infantile periods of society the just conceptions of the present day in geography and astronomy, give to them a degree of folly and inconsistency with which they cannot justly be charged.[2]

The earliest view of Grecian cosmology that we possess, is that contained in the poems of Homer. Next in antiquity is that of the poems of Hésiod, who flourished somewhat later, for he displays a much more extended knowledge of the earth than Homer appears to have possessed.

As navigation and the intercourse with foreign countries increased, just ideas respecting the more distant regions became more common among the Greeks, and districts were continually reclaimed from fable, and brought into the circuit of truth and knowledge. Not to speak of the philosophers and historians, we may discern in the poets of each succeeding age the progressively

---

[1] On the subject of this section see Müller, *Proleg.* 81 *seq.*

[2] We recommend the excellent works of Völcker on the Homeric and Mythic Geographies; and also that of Ukert on the Geography of the Greeks and Romans.

extending knowledge of the real character of distant lands. Yet still we must not always expect to find in poets all the knowledge of the age they live in; they love to imitate their predecessors, they often are unacquainted with the advance of knowledge, they write for the people, who still retain old prejudices. It is thus that in the poets of the Augustan age we shall find the Homéric ideas of the universe, just as in some modern poets we may meet the Ptolemaïc astronomy and judicial astrology, after both had been exploded.

The Greeks of the days of which Homer sings, or rather of the poet's own time, though well acquainted with navigation, do not appear to have been in the habit of making distant voyages. The Krétans and the Taphians (a people who inhabited some small islands in the Iónian Sea) perhaps form an exception. We read in the Odyssey of their piracies committed on Egypt and Sidón,[1] and of their bartering voyages to Temesa[2] (perhaps the place of that name in Italy), where they exchanged iron for copper. But the great authorities of the Greeks respecting foreign lands were probably the Phœnicians, who in the most distant ages visited Africa, Spain, and possibly the shores of the Atlantic; and it is likely that, after the fashion of travellers and sailors, mingling truth and fiction, they narrated the most surprising tales of the marvels of the remote regions to which they had penetrated.

According to the ideas of the Homéric and Hésiodic ages, it would seem that the *World* was a hollow globe, divided into two equal portions by the flat disk of the Earth.[3] The external shell of this globe is called by the poets *brazen*[4] and *iron*,[5] probably only to express its solidity. The superior hemisphere was named Heaven, the inferior one Tartaros. The length of the diameter of the hollow sphere is given thus by Hésiod.[6] It would take, he says, nine days for an anvil to fall from Heaven to Earth; and an equal space of time would be occupied by its fall from Earth to the bottom of Tartaros. The luminaries which gave light to gods and men shed their radiance through all the interior of the upper hemisphere; while that of the inferior one was filled with eternal gloom and darkness, and its still air unmoved by any wind.

The *Earth* occupied the centre of the *World* in the form of a round flat disk,[7] or rather cylinder, around which the *river* Ocean

---

[1] *Od.* xiv. 252 *seq.*, 452; xv. 425 *seq.*   [2] *Od.* i. 184.
[3] *Il.* viii. 16.   Hés. *Theog.* 720.
[4] *Il.* v. 504; xvii. 425.   *Od.* iii. 2.   Pind. *Pyth.* x. 27 (42).   *Nem.* vi. 3 (6).
[5] *Od.* xv. 329; xvii. 565.   [6] *Theog.* 722.
[7] Called by the Latins *Orbis terrarum*. The Greeks do not appear to have had any corresponding expression.

flowed.[1] Hellas was probably regarded as the centre of the Earth but the poets are silent on this point. They are equally so as to the exact central point, but probably viewed as such Olympos, the abode of the gods. In after times Delphi became the *navel of the earth*.[2] The Sea divided the terrestrial disk into two portions, which we may suppose were regarded as equal. These divisions do not seem to have had any peculiar names in the time of Homer. The northern one was afterwards named Europe;[3] the southern, at first called Asia alone, was in process of time divided into Asia and Libya,[4] the former comprising all the country between the Phasis and the Nile, the latter all between this river and the western Ocean.[5]

In the Sea the Greeks appear to have known to the west of their own country southern Italy and Sicily, though their ideas respecting them were probably vague and uncertain; and the imagination of the poets, or the tales of voyagers, had placed in the more remote parts of it several islands, such as the O'gygian the isle of Kalypsó, the Ææan that of Kirké, the Æolian that of Æolos, Scheria the abode of the Phæakians,—islands in all probability as ideal and as fabulous as the isles of Panchaia, Lilliput, or Brobdingnag, though both ancients and moderns have endeavoured to assign their exact positions. Along its southern coast lay, it would appear, the countries of the Lótos-eaters, the Kyklópes, the Giants, and the Læstrigonians. These isles and coasts of the western part of the Sea were the scenes of most of the wonders of early Grecian fable. There, and on the isles of the Ocean, the passage to which was supposed to be close to the island of Kirké, dwelt the Sirens, the Hesperides, the Grææ, the Gorgons, and the other beings of fable.

[1] See *Il.* xviii. 607, 608. *Æsch. From.* 138. Ov. *Met.* i. 30.

[2] Ὄμφαλος τῆς γῆς, Pind. *Pyth.* iv. 74 (131); vi. 3. Paus. x. 16, 3. There may be some connection between Delphi and δελφύς, *womb*, which gave occasion to the notion. Welcker (*Kret. Kol.* 45.) makes Δέλφος equivalent to Τήλεφος. The habit of regarding their own country as the centre of the earth prevails at the present day among the Chinese and the Hindús. The Rabbin held the same of Jerusalem (Buxtorf, *Lex. Chald.* 854.); it was also a principle in the cosmogony of the ancient Persians and Scandinavians.

[3] The term Europe first occurs in the Homeridian hymn to Apolló (*v.* 251), where it is opposed to the Peloponnése and the islands, and apparently denotes continental Greece. It would seem therefore to come from εὐρύς, and to signify *mainland*. (See Völck. *Hom. Geog.* 103.) Bochart, Buttmann (*Mythol.* ii. 176) and others derive it from the Hebrew 'Ereb (עֶרֶב), *evening*, as signifying the West. See Welcker, *Kret. Kol.* 55.

[4] See our note on Sall. *Jug.* xiv. 3.

[5] Asia seems to have been at first nothing more than the rich land on the banks of the Kaÿster. (*Il.* ii. 461. Heyne *in loco.*) Libya is in Homer merely a district to the west of Egypt.

The only inhabitants of the northern portion of the earth mentioned by Homer are the Hellénes and some of the tribes of Thrace. But Hésiod[1] sang of a happy race, named the Hyperboreans, dwelling in everlasting bliss and spring beyond the lofty mountains, whose caverns were supposed to send forth the piercing blasts of the north wind,[2] which chilled the people of Hellas. According to Pindar,[3] the country of the Hyperboreans, from which the river Istér flowed, was inaccessible either by sea or land. Apolló was their tutelar deity, to whom they offered asses in sacrifice, while choirs of maidens danced to the sound of lyres and pipes, and the worshippers feasted having their heads wreathed with garlands of the god's favourite plant, the bay. They lived exempt from disease or old age, from toils and warfare, and, conscious of no evil thoughts or acts, they had not to fear the awful goddess Nemesis.[4]

On the south coast of the Sea, eastwards of the fabulous tribes above enumerated, lay Libya and Egypt. The Sidónians, and a people named the Erembians,[5] are also mentioned by Homer, and the Greeks appear to have been well acquainted with the people of the west coast of Lesser Asia. They do not seem to have navigated the Euxine at this time, though they were doubtless not ignorant of it, as Homer names some of the peoples on its southern coast. They must of course have regarded it as a portion of the Sea. We have no means of ascertaining whether they supposed it to communicate with the Ocean, like the western part of the Sea. Of Kolchis and Kaukasos they appear to have had no knowledge whatever in these early ages. They were equally ignorant of the interior of Asia.

On the eastern side of the earth, close to the stream of Ocean, dwelt a people happy and virtuous as the Hyperboreans. They were named the Æthiopians :[6] the gods favoured them so highly that they were wont to leave at times their Olympian abodes and go to share their sacrifices and banquets.[7] A passage of the Odyssey[8] divides the Æthiopians into two tribes, the one on the eastern, the other on the western margin of the earth.[9] In later ages, when knowledge of the earth had increased, the Æthiopians or sun-burnt men were placed in the south; but this is contrary

---

[1] Hérod. iv. 32.
[2] 'Ρῖπαι, blasts, whence these mountains were named Rhipæans.
[3] Pind. Ol. iii. 13 (24) seq.; viii. 47 (63). Pyth. x. 30 (50) seq. Isth. vi. 23 (33).
[4] See Appendix A.
[5] Perhaps the Syrians (Aram) or the Arabs: see Strab. i. 2, 34, p. 42; xvi. 4. 27. p. 784.
[6] That is, black or sun-burnt men, from αἴθω, to burn.
[7] Il. i. 423; xxiii. 205. Od. i. 22; v. 282.
[8] Od. i. 23, 24.
[9] See Appendix B.

to the views of Homer,[1] who assigns the southern portion of the
terrestrial disk to a nation of dwarfs named, from their diminutive
stature,[2] Pygmies, to whose country the cranes used to migrate
every winter, and their appearance was the signal of bloody warfare to the puny inhabitants, who had to take up arms to defend
their corn-fields against the rapacious strangers.

On the western margin of the earth, by the stream of Ocean,
lay a happy place named the E'lysian Plain, whither the mortal
relatives of the king of the gods were transported without tasting
of death, to enjoy an immortality of bliss.   Thus Próteus says to
Meneláos,[3]

> But thee the ever-living gods will send
> Unto the Élysian Plain, and distant bounds
> Of earth, where dwelleth fair-hair'd Rhadamanthys:
> There life is easiest unto men; no snow,
> Or wintry storm, or rain, at any time
> Is there; but Ocean evermore sends up
> Clear-blowing western breezes to refresh
> The habitants; because thou hast espoused
> Helené, and art son-in-law of Zeus.

In the time of Hésiod [4] the E'lysian Plain was become the Isles
of the Blest; but Pindar [5] appears to reduce the number of these
happy isles to one.

We thus see that the Greeks of the early ages knew little of any
real people except those to the east and south of their own country,
or near the coast of the Mediterranean.   Their imagination meantime had peopled the western portion of this sea with giants,
monsters, and enchantresses; while they placed around the edge
of the disk of the earth, which they probably regarded as of no
great width, nations enjoying the peculiar favour of the gods, and
blessed with happiness and longevity,—a notion which continued
to prevail even in the historic times.[6]

We have already observed that the Ocean of Homer and Hésiod
was a river or stream.   It is always so called by these poets,[7] and
they describe the sun and the other heavenly bodies as rising out

---

[1] *Il.* iii. 3-7.   Heyne doubts of the genuineness of this passage.   Payne
Knight would be content with rejecting *vv.* 6 and 7.   It is to be observed that
it is not Homer's custom to use two particles of comparison (ὥς and ἠΰτε)
together, and that the Pygmies seem to contradict the analogy which places
races superior to ordinary men on the shores of Ocean.

[2] That is, men only as tall as the fist, from πυγμή. *fist*, like our Tom Thumb.

[3] *Cd.* iv. 563.   [4] Ἔργ. 169.   [5] *Ol.* ii. 70 (129).   [6] Hérod. iii. 106.

[7] Πϑταμὸς, ῥόος, ῥοαί, *Il.* iii. 5; xiv. 245; xvi. 151; xviii. 240, 402, 607;
xix. 1; xx. 7.   *Od. x.* 21. 639; xii. 1; xxii. 197; xxiv. 11.   Hés. Ἔργ. 566
Theog. 242, 841.

of and sinking into its placid current.[1] Its course was from south
to north up the western side of the earth. It flowed calmly and
equably, unvexed by tempests and unnavigated by man. It was
termed *back-flowing, deep-flowing, soft-flowing,* from its nature.[2]
Its waters were sweet, and it was the parent of all fountains and
rivers on the earth. As it was a stream, it must have been conceived to have a further bank to confine its course, but the poet of
the Odyssey alone notices the transoceanic land, and that only in
the western part. He describes it as a region unvisited by the
sun, and therefore shrouded in perpetual darkness, the abode of
a people whom he names Kimmerians. He also places there Erebos,
the realm of Aïdés and Persephoneia, the final dwelling of all the
race of man, a place which the poet of the Ilias describes as lying
within the bosom of the earth.[3]

As Homer[4] represents the heaven as resting on pillars kept by
Atlas, and which were on the earth, and Hésiod[5] describes the
extremities of heaven, earth, sea ($\pi\acute{o}\nu\tau os$), and Tartaros as meeting,
it would seem to follow that the Ocean lay outside of the hollow
sphere of the world, and encompassed the middle of it like a rim;
and the armillary sphere would thus give us an idea of the Homeric
world. But to this hypothesis it may be justly objected that the
celestial bodies all rose out of and sank into the Ocean-stream.

The portion of the hollow sphere above the earth contained
Olympos, the abode of the gods; but there is great difficulty in
ascertaining its exact nature and situation. As it is always represented as a mountain, it must have rested on the earth, and yet
one passage of the Ilias[6] would seem plainly to speak of it as

---

[1] *Il.* vii. 422; viii. 485; xviii. 239; *Od.* iii. 1; xix. 433; xxiii. 242, 347.
Hés. Ἔργ. 566. Thus Milton also, *Par. Lost,* v. 139.

> . . . . the sun, who scarce uprisen,
> With wheels yet hovering o'er the ocean brim,
> Shot parallel to the earth his dewy ray ;

and Tasso, *Ger. Lib.* i. 15.

> Sorgeva il novo sol dai lidi Eoi,
> Parte già fuor, ma 'l più ne l' onde chiuso.

[2] Ἀψόῤῥοος, *Il.* xviii. 399. *Od.* xx. 65. (ἂψ ἀνασειράζοντος ἑὸν ῥόον εἰς
ἑὸν ὕδωρ, Nonn. xxxviii. 317.) Hés. *Theog.* 776. βαθύῤῥοος, *Il.* vii. 422;
xiv. 311. *Od.* xi. 13; xix. 434. βαθυῤῥείτης, *Il.* xxi. 195. Hés. *Theog.* 265;
ἀκαλαῤῥείτης, *Il.* vii. 422. *Od.* xix. 434. An epithet of O'keanos in Hésiod
(*Theog.* 274, 288, 294) is κλυτὸς, *illustrious,* or rather *bright.* See Appendix C.
[3] *Il.* iii. 278; ix. 568; xix. 259; xx. 61; xxii. 482; xxiii. 100.
[4] *Od.* i. 54.   [5] Theog. 736.
[6] *Il.* viii. 18–26. Zenodotos, however, rejected *vv.* 25, 26, in which all the
difficulty lies: see Schol. *in loco.* There is also a difficulty in *Il.* v. 750 com-

distinct from the earth; and the language of the Odyssey respecting it is still more dubious.[1]

Were we to follow analogy, and argue from the cosmology of other races of men, we would say that the upper surface of the superior hemisphere was the abode of the Grecian gods. The Hebrews seem, for example, to have regarded the concave heaven as being solid (hence the threat, that Jehovah would make their neaven brass and their earth iron),[2] and its upper surface as the abode of Jehovah and his holy angels, the place where he had formed his magazines of hail, rain, snow, and frost.[3] According to the notions of the ancient Scandinavians the heaven was solid, and its upper surface, which they named Asgardr (*God-abode*), was the dwelling of their gods, and the place to which the souls of the virtuous and the valiant dead ascended along the celestial bridge Bifröst, i.e. the Rainbow. The ideas of the ancient Italians and other peoples seem to have been similar. Hence we might be led to infer that Olympos, the abode of the Grecian gods, was synonymous with Heaven, and that the Thessalian mountain, and those others which bore the same name, were called after the original heavenly hill.[4] A careful survey, however, of those passages in Homer and Hésiod in which Olympos occurs, will lead us to believe that the Achæans held the Thessalian Olympos, the highest mountain with which they were acquainted, to be the abode of their gods.[5]

The entrance to the city or palace of the gods on Olympos was closed by a gate of clouds kept by the goddesses named the Seasons; but the cloudy valves rolled open spontaneously to permit the greater gods to pass to and fro on their visits to the earth.[6]

---

pared with v. 754; but this may be explained by supposing that the abode of the gods occupied only a part of Olympos.

[1] Nitzsch rejects *Od.* xi. 314, 315.   [2] *Deut.* xxviii. 23.

[3] See Job, xxxviii. 22. The very rational supposition of some learned and pious divines, that it did not suit the scheme of Providence to give the Israelites more correct ideas on natural subjects than other nations, relieves Scripture from many difficulties.

[4] The Scholiast on Apollonios Rhodios (i. 599) enumerates six, namely in Macedonia, Thessaly, Mysia, Kilikia, Élis, Arkadia; to which are to be added those of Kypros, Lesbos, Akarnania, and Lakónia. (Polyb. ii. 65; v. 24.) We may here observe that v. 128 of the Theogony is probably an interpolation.

[5] See particularly *Il.* xiv. 225 *seq.* The Hindú Merú and the Persian Elburs were in like manner on the earth.

[6] *Il.* v. 749; viii. 393. Thus Milton:

> Heaven opened wide
> Her ever-during gates, harmonious sound
> On golden hinges moving, to let forth
> The king of glory.—*Par. Lost,* vii. 205.

It is an utterly unfounded supposition of the learned Voss,[1] that there were doors at the eastern and western extremities of the heaven, through which the sun-god and other deities ascended from and went down into the stream of Ocean. The celestial luminaries seem rather, according to Homer and Hésiod, to have careered through void air, 'bringing light to men and gods.' When in after times the solid heaven was established as the abode of the gods, the necessity for these doors was perhaps felt; and they were accordingly invented by those who were resolved to leave nothing unexplained.

The stars appear to have been regarded as moving under the solid heaven, for they rose out of and sank into the Ocean-stream. The only ones mentioned by name by Homer and Hésiod are the constellations Oríon, the Bear, the Pleiades, and the Hyades, the single stars Boótés or Arktúros, and Seirios, and the planet Venus, which they seem to have viewed as two distinct stars, in its characters of Morning-star (*Eósphoros*), and Evening-star (*Hesperos*). There is no reason to suppose the Greeks to have had any knowledge of the signs of the Zódiac until after their intercourse with Asia and Egypt had commenced.

Tartaros was, as we have already remarked, unvisited by the light of day. It was regarded as the prison of the gods, and not as the place of torment for wicked men, being to the gods what Erebos was to men—the abode of those who were driven from the supernal world.[2] The Titans when conquered were shut up in it, and in the Ilias [3] Zeus menaces the gods with banishment to its murky regions.

Such were the opinions respecting the world and its parts held by the Greeks of the heroic times, and even some ages later. With the advance of knowledge, however, their ideas altered, and they began to conceive more justly on these subjects. The voyages of the Samians and the Phokæans to the West, and the establishment of the Milésian colonies on the shores of the Euxine, and the

And again, *v.* 374:

> He through heaven,
> That opened wide her blazing portals, led
> To God's eternal house direct the way.

---

[1] *Mythol. Briefe*, i. 190. Note on Verg. *Geor.* iii. 261. The passages there quoted (Pind. *Fr. incert.* 100. Apoll. Rh. iii. 159, and Q. Smyrnæus, xiv. 225), as is too often the case with him, by no means bear him out in his theory. Statius is the earliest poet who speaks of these gates: see Theb. i. 158; vi. 35; x. 1. Nonnos (xxvii. 2) describes Éós as opening the gates of the east.

[2] *Il.* viii. 478 *seq.* Hés. *Theog.* 717 *seq.*   [3] Il. viii. 13.

interoourse thus opened with the interior of Asia, led to the supposition that the earth was *oval* rather than round, its greater diameter running east and west.[1] In like manner in the time of Pindar[2] and Æschylos[3] the Ocean had increased to the dimensions of a sea, and Hérodotos[4] derides those who still regarded it as a river. Finally, the change of religious ideas gradually affected Erebos, the abode of the dead. The E'lysian Plain was moved down to it as the place of reward for the good, and Tartaros was raised up to it to form the prison in which the wicked suffered the punishment due to their crimes.[5]

Cosmogony and Theogony.

The origin of the world and the origin of the gods, i.e. cosmogony and theogony, are in the Grecian system, as in those of some other nations, closely united. The sages of antiquity seem to have had a strong persuasion that, to bring creation and similar acts down to the comprehension of tribes led by the senses, it was necessary to represent natural agents as living and active persons; or they felt a pleasure in exciting admiration, by the narration of the strange and wonderful adventures of beings older and more powerful than mankind;[6] or finally such was the natural tendency of the human mind in those remote ages.[7]

The lively and creative genius of the Greeks seems particularly to have delighted in this species of fiction. They loved to represent the origin, the union, and the changes of the various parts of nature, under the guise of matrimony and birth (their more cheerful system, unlike those of Asia and Scandinavia, excluding the idea of the death of a god); and causes with them became parents, effects children, the production of an effect the birth of a divine child.

Every cosmogonic system commences with a Chaos, or state of darkness and confusion. The chief difference among these systems lies in the circumstance that some viewed the earth, others the water, as the immediate origin of organised bodies. In Grecian cosmogony Homer would appear to have followed the latter, for he terms O'keanos the origin of all;[8] while the former is the theory

[1] Strabó (ii. 5, 14, p. 118) makes the earth the shape of a *chlamys*.
[2] *Pyth.* iv. 251 (447).   [3] *Prom.* 431.   [4] Hérod. ii. 23; iv. 8, 36, 45.
[5] Æschylos (*Prom.* 152) still places it under Erebos; in Hésiod's 'Aσπίs, vv. 254, 255, it is placed in the realm of Aïdés,—a proof among many that critics are right in assigning a later age to that part of the poem.
[6] See Müller, *Proleg.* 270.
[7] What is called the Wisdom of the Ancients is in reality nothing but the art of personifying or investing in figurative language simple, moral, and physical ideas.   *Il.* xiv. 201.

adopted in the Theogony of Hésiod. Thalés and the Iónian school of philosophy followed the Homeric cosmogony. In the Timæos of Plató it is said that the offspring of Heaven and Earth were O'keanos and Téthys, and that from these sprang Kronos, Rhea, and the other deities. This is apparently, however, an attempt at bringing Homer and Hésiod into harmony.

The venerable Theogony of Hésiod is evidently the parent of all the succeeding ones, and is itself but the echo of those of bards of far higher antiquity than the Askræan to whom it is ascribed, and who often was ignorant of the meaning of what he delivered; it has further been largely interpolated. We will here relate the portion of it which extends from Chaos to the establishment of the empire of Zeus and origin of the gods worshipped in Greece.

Chaos[1] (*Void Space*) was first: then came into being 'broad-breasted' Earth, the gloomy Tartaros, and Love. Chaos produced Erebos and Night, and this last bore to Erebos Day and Æther.

Earth now produced Uranos (*Heaven*), of equal extent with herself, to envelope her, and the Mountains and Pontos (*Sea*).[2] She then bore to Uranos a mighty progeny: the Titans; six males, O'keanos, Kœos, Krios, Hyperión, Iapetos, and the youngest of them Kronos; and six females, Theia, Rheia (or Rhea), Themis, Mnémosyné, Phœbé, and Téthys. She also bore the three Kyklópes, Brontés, Steropés, and Argés,[3] and the three Hundred-handed (ἑκατόγχειρες), Kottos, Briareós, and Gyés. These children were hated by their father, who, as soon as they were born, thrust them out of sight into a cavern of Earth,[4] who, grieved at his unnatural conduct, produced the 'substance of hoary steel,' and forming from it a sickle, roused her children, the Titans, to rebellion against him: but fear seized on them all except Kronos, who lying in wait with the sickle with which his mother had armed him, mutilated his

---

[1] From χάω, *to gape*. Ginnunga Gap (*Swallowing Throat*) is the Chaos of Scandinavian mythology.

[2] Perhaps the *bed* of the sea, and akin to the Latin *fundus;* the Teutonic *boden, bottom.* Earth would thus have at first produced the elevations of her surface and the *one* great depression of it; for there was only *one* sea: see below, chap. xvii. *Néreus.*

[3] Göttling (on *v.* 501) asserts that the Kyklópes were the progeny of Earth alone. He says that this is proved by a comparison of *v.* 139

Γείνατο δ' αὖ Κύκλωπας, κ. τ. λ.

with *v.* 147.

῎Αλλοι δ' αὖ Γαίης τε καὶ Οὐρανοῦ ἐξεγένοντο.

We do not see the force of this argument.

[4] Apollodóros says that it was the Kyklópes and Hundred-handed alone whom Uranos thus treated. Völcker (*Myth. der Jap.* 283) says that the Titans were also hut up.

unsuspecting sire. The drops which fell on the earth from the wound gave birth to the Erinnyes, the Giants, and the Melian nymphs: from what fell into the sea sprang Aphrodíté, the goddess of love and beauty.

Earth bore to her other son Pontos the 'truth-speaking' Néreus, Thaumas (*Wonder*), Phorkys, 'fair-cheeked' Kétó, and Eurybia. Néreus had by Dóris, a daughter of the Titan O'keanos, the fifty Néréides or sea-nymphs. Thaumas was by E'lektra (*Brightness*), another daughter of O'keanos, father of the swift Iris (*Rainbow*), and of the 'well-haired' Harpies. Kétó bore to her brother Phorkys the Grææ, the Gorgons, the Echidna, and the serpent that guarded the golden apples of the Hesperides.

Earth finally, after the overthrow of the Titans, bore by Tartaros her last offspring, the hundred-headed Typhóeus, the father of storms and whirlwinds, whom Zeus precipitated into Tartaros.

The progeny of the Titans was numerous. O'keanos had by his sister Téthys all the rivers that flow on the earth, and the Ocean-nymphs, three thousand in number. Theia bore to Hyperíón, Hélios (*Sun*), Seléné (*Moon*), and E'ós (*Dawn*); and Phœbé to Kœos, Asteria (*Starry*) and Létó. Krios had by Eurybia (*Wide-strength*), the daughter of Pontos, Astræos (*Starry*), Pallas, and Persés. To Astræos E'ós bore the winds Zephyros, Boreas, and Notos, and E'ósphoros (*Dawn-bearer*), or Morning-star, and the stars of heaven. Styx, a daughter of O'keanos, was by Pallas the mother of Envy and Victory, Strength and Force: and Asteria, the daughter of Kœos, bore to Persés Hekaté.

The fifth Titan, Iapetos, was by Klymené, a daughter of O'keanos, the father of four sons, Atlas, Menœtios, Prométheus, and Epimétheus.

Rhea was united to Kronos, and their offspring were Hestia, Démétér, Héra, Aïdés, Poseidón, and Zeus. Kronos, having learned from his parents, Heaven and Earth, that he was fated to be deprived by one of his sons of the kingdom which he had taken from his father, devoured his children as fast as they were born. Rhea, when about to be delivered of Zeus, besought her parents to teach her how she might save him. Instructed by Earth, she concealed him in a cavern of Kréte, and gave a stone in his stead to Kronos. This stone he afterwards threw up,[1] and with it the children whom he had devoured. When Zeus was grown up, he and the other children of Kronos made war on their father and the

---

[1] It was shown in after times in the neighbourhood of Delphi (Hés. *Theog.* 498. Pausanias, x. 24, 6), the legend having been transplanted thither from Créte, its original soil. The whole fable seems to have been unknown to Homer, who always speaks of Zeus as the eldest son of Kronos.

Titans. The scene of the conflict was Thessaly; the former fought from Olympos, the atter from Othrys. During ten entire years the contest was undecided; at length by the counsel of Earth the Kronids released the Hundred-handed, and called them to their aid. The war was then resumed with renewed vigour, and the Titans were finally vanquished and imprisoned in Tartaros under the guard of the Hundred-handed. The Kronids then, by the advice of Earth, gave the supreme power to Zeus, who in return distributed honours and dominion among the associates of his victory.

In this theogony order and philosophic consequence are plainly discernible. We find it faithfully adhering to the cosmologic ideas above developed.[1] Void Space must naturally have been first: Earth, was to occupy the centre of the World; Tartaros, the lowest and deepest gloom; and Love, the generating principle of life and motion. follow in their due order.[2] As in all cosmogonies darkness precedes light. so Erebos and Night, the one the darkness beneath, the other that above the earth, succeed, and from them spring Day the Lower, and Æther the higher light above the earth. Without the intervention of Love, Earth now produces the Heaven, which arches over her; the Mountains which rise on her surface and support the heaven; and the barren salt Sea, or the cavity in which its waters repose. United then by Love with Uranos, she gives birth to the Titans, the origins of gods and men, of the celestial luminaries, and the fructifying streams.

The making thunder, lightning, and other celestial phænomena to be children of Heaven and Earth might seem to imply a deeper knowledge of physics than can be justly assigned to these early ages. The cause, however. would appear to have been a simple one. Uranos being masculine could not produce of himself, and Earth was the only female being that could be united with him; but it will presently appear that Earth was their appropriate mother. The Kyklópes, that is the *Whirlers*,[3] whose individual

---

[1] For the explanation of the Theogony see Hermann, *De Antiq. Græcor. Mythologia* (Opusc. vol. ii. 167 seq.), *Briefe an Creuzer*, and *Ueber das Wesen und die Behandlung der Mythologie:* see also Müller, *Proleg.* pp. 371–379.

[2] So in Hindú cosmogony, when Brahma began to view himself in the light of Maya (*Illusion*) his contemplation caused the surrounding darkness to divide, and Cama (*Love*) came into productive energy. Bohlen, *Das Alte Indien*, i. 161. A similar energy is assigned to Πόθος (*Desire*), in the Phœnician cosmogony of Sanchoniathón.

[3] Κύκλωψ, rendered by Hermann *Volvulus*. from κύκλος, is a simple, not a compound substantive, of the same class with μώλωψ, with Κέρκωψ, Κέκρωψ, Πέλοψ, &c.: see p. 15. Like *Argiletum* (above, p. 9), its form admitting of decomposition gave origin to the one-eyed giants of the Odyssey, who were also known to the author of the Theogony: see v. 143. The next three lines are an interpolation.

names signify Thunder, Lightning, and Brightness, or Swiftness, represent one kind of celestial phænomena, and the Hundred-handed must therefore be the personifications of another, but what kind is more difficult to ascertain. It is however, probable that they refer to the winter, as the Kyklópes seem more especially related to the *œstas* or warm portion of the year;[1] and that they are the hail, rain and snow of that season: Kottos, that is *Smiter,* being the hail; Gyés, the *Furrower,* the rain; and Briareós, the *Presser,* the snow, which lies deep and heavy on the ground;[2] and they were naturally named Hundred-handed, from their acting so extensively at the same moment of time.[3]

Of the Titans we shall presently treat at length, and the progeny of Earth and Pontos will be noticed in another place.[4] There remain therefore only to be considered the beings which sprang from the blood of the mutilated Uranos. These are the Erinnyes, the Giants, and the Melian nymphs. Productiveness is the consequence of that act, for which analogy would incline us to look; and when we divest our mind of the idea of the Giants given by Homer, and which became the prevalent one, we may without difficulty find that they simply signify *Producers.*[5] By the Melian nymphs may possibly be signified the producers of fruits or of cattle.[6] The Erinnyes offer most difficulty; they may be, as some think, chthonic powers,[7] and have undergone a change of character like the Giants, Hermés, and other similar beings; of their late character—that of punishers of the violators of the order of nature—may have been their original one, and their origin have been ascribed to the first violation of filial duty.

---

[1] See our note on Vergil, *Geor.* ii. 322.

[2] Κόττος, from κόπτω, *to smite;* Γύης (Γύγης is wrong, see Göttling *in loc.*) is the *buris* or plough-beam: see our Vergil, Terms of Husb. *s. v.;* Βριάρεως is akin to Βριάω, Βριαρὸς, Βρίθω, Βριθὺς, all denoting *weight* and strength.

[3] The above explanation is that given by Hermann (*Ueber das Wesen,* &c. p. 84). He had given a different one previously (*De Myth. Ant.* Opusc. ii. 176), which he rejected for the present more probable one. Welcker also (*Tril.* 147) understands by the Hundred-handed the *water,* under its various forms. Lauer (*System der Griech. Myth.* 162) says they are the sea.

[4] See below, chap. xvii. and xviii.

[5] Γίγαντες, *Genitales,* from ΓΑ΄Ω, ΓΕ΄ΝΩ, γίγνω, γιγνάω. Hermann, *ut sup.* Opusc. ii. 177. Völcker, *Myth. der Jap.* 272, *note.* From ΓΑ΄Ω would come regularly a verb in μι, ΓΙ΄ΓΗΜΙ, of which γίγας is the present participle.

[6] Μελίαι, from μῆλον, *sheep,* or *apple, pomum* (Völcker, *ut sup.*). Others understand by them Ash-nymphs, from μελία. In this last case they might denote the production of timber-trees. Hermann renders μελίαι *Cicurinæ,* deriving it from the same root with μειλίσσειν.

[7] Völcker, *ut sup.,* from ἐν ἔρᾳ ναίειν (Tzetz. *Lyc.* 152), referring to Démétér Erinnys. According to Hermann ἐριννύες is *quasi* ἐλιννύες, *Maturnæ,* from ἐλιννεύω.

We now proceed to the important mythe of the Titans, and as the view of it given by Völcker seems to us to come nearer to the truth than any preceding one, we will lay it before our readers.[1]

The six sons and six daughters of Heaven and Earth above enumerated alone are Titans, and the most probable derivation of the name he thinks is that which makes it equivalent to *Earth-born*.[2] The germs of all beings afterwards to be formed lie in them, but they are enclosed within the earth, and cannot act till Uranos is deprived of his procreative power, and Aphrodíté is produced. Then the Titans O'keanos and Téthys give origin to the rivers and streams of the earth; from Kœos, Krios, Hyperíón, Theia, and Phœbé, spring the sun, moon, and other luminaries and light-beings; and the material world being thus completed, Kronos and Rhea give birth to the gods, and Iapetos becomes the father of men.[3] Their task being thus completed, and the earth replenished with its fitting inhabitants, the Titans are dismissed, to remain inactive in Tartaros.

The Titan-war therefore, in the opinion of this critic, could have formed no part of the original mythe. It had its origin in the figurative terms *bind* and *loose*, used to signify the checking and permitting of the productive powers of the Titans. Homer knows nothing of this war; he merely says that Zeus placed Kronos beneath 'the earth and the barren sea,'[4] and in him the opposition between the Olympian gods and the Titans is merely a local one; the one being the dwellers of the brilliant Olympos, the other the inmates of the gloomy Tartaros.[5] Hésiod, who evidently misunderstood the sense of the mythe, first gave it the form of a war, and narrated its details in splendid poetry; but the contradictions and variations in his narrative give convincing proof of its being alien from the ancient cosmogonic mythe. In the hands of the logographers and poets, such as Æschylos, the cosmogony becomes the history of a series of dynasties, and, contrary to Hésiod, the children of all the Titans, except Kronos and

---

[1] *Myth. der Jap.* 280 *seq.*

[2] Namely, that given by Diodóros (iii. 57) from τιταία, same as γῆ: and supposing the root to be αἶα, ταῖα (by reduplication τιταία) would come as easily from it as γαῖα and δαῖα. Völcker gives (285, *note*) a long list cf cognate terms.

[3] Kronos and Iapetos are joined together by Homer (*Il.* viii. 479). In the hymn to Apollo, *vv.* 336, 337, we read

Τιτῆνές τε θεοί, τοὶ ὑπὸ χθονὶ ναιετάοντες
Τάρταρον ἀμφὶ μέγαν, τῶν ἔξ ἄνδρες τε θεοί τε.

A similar view is given in the 37th Orphic hymn.

[4] *Il.* xiv. 203. [5] *Il.* xv. 225, *et seq.*

Rhea, are counted among the Titans, and set in hostility with the Kronids. Thus Pherekýdés[1] commences with saying that Uranos reigned first, and had by Earth the Kyklópes and the Hundred-handed. He casts all these into Tartaros, and then the Titans are born; who all, except O'keanos,[2] at the instigation of their mother, fall on their sire, whom Kronos mutilates. They liberate their imprisoned brethren; but Kronos, to whom the kingdom is given, binds them again in Tartaros. Then follows the account of the birth of the Kronids, who by freeing the Kyklópes and their brethren win the victory, and the three brothers divide the dominions of their father among them by lot.[3]

The Titan-war, as this critic thinks, had its origin and example in those of Typhón, the Alóeids, and the Giants against the gods. The circumstance of Zeus being termed King (though for another reason), the change of the three celestial sovereigns, and the mutilation of Uranos, aided in making the mythe take this form. The question how Zeus came to the throne was naturally answered by the tale of a revolution and hostility between the two classes of gods. Imitation is also everywhere to be traced. Zeus is made to mutilate Kronos as Kronos mutilated Uranos.[4] The latter hides his children under the earth, the former swallows his. Kronos is the youngest child, so is Zeus; the Titans divide the dominion of the world, the Kronids do the same. As Kronos devours his children for fear of their dethroning him, so something similar is recorded of Zeus.[5] Earth always gives the counsel;[6] and in the Ilias an attempt of the Olympians to bind Zeus is mentioned, in which Briareós again comes to his aid.[7]

Such is the theory of this most able mythologist. Instead of examining it critically, we will briefly state the conclusions at which we have ourselves arrived on this rather abstruse subject.

[1] That is, supposing (as there is every reason to do) that Apollodóros followed him in his theogony.

[2] The Titanesses are evidently also to be excepted.

[3] See *Il.* xv. 187 *seq.*

[4] Timæos, *ap. Sch. Apoll. Rh.* iv. 913. Tzetz. *Lyc.* 762, 869. This, however, seems to be a very late fiction.

[5] *Theog.* 886 *seq.*   [6] *Ib.* 159, 475, 626, 891.

[7] *Il.* i. 396 *seq.* Hermann (*Ueber das Wesen*, &c., 85) gives the following, more ingenious perhaps than solid, explanation of this celebrated mythe. Héra, Poseidón, and Athéna set about binding Zeus; that is, mankind would wish to keep summer always for their agriculture (Héra, the earth), their navigation, and their civil institutions and occupations, and have no winter. But Thetis, *the S other* (θέω), who reduces all strife to peace and order, calls Briareós up to heaven, and men must now give over their thoughts of getting the fine weather into their power.

The Titans—which name we would render the *Strivers* or *Exerters*[1]—are the *earliest* offspring of Heaven and Earth, whom it is their office to replenish with animated and intelligent beings, with light and with water. Contrary, therefore, to the current opinion of their representing the wild and turbulent powers of nature, they are to be regarded as beneficent agents, and the period of their dominion as the Golden Age, during which, under the rule of Kronos, there prevailed a perpetual spring. At the commencement of their sway, the Giants and other beings, probably the origin of vegetation and of the inferior animals, had come into existence, and thus creation was complete. But Heaven and Earth had other children, the Kyklópes and the Hundred-handed, which their sire had enclosed within the earth. For as they represent the celestial phænomena which have their origin in the vapours which earth sends up to form the clouds, whence they descend, it was necessary that they should be inactive during that brilliant season. But this happy condition was not to be of perpetual duration. Zeus and his brethren, as the representatives of another order of things, release these beings; that is, the earth now begins to send up vapours, and thunder and the other celestial phænomena come into activity, and the change of seasons commences.[2] The *war* was therefore a component part of the original mythe, and the Titans could not have been imprisoned by their sire. But further changes menaced the course of nature now established. Earth and Tartaros give origin to the terrific Typhóeus, whom Zeus, after a long and severe conflict, reduces and confines; that is, volcanoes and other phænomena, which have their origin in the *interior* of the earth[3] (hence his sire is Tartaros), menace the regular course of the seasons, with their aërial phænomena, which now prevails; but they are placed under restraint, and there are consequently no further wars or changes of dynasty, nature having arrived at her destined and final condition.

There would also appear to have been some other ancient system of the celestial dynasties, which assigned the place of Uranos and Gæa to Ophíon and Eurynomé. As this last is said to be an O'keanis, and the former name is manifestly derived from the symbol for the earth,[4] it would seem to have been one

---

[1] From ΤΑΩ, ΤΙΤΑΩ, τιταίνω (see *Theog.* 209), to express their procreat.ve *efforts*. Τιτὰν would come from ΤΙΤΑΩΝ, as Πὰν from πάων, 'Αλκμὰν from 'Αλκμάων, &c.

[2] Jupiter antiqui contraxit tempora veris,
　　 Perque hiemes, æstusque et inæquales autumnos,
　　 Et breve ver spatiis exegit quatuor annum.—Ov. *Met.* i. 116.

[3] Τυφωεὺς, from τύφω, to *smoke*.   [4] Ὄφις, a *serpent*.

of the systems in which earth and water were regarded as the origin of all beings. It reverses however the usual order, the earth being generally looked on as the female principle. We find no traces of it anterior to the Alexandrian period, when it is noticed by Lykophrón[1] and Apollónios.[2] At a much later age it is alluded to by Nonnos.[3] Milton, who, like the Alexandrians, loved to bring forward recondite mythes and traditions, nearly translates the Rhodian poet in the following lines:

> And fabled how the serpent, whom they called
> Ophion, with Eurynome,—the wide-
> Encroaching Eve perhaps,—had first the rule
> Of high Olympos, thence by Saturn driven
> And Ops, ere yet Dictæan Jove was born.—*Par. Lost*, x. 580

CHAPTER IV.

THE TITANS AND THEIR OFFSPRING:—NIGHT, OKEANOS AND TETHYS, HYPERION AND THEIA, HELIOS, SELENE, EOS, KŒOS AND PHŒBE, KRIOS, HEKATE, KRONOS AND RHEA.

WE are now to consider the Titans and their offspring in particular, omitting Iapetos, who will find his appropriate place at the head of mankind. Though Night, ' eldest of things,' does not belong to the Titans, we will commence with an account of her.

Νύξ. (*Nox.* 𝔑𝔦𝔤𝔥𝔱.)

In the Theogony Night is the daughter of Chaos, and sister of Erebos, to whom she bore Day and Æther.[4] She is then said to have produced without a sire Fate (Μόρος) and Kér, Death, Sleep and Dreams, Momos (*Mockery*), Woe, the Hesperides, Nemesis, Deceit, Love (Φιλότης), Old-age, and Strife.[5] Euripidés[6] says that Madness (Λύσση) was the offspring of Night and Heaven.

It is not difficult to discern the reasons for giving this progeny to Night. It is a principle of all cosmogony that darkness preceded light, which sprang from it; a truth here expressed by

[1] *Cassandra*, 1192, with the note of Tzetzés.
[2] *Argonaut.* i. 503 *seq.* It is remarkable that there is no scholion on the passage.
[3] Dionys. ii. 573; viii. 161 ; xii. 44 ; xli. 352.   [4] *Theog.* 123.
[5] *Theog.* 211 *seq.* The verse containing Deceit and Love (*v.* 224) is regarded as an interpolation. Another certain interpolation is *vv.* 217-222, in which the Mœræ and Kéres are classed among the offspring of Night.
[6] *Her. Fur.* 844.

making Night the parent of Day and Æther. Night is also naturally regarded as the parent of Death, Sleep, Dreams, and their kindred ideas. Philotés, or the union of love, is also for a similar reason the child of Night.[1] Deceit, Age, Strife, and Woe are figuratively her offspring, and so perhaps is Mockery, on account of its dark covert nature, as opposed to the openness of truth and candour; and Madness as being an obscuration of the mind, which perhaps is indicated in making her sire the clear lucid Heaven; the Hesperides are children of Night because their abode was near hers in the West. Nemesis is probably a daughter of Night to indicate the secret concealed path which the divine justice often treads to inflict the punishment due to vice.

Hésiod places the cave which was the abode of Night in the West, behind where Atlas supports the heavens.[2] Night and Day, he says, are there by turns; when one goes in the other goes out. Day bears light to mortals; Night, 'wrapt in a sable cloud, carries Sleep in her arms.' It is not quite clear whether the poet places the dwelling of Night on this side of or beyond the Ocean;[3] Stésichoros, as we shall presently see, seems to assign its position to the other side of that stream.

In Homer Sleep says to Héra that, when once at her desire he had cast Zeus into a slumber, the god on waking sought him, and would have flung him from the sky down into the sea, but that he took refuge with Night, 'the subduer of gods and men,' whom Zeus revering remitted his anger.[4] The poet gives here no intimation of any kindred between Night and Sleep. The dwelling of both would seem to be on Olympos.

Alkman[5] and Sophoklés[6] speak of the abode or *springs* of Night in the North, whilst Apollónios[7] appears to place them within the earth.

It was, as we shall see, the custom of the poets (or perhaps such had been previously the popular creed) to bestow chariots and horses on those deities who had a long course to perform. We do not however find a vehicle assigned to Night by Homer or Hésiod; but succeeding poets furnished her with one. Æschylos[8] speaks of her 'dark chariot;' Euripidés[9] describes her as driving through Olympos,—the sky according to the views of his time; Theokritos[10] calls the stars 'the attendants on the car of

---

[1] Ἐν φιλότητι μιγεῖσα and ἐν φιλότητι καὶ εὐνῇ are contant phrases in Homer and Hésiod.   [2] *Theog.* 746 *seq.*
[3] See Völcker, *Hom. Geog.* p. 39.   [4] *Il.* xiv. 249 *seq.*
[5] Fr. 123. Welcker.   [6] *Fr. Incert.* 93.   [7] *Argonaut.* iv. 630.
[8] *Choëph.* 660.   [9] *Fr Androm.* 28.   [10] *Idyll.* ii. 166.

quiet Night;' Apollónios[1] represents Night as yoking her horses at sunset; and Statius[2] makes Sleep her charioteer.   Night was called by the poets,[3] 1. *Black-robed*; 2. *Black-winged.*

As the name of this deity is common to most of the languages which are akin to the Greek,[4] its derivation is not perhaps to be found in any of them.

Ὠκεανὸς καὶ Τηθύς.   *Oceanus et Tethys.*

O'keanos, the first-born of the Titans, espoused his sister Téthys.   Their offspring were the rivers of the earth, and three thousand daughters, named O'keanides, or Ocean-nymphs.[5]   This is all the account of O'keanos and Téthys given in the Theogony; elsewhere[6] Hésiod makes them to be the parents of Helené. Homer speaks of them as the origin of the gods.[7]   When Zeus, he says, placed his sire in Tartaros, Rhea committed her daughter Héra to the charge of O'keanos and Téthys, by whom she was carefully nurtured.[8]   Euripidés[9] terms O'keanos as being a river-god, *bull-headed* (ταυρόκρανος).

The abode of O'keanos was at the end of the earth, probably in the West.[10]   He dwelt, according to Æschylos, in a grotto-palace; beneath his stream, as it would appear.[11]   In the Prométheus Bound of this poet O'keanos comes borne through the air on a griffon, to console and advise the lofty-minded sufferer; and from the account which he gives of his journey it is manifest that he came from the West.   When Héraklés was crossing his stream in the cup of the sun-god to fetch the oxen of Géryones, O'keanos rose, and by agitating his waters tried to terrify him, but on the hero's bending his bow at him he retired.[12]   In the Ilias[13] O'keanos is said to dread the thunder of Zeus.   As in similar cases, it is not always easy to distinguish the god from the stream over which he rules.

The name O'keanos is apparently connected with a family of

---

[1] *Argonaut.* iii. 1193.   [2] *Theb.* ii. 59.

[3] 1. μελάμπεπλος (Eur. *Ion*, 1150).   2. μελανόπτερος (Aristoph. *Av.* 695).

[4] *Nis* Sanscr., *Nox* Lat., *Night* Eng., *Nacht* Germ., *Nátt, Nat, Natt*, Scandinav.

[5] *Theog.* 337 *seq.*   Comparing *v.* 338 *seq.* with *v.* 367 *seq.* we feel inclined to regard the catalogue of the rivers in the former place as a late addition.

[6] Sch. *Pind. Nem.* x. 80 (150).

[7] *Il.* xiv. 201, 302.   In *v.* 246, he is called the origin of all (πάντεσ τ.)— whether gods or things is uncertain.

[8] *Il.* xiv. 202, 303.   [9] *Or.* 1377.

[10] *Il.* xiv. 200, 301.   [11] *Prom.* 300.

[12] Pherekýdés *ap. Athén.* xi. 470.   [13] *Il.* xxi. 195.

words signifying *water*;[1] that of Téthys seems to express the *Rearer*, the *Nurse*, or *Grandmother*;[2] and some understand by it Mother Earth.[3] O'keanos and Téthys might thus answer to Poseidón and Démétér in some mythes of production where rivers are the offspring. But as the chief products of their union are the numerous Ocean-nymphs, denoting in general qualities of the Ocean-stream, Téthys may perhaps be merely the expression of its calm, equable and constant current. It seems in fact to be only another form of Thetis, the name of a Néréis.[4]

Ὑπερίων καὶ Θείη. *Hyperion et Theia.*

Hyperión and Theia are in the Theogony[5] the parents of the Sun, Moon, and Dawn. In Homer Hyperión is equivalent to Hélios.[6] Pindar extols Theia as the bestower of wealth on mortals.[7]

The interpretation given by the ancients of Hyperión as *Overgoer*, seems liable to little objection.[8] Some interpret Theia *Swift*;[9] Müller renders it *Bright*.[10]

Ἥλιος, Ἥλιος. (*Sol.* 𝔖un.)

Hélios was the son of Hyperión by Theia, or according to a Homeridian hymn by Euryphaessa (*Wide-shining*). His office was to give light to men and gods during the day.

In the Odyssey, when Hélios ends his diurnal career, he is said to go under the earth:[11] it is not easy to determine whether the poet meant that he then passed through Tartaros back to the East during the night. At all events neither Homer nor Hésiod evinces

---

[1] See Appendix D.

[2] Akin to τηθή or τιτθή, nurse or grandmother, τιτθή nipple, τιθήνη, nurse, &c. Hermann renders it *Alumnia*.

[3] Schwenck, 102.

[4] From θέω, the endings θυς and τις being merely formative: see p. 15.

[5] *Theog.* 371 seq.

[6] *Il.* xix. 398 (comp. vi. 513). *Od.* i. 24. Ὑπερίων ἠέλιος occurs in *Il.* viii. 480. *Od.* i. 8; xii. 133, 263, 346, 374. It is possible that Ὑπερίων is the contraction of Ὑπεριονίων (see Passow s. v. Völcker, *Hom. Geog.* 26); but it is simpler to take it as an epithet of the Sun made his sire, as another epithet Φαέθων is made his son.

[7] *Isth.* v. 1.

[8] This is adopted by Völcker, *ut sup.*, and Müller, *Proleg.* 375. Hermann renders it *Tollo* (subst.).

[9] From θέω. Völcker, *ut supra*. Hermann makes it *Ambulona*.

[10] *Proleg. ut sup.*, regarding it probably as the same with δῖα: see Appendix C.

[11] *Od.* x. 191: comp. Apoll. Rh. iii. 1191.

any knowledge of the beautiful fiction of the solar cup or basin.[1] The origin of this seems to lie in the simple fact that men. seeing the sun rise in the east and set in the west each day, were naturally led to inquire how his return to the east was effected. If then, as there is reason to suppose, it was the popular belief that a lofty mountainous ring ran round the edge of the earth, it was easy for the poets to feign that on reaching the western stream of Ocean Hélios himself, his chariot and his horses, were received into a magic *cup* or *boat* made by Héphæstos, which, aided by the current, conveyed him during the night round the northern part of the earth, where his light was only enjoyed by the happy Hyperboreans, the lofty Rhipæans concealing it from the rest of mankind.[2]

The *cup* ($\lambda\acute{\epsilon}\beta\eta\varsigma$ or $\delta\acute{\epsilon}\pi\alpha\varsigma$) of the Sun-god appeared first, we are told, in the Titanomachia of Arktínos or Eumélos.[3] Peisander, in his Hérakleia,[4] represented O'keanos giving the hero the Sun-god's cup to pass over to Erytheia; and Stésichoros said in his Géryonéis,[5] that

> Hélios Hyperionidés
> Into the golden cup went down;
> That, through the Ocean having passed,
> He to the depths of dark sacred Night might come,
> Unto his mother and unto his wedded wife,
> And his dear children; but the grove shaded with laurel
> Entered the son of Zeus.

Mimnermos had the following lines in his poem named Nannó:[6]

> Hélios is doomed to labour every day;
>   And rest there never is for him
> Or for his horses, when rose-fingered Éós
> Leaves Ocean and to heaven ascends.

---

[1] The most learned of poets is the only one that has alluded to this fiction in modern times. He evidently had it in view in the following lines:

> . . . The gilded car of day
> His glowing axle doth allay
> In the steep Atlantic stream;
> And the slope sun his upward beam
> Shoots against the *dusky pole*,
> Pacing toward the other goal
> Of his chamber in the east.—*Comus*, 95.

In the Cambridge MS. the reading in *v*. 99 is *northern pole*.

[2] They must also have supposed that the cup continued its course during the day, thus compassing the earth every twenty-four hours.

[3] Athén. xi. 470.   [4] Id. *l. c.*

[5] Id. *l. c.* The grove, Müller (*Dorians*, i. 536) thinks, was in the country of the Hyperboreans.   [6] Id. *l. c.*

For through the waves his loved bed beareth him,
    Hollow and formed of precious gold
By Héphæstos' hand, and winged; the watei's top
    Along, it bears the sleeping god,
From the Hesperides' to the Æthiops' land,
    Where stand his horses and swift car
Until the air-born Éós goes forth :
    Then Hélios mounts another car.

In these lines of Mimnermos, the god, as described above, is carried round the earth during the night; and in the following passage of the same poet [1] his palace is evidently situated in the East.

    Æétés' city, where swift Hélios' beams
        Within his golden chamber lie,
    By Ocean's marge, whither bold Iasón went.

It is also in the East that 'the stables' of Hélios are placed by Euripidés in his Phaethón; [2] while in another passage [3] he speaks of the 'dark stable' of the Sun-god, doubtless meaning the West. In Stésichoros, as we may observe, the abode of Hélios would seem to be in the realm of Night, beyond Ocean. Alexander the Ætolian, [4] when speaking of the plant by means of which Glaukos became a sea-god, says that it grew for Hélios in the Isles of the Blest, and that he gave his horses their evening meal (δόρπον) of it to recruit their vigour. Ovid also, [5] the faithful follower of the Greeks, places the pastures of the solar steeds in the West, where they have ambrosia for grass; and Statius, [6] in a beautiful passage, describes the Sun as losing his steeds on the margin of the western sea, where the Néréides and Seasons take off their harness. In Nonnos, [7] when the god arrives in the West, Phósphoros unyokes the sweating steeds, washes them in the waves of Ocean, and then leads them to their stalls; and when they are rested the god drives them round the Ocean to the East. In two other passages of his wild poem [8] Nonnos places the abode of the Sun in the East. It is remarkable that neither he nor the Latin poets ever allude to the cup. The park and gardens of Hélios are thus richly described by Claudian: [9]

    Thus having said, his gardens all bedewed
    With yellow fires he (*Sol*) enters, and his vale,
    Which a strong-flaming stream surrounding pours
    Abundant beams upon the watered grass,

---

[1] Strab. i. 2, 40, p. 47.   [2] Fr. Phaethón.   [3] *Alcést.* 591.
[4] Athén. *l. c.*   [5] *Met.* iv. 214.   [6] *Theb.* iii. 407 *seq.*
[7] *Dionys.* xii. 1 *seq.*   [8] Ib. xxxii. 51 · xxxviii. 297.
[9] *In Prim. Cons. Stil.* ii. 467

E

On which the Sun's steeds pasture. There he binds
With fragrant wreaths his locks, and the bright manes
And yellow reins of his wing-footed steeds.

He does not, however, tell the site of this brilliant spot; but as
the Sun sets out from it on his diurnal course, when his steeds'
manes have been adorned by Lucifer and Aurora, we may presume
that it was in the East. It is also in the East that Ovid places the
splendid palace of the Sun, where the lucid god sat enthroned,
surrounded by the Days, Months, Years, Seasons, Ages, and Hours.[1]

From a consideration of all these passages it may seem to follow,
that the ideas of the poets on this subject were very vague and
fleeting. Perhaps the prevalent opinion was that the Sun rested
himself and his weary steeds in the West, and then returned to
the East. We are to recollect that the cup was *winged*, that is,
endowed with magic velocity.

Neither Homer nor Hésiod speaks of the chariot of the Sun;
but as the former poet names the horses of E'ós, he must naturally
have supposed Hélios to have driven similar steeds along the sky.
In the Hymns[2] Hélios appears in a chariot; Pindar[3] calls him
‘the ruler of fire-breathing steeds.’ It is probable that, like the
other Homeric gods, Hélios had originally only two horses; but
Euripidés and the succeeding poets[4] give him four, which, according to the Latin poets, are of a dazzling white colour.[5] Their
names are E'ós or E'óos (*Eastern*), Æthón or Æthiops (*Burning*),
Bronté (*Thunder*), Astrapé or Steropé (*Lightning*).[6]

On the Thrinakian island, says Homer,[7] fed the flocks and herds
of Hélios, under the charge of his daughters, the nymphs Phaethusa
and Lampetié (*Shining* and *Gleaming*). These were seven herds
of oxen, and as many flocks of sheep, fifty in each flock and herd.
They neither bred nor died; and probably as the oxen are termed
black, and the sheep *fair* or *bright* (καλὰ), they denote the days and
nights of the year.[8] At Tænaron also this god had a flock of ‘long-
wooled’ sheep;[9] he had also herds of oxen at Gortýna in Kréte,[10]
and sacred sheep at Apollonia in E'peiros.[11]

The Sun was not singular in this circumstance of possessing
sacred cattle, but they were dedicated to him more frequently than

---

[1] *Met.* ii. 1 *seq.*   [2] *Hymn to Démétér*, 88, 89.   [3] *Ol.* vii. 71 (130).
[4] Eur. *Ión*, 82. *Electr.* 866. *Fr. Archelaos*, 2. *Fr. Phaethón*, 1.
[5] Accius, Fr. in Porson's note on Eur. *Phœn.* 1. Ov. *Amor.* ii. 1, 24. Comp.
Propert. ii. 15, 32.
[6] Hygin. 183. Sch. Eur. *Phœn.* 1. For Bronté and Steropé, Ovid (*Met.* ii.
153) gives Pyroeis (*Fiery*), and Phlegón (*Burning*).
[7] *Od.* xii. 127 *seq.*   [8] See Schol. *in loco.*
  Hom. *Hymn to Apoll.*, 233.   [10] Servius, *Verg. Buc.* vi. 60.
[11] Hérod. ix. 93.

t: other deities for obvious reasons, such as his being, as it were, the celestial shepherd or overseer of the stars, which he pens up and lets forth at morn and eve,[1] and being the god who gave increase to the earth.[2]

By Perséis or Persé (*Brightness?*), a daughter of O'keanos, Hélios was father of Æétés, and his sister Kirké the great enchantress,[3] and of Pasiphaé, who espoused Minós the son of Zeus.[4] The nymphs just mentioned, who kept his cattle, were his children by Neæra (*Newness?*).[5] Augeas (*Bright-one*), king of E'lis, so rich in flocks and herds, was said to be the offspring of the Sun-god by Iphiboé[6] (*Strong-cow*). By the nymph Rhodos, the daughter of Aphrodíte, Hélios had the seven Héliades, who were the first inhabitants of the isle of Rhodes.[7] The Charites are also said to have been daughters of Hélios by Æglé (*Splendour*).[8]

The Ocean-nymph Klymené (*Bright?*) bore to Hélios a son named Phaethón (*Gleaming*). The claims of this youth to a celestial origin being disputed by Epaphos the son of Zeus, he journeyed to the palace of his sire, from whom he extracted an unwary oath that he would grant him whatever he asked. The ambitious youth instantly demanded permission to guide the solar chariot for one day, to prove himself thereby the undoubted progeny of the Sun-god. Hélios, aware of the consequences, remonstrated, but to no purpose. The youth persisted, and the god, bound by his oath, reluctantly committed the reins to his hands, warning him of the dangers of the road, and instructing him how to avoid them. Phaethón grasps the reins, the flame-breathing steeds spring

---

[1] Modern poets follow Ovid (*Met.* ii. 114) in assigning this office to the Morning-star:

> They sighing left the land his silver sheep
> Where Hesperus doth lead, doth fold, doth keep (i.e. the sky).
> Fairfax, *Godf. of Bouillon*, ix. 65.

> Phosphor his gold-fleeced droves folds in their bowers,
> Which all the night had grazed about the Olympic towers.
> Ph. Fletcher, *Purp. Island*, ix. 1.

> Surgit odoratis pariter formosus ab Indis
> Ætherium pecus albenti qui cogit Olympo.
> Mane vocans et serus agens in pascua cœli.
> Milton, *Natur. non pati sen.* 45.

> His countenance as the morning star that guides
> The starry flock.—Id. *Par. Lost*, v. 708.

Rossetti, however (*Salterio* II. ix. 1), terms the sun *Il duce degli astri.*

[2] Πλὴν τοῦ τρέφοντος Ἡλίου χθονὸς φύσιν.—Æsch. *Agam.* 633.
[3] *Od.* x. 137. Hés. *Theog.* 956 seq. [4] Apollod. i. 9. 1.
[5] *Od.* xii. 133. [6] Apoll. Rh. i. 172. Apollod. ii. 5, 5. Tzetz. Lyc. 41
[7] Pind. *Ol.* vii. 14 (25) *seq.* [8] Antimachos *ap. Paus.* ix. 35, 38.

forward; but soon aware that they are not directed by the well-known
hand they run out of the course; the world is set on fire, and a
total conflagration would have ensued, had not Zeus, at the prayer
of Earth, launched his thunder, and hurled the terrified driver from
his seat. He fell into the river E'ridanos. His sisters, the Héliades,
as they lamented his fate, were turned into poplar trees [1] on its
banks, and their tears, which still continued to flow, became amber
as they dropped into the stream. Kyknos, the friend of the ill-
fated Phaethón, also abandoned himself to mourning, and at
length was changed into a swan (κύκνος).[2]

The age of this story is uncertain,[3] but it has all the appearance
of being a physical mythe devised to account for the origin of the
electron or amber,[4] which seems to have been brought from the
Baltic to Greece in the very earliest times. In the opinion of
Welcker,[5] it is only the Greek version of a German legend on that
subject; for the tradition of the people of the country was said to
be,[6] that the amber was produced from the tears of the Sun-god,
that is Phœbos-Apolló according to the Greeks who added that he
shed these tears when he came to the land of the Hyperboreans,
an exile from heaven on account of the fate of his son Asklépios.
But as this did not accord with the Hellenic conception of either
Hélios or Apolló, the Héliades were devised to remove the incon-
gruity. The foundation of the fable lay in the circumstance of
amber being regarded as a species of resin which drops from the
trees that yield it. The tale of Kyknos is only one of the numerous
legends devised by the Greeks to account for the origin of remarkable animals. The E'ridanos is said to have been a mere poetic
name, there being no stream actually so called; though it was
afterwards given by the poets to the Rhine, the Rhodanus or
Rhone, and the Padus or Po, on the banks of which last stream
the fable of Phaethón was localised.

[1] Vergil in one place (*Æn.* x. 190) says *poplars*, in agreement with the
current of authorities; in another (*Buc.* vi. 62) he calls them *alders*.

[2] Apoll. Rh. iv. 597 *seq.* Ov. *Met.* i. 750 *seq.;* ii. 1 *seq.* Hygin. 152, 154.
Nonn. xxxviii. 105, 439. Sch. *Od.* xvii. 208. Verg. *Buc.* vi. 62. (Servius
and Voss, *in loc.*) *Æn.* x. 189. Serv. *in loc.* Lucret. v. 397 *seq.* Lucian,
Deor. Dial. 25.

[3] There are still some fragments remaining of the Héliads of Æschylos and
the Phaethón of Euripidés. Ovid appears to have followed closely the former
drama. Hyginus and the Scholiast on Homer (*Od.* xi. 325) give Hésiod as
their authority, but it was probably the Astronomy ascribed to that poet, a
late production, to which they referred.

[4] Ἤλεκτρον, as Welcker observes, resembles ἠλέκτωρ, an epithet of the Sun.
Buttmann (*Ueber das Elektron, Mytholog.* ii. 337 *seq.*) derives ἔλεκτρον from
ἕλκω, *to draw.*

[5] *Tril.* 566 *seq.*   [6] Apoll. Rh. iv. 611 *seq.*

According to another legend, Klytia (*Bright?*), a daughter of O'keanos, was beloved by the Sun-god; but he transferred his affections to Leukothea, daughter of Orchamos (*Ruler*), king of the eastern regions. The god visited her during the night, in the form of her mother. The virgin was obliged to comply with his wishes, and Klytia filled with jealous rage discovered the secret to Orchamos, who buried his hapless daughter alive. The god, unable to save her, turned her into the frankincense plant, and the neglected Klytia pining away became a sunflower.[1]

Here also we have one of the legendary origins of natural productions. The date of the tale is unknown, but it is probably not very ancient; it is only to be found at present in the Latin poet Ovid;[2] but beyond question he took it from a Greek original.

Hélios, as the god whose eye surveyed all things,[3] was invoked as a witness to solemn oaths.[4] Not being one of the Olympian gods, he was not honoured with temples in Greece, but he had altars at Corinth, Argos, and some other places. The chief seat of his worship was the isle of Rhodes, where stood the celebrated Kolóssos, or statue of brass seventy cubits high, in his honour.[5] The legend said[6] that, when Zeus and the other Immortals were dividing the earth among them by lot, the Sun happening to be absent got no share. On his reminding Zeus of this, the god was about to make a new allotment, but Hélios would not suffer him, saying that he had seen a fertile land lying beneath the ' hoary sea,' with which he would be content. The gods then swore that it should be the undisturbed possession of the Sun-god, and the isle of Rhodes emerged from the deep.

Hélios is represented by artists driving his four-horse chariot, his head surrounded with rays, a whip in his hand, and preceded by E'ósphoros. Sometimes he is standing with a flambeau in his hand, and two of his horses near him.

This god was styled,[7] 1. *Mortàl-delighting;* 2. *Mortal-illuming;* 3. *Unwearied,* &c.

The name Hélios ("Ηλιος) is perhaps derived from ἔλα, ἔλη, *brightness.* It seems, however, akin to the names of the Sun, in the languages which are of the same family with the Greek.[8]

---

[1] Ov. *Met.* iv. 190 *seq.*
[2] Lactantius Placidus, in his Arguments of Ovid's Metamorphoses, quotes Hésiod for this story.　　　[3] *Hymn to Démétér,* 62.
[4] *Il.* iii. 277; xix. 259. Comp. Verg. *Æn.* xii. 176.
[5] Plin. *Nat. Hist.* xxxiv. 7.　　　[6] Pind. *Ol.* vii. 54 (100) *seq.*
[7] 1. τερψίμβροτος : 2. ψαεσίμβροτος ; 3. ἀκάμας,
[8] When we recollect that *s* and *h* are commutable (ἐπτὰ, *septem,* ὕλη, *silva*),

Σελήνη. (*Luna.* 𝔐𝔬𝔬𝔫.)

Seléné, the sister of Hélios, drove her chariot through the sky while he was reposing after the toils of the day. There is, however, no allusion in Homer or Hésiod to the chariot of Seléné; but one of the Hymns[1] describes her as bathing in Ocean, putting on gleaming raiment, and then ascending a chariot drawn by glittering steeds. Theokritos[2] also gives Seléné horses; but we do not meet with any other mention of her chariot and horses in the Greek poets. In Ovid[3] her steeds are snow-white; Statius[4] places her in a car drawn by two horses. Pausanias[5] says that one of the figures on the base of the throne of Zeus at Olympia was Seléné driving a single horse, as it appeared to him; but that others said it was a mule, and they had a silly legend respecting it. We find this lunar mule also spoken of elsewhere.[6]

The later poets make steers or heifers the draught-cattle of Seléné.[7] This notion had its very natural origin in the contemplation of the *horned* moon.[8]

In the general and natural mode of representation Seléné is the sister of Hélios, but another view of the subject made her his daughter, he being the source of her light;[9] while a third view

---

as also the semivowels *l, n, r* (Panormus, *Palermo*, &c.), we may perhaps say that *Hélios, Sol* (Latin and Scandinav.), *Sonne, Sun* (Germ. and Eng.), *Surya* (Sanscrit), are akin. This last term is said to signify *divine*.

[1] Hom. *Hymn* xxxii. 7.   [2] *Idyll.* ii. 163.
[3] *Rem. Amor.* 258. *Fast.* iv. 374.
[4] *Theb.* i. 336. See also viii. 271.   [5] Paus. v. 11, 8.
[6] " Mulus vehiculo Lunæ adhibetur quod tam sterilis ea sit quam mulus, vel quod ut mulus non suo genere sed equi creetur, sic ea solis, non suo, fulgore luceat."—Paul. Diac. *v.* Mulus. See Voss, *Myth. Br.* ii. 7, 8. This able critic makes two most extraordinary mistakes on this subject. He says that Euripidés gives Seléné a chariot (*Phœn.* 178 *seq.*), whereas the poet in that place is evidently speaking of the chariot of Amphiaraos. Again, he says, " In Nonnos (vii. 244) she drives in a silver car with unbridled mules." It is the chariot of Semelé, not of Selené, that is described by that poet.
[7] Nonn. i. 331, 455; ii. 405; vii. 247; xi. 186; xii. 5; xlviii. 320. (βοῶν ἐλάτειρα Σελήνη is his usual expression). Claudian, *Rapt. Pros.* iii. 403. *Eidyl.* i. 60. Anthol. Lat. i. 1. 56. See also the epigram in the fragments of Ovid.
[8] Moschos (*Idyll.* ii. 87), when describing the bull into which Zeus changed himself in order to carry off Európa, says,

Ἴσά τ᾽ ἐπ᾽ ἀλλήλοισι κέρα ἀνέτελλε καρήνου
ἄντυγος ἡμιτόμου κεραῆς ἅτε κύκλα σελήνης.

It may be that a similar view was also the origin of the epithet ταυροπόλος given to Artemis at Athens (Eur. *Iph. in Taur.* 1469. Aristoph. *Lys.* 447), and to Athéna (another moon-goddess) according to Xenomédés (Sch. Lys. *l. c.*).
[9] Eur. *Phœn.* 175. Nonn. v. 166 *et alibi.* The Scholiast on Euripidés (*l. c.*) says that " Æschylos and the φυσικώτεροι say she is his daughter, because she

made her by him the mother of the four Seasons.[1] In one of the Homeridian Hymns[2] Seléné is called the daughter of Pallas, son of Megamédés.

It was said that Seléné was enamoured of Endymión, on whom Zeus had bestowed the precious gift of perpetual youth, but united with perpetual sleep; and that she used to descend to him every night on the summit of Mount Latmos, the place of his repose.[3] The god Pan was also said to have gained her love under the form of a snow-white ram.[4] She bore to Zeus a daughter named Pandia;[5] and Ersa (*Dew*) was also the offspring of the king of heaven and the goddess of the moon.[6]

This last is a pleasing fiction of the lyric poet Alkman. The moon was naturally, though incorrectly, regarded as the cause of dew;[7] and nothing therefore was more obvious than to say that the dew was the progeny of the moon and sky personified after the usual manner of the Greeks.

In the Homeridian Hymn to Seléné she is styled:[8] 1. *White-*

---

partakes of the solar light, and changes her form according to the solar positions," or "because she thence, as from a fount, draws light." This, by the way, strongly resembles Milton's

> Hither as to their fountain other stars
> Repairing in their golden urns draw light."—*Par. Lost*, vii. 364.

[1] Quintus Smyrnæus, x. 334 *seq.*   [2] *Hymn* iii. 100.
[3] See below, Part II. chap. x. *Endymión.*
[4] Verg. *Geor.* iii. 391.   Philargyrius (*in loc.*) and Macrobius (v. 22) say that the fable was related by Nikander.
[5] Hom. *Hymn* xxxii. 15.   Πανδία, *all-divine*, or *all-bright*, is plainly the Moon.
[6]   Διὸς θύγατερ ἔρσα τρέφει καὶ Σελάνας δίας
are the words of Alkman, as quoted by Plutarch, *Quæst. Nat.* 24.   *De Fac. in Orb. Lunæ*, 25.   *Sympos.* iii. 10, 3.
[7] "Roscida Luna." Verg. *Geor.* iii. 335.   In the Icaromenippos (13) of the witty Lucian, Empedoklés lives in the moon, where he feeds on *dew;* and in the same writer's True History (i. 20) the Selénites agree to pay the Héliótes an annual tribute of 10,000 urns of *dew.*   The same notion will be found in modern poets.   Thus Tasso,—

> E già spargea rai luminosi e gelo
> Di vive perle la sorgente Luna.— *Ger. Lib.* vi. 103.

Shakspeare (*Midsum. Night's Dream*, ii. 1) speaks of ' Cupid's fiery dart,'

> Quenched in the chaste beams of the watery moon;

and Fletcher (*Faith. Shep.* A. iv.) says,

> . . . . letting fall apace
> From those two little heavens upon the ground
> Showers of more price, more orient and more round
> Than those that hang upon the moon's pale brow.

[8] 1. λευκώλενος ; 2. εὐπλόκαμος.

armed; 2. *Well-tressed,*—two of the usual epithets of the god-desses.

Empedoklés[1] and Euripidés[2] give the Moon an epithet (γλαυκ-ῶπις) usually appropriated to Pallas-Athéné, and of which we shall treat in its due place.

The name Seléné (Σελήνη) is plainly derived from σέλας, *bright-ness,* and is one of the large family of words of which ἔλα or ἔλη (*Helle*, Germ.) may be regarded as the root.

'Hώς. (*Matuta. Aurora.* 𝔇𝔞𝔴𝔫.)

The third of the children of Hyperíon and Theia was E'ós, or the Dawn. Like Seléné she was named by later poets[3] from Pallas, and their reason for so doing is not so easy to be discerned. Æs-chylos would seem to term her the child of Night,[4]—a very obvious and natural genealogy.

In Homer and Hésiod E'ós is simply the goddess of the dawn, but in the works of succeeding poets she is identified with Hémera, or the Day.[5]

Homer who is silent respecting the chariots of Hélios and Seléné, names the steeds which drew that of E'ós. He calls them Lampos (*Shining*) and Phaethón (*Gleaming*).[6] Æschylos[7] and Theokritos[8] name the goddess 'white-horsed,' and Euripidés[9] describes the 'white-winged' Hémera carrying off Tithónos in her golden four-horsed chariot. In another passage of this poet[10] we meet with the 'one-horsed' E'ós, whether riding or driving is not said; but we may assume the latter, as such was the practice of Seléné. Lykophrón[11] gives her the winged horse Pégasos for her steed, and the scholiasts inform us that, when this horse had thrown Bellerophontés down to earth, E'ós asked and obtained him from Zeus.[12]

---

[1] Plut. *De Fac. in Orb. Lunæ,* 16, 21.
[2] *Fr. Incert.* 209 : comp. Nonn. v. 70.
[3] Ov. *Met.* ix. 420 ; xv. 191, 700. *Fast.* iv. 373. The title Pallantias given here to Aurora is, we believe, only to be found in this poet, but he probably had Greek authority for it.   [4] *Agam.* 275.
[5] Æsch. *Pers.* 386. Eur. *Tróad.* 847. Bion, *Idyll.* vi. 18. Quint. Smyrn. i. 119, 827 ; v. 62. Nonn. vii. 286, 294 ; xxv. 567. Musæos, 110. Tryphiodor. 204. Verg. *Æn.* vi. 535. Val. Flac. *Arg.* i. 283.   [6] *Od.* xxiii. 245.
[7] *Ut supra.*   [8] *Idyll.* xiii. 11. Comp. Quint. Smyrn. i. 49.
[9] *Troad.* 843. For χρύσεος Barnes reads κρόκεος, which reading is followed by Voss, *Myth. Br.* ii. 79.
[10] *Orest.* 1001.   [11] *Cass.* 16, 17.
[12] Sch. *Il.* vi. 155. Sch. *Eur. Orest. ut supra.* Tzetz. *Lyc. ut supra.* Eudocia, 89.

E'ós was, by A*iræos, the mother of the winds Boreas, Zephyros and Notos, and of the stars of heaven.[1]

The lovely goddess of the dawn was more than once smitten with the love of mortal men. She carried off O'ríón, and kept him in the isle of Ortygia, till he was slain there by the darts of Artemis.[2] Kleitos (*Bright?*), the son of Mantios, was for his exceeding beauty snatched away by her, 'that he might be among the gods.'[3] She also carried off Kephalos, and had by him a son named Phaëthón,[4] whom Aphrodité in like manner snatched away, and made him the nocturnal guardian of one of her temples. But her strongest affection was for Tithónos, son of Laomedón, king of Troy. When she had carried him off, she besought Zeus to bestow on him immortality. The sovereign of Olympos assented, and Tithónos became exempt from death; but the love-sick goddess, having forgotten to have youth joined in the gift, began with time to discern old-age creeping over the visage and limbs of her beautiful lover. When she saw his hairs blanching, she abstained from his bed, but still kept him and treated him with due attention in her palace on the eastern margin of the Ocean-stream, 'giving him ambrosial food and fair garments.' But when he was no longer able to move his limbs, she deemed it the wisest course to shut him up in his chamber, whence his feeble voice was incessantly heard.[5] Later writers say that out of compassion she turned him into a tree-cricket (τέττιξ, *cicada*).[6] In Homer the goddess is less fastidious, and she is described as rising from the bed of the 'illustrious Tithónos, to bear light to mortals and immortals.'[7] Memnón and Æmathión were the children whom E'ós bore to Tithónos.[8]

In the works of the artists E'ós drives a four-horsed car. Night, the moon, and the stars retire before her. Sometimes she is winged, at other times not.

E'ós was styled by the poets,[9] 1. *Rose-fingered*; 2. *Rose-armed*;

---

[1] Hés. *Theog.* 378.   [2] *Od.* v. 121.   [3] *Od.* xv. 250.
[4] Hés. *Theog.* 986. Eur. *Hip.* 456. See Part II. ch. v. *Ceph.* and *Proc.*
[5] Hom. *Hymn to Aphrodité*, 218 *seq.*
[6] Sch. Il. xi. 1. Tzetz. Lyc. 18.
[7] *Il.* xi. 1. *Od.* v. 1. Propert. ii. 18, 7 : comp. Nonn. xxvii. 3.
[8] Hés. *Theog.* 984. The taking away by the Dawn of O'ríón (the constellation), and of Kephalos (κνέφαλος, *darkness*), is easy of explication. That of Kleitos may signify the union of the dawn with light. The tale of Tithónos has the air of a mere poetic fiction, devised perhaps to give a mythic origin to the *tettix*. There is possibly a connection between Τιθ-ωνὸs and τέτ-τιξ.
[9] 1. ῥοδοδάκτυλος: 2. ῥοδόπηχυς: 3. κροκόπεπλος: 4. χρυσόθρονος: 5. ἐΰθρονος: 6. ἐΰπλόκαμος: 7. χιονοτέζα: 8. καλλιφεγγής: 9. φαεσίμβρο-τος: 10. πολυδερκής: 11. ἠριγένε *.

3. *Yellow-robed;* 4. *Gold-seated;* 5. *Well-seated;* 6. *Well-tressed;*
7. *Snow-footed;* 8. *Fair-lighting;* 9. *Mortal-illuming;* 10. *Much-
seeing;* 11. *Air-born,*[1] &c.

The most probable derivation of the name E'ós ('Ηὼς, Dor. 'Αὼς)
seems to be that from ἄω, *to blow,* regarding it as the cool morning
air, whose gentle breathing precedes the rising of the sun.[2]

Κοῖος καὶ Φοίβη.   Kœos et Phœbe.

The offspring of this pair of Titans were 'sable-vested' Létó,
and ' well-named ' Asteria,'[3] which last espoused Persés, the son of
Krios.   Létó was destined to be the mother of Apolló and Artemis
under the new order of things, which succeeded the time of the
Titans.

The name Phœbé plainly signifies *Lucid,*[4] and a very obvious
etymon will give a similar signification for that of Kœos.[5]   They
may then denote light or day viewed as the precursor or origin of
night or darkness; but only in a sensible and poetic, not cosmogonic, sense.

Κρῖος.   Krios.

This Titan is in the Theogony[6] said to be the sire of Astræos,
Pallas and Persés, by Eurybia (*Wide-force*), a daughter of Pontos
and Earth.[7]   Astræos, as we have just seen, was by E'ós the father
of the Winds and Stars.   Pallas had by Styx the Ocean-nymph,
Envy and Victory, Strength and Force; and Persés married
Asteria the daughter of Kœos and Phœbé, by whom he had a
daughter named Hekaté.

There is some difficulty about these personages, who are hardly
ever mentioned by the poets.   The origin of the name Krios is
not apparent.[8]   Pallas (*Shaker ?*) would seem from the names of

---

[1] See Appendix E.   Hence perhaps it is that E'ós and Astræos are the
parents of the Winds.
[2] Hermann, *Ueber d ıs Wesen,* &c., 98.   The Latin Aurora is similarly
related to *aura.*   [3] Hés. *Theog.* 404.
[4] From φάω, *to shine.* Phœbé, according to Hermann, is *Februa, Purger,* and
Kœos, *Turbulus.*   [5] From καίω, *to burn.*
[6] *Theog.* 375.   [7] Ib. 239.
[8] Hermann renders it *Sejugus,* from κρίνω, *to separate.*   There is usually,
as we may see, an analogy between the names of the Titans and those of their
wives and children.   Hence Κρῖος may be connected with κριὸς, r *m,* and both
be derived from some root signifying *strength* or *power,* or perhaps *pre-eminence,*
and so be connected with κάρα.   Lauer, (*System,* &c. 159) who writes the
name Κρεῖος, renders it *powerfu!,* and understands it of the *sea.*

his offspring to be of a moral. not of a physical nature, unlike the progeny of the three preceding Titans. With Astræos (*Starry*) and Persés (*Bright ?*). and their children, the difficulty is much less, for they are all physical beings.

We cannot avoid here intimating our suspicion that the two moral beings Themis and Mnémosyné[1] were not originally among the Titans. According to all analogy the sage or poet who devised the mythe of the six male and six female Titans must have intended to employ them in pairs in the task of production; and yet we find Krios united with a daughter of Pontos and Earth, one of a class of beings quite alien from the Titans, and Iapetos with an Ocean-nymph; while Themis and Mnémosyné are reserved to be the parents of moral beings by Zeus in the new order of things. This is surely not the order one might have anticipated. It is now, we apprehend, hardly possible to rectify the error, if it should be such.

Ἑκάτη. Hekate.

In the Theogony[2] this goddess is the daughter of Persés and Asteria. Bakchylidés made her a daughter of Night, and Musæos gave her Zeus for a sire in place of Persés,[3] while others said that she was the offspring of the Olympian king by Pheræa, the daughter of Æolos,[4] or by Démétér.[5] According to Pherekýdés her sire was Aristæos.[6]

It is said in the Theogony[7] that Hekaté was highly honoured by Zeus, who allowed her to exercise extensive power over land and sea, and to share in all the honours enjoyed by the children of Heaven and Earth. She rewards sacrifice and prayer to her with prosperity. She presides over the deliberations of the popular assembly, over war, and the administration of justice. She gives success in wrestling and horse-racing. The fisherman prays to her and Poseidón; the herdsman, to her and Hermés,—for she can increase and diminish at her will. Though an only child (in contrast to Apolló and Artemis, who have similar power) she is honoured with all power among the immortals, and is by the

---

[1] Hermann. however, makes them both natural beings, rendering Themis, *Statina*, and Mnémosyné, *Moneta*, or *Mover*.

[2] *Theog.* 411.　　　　　　　　[3] Sch. *Apoll. Rh.* iii. 467.

[4] Tzetz. *Lyc.* 1180. Hecaté was worshipped at Pheræ in Thessaly, hence this genealogy.

[5] Sch. *Theocr.* ii. 12, as being the same with Persephoné.

[6] Sch. *Apoll. Rh. l. c.* Perhaps Zeus-Aristæos, which also would identify her with Persephoné.

[7] *Theog.* 411 *seq.*

appointment of Zeus the rearer of children, whom she has brought to see the light of day.

This passage is, however, plainly an interpolation in the Theogony, with which it is not in harmony. It has all the appearance of being an Orphic composition, and is perhaps the work of the notorious forger Onomakritos.[1]

The name Hekaté is the feminine of Hekatos, one of the epithets of Apolló,[2] and is itself an epithet of his sister Artemis.[3] It was, as we have seen,[4] a common practice with the Greeks to form from the epithets of a deity other similar deities, or even hostile and rival beings, sometimes nymphs, or other companions of the original deity. In this manner, supposing Artemis to have been an original moon-goddess, her epithet of *Far-shooter* (ἐκάτη) may have separated from her, and have become another moon-goddess, for such is the real character of Hekaté; or Hekaté may have been the primitive name of the moon-goddess with one of the tribes of Greece.

The system of *Theocrasy* which we have already mentioned frequently confounded deities who were originally distinct, but it sometimes only re-united those which were really the same, but which had been separated in the progress of time. In Hekaté we seem to have instances of both processes; she was identified with Seléné, Artemis, and Eileithyia, all probably moon-goddesses, and with Persephoné, of whom the original conception was totally different.

In consequence of this confusion Hekaté became the patroness of magic and mistress of the under-world.[5] She was invoked as the triple goddess,[6] and believed to wander by night along the earth, seen only by the dogs, whose baying announced her approach. She was regarded as beneficent, and as the averter of evil, and was honoured with altars and temples.[7] Her statues, which were dog-headed,[8] were set up at Athens and elsewhere in the market-places and at cross-roads; and at the time of new moon the wealthy persons used to send suppers to be placed before her, which the

---

[1] See Göttling *in loc.* Thiersch, *Ueber Hésiodos*, p. 24.

[2] Ἕκατος, *Far-shooter* (from ἑκάς). *Il.* vii. 83; xx. 295.

[3] Ἄρτεμιν δ' ἑκάταν, Æschyl. *Sup.* 690.

[4] See above, p. 18.

[5] Apoll. Rh. iii. 862. Ov. *Met.* vii. 194 *seq.*

[6] Verg. *Æn.* iv. 511. Servius, *in loc.* The fish called τρίγλη was offered to her, διὰ τὴν τῆς ὀνομασίας κοινότητα; she was τριοδῖτης and τρίγληνος; and her suppers were on the thirtieth of the month (ταῖς τριάκασι). Athén. vii. 325.

[7] Sch. *Aristoph. Wasps*, 804. Cic. *De Nat. Deor.* iii. 18.

[8] Aristoph. *ap. Eustath.* p. 1467. 1. 35. (*Fr. Incert.* 133.) Euripidés *ap. Plut. de Is. et Os.* 71.

poor would then come and eat, saying that Hekaté had eaten them.[1]
The reason of this offering is said to have been that she might
prevent the souls of the dead from appearing.[2]

A name of this goddess was Brimó.[3] This seems to have been
chiefly employed to denote her terrific appearance, especially
when she came summoned by magic arts. Apollónios[4] describes
her as having her head surrounded by serpents twining through
branches of oak, while torches flamed in her hands, and the infernal dogs howled around her. Lucian's 'liar of the first magnitude,' Eukratés,[5] gives a most terrific description of her appearance. In this character she was also sometimes called Empusa.[6]
These were evidently all comparatively late ideas and fictions.

Κρόνος καὶ 'Ρείη ἢ 'Ρέα. (Saturnus et Ops.)

We are now arrived at the immediate origin of the Olympians,
the gods worshipped throughout all Greece.

The mutilation of Uranos by his youngest son Kronos, and
the overthrow of the latter by Zeus and his other children, the
Kronids, have been already narrated. According to the Theogony,[7] all the Titans (O'keanos, it would appear, excepted) were
on this occasion shut up in Tartaros. Homer only names Kronos
and Iapetos,[8] but he evidently included the others in his view of
the subject.[9] At a later period it was said that Zeus had released
the Titans.[10] Hésiod in his didactic poem says that Kronos ruled
over the Isles of the Blest at the end of the earth by the 'deep-
eddying' ocean;[11] and Pindar[12] gives a luxuriant description of
this blissful abode, where the departed heroes of Greece dwelt
beneath the mild rule of Kronos and his assessor Rhadamanthys.
In the Prométheus Loosed of Æschylos[13] the chorus consisted
the twelve Titans, and they came as it would appear from the
eastern part of the Ocean-stream.

It was fabled at a late period that Kronos lay asleep, guarded
by Briareós, in a desert island near Britannia in the Western
Ocean.[14]

---

[1] Sch. *Aristoph. Plut.* 594. Eudocia, 144.
[2] See Voss, *Myth. Br.* iii. 190 *seq.*   [3] *Roarer*, from βρέμω, to roar.
[4] *Argonaut.* iii. 1214 *seq.*   [5] *Philopseud.* 22–24.   [6] Eudocia, 147.
[7] *Theog.* 716 *seq.*   [8] *Il.* viii. 479.   [9] *Il.* xiv. 274 ; xv. 225.
[10] Pind. *Pyth.* iv. 291 (518).
[11] Ἔργ. 167 *seq.* This probably originated in the notion of the golden age
among men having been during the reign of Kronos: see p. 43.
[12] *Ol.* ii. 68 (123) *seq.*   [13] Æschyl. *Fr.* 178. Welcker, *Tril.* 35 *seq.*
[14] Plut. *de Defect. Orac.* 18. *De Fac. in Orb. Lunæ*, 26. Procopius, *Bell.
Goth.* iv. 20. "On the coast of the ocean opposite Britannia," says Tzetzés
(*Lyc.* 1204), "dwell fishermen who are subjects of the Franks, but they pay

The Golden Age, so celebrated by poets, is said to have been in the reign of Kronos, when, according to Hésiod,[1]

> Men lived like gods, with minds devoid of care,
> Away from toils and misery: then was not
> Timid old-age, but aye in feet and hands
> Equally strong the banquet they enjoyed,
> From every ill remote. They died as if
> O'ercome with sleep, and all good things were theirs.
> The bounteous earth did of herself bring forth
> Fruit much and plenteous, and in quietness
> Their works midst numerous blessings they pursued.

According to a fragment of the poetic philosopher Empedoklés, Kronos married the 'blooming' Euonymé, who bore to him 'beautiful-haired golden' Aphrodíté, the 'deathless' Fates, and the 'variety-bestowing' Erinnyes.[2]

The only adventure recorded of this god is his amour with the Ocean-nymph Philyra, whom, dreading the jealousy of his wife Rhea, he turned into a mare, and himself into a horse. The produce of their love was the Kentaur Cheirón, half-man half-horse. Vergil,[3] in describing a horse of perfect strength and beauty, says,

> Such, at the coming of his wife, the swift
> Saturnus' self upon his equine crest
> Poured out a mane, and lofty Pelion filled
> With his shrill neighings as away he fled.

---

them no tribute, on account, as they say, of their ferrying over the souls of the departed. They go to sleep in their houses in the evening, but after a little time they hear a knocking at the doors, and a voice calling them to their work. They get up and go to the shore, not knowing what the need is; they see boats there, but not their own, with no one in them; they get in, row away, and perceive that they are heavy as if laden with passengers, but they see no one. In one pull (ῥοπῇ) they reach the isle of Britannia, which with their own boats they can hardly reach in a day and a night. They still see no one. but they hear the voices of those that receive their passengers, and name their fathers and mothers and themselves, and their ranks and occupations. They then return with their boats much lighter, and in one pull they reach their homes." There is a curious legend somewhat similar to thi, in the *Fairy Mythology* (i. 202, p. 127, new edit.), the scene of which is in nearly the same spot.

[1] Ἔργ. 112 *seq.* Göttling rejects *v.* 111,

Οἱ μὲν ἐπὶ Κρόνου ἦσαν ὅτ᾽ οὐρανῷ ἐμβασίλευεν,

as not Hésiodic. It may be noticed here that the Quetzalcoatl of the Mexicans had some points of resemblance, accidental of course, with Kr nos and Saturnus.

[2]
Γήματο δ᾽ Εὐονύμην θαλερὸν Κρόνος ἀγκυλομήτης,
ἐκ τοῦ καλλίκομος γένετο χρυσῆ Ἀφροδίτη,
Μοῖραί τ᾽ ἀθάνατοι καὶ Ἐριννύες αἰολόδωροι.—Tzetz. *Lyc.* 406.

There does not appear the slightest allusion to this strange genealogy anywhere else. We should perhap, read Eurynomé for Euonymé, and then Kronos might take the place of Ophíon.   [3] *Geor.* iii. 193.

This legend, it is said, first appeared in the poem of the Gigantomachia;[1] it is also noticed by Pindar[2] and by Apollónios.[3] Probably the praise of Cheirón by Homer[4] for his love of justice, led to the making him the offspring of the god who ruled over the golden race of men; and if, as it would appear, he taught his heroic pupils music as well as other accomplishments, a more suitable mother could not be assigned him than the nymph Lyreloving.[5]

It is highly probable that the whole history of this god was originally merely a philosophic mythe. Kronos would evidently appear to signify *time* :[6] he is the son of Heaven, by the motion of whose luminaries time is measured; he is married to Rhea (ῥέα, *flowingly*), and time flows; he devours his own children, and time destroys what it has brought into existence.[7]

Perhaps, as has been ingeniously conjectured,[8] Zeus, the god of the heaven, was poetically named Kroníon, that is the Son of Time, and this led to the giving a separate and distinct existence to this deity.

Kronos was in after times confounded with the grim deity Moloch, to whom the Tyrians and Carthaginians offered their children in sacrifice. The slight analogy of this practice with the legend of Kronos devouring his children, may have sufficed for the Greeks to infer an identity of their ancient deity with the object of Phœnician worship. It was not improbably the circumstance of both gods being armed with a sickle, which led to the inference of Kronos being the same with the Saturnus of the Latins.[9] The fabled flight of this last from Olympos to Hesperia, and his there establishing the golden age, may have been indebted for its origin to the legend of the reign of Kronos over the Islands of the Blest in the western stream of Ocean.

There do not appear to have been any temples of Kronos in

---

[1] Sch. *Ap. Rh.* iii. 554.   [2] *Pyth.* iii. 1 *seq.*   [3] *Arg.* ii. 1232.
[4] *Il.* xi. 832.

[5] Φιλύρα, *quasi* φιλίλυρα. Welcker, *Nachtrag zur Tril.* 53, note.

[6] There is scarcely any difference between Κρόνος and χρόνος. " Χρόνος ὁ πάντων πατήρ." Pind. *Ol.* ii. 17 (32). Hermann renders Kronos *Perficus* from κραίνω.

[7] In like manner Sanis the Hindú god of time is represented as devouring his children.

[8] Welcker, *Tril.* 96. We cannot, however, agree with this critic that Rhea is equivalent to Gæa, *Earth*. Further, if our theory of terminations (see p. 15) be correct, Kroníon is rather *maker of time*. Lauer too (*System*, &c.) regards Kronos and Rhea as forms of Heaven and Earth.

[9] See below, Mythology of Italy, *Saturnus;* and Buttmann, *Ueber den Kronos oder Saturnus, Mytholog.* i. 28 *seq.*

Greece;[1] but the Athenians had a festival in his honour named the Kronia, which was celebrated on the twelfth day of the month Hecatombæón, i.e. in the end of July,[2] and which, as described to us, strongly resembles the Italian Saturnalia.[3]

The only epithet given to Kronos by the elder poets is *Crooked-counselled*.[4] This probably refers to his art in mutilating his sire.

CHAPTER V.

THE HOMERIC GODS IN GENERAL.

FAMILIARITY, it is known but too well, is productive of indifference, and the greatest charms of nature and art lose most of their attractions in the eyes of those who are long and intimately acquainted with them. This is particularly the case with the beautiful mythology of Greece: we are in general familiar with its legends from an early age, but we view them detached and unconnected, ignorant of their real meaning, and of their place and importance in the system (though a loose one) to which they belong; and they therefore rarely produce their full effect on our minds. But did the Grecian mythology not enter into our literature, and were we to remain unacquainted with it till we should open the volumes of Homer, and peruse works like the present,

---

[1] There was a chapel of Kronos and Rhea at Athens (Paus. i. 18, 7), and sacrifices were made to him on the Kronian hill at Olympia (Id. vi. 20. 1): see also Ceb. *Tab. init.*   [2] Demosth. *Timocr.* 708.

[3] Philochorus (*ap. Macrob.* i. 10) says: "Saturno et Opi primum in Attica statuisse aram Cecropem......instituisseque ut patres familiarum et frugibus et fructibus jam coactis passim cum servis vescerentur...delectari enim deum honore servorum contemplatu laboris." Macrobius also (i. 7) gives the following lines from the Annals of the old poet Accius :—

> Maxima pars Graium Saturno et maxime Athenæ
> Conficiunt sacra quæ Cronia esse iterantur ab illis:
> Cumque diem celebrant, per agros urbesque per omnes
> Exercent epulas læti, famulosque procurant
> Quisque suos. Nostrisque itidem est mos traditus illinc
> Iste, ut cum dominis famuli epulentur ibidem.
>
>   Comp. Athen. xiv. 44, 45.

It seems, however, hardly credible that so remarkable a festival should be unnoticed by all the extant Greek writers; and we cannot help thinking that the Greeks of the later times attempted to pass off their Kronia as the origin of the Saturnalia. Surely the vintage was not over in July. When Athénæos (xiv. 639) is enumerating the various festivals which resembled the Saturnalia he makes no mention of the Attic Kronia.

[4] Ἀγκυλομήτης. Nonnos (xxiv. 234) calls him *Broad-bearded* (εὐρυγένειος)

what a new world would burst on our sight,—how splendid would Olympos and its dwellers then arise to view! To present the gods in their Olympian abode, and exhibit a sketch of their life and occupations, are the objects of the present chapter.[1]

As has been already stated, the Greeks of the early ages regarded the lofty Thessalian mountain named Olympos as the dwelling of their gods. In the Odyssey, where the deities are of a character far more dignified and elevated than in the Ilias, the place of their abode shares in their exaltation; and it may almost be doubted if the poet who drew the following picture of Olympos could have conceived it to be no more than the summit of a terrestrial mountain.

> Olympos, where they say the ever-firm
> Seat of the gods is, by the winds unshaken,
> Nor ever wet with rain, nor ever showered
> With snow, but cloudless æther o'er it spreads,
> And glittering light encircles it around,
> On which the happy gods aye dwell in bliss.[2]

We have observed above, that man loves to bestow his own form upon his gods, as being the noblest that he can conceive. Those of Homer are therefore all of the human form, but of far larger dimensions than men;[3] great size being an object of admiration both in men and women in those early and martial ages. Thus when the goddess Athéna[4] ascends as driver the chariot of Diomédés,

> Loud groan'd the beechen axle with the weight,
> For a great god and valiant chief it bore;

when in the battle of the gods[5] Arés is struck to the earth by this goddess, he is described as covering seven plethra of ground; the helmet of the goddess herself would, we are told,[6] cover the footmen of a hundred towns; when Héra is about to make an oath she lays one hand on the earth, the other on the sea;[7] the voices of Poseidón and Arés are as loud as the shout of nine or ten thousand men.[8]

The gods can however increase or diminish their size, assume the form of particular men,[9] or of any animals,[10] and make them-

---

[1] Compare Grimm, *Deutsche Mythologie*, chap. xiv., and Bohlen, *Das alte Indien*, i. 182 *seq.* for the analogous ideas of the Scandinavians and Hindús.

[2] *Od.* vi. 42 *seq.* : comp. Lucret. iii. 18 *seq.*

[3] See *Il.* xviii. 519. Even in the historic days the gods were in the popular idea of larger size than men: see Héród. i. 60.

[4] *Il.* v. 837 : see Hom. Hymn iv. 276.

[5] *Il.* xxi. 407.

[6] *Il.* v. 744. Heyne, *in loc.*

[7] *Il.* xiv. 272.

[8] *Il.* v. 860; xiv. 148.

[9] *Il.* iv. 86; xiii. 45, 216. *Od.* i. 105; ii. 268.

[10] *Il.* vii. 58; xiv. 290. *Od.* iii. 371; xxii. 240: comp. Milt. *Par. Lost,* iv. 196. Heyne, however (on *Il.* vii. 58), denies these changes.

F

selves visible and invisible at their pleasure.[1] Their bodies are also of a finer nature than those of men. It is not blood, but a blood-like fluid named *ichór*, which flows in their veins.[2] They are susceptible of injury by mortal weapons: the arrows of Héraklés violate the divine bodies of Héra and Hadés;[3] Diomédés wounds both Aphrodíté and Arés.[4] They require nourishment as men do; their food is called Ambrosia, their drink Nectar.[5] Their mode of life exactly resembles that of the princes and nobles of the heroic ages. In the palace of Zeus on Olympos they feast at the approach of evening, and converse of the affairs of heaven and earth; the nectar is handed round by Hébé (*Youth*), Apolló delights them with the tones of his lyre, and the Muses in responsive strains pour forth their melodious voices in song; when the sun descends, each god retires to repose in his own dwelling.[6] They frequently partake of the hospitality of men,[7] travel with them,[8] and share in their wars and battles.[9]

With the form, the Homeric gods also partake of the passions of men. They are capricious, jealous, revengeful, will support their favourites through right and wrong, and are implacable toward their enemies, or even those who have slighted them.[10] Their power was held to extend very far; men regarded them as the authors of both good and evil; all human ability and success was ascribed to them. They were believed to have power over the thoughts of men, and could imperceptibly suggest such as they pleased.[11] They required of men to honour them with prayer, and the sacrifice of oxen, sheep, goats, lambs and kids, and oblations of wine and corn, and fragrant herbs.[12] When offended, they usually remitted their wrath if thus appeased.[13]

The Homeric gods have all different ranks and offices; Olympos being, in fact, regulated on the model of a Grecian city of the heroic ages. Zeus was king of the region of the air and clouds which had fallen to him by lot on the dethronement of his father Kronos; the sea was the realm of his brother Poseidón; the under-world fell to Aïdés, in the division of their conquests; Earth and

---

[1] *Il.* i. 198.   [2] *Il.* v. 340, 416.
[3] *Il.* v. 392, 395.   [4] *Il.* v. 335, 855.
[5] A passage in the Odyssey (xii. 63) would seem to say that the ambrosia was brought each day by pigeons to Olympos from the shores of Ocean in the blissful West : see Appendix F. It would also appear that the partaking of this food conferred immortality : see Part II. ch. x. *Tantalos.*
[6] *Il.* i. 601 *seq.*
[7] *Il.* i. 423. *Od.* i. 26, 125 *seq.*; vii. 201 *seq.* (Nitzsch *in loc.*)
[8] *Od.* ii. 399 *seq.*   [9] *Il.* v. 592 *seq.*; xiii. 43 *seq.*   [10] *Il.* ix. 558.
[11] *Il.* i. 55; viii. 218; xiii. 794; xvii. 469.
[12] *Il.* iv. 49; xxiv. 70.   [13] *Il.* ix. 497.

Olympos were common property.[1] Zeus, however, as eldest brother,[2] exercised a supremacy, and his power was the greatest. The other inhabitants of Olympos were Héra the sister and spouse of Zeus, Apolló the god of music and archery, his sister Artemis the goddess of the chase, and their mother Létó, Aphrodíté goddess of love, and her mother Dióné, Arés god of war, Pallas-Athéné goddess of prudence and skill, Themis goddess of justice, Hermeias god of gain, Hébé the attendant of the Olympian king and queen, and Iris their messenger, Héphæstos the celestial artist and Pæéón the physician, and the Muses, the Graces, and the Seasons. Poseidón was frequently there; but Démétér the goddess of agriculture, and Dionýsos the god of wine, do not appear among the residents of Olympos. The Nymphs and the River-gods occasionally visited or were summoned to it.[3] E'ós, Hélios, and Seléné rose every day out of the Ocean-stream, and drove in their chariots through the air, shedding their cheering beams abroad.

Of the residents of Olympos, its king and his son Héphæstos[4] alone knew the pleasures or the pains of the wedded state. Arés and Hermeias intrigued occasionally with mortal women, but the character of Phœbos-Apolló was of unstained purity.[5] Of the goddesses, Aphrodíté alone could be charged with breach of chastity;[6] Artemis, Pallas-Athéné, Hébé, and Iris, were all spotless virgins.

All the dwellings of the gods upon Olympos were of brass or copper (χαλκός), the metal which was in the greatest abundance in Greece. Héphæstos was architect and smith; he formed all the arms, household furniture, chariots, and other articles in use among the Celestials; but their dress, especially that of the goddesses, appears to have been the workmanship of Pallas-Athéné or the Graces.[7] The gold which proceeded from the workshop of Héphæstos was filled with automatic power; his statues were endowed with intelligence;[8] his tripods could move of themselves; he made the golden shoes, or rather soles (πέδιλα)[9] with which the

---

[1] Il. xv. 193.
[2] Il. xx. 7.
[3] Il. xiii. 355; xv. 164 seq.
[4] Il. xviii. 382. Od. viii. 266 seq.
[5] We shall give in the sequel some reasons for regarding Il. ix. 559–564, as an interpolation.
[6] Od. viii. ut supra. Il. v. 247, 248
[7] Il. v. 735; xiv. 178.
[8] Il. xviii. 417.
[9] . . . . . Ὑπὸ ποσσὶν ἐδήσατο καλὰ πέδιλα
ἀμβρόσια, χρύσεια, τά μιν φέρον ἠμὲν ἐφ' ὑγρὴν,
ἠδ' ἐπ' ἀπείρονα γαῖαν ἅμα πνοιῇς ἀνέμοιο.
Il. xxiv. 340. Od. i. 96; v. 44.

It is upon these verses that Voss founds his favourite theory (of which the idea appears to have been given by Eustathius) of these soles having a magic power, and of the gods being transported by them. But all that seems to be meant by the poet is that the gods, like men, put on their shoes when about to go any-

F 2

gods trod the air and the waters, or strode, with the speed of winds or even of thought,[1] from mountain to mountain upon the earth, which trembled beneath their weight.[2] The chariots of the gods and their appurtenances were formed of various metals. That of Héra, for example, is thus described:[3]

> Then Hébé quickly to the chariot put
> The round wheels, eight-spoked, brazen, on the strong
> Axle of iron. Gold their fellies were,
> And undecaying, but thereon of brass
> The tires[4] well fitting, wondrous to behold.
> Of silver was the rounded nave of each;
> The body was hung by gold and silver cords,
> And two curved sides encompass'd it about.
> The pole was silver, and upon its end
> She tied the beauteous golden yoke, and bound
> On it the golden braces fair: the steeds
> Swift-footed then beneath the yoke were led
> By Héra, eager for the war and strife.

These chariots were drawn by horses of celestial breed,[5] which could whirl them to and fro between heaven and earth through the yielding air, or skim with them along the surface of the sea without wetting the axle. They were only used on occasions of taking a long journey, as when Héra[6] professes that she is going to the end of the earth to make up the quarrel between O'keanos and Téthys; or on occasions in which the gods wished to appear with state and magnificence.[7] On ordinary occasions the gods moved by the aid of their golden shoes: when at home in their houses, they, like the men of those ages, went barefoot.

The Titans, as we have seen, were twelve in number, six of each sex. In like manner we find twelve Olympians, similarly divided. The gods were Zeus, Poseidón, Héphæstos, Hermés, Apolló, Arés;

---

where on foot. Another notion of his, that the horses of the gods were shod by Héphæstos, is certainly erroneous, for the Greeks did not shoe their horses.

[1] *Il.* xv. 80.   [2] *Il.* xiii. 18.   [3] *Il.* v. 722 *seq.*

[4] The old, now provincial, term *streaks* (German *Striche*), signifying the separate pieces of iron which were nailed round the wheels of vehicles, seems exactly to correspond to the Greek ἐπίσσωτρα. We can hardly suppose the smiths of Homer's days to have understood the mode of shoeing in a hoop.

[5] The earliest instances to be found of any other species of animal drawing the chariot of the gods are in Sapphó's Hymn to Aphrodíté, where she describes the chariot of that goddess as drawn by sparrows; and in that of Alkæos to Apolló (below, ch. viii.), where the god has a team of swans.

[6] *Il.* xiv. 300.

[7] *Il.* viii. 41 *seq.*; xiii. 23 *seq.* It is worthy of notice that while the chariots of men had sometimes three horses (*Il.* viii. 80 *seq.*; xvi. 148 *seq.*), or perhaps even four (viii. 185), those of the gods had never more than two *Il.* v. 768; viii. 41 *seq.*; xiii. 23. *Od.* xxiii. 245.

the goddesses were Héra, Démétér, Hestia, Athéna, Aphrodíté, and Artemis.[1] This arrangement could hardly have been known to Homer, who never mentions Hestia, and but incidentally Démétér. The earliest writer by whom we find the twelve gods noticed is Hellaníkos, who says [2] that Deukalión built altars to them after the flood. It was perhaps the number of the months of the year that caused twelve to be fixed on as that of the Titans and the Olympians; [3] or it may have been because twelve was the political number of the Ionian race, for it seems probable that it was only among them, particularly at Athens,[4] that altars were erected to these twelve gods. At Olympia there were six altars to six pairs of deities, but they were not exactly the same with those above enumerated.[5] In later times it became a common practice to raise altars to the twelve gods.[6]

CHAPTER VI.

THE KRONIDS:—ZEUS, POSEIDÓN, HADÉS, HESTIA.

THE Kronids, or children of Kronos and Rhea, were Zeus, Poseidón, Hadés, Hestia, Héra, and Démétér. The first four we shall place here: the last two, as wives of Zeus, will find their more appropriate situation along with their children.

Ζεύς. (Jovis, Jupiter.)

Zeus is in the Ilias the eldest son of Kronos and Rhea. He and his brothers, Poseidón and Hades, divided the world by lot among them, and the portion which fell to him was the ' extensive heaven in air and clouds.'[7] All the aërial phænomena, such as thunder and lightning, wind, clouds, snow, and rainbows, are therefore ascribed to him; [8] and he sends them either as signs [9] and warnings, or to punish the transgressions of man, especially the perversions of law and justice, of which he is the fountain.[10] Zeus is called the ' father of men and gods' : [11] his power over both is

---

[1] Sch. *Apoll. Rh.* ii. 532.   [2] Id. iii. 1085. Eudocia, 108.
[3] Comp. Welcker, *Tril.* 180. Böttiger, *Kunst-Myth.* ii. 52.
[4] Hérod. ii. 7; vi. 108. Thuc. vi. 54. Plato, *Laws*, v. 745.
[5] They were Zeus and Poseidón, Héra and Athéna, Hermés and Apolló, the Graces and Dionýsos, Artemis and Alpheios, Kronos and Rhea. Hérodóros, *ap. Sch. Pind. Ol.* v. 5 (10).
[6] See Polyb. iv. 39. Diodór. xvi. 92 ; xvii. 95.   [7] *Il.* xv. 187 *seq.*
[8] *Il.* v. 522 ; vii. 479; x. 5 *seq.*; xii. 252, 278 *seq.*; xiii. 242, 796; xvii. 547; xix. 357.   [9] *Il.* iv. 75; xi. 53; xiii. 244; xvii. 548.
[10] *Il.* i. 238, 239.   [11] Πατὴρ ἀνδρῶν τε θεῶν τε.

represented as supreme,[1] and his will is fate. Earthly monarchs obtain their authority from him;[2] they are but his vicegerents, and are distinguished by epithets derived from his name.[3] In his palace on Olympos Zeus lives after the fashion of a Grecian prince in the midst of his family; altercations and quarrels occur between him and his queen, Héra;[4] and, though in general kind and affectionate to his children, he occasionally menaces or treats them with rigour.[5]

In the Odyssey the character of this god is, agreeably to the more moral tone of that poem, of a higher and more dignified order. No indecent altercations occur; both gods and men submit to his power without a murmur, yet he is anxious to show the equity of his decrees and to 'justify his ways.'[6]

The Theogony, as we have seen, represents Zeus as the last-born child of Kronos and Rhea, and according to it the supreme power was freely conferred on him by his brother, and he thus became the acknowledged head of the Olympian gods, the objects of Grecian worship.

Though Homer names the parents of nearly all the gods who appear in his poems, and it follows thence that they must have been born in some definite places, he never indicates any spot of earth as the natal place of any of his deities.[7] A very ancient tradition, however, (for it occurs in Hésiod) made the isle of Kréte the scene of the birth of the monarch of Olympos. According to this tradition, Rhea, when about to be delivered of Zeus, retired to a cavern near Lyktos or Knóssos in Kréte. She there brought forth her babe, whom the Melian nymphs received in their arms; Adrasteia rocked him in a golden cradle, he was fed with honey and the milk of the goat Amaltheia, while the Kurétes[8] danced about him clashing their arms to prevent his cries from reaching the ears of Kronos.[9] According to another account, the infant deity was fed on ambrosia brought by pigeons

---

[1] *Il.* ii. 116; iv. 55; v. 877; viii. 5 *seq.*, 210; ix. 25; xii. 242; xiii. 355.
[2] *Il.* ii. 197, 205.
[3] *Zeus-sprung* (Διογενής), *Zeus-reared* (Διοτρεφής), *Zeus-loved* (Διόφιλος).
[4] *Il.* i. 540 *seq.*   [5] *Il.* v. 888 *seq.*   [6] *Od.* i. 32 *seq.*
[7] The notion of Voss that the gods were all born in the Island of the Blest at the Fount of Ocean, appears to us to be quite unsupported by evidence. He founds it on *Il.* xiv. 201.
[8] These beings, which have been confounded with the Corybantes and others, and made the subjects of much mystery, seem to be nothing but the Krétan young men (κοῦροι), who used to dance the Pyrriché, or war-dance, thrown back to the mythic times, and associated with the deity in whose honour they performed their dance: see Lobeck, *Aglaoph.* 1111 *seq.*
[9] Kallimachos, *Hymn to Zeus.*

from the streams of Ocean, and on nectar which an eagle drew each day with his beak from a rock.[1] This legend was gradually pragmatised; Zeus became a mortal king of Kréte, and not merely the cave in which he was reared, but the tomb which contained his remains, was shown by the 'lying Kretans.'[2]

The Arcadians, on the other hand, asserted that Zeus first saw the light among their mountains. Rhea, they said, came to Mount Parrhasion, amongst whose thickets she brought forth her divine son. She sought for water to wash the new-born babe, but in vain, for Arcadia was then a land unwatered by streams; the Ladón, the Alpheios, and their kindred floods not having yet appeared. "Dear Earth! do thou too bring forth," said the goddess, and smiting the mountain with her staff she caused to gush from it a copious flow of water, which she named the Neda, from one of the nymphs who assisted at her labour, and who then conveyed the babe to Knóssos in Kréte.[3] The more general tradition, however, was that the nymph Neda and her sisters, Theisoa and Hagnó, reared the infant deity in a cavern of Mount Lykæon, where there was a place named Krétea, as other spots in Arcadia were designated by names belonging to places in Kréte.[4]

All, therefore, that we can collect with safety from these accounts is that the worship of the Diktæan Zeus in Kréte, and of the Lykæan Zeus in Arcadia, was of the most remote antiquity, and that thence, when the Euhemeristic principle began to creep in among the Greeks, each people supposed the deity to have been born among themselves. The Kretan legend must however be regarded as the more ancient, for the Arcadians evidently attempted to transfer the names of places in it to their own country, a practice of which as we proceed we shall meet with other instances.

In the Theogony the celestial progeny of Zeus are enumerated in the following order.[5]

Zeus first espoused Métis (*Prudence*), who exceeded gods and men in knowledge. But Heaven and Earth having told him that her first child, a maid, would equal himself in strength and counsel, and her second, a son, would be king of gods and men, he

Τὸν μὲν ἄρα τρήρωνες ὑπὸ ζαθέῳ τράφον ἄντρῳ,
ἀμβροσίην φερέουσαι ἀπ' Ὠκεανοῖο ῥοάων·
νέκταρ δ' ἐκ πέτρης μέγας αἰετὸς αἰὲν ἀφύσσων
γαμφλῆς φορέεσκε ποτὸν Διὶ μητιόεντι.
Mœró of Byzantion *ap. Athen.* xi. 490.

[2] Κρῆτες ἀεὶ ψεῦσται. Kallim. *ut supra*, v. 8.
[3] Kallim. *ut supra*. The real root of Neda (Νέδα) is probably νάω, *to flow.*
[4] Paus. viii. 31, 4; 38, 3; 47, 3. Theisoa was the name of a place and Hagnó of a spring on Mount Lykæon.   [5] *Theog.* 886 *seq.*

cajoled her when she was pregnant, and swallowed her; and after
a time the goddess Pallas-Athéné sprang forth from his head.
He then married, Themis, who bore him the Seasons and
Fates. The O'keanis Eurynomé next produced him the Charites
or Graces; Démétér was then by him the mother of Persephoné,
Mnémosyné of the Muses, and Létó of Apolló and Artemis. His
last spouse was Héra, who bore him Hébé, Arés, and Eileithyia.

According to Homer,[1] Héphæstos was the son of Zeus by Héra,
and Aphrodíté his daughter by Dióné. The Theogony further says
that Maia, the daughter of Atlas, bore him Hermés.[2] A later
fable said that Asteria, the sister of Létó, flying the love of Zeus,
flung herself from heaven down to the sea, and became the isle
afterwards named Délos.[3]

Mortal women also bore a numerous progeny to this amorous
monarch of the gods, and every species of transmutation and
disguise was employed by him to accomplish his object. He
assumed the form of her husband Amphitryón to deceive the
modesty of Alkméné, who became the mother of Héraklés. Léda
was beguiled by him in the shape of a beautiful white swan.
Under the form of a shower of gold he penetrated the brazen
prison in which Danaé was inclosed, and became the father of
Perseus. Antiopé, the mother of Amphíón and Zéthos, was
forced by him in the guise of a satyr. To seduce the Arcadian
nymph Kallistó he presumed to take the form of Artemis, the
goddess of chastity. A bull was the form in which he carried off
Európé, the sister of Kadmos; and a flame of fire or the plumage
of an eagle disguised the god from Ægína, the mother of Æakos.
By Semelé he was the father of Dionýsos, who became a god. By
Ió he had a son named Epaphos. Many other heroes could also
boast of being the sons of Zeus by different mothers. Of all
these mortal loves we shall give a detailed account when we come
to speak of the heroes who sprang from them.

The love of Zeus (and in this there lies a moral) was not
always a source of happiness to those whom he honoured with it.
Ió, for example, underwent a dreadful persecution from Héra, as
also did Létó; Semelé perished in the flames which invested the

---

[1] *Il.* i. 572; v. 370, 371.   [2] *Theog.* 938.
[3] In the text we have followed Kallimachos (*Hymn* iv. 37 *seq.*), who says,
alluding to her name, that she came down "like a star." This was probably
the more ancient version, but it was also said that she took the form of a
quail, ὄρτυξ (see Apollod. i. 4, 1. Hygin. 53. Serv. *on Æn.* iii. 73), whence the
isle was named Ortygia. This identification of Délos and Ortygia was, however, certainly later than the time of Pindar, who (Nem. i. 4) calls them sisters.
(See below, chap. viii.) The whole legend seems to owe its origin to the
affinity of sense between the words Asteria and Délos.

lord of the thunder and lightning: Danaé and her babe were abandoned to the waves of the sea.

We shall presently show that the name Zeus signifies God. When, therefore, we recollect how usual it was in the oriental and early Greek style to represent magnitude or excellence by associating it with the name of the deity,[1] it need not surprise us to meet so many *Zeus-sprung* heroes in the mythology of Greece.[2] A mere epithet might have been the germ of the mythe; Zeus was then placed at the head of a genealogy; and last came the poets, who detailed the amorous history. This theory, however, goes on the supposition of these heroes having been real personages, whereas, as we proceed, we shall find reasons for regarding them in general as mere personifications.

It seems to have been an ancient opinion that the gods used to assume the human form and go among mankind to mark their conduct.[3] To this notion—which carries our minds back to those happy ages commemorated in the Book of Genesis, ' when angels dwelt and God himself with man'—we are indebted for some interesting legends told by poets, of Zeus taking the human form, and coming down to view more closely the conduct of mankind over whom he ruled. Such was his visit to Lykáón king of Arcadia, whom he punished for his impiety; and that on occasion of which the piety of Hyrieus was rewarded by the birth of O'ríon. The most pleasing tale is that of Philémón and Baukis, narrated by Ovid in his most agreeable manner, to the following effect.[4]

Zeus and Hermés came one time in the form of men to a town in Phrygia. It was evening; they sought for hospitality, but every door was closed against them. At length they approached a humble cottage where dwelt an aged man, named Philémon, with Baukis his wife, of equal years, by whom the wayfarers were gladly received. The poet pleases his imagination amidst the luxury of Rome in describing the furniture of their simple abode, and the homely fare, though their best, which they set before their celestial guests, whose quality was at length revealed by the miracle of the wine-bowl being spontaneously replenished as fast

---

[1] In Hebrew (*Ps.* lxxx. 11) *Cedars of God* are *lofty* cedars. Commentators usually regard the *Sons of God* in *Gen.* vi. 2, as being, to use the words of Milton,

. . . that sober race of men, whose lives
Religious titled them the Sons of God.

See Heyne *on Apollod.* i. 7, 5.

[2] In the Ilias, when Hectór is routing the Greeks, Poseidón says of him (xiii. 54) ὃς Διὸς εὔχετ' ἐρισθενέος παῖς εἶναι.

[3] *Od.* xvii. 484 *seq.* Hésiod, Ἔργ. 249 *seq.*

[4] *Met.* viii. 620 *seq.* We have been unable to discover his Greek original.

as it was drained.   They told their hosts that it was their intention to destroy the godless town, and desired them to leave their
house and ascend the adjacent hill.   The aged pair obeyed; but
ere they reached the summit they turned round to look, and beheld a lake where the town had stood.   Their own house remained,
and, as they gazed and deplored the fate of their neighbours, it
became a temple.   On being desired by Zeus to express their
wishes, they prayed that they might be appointed to officiate in that
temple, and that they might be united in death as in life.   Their
prayer was granted, and as they were one day standing out before
the fane, they were suddenly changed into an oak and a lime-tree.[1]

It was the habit of the Greeks to appropriate particular plants
and animals to the service of their deities.   There was generally
some reason for this, founded on physical or moral grounds, or
on both.   Nothing therefore could be more natural than to assign the oak,[2] the monarch of trees, to the celestial king, whose
ancient oracle moreover was in the oak-woods of Dódóna.[3]   In like
manner the eagle was evidently the bird best suited to his service.[4]

The celebrated Ægis,[5] the shield which sent forth thunder,
lightning, and darkness, and struck terror into mortal hearts,
was formed for Zeus by Héphæstos.[6]   In Homer we see it sometimes borne by Apolló[7] and by Pallas-Athéné.[8]

The most famous temple of this god was at Olympia in E'lis,
where every fourth year the Olympian games were celebrated in
his honour: he had also a splendid fane in the isle of Ægína.
But, though there were few deities less honoured with temples
and statues, all the inhabitants of Hellas combined in the duty
of doing homage to the sovereign of the gods.   His great oracle
was at Dódóna, where, even in the Pelasgian period, his priests,
the Selli, announced his will and futurity.[9]

Zeus was represented by the artists as the model of dignity
and majesty of mien; his countenance grave but mild.   He is

---

[1] The reader will doubtless have observed the resemblance between this
legend and the account of Lot and the angels in the book of Genesis, which
last may have been carried to Greece, or have been learned by the Greeks at
Alexandria.   See Leclerc's Dissertatio de Sodoma, etc. in his *Mosis Prophetæ
V. Libri*, etc.   In the Fairy Mythology will be found a Swiss version of this
legend.   [2] Φηγὸς, *Quercus æsculus*.   See *Il.* vii. 60.
[3] *Il.* xvi. 233.   *Od.* xiv. 327; xix. 296.   Hés. *Fr.* 54.
[4] *Il.* viii. 247 *seq.*; xii. 200 *seq.*   *Od.* ii. 146.
[5] This word is derived from ἀΐσσω *to excite*; but as it greatly resembles the
Greek word for *goat* (αἴξ, αἰγὸς), the legend of its being covered with the skin
of the goat which nursed the god was devised at a subsequent period : see
Heyne *on Il.* ii. 148, 448.   Welcker, *Tril.* 153.   Böttiger, *Kunst-Myth.* ii. 88.
[6] *Il.* xv. 310.   [7] *Il.* xv. 229, 368.
[8] *Il.* v. 738; xviii. 203.   *Od.* xxii. 297.   [9] *Il.* xvi. 233.

seated on a throne, and grasping his sceptre and the thunder. The eagle is standing beside the throne.

The epithets of this god in Homer are,[1] 1. *Ægis-holding ;* 2. *Cloud-collecting ;* 3. *Black-clouding ;* 4. *Thunder-loving ;* 5. *High-seated ;* 6. *Lightening ;* 7. *Counselling ;* 8. *Wide-seeing* or *Wide-thundering ;* and others of similar signification.

The epithets of Zeus derived from his offices, such as Xenios, as protector of strangers, Horkios, the guardian of oaths, were numerous. He was also named like the other gods from the places where he was worshipped, ex. gr. Klarios, Kithærónios. Toward the end of the month Anthestérión (beginning of March), a festival named the Diasia was held at Athens, in which offerings were made to Zeus, the *Mild* or *Appeased* ($\mu\epsilon\iota\lambda\iota\chi\iota\sigma$),[2] answering to the sin-offerings of the Mosaic law. At Argos there was an ancient wooden statue ($\xi\delta\alpha\nu\sigma\nu$) of Zeus, which had a third eye in its forehead. The tradition was that it had been the domestic image of Priamos, and had been brought from Troy by Sthenelos. The three eyes are rightly explained by Pausanias as indicative of the dominion of Zeus (the God) over heaven, earth (land and water), and the under-world.[3]

A very simple process will lead us to the true signification of the name of this deity. Its Æolic form is Δεύς, which is almost the same as the *deus* of the Latin, the affinity of which language to the Æolic Greek is well known.[4] Zeus (Ζεύς) therefore is *God,* the same as θεός, *deus,* and akin to the Persian *Deev* or *Dew,* and the Sanscrit *Dyaus.* Perhaps it is also akin to *dies, day* (as in Diespiter); and hence Zeus is the Heaven, the god who gives light from heaven, and fertility to the earth.[5] The oblique cases of Zeus come from Δίς and Ζὴν, or Ζὰν, the former of which is manifestly equivalent to Ζεύς, and the latter is probably a contraction of the participle ζάων, *living.*

Ποσειδάων, Ποσειδῶν. (*Neptunus.*)

This son of Kronos and Rhea became the ruler of the sea. His queen was Amphitríté, one of the daughters of Néreus and Dóris.[6]

---

[1] 1. αἰγίοχος : 2. νεφεληγερέτης : 3. κελαινεφής : 4. τερπικέραυνος : 5. ὑψίζυγος : 6. ἀστεροπητής : 7. μητίετης : 8. εὐρύοπα.
[2] Thuc. i. 126.   [3] Paus. ii. 2+, 3, 4.
[4] See Aristoph. *Achar.* 911. The Greek ζ (*i. e.* δσ) is frequently *d* in the corresponding Latin term ; thus ῥίζα, *radix,* ὄζω, *odor :* see Müller, *Proleg.* 289.
[5] In Sanscrit *Deev* is 'bright-shining,' and hence ' heaven.'
[6] Hés. *Theog.* 243, 930 : see also *Od.* v. 422 ; xii. 60, 97. Apollodóros (i. 4, 4), says she was an Okeanis. Her name is apparently of the same origin as that of Tritón, signifying *Corroder, Wearer-away :* see below, chap. xvii.

Their children were Tritón[1] and Rhodé, or Rhodos, which last became the bride of Hélios.[2] A late legend said that Amphitríté fled the love of the god, but that he came riding on a porpoise (δελφὶν), and thus won her affection; and for his service he placed the porpoise among the stars.[3]

Poseidón, like his brother Zeus, had a numerous progeny both by goddesses and mortals. The fleet steed Areión was the offspring of the sea-god and Démétér, both having assumed the equine form.[4] According to one account the nymph Rhodos was his daughter by Aphrodíté.[5]

Tyró, the daughter of Salmóneus, the wife of Krétheus, loved the river Enípeus, and frequented his stream; Poseidón, under the form of the river-god, 'mingled in love' with her, and she became the mother of Pelias and Néleus.[6] Iphimédeia bore him O'tos and Ephialtés, those gigantic babes, who in their ninth year attempted to scale heaven.[7] As a ram, he was by Theophané, daughter of Bisaltos, the sire of the gold-fleeced ram which carried Phrixos to Kolchis.[8] The sea-nymph Thoósa bore him the huge Kyklóps Polyphémos.[9] The invulnerable Kyknos, who was slain by Achilleus, was also the offspring of this deity:[10] so also were Théseus, Eumolpos, and other heroes. The children of the sea-god were in general noted for violence and turbulence of character, indicative of the nature of their sire. This, however, does not apply to those whom we meet with in the mythology of Attica, where, agreeably to the character of the people, everything bears a mild and gentle aspect.

Poseidón was worshipped in Arcadia under the title of Hippios.[11] One legend of that country made him the sire of the steed Areión;[12] and another said that when Rhea brought him forth, she pretended to Kronos that she had been delivered of a foal, which she gave him to devour.[13] The origin of the horse was also ascribed to this god. According to a Thessalian legend, he smote a rock in that country with his trident, and forth sprang the first horse, which was named Skyphios.[14] The vain people

---

[1] *Theog.* 931.   [2] See above, p. 51.
[3] Eratosth. *Catast.* 31.   Hygin. *Poet. Astr.* i. 17.   [4] See below, chap. xi.
[5] Hérophilos *apud Sch. Pind. Ol.* vii. 13 (24).   [6] *Od.* xi. 235 *seq.*
[7] *Od.* xi. 305 *seq.*   [8] Hygin. 188.   Ov. *Met.* vi. 117.
[9] *Od.* i. 71.   [10] Ov. *Met.* xii. 72.   Sch. *Theocr.* xvi. 49.
[11] ῞Ιππιος, from ῞ιππος, *a horse.*   Paus. viii. 10, 2 ; 14, 5 ; 25, 7 ; 36, 2 , 37, 10.   [12] See below, chap. ix.
[13] Paus. viii. 8, 2.   The legend added that Rhea put her new-born babe among the lambs (ἄρνες) that pastured thereabouts, whence an adjacent spring was named Arné.
[14] Sch. *Pind. Pyth.* iv. 139 (246).   Probus *on Geor.* i. 13.   Lucan, *Phars* vi. 396.   Skyphios is evidently related to σκάφος and to *skiff, ship.*

of Attica affected to believe that it was on their soil that the
sea-god first presented the horse to mankind.[1]   The winged steed
Pégasos is also the offspring of Poseidón.[2]   In the Ilias, when
Zeus returns from Ida to Olympos, it is Poseidón that unyokes
his horses;[3] the same god is said to have given the Harpy-born
steeds of Achilleus to Péleus;[4] he is joined with Zeus as the
teacher of the art of driving the chariot;[5] and when Meneláos
charges Antilochos with foul play in the chariot-race, he requires
him to clear himself by an oath to Poseidón.[6]

All this indicates a close connection between the sea-god and
the horse. The usual solution given is, that as, according to
Hérodotos, the worship of Poseidón came from Libya to Greece,
and as the Libyans were an agricultural, not a seafaring people,
the agents must have been the Phœnicians; but this people, we
are assured, also brought the first horses into Greece (as the
Spaniards did into America, and as much to the astonishment of
the rude natives), and thus the knowledge of the horse and of
Poseidón came together, and they were consequently associated in
the popular mind.[7]

This, we may observe, is all merely gratuitous hypothesis. The
absurd passion of Hérodotos for deducing the religion of Greece
from abroad is so notorious, that few, we should suppose, would
lay any stress on his testimony in these matters. Had a god of
the sea been worshipped in Egypt, beyond question the historian
would have derived Poseidón from that country. Again, what can
be more absurd than to suppose that Greece, a portion of the continent of Europe, to the north of which dwelt the Thracians and
Scythians, renowned in all ages for their horses,[8]—Upper Asia
being, as zoologists assert, the original seat of these animals—
should have first received them from the coast of Africa? We
may therefore, we think, safely dismiss this hypothesis, and look
for an explanation of the phænomenon elsewhere.

The horse is the principal means of transport by land, as the
ship is by sea; the one name might therefore be metaphorically
employed for the other. Thus in Homer[9] Pénelopé says,

> Why, herald, is my son gone? for no need
> Had he to mount the swift-coursed ships, which are
> For men the horses of the sea, and pass
> O'er the great deep;

in Plautus[10] one of the characters says, "That is to say, you have

---

[1] Soph. *Œd. Col.* 714.   Serv. *Geor.* i. 13.   [2] Hés. *Theog.* 278 *seq.*
[3] *Il.* viii. 440.   [4] *Il.* xxiii. 277.   [5] *Il.* xxiii. 307.   [6] *Il.* xxiii. 584.
[7] See Böttiger, *Kunst-Myth.* ii. 325 *seq.*   [8] See *Il.* xiii. 4 *seq.*
[9] *Od.* iv. 707.   [10] *Rudens*, i. 5, 10.

been carried on a *wooden horse* along the azure road;" and the
Arabs call their camel *the ship of the desert.* This seems to offer
a natural solution of the difficulty, the sea-god being regarded as
the author of ships, the horses of the sea, and thence by an easy
transition of the real animals.[1] But still when we reflect how
widely spread was the habit of regarding the horse as in some mysterious manner connected with the water,[2] we may hesitate to give
our full assent to this theory.

It is rather curious to observe the manner in which Poseidón
and Pallas-Athéné are associated. They were worshipped together,—he as Hippios, she as Hippia,—at Kolónos near Athens,[3]
and we also find them united in the legend of Bellerophontés;[4]
they contended for the possession of Attica[5] and Trœzén;[6] in the
former case the sea-god was forced to yield, in the latter Zeus
decided that they should hold the dominion in common. In like
manner Poseidón is said to have contended with Héra for Argos,[7]
and with Hélios for Corinth;[8] with Zeus for Ægína,[9] and with
Dionýsos for Naxos;[10] and to have exchanged Delphi and Délos
with Létó and Apolló for Kalaureia and Tænaron.[11] Mythes of
this kind, it is evident, merely indicate a change or a combination of the worship of the deities who are the subjects of them,
in the places where the scenes of the supposed contests are
laid.[12]

Beside his residence on Olympos, Poseidón had a splendid palace
beneath the sea at Ægæ.[13] Homer gives a noble description of
his passage from it on his way to Troy, his chariot-wheels but
touching the watery plain, and the monsters of the deep gamboling
around their king. His most celebrated temples were at the
Corinthian isthmus, Onchéstos,[14] Heliké,[15] Trœzén, and the pro-
montories of Sunion, Tænaron, Geræstos, and other headlands.[16]

Poseidón is represented, like Zeus, of a serene and majestic
aspect; his form is strong and muscular. He usually bears in

---

[1] See in Völcker (*Myth. der Jap.* 133 *seq.*) an excellent discussion of this
subject.
[2] In the *Tales and Popular Fictions,* 79 *seq.* will be found some instances;
see also *Fairy Mythology, passim.*

[3] Paus. i. 30, 4.   [4] See Part II. chap. vi. *Bellerophontés.*
[5] See Part. II. ch. v. *Cecrops.*   [6] Paus. ii. 30, 5.
[7] Id. ii. 15, 5.   [8] Id. ii. 1, 6.
[9] Plut. *Symp.* ix. 6.   [10] Plut. *l. c.*
[11] Paus. ii. 33, 2.   Strab. viii. 6, 14, p. 374. It was Hélios, not Apolló,
that was the possessor of Tænaron. Hom. *Hymn to Apolló,* 411.
[12] See Müller, *Æginetica,* 26 *seq.*   [13] *Il.* xiii. 21.   *Od.* v. 381.
[14] Hom. *Hymn to Apolló,* 230.   [15] *Il.* viii. 203; xx. 404.
[16] Apoll. Rh. iii. 1240 *seq.*

his hand the trident, the three-pronged symbol of his power: the porpoise and other marine objects accompany his images.

The poetic epithets of Poseidón are,[1] 1. *Earth-holding*; 2. *Earth-shaking*; 3. *Dark-haired*; 4. *Wide-ruling*; 5. *Loud-sounding*; &c.

In Poseidón we may discern the original god of water in general, of springs and rivers as well as of the sea. The legends respecting him (his amour with Démétér, the *earth*, for instance), are on this supposition easy of explanation. The simple Doric form of his name, Ποτίδας, shows its true origin to be from the root ΠΟΩ, and that it is of the same family with πότος, πόντος, ποταμὸς, all relating to water and fluidity.[2]

'Αῖς, 'Αίδης, 'Αϊδωνεὺς, Ἄδης, Πλούτων. (*Orcus, Dis.*)

Hadés, the brother of Zeus and Poseidón, was lord of the subterrane region, the abode of the dead. He is described as being inexorable and deaf to supplication,—for from his realms there is no return,—and an object of aversion and hatred both to gods and men.[3] All the latter were sure to be sooner or later collected into his kingdom. His name appears to denote *invisibility*,[4] significatory of the nature of the realm over which he ruled. At a later period he received the appellation of Plutón,[5] as mines within the earth are the producers of the precious metals. This notion, Voss[6] thinks (but, as is too often the case, on insufficient evidence [7]), began to prevail when the Greeks first visited Spain, the country most abundant in gold.

The adventures of this god were few, for the gloomy nature of himself and his realm did not offer much field for such legends of the gods as Grecian fancy delighted in; yet *he* too had his love-adventures. The tale of his carrying off Persephoné (which we shall relate at length in the sequel) is one of the most celebrated

---

[1] 1. γαιήοχος: 2. ἐννοσίχθων, ἐννοσίγαιος: 3. κυανοχαίτης: 4. εὐρυμέδων, εὐρυκρείων, εὐρυσθενής: 5. βαρυσμάραγος, βαρύδουπος, βαρύκτυπος, ἐρίκτυπος.

[2] See Müller, *Proleg.* 289.

[3] *Il.* ix. 158, 159.

[4] From α and εἴδω, *to see.* The names of the gods, however, are rarely compounds.

[5] Πλοῦτος, *wealth.*

[6] *Myth. Br.* ii. 175. Heyne (*on Apollod.* p. 780) is of opinion that it was first given in the Mysteries. It is employed occasionally by the Attic dramatists (Soph. *Antig.* 1200. Eur. *Alc.* 360. Aristoph. *Frogs, passim*), and became the prevalent one in later times, when Hadés came to signify a place rather than a person. It was very rarely used by the Latin writers.

[7] Surely the Greeks knew the gold-mines of Thrace, and the silver-mines of Attica before those of Spain.

in antiquity. He loved, we are told,[1] and carried off to Erebos the O'keanis Leuké; and when she died, he caused a tree, named from her (λεύκη, *white poplar*) to spring up in the E'lysian Plain. Another of his loves was the nymph Mentha, whom Persephoné out of jealousy turned into the plant which bears her name.[2]

Hadés, Homer tells us,[3] was once wounded in the shoulder by the arrows of Héraklés; but from the ambiguity of the phrase used by the poet (ἐν πύλῳ) it is difficult to determine the scene of the conflict. Some say it was at the *gate* of the nether world, when the hero was sent to drag the dog of Hadés to the realms of day;[4] others that it was in Pylos, where the god was aiding his worshippers against the son of Zeus.[5]

The region over which Hadés presides is represented in the Ilias and in the Theogony[6] as being within the earth : in the Odyssey[7] it is placed in the dark region beyond the stream of Ocean. Its name is Erebos ;[8] the poets everywhere describe it as dreary, dark, and cheerless. The dead, without distinction of good or evil, age or rank, wander about there, conversing of their former state on earth : they are unhappy, and they feel their wretched state acutely. Achilleus, the son of a goddess, declares to Odysseus that he would rather be a day-labourer to the poorest cultivator on earth than a king in those regions. They have no strength or power of mind or body.[9] Some few, enemies of the gods, such as Sisyphos, Tityos, Tantalos, are punished for their crimes, but not apart from the

---

[1] Servius *on Virg. Buc.* vii. 61.

[2] Strab. viii. 3, 14, p. 344. Sch. *Nicand. Alex.* 374. Oppian. *Hal.* iii. 486. Ov. *Met.* x. 728.

[3] *Il.* v. 395 *seq.*

[4] Sch. *Il.* v. 395, 397. Sch. *Od.* xi. 605. Eudocia, 207. The other authorities are collected by Heyne in his note on *Il.* v. 397. Voss translates in this sense.

[5] Apollod. ii. 7, 3. Paus. vi. 25, 2. Seneca, *Herc. Furens*, 560 *seq.* : see Pind. *Ol.* ix. 33 (50), with the Scholia. Heyne, Müller, and Buttmann are in favour of this sense of the phrase.

[6] *Il.* iii. 278; ix. 568 *seq.* ; xx. 61 *seq.;* xxiii. 100. *Theog.* 455, 767. Such was also the site of the Hebrew Sheol : see *Numb.* xvi. 30 *seq.;* 1 *Sam.* xxviii. 13.

[7] *Od.* x. 508 *seq.* ; xi. 1 *seq.* ; 635 *seq.;* xii. 81. The poet terms the place whence the dead come to Odysseus δόμον and δόμους 'Αΐδαο. He may therefore have regarded Erebos as a huge mansion or town in the land beyond the Ocean : comp. Ov. *Met.* iv. 432 *seq.*

[8] It is well known that Hadés became afterwards synonymous with Erebos : see Appendix G. Heyne (*on Il.* viii. 368) makes a strange mistake in saying that Erebos lay between the Earth and Hadés, beneath which was Tartaros. Passow (*v.* ἔρεβος) adopts this notion, and adds that Erebos was but a *passage* to Hadés, from which, he says, it is expressly distinguished in *Il.* viii. 368 (as person and place certainly). It is plain that neither of these writers had correct ideas on this subject. [9] *Od.* xi. 393.

re.:t of the dead.[1] Nothing can be more gloomy and comfortless than the whole aspect of the realm of Hadés as pictured in the Odyssey. It is in fact surprising that men who had such a dreary prospect before them should not have been more attached to life, and more averse from war and everything that might abridge its period, than the ancient Greeks were.[2]

In process of time, when communication with Egypt and Asia had enlarged the sphere of the ideas of the Greeks, the nether-world underwent a considerable change. It was now divided into two separate regions: Tartaros, which in the time of Homer and Hésiod was thought to lie far beneath it, and to be the prison of the Titans, became one of these regions, and the place of punishment for wicked men; and the Elysian Plain, which lay on the shore of the stream of Ocean, the retreat of the children and relatives of the king of the gods, was moved down thither to form the place of reward for good men. A stream encompassed the domains of Hadés,[3] over which the dead, on paying their passage-money ($\nu\alpha\hat{v}\lambda o\nu$), were ferried by Charón;[4] the three-headed dog Kerberos guarded the entrance;[5] and the three judges, Minós, Æakos, and Rhadamanthys, allotted his place of bliss or of pain to each of the dead who was brought before their tribunal.[6] *The river of Oblivion* ($\acute{o}$ $\tau\hat{\eta}s$ $\lambda\acute{\eta}\theta\eta s$

[1] The genuineness of the passage (*Od.* xi. 564–626) in which these personages are mentioned was doubted of by Aristarchos. Notwithstanding the arguments of Payne Knight (*Proleg.* § xix.) in defence of it, we incline to the opinion of the Alexandrian critic.

[2] See Plato, *Rep.* iii. 386, b. Voss, *Anti-Symb.* i. 203, 204. The ancient Hebrews seem also to have had gloomy ideas of Sheól, their under-world (see Hezekiah's song, *Is.* xxxviii. 10 *seq.*); the Celtic and Germanic tribes the contrary.

[3] The *river* which was to be passed is mentioned, *Il.* xxiii. 73. It would seem to be the Styx : see *Il.* viii. 369.

[4] See Pind. *Fr. Incert.* 4. Æschyl. *Seven ag. Thebes*, 856 *seq.* *Agam.* 1557. Eur. *Alc.* 361, 439. Aristoph. *Plut.* 278. *Frogs*, 183. *Lys.* 606. The earliest mention of Charón in Grecian poetry seems to have been in the ancient poem of the Minyas, quoted by Pausanias, x. 28.

[5] Apollod. ii. 5, 12. Homer (*Il.* viii. 368) mentions the *dog* of Hadés. Hésiod (*Theog.* 311) names him Kerberos, and gives him fifty heads. See also *Theog.* 769 *seq.* Others gave him one hundred heads. Pind. *Fr. Incert.* 27. Hor. *Carm.* ii. 13, 34.

[6] This is probably founded on the passage in the Odyssey (xi. 568) where the hero says he saw Minós judging in Erebos, but he only judged there as O'ríón hunted, *i. e.* pursued his occupation as when on earth. According to the fine mythe in Plató (*Gorgias*, 523), Æakos and Rhadamanthys sit at the point in the mead ($\tau\rho\iota\acute{o}\delta\varphi$) where the path branches off to the Isles of the Blest and to Tartaros (see Verg. *Æn.* vi. 540); the former judges the dead from Europe, the latter those from Asia (above, p. 30). If any case proves too difficult for *them*, it is reserved for the decision of Minos.

ποταμὸς)[1] was added to those of Homer's trans-Oceanic region,[2] of whose waters the dead were led to drink previous to their returning to animate other bodies on earth.[3] In the sixth book of Vergil's Æneïs will be found the richest and fullest description of the new-modified under-world, and for those who love to trace the progress and change of ideas, it will not be an uninteresting employment to compare it with that in the eleventh book of Homer's Odyssey. The poet Claudian[4] too has, with his usual elegance, drawn a luxuriant description of the blissful scenes which the under-world would present, to console and reconcile its future mistress.

In reading the 'portentous lies' (as they have well been termed)[5] of the Egyptian priests on this subject, one is at a loss which most to admire, *their* audacity, or the credulity of the Greeks. For the former asserted, and the latter believed, that Orpheus and Homer had both learned wisdom on the banks of the Nile; and that the Erebos of Greece, and all its parts, personages and usages, were but transcripts of the mode of burial in Egypt. Here the corpse was, on payment of an obelos, conveyed by a ferryman (named Charón in the language of Egypt) over the Acherusian lake, after it had received its sentence from the judges appointed for that purpose. O'keanos was but the Egyptian name of the Nile; the Gates of the Sun were merely those of Héliopolis; and Hermés, the conductor of souls,[6] was familiar to the Egyptians; and thus they appropriated all the mythic ideas of Greece. It may give some idea of their hardihood, to observe that they affirmed, on the authority of their sacred books and temple-archives, that Orpheus, Musæos, Melampus and Dædalos—not one of whom probably ever existed—had all visited Egypt.[7] But enough of such mendacity; we should not have noticed it, were it not that the fashion of tracing the religion and institutions of Greece to Egypt is not yet extinct.

Before we quit Aïdóneus and his realms, we must call attention to the circumstance of a large portion of the human race agreeing

---

[1] *Fluvius, amnis, flumen Lethæus-um*, Verg. *Æn.* vi. 705, 714, 749. *Lethæus* is in these places and in *Geor.* i. 78, iv. 545, simply the Greek adj. ληθαῖος, *obliviosus.* By taking in like manner *Actæus* in *Buc.* ii. 24, as a common adj. ἀκταῖος, we have succeeded in giving an easy and natural sense to that passage. We may here add that as ἠλύσιος is an adj., *campum* is to be understood with *Elysium* in *Æn.* vi. 744.

[2] These were Acherón, Pyriphlegethón, and Kokýtos. *Od.* x. 513, 514.

[3] Verg. *Æn. ut supra.* It is not known how or when the doctrine of the Metempsychosis came into Greece. We first meet with it in Pindar, *Ol.* ii. 68 (123). *Fr. Thrén.* 4.

[4] *Rapt. Pros.* ii. 282 *seq.*: see also Sil. Ital. xiii. 550 *seq.* and Tibull. i. 3, 59 *seq.*

[5] Lobeck, *Aglroph.* 811.   [6] See *Od.* xxiv. 1 *seq.*   [7] Diodór. i. 92, 96.

to place the abode of departed souls either beneath the earth, or in the remote regions of the West. The former notion, it is probable, owes its origin to the simple circumstance of the mortal remains of man being deposited by most nations in the bosom of the earth; and the habits of thinking and speaking which thence arose, led to the notion of the soul also being placed in a region within the earth. The calmness and stillness of evening succeeding the toils of the day, the majesty of the sun sinking as it were to rest amid the glories of the western sky, exert a powerful influence over the human mind, and lead us almost insensibly to picture the West as a region of bliss and tranquillity. The idea of its being the abode of the departed good, where in calm islands they dwelt 'from every ill remote,' was therefore an obvious one.[1] Finally, the analogy of the conclusion of the day and the setting of the sun with the close of life, may have led the Greeks,[2] or it may be the Phœnicians or Egyptians,[3] to place the dwelling of the dead in general in the dark land on the western shore of Ocean.

Hadés, we are told by Homer, possessed a helmet which rendered its wearer invisible: it was forged for him by Héphæstos, the later writers say, in the time of the war against the Titans. Pallas-Athéné, when aiding Diomédés, wore it to conceal her from Arés.[4] When Perseus went on his expedition against the Gorgons, the helm of invisibility covered his brows.[5] This helmet of Hades will find its parallel in tales both of the East and the West, now consigned to the nursery.

By artists, the god of the nether-world was represented similar to his brothers, but he was distinguished from them by his gloomy and rigid mien. He usually bears a two-pronged fork in his hand.

The poets called Hadés,[6] 1. *Subterranean Zeus*;[7] 2. *People-*

---

[1] Some tribes of the North American Indians place the happy hunting-grounds of the departed far away beyond a stream in the West. The ideas of the Greenlanders, and of some of the tribes of South America are similar: see Völcker, *Hom. Geog.* 142. Even the rude aborigines of Australia are said to regard the West as the abode of the departed.

[2] This notion seems almost peculiar to the Odyssey; the only allusion to it that we have met with elsewhere is in Sophoklés (*Œd. Tyr.* 176), where Hadés is called 'the western god' (ἀκτὰν πρὸς ἑσπέρου θεοῦ).

[3] See Part II. ch. xii.   [4] *Il.* v. 845.   [5] Apollod. i. 6, 2.

[6] 1. Ζεὺς καταχθόνιος: 2. ἀγεσίλαος: 3. πολυδέγμων, πολυδέκτης: 4. πυλάρτης: 5. ἀγέλαστος: 6. κλυτόπωλος: 7. ἀδάμαστος (fortis tanquam Orcus. Petron. 62): 8. ἴφθιμος: 9. στυγερὸς: 10. κρυερός.

[7] We agree with Heyne and Payne Knight in regarding the line of the Ilias (ix. 457) where this epithet occurs as spurious. It is contrary to the analogy of the whole poem. We however doubt of the genuineness of much of this ninth book.

collecting; 3. *Much-receiving*; 4. *Gate-keeping*; 5. *Laughterless* 6. *Horse-renowned*; 7. *Invincible*; 8. *Strong*; 9. *Hateful*; 10. *Cold*; &c.

At Hermioné in Argolis Hadés was worshipped under the name of *Illustrious* (κλύμενος),[1] and Persephoné under that of *Subterrane* (χθονία). The former would seem to have been placatory, like *Eumenides* that of the Erinnyes.

The epithet *People-collecting*, or *driving*, seems to refer to an office of Hadés, which was afterwards transferred to Hermés. In the original conception of the god of the under-world, he was probably supposed to be himself the agent in removing from the realms of day those who were to be his subjects. Pindar speaks of the staff of Hadés, with which he *drives down* (κατάγει) the dead along the hollow way to Erebos.[2] It is in fact not an improbable supposition that Hadés, like the Latin Orcus, may have been originally identical with Death. His name, we may remark, often has that signification in the Attic dramatists.[3]

In the Alkéstis of Euripidés we meet with the first mention of a very remarkable notion of the Greeks. The dead seem to have been regarded in the light of victims offered to Hadés;[4] and as it was the custom in commencing a sacrifice to pluck some hairs from the forehead of the victim and burn them on the altar, so Death is here represented as coming to cut off a lock of the hair of Alkéstis.[5] Of this rite, however, no other mention is, we believe, to be found in Grecian literature. If we may trust to the Latin poets,[6] the duty of performing it belonged to Persephoné, a view which seems to contradict all analogy.

---

[1] Paus. ii. 35, 9, 10. Ov. *Fast.* vi. 757.

Δάματρα μέλπω κόραν τε Κλυμένοιο ἄλοχον Μελίβοιαν.
Lasos of Hermioné, *Hymn to Démétér* (Athén. x. 455; xiv. 624).

Τῇ χθονίῃ μυστικὰ Δήμητρί τε καὶ Περσεφόνῃ καὶ Κλυμένῳ τὰ δῶρα.
Philikos of Kerkýra (Héphæstión, ch. ix.).

[2] *Ol.* ix. 33 (50) *seq.* Compare Simonidés *Fr.* iv. 14. In the Sanscrit poem named Savítrí, Yama, the Hindú Hadés, comes himself to take away the soul of a dying prince: see Bopp, *Diluvium*, etc. The modern Greeks assign this office to Χάρος, *i. e.* Χάρων, who rides on a horse with the young people up before him, the aged behind him, and the children with him on the saddle.—Grimm, *Deut. Mythol.* p. 804.

[3] See Æsch. *Agam.* 667. Soph. *Œd. Col.* 1440. Eur. *Alc.* 13, 268, 843 *Hip.* 1047, 1366. *Iph. Taur.* 486.

[4] " Victima nil miserantis Orci."—Hor. *Carm.* ii. 3, 24.

[5] *v.* 74 *seq.* It is worthy of notice that Macrobius, when speaking of this drama (*Sat.* v. 19), renders Θάνατος by *Orcus.*

[6] Verg. *Æn.* iv. 698 *seq.* Hor. *Carm.* i. 28, 19, 20   Stat. *Silv.* ii. 1, 147.

'Ιστία, 'Εστία. (*Vesta*.)

An idea of the sanctity of the domestic hearth (ἑστία), the point of assembly of the family, and the symbol of the social union, gave the Greeks occasion to fancy it to be under the guardianship of a peculiar deity, whom they named from it, Hestia. This goddess does not appear in the poems of Homer. though he had abundant opportunities of noticing her. By Hesiod [1] she is said to have been the daughter of Kronos and Rhea.

The hymn to Aphrodíté relates that Hestia, Artemis, and Athéna were the only goddesses who escaped the power of the queen of love. When wooed by Poseidón and Apolló, Hestia, placing her hand on the head of Zeus, vowed perpetual virginity. Zeus, in place of marriage, gave her to sit in the middle of the house 'receiving fat,' and to be honoured in all the temples of the gods.

In the Prytaneion of every Grecian city stood the *hearth*, on which the sacred fire flamed, and where the offerings were made to Hestia.[2] In that of Athens there was a statue of the goddess.[3] The name Hestia evidently comes from the root ΣΤΑ, and indicates the fixed steady position of the hearth in the centre of the room where the family assembled.

CHAPTER VII.

HERA:—ARES, HEPHÆSTOS, HEBE.

"Ηρη, "Ηρα. (*Juno*.)

IN Homer this goddess is one of the children of Kronos and Rhea, and wife and sister to Zeus.[4] When the latter placed his sire in Tartaros, Rhea committed Héra to the care of O'keanos and Téthys, by whom she was carefully nurtured in their grotto-palace.[5] She and Zeus had however previously 'mingled in love unknown to their parents.[6] Hésiod, who gives her the same parents, says that she was the last spouse of Zeus.[7] According to the Argive legend,[8] Zeus, who had long secretly loved his sister, watched one day when she was out walking alone near Mount Thronax, and raising a great storm of wind and rain fled shivering and trembling, under the form of a cuckoo, to seek

[1] *Theog.* 454.　　[2] Pind. *Nem.* xi. 1 *seq.*　　[3] Paus. i. 18, 3.
[4] *Il.* iv. 59.　　[5] *Il.* xiv. 202 *seq.*　　[6] *Il.* xiv. 295.
[7] *Theog.* 921.　　[8] Sch. *Theocr.* xv. 64. from Aristotle. Paus. ii. 17, 4.

shelter on the knees of the unsuspecting maiden. She covered the poor bird, as she thought him, with her mantle, and Zeus then resuming his proper form accomplished his wishes. But when she had implored him in the name of her mother to spare her, he gave her a solemn promise to make her his wife,—a promise which he faithfully performed. Henceforth the hill Thronax was named Kokkygion, i.e. *Cuckoo-Hill.*

In the Ilias (for she does not appear in the Odyssey) Héra, as the queen of Zeus, shares in his honours. The god is represented as a little in awe of her tongue, yet daunting her by his menaces. On one occasion he reminds her how once, when she had raised a storm, which drove his son Héraklés out of his course at sea, he tied her hands together and suspended her with anvils at her feet between heaven and earth;[1] and when her son Héphæstos would aid her, he flung him down from Olympos.[2] In this poem the goddess appears dwelling in peace and harmony with Létó, Dioné, Themis and their children: later poets speak much of the persecution which Létó underwent from the enmity of Héra, who also, as shall hereafter be related, made Ió, Semelé, Alkméné and other women, pay dear for their intrigues with the Olympian king.

The children of Zeus and Héra were Arés, Hébé, Eileithyia or the Eileithyiæ, to which some added the Charites or Graces.[3] Héphæstos was the progeny of Héra without a sire; she was also said to have given origin to the monster Typháón.[4]

In the mythic cycles of Dionýsos and Héraklés Héra acts a prominent part as the persecutor of the heroes, who were the offspring of Zeus by mortal mothers. In like manner, as the goddess of Argos, she is active in the cause of the Achæans in the war of 'Troy divine.' In the Argonautic cycle she was the protecting deity of the adventurous Iasón. There is, in fact, none of the Olympian deities more decidedly Grecian in feeling and character than this goddess.

The chief seats of the worship of Héra were Argos, Samos, and Platææ. She was also honoured at Sparta, Corinth, Kerkýra, and other places. The victims offered to her were kine, ewe-lambs and sows. The willow, the pomegranate, the dittany, the lily, were her sacred plants. Among birds, the cuckoo, and afterwards the gaudy stately peacock, were appropriated to the Olympian queen.

According to the legend the goddess herself formed this last

---

[1] *Il.* xv. 18 *seq.*
[2] *Il.* i. 590 *seq.* compared with xv. 22.
[3] Coluth. *Rapt. Hel.* 88, 173.
[4] Hom. *Hymn to Apolló.* 305 *seq.*

bird from the many-eyed Argos, whom she had set as keeper over the transformed Ió. Moschos[1] (in whom we first meet with this legend), when describing the basket which Európé had in her hand when, as she was gathering flowers, she was carried off by Zeus, says,

> Around, beneath the curved basket's rim
> Was Hermés formed, and near to him lay stretched
> Argos, with ever-sleepless eyes supplied;
> Out of whose purple blood was rising up
> A bird, whose wings with many colours glowed:
> Spreading his tail, like a swift-sailing ship,
> The golden basket's edge he covered o'er.

Ovid[2] says that Héra planted the eyes of Argos in the tail of her favourite bird: and Nonnos[3] asserts that Argos himself was turned into this bird.

The peacock (ταώς), we must observe, was unknown in the days of Homer, when, as we have already shown, the gods had not as yet any favourite animals. It is an Indian bird, and was according to Theophrastos introduced into Greece from the East.[4] Peafowl were first brought to Samos, where they were kept at the temple of Héra; and gradually the legend was spread that Samos was their native place, and that they were the favourite birds of its goddess. The comic poet Antiphanés, a contemporary of Sókratés, says,[5]

> 'Tis said the phœnixes are all born in
> The City of the Sun; at Athens, owls;
> Excellent pigeons Kypros hath; and Héra
> Of Samos owns, they say, the golden breed
> Of birds, the fair-form'd much-admired peafowl.

Whole flocks of them were fed in the sacred grove of the goddess. They were gradually but slowly spread through Greece. The Roman poet Ovid yokes them to the chariot of Héra:

> The sea-gods granted: in her easy car,
> By painted peabirds drawn, Saturnia moves
> Through the clear air. [6]

We have not met with any Greek authority on this subject, and suspect that he had none but that of his own rich imagination.

---

[1] *Idyll.* ii. 55 *seq.* [2] *Met.* i. 722. [3] *Dionys.* xii. 72.
[4] Its Arabic and Persian name at the present day is *Taús,* similar to the Greek ταώς, properly ταFώς, whence the Latin *pavo.* It is called *sikhi* in Sanscrit, and is supposed to be the Hebrew *tukee* (תֻּכִּי, 1 *Kings,* x. 22), which, however, may have been the parrot, whose name in Persian is *tútee.*
[5] Athén. xiv 655. [6] Ov. *Met.* ii. 531.

Few passages in the Ilias are more celebrated than the follow·
ing picture of the love-union of Zeus and Héra on the summit of
Ida:[1]

> He said ; and in his arms Kroníon seized
> His spouse. Beneath them bounteous earth sent up
> Fresh-growing grass : there dewy lotus rose,
> Crocus and hyacinth, both thick and soft,
> Which raised them from the ground. On this they lay,
> And o'er them spread a golden cloud and fair,
> And glittering drops of dew fell all around.

This is, we think justly, regarded as a sportive adaptation by
the epic poet of an ancient physical mythe of the union of Zeus
and Héra (heaven and earth, as we shall presently show) in
spring-time producing vegetation. It is in effect the *Sacred
Marriage* (ἱερὸς γάμος) of these deities, which, as we will now
proceed to explain, was represented in those places where Héra
was principally worshipped.

We have above related the Argive legend in which the cuckoo,
the herald of the spring, appears as the agent in the loves of the
two deities. There was a fount at Nauplia near Argos named
Kanathos, by bathing in which Héra, the legend said, renewed
each year her virginity.[2] In the temple of this goddess near
Mykénæ (in which stood her statue, the far-famed labour of
Polykleitos) was shewn her bed;[3] a stream called Asterión ran by
the temple, and on its banks grew the plant of the same name,
which was used for weaving the (bridal?) coronals of the goddess.[4]
The garland of Héra was termed πυλεὼν by the Spartans, and
was formed of the plant named Kyperos, and of the Helichrysos,
which is of the same *genus* with the Asterión.[5] At Argos there
was a temple of Héra Antheia (*Flowery*).[6] In all these usages
and circumstances the idea of the marriage of Héra, and its being
the cause of the spring of plants, may, we think, be discerned.

The tradition of Stymphálos in Arkadia was,[7] that Héra had
been brought up there by Temenos, who raised three temples to
her, under the names of *Virgin, Married* (τελεία), and *Widow;* the
first while she was a maid, the second when she married Zeus,
the third when she separated from him. The real cause of these
names will however appear from a comparison of this legend
with the one just given, and with those which are to follow.

At Samos the temple of Héra stood on the banks of the Imbrasos, and within its precincts was shown a willow (λύγος), be·
neath whose shade, according to the temple legend, the goddess

---

[1] *Il.* xiv. 345. [2] Paus. ii. 38, 2. [3] Id. ii. 17, 3.
[4] Id. ii. 17, 2. [5] Alcman, *Fr.* 29. [6] Paus. ii. 22, 1. [7] Id. viii. 22, 2.

was born.[1] Another name of the Imbrasos was said to be Parthenios.[2] Every year an ancient wooden image (βρέτας) of Héra disappeared from the temple: it was then diligently sought for, and was always found on the sea-shore bound to a willow, whose longest branches were drawn down so as to envelope it. The priestess then loosed it; it was washed; a kind of cakes were set before it, and it was brought back to the temple.[3] In this ceremony also may be discerned a reference to the marriage of Héra. The disappearance of the image looks like the carrying away of the betrothed maiden; the willow bed, for such it apparently is, refers perhaps to the chastity of the goddess, the willow being regarded as a great promoter of this virtue;[4] she is bound to it probably to prevent her flight from Zeus. The cakes may have had some analogy with the *confarreatio* of the Romans,[5] or our own usage of bride cakes. In the temple there was a statue of the goddess in the bridal-dress,[6] and a new bridal-robe was woven for it every year.[7]

Like most of the usages and ceremonies of Greece, this Samian custom was pragmatised.[8] The temple, it was said, had been built by the Leleges and the Nymphs: Admété, daughter of Eurystheus, fled thither from Argos; the goddess appeared in a vision to her, and she became priestess of the temple. Some Tyrrhénian pirates, at the instigation of the Argives, stole the image, in order to draw down the vengeance of the people on Admété. But lo! their ship became motionless when the sacred image was brought on board. In terror the pirates carried it back to the shore, and made an offering of cakes to appease it. They then departed, and next day the rude ignorant people of the isle, in their search after it, finding it on the sea-shore, thought it had run away of itself, and bound it to a willow to prevent its doing so again. Admété then loosed it and restored it to its place in the temple, and hence, it was said, arose the annual ceremony.

In the name Admété, it will be observed, we have again a reference to the chastity of the goddess. The making her an Argive, and daughter of Eurystheus, appears also to intimate

---

[1] Paus. vii. 4, 4.
[2] Strab. x. 2, 17, p. 457. Sch. *Apoll. Rh.* i. 187. Διὰ τὸ ἐκεῖ παρθένον οὖσαν τετράφθαι τὴν Ἥραν. The island itself was thence named Parthenia. Id. *ib.*, Kallim. iv. 49. Another of its names was Anthemis or Anthemus (*Flowery*), Strab. *ut sup.*
[3] Ménodotos *ap. Athén.* xv. p. 672.
[4] Plin. *Nat. Hist.* xxiv. 9.
[5] " Novæque nuptæ farreum præferebant."—Plin. *Nat. Hist.* xviii. 3.
[6] " Nubentis habitu."—Varro.
[7] In Élis it was woven every fifth year. Paus. v. 16, 2.
[8] Athén. *ut sup.*

that the worship of Héra came to Samos from Argos, and that it
belonged to the ante-Dórian period.

In Bœótia the popular mythe had taken a somewhat different
view of the character of Héra, and she appears as the jealous wife,
such as she is represented in the Ilias.

Héra, the legend said, offended for some cause or another with
Zeus, renounced his bed and society. The god in perplexity sought
advice from the autochthon Alalkomenos, and by his counsel gave
out that he was going to marry another; and cutting down a handsome tree, they shaped it into the form of a woman, naming it
Dædala, and arrayed it in the bridal habit. The bridal hymn was
sung, the nymphs of the Tritón furnished the bath, Bœótia gave
pipes and dances, and the pretended bride was placed on a car
drawn by kine. When this reached the ears of Héra she could not
contain herself, but coming down in a rage from Kithærón, followed
by the women of Platææ, she rushed to the car, seized the supposed bride, and tore off her dress. Then discovering the heat, she
became reconciled to her lord, and with joy and laughter took herself the place of the bride, and committed the image to the flames.[1]

This legend was invented to explain the origin of a national
festival of Bœótia named the Dædala. Of this there were two
kinds, the Small, celebrated every seven, the Great, every sixty
years. According to Pausanias, there was a wood near Alalkomenæ where grew the finest oaks in Bœótia, to which the Platæans
repaired, and setting some dressed meat before it, and watching
the ravens, marked which of them took the meat, and on what
tree he sat. They then cut down that tree and made an image
from it. It is probable that the other cities of Bœótia did the
same; and this was called the Little Dædala. When the time of
the Great Dædala came, there were fourteen images ready (one
for each of the cities of Bœótia), with which they repaired to the
banks of the Asópos. Each image was placed on a car, and a
bride-maid (νυμφεύτρια) set beside it. The procession then moved
on, each car taking its place by lot, and ascended to the summit
of Kithærón, where an altar of wood stood ready prepared; a bull
was there sacrificed to Zeus, and a cow to Héra; and other victims,
with wine and perfumes, were cast on the altar, as also were the
images, and the whole was set on fire, and a flame thus raised was
visible to a great distance.[2]

From the very confused account of this festival which has been
transmitted to us, it is a matter of much difficulty to ascertain its
real character. It seems most probable, however, that it was

---

[1] Plut. *Fr.* ix. 6.　Paus. ix. 3.　　　　[2] Paus. *ut supra.*

designed to form an astronomic cycle, and to serve as a calendar of time, and also to operate as a bond of union among the Bœótian states. For our present purpose it is sufficient to remark the union expressed in it of Zeus and Héra, and the sacrifice of the bull and cow to these deities.

There was another legend of Zeus and Héra, of which Kithæ-rón was also the scene. The maiden Héra, it said, was reared in Eubœa; but Zeus stole her away, and Kithærón gave him a shady cavern to conceal her in. When her nurse Makris came in quest of her charge and wanted to search the cavern, Kithærón would not permit her, saying that Zeus was abiding there with Létó. The nurse then went away, and Héra in consequence of this associated Létó with herself in her temple and altar under the title *Of-the-Recess* (μυχία).[1]

Here again we meet with the Sacred Marriage performed in secret, as at Argos. In Eubœa, Héra was called *Virgin* (πάρ-θενος);[2] and a place there sacred to her was named Parthenion. Makris (which we find personified in the legend) was a name of that island.

The marriage of Zeus and Héra was viewed as the pattern of those of mankind, and the goddess was held to preside over the nuptial league. Hence she was named the *Yoker* (ζυγία), the *Consecrator* (τελεία), the *Marriage-goddess* (γαμήλιος).

As we have already hinted, we are inclined to assent to the opinion of those who view in Zeus the heaven, and in Héra the earth, and regard this holy marriage so continually renewed, and of which the memory was kept up in so many places, as that of heaven and earth in the spring of each returning year, when the showers descend, and foliage, herbage, and flowers cover the face of nature.[3] As the earth exhibits no symptoms of becoming effete, but brings forth her progeny with undiminished vigour in each succeeding year, the early sages of Greece devised the mythe of the perpetually renewed virginity of the goddess.[4] The physical union of earth and heaven is, we think, plainly dis-

---

[1] Plut. *Fr.* ix. 3. [2] Eustath. *Il.* ii. p. 286.
[3] See Welcker *in Schwenk.* 267 *seq.* A German poet of the 17th century says prettily of May —

> Dieser Monat ist ein Kuss
> Das der Himmel gibt der Erde,
> Dass sie jetzo eine Braut,
> Künftig eine Mutter werde.

Empedoklés (*ap. Athenag. Leg.* 18) termed Héra (earth) φερέσβιος, and Nennos (viii. 168) names her παμμήτωρ.
[4] "Tellurem, quæ divinam et æternam juventam sortita communis omnium parens dicta sit."—Colum. i. pr.

cernible in the beautiful passage of Homer above noticed. It is given without any disguise by Euripidés;[1] in whose time the deities of the popular creed were generally regarded as personifications of physical objects and powers; and he has been imitated by the Latin Epicurean poets Lucretius[2] and Vergil.[3] It may finally be observed that in the mythology of Scandinavia, Odin, the god of heaven, is married to Frigga, the goddess of the vernal flowering earth.

The consecration of the cow to Héra is also to be considered as a proof of her being regarded as the earth ; for in the religion of the ancient Germans (which was akin to that of the Greeks) the cow was assigned to the service of the goddess Hertha, or Earth.[4] In India this animal is a symbol of the earth and of Lakshmi or Srees, the goddess who blesses it with abundance;[5] in Egypt it was sacred to Isis, whom Hérodotos identifies with the Démétér of Greece.[6] At Argos the chariot in which the priestess of Héra rode was drawn by oxen,[7] so too were the cars in the procession of the Dædala, where a cow also was the victim. It has likewise been supposed, not without reason, that the ancient epithet of the goddess, Ox-eyed or Cow-eyed (βοῶπις), refers to this connection between her and that animal.[8]

Héra was represented by Polykleitos seated on a throne, holding in one hand a pomegranate, the emblem of fecundity in the other a sceptre, with a cuckoo on its summit.[9] Her air is dignified and matronly, her forehead broad, her eyes large, and her arms finely formed; she is dressed in a tunic and mantle.

By Homer and Hésiod Héra is styled,[10] 1. Ox-eyed; 2. White-armed; 3. Gold-seated; 4. Gold-shod; 5. Majestic.

---

[1]
Γαῖα μεγίστη καὶ Διὸς αἰθήρ·
ὁ μὲν ἀνθρώπων καὶ θεῶν γενέτωρ,
ἡ δ' ὑγροβόλους σταγόνας νοτίους
παραδεξαμένη τίκτει θνατοὺς
τίκτει δὲ βορὰν φῦλά τε θηρῶν·
ὅθεν οὐκ ἀδίκως.
μήτηρ πάντων νενόμισται.—Fr. Chrys.: see also Æsch. Fr. 38.

[2] De Rer. Nat. i. 251 seq.; ii. 991 seq. This poet nearly translates the preceding lines of Euripidés.
[3] See the beautiful passage, Geor. ii. 325 seq.
[4] Tac. Germ. 40.   [5] See Bohlen, Das alte Indien, i. 254.
[6] Hérod. ii. 44, 156. Σύμβολον (Αἰγυπτίοις) γῆς τε αὐτῆς καὶ γεωργίας καὶ τροφῆς ὁ βοῦς.—Clem. Alex. Strom. v. p. 413 Sylb.
[7] Hérod. i. 31.
[8] Müller, Proleg. 262. He renders it cow-formed with reference to Ió.
[9] Paus. ii. 17, 4.
[10] 1. βοῶπις: 2. λευκώλενος: 3. χρυσόθρονος: 4. χρυσοπέδιλος: 5. πότνια.

The origin of the name Héra is somewhat difficult to determine. We may venture to reject the derivations from ἀήρ, *air*, and from ἐράω, *to love*,[1] of which the former refers to a physical theory, according to which Héra was the air and Zeus the æther; and the latter to that part of her character by which she was the goddess presiding over the nuptial union. As the goddess of the earth in the religion of Argos, her name would seem to come very simply from ἔρα, *earth*; yet there is great plausibility in the theory of Ἥρα being the feminine of Ἥρως, anciently Ἥρος,[2] and that these terms answered to each other as the Latin *herus, hera*, and the German *Herr, Herrin*, and therefore signified *Master* and *Mistress*.[3] It is possible, however, that the two derivations may in a certain sense be correct. The goddess may have been originally merely *Earth*, and then, as she separated from the object over which she presided and became the Olympian queen, she may have been regarded as the great Mistress.[4]

Ἄρης. (*Mars.*)

Arés, the god of war, is in Homer and Hésiod the son of Zeus and Héra.[5] His delight was in tumult and strife; yet his wild fury was always forced to yield to the skill and prudence of Pallas-Athéné, guided by whom Diomédés wounds and drives him from the battle;[6] and in the conflict of the gods,[7] this goddess herself strikes him to the earth with a stone. To give an idea of his huge size and strength, the poet says in the former case that he roared as loud as nine or ten thousand men; and in the latter, that he covered seven plethra of ground. On another occasion Arés received a wound from the spear of Héraklés;[8] he was also shut up in prison by the gigantic youths, Otos and Ephialtés.[9]

Terror and Fear (Δειμὸς and Φόβος), the sons of Arés, and Strife (Ἔρις) his sister, accompany him to the field when he seeks the battle.[10] Another of his companions is Enyó[11] (Ἐννώ), the daughter of Phorkys and Kétó[12] according to Hésiod, a war-goddess answering to the Bellona of the Romans. The name Enyalios,

---

[1] Plato, *Cratyl.* 404.

[2] The Ἔρος of Hésiod is Ἔρως in the subsequent writers.

[3] Müller, *Proleg.* 244. Böttiger, *Kunst-Myth.* ii. 222, 223. Δέσποινα and ἄνασσα were titles frequently given to the goddesses; the former in particular belonged to Démétér and her daughter.

[4] See above, p. 9. For further information on the subject of Héra the reader s referred to Welcker, *ut supra*, and to Böttiger's *Kunst-Myth.* ii. 213 *seq.*

[5] *Il.* v. 892, 896. *Theog.* 922.   [6] *Il.* v. 855.   [7] *Il.* xxi. 403 *seq.* Hés. Ἀσπίς, 460.   [9] *Il.* v. 385.   [10] *Il.* iv. 440.

[11] *Il.* v. 333. Probably the *Inciter* from ΝΥΩ, νύσσω, *to prick, to goad.*

[12] *Theog.* 273.

which is frequently given to him in the Ilias,[1] corresponds with hers.

The figurative language, which expresses oiigin and resemblance by terms of paternity, may have given a mortal progeny to Arés. As a person who came by sea was figuratively called a son of Poseidón, so a valiant warrior was termed *a son*, or, as it is sometimes expressed by Homer, *a branch* or *shoot of Arés* (ὄζος ῎Αρηος). But the only tale of his amours related at any length by the poets is that of his intrigue with Aphrodíté.

Arés—so sang Démodokos to the Phæakians [2]—loved Aphrodíté, the beautiful but frail spouse of Héphæstos, and often visited her in the absence of her unsightly husband. These visits were not unobserved by Hélios (for what can escape the piercing eye of the Sun-god?), and he gave information to the injured artist. Héphæstos dissembled his rage, and going to his workshop forged a net so subtile as to be invisible, so strong as to be infrangible by even the god of war. He disposed it in such a manner as to catch the lovers: then feigning a journey, set out as it were for Lémnos. Arés, who was on the watch, flew to his expecting mistress: the heedless lovers were caught in the net: the Sun-god gave notice; the husband returned, and standing at his door called all the gods to come and behold the captives. The dwellers of Olympos laughed heartily, and some jokes were passed on the occasion. Poseidón however took no part in the mirth, but drawing Héphæstos aside pressed him to accommodate the affair. The artist, doubtful of the honour of the soldier, was loath to assent, till Poseidón pledged himself to see him paid. He then yielded, and released his prisoners. Arés hastened away to his favourite region of Thráke: Aphrodíté fled to hide her shame in her beloved isle of Kypros.

This tale is an evident interpolation in the part of the Odyssey where it occurs. Its date is uncertain; but the language, the ideas, and the state of society which it supposes, might almost lead us to assign its origin to a comparatively late period. It may be, as is generally supposed, an ancient physical mythe, or rather a combination of two such mythes; for beauty might naturally have been made the spouse of the god from whose workshop proceeded so many elegant productions of art, and, as we are about to show, another physical view led to the union of Arés and Aphrodíté. Still, we cannot avoid regarding the present tale rather as a sportive effusion of Grecian wit and satire, though it may have been founded on those mythic views. In Greece, as

---

[1] *Il.* vii. 166; viii. 264; xiii. 519; xvii. 259; xviii. 309; xx. 69; xxii. 132.
[2] *Od.* viii. 266 *seq.* Ov. *Art. Amat.* ii. 561.

everywhere else, wealth and beauty were occasionally united in wedlock : and there too, as elsewhere, martial renown and showy exterior were passports to the hearts of the fair. If the tale was framed on the coast of Asia, we know that warfare was frequent enough among the Grecian cities there to allow of reputation being gained by deeds of valour.[1]

To the above tale has also been appended by later writers a legendary origin of the cock (ἀλεκτρυών). It is said that Alektryón was a youth whom Arés placed to watch while he was with Aphrodíté; and, for neglect of his task, he was changed by the angry god into the bird of his name.[2]

Hésiod says[3] that Harmonia (*Order*) was the daughter of Arés and Aphrodíté. This has evidently all the appearance of a physical mythe, for from Love and Strife (i.e. attraction and repulsion) it is clear, arises the order or *harmony* of the universe.[4] Terror and Fear are also said by Hésiod[5] to have been the offspring of Arés and Aphrodíté, of whose union with Héphæstos (to whom he gives a different spouse) he seems to have known nothing. In the Ilias we may observe that Arés and Aphrodíté are spoken of as brother and sister, much in the same manner as Apolló and Artemis.[6]

The best known of the children of this god by mortal women are Askalaphos and Ialmenos,[7] Œnomaos king of Pisa, Diomédés of Thráke, Kyknos, Phlegyas, Dryas, Parthenopæos, and Téreus; he was also said to have been the sire of Meleagros and other hero-princes of Ætolia.[8] His children, like those of Poseidón, were usually of a violent character.

The Hill of Ares (Ἄρειος πάγος), at Athens, is said to have derived its appellation from the following circumstance. Halirrhothios, a son of Poseidón, had offered violence to Alkippé, the daughter of Arés. Her father killed the offender, and he was summoned by Poseidón before a court of justice for the murder. The trial was held on this hill, the twelve gods sat as judges, and Arés was acquitted.[9] Another tradition derived the name of the hill from the Amazons having there offered sacrifices to Arés, their sire.[10] It is quite manifest therefore that the real origin of the name was unknown.

The temples and images of Arés were not numerous. He is

---

[1] See Hérod. vi. 42.
[2] Sch. *Aristoph. Birds,* 836. Lucian, *Alectr.* 3. Eudocia, 34.   [3] *Theog.* 937.
[4] Plut. *de Is. et Os.* 48. Arist. *Pol.* ii. 6. Macrob. *Sat.* i. 19. Welcker, *Kret. Kol.* 40.   [5] *Theog.* 934.   [6] *Il.* v. 359 *seq.* ; xxi. 416 *seq.*
[7] *Il.* ii. 512.   [8] For all these sons of Arés see Apollodóros, *passim.*
[9] Eur. *Elec.* 1257. Apollod. iii. 14, 2. Sch. *Eur. Orest.* 1650.
[10] Æsch. *Eum.* 689.

represented as a warrior, of a severe menacing air, dressed in the heroic style, with a cuirass on, and a round Argive shield on his arm. His arms are sometimes borne by his attendants.

The epithets of Arés were all significative of war. He was styled by Homer and Hésiod,[1] 1. *Blood-stained*; 2. *Shield-borer*; 3. *Man-slaying*; 4. *Town-destroyer*; 5. *Gold-helmed*; 6. *Brazen*; 7. *People-rouser*; 8. *Impetuous*, &c.

The name Arés ("Αρης) would appear to be connected with ἀνήρ, ἄρρην and ἀρετὴ (*valour*), and therefore to be significant of the character of the god. But some late critics[2] seem rather to look to ἔρα, *earth*, for its origin, and to regard him as having been one of the chthonic powers in the Pelasgian creed, and to think that, like those of Hermés and Pallas-Athéné, his character changed with the change of manners in Greece. In like manner the Latin Mars and the Hindú Kartekeya seem to have had originally a different character from the martial one.[3] Perhaps the original conception of Arés and Aphrodíte was physical and cosmogonic, answering, as we have intimated above, to the Strife and Love (νεῖκος and φιλότης) of Empedoklés, the repulsion and attraction of modern physics. In that case ἔρις might be the root of his name.

"Ηφαιστος. (*Vulcanus*.)

Héphæstos, the Olympian artist, is in Homer the son of Zeus and Héra.[4] According to Hésiod[5] he was the son of Héra alone, who was unwilling to be outdone by Zeus when he had given birth to Pallas-Athéné.[6] He was born lame, and his mother was so displeased at the sight of him that she flung him from Olympos. The Ocean-nymph Eurynomé and the Néréis Thetis saved and concealed him in a cavern beneath the Ocean, where during nine years he employed himself in manufacturing for them various ornaments and trinkets.[7] We are not informed how his return to Olympos was effected, but we find him in the Ilias firmly fixed there; and all the houses, furniture, ornaments, and arms of the Olympians were the work of his hands.

It would be an almost endless task to enumerate all the articles formed by Héphæstos; we shall however notice some of the chief of them. One thing is remarkable concerning them, that they

---

[1] 1. μιαίφονος: 2. ῥινοτόρος: 3. ἀνδρειφόντης, βροτολοιγός; 4. πτολιπόρθος 5. χρυσεοπήληξ; 6. χάλκεος: 7. λαοσσόος: 8. θοῦρος.
[2] Welcker *in Schwenk*. 232 *seq.* Völcker, *Myth. der Jap.* 79.
[3] See Mythology of Italy, *Mars.*   [4] *Il.* i. 572, 578.   [5] *Theog.* 927
[6] As *she* was the celestial, *he* the terrestrial heat, they are assigned their appropriate parents.   [7] *Il.* xviii. 394 *seq.*

were all made of the various metals; no wood, or stone, or any other substance, entering into their composition : they were moreover frequently endowed with automatism.

All the habitations of the gods on Olympos were made by Héphæstos, and were all composed of metal; as also were their chariots and arms. He made armour for Achilleus and other mortal heroes.[1] The fatal collar of Harmonia was the work of his hands.[2] The brass-footed, brass-throated, fire-breathing bulls of Æétés king of Kolchis were the gift of Héphæstos to Æétés' father Hélios ;[3] and he made for Alkinoos, king of the Phæacians, the gold and silver dogs which guarded his house.[4] For himself he formed the golden maidens, who waited on him, and whom he endowed with reason and speech.[5] He gave to Minós, king of Kréte, the brazen man Talós, who each day compassed his island three times, to guard it from the invasion of strangers.[6] The brazen cup in which the Sun-god and his horses and chariot are carried round the earth every night was also the work of this god.[7]

The only instances we meet of Héphæstos' working in any other substance than metal are in Hésiod, where at the command of Zeus he forms Pandóra of earth and water,[8] and where he uses gypsum and ivory in the formation of the shield which he makes for Héraklés.[9] That framed by him for Achilleus in the Ilias is all of metal.

In the Ilias[10] the wife of Héphæstos is named Charis; in Hésiod,[11] Aglaia, the youngest of the Charites ; in the interpolated tale in the Odyssey, Aphrodíté the goddess of beauty.[12] He is said to have asked Pallas-Athéné in marriage of Zeus, who gave him permission to win her if he could. Héphæstos was a rough wooer, and attempted to offer violence to the goddess. An Athenian legend refers the birth of Erichthonios, one of the mythic kings of Attica, to this circumstance.[13]

The favourite haunt of Héphæstos on earth was the isle of Lémnos. It was here he fell when flung from heaven by Zeus for attempting to aid his mother Héra, whom Zeus had suspended in the air with anvils fastened to her feet. As knowledge of the earth advanced, Ætna,[14] Hiera (one of the Liparæan isles),[15]

---

[1] *Il.* viii. 195. [2] Apollod. iii. 4, 2. [3] Apoll. Rh. iii. 230.
[4] *Od.* vii. 91. Nitzsch *in loc.* [5] *Il.* xviii. 419.
Apollod. i. 9, 26. See Part II. chap. xii. *Minós.*
[·] See above, p. 48. [8] Ἔργ. 60.
[9] Ἀσπίς, 141. Thiersch and Göttling, we think justly, regard *vv.* 141--317 as the interpolation of a poet of a much later age.
[10] *Il.* xviii. 382. [11] *Theog.* 945. [12] See above, p. 94.
[13] See below, Part II. chap. vi. [14] Æsch. *Prom* 366.
[15] Kallim. iii. 47. Strab. vi. 2, 10, p. 275. Sch. *Apoll. Rh.* iii. 42.

H

and all other places where there was subterranean fire, were regarded as the forges of Héphæstos; and the Kyklópes were associated with him as his assistants. In Homer, when Thetis wants Héphæstian armour for her son, she seeks Olympos, and the armour is fashioned by the artist god with his own hand. In the Augustan age, Venus prevails on her husband, the master-smith, to furnish her son Æneas with arms; and he goes down from Heaven to Hiera, and directs his men, the Kyklópes, to execute the order.[1] It is thus that mythology changes with modes of life.

Héphæstos and Pallas-Athéné are frequently joined together as the communicators to men of the arts which embellish life and promote civilization.[2] The philosophy of this view of the two deities is correct and elegant; as also is that of the union of Héphæstos with Aphrodíté or a Charis indicative of the elegance and beauty of his works.[3]

The artist-god is usually represented as of ripe age, with a serious countenance and muscular form: his hair hangs in curls on his shoulders. He generally appears with hammer and tongs at his anvil, in a short tunic, and his right arm bare, sometimes with a pointed ap on his head. The Kyklópes are occasionally placed with him.

The poetic epithets of Héphæstos were derived either from his lameness or from his skill. He was called,[4] 1. *Both-feet-lame*; 2. *Lame-foot*, or *Weak-ankled*; 3. *Feeble*; 4. *Renowned-* or *Bright-artist*; 5. *Very-renowned*, or *Very-bright*; 6. *Wise*, etc.

Héphæstos must have been regarded originally as simply the fire-god, a view of his character which we find even in the Ilias.[5] Fire being the great agent in reducing and working the metals, the fire-god naturally became an artist. The former was probably Héphæstos' Pelasgian, the latter his Achæan character. The simplest derivation of his name therefore seems to be that which,

---

[1] *Æneis*, viii. 407 *seq*.

[2] *Od.* vi. 233; xxiii. 160. Hom. *Hymn* xx. Solón, v. 41. Plato, *Politic.* p. 177. Völcker, *Myth. der Jap.* 21 *seq*.

[3] In Gen. iv. 22, Na'amah (*beautiful*) is the sister of Tubalcain (*copper-smith*?), the "instructor of every artificer in brass and iron." The coincidence is curious.

[4] 1. ἀμφιγυήεις: 2. κυλλοποδίων: 3. ἠπεδανός: 4. κλυτοτέχνης, κλυτοεργός: 5. ἀγακλυτὸς, περικλυτός: 6. πολύμητις, πολύφρων. In ἀμφιγυήεις and some other compounds ἀμφὶ is i. q. ἄμφω, as in some Latin compounds *ambi* is i. q. *ambo*.

[5] *Il.* xx. 73; xxi. 330 *seq*. His name is also synonymous with *fire*, ix. 468; xvii. 88; xxiii. 33.

regarding the first letter as euphonic, and Héphæstos as Phæstos (Φαῖστος), deduces it from φάω, *to give light*.[1]

Some of the epithets given to Héphæstos are calculated to excite our surprise. The deities of Olympos are usually represented as endowed with perfect beauty and vigour, and yet here is one of them to whom is ascribed a physical defect of no small magnitude—the want of the power of free and independent motion. Nowhere then does the necessity of regarding the gods as mere personifications more appear than in this remarkable instance. On all other theories the difficulty seems inexplicable; while, if we regard Héphæstos as the fire-god, *i. e.* as the fire, a simple and obvious solution presents itself. Fire, as compared with air and water, is fixed and stationary, incapable of advancing or even of sustaining itself without the aid of other substances. This the personifying genius of antiquity seems to have expressed by making the fire-god weak in the ankles, and therefore in general r quiring support; for which purpose the poet gives him golden hand-maidens, as in those days the domestic servants were always females.[2]

Ἥβη. (*Juventas.* 𝔜𝔬𝔲𝔱𝔥.)

Hébé was one of the children of Zeus and Héra.[3] In Olympos she appears as a kind of maid-servant; she hands round the nectar at the meals of the gods;[4] she makes ready the Chariot of Héra,[5] and she bathes and dresses Arés when his wound had been cured.[6] When Héraklés was assumed to the abode of the gods, Youth was given to him in marriage.[7]

It was apparently to bring the life of the gods more into harmony with that of men, that the office of cup-bearer was

---

[1] Plato, *Cratyl.* 407.

[2] This explanation, though our own, cannot lay claim to perfect originality; or see Sch. *Od,* viii. 300. Phornutus also (*N. D.* 19) made an approach to it, when he said that the lameness meant that he could not go without a stick, and Eméric-David says, "Attendu la marche inégale et vacillante de la famme."—*Vulcain,* etc. Paris, 1838.

[3] *Od.* xi. 604. Hés. *Theog.* 922. Her parentage is not mentioned in the lias. Ovid, we know not on what authority, calls her (*Met.* ix. 415) the step-daughter of Zeus.

[4] *Il.* iv. 2. (Heyne *in loc.*) This is also the office of the Valkyries in the Asgard of Scandinavian mythology.

[5] *Il.* v. 722.

[6] *Il.* v. 9 5. This however, was not a servile office; the daughter of Nestór renders it to Télemachos (*Od.* iii. 464), as Angelica the Fair does to Orlando *Orl. Innam.* I. xxv. 38: comp. *Don Quixote,* Part I. ch. 50), and as, we believe, still done by maidens in some remote parts of Scandinavia.

[7] *Od.* xi. 604.

afterwards transferred to Ganymédés.[1]   Alkæos and Sapphó give
it to Hérmes, the celestial herald,[2] it being the office of the heralds
in Homer.   A poet named Kapito bestowed it (we know not for
what reason) on Harmonia.[3]

At Phlius in the Peloponnése a goddess was worshipped, whom
the ancient Phliasians, Pausanias says,[4] called Ganymédé, but in
his time she was named Hébé ; Strabó says[5] that Hébé was worshipped at Phlius and Sikyón under the name of Dia.   It is not
improbable that from the name Ganymédés (*Joy-promoter*), so well
suited to a cup-bearer, a feminine title had been formed for Hébé.

Hébé was called by the poets,[6] 1. *Fair-ankled*; 2. *Gold-wreathed*;
3. *Bright-limbed*.   The epithet πότνια, given to Hébé by Homer,
may perhaps best be rendered by *dignified;* its root is *pot-*, as it
appears in πόσις and *potens.*

CHAPTER VIII.

LETO :—PHŒBOS-APOLLO, ARTEMIS.

Λητώ.   (*Latona.*)

LÉTÓ was daughter of the Titans Kœos and Phœbe.[7]   In Homer
she appears as one of the wives of Zeus, and there occur no trace
of enmity between her and Héra.   Posterior poets, however, fabl
much of the persecution she underwent from that goddess.[9]   He
children by Zeus were Phœbos-Apollo and Artemis.

While wandering from place to place with her children, Lét
says a legend most prettily told by Ovid,[10] arrived in Lykia.   Th
sun was shining fiercely, and the goddess was parched with thirs
She saw a pool, and knelt down at it to drink.   Some clowns, wh
were there cutting sedge and rushes, refused to allow her to slak
her thirst.   In vain the goddess entreated, representing tha
water was common to all, and appealing to their compassion fc
her babes.   The brutes were insensible : they not only mocked ;
her distress, but jumped into and muddied the water.   The goddes

---

[1] *Il.* xx. 234 ; in direct opposition with iv. 2.   [2] Athén. x. 425.
[3] Id. *ib.*   [4] Paus. ii. 13, 3.   [5] *Geog.* viii. 6, 24, p. 382.
[6] 1. καλλίσφυρος : 2. χρυσοστέφανος : 3. ἀγλαόγυιος.
[7] See above, p. 58.   [8] *Il.* xxi. 499.
[9] Hésiod also could have known nothing of this enmity, as (*Theog.* 918)
makes her marriage with Zeus precede that of Héra.
[10] *Met.* vi. 313 *seq.* from Nicander ; see Anton. Lib. 35.   Vergil also see
to allude to it, *Geor.* i. 378.   This is surely one of those legends which a
mere sports of fancy.

though the most gentle of her race, was roused to indignation: she raised her hand to heaven and cried, " May you live for evei in that pool!" Her wish was instantly accomplished, and the churls were turned into frogs.

Niobé, the daughter of Tantalos and wife of Amphíon, proud of her numerous offspring, ventured to set herself before Létó : the offended goddess called upon her children Apolló and Artemis, and soon Niobé was by the arrows of these deities made a childless mother, and stiffened into stone with grief.[1] Tityos, a son of Earth, having attempted to offer violence to this goddess, also fell by the arrows of her children.[2]

Létó was called,[3] 1. *Fair-ankled* ; 2. *Sable-vested* ; 3. *Gold-tressed* ; 4. *Much-honoured.*

With respect to the origin of this goddess and her name, the most simple hypothesis, in our opinion, is that which regards herself as Night, and esteems her name to be of the same family of words with λήθω, λήθη, and with the Latin *lateo* and *Laverna*, and, therefore, to signify *the Concealer*, i.e. *darkness*. The parents assigned to her correspond with this hypothesis; for light, which is made to spring from darkness, may, in a reversed order, be regarded as its origin. The epithet 'sable-vested'[4] and the mildness of character usually ascribed to this goddess,[5] also accord with Night (εὐφρόνη); and if it should appear that the children of Létó were Sun and Moon, there can hardly remain a doubt of this being her true nature.

Φοῖβος 'Απόλλων. (*Apollo.*)

Phœbos-Apollo was the son of Zeus and Létó. In Homer he is the god of archery, music, and prophecy.[6] His arrows were not merely directed against the enemies of the gods, such as O'tos and Ephialtés :[7] all sudden deaths of men were ascribed to his darts ; sometimes as a reward, at other times as a punishment. He was

---

[1] See below, Part II. ch. iv. *Zethos and Amphíon.*

[2] See Part II. ch. iv. *Tityos.*

[3] 1. καλλίσφυος : 2. κυανόπεπλος : 3. χρυσοπλόκαμος : 4. ἐρικυδής.

[4]   " Sable-vested Night, eldest of things."
          Milton, *Par. Lost*, ii. 962. See the epithets of Night, above, p. 46.

[5] In Plato (*Cratyl.* 406) her name is deduced ἀπὸ τῆς πραότητος τῆς θεοῦ, apparently from λῶ or λεῖος.

[6] Thus in the Hymn presently to be quoted, the new-born deity says, *v.* 131—

          Εἴη μοι κιθαρίς τε φίλη καὶ κάμπυλα τόξα,
          χρήσω δ' ἀνθρώποισι Διὸς νημερτέα βουλήν.

[7] *Od.* xi. 318.

uiso by his shafts the sender of pestilence, and he removed it
when duly propitiated.   At the banquets of the gods on Olympos,
Apolló played on his *phorminx* or lyre, while the Muses sang.[1]

> Thus they the whole day long till set of sun
> Feasted ; nor wanted any one his part
> Of the equal feast, or of the phorminx fair
> Which Phœbos held, or of the Muses' lay,
> Who sang responding with melodious voice.

Eminent bards, such as Démodokos,[2] were held to have derived
their skill from the teaching of Apolló or the Muses.   Prophets
in like manner were taught by him; at Pythó he himself revealed
the future.[3]

As in Homer and Hésiod no birth-place of any of the gods is
noticed, we must regard the tale of the birth of Phœbos-Apolló
in the isle of Délos as being posterior to the time of these poets.
According to the Homeridian hymn in his honour, it took place
in the following manner.   Létó, persecuted by Héra, besought all
the islands of the Ægæan to afford her a place of rest; but all
feared too much the potent queen of heaven to assist her rival.
Délos alone consented to become the birth-place of the future
god, provided Létó would pledge herself that he would not con-
temn her humble isle, and would erect there the temple vowed by
his mother.   Létó assented with an oath, and the friendly isle
received her.   For nine days and nights the pains of labour continued.   All the goddesses, save Héra and Eileithyia (whom the
art of Héra kept in ignorance of this great event), were assembled
in the isle.   Moved with compassion for the sufferings of the
travailing goddess, they despatched Iris to Olympos, who brought
Eileithyia secretly to Délos.   Létó then grasped a palm-tree in
the soft mead, on the banks of the Inópos, Earth smiled around,
Apolló sprang to light, and the goddesses shouted aloud to celebrate his birth.   They washed and swathed the infant deity, and
Themis gave him nectar and ambrosia.   As soon as he had tasted
the divine food, his bands and swaddling-clothes no longer retained him : he sprang up, and called to the goddesses to give
him a lyre and a bow, adding that he would thenceforth declare
to men the will of Zeus.   He then, to the amazement of the assembled goddesses, walked firmly on the ground; and Délos,
exulting with joy, became covered with golden flowers.[4]

---

[1] *Il.* i. 601.   [2] *Od.* viii. 488.   [3] *Ib.* 79.

[4] *Hymn to Apolló :* see Theognis, 5 *seq.* Eur. *Hec.* 457 *seq.* We may
observe that the tale of Délos having been an invisible or floating island, does
not appear to have been devised when this hymn was composed.   We meet
with the latter notion first in Pindar, *Fr. Prosod.* 1.

Kallimachos[1] relates the birth of Apolló somewhat differently. According to him, Héra, knowing that the son of Létó would be dearer to Zeus than her own son Arés, was resolved, if p ssible, to prevent his birth. Determined, therefore, that no place should receive the travailing goddess, she took her own station in the sky : she placed her son Arés upon the Thracian mountain Hæmos, and her messenger Iris on Mount Mimas, to watch the islands. All the lands, hills, and rivers of Hellas refused to hearken to the prayers of the goddess. Moved with wrath, the unborn Apolló menaced Thébes for her discourteous refusal, and foretold the future fate of the children of Niobé. The river-god Péneios alone valued justice and humanity more than the wrath of Héra : he checked his stream to give a shelter to the goddess ; but instantly Arés arose, clashed his arms, that the mountains and all Thessaly trembled at the sound, and was about to fling the peaks of Pangæos on the generous stream, who undauntedly awaited the issue ; when Létó passed further on, entreating him not to expose himself to danger on her account. She now turned to the islands, but none would receive her ; and the unborn god called out to her that a floating island was to be his birth-place. At length she met Délos, then called Asteria, which floated among the Kyklades.[2] Délos generously invited the wearied goddess to enter her, expressing her willingness to encounter the anger of Héra. This last goddess, however, when informed by her messenger, remits her anger ; Apolló is born ; a choir of swans comes from the Mæonian Paktólos, and flies seven times around the isle to celebrate his birth ; the Délian nymphs receive and sing the sacred verses of Eileithyia ; the sky gives back the joyful cry ; and Délos, as before, becomes invested in gold.

In the Homeridian hymn to Apolló, the manner of his first getting possession of Pythó is thus related. When Apolló resolved to choose the site of his first temple, he came down from Olympos into Pieria : he sought throughout all Thessaly ; thence went to Eubœa, Attica, and Bœótia, but could find no place to his mind. The situation of Tilphussa, near Lake Kópäïs, in Bœótia, pleased him ; and he was about to lay the foundations of his temple there, when the nymph of the place, afraid of having her own fame eclipsed by the vicinity of the oracle of Apolló, dissuaded him, by representing how much his oracle would be disturbed by the noise of the horses and mules coming to water at her stream. She recommends to him Krissa, beneath Mount Parnassos, as a quiet sequestered spot, where no unseemly sounds would disturb the holy silence demanded by an oracle. Arrived

---

[1] *Hymn to Délos.* [2] Comp. Verg. *Æn.* iii. 75

at Krissa, the god is charmed by the solitude and sublimity of the scene. He forthwith sets about erecting a temple, which the hands of numerous workmen speedily raise, under the direction of the brothers Trophónios and Agamédés. Meanwhile the god slays with his arrows the monstrous serpent which abode there and destroyed the people and cattle of the vicinity. As she lay expiring, the exulting victor cried, "Now *rot* (πύθεν) there on the man-feeding earth;" and hence the place and oracle received the appellation of Pythó. The fane was now erected, but priests were wanting. The god as he stood on the lofty area of the temple, cast his eyes over the sea, and beheld far off, south of the Peloponnése, a Krétan ship sailing for Pylos. He plunged into the sea, and in the form of a porpoise sprang on board the ship. The crew sat in terror and amazement; a south wind carried the vessel rapidly along: in vain they sought to land at Tænaron; she would not obey the helm. When they came to the bay of Krissa a west wind sprang up, and speedily brought the ship into port; and the god in the form of a blazing star left the vessel, and descended into his temple. Then, quick as thought, he came as a handsome youth with long locks waving on his shoulders, and accosted the strangers, inquiring who they were and whence they came. To their question in return, about what that place was to which they were come, he replies by informing them who he is, and what his purpose was in bringing them thither. He invites them to land, and says, that as he had met them in the form of a porpoise (δελφὶν) they should worship him as Apolló Delphinios, whence the place should also derive its name.[1] They now debark: the god playing on his lyre precedes them, and leads them to his temple, where they become his priests and ministers.[2]

As might be expected, the legends of so celebrated an event as the establishment of the oracle of Apolló at Delphi, the sacred counsellor of all Greece, are various. The names Pythó and Delphi alone sufficed to give a foundation for some of them. The former, which evidently signifies the *Place of Enquiry*, a title well suited to an oracle, gave occasion to the legend above related,

---

[1] "There is a kind of phonetic symbols of towns and districts, according to which an animal or plant, whose name sounds like theirs, becomes as it were their arms. In the department of figures this has been long since recognised from the medals, but it also frequently appears in the mythic form, and in this it in some cases loses itself in the most remote antiquity."— Welcker, *Kret. Kol.* 72.

[2] See Müller, *Proleg.* 209 *seq.* He thinks that this hymn was composed before the destruction of Kirrha (Ol. 47). He also thinks (*Dor.* i. 241) that the worship of Apolló at Delphi was established by Dórians from Parnassos and Krétans from the island, about 200 years before the Dórian migration.

and also to one of a huge serpent named Pythón,[1] which it is said, came out of his den and attacked Létó when she was going by with her children in her arms; she stood then on a rock, holding the infant Artemis, and urged on her son by calling to him, ἴε, παῖ, and he despatched the monster with his arrows.[2] This serpent, another version of the legend says, was named Delphíné,[3] for the formation of which name, as we may perceive, Delphi probably gave its aid, as it did also for that of the change of the god into the porpoise, and for his title Delphinios.

The Homeric Apolló is a being of remarkable purity, and the poet seems to have had a strong feeling of the dignity of his character, for he never ventures to use the same familiarity with him as with the other gods, Zeus himself not excepted. Apolló is the friend of man, he protects his worshippers, and he punishes the unjust and impious. At all periods of Grecian literature we find the character of the 'pure (ἁγνὸς) god,' as he was emphatically called, still the same. There is a serene cheerfulness always ascribed to him, he is averse from gloom, and the promoter of joy and innocent pleasure;[4] but at the same time dignified in his sentiments and actions. The purity of his character appears also in this, that no amours with either goddesses or mortals are ascribed to him in the Homeric poems.[5] When, however, in subsequent times, heroes and heroic families were made to derive their lineage from the residents of Olympos, Phœbos-Apolló was also provided with his love-adventures by the poets; yet it is observable that he was not remarkably happy in his love, either meeting with a repulse, or having his amour attended with a fatal termination, and that none of these heroic families could claim him as the head of their genealogy.

"The first love of Phœbos," says Ovid, "was Daphné, the daughter of Péneios." Apolló, proud of his victory over the Pythón, beholding Erós bending his bow, mocked at the efforts of the puny archer. Erós incensed flew, and taking his stand on Parnassos shot his golden arrow of love into the heart of the son of Létó, and discharged his leaden one of aversion into the bosom of the nymph of Péneios. Daphné loved the chase, and it alone, indifferent to all other love. Phœbos beheld her, and burned with passion. She flies, he pursues: in vain he exhausts his eloquence, magnifying his rank, his power, his possessions; the nymph but

---

[1] Yet in the Semitic languages *Pethen* (פֶתֶן) is a snake, an adder.

[2] Eur. *Iph. Taur.* 1245 *seq.* Klearchos of Soli *ap. Athén.* xv. 701. Hygin. 140. Ov. *Met.* i. 439.   [3] Apoll. Rh. ii. 706.

[4] See Æschyl. *Agam.* 1075 *seq.* Kallim. *Hymn to Apolló,* 20 *seq.* Plut. *De Ei.* 20.   [5] *Il.* ix. 557 *seq.,* may seem to form an exception, but see Appendix H.

urges her speed the more. Fear gave wings to the nymph, love to the god. Exhausted and nearly overtaken, Daphné on the banks of her father's stream stretched forth her hands, calling on Péneios for protection and change of form. The river-god heard; bark and leaves covered his daughter, and Daphné became a bay-tree (δάφνη, laurus). The god embraced its trunk, and declared that it should be ever afterwards his favourite tree.[1]

Of this legend we need only observe, that it is one of the many tales devised to give marvel to the origin of natural productions, and that its object is to account for the bay-tree being sacred to Apolló.

Apolló, it is also said by the same poet, thought himself happy in the love and fidelity of Korónis, a maiden of Larissa. His ignorance was his bliss, for the nymph was faithless. The crow,[2] the favourite bird of the god, and then white as his swans, saw the maiden in the arms of a Hæmonian youth, and bore the tidings to his master, who immediately discharged one of his inevitable arrows into the bosom of the frail fair one. Dying she deplores the fate, not of herself, but of her unborn babe. The god repents when too late; he tries in vain his healing art, and dropping celestial tears, places her on the funereal pyre: extracting the babe, he gave him to be reared by Cheirón, the Kentaur. To punish the crow, he changed his hue from white to black.[3]

This is probably a legend of some antiquity, for in a fragment of one of the poems ascribed to Hésiod,[4] it is said that the crow brought tidings to Phœbos of the marriage of Ischys, the son of Eilatos, with Korónis, the daughter of Phlegyas. The tale is also told by Pindar,[5] but he says nothing of the crow, making the god himself, though at Pythó, discover what was done through his divine power. At his desire Artemis shot the fair offender with her arrows.

Marpéssa, the daughter of Euénos, was beloved by Apolló, whose suit was favoured by her father. Idas, another lover, having obtained a winged chariot from Poseidón, carried off the appa-

---

[1] Ov. Met. i. 452 seq. Hygin. 203. The great majority of the authorities place the legend in Arcadia, making Daphné the daughter of the Ladón by Earth (the natural parent of a plant), and add that it was her mother that changed her on her prayer. Paus. viii. 20, 4. Nonn. xlii. 387. Eudocia, 106, 273. Sch. Il. i. 14. Stat. Theb. iv. 289. Serv. Buc. iii. 63. Lucian, De Salt. 48. Apolló was, however, much more closely connected with the Péneios and Tempé than with the Ladón and Arcadia.

[2] Κόραξ, corvus. We have proved this to be the crow: see our Vergil, Ex-curs. VI.; κορώνη, cornix, raven, would come nearer the name of Korónis, but perhaps an opposition was intended.   [3] Ov. Met. ii. 542 seq.

[4] Ap. Sch. Pind. Pyth. iii. 8 (14), 27 (48).   [5] Pyth. iii. 8 (14) seq.

rently not reluctant maid. Her father pursued the fugitives, but coming to the river Lykormas, and finding his progress stopped by it, he slew his horses and cast himself into the stream, which from it derived its name Euénos.[1] Meantime Apolló met and took the fair prize from Idas. The matter being referred to Zeus, he allowed the maiden to choose for herself; and fearing that when she grew old Apolló would desert her, she wisely chose to match with her equal, and gave her hand to her mortal lover.[2]

Cassandra, daughter of Priamos king of Troy, also attracted the love of this god: the price she set on her favours was the gift of prophecy. The gift was freely given, but the royal maid refused the promised return; and the indignant deity, unable to recall what he had bestowed, made it useless by depriving her predictions of credit.[3]

Kyréné, a daughter of the river Péneios, was another of the loves of Phœbos; he carried her in his golden chariot over the sea to Libya, where she bore him a son named Aristæos.[4]

By Kreüsa, daughter of Erechtheus king of Attica, Apolló was the sire of Ión, from whom the Iónians derived their origin.[5]

The only celestial amour recorded of Apollo is that with the muse Kalliopé, of which the fruit was Orpheus.[6] No parents more suitable could be assigned to the poet, whose strains could move the woods and rocks, than the god of poetry and the muse *Fair-voice*.

Kyparissos and Hyakinthos were two beautiful youths, favourites of Apolló; but that favour availed not to avert misfortune. The former, having by accident killed a favourite stag, pined away with grief, and was changed into the tree which bears his name.[7] The latter, a youth of Amyklæ, was playing one day at discus-throwing with the god. Apolló made a great cast, and Hyakinthos running too eagerly to take up the discus, it rebounded and struck him in the face. The god, unable to save his life, changed him into the flower which was named from him, and on whose petals Grecian fancy saw traced αἲ, αἲ, the notes

---

[1] *i. e.* from εὖ and ἠνία, the name of the river giving origin to the legend. Euenos may come from εὖ and ἄω, *to breathe*, or *to satiate*.

[2] Apollod. i. 7, 8. Sch. *Il.* ix. 557. This is alluded to, we may perceive, in the Ilias, and it is the only love-tale of Apolló in Homer. In the Hindú poem of Nalas, the heroine Damayanti acts in the same manner as Marpéssa, and on the same principle.

[3] Æsch. *Ag.* 1211. Apollod. iii. 12, 5.

[4] Pindar, *Pyth.* ix. : see Part II. chap. iv. *Autonoé*, etc.

[5] See Part II. chap. v. *Creüsa*, etc.   [6] See below, ch. xii. *Muses*.

[7] Ov. *Met.* x. 106 *seq.* Serv. *Æn.* iii. 64. . We have not met with any Greek authority for this legend, and the same story is told of the Ital.an god Silvanus. Serv. *Geor.* i. 20.

of grief.[1] Other versions of the legend say that Zephyros (*West-wind*), enraged at Hyakinthos' having preferred Apolló to himself, blew the discus, when flung by Apolló, against the head of the youth, and so killed him.[2] A festival called the Hyakinthia was celebrated for three days in the summer of each year at Amyklæ, in honour of the god and his unhappy favourite.[3]

The babe saved from the pyre of Korónis was Asklépios, who became so famous for his healing powers. Extending them so far as to restore the dead to life, he drew on himself the enmity of Hadés, on whose complaint Zeus with his thunder deprived him of existence. Apolló incensed slew the Kyklópes who had forged the thunderbolts, for whicn bold deed Zeus was about to hurl him down to Tartaros, but, on the entreaty of Létó, he was so far mollified as to be content with the offender's becoming a servant to a mortal man for the space of a year. Admétos, king of Pheræ, in Thessaly, was the person selected to be honoured by the service of the god, who, according to the more dignified and probable view of the mythe, pastured this prince's flocks and herds on the verdant banks of the river Amphrýsos, making the kine under his charge all bear twins;[4] while according to another he discharged for him even the most servile offices.[5] When the term of his servitude was expired he was permitted to return to Olympos.[6]

In this mythic tale of Apolló serving Admétos Müller sees matter of deeper import than might at first sight be suspected. According to the Delphian tradition, it was for slaying the Pythón that the god was condemned to servitude. Every eighth year the combat with this being was the subject of a mimic representation at Delphi. A boy who personated Apolló, having in

---

[1] Eur. *Hel.* 1469 *seq.* Apollod. i. 3, 3, iii. 10, 3. Ov. *Met.* x. 162 *scq.*

[2] Eudocia, 408. Nonn. x. 253 *seq.;* xxix. 95 *seq.* Lucian, *Dial. Deor.* 14; *De Salt.* 45.

[3] See Müller, *Dorians,* i. 373. This critic gives strong reasons for supposing the Hyakinthia to have been originally a feast of Démétér. The legend in the text was merely invented to give a mythic account of its origin.

[4] Apollod. i. 9, 15; iii. 10, 4. Eur. *Alc.* Prol. *cum schol.*, in which Hésiod and Pherekýdés are quoted as authorities. Hygin. 49, 50. Diodór. iv. 71. Verg. *Geor.* iii. 2. Voss, *in loc.* The Alexandrians, namely Rhianos (*ap. Sch. Eur. Alc.* 1) and Kallimachos (*Hymn to Apolló,* 49), say that it was out of love he served Admétos.

[5] That is if critics be right in referring the following line of Sophoklés (*ap.* Plut. *de Def. Orac.* 14) to this subject.

Οὑμὸς δ' ἀλέκτωρ (*husband*) αὐτὸν ἦγε πρὸς μύλην.

These, Müller (*Dor.* i. 339) says, are the words of Alkéstis in a drama named, it would seem, Admétos.   [6] See Part II. chap. ii. *Admétos.*

mimic show slain the Pythón, fled and took his way along the Sacred Roaa to the vale of Tempé in the north of Thessaly, to be purified as it were from the guilt of the bloodshed; and having there plucked a branch of bay, in imitation of the act of the god, he returned to Delphi at the head of a *theoria*.[1] This mimic flight also represented the servitude of the god, which the legend placed at Pheræ in Thessaly.[2] Müller, therefore, who views in the whole transaction a deep moral sense, and a design to impress upon the minds of men a vivid idea of the guilt of bloodshed, by representing even the pure god Apolló as being punished for slaying the Pythón, a being of demon origin, deems the original legend to have been a still bolder stretch of fancy, and that it was to the god of the under-world, to Hades himself, that Apolló was obliged to become a servant.[3] This hypothesis he thinks is confirmed by the names which occur in the legend: for Admétos,[4] he says, must have been an epithet of Hadés; Klymené, the name of Admétos' mother, is one of Persephoné; and Pheræ was a town sacred to the goddess Hekaté, who was connected with the lower-world.[5]

It cannot be said positively whether this mythe (which is apparently a temple legend of Delphi) was known to Homer. In the Catalogue,[6] the mares of Eumélos Pherétiadés are highly praised for their beauty and swiftness, and it is added that Apolló had reared them in Pieria.[7] At the funeral-games, toward the close of the poem,[8] Eumélos, named Pherétiadés and son of Admétos, is one of the competitors in the chariot-race. These notices, however, we may observe, occur in the parts of the Ilias of which the antiquity is most dubious. It may also be doubted if the temple legend of Delphi could be as old as the age to which Homer is usually referred. In another of the latter books of the Ilias it is said that Poseidón and Apolló, by the command of Zeus (we know not why given), served Laomedón, king of Troy, for a year; at the end of which time he refused to pay them their wages, and threatened to cut off the ears of both, and even to sell the latter for a slave. The task of Apolló had been to tend the herds of the Trojan king in the valleys of Ida.[9]

[1] Pindar and Kallimachos *ap.* Tertul. *De Cor. Mil.* 7. Luc. *Phar.* vi. 409.
[2] Plut. *de Def. Orac.* 15, 21. *Quæst. Gr.* 12. Ælian. *Var. Hist.* iii. 1.
[3] The same notion is expressed in Plutarch (*De Def. Or.* 21) if the reading given by Wyttenbach from Eusebius be the true one, as it most probably is.
[4] Equivalent with 'Αδάμαστος, see p. 83.
[5] Müller, *Proleg.* 300 *seq. Dorians,* i. 338. *Eumen.* 152, 159. [6] *Il.* ii. 763.
[7] The Venetian MS. (which is followed by Wolf) reads Πηερίη for Πιερίη: see Heyne *in loco.* According to the hymn to Hermés (*v.* 22, 70 *seq.*) the herds of the gods fed in Pieria under the care of Apolló. [8] *Il.* xxiii. 288.
[9] *Il.* xxi. 442 *seq.* Any one who reflects on the exalted characters of these

Apolló, it is said,[1] was taught divination by Pan, the son of Zeus and Thymbris. For his musical instrument he was indebted to the invention of his half-brother Hermés. Pan, the god of shepherds, venturing to set his reed-music in opposition to the lyre of Apolló, was pronounced overcome by Mount Tmólos, who had been chosen judge; and all present approved the decision except king Midas, whose ears were, for their obtuseness, lengthened by the victor to those of an ass.[2] The Silén [3] Marsyas, having found the pipe which Athéna for fear of injuring her beauty had flung away, contended with Apolló before the Muses, and was by him flayed for his temerity when vanquished; and the tears of the nymphs and rural gods for the fate of their companion gave origin to the stream which bore his name.[4]

This last legend admits of a very simple explanation. Marsyas was a river-god of Phrygia, the country in which the music of wind-instruments was employed in the service of the gods; while the lyre was used by the Greeks in that of Apolló.[5] Hence, to express the superiority of the latter, a contest was feigned between Apolló and Marsyas. At the cavern in the town of Kelænæ in Phrygia, whence the stream Marsyas issues, was hung, for some reason which is not very clear, a leathern bag,[6] and hence it was fabled that Apolló flayed his vanquished rival.[7]

The Homeric Apolló is a divinity totally distinct from Hélios, though probably, as will shortly appear, originally the same. When mysteries and secret doctrines were introduced into Greece, these deities were united, or perhaps we might say re-united. Apolló at the same period also took the place of Pæéon, and became the god of the healing art.[8]

---

two gods in the undoubtedly genuine parts of the poem, must have some suspicion of this legend. The building of the wall is spoken of elsewhere (vii. 452), and it is said to have been the work of *both* the gods: comp. Eur. *Tróad.* 4 *seq.*

[1] Apollod. i. 4, 1. Some MSS. for Θύμβρεως read "Υβρεως: others for Πανὸς read πατρὸς : see Heyne *in loc.* This critic seems disposed to read μαθὼν παρὰ τοῦ πατρὸς, in favour of which is all mythic analogy. According to Nicander (in Athén. vii. 296), the sea-god Glaukos was the instructor of Apolló.
[2] This legend is only to be found in Ovid (*Met.* xi. 153 *seq.*).
[3] Hérodotos thus justly names him. See below, chap. xvi. *Silenos.*
[4] Hérod. vii. 26. Apollod. i. 4, 2. Paus. ii. 7, 9. Plut. *de Fluv.* 10. Diodór. iii. 59. Hygin. 165. Ov. *Met.* vi. 382 *seq.* ; *Fast.* vi. 703 *seq.*
[5]   Sonante mixtum tibiis carmen lyra,
              Hac Dorium, illis Barbarum.—Hor. *Epod.* ix. 5.
[6] Hérod. *ut supra.* Xen. *Anab.* i. 2, 8. Ælian, *Var. Hist.* xiii. 20.
[7] See Müller, *Proleg.* 113.
[—] Eur. *Alc.* 970. Plato, *Critias.* Hermann, *Ueber das Wescn,* etc., 108. In the Ilias, however (v. 445 *seq.*), Æneias is cured of his wound by Létó and Artemis

This god was a favourite object of Greci∋n worship, and his temples were numerous. Of these the most celebrated were that of Delphi in Phókis,—his acquisition of which we have above re-lated, and where, as the mythe of Pythón would seem to intimate, a conflict took place between the religion of Apolló, proceeding southwards from Pieria, or westwards from Délos, and the ancient religion of the place, the worship of Gæa or Themis,[1]—and those of Délos, of Patara in Lykia, Klaros in Iónia, Grynion in Æolis, Didyma at Milétos; in all of which his oracles revealed the future.

A very able mythologist of the present day[2] maintains that the worship of Apolló was originally peculiar to the Dórian race, who were at all times his most zealous votaries. As the Homeric poems prove the worship of this deity to have been common to the Achæan race, and well known on the coasts of Asia long before the Dórian migration, the critic is forced to have recourse to the not very probable supposition of a Dórian colony having left the mountains of Thessaly many years before the Trojan war, and carried the Apolló-religion to Kréte, whence it was spread to the coast of Asia, and also conveyed to Délos and Delphi. We cannot assent to this theory. Apolló seems to have been one of the original gods of the Grecian race; and he was worshipped by one people more than another, on the same principle as in India Vishnú is in some places more worshipped than Seeva; Thor was most honoured by the ancient Norwegians, and Odin by the Swedes; Sant' Iago is more frequently invoked in Spain, and St. Antony in Italy,—without the existence and the rights of the others being denied.[3]

Apolló was supposed to visit his various favourite abodes at different seasons of the year :

> Such as, when wintry Lykia and the streams
> Of Xanthos fair Apolló leaves, and comes
> To his maternal Délos, and renews
> The dances ; while round his altars shout
> Kretans, Dryopians, and the painted race
> Of Agathyrsians ; he, along the top
> Of Kynthos walking, with soft foliage binds
> His flowing hair, and fastens it in gold ;
> His arrows on his shoulders sound.[4]

One of the most beautiful descriptions of these progresses of Apolló was that given by the lyric poet Alkæos. The poem has

---

:n the temple of Apolló, and (xv. 254 *srq.*) that god himself restores vigour to Hectór. Pæéón may come from παίω, and express the effect of the sun-beams.
[1] See Æsch. *Eumen.* 1 *seq.* Sch. *in loc.*   [2] Müller, *Dórians*, vol. i. book ii.
[3] See Höck, *Kreta*, vol. ii.   [4] Verg. *Æn.* iv. 143.

unfortunately perished, but we find the following analysis of it in the works of the sophist Himérios.[1]

"When Apolló was born, Zeus adorned him with a golden head-band and lyre, and gave him moreover a team to drive (the team were swans).[2] He then sent him to Delphi and the streams of Kastalia, thence to declare prophetically right and justice to the Hellénes. He ascended the car, and desired the swans to fly also to the Hyperboreans.[3] The Delphians, when they perceived this, arranged a Pæan and song, and setting choirs of youths around the tripod, called on the god to come from the Hyperboreans. Having given laws for a whole year among those men, when the time was come which he had appointed for the Delphic tripods also to resound, he directed his swans to fly back from the Hyper-boreans. It was then summer, and the very middle of it, when Alkæos leads Apolló back from the Hyperboreans; for when summer shines and Apolló journeys, the lyre itself whispers in a summer-tone of the god. The nightingales sing to him, as the birds should sing in Alkæos; the swallows and cicadas also sing, not narrating their own fate when among men, but tuning all their melodies to the god. Kastalia too flows with poetic silver streams, and Kephissos swells high and bright with his waves, emulating the Enipeus of Homer. For, like Homer, Alkæos ventures to make the very water capable of perceiving the access of the god."

It was probably on account of their pure white hue that the swans were assigned to the pure god Phœbos-Apolló; and this connection with the god of music gave origin to the fable, as it is esteemed, of the melody of these birds.[4] The wolf was also assigned to this deity, on account of his bright colour, as some think, but it is far more likely that it was the similitude of his name to an epithet of the god which gave occasion to it. The noisy chirping *tettix* (*cicada*), or tree-cricket, was naturally associated with the god of music; and as the god of augury Apolló was the patron of the hawk and crow. The bay-tree was the plant dedicated to this deity.

---

[1] *Or.* xiv. 10. Voss, *Myth. Br.* ii. 109.
[2] Claudian (*De VI. Con. Honor.* 30) makes his team on this occasion griffons.
[3] See above, p. 30.
[4] There seems, however, to be some foundation for it. A naturalist of the present day says, "This species of swan deserves the title *Musicus ;* for when in small troops they fly aloft in the air their melodious melancholy voices sound like trumpets heard in the distance."—Faber, *Geschichte der Vögel Islands,* 1822, quoted by Finn Magnusen (*Edda Sœmundar,* iii. 530), whose own words are, " Cygnorum cantus dulcissimus in Islandia, Scotia, et pluribus regionibus sæpissime auditur, *quod etiam nosmet, propria experientia edocti, attestari possumus.*" We have ourselves heard the trumpet-tones of a swan. See Voss, *Myth. Br.* ii. 132.

Apollŏ was represented by the artists in the perfection of united manly strength and beauty. His long curling hair hangs loose, or bound with the *strophium* behind; his brows are wreathed with bay; in his hands he bears his bow or lyre. The wonderful Apollŏ Belvidere shows at the same time the conception which the ancients had of this benign deity, and the high degree of perfection to which they had attained in sculpture.

Few deities had more appellations than the son of Létŏ. He was called Délian, Delphian, Pataræan, Klarian, &c., from the places of his worship; and Smynthian from a Phrygian word signifying *mouse*, of which animal a legend said he had been the destroyer in Tróas. He was also styled,[1] 1. *Crooked*, or *Bending*, probably from the position of the archer when shooting;[2] 2. *Herding*, as keeping the flocks and herds of the gods, or those of Admétos; and by the poets, 3. *Silver-bowed*; 4. *Far-shooter*; 5. *Gold-sworded*, or *Gilder*; 6. *Well-haired*, and *Gold-haired*; 7. *Unshorn-locked*; 8. *People-rouser*, &c.

This god had several epithets apparently connected with the Greek name of the wolf (λύκος); but as there was an ancient Greek word signifying *light* (ΛΥΚΗ),[3] of a similar form, the great probability, in the eyes of all who regard Apollŏ as the sun-god, or as a moral being of great purity, will be that this last is the real root of these names, and that, as we said above, it was merely similarity of sound that caused the wolf, or the country Lykia, to be regarded as their origin. Thus the god is called by Homer λυκηγενὴς, which may be rendered with the utmost propriety *Light-born*,[4] or *Light-producing*, whereas the usual interpretation, *Lykia-born*, contradicts the fact of the Homeric gods not having birth-places on earth. Two other epithets of Apollŏ, λύκιος and λύκειος, which are usually rendered *Lykian*, or *Wolf-destroying*, or rather *Wolfish*, may signify *Lighted*, or *Lighting*. There are two others, λυκοκτόνος, which evidently signifies *Wolf-killing*, and λυκοεργὴς, which is apparently *Wolf-restraining*, or *-destroying*,[5]

---

[1] 1. λοξίας: 2. νόμιος: 3. ἀργυρότοξος: 4. ἕκατος, ἑκατηβελέτης, ἑκαέργος, ἤϊος: 5. χρυσάορος, χρυσάωρ: 6. εὐχαίτης, χρυσοχαίτης: 7. ἀκερσεκόμης: 8, λαοσσόος.

[2] Müller, *Dór.* i. 328. It is usually derived from the *crooked* ambiguous nature of oracular responses; but Artemis, who never gave oracles, was named Loxó.

[3] This word is connected with λευκὸς, *white*, and with the Latin *lux*, *luceo*, and the Teutonic *Licht* and *Light*. The terms ἀμφίλυκη and λυκάβας prove, we think, the former existence of ΛΥΚΗ. See Müller, *ut sup.* 325 *seq.*

[4] Some would derive it from λύγη, *darkness*.

[5] It might, however, be *Light-produced* or *-producing*; or, if λύγη be the origin, both epithets might signify *darkness-destroying*.

I

but they are probably of late origin, and formed after the derivation from λύκος, *wolf*, had become the prevalent one.

Apolló was also named Agyieus (ἀγυιεὺς), as the guardian of
the streets and roads (ἀγυιαί). Stone-pillars with pointed heads,
placed before the doors of the houses, were the images of the god
under this name. This practice was peculiar to the Dórians.[1]
Apolló was called Pæan, either from his healing power (from
παύω or ΠΑΩ), in which case he would be identical with Pæéon ;
or from his protecting and avenging character (from παίω). The
hymn sung to him on the cessation of a plague, or after a victory,
was thus named.

The name Phœbos-Apolló is generally regarded as of Grecian
origin. The former part critics are unanimous in deriving from
φάω, *to shine;* of which the advocates for the original identity of
this deity with Hélios see at once the appropriateness : the maintainers of the contrary system interpret Phœbos *pure, unstained,*
making it equivalent to the ἀγνὸς θεὸς, as he is sometimes called.[2]
Apolló is by some derived from ὅλω, *to destroy;* by others from an
old verb ἀπέλλω, akin to the Latin *pello, to drive away;* by others
again from ἀέλιος, *the sun*, with the digamma F between the first
two vowels. The strangest etymon of all is that of Buttmann,
who, taking the Krétan form 'Αβέλιος to be the original one,
deduces it, according to his system of tracing the Greek religion
from the East, from Jabal and Jubal, the first musician and first
herdsman according to Scripture.[3]

῎Αρτεμις. (*Diana.*)

Artemis was daughter of Zeus and Létó, and sister to Apolló.
She was the goddess of the chase ;[4] she also presided over health.
The sudden deaths of women were ascribed to her darts,[5] as those
of men were to the arrows of her brother, of whom she forms the
exact counterpart.[6] Artemis was a spotless virgin; her chief joy
was to speed like a Dórian maid over the hills, followed by a train
of nymphs in pursuit of the flying game.[7]

> As arrow-joying Artemis along
> A mountain moves, either Taÿgetos high,

---

[1] Sch. *Aristoph. Wasps,* 870.　Sch. *Eurip. Phœn.* 631.
[2] See Müller, *Dórians,* i. 324.　Pindar (*Ol.* vii. 60 (108)) terms Hélios ἀγνὸν
θεόν, and Æschylos (*Prom.* 22) speaks of his φοίβη φλόξ.
[3] *Mytholog.* i. 167 *seq.*　　　　　[4] *Il.* v. 51; xxi. 485.　*Od.* vi. 102 *seq.*
[5] *Il.* vi. 428 ; xix. 59.　*Od.* xi. 172 ; xv. 478.
[6] Claud. *Rapt. Pros.* ii. 27 *seq.*
[7] *Od.* vi. 102.　Comp. *Hymn to Aphrodíte,* 16 *seq.* and Apoll. Rh. iii. 876 *seq*

Or Erymanthos, in the chase rejoiced
Of boars and nimble deer ; and with her sport
The country-haunting nymphs, the daughters fair
Of Ægis-holding Zeus, while Létó joys ;
O'er all she high her head and forehead holds,
Easy to know, though beautiful are all.

The Homérids have also sung the huntress-goddess: cne of them in his hymn to her thus describes her occupations:[1]

Along the shady hills and breezy peaks,
Rejoicing in the chase, her golden bow
She bends, her deadly arrows sending forth.
Then tremble of the lofty hills the tops ;
The shady wood rebelloweth aloud
Unto the bowstring's twang; the earth itself
And fishy sea then shudder : but she still
A brave heart bearing goeth all around,
Slaughtering the race of salvage beasts.   But when
Beast-marking, arrow-loving Artemis
Would cheer her soul, relaxing her curved bow
She to her brother Phœbos-Apolló's house
Ample repaireth, to the fertile land
Of Delphi, there to arrange the lovely dance
Of Muses and of Graces ; then hangs up
Her springy bow and arrows, and begins
To lead the dance ; her body all arrayed
In raiment fair.   They, pouring forth their voice
Divine, sing Létó lovely-ankled, how
She brought forth children, 'mid the Deathless far
The best in counsel and in numerous deeds.

Kallimachos thus relates the early history of the goddess.[2]

Artemis while yet a child, as she sat on her father's knee, besought him to grant her permission to lead a life of perpetual virginity,[3] to get a bow and arrows formed by the Kyklópes, and to devote herself to the chase.   She further asked for sixty Ocean-nymphs as her companions, and twenty nymphs from Amnísos in Kréte as her attendants.   Of towns and cities she required not more than one, satisfied with the mountains, which she never would leave but to aid women in the pains of childbirth.   Her indulgent sire assented with a smile, and gave her not one but thirty towns.   She speeds to Kréte, and thence to Ocean, and selects all her nymphs.   On her return she calls at Lipara on Héphæstos and the Kyklópes, who immediately lay aside all their work to execute her orders.   She now proceeds to Arkadia, where

---

[1] *Hymn* xxvii.   [2] *Hymn to Artemis.*
[3] The purity and chastity generally ascribed to Artemis may, as some think, have their origin in the pure unsullied light of the moon in southern regions ; but may as well have had a moral origin in the character of those maidens who devoted themselves to rural pursuits.

Pan, the chief god of that country, supplies her with dogs of an excellent breed. Mount Parrhasios then witnessed the first exploit of the huntress-goddess. Five deer larger than bulls, with horns of gold, fed on the banks of the ' dark-pebbled ' Anauros at the foot of that hill : of these the goddess unaided by her dogs caught four, which she reserved to draw her chariot : the fifth, destined by Héra for the last labour of Héraklés, bounded across the Keladón and escaped.

According to the same poet, the chariot of Artemis and the harness of her deer are all of gold. When she drives to the house of Zeus, the gods come forth to meet her. Hermés takes her bow and arrows, and Apolló used to carry in her game, till Héraklés was received into Olympos, when for his strength that office devolved on him. He carries in the bull, or boar, or whatever else she may have brought, exhorting the goddess to let the hares and small game alone, and attach herself to the boars and oxen; for Héraklés, the poet observes, though deified, still retains his appetite. The Amnisiades then unyoke her stags, and bring to them from Héra's mead some of the trefoil on which the horses of Zeus feed, and fill their golden troughs with water. The goddess herself meantime enters the house of her father, and sits beside her brother Apolló.

The adventures of Artemis were not numerous. She turned, as we shall relate below, Aktæón into a stag, for having unconsciously beheld her when bathing.[1] Kallistó was changed by her into a bear, for breach of chastity.[2] O'ríón perished by her arrows ;[3] as also did Chioné the daughter of Dædalión, who set her beauty above that of the goddess.[4] With her brother she destroyed the children of Niobé, who had presumed to prefer herself to Létó ;[5] and in a fable later than Homer she is said to have detained the Grecian fleet at Aulis, in consequence of Agamemnón's having killed a hind which was sacred to her, and to have required the sacrifice of his daughter Iphigeneia. The Alóeids, O'tos and Ephialtés, it was said, sought in marriage Héra and Artemis : the latter goddess, changing her form into that of a hind, sprang out between the two brothers, who aiming their darts at the supposed beast, by her art pierced each other and died.[6]

We have already noticed the practice of the Greeks to unite similar deities, or to make one of them principal, and the others companions or attendants ; and also to form nymphs and other subordinate beings attached to the service of the gods out of their

[1] See Part II. chap. iv. *Autonoé.*   [2] Part II. chap. viii. *Kallistó.*
[3] *Od.* v. 123.   [4] Ov. *Met.* xi. 321.   [5] *Il.* xxiv. 602
[6] Apollod. i. 7, 4. Kallim. *Hymn* iii. 264 : see Part II. chap. iv. *O'tos.*

epithets. Of these practices Artemis furnishes more examples perhaps than any other deity.

The Krétans worshipped a goddess the same as or very similar to Artemis, whom they named Britomartis, which in their dialect signified *Sweet-Maid*.[1] She was also called Diktynna, a goddess of that name, and of a similar nature, having been perhaps united with her. There was a similar deity named Aphæa, worshipped at Ægína, and they were all joined in a legend in the following manner.

The Krétan nymph Britomartis, the daughter of Zeus and Charmé, was a favourite companion of Artemis. Minós falling in love with her, pursued her for the space of nine months, the nymph at times concealing herself from him amidst the trees, at times among the reeds and sedge of the marshes. At length, being nearly overtaken by him, she sprang from a cliff into the sea, where she was saved in the nets (δίκτυα) of some fishermen. The Krétans afterwards worshipped her as a goddess under the name of *Diktynna*, from the above circumstance, which also was assigned as the reason of the cliff from which she threw herself being called *Diktæon*. At the rites sacred to her, wreaths of pine or lentisk were used instead of myrtle, as a branch of the latter had caught her garments and impeded her flight. Leaving Kréte, Britomartis then sailed for Ægína in a boat: the boatman attempted to offer her violence, but she got to shore and took refuge in a grove on that island, where she became invisible (ἀφανής): hence she was worshipped in Ægína under the name of Aphæa.[2]

The well-known legend of Alpheios and Arethusa offers another remarkable instance of this procedure.

Arethusa, it is said, was an Arcadian nymph, and a companion of the huntress-goddess. As she was one day returning from the chase she came to the clear stream of the Alpheios, and enticed by its beauty stripped herself and entered it, to drive away the heat and the fatigue. She heard a murmur in the stream, and terrified sprang to land. The river-god rose; she fled away, naked as she was; Alpheios pursued her. She sped all through Arcadia, till with the approach of evening she felt her strength to fail, and saw that her pursuer was close upon her. She then prayed to Artemis for relief, and was immediately dissolved into a fountain. Alpheios resumed his aqueous form, and sought to mingle his waters with hers. She fled on under the earth and through the sea, till she

---

[1] Βριτόν, ἀγαθόν, Et. Mag. *v.* Βριτόμαρτις.
[2] Kallim. *Hymn* iii. 189. Diodór. v. 76. Anton. lib. 40. Strab. x. 4, 12, p. 479. Paus. ii. 30, 3. Diktynna (like δίκτυον) apparently comes from δίκω, *to cast*, and alludes to the moonbeams; Aphæa evidently comes from φάω, *to shine*.

rose in the isle of Ortygia at Syracuse, still followed by the amorous stream.[1]

The explanation of this mythe is as follows.[2] Artemis was worshipped in E'lis under the titles of Alpheiæa, Alpheióa, Alpheiónia, and Alpheiusa;[3] and there was a common altar to her and Alpheios within the precincts of the Altis at Olympia.[4] When in the fifth Olympiad Archias the Corinthian founded the colony of Syracuse in Sicily, there were among the colonists some members of the sacerdotal family of the Iamids of Olympia.[5] These naturally exercised much influence in the religious affairs of the colony, whose first seat was the islet of Ortygia. A temple was built there to Artemis Of-the-Stream (ποταμία),[6] to which perhaps the proximate inducement was the presence of the fount Arethusa, which contained large fishes, and sent forth a copious stream of water into the sea.[7] From the original connection between Alpheios and Artemis, the notion gradually arose, or it was given out, that the fount contained water of the Alpheios, and thence came the legend of his course under the sea.[8] Eventually, when the poetic notion of Artemis as a love-shunning maiden became the prevalent one,[9] the goddess was made to fly the pursuit of Alpheios.[10] The legend at Letríni was[11] that he fell in love with her, but seeing no chance of success in a lawful way he resolved to force her. For this purpose he came to Letríni, where she and her nymphs were celebrating a pannychis or wake, and mingled with them. But the goddess, suspecting his design, had daubed her own face and those of her nymphs with mud, so that he was unable to distinguish her, and thus was foiled. Finally she was converted into the coy nymph Arethusa.[12] A late pragmatising form of the pleasing mythe was, that Alpheios was a hunter who was in love with the huntress Arethusa. To escape from his importunities

[1] Ov. Met. v. 572 seq. Moschos, Idyl. vii.
[2] See Müller, Proleg. 135. Dórians, i. 393.
[3] Paus. vi. 22, 8–10. Strab. viii. 3, 12, p. 343. Athen. viii. 346.
[4] Above, p. 69.   [5] Pind. Ol. vi. 6 (8).
[6] Id. Pyth. ii. 4 (7), cum Sch.
[7] Id. Pyth. ii. 7 (11). Ibycos ap. Sch. Pind. Nem. i. 1. Diodór. v. 3. Strab. vi. 2, 4, p. 270. Cic. Verr. iv. 53.
[8] Ibycos ap. Sch. Theocr. i. 117. Pind. Nem. i. 1.
[9] Thus when Artemis had become the huntress, the Eleians changed the name of the Alpheiæa of the Letrinæans to Elaphiæa (from ἔλαφος), Paus. ut sup.
[10] Pind. ut sup.   [11] Paus. ut sup.
[12] It is uncertain when this change took place; it is the goddess who is pursued in Telesilla, ut sup. (Ol. 64). The oracle given to Archias (Paus. v. 7, 3) is probably a late fiction, as it speaks of the fount of Arethusa. Welcker (Schwenk. 263) regards this name as being ἀρι-θοῶσα. We shall presently offer what we deem a more likely etymon.

the passed over to Ortygia, where she was changed into a fountain, and Alpheios became a river.[1]

In proof of the truth of this fable, it was asserted that a cup (φιάλη) which fell into the Alpheios rose in Arethusa, whose pellucid waters also became turbid with the blood of the victims slain at the Olympic games.[2]

We may here observe, that in the Peloponnése the relation between Artemis and the water was very intimate. She was worshipped in several places as Limnátis and Heleia, and there were frequently fountains in her temples. She was therefore probably regarded as a goddess of nature, that gave vigour and growth to plants and animals by the means of moisture.[3]

Among the various titles of Artemis were Loxó, Hekaergé, Argé, and O'pis, or Upis.[4] She bore the first two as the sister of Apolló Loxias and Hekaergos. She was styled Argé as the *swift* or the *bright* goddess, and Upis or O'pis probably as her whose *eye* was over all. In the isle of Délos however were shown the tombs of O'pis and Argé behind the temple of Artemis, and the tradition of the place was, that they, who were two Hyperborean maidens, had been the companions of Apolló and Artemis when they first came to Délos.[5] According to another account, these Hyperborean maidens were three in number, and named Upis, Loxó, and Hekaergé,[6] while a third named only O'pis and Hekaergé.[7] There was also a legend of a nymph Argé, who when pursuing a buck cried out to him, "Though you should follow the course of the Sun I will overtake you," at which the Sun being offended, turned her into a doe.[8] Another legend said that Zeus carried away the nymph Argé from Lyktos in Kréte to a hill named Argillos on the banks of the Nile, where she became the mother of Dionýsos.[9]

If Artemis was merely one of the names under which the moon was worshipped, it need not surprise us to find her identified with Seléné, with Hekaté, and even with Persephoné the goddess of the under-world, and to be thence called the *three-formed* goddess,[10] ruling as Seléné in the sky, as Artemis on earth, as Persephoné in Erebos. This will also give a very simple reason for her being like Eileithyia, the aider of women in labour. If Artemis was not originally a moon-goddess, these identifications become somewhat difficult of solution.[11]

[1] Paus. v. 7, 2.
[2] Ibycos *ut sup.* Strab. *ut sup.* Mela, ii. 7. Plin. *Nat. Hist.* ii. 103.
[3] Comp. Müller, *Dórians*, i. 392. [4] Alex. Ætol. *ap. Macrob.* v. 22.
[5] Hérod. iv. 35. [6] Kallim. *Hymn to Délos*, 292.
[7] Melanópos of Kymé *ap. Paus.* v. 7, 8. [8] Hygin. 205.
[9] Plut. *de Fluv.* xvi. 3. [10] See below, chap. xii. *Eileithyiæ.* [11] Of Artemis-Callistó and Artemis-Iphigeneia, or Orthia, we shall treat in the Second Part.

Artemis was also confounded with the goddess worshipped on the Tauric Chersonése, whose altars were stained with the blood of such unhappy strangers as were cast on that inhospitable shore.[1] She was identified too with the goddess of nature adored at Ephesos, whose symbolic figure, by its multitude of breasts and heads of animals hung round it, denoted the fecundity of nature. In Magnésia on the Mæander there was a most stately temple of Artemis-Leukophryné (*White-browed*),[2] in which was shown the tomb of a maiden named Leukophryne,[3] who was probably regarded as bearing a relation to the goddess similar to that borne by Upis and Argé at Délos. Leukophryné was therefore no more than an epithet of Artemis, who had also a temple at Leukophrys on the coast;[4] and it becomes a question whether (like Artemis of Ephesos, with whom she must have been identical) she derived her appellation from that town, whose name probably corresponded with its situation on a chalk-cliff; or whether it was expressive of her beauty. As however beauty was not an attribute of the Asiatic goddess, the former is more likely to be the true supposition.[5]

No spot on earth is assigned as the birth-place of Artemis by Homer, in whose time, as we have more than once observed, that practice had not yet commenced; but as he mentions the island Ortygia as that in which she shot O'rión,[6] succeeding poets fabled that she was born there.[7] This island was described by Homer as lying in the western sea, the scene of all wonders, and was probably as imaginary as the O'gygian isle of Kalypsó; but when at a later period the Greeks grew more familiar with those distant regions, zeal for the honour of the poet who had sung so well the wanderings of Odysseus, and the love of definiteness, led them to affix the names which he employs to various places really to be found, and the islet at the port of Syracuse was determined to be the Ortygia of the Odyssey.[8]

Artemis is generally represented as a healthy, strong, active maiden,—handsome, but with no gentleness of expression. She wears the Krétan hunting-shoes (ἐνδρομίδες), and has her garment tucked up for speed. On her back she bears a quiver, and in her hand a bow or a hunting-spear. She is usually attended by a dog.

At Trœzén there was a temple of Artemis-Lykæa, the erection of which was ascribed to Hippolytos, but the guides could give

[1] Hérod. iv. 103. Eurip. *Iph. in Taur.*   [2] Tacitus, *Ann.* iii. 62.
[3] Clem. Alex. *Protrept.* p. 20. Arnob. *adv. Gentes*, 6.
[4] Xen. *Hell.* iii. 2, 19; iv. 8, 17.   [5] Comp. Buttmann, *Mythol.* ii. 133 *seq.*
[6] *Od.* v. 121.
[7] Hom. *Hymn to Apolló*, 16. Pind. *Nem.* i. 1. Orph. *Hymn* xxxv. 5.
See below, chap. xix. *Ortygia.*

Pausanias no account of the unusual title Lykæa.[1] Another ambiguous name of this goddess was that of Tauropolos.[2] The chief titles given to Artemis by the poets were,[3] 1. *Arrow-joying;* 2. *Gold-bridled;* 3. *Gold-shafted;* 4. *Deer-slayer;* 5. *Beast-marking;* 6. *Rushing;* 7. *Holy;* 8. *Horse-urger,* etc.

The name Artemis seems to be, as Buttmann thinks, identical with ἀρτεμής, *integer, whole, uninjured,* and therefore *sound* and *pure,* and to refer to the virginity of the goddess. Welcker regaids it as an epithet of the goddess of nature, similar to O'pis and Nemesis, and he says that it is ἄρι-Θέμις.[4] Neither of these derivations appears to us to be satisfactory; and the following may seem perhaps to come nearer to the truth.

Artemis is *quasi* Althemis or Aldemis or Ardemis, from ἄλθω ᾽ΑΛΔΩ (ἀλδαίνω), *to nourish* or *cause to grow,* or ἄρδω *to water* and thence *to nourish.* This perfectly unforced etymology accurately accords with the moon, whose influence on vegetation and growth in general the ancients held to be so very considerable, and which they regarded as the mother of dews. Another name of the goddess may have been ἡ ἀλθέουσα, ἀλδέουσα or ἀρδέουσα, and δ and φ being commutable (as θήρ, φήρ), the name may have become ἀλφείουσα, etc., to which ᾽Αλφειὸς (ἀλθειὸς *the nourisher*) would correspond as a masculine power, and therefore an appropriate name for a river. Altheüsa, it is plain, might easily become Arethusa. Possibly too Εἰλείθυια, which has the form of a *perf. part.,* may have come from ἠλθηνῖα, or some word of similar form and signification.

Mythologists are divided into two parties respecting the original nature of Létó and her children, the one regarding them as physical, the other as ethical beings. Both, however, are agreed that the latter is their character in the Homéric and Hésiodic poetry, where, as we have seen, Apolló appears only as the god of prophecy, music and archery, and Artemis as his counterpart in this last office. Voss[5] therefore (with whom agree Wolf,[6]

[1] Paus. ii. 31, 4. It evidently, however, refers to light.

[2] Soph. *Ajax,* 172. Eur. *Iph. Taur.* 1457. Aristoph. *Lys.* 447, the scholiast on which says, that according to Xenomédés it was sometimes given to Athéna; also, as we shall see, a moon-goddess. *Steer-driver* seems to us the most probable signification (see above, p. 54). By some (among whom Euripidés may perhaps be classed) it is held to relate to the worship of the goddess by the Taurians.

[3] 1. ἰοχέαιρα: 2. χρυσήνιος: 3. χρυσηλάκατος: 4. ἐλαφηβόλος: 5. θηρο-σκόπος: 6. κελαδεινή: 7. ἁγνή: 8. ἱπποσόα. A number of others will be found in Aristophanés.   [4] *In Schwenk.* 263.

[5] *Myth. Br.* ii. 385; iii. 53 *seq.*   [6] *On Il.* i. 43, 50.

Lobeck,[1] Hermann,[2] Völcker,[3] Nitzsch,[4] and Müller),[5] maintains such to have been the original conception of these deities, while Heyne,[6] Buttmann,[7] Welcker,[8] and Lauer,[9] together with Creuzer and the whole body of the mystics, think that in the *theocrasy* of the ancients, by which Apolló and Artemis were identified with Hélios and Seléné, they were only restored to their original nature and character. We have more than once hinted our inclination to regard the latter as the more correct hypothesis. We will now briefly state the principal arguments on both sides.

In favour of the theory of Apolló and Artemis being sun and moon, it is alleged that they were early so considered. Thus we find the Persian general of Darius sparing the isle of Délos on their account, and making offerings to them evidently as gods of the two great luminaries (Mithras and Mitra in the Persian system).[10] We also meet with this view in Plató[11] and Euripidés;[12] and in the Alexandrine period it was so prevalent, that Kallimachos[13] blames those who separate these deities from the sun and moon. This however might have been nothing more than the arbitrary procedure of priests and philosophers, and more sure grounds must be sought in the attributes and epithets of these deities anterior to the time of theocrasy.

Apolló and Artemis, then, are brother and sister, the children of Zeus (that is, the deity) and Létó, whose name, by a perfectly unstrained etymology, may be rendered *Night;* and the origin of the sun and moon, and their affinity, could not be more appropriately described. Apolló is represented as full of manly vigour, with long unshorn locks, armed with a golden sword and a bow and quiver, from which he sends forth deadly arrows. These waving locks are a simple representation of the eams of the sun,[14] who in the Psalms is described as 'a bridegroom coming out of his chamber, and rejoicing to run his race;' a golden sword is the weapon of Freyr, the sun-god of Scandinavian mythology;[15] and the arrows may well express the penetrating beams of the sun, or the *coups de soleil* and diseases caused by his action. For a similar

[1] *Aglaoph.* 79.
[2] *Ueber das Wesen,* etc., 106 *seq.*
[3] *Myth. der Jap.* 306.
[4] *On Od.* iii. 279.
[5] *Dórians,* i. 309 *seq.*
[6] *On Il.* i. 50; and iv. 101.
[7] *Mythol.* i. 1. "Apollon und Artemis."
[8] *Tril.* 41, 65, 222.
[9] *System,* etc., 253.
[10] Hérod. vi. 97. In the Eddaic system Freyr and Freya are brother and sister, and sun and moon.
[11] *Laws,* xii. 3.
[12] *Fr. Phaëthon.* 10.
[13] *Fr.* 48.
[14] In Persian poetry the sun of spring is termed a golden-haired youth.
[15] The epithet χρυσάωρ, χρυσάορος, may, however, merely signify *gilder* see below, chap. xviii. *Gorgons.*

reason arrows were given to the goddess of the moon.[1] The names Phœbos and Artemis, as above explained, agree perfectly with the sun and moon. Apolló being conceived armed with bow and arrows, was naturally held to be the god of archery; and the sun, whose eye surveys everything, might be looked on as the most suitable revealer of the will of Zeus to men, and thence Apollo be the god of prophecy. The cheerfulness which the appearance of the sun induces over all nature, vivified and refreshed by the repose of the night, and the songs of birds which precede or accompany his rising, and which poets of all countries have noticed and sung,[2] might easily cause the sun-god to be regarded as the god of music, though it is more likely that Apolló owes this character to the employment of the lyre in his worship. Artemis may in like manner have been regarded as the goddess of the chase from her being armed with arrows, or as the beasts of venery feed by night and sleep by day,[3] or as the moon-goddess was held to preside over the birth and growth of animated beings. Finally, the offering of ripe ears of corn, the 'golden summer,' to Apollo, and his being prayed to as the averter of mildew and the destroyer of mice and grasshoppers, are reasons for viewing him as a god of nature.[4]

[1] "The sun shall not smite thee by day, nor the *moon* by night." *Ps.* cxxi. 6. "A man subject to the rays of the moon and the night-damp air after the burning heat of the day, was almost sure of a fever. The moon, both here (coast of Africa) and in the West Indies, is more powerful than the sun ; meat hung in the rays of the former becomes tainted sooner than if exposed to the latter." Chamier, *Life of a Sailor*, i. 270 : see Plut. *Sympos.* iii. 10. The effect, however, is produced by the atmosphere, and not by the moonbeams. See Notes and Queries, 3 S. xi. 8.

The Spanish women (we have read) will expose themselves without fear to the rays of the sun, but they cover themselves up against those of the moon.

[2]
> Ὡs ἡμῖν ἧδε λαμπρὸν ἠλίου σέλας
> ἐῷα κινεῖ φθέγματ' ὀρνίθων σαφῆ.—Soph. *Elect.* 17.

> Non si destò fin chè garrir gli augelli
> Non sentì lieti e salutar gli albori,
> E mormorare il fiume e gli arboscelli,
> E con l' onda scherzar l' aura e co' fiori.—Tasso, *Ger. Lib.* vii. 5.

> Sweet is the breath of morn, her rising sweet,
> With charm of earliest birds.—Milton, *Par. Lost*, iv. 640.

The poets of the Spanish peninsula, who are so distinguished for their love of external nature, have numerous descriptions of this kind, *ex. gr.*:

> Os passaros voando
> De raminho em raminho vão saltando,
> E com suave e doce melodia
> O claro dia estão manifestando.—Camões, *Canç.* iii. 1.

[3] "Nemoribus quoque adesse dicitur (Diana) quod omnis venatio nocte pascatur dieque dormiat." Fulgent. ii. 19. Eudocia, 148.

[4] See Müller, *Dórians*, i. 309.

Against all this it is alleged that these identifications were merely the work of the philosophers of the Iónic school, who sought to assimilate all the deities of the popular creed with material powers or with the attributes of the universal intellect; that the epithets and attributes of Apolló all answer to a moral being of great purity, while the bow and arrows are a natural symbol of the god who sends death from afar; that nothing can be concluded from his being a patron and protector of agriculture, as he is such as the averter of misfortune in general; that in his religious character he is no god of nature, not being a deity of generation and production, but represented as ever youthful and unmarried, the tales of his amours being all of a late age, and having no connexion with his worship. Finally, great stress is laid on the fact of Apolló and Artemis being so totally distin:t from the sun and moon in all the elder poetry.[1]

CHAPTER IX.

DIONE:—APHRODITE, EROS.

Διώνη. Dione.

IN the Ilias[2] Dioné is a wife of Zeus, and mother of Aphrodíte. The name Dioné also occurs among the Ocean-nymphs,[3] the Néréides[4] and the Hyades.[5] At Dodona this goddess shared in the honours and the worship of Zeus, being regarded as his queen.[6] Her name is apparently the feminine of his, and probably signified simply *goddess*.[7]

'Αφροδίτη. (*Venus.*)

The Aphrodíte of the Ilias[8] is the daughter of Zeus and Dióné, and by the Alexandrian and the Latin poets[9] she is sometimes

---

[1] See Müller, *Dórians, ut sup.; Proleg.* 262. Hermann, *ut sup.* 110 *seq.*
[2] *Il.* v. 370.   [3] Hés. *Theog.* 353.
[4] Apollod. i. 2, 6. He also places her among the Titanesses, i. 1, 3.
[5] Pherekýdés *ap. Sch. Il.* xviii. 486.
[6] Démosth. *False Emb.* 427; *Meidias* 531; *Epist.* 10.
[7] From Δίς, Διός, as from the Dóric Ζάν, Ζανώ, from *Jovis, Jovino, Juno.*
[8] *Il.* v. 370.
[9] Theocr. vii. 116. Bion, i. 93. Ov. *Art. Amat.* iii. 3, 769. *Fast.* ii. 461. Stat. *Silv.* ii. 7, 2. *Achil.* ii. 340. *Pervig. Veneris, passim.* Servius (*on Æn.* iii. 466) even calls Dióné Venus. Διώνη might possibly be a contraction of Διωνίνη, formed like 'Ωκεανίνη.

called by the same name as her mother. Hésiod[1] says she sprang from the *foam* (ἀφρὸς) of the sea, into which the mutilated part of Uranos had been thrown by his son Kronos. She first, he adds, approached the land at the island of Kythéra, and thence proceeded to Kypros, where grass grew beneath her feet, and Love and Desire attended her.

One of the Homérids[2] sings, that the moist-blowing west-wind wafted her in soft foam along the waves of the sea, and that the gold-filleted Seasons received her on the shore of Kypros, clothed her in immortal garments, placed a golden wreath on her head, rings of orichalcum and gold in her pierced ears, and golden chains about her neck, and then led her to the assembly of the Immortals, every one of whom admired, saluted, and loved her, and each god desired her for his wife.

Empedoklés said that Aphrodíté was the daughter of Kronos.[3]

The husband assigned to this charming goddess is usually the lame artist Héphæstos. Her amour with Arés we have already narrated; and Hermés, Dionýsos, and Poseidón, it is said, could also boast of her favours. Among mortals, Anchísés and Adónis are those whose amours with her are the most famous. The tale of her love-adventure with the former is noticed by Homer,[4] and it is most pleasingly told by a Homérid; the following is an analysis of his hymn.

Aphrodíté had long exercised uncontrolled dominion over the dwellers of Olympos, uniting in cruel sport both males and females with mortals. But Zeus resolved that she should no longer be exempt from the common lot. Accordingly he infused into her mind the desire of a union of love with mortal man. The object selected was Anchísés, a beautiful youth of the royal house of Troy, who was at that time with the herdsmen feeding oxen among the hills and valleys of Ida.

The moment Aphrodíté beheld him she was seized with love. She immediately hastened to her temple in Kypros, where the Charites dressed and adorned her, and then in the full conscious-ness of beauty she proceeded through the air. When she came to Ida, she advanced toward the stalls, and was accompanied on her way by all the wild beasts of the mountains, whose breasts the exulting goddess filled with love and desire.

Anchísés happened to be alone in the cotes at this time, and was amusing his leisure by playing on the lyre. When he beheld the goddess, who had divested herself of the usual marks of

---

[1] *Theog.* 188 *seq.*
[3] See above, p. 62.
[2] *Hymn* vi.
[4] *Il.* v. 247, 313.

divinity, he was amazed at her beauty and the splendour of her attire. He could not avoid regarding her as something more than human; he accosts her as one of the Immortals, vows an altar to her, and beseeches her to grant him a long and a happy life. But Aphrodíté denies her heavenly origin, and feigns that she is a mortal maid and daughter to Otreus king of Phrygia, adding, that while she was dancing, in honour of Artemis, with the nymphs and other maidens, and a great crowd was standing around, Hermés had snatched her away, and carried her through the air over hills and dales and plains, till he had brought her to Ida, where he informed her that she was to be the wife of Anchísés; and then, having instructed her in what she was to do, had departed, leaving her alone in the mountains. She earnestly entreats the Trojan youth to conduct her unsullied to his family, and to dispatch a messenger to her father to treat of the marriage and the dower.

But while thus speaking, the artful goddess filled the heart of the youth with love. Believing her now to be mortal, all his veneration vanishes, and he declares that not even Apolló should prevent his taking advantage of the favourable moment. He seized the hand of the goddess, and 'led her blushing like the morn' into the rustic shed.

When evening approached, and the arrival of the herdsmen with the sheep and oxen was at hand, the goddess poured a profound sleep over Anchísés. She arose from the skin-strewn couch, and prepared to depart. Resuming the marks of divinity, the brilliant eyes and rosy neck, she stood at the door and called to her slumbering lover to awake and observe the change. Filled with awe, he conceals his face in the clothes and sues for mercy; but the goddess reassures him, and informs him that she will bear a son, whom she will commit to the mountain-nymphs to rear, and will bring to him when in his fifth year. He is then to feign that the child is the offspring of one of the nymphs; but the secret of the goddess is to remain inviolate, under pain of his being struck with lightning by Zeus.

> So saying unto breezy Heaven she sped.
> Hail, goddess, who o'er well-dwelt Kypros rulest!
> But I will pass from thee to another hymn,

concludes the poet, according to the regular practice of his brethren.

Myrrha, the daughter of Kinyras, having offended Aphrodíté,[1]

[1] By asserting that her hair was more beautiful than that of the goddess. Sch. *Theocr.* i. 109.

was by her inspired with a passion for her own father. After a long struggle against it, she gratified it by the aid of her nurse, unknown to its object.[1] When Kinyras found what he had unwittingly done, he pursued his daughter with his drawn sword, to efface her crime in her blood. He had nearly overtaken her, when she prayed to the gods to make her invisible, and they in pity changed her into a myrrh-tree. In ten months afterwards the tree opened, and the young Adónis came to light. Aphrodíté, delighted with his beauty, put him into a coffer, unknown to all the gods, and gave him to Persephoné to keep. But the goddess of the under-world, as soon as she beheld him, refused to part with him; and the matter being referred to Zeus, he decreed that Adónis should have one third of the year to himself, be another third with Aphrodité, and the remaining third with Persephoné. Adónis gave his own portion to Aphrodité, and lived happily with her; till having offended Artemis, he was torn by a wild boar [2] and died.[3] The ground where his blood fell was sprinkled with nectar by the mourning goddess, and the flower called the anemone or wind-flower sprang up from it, which by its caducity expresses the brief period of the life of the beautiful son of Myrrha.[4] The rose also derived its present hue from this fatal event; for as the distracted goddess ran barefoot through the woods and lawns to the aid of her lover, the thorns of the rose-briars tore her delicate skin, and their flowers were thenceforth tinged with red.[5] Other accounts, however, say that the goddess changed Adónis himself into this fragrant flower.[6]

The tale of Adónis is evidently an Eastern mythe; for both his own name and those of his parents refer to that part of the

---

[1] Hésiod (ap. Apollod. iii. 14, 3) said that Adónis was the son of Phœnix and Alphesibœa. It is uncertain whether he made the latter daughter of the former or not. Panyasis (Id. ib.) made him the offspring of Theias, king of Assyria, by his own daughter Smyrna.

[2] Arés, out of jealousy, took, it is said, the form of a boar for the purpose of killing him. Sch. Theocr. iii. 47. Eudocia, 24. Tzetz. Lyc. 831. Nonn. xxix. 135; xli. 210.

[3] Apollod. ut supra. Ov. Met. x. 298, seq. Eudocia and Tzetzés, ut supra. Anton. Liberal. 34. Bion, i.

[4] Nicander ap. Sch. Theocr. v. 92. Ov. Ib. 731. Others said that the anemone, which was white before, was turned red by the blood of Adónis. Eudocia and Tzetzés, ut supra.

[5] Eudocia and Tzetzés, ut supra.

[6] Serv. Buc. x. 18. Bion (i. 65) ascribes the origin of the rose to the blood, that of the anemone to the tears of the goddess:

Αἷμα ῥόδον τίκτει, τὰ δὲ δάκρυα τὰν ἀνεμώναν.

For a less elegant Mohammedan legend of the origin of the rose, see above, p. 7

world.[1] He appears, in fact, to be the same with the Thammuz
mentioned by the prophet Ezekiel,

> Whose annual wound in Lebanon allured
> The Syrian damsels to lament his fate,
> While smooth Adonis from his native rock
> Ran purple to the sea, supposed with blood
> Of Thammuz yearly wounded;

and to be a Phœnician personification of the sun, who during a
part of the year is absent, or as the legend expresses it, with the
goddess of the under-world; during the remainder with Astarté,
the regent of heaven. A festival in honour of Adónis was annually celebrated at Byblos by the Phœnician women during two
days; the first of which was spent in grief and lamentation, the
second in joy and triumph. In Greece, whither these rites were
transplanted, the festival was prolonged to eight days. It is uncertain when the Adónia were first celebrated in that country;
but we find Plató[2] alluding to the Gardens of Adónis, as pots
and boxes of growing herbs used in them were called, and the
ill fortune of the Athenian expedition to Sicily was in part
ascribed to the circumstance of the fleet having sailed during
that festival.[3] The Idyll of Theokritos called the Adóniazusæ
describes in admirable dramatic style the magnificence with
which the feast of Adónis was celebrated in the Græco-Ægyptian
city of Alexandria.

This notion of the mourning for Adónis being a testimony of
grief for the absence of the sun during the winter, is not, however, to be too readily acquiesced in. Lobeck[4] for example asks,
with some appearance of reason, why those nations whose heaven
was mildest, and their winter shortest, should so bitterly bewail
the regular changes of the seasons, as to feign that the gods
themselves were carried off or slain; and he shrewdly observes,
that in that case the mournful and the joyful parts of the festival
should have been held at different times of the year, and not
joined together as they were. He further inquires, whether the
ancient nations, who esteemed their gods to be so little superior
to men, may not have believed them to have been really and not
metaphorically put to death. And in truth it is not easy to

[1] Adónis is the Semitic אֲדוֹן (Adôn) Lord. Kinyras comes from כִּנּוֹר
'Kinnôr), the Greek κινύρα, whence κινυρίζω, to lament, as in the Irish keening.
Myrrha is מוֹר (Môr) Myrrh.
[2] Phædrus, § 138. Spenser, who treats the Grecian Mythology in the most
arbitrary manner, gives, in the Faerie Quene, a peculiar view of the Gardens
of Adónis. See also Milton, Comus, 992 seq. The Italian poet Marini has
made Adónis the hero of a long and tedious poem.   [3] Plut. Nikias, 13.
[4] Aglaophamus, p. 691. See Plut. de Is. et Os 70.

give a satisfactory answer to these questions.[1] Still it may be observed that the earth being the object principally in view, the failure of her productive power during the winter may have been ascribed to the want of fecundating energy in the sun, expressed here by the death of Adónis, in the Phrygian system by the mutilation of Attis.

According to Homer, Aphrcdíté possessed an *embroidered girdle* (κεστὸς ἱμάς), which had the gift of inspiring love and desire for the person who wore it. Héra, when about to lull Zeus to sleep by filling him with these affections, borrowed the magic girdle from Aphrodíté.[2]

The animals sacred to Aphrodíté were swans, doves, and sparrows. Horace[3] places her in a chariot drawn by swans, and Sapphó[4] in one whose team were sparrows. In one of the odes ascribed to Anakreón a dove announces herself as a present from the goddess to the bard. The bird called Iynx or *Fritillus*, of which so much use was made in amatory magic, was also sacred to this goddess;[5] as was likewise the swallow, the herald of spring, the season of love. Her favourite plants were the rose and the myrtle. She was chiefly worshipped at Kythéra and Kypros;[6] in which latter isle her favourite places were Paphós, Golgœ, Idalion, and Amathus; and also at Knidos, Milétos, Kós, Corinth, Athens, Sparta, etc.

In the more ancient temples of this goddess in Kypros she was represented under the form of a rude conical stone. But the Grecian sculptors and painters, particularly Praxitelés and Apellés, vied with each other in forming her image the *idéal* of female beauty and attraction. She appears sometimes rising out of the sea and wringing her locks; sometimes drawn in a conch by Tritons, or riding on some marine animal. She is usually naked, or but slightly clad. The Venus de' Medici remains to us a noble specimen of ancient art and perception of the beautiful.

The most usual epithets of Aphrodíté were,[7] 1. *Smile-loving;* 2. *Well-garlanded;* 3. *Golden;* 4. *Quick-winking;* 5. *Well-tressed;* 6. *Care-dissolving;* 7. *Artful;* 8. *Gold-bridled;* etc.

There is none of the Olympians of whom the foreign origin is

---

[1] There were, however, in antiquity some who viewed the mythe of Adónis as similar to that of Persephoné, referring to the growth of corn: see Winer, *Realwörterbuch s. v.* Thammus. This idea had presented itself to our own mind before we met with this place of Winer.

[2] *Il.* xiv. 214.　　　　　　　　　　　[3] *Carm.* iii. 28, 15, iv. 1, 10.

[4] In the ode preserved by Dion. Hal. *Γε compos. verborum.*

[5] See Pind. *Pyth.* iv. 214 (380) *cum schol.*

[6] The goddess of Kypros was plainly the Phœnician Astarté.

[7] 1. φιλομμειδής: 2. εὐστέφανος: 3. χρυσέη: 4. ἑλικοβλέφαοος, ἑλικῶπις
5. εὐπλόκαμος: 6. λυσιμελής: 7. δολόμητις: 8. χρυσήνιος, etc.

ᴋ

so probable as this goddess. She is therefore in general regarded as being the same with the Astarté of the Phœnicians. There can, we freely confess, be little doubt of the identification of this last with the Grecian Aphrodíte, for the tale of Adónis sufficiently proves it; and that this took place at a very early period, the name Kypris, given to Aphrodíte so frequently by Homer, evinces. Still we look on Aphrodíte to be (as her name seems to denote[1]) an original Grecian deity; at first, probably, merely cosmogonic, but gradually adopted into the system of the Olympians, and endowed with some of the attributes of Héra (who was also identified with Astarté), and thus becoming the patroness of marriage.[2] It was probably on account of her being esteemed the same with Astarté, the moon-goddess and queen of heaven, that Aphrodíte was so frequently styled the *Heavenly* (Urania). It is very important to observe that she was so named at her temple in Kythéra, which was regarded as the holiest and most ancient of her fanes in Greece, and was perhaps a Phœnician foundation like that on Mount Eryx in Sicily.[3] Her antique wooden statue (ξόανον) in this temple was armed, as it also was at Sparta and Corinth.[4] In this last city she was also styled Urania,[5] and her worship there was eminently Asiatic in character.

Lauer, who however has not developed his theory, appears to have regarded Aphrodíte as the verdant flowery earth. In this view she would coincide with the Frigga of Northern mythology, and the reason for transferring to her the mythe of Adónis would be apparent. But we see nothing in her mythology to justify this view.

Ἔρος, Ἔρως. (Cupido, Amor. 𝕷𝖔𝖇𝖊.)

This deity is unnoticed by Homer; in the Theogony of Hésiod[6] he is one of the first of beings, and produced without parents; in those of the comic poets Aristophanés and Antiphanés he is the offspring of Night;[7] in the Orphic poems he was the son of Kronos.[8] Sappho[9] made him the progeny of Heaven and Earth, while Simónidés assigned him Aphrodíte and Arés for parents.[10] In O'lén's hymn to Eileithyia[11] that goddess was termed the mother of Love, and Alkæos said that 'well-sandalled Iris bore Love to gold-locked Zephyros.'[12]

---

[1] Ἀφροδίτη, *quasi* Ἀφροδύτη, *Foam-sprung.*   [2] *Il.* v. 429.
[3] See our note on Ov. *Fasti,* iv. 871.
[4] Paus. iii. 23, 1; and ii. 5, 1; iii. 15, 10.
[5] Pind. Fr. Schol. 1. Boeckh and Dissen. *in loc.*: comp. Jacobs *Anthol.* xvii. p 377.   [6] Theog. 120.
[7] Aristoph. *Birds,* 695. Jablonski, *Panth. Ægypt.* i. 14.
[8] Sch. *Apoll. Rh.* iii. 26.   [9] Id. *ib.*   [10] Id. *ib.*   [11] Paus. ix. 27, 2.
[12] *Ap.* Plut. *Amator.* 20. Nonn. xxxi. 110, 111. This strange poet had a little before (xxix. 334) called Héphæstos the sire of Love.

The cosmogonic Erós is apparently a personification of the principle of attraction, on which the coherence of the material world depends. Nothing was more natural than to term Aphrodíté the mother of Love, but the reason for so calling Eileithyia, the president of child-birth, is not equally apparent. It may be perhaps that in the hymn ascribed to O'lén this goddess was identified with Aphrodíté Archæa, to whom Théseus was said to have dedicated an altar at Délos:[1] possibly it was meant to express the increase of conjugal affection produced by the birth of children. The making Love the offspring of the West-wind and the Rainbow would seem to be only a poetic mode of expressing the well-known fact, that the spring, the season in which they most prevail, is also that of Love.[2] In the bucolic and some of the Latin poets the Loves are spoken of in the plural number, but no distinct offices are assigned them.[3]

Thespiæ in Bœótia was the place in which Erós was most worshipped. The Thespians used to celebrate games in his honour on Mount Helikón. The oldest image of the god in their city was of plain stone, but Praxitelés afterwards made for them one of Pentelican marble of rare beauty.[4] Erós also had altars at Athens and elsewhere.

The poetic epithets of this deity were,[5] 1. *Gold-haired*; 2. *Gold-winged*; 3. *Sweet-minded.*

The god of love was usually represented as a plump-cheeked boy, rosy and naked, with light hair floating on his shoulders. He is always winged, and armed with a bow and arrows.[6]

[1] Müller, *Dor.* i. 333.

[2]
Ωραῖος καὶ Ἔρως ἐπιτέλλεται, ἡνίκα περ γῆ
ἄνθεσιν εἰαρινοῖς θάλλει ἀεξομένη.—Theognis, 1275.

See Plut. *ut supra*, for another explication of this fiction. Vasanta (*Spring*) is one of the companions of Cama, the Hindoo Erós.

[3] Theocr. vii. 96. Bión, i. *passim.* Hor. *Carm.* i. 19, 1.

[4] Paus. ix. 27, 1; 31, 3.

[5] 1. χρυσοκόμης; 2. χρυσόπτερος; 3. γλυκύθυμος.

[6] Nonnos (vii. 194) seems to represent his arrows as tipt with flowers. The arrows of the Hindoo Cama are thus pointed, and the Portuguese poet Camões seems to have had a similar conception, for when enumerating flowers (*Eleg.* vi.) he says that of them Cupid

> Muitas capellas tece, que de settas
> Lhe servem contra peitos de donzellas.

The Scottish song, on the other hand, says that

> Love tips his arrows with woods and parks,
> And castles and riggs and muirs and meadows.

(In the earlier poets as well as in the most ancient works of art Erós is not represented as a boy, but as a full-grown youth.—Ed.)

There was a being named Anterós (ἀντὶ ἔρως), who was in some cases viewed as the avenger of slighted love;[1] in others as the symbol of reciprocal affection.[2] The Platónic philosopher Porphyrius tells the following pretty legend.

Aphrodíté, complaining to Themis that her son Erós continued always a child, was told by her that the cause was his being solitary, and that if he had a brother he would grow apace. Anterós was soon afterwards born, and Erós immediately found his wings enlarge, and his person and strength greatly increase. But this was only when Anterós was near; for if he was at a distance, Erós found himself shrink to his original dimensions. The meaning of this fable is so apparent that it needs not explication.

At the time when it had become the mode to exalt the characters of philosophers by ascribing to them all kinds of wonderful works, the sophist Eunapius told the following curious legend in his life of Jamblichus, the author of as marvellous a life of Pythagoras. Jamblichus and his companions having gone to the warm baths of Gadara in Lykia, and bathed in them, a conversation arose among them on the nature of the baths. The philosopher smiled and said, "Though it is not strictly right in me to do so, yet I will show you something new." He then desired them to inquire of the inhabitants, what were the traditional names of two of the smaller but handsomer of the warm springs. They replied that one of them was called Erós and the other Anterós, but that they knew not the cause of their being so styled. Jamblichus, who was just then standing at the brink of the fount of Erós, touched the water, and murmured a few words over it. Immediately there rose from the bottom a little boy of a fair complexion and moderate size: his hair, of a rich golden hue, hung down his back, which was bright and clean as that of a person who had just bathed. All present were in amazement: the philosopher then leading them to the other spring did as he had done before; and instantly another Love, similar to the first, except that his hair was of a bright dark hue, rose to light. The two embraced, and clung round the philosopher as if he had been their father; and after caressing them for some time, he restored them to their native element. His companions, who had been previously disposed to regard him as an impostor, convinced by this wonder, henceforth received his words as those of a divinity.

The adventures of Erós are not numerous. Some pretty little trifles respecting him will be found in the bucolic poets, and his adventure with Apolló has been already noticed. The most

[1] Paus. i. 30, 1.   Plut. *Amat.* 20.   [2] Plato, *Phædr.* 255.   Paus. vi. 23, 4.

celebrated is that contained in the agreeable tale of his love for Psyché (ψυχὴ, *the soul*), preserved by Apuleius in his Metamorphoses, and which we will here give in an abridged form.

There were one time a king and a queen who had three daughters, of whom the youngest named Psyché was one of the loveliest creatures earth ever beheld. People crowded from all parts to gaze upon her charms, altars were erected to her, and she was worshipped as a second Venus. The queen of beauty was irritated on seeing her own altars neglected, and her adorers diminishing. She summoned her son; and conducting him to the city where Psyché dwelt, showed him the lovely maid, and ordered him to inspire her with a passion for some vile and abject wretch. The goddess departed, leaving her son to execute her mandate. Meantime Psyché, though adored by all, was sought as a wife by none. Her sisters, who were far inferior to her in charms, were married, and she remained single, hating that beauty which all admired.

Her father consulted the oracle of Apolló, and was ordered to expose her on a rock, whence she would be carried away by a monster, the terror of heaven, earth, and hell. The oracle was obeyed, and Psyché amidst the tears of the people placed on a lofty rock. Here, while she sat weeping, a Zephyr sent for the purpose gently raised and carried her to a charming valley. Overcome by grief she falls asleep, and on awaking beholds a grove with a fountain in the midst of it, and near it a stately palace of most splendid structure. She ventures to enter this palace, goes over it lost in admiration at its magnificence; when suddenly she hears a voice, telling her that all there is hers, and all her commands will be obeyed. She bathes, sits down to a rich repast, and is regaled with music by invisible performers. At night she retires to bed; an unseen youth addresses her in the softest accents, and she becomes his wife.

Her sisters had meanwhile come to console their parents for the loss of Psyché, whose invisible spouse informs her of this event, and warns her of the danger likely to arise from it. Moved by the tears of his bride, he however consents that her sisters should come to the palace. The obedient Zephyr conveys them thither. They grow envious of Psyché's happiness, and try to persuade her that her invisible lord is a serpent, who will finally devour her. By their advice she provides herself with a lamp and a razor to destroy the monster. When her husband was asleep she arose, took her lamp from its place of concealment, and approached the couch; but there she beheld, instead of a dragon, Love himself. Filled with amazement at his beauty, she leaned in rapture over his charms; a drop of oil fell from the lamp on the shoulder of the god; he awoke, and flew away. Psyché caught his leg as he rose, and was raised into the air, but fell; and as she lay, the god reproached her from a cypress for her breach of faith.

The abandoned Psyché attempted to drown herself in the neighbouring stream : but, fearing Love, it cast her upon a bank of flowers, where she was found and consoled by the god Pan. She now goes through the world in search of Cupid : she arrives at the kingdom of her sisters; and, by a false tale of Cupid's love for them, causes them to cast themselves from the rock on which she had been exposed, and through their credulity they perish. She still roams on, persecuted and subjected to numerous trials by Venus. Pitied but unaided by the higher goddesses Ceres and Juno, the plants and the animals, the reed, the owl, and the eagle, give her their advice and assistance. Venus, bent on her destruction, dispatches her to Proserpina with a box to request some of her beauty. Psyché, dismayed at the peril of the journey to the lower regions, ascends a tower, determined to cast herself from it and end her woes; but the tower pities her, and instructs her how to proceed. She accomplishes her mission in safety. As she is returning, she thinks she may venture to open the box and take a portion for herself, that she may be the more pleasing to her husband. She opens the box, when instead of beauty there issues from it a dense black exhalation, and the imprudent Psyché falls to the ground in a deep slumber from its effects. In this state she is found by Cupid, who had escaped by the window of the chamber where he had been confined by his mother; he awakens her with the point of one of his arrows, reproaches her with her curiosity, and then proceeds to the palace of Jupiter to interest him in her favour. Jupiter takes pity on her, and endows her with immortality; Venus is reconciled, and her marriage with Cupid takes place. The Hours shed roses through the sky, the Graces sprinkle the halls of Heaven with fragrant odours, Apollo plays on his lyre, the Arcadian god on his reeds, the Muses sing in chorus, while Venus dances with grace and elegance to celebrate the nuptials of her son. Thus Cupid was at length reunited to his long-lost Psyché, and their loves were speedily crowned by the birth of a child, whom his parents named Pleasure.[1]

This beautiful fiction is perhaps a philosophic allegory, intended by its inventor for a representation of the mystic union between the divine love and the human soul, and of the trials and purifi

[1] And from her fair unspotted side
Two blissful twins are to be born
Youth and Joy, so Jove hath sworn.—*Comus*, 1009

cations which the latter must undergo, in order to be perfectly fitted for an enduring union with the divinity. It is thus explained by the Christian mythologist Fulgentius.[1] "The city in which Psyché dwells is the world; the king and queen are God and matter; Psyché is the soul; her sisters are the flesh and the free-will: she is the youngest, because the body is before the mind; and she is the fairest, because the soul is higher than free-will, more noble than the body. Venus, i. e. lust, envies her, and sends Cupido, i. e. desire, to destroy her; but as there is desire of good as well as of evil, Cupid falls in love with her: he persuades her not to see his face, that is, not to learn the joys of desire; just as Adam, though he could see, did not see that he was naked until he had eaten of the tree of desire. At the impulsion of her sisters she put the lamp from under the bushel, that is, revealed the flame of desire which was hidden in her bosom, and loved it when she saw how delightful it was; and she is said to have burned it by the dripping of the lamp, because all desire burns in proportion as it is loved, and fixes its sinful mark on the flesh. She is therefore deprived of desire and her splendid fortune, is exposed to perils, and driven out of the palace."

This fanciful exposition will probably not prove satisfactory to many readers. The following one of a modern writer[2] may seem to come nearer the truth. "This fable, it is said, is a representation of the destiny of the human soul. The soul, which is of divine origin, is here below subjected to error in its prison the body. Hence trials and purifications are set before it, that it may become capable of a higher view of things, and of true desire. Two loves meet it,—the earthly, a deceiver who draws it down to earthly things; the heavenly, who directs its view to 'the original fair and divine, and who gaining the victory over his rival, leads off the soul as his bride."

According to a third expositor[3] the mythe is a moral one. It is intended to represent the dangers to which nuptial fidelity was exposed in such a country as degenerate Greece, and at the same time to present an image of a fidelity subjected to numerous temptations and victorious over them all.

The interpretation of an allegory is always hazardous; for fancy presided over its birth, and fancy must always have a large share in the attempts made to develope its secret and real nature. All, therefore, that we should ever hope to arrive at is a view of the general sense and meaning. In truth many a tale seems to be allegoric which was never meant to be so by its author, and

[1] *Mythologicon*, iii. 6.   [2] Hirt. *ap.* Creuzer, *Symbolik*, iii. 573.
[3] Thorlacius, *ap. eundem, ib.*

many a tale *is* allegoric in which the vulgar discern nothing but amusing narrative   The story of Cupid and Psyché may after all have been, as some think, nothing more than a Milésian tale like that, for instance, of the Matron of Ephesos.[1]   We ourselves long inclined to the current opinion of its having been originally a philosophic allegory, but we now feel disposed to regard it as merely a tale of fancy.

Ere we quit this subject we must observe, that a Greek name for the *moth* was Psyché (ψυχή).   The fondness of this insect for approaching at night the flame of the lamp or candle, in which it so frequently finds its death, reminds a mystic philosopher of the fate of the soul destroyed by the desire of knowledge, or absorbed and losing its separate existence in the deity, who dwells in light according to the philosophy of the East.   But further, the world presents no illustration so striking or so beautiful of the immortality of the soul, as that of the moth or butterfly bursting on brilliant wings from the dull groveling caterpillar- or larva-state in which it had previously existed, fluttering in the blaze of day, and feeding on the sweetest and most fragrant products of the spring. Hence it was, in all probability, that the Greeks named the butterfly the *soul*.[2]

The fable of Love and Psyché has been the original of many a pleasing fairy-tale.   It forms an episode in the Adone of the Italian poet Marini ; it has been told in French prose by the *naï* and charming La Fontaine ; and the united powers of Corneille Molière, and Quinault produced a *tragédie-ballet* named Psyché for the amusement of the court of Louis XIV.   In English, the amiable and accomplished Mrs. H. Tighe has narrated the tale of Psyché and her celestial lover in elegant and harmonious Spenserian verse.

Chapter X.

PALLAS-ATHÉNÉ, AND HERMÉS.

We place these deities together, dissimilar as they may appear in office and character, as they form two remarkable instances of gods altering their characters and attributes with a change of manners or institutions in the people.

----

[1] See Paldamus, *Römische Erotik*, p. 92 *seq.*

[2] The earliest instance of this mode of thought that we have met with is the following passage of Dante :

> Non v' accorgete voi che noi siam vermi,
> Nati a formar l' angelica *farfalla*
> Che vola a la giustizia senza schermi.—*Purg.* x. terz. 42.

Παλλὰς ᾿Αθηναίη, καὶ ᾿Αθήνη, ᾿Αθηνᾶ. (*Minerva.*)

The Pallas-Athéné of both the Homéric poems is the daughter of Zeus; in one place[1] it seems to be intimated that she had no other parent. In the Theogony Zeus swallows Métis, and the 'blue-eyed Tritogeneia' is born from his head,[2] which, Pindar[3] says, Héphæstos opened with a brazen axe; Athéna then, the poet adds, sprang forth with a shout which terrified Heaven and Mother Earth, while the king of the gods poured a shower of gold on Rhodes, the sacred isle of the Sun-god. Stésichoros[4] had already sung how the goddess issued from the head of her sire in perfect panoply,—a circumstance however evidently to be understood in the narrative of Pindar. According to the Homérid[5] Olympos shook at the divine birth, the earth resounded, the sea was moved, and Hélios checked his steeds in their career till the new-born goddess took off her radiant armour. Later authorities assign the task of opening the head of Zeus to Prométheus,[6] or Hermés.[7] It was even added that she issued from the head of her sire, not only armed, but furnished with a war-car and horses.[8] According to Hérodotos[9] the goddess was the offspring of Poseidón and the nymph Tritónis.

Pallas-Athéné is in Homer, and in the general popular system, the goddess of wisdom and skill. She is in war opposed to Arés, the wild war-god, as the patroness and teacher of just and scientific warfare. She is therefore on the side of the Greeks, and he on that of the Trojans. But on the shield of Achilleus, where the people of the besieged town are represented as going forth to lie in ambush, they are led by Arés and Athéna together,[10] possibly to denote the union of skill and courage required for that service.[11] Every prudent chief was esteemed to be under the patronage of Athéna, and Odysseus was therefore her especial favourite, whom she relieved from all his perils, and whose son Télemachos she also took under her protection, assuming a human form to be his

[1] *Il.* v. 875 *seq.*
[2] Th. 886 *seq.* 924. The scholion on *v.* 890 is as follows: Λέγεται ὅτι ἡ Μῆτις τοιαύτην εἶχε δύναμιν ὥστε μεταβάλλειν εἰς ὁποίαν ἂν ἐβούλετο. Πλανήσας οὖν αὐτὴν ὁ Ζεὺς καὶ πικρὰν ποιήσας κατέπιεν ἔγκυον οὖσαν. For πικρὰν, which gives little or no sense, Lobeck (*Aglaoph.* p. 613) would drea μυῖαν; we however prefer μικρὰν, which Göttling proposes. This critic points out the similarity between this fiction and that of Puss in Boots and the Ogre. See above, p. 71.

[3] *Ol.* vii. 34 (63) *seq. cum Schol.*
[4] Sch. *Apoll. Rh.* iv. 1310.
[5] Hom. *Hymn* xxviii.
[6] Eur. *Ión.* 455. Apollod. i. 3.
[7] Sch. *Pind. ut supra.*
[8] Et. Mag. *v.* ἱππία.
[9] Hérod. iv. 180.
[10] *Il.* xviii. 516: comp. *Od.* xiv. 216.
[11] *Il.* xiii. 277. *Od.* xiv. 217.

guide and director.   In like manner Kadmos, Héraklés, Perseus, and other heroes were, as we shall see, favoured and aided by this goddess.

As the patroness of arts and industry in general, Pallas-Athéné was regarded as the inspirer and teacher of able artists.   Thus she taught Epeios to frame the wooden horse, by means of which Troy was taken ;[1] and she also superintended the building of the ship Argó.[2]   Athéna was likewise expert in female accomplishments; she wove her own robe and that of Héra, which last she is said to have embroidered very richly.[3]   When the hero Iasón was setting forth in quest of the Golden Fleece, Athéna gave him a cloak wrought by herself.[4]   She taught this art to mortal females who had won her affection.[5]   When Pandóra was formed by Héphæstos for the ruin of man she was attired by Pallas-Athéné.[6]

By the Homérid[7] Athéna and Héphæstos are united as the benefactors and civilisers of mankind by means of the arts which they taught them, and we shall find them in intimate union in the mythic system of Attica.   This goddess is in various mythes also united with Poseidón.[8]

Homer[9] thus describes Pallas-Athéné arraying herself in the arms of Zeus, when preparing to accompany Héra to the plain where the Greeks and Trojans were engaged in conflict.

> But Athénæé, child of Zeus supreme,
> The ægis-holder, on her father's floor
> Let fall her peplos various, which she
> Herself had wrought, and laboured with her hands.
> The tunic then of cloud-collecting Zeus
> She on her put, and clad herself in arms
> For tearful war ; and round her shoulders cast
> The fringed ægis dire, which all about
> Was compassed with fear. In it was Strife,
> In it was Strength, and in it chill Pursuit ;
> In it the Gorgon-head, the portent dire,—
> Dire and terrific, the great prodigy
> Of ægis-holding Zeus.   Upon her head
> She placed the four-coned helmet formed of gold,
> Fitting the foot-men of a hundred towns.
> The flaming car she mounted, seized the spear,
> Great, heavy, solid, wherewith the strong-sired
> Maiden the ranks of heroes vanquisheth,
> With whom she is wroth.

A Mæonian maid named Arachné, proud of her skill in weaving

---

[1] *Od.* viii. 493.   Hésiod ('Εργ. 428) terms a carpenter 'Αθηναίας δμωός.
[2] See also *Il.* v. 61 ; xv. 412.   [3] *Il.* v. 735 ; xiv. 178.
[4] Apoll. Rh. i. 721.   [5] *Od.* xx. 72.   [6] Hés. *Theog.* 573.   [7] See above, p. 98.
[8] See above, p. 78, and Part II. ch. vi. *Bellerophontés.*   [9] *Il.* v. 733.

and embroidery, in which arts the goddess had instructed her, ventured to deny her obligation, and challenged her patroness to a trial of skill. Athéna, assuming the form of an old woman, warned her to desist from her boasting; and when she found her admonitions were vain, she resumed her proper form and accepted the challenge. The skill of Arachné was such, and the subject she chose (the love-transformations of the gods) so offensive to Athéna, that she struck her several times on the forehead with the shuttle. The high-spirited maid unable to endure this affront hung herself, and the goddess relenting changed her into a *spider* (ἀράχνη).[1]

The invention of the flute or pipe (αὐλός) is also ascribed to this goddess. When Perseus, says Pindar,[2] had slain Medusa, her two remaining sisters bitterly lamented her death. The snakes which formed their ringlets mourned in concert with them, and Athéna hearing the sound was pleased with it, and resolved to imitate it: she in consequence invented the pipe, whose music was named *many-headed* (πολυκέφαλος), on account of the number of the serpents whose lugubrious hissing had given origin to it. Others[3] say that the goddess formed the pipe from the bone of a stag, and bringing it with her to the banquet of the gods began to play on it. Being laughed at by Héra and Aphrodíté, on account of her green eyes and her swollen cheeks, she went to a fountain on Mount Ida, and played before the liquid mirror. Satisfied that the goddesses had had reason for their mirth, she threw her pipe away: Marsyas unfortunately found it, and learning to play on it, ventured to become the rival of Apolló. His fate has been already related.

The favourite plant of Athéna was the olive, to which she had given origin. Among animals the owl and the serpent were sacred to her. Athéna was most honoured in Athens ('Αθῆναι), the city whence she probably derived her name, and where the splendid festivals of the Panathénæa were celebrated in her honour. She had also temples at Thébes, Argos, Sparta, and elsewhere. At Tegea she was worshipped under the title of Alea. She contended,

---

[1] Ov. *Met.* vi. 1 *seq.*,—the name as usual giving origin to the fable. In the Semitic languages *arag* (אָרַג) is, to weave, and it is used of the spider, *Is.* lix. 5. Our own *spider* (Germ. *spinne*) is evidently a corruption of *spinner*, or possibly *spinder*. We know not what Greek authority Ovid followed, probably Nicander. Vergil alludes to this legend,

aut invisa Minervæ
Laxos in foribus suspendit aranea casses.—Geor. iv. 246.

See Servius and Probus *in loc.*

[2] *Pyth.* xii. 7 (15) *seq. cum Sch* Non xxiv. 37 ; xl. 227 *seq.*

[3] Hygin. *Fab.* 165.

as we have seen, with Poseidón for Athens and Trœzén, and, according to one account, for Argos.

This goddess is represented with a serious thoughtful counte-nance, her eyes are large and steady, her hair hangs in ringlets on her shoulders, a helmet covers her head ; she wears a long tunic and mantle, she bears the ægis on her breast or on her arm, and the head of the Gorgón is on its centre.   She often has bracelets and ear-rings, but her general air is that of a young man in female attire.

Pallas-Athéné was called by the poets,[1] 1. *Owl-* or *Green-eyed;*[2] 2. *Town-destroying;*   3. *Town-protecting;*   4. *Plundering;*   5. *Un-wearied* or *Invincible;*   6. *People-rouser,* &c.

We are now to inquire into the signification of the name of this goddess and her original nature.

The simplest and most natural interpretation of Pallas-Athénæé appears to be Athenian Maid, and she thus forms a parallel to the Eleusinian Maid (Κόρη), Persephoné.[3]   As this is her constant title in Homer, it is manifest that she had long been regarded as the tutelar deity of Athens.   We may therefore safely reject the legends of her being the same with the Néith of Saïs in Egypt, or a war-goddess imported from the banks of the lake Tritónis in Libya, and view in her one of the deities worshipped by the agri-cultural Pelasgians, and therefore probably one of the powers engaged in causing the productiveness of the earth.   Her being represented in the poe‘ic creed as the goddess of arts and war alone, need not cause us any hesitation, as that transition from physical to moral agents, of which we shall presently give an ex-planation, was by no means uncommon.   It is to the ethic side of her character that the mythe of her birth from the head of her sire belongs.

The most probable theory, in our opinion, is that which views in Pallas-Athéné the temperate celestial heat and its principal agent on vegetation, the moon.[4]   This idea was not unknown to the ancients ; Athéna is by Aristotle expressly called the moon ;[5] on the coins of Attica, anterior to the time of Periklés, there was a moon along with the owl and olive-branch ;[6] there was a torch-

[1] 1. γλαυκῶπις: 2. πολιπόρθος: 3. πολιοῦχος, ἐρυσίπτολις: 4. ἀγελεία: 5. ἀτρυτώνη: 6. λαοσσόος.
[2] More probably *Bright-eyed :* see Appendix C.
[3] Müller, *Proleg.* 244. See also Eudocia, 4. Schwen‘:. ‘30. Welcker, *Tril.* 282. Müller says that Παλλάς is the same as πάλλα   originally *maid ;* the terms are to each other as γυνή and ΓΤΝΑΙΞ. There was a temple of Athéna Koria near Cleitór in Arcadia. Paus. viii. 21, 4.
[4] Müller, *Minervı Polias,* 5.   *Proleg.* 213. Welcker, *Tril.* 277 seq.
[5] Arnob. iii. 31.   [6] See Eckhel, *Doct. Num.* ii. p. 163, 209.

race (λαμπαδοφορία) at the Panathénæa, a contest with which none but light-bearing deities were honoured;[1] at the festival of the Skira or Skirophoria the priest of the Sun and the priestess of Athéna went together in procession beneath the shade of a large white umbrella (σκίρον);[2] a title of Athéna was *All-dew* (Pandrosos);[3] in the ancient legend of Athens there was a Sacred Marriage between Athéna and Héphæstos,[4] in whose temple stood a statue of the goddess:[5] she was also said to have given fire to the Athenians;[6] and a perpetual flame was maintained in her temples at Athens and Alalkomenæ.[7] It could hardly have been from any other cause than that of her being regarded as the moon, that the nocturnal owl, whose broad full eyes shine so brightly in the dark, was consecrated to her; the shield or corselet with the Gorgón's head on it seems to represent the full-orbed moon; and finally the epithet *Glaukópis*, which is as it were appropriated to Athéna, is also given to Seléné.[8]

To these proofs respecting the Athenian goddess we may add that at Tegea Athéna was called Alea, that is probably *Warmer;*[9] a festival with a lamp-race was celebrated at Corinth in honour of Athéna Hellótia;[10] at Sparta she was named Ophthalmitis or *Eyed*, and at Argos *Quick-seer* (ὀξυδερκώ).[11]

If this theory be correct, the best explanation of the perplexing epithet Tritogeneia might seem to be that which derives it from the *three* phases of the moon.[12] There are two other interpretations of this name which have had more general currency. The one supposes it to signify *Head-sprung*, as the word τριτώ is said to have signified *Head* in some of the obscurer dialects of Greece.[13] But accounts like this are very suspicious, and the later Greeks would have made little scruple about coining a term if they wanted

---

[1] Pan, Artemis, Athéna, Héphæstos, Prométheus: see Müller, *Min. Pol. ut supra.*

[2] Harpocrat. *v.* Σκίρα. Hence the goddess was named Σκιράς, and the month (about midsummer) Σκιροφοριών.

[3] Sch. *Aristoph. Lys.* 440.   [4] See Part II. chap. v. *Erichthonios.*
[5] Paus. i. 14, 5.   [6] Plut. *Cim.* 10.
[7] Paus. i. 26, 7; ix. 34, 1.

[8] See above, p. 56, and Appendix C. Lauer labours to prove that Athéna was the clouds, but everything that he alleges applies as well or better to the moon; besides the clouds could hardly be regarded as a unity, as they generally present a scattered appearance.

[9] Paus. viii. 4, 3; 9, 3.   [10] Sch. *Pind. Ol.* xiii. 40 (56).
[11] Paus. ii. 24, 2; iii. 18, 2.

[12] Τριπλόον εἶδος ἔχουσα πέλει Τριτωνὶς Ἀθήνη. Nonn. v. 73.

[13] That of the Athamanes, according to Nikander of Kolophón, Hésych. *s. v.* Etym. Mag. and Photius, *s. v.*; that of the Crétans, Eustath. *on Il.* iv. p. 524, viii. p. 696, *Od.* iii. p. 1473; that of the Bœótians, Tzetz. *Lyc.* 519.

it to suit any purpose. The other interpretation, which makes the banks of the river or lake Tritón the birth-place of Athéna has found a greater number of supporters; but as so many countries sought to appropriate the Tritón to themselves,[1] the choice among them might seem difficult. The contest, however, has lain between the river or lake Tritón in Libya and a small stream of the same name in Bœótia. The ancients in general were in favour of the former; but as there is no reason to suppose that the Greeks knew anything of the Libyan Tritón in the days of Homer, or probably till after the colony had been settled at Kyréné, this theory seems to have little in its favour. Müller[2] therefore at once rejects it, and fixes on the banks of the Bœótian brook as the natal spot of the goddess. Here, however, again Homer presents a difficulty, for, as we have already observed, the practice of assigning birth-places on earth to the gods does not seem to have prevailed in his age. Indeed, we strongly suspect that the streamlet that flowed by Alalkomenæ got its name in the same manner as the hill Délos at Tegyra, and the grove Ortygia at Ephesos.[3] Lauer, regarding as correct the account of this goddess, i.e. the cloud, being the daughter of Poseidón, renders Tritogeneia *Water-born*.[4] After all we fear that the term is one of those which are fated never to be satisfactorily explained.

The moon-goddess of the Athenians may have come by her moral and political character in the following manner.[5] It was the practice of the different classes and orders in a state to appropriate the general tutelar deity to themselves by some suitable appellation. The Attic peasantry, therefore, named Athéna the *Ox-yoker* ($\beta o \nu \delta \epsilon i a$), the citizens called her *Worker* ($\epsilon \rho \gamma \acute{a} \nu \eta$), while the military class styled her *Front-fighter* ($\pi \rho \acute{o} \mu a \chi o s$). As these last were the ruling order, their view of the character of the goddess became the prevalent one; yet even in the epic poetry we find the idea of the goddess presiding over the arts still retained.

Some of the ancients regarded Athéna as the air,[6] others as the earth.[7] There are some mythes which can be explained with so much more ease on this last hypothesis, that we think it not im-

---

[1] There were Tritóns in Bœótia, Thessaly (Sch. *Apoll. Rh.* i. 109), Arcadia (Paus. viii. 26, 6), Krété (Diodor. v. 72), Thrace (Interp. to *Vib. Sequester*, p. 285).   [2] *Orchom.* 355.

[3] See below, chap. xv., *Artemis of Ephesos*.

[4] *System*, etc., 315. He makes a verb ΤΡΙΩ, i. q. $\rho \epsilon \omega$, and thence τριτὰ, i. q. $\rho \epsilon \tilde{v} v a$.

[5] See Müller, *Min. Pol.* p. 1.

[6] Diodor. i. 12. Tzetz. *Lyc.* 519.

[7] Heraklid. *Alleg. Hom.* p. 444. Völcker, *Myth. der Jap.* 191.

probable that the Pelasgian goddess of Argos and other places, who had been identified with the Athenian Maid, may have originally been the same with Héra and Démétér.[1]

Ἑρμείας, Ἑρμῆς, Ἑρμάων. (*Mercurius.*)

Hermeias (as Homer always names this god)[2] is in one place of the Ilias called the son of Zeus,[3] but his mother is unnoticed. When, in the same poem, Dioné is consoling her wounded daughter,[4] she reminds her how others of the Celestials had suffered similar calamities inflicted by mortals. Thus Arés, she says, was once shut up in a brazen prison by O'tos and Ephialtés, where he languished till Hermeias, being informed of his state, contrived to steal him out of his dungeon. Elsewhere the poet tells us that of all the Trojans Hermeias most loved Phorbas (*Feeder*), *rich in sheep*, and bestowed on him wealth (κτῆσιν) ;[5] and that Eudóros (*Wealthy* or *Munificent*) was the son of Hermeias by Polymélé (*Sheep-full*), the daughter of Phylas (*Keeper*).[6]

Hermeias is opposed in the battle of the gods to Létó, but declines the combat on the plea of the impolicy of making an enemy of one of the consorts of Zeus; at the same time courtier-like telling her that, if she pleases, she may boast of having vanquished him by main strength.[7] When the corse of Hektór was exposed by Achilleus, the gods, pitying the fate of the hero, urged Hermeias to *steal* it away. On king Priamos' setting forth to ransom the body of his son, Zeus desires Hermeias to accompany him, reminding him of his fondness for associating with mankind.[8] The god obeys his sire, puts on his 'immortal golden sandals, which bear him over the water and the extensive earth like the blasts of the wind,' and takes 'his rod, with which he lays asleep the eyes of what men he will, and wakes again the sleepers.' He accompanies the aged monarch in the form of a Grecian youth, telling him that he is the son of a wealthy man named Polyktór (*Much-possessing*).

In the Odyssey Hermeias takes the place of Iris, who does not appear at all in this poem, and becomes the messenger of Zeus. He still retains his character of a friend to man, and comes unsent to point out to Odysseus the herb *Moly*, which will enable him to escape the enchantments of Kirké.[9] Eumæos the swine-herd

---

[1] For Athéna Hippia and Gorgó, see below, Part II. *Bellerophontés* and *Perseus.*

[2] Wherever the form Ἑρμῆς occurs, the passage may be regarded as an interpolation.   [3] *Il.* xxiv. 333.   [4] *Il.* v. 390.   [5] *Il.* xiv. 490.

[6] *Il.* xvi. 179. Perhaps Phylas, like φυλλάς, φύλλον, comes from φύω.

[7] *Il.* xx. 35; xxi. 498.   [8] *Il.* xxiv. 333.   [9] *Od.* x. 277 *seq.*

makes an offering to Hermés and the nymphs.[1] At the commencement of the spurious twenty-fourth book, Hermeias appears
in his character of conveyer of souls to the realms of Hadés.

Hésiod says,[2] that the Atlantis Maia bore to Zeus the 'illustrious Hermés, the herald of the Immortals.' In another place
he speaks of him very explicitly as the deity presiding over flocks
and herds, saying that the herdsmen prayed to him and Hekaté.
This poet also ascribes to him the only act injurious to man with
which he is charged, namely, a share in the formation of the
fatal Pandóra, to whom he gave her 'currish mind and artful
disposition.'[4]

One of the last of the Homérids thus sang the story of the
birth and first exploits of this sly deity.

Hermés was born of the mountain-nymph Maia, in a cavern of
Mount Kylléné in Arcadia. He had scarcely been laid in his
cradle, when he got up and set off for Pieria to steal cows from
Apolló. As he was going out he met a tortoise, which he caught
up and carried back into the cave; where quick as thought he
killed the animal, took out the flesh, adapted reeds and strings to
the shell, and formed from it the phorminx or lyre, on which he
immediately played with perfect skill. He then laid it up in his
cradle, and resumed his journey.

He arrived by sunset in Pieria, where the oxen of the gods fed
under the care of Apolló. He forthwith separated fifty cows
from the herd and drove them away, contriving to make them go
backwards; and throwing away his sandals, bound branches of
myrtle and tamarisk under his feet, that the herdsman-god might
have no clue by which to trace his cattle. As he passed by
Onchéstos in Bœótia, he saw an old man engaged in planting his
vineyard, whom he straitly charged not to tell what he had seen.
He then pursued his way by 'shady hills, resounding vales, and
flowery plains,' and as the moon was rising arrived with his booty
on the banks of the Alpheios in the Peloponnése. He there fed
and stalled the kine, made a fire, killed, cut up, and dressed
two of them, and even made black-puddings of their blood, and
then thriftily spread their skins to dry on a rock. He burned the
heads and feet, and put out the fire, effacing all signs of it, and
flung his twig-sandals into the river. With day-break he slank
home and stole into his cradle, not unobserved by his mother,
who reproached him with his deeds; but he replied, that he was

---

[1] *Od.* xiv. 435. This verse, however, is manifestly spurious.
[2] *Theog.* 938. Ἑρμῆν.   [3] *Theog.* 444. Ἑρμῇ. See above, **p. 59.**
[4] Ἑργ. 67. Ἑρμείαν.

resolved by his actions to procure admission for her and himself to the assembly of the gods.

In the morning Apolló missed his kine : he set out in search of them, and met the old man, who informed him of his having seen a child driving cows along. He comes to Pylos, where he sees the traces of his cattle, but is amazed at the strange footprints of their driver. He proceeds to the fragrant cave of the nymph, and Hermés on seeing him gathers himself up under the clothes, afraid of the god. Apolló takes the key, opens and searches the three closets where the nymph kept her clothes, ornaments, and food, but to no purpose. He then threatens the child that he will fling him into Tartaros unless he tells him where the cows are : but Hermés stoutly denies all knowledge of them, and even very innocently asks what cows are. Apolló pulls him out of his cradle, and they agree to go and argue the matter before Zeus. Arrived in Olympos, Apolló relates the theft, and tells what reasons he had for suspecting the baby of being the thief. All this is, to the great amusement of the Celestials, manfully denied and its absurdity shown by the little fellow, who still has his cradle-clothes about him. Zeus however gives it against him, and the two brothers are sent in quest of the missing kine. They come to Pylos, and Hermés drives the cattle out of the cave : Apolló misses two of them ; to his amazement he sees their skins upon the rock, and is still more surprised, when, on going to drive the others on, he finds that the art of Hermés had rooted their feet to the ground. Hermés then begins to play on his lyre, the tones of which so ravish Apolló that he offers him the cows for it. The young god gives him the lyre, and receives the cattle. The divine herdsman also bestows on him his whip, and instructs him in the management of the herds.

They now proceed together to Olympos, where Apolló, still suspicious, exacts an oath from Hermés that he will never steal his lyre or bow ; and this being complied with, he presents him with ' a golden, three-leafed, innocuous rod,' the giver of wealth and riches.

The stealing of the cattle of Apolló is somewhat differently related by other writers. According to them,[1] Apolló, delighted with the society of Hymenæos son of Magnés, a Thessalian youth,

---

[1] Ant. Lib 23. He quotes as his authorities Hésiod in the Eœæ, Nikander, Didymarchos and Antigonos in their respective Metamorphoses, and Apollónios Rhodios in his Epigrams. It is uncertain which of these authorities Ovid followed (*Met.* ii. 676 *seq.*) ; his narrative differs in some points from that in the text ; in particular, he makes Élis and Messéné the scene of Apolló's pastoral life, *v.* 679.

L

neglected the care of his oxen, which pastured along with those of Admétos. Hermés, who in this version of the legend is not a babe, thought the opportunity favourable for stealing a few of the heedless herdsman's cattle. He first cast the dogs into a deep slumber, and then drove off twelve heifers, a hundred unyoked cows, and a bull. He took the precaution of tying a bundle of twigs to the tail of each to efface their footprints, and brought his prize safely on to the place called the Look-out of Battos, in the Peloponnése. Hearing the lowing of the kine, Battos ran out to look, and immediately knew them to be stolen, but agreed for a certain reward not to give information to any one respecting them. Hermés having arranged this matter drove on, and concealed his stolen kine in a cavern. He then resolved to make trial of the fidelity of Battos, and changing his form, came and inquired if he had seen any one driving stolen cattle by, offering a cloak as a reward for intelligence. The covetous Battos took the cloak, and turned informer: the god, incensed at his duplicity, struck him with his rod and changed him into a rock, ' which the cold or the heat never leaves.'

The following prank is also said to the charge of this roguish deity. Watching one day hi· .nother and her sisters when they went to bathe, he stole their clothes, and did not return them till he had amused himself well with laughing at their perplexity.[1]

A god with so many agreeable qualities as Hermés was not very likely to fail of success with the fair sex, both among gods and mankind. Homer, as we have observed above, says that Eudóros, one of Achilleus' captains, was the son of Hermés by Polymélé the daughter of Phylas. The god having seen her, singing in the choir of Artemis, had fallen in love with her. She bore him privately a son, who was reared by her father, herself having married Echeklés. By Chione (*Snowy*) the daughter of Dædalión,[2] or as others said by Stilbé or Télaugé the daughter of E'ósphoros,[3] Hermés was the father of Autolykos the noted cattle-stealer. The Thessalian maiden Antianeira bore him two sons, ' rich in corn-fields,' Echíón and Eurytos.[4] Myrtilos, the charioteer of Œnomaos, was the son of Hermés by one of the daughters of Danaos.[5] The celebrated Sicilian shepherd Daphnis was the offspring of this god and one of the nymphs.[6]

One day Hermés beheld Hersé, the daughter of Kekrops,

[1] Sch. *Il.* xxiv. 24.
[2] Pherekýd. *ap. Sch. Od.* xix. 432. Hygin. 200. Ov. *Met.* xi. 312.
[3] Sch. *Il.* x. 267.   [4] Pind. *Pyth.* iv. 178 (318). Apoll. Rh. i. 51 *seq.*
[5] Sch. *Eur. Orest.* 991.
[6] Diodor. iv. 84. Parthénios, *Erot.* 24,—both from Timæos.

among the maidens who were carrying the sacred baskets to the temple of Pallas-Athéné. Smitten with her charms, he entered the royal abode, where the three sisters, Aglauros, Pandrosos and Hersé, occupied three separate chambers. That of Hersé was in the middle, that of Aglauros on the left. The latter first saw the god, and enquired of him who he was and why he came. Hermés immediately informed her of his rank, and his love for her sister, entreating her good offices in his suit. These she promised on the condition of receiving a large quantity of gold, and drove him out of the house till he should have given it. Pallas-Athéné, incensed at her unhallowed cupidity, and provoked with her also for other causes, sent Envy to fill her bosom with that baleful passion. Unable then to endure the idea of the felicity of her sister, she sat down at the door, determined not to permit the god to enter. Hermés exerted his eloquence and his blandishments on her in vain; at length, provoked by her obstinacy, he turned her into a black stone. Hersé became the mother of Kephalos.[1]

The only amour of Hermés with any of the dwellers of Olympos was that with Aphrodíté, of which the offspring was a son named Hermaphrodítos, from the names of his parents, and whose adventure with the Naïs Salmakis is narrated by Ovid in his Metamorphoses.[2] Hermés is in some legends said to be the father of the Arcadian god Pan,[3] and he is even charged with being the sire of the unseemly god of Lampsakos.[4] Both, it may be observed, were rural deities.

At Tanagra in Bœótia Hermés was worshipped under the names of *Ram-bearer* (κριοφόρος) and *Defender* (πρόμαχος): the former was given him for having delivered the citizens from a pestilence, by carrying a ram round the walls; and on the festival of Hermés, the most beautiful of the Tanagrian youths bore a lamb on his shoulders round the walls in honour of the god. The latter title was conferred on him because, when the Eretrians attacked the Tanagrians, Hermés as a young man, and armed with a curry-comb, led the latter to victory.[5]

Hermés was regarded as the god of commerce, of wrestling

---

[1] Apollod. iii. 14, 3. Ov. *Met.* ii. 708 *seq.* Hyginus (160) says that Kephalos was the son of Hermés by Kreüsa, the daughter of Erechtheus.
[2] *Met.* iv. 285. [3] See below, chap. xvi. [4] Hygin. 160.
[5] Paus. ix. 22. These are both silly expositions; the first is confuted by the fact that in the Karnasian grove in Messéné there was a statue of Hermés carrying a ram (Paus. iv. 33, 4), and a similar statue at Olympia (Id. v. 27, 8). At Corinth there was a ram beside his statue, ὅτι μάλιστα δοκεῖ θεῶν ἐφορᾶν al αὔξειν ποίμνας (Id. ii. 3, 4.).

and all the exercises of the palæstra, of eloquence, even of thieving
in short, of everything relating to gain or requiring art and
ingenuity. A certain good-humoured roguery was at all times
a trait in his character. In the pleasing tale of Arés and Aphro
díté already noticed, the gallant reply of Hermés to the question
of Phœbos-Apolló called forth the laughter of the Olympians.

This god is usually represented with a *chlamys* or cloak neatly
arranged on his person, with his *petasus* or winged hat, and the
talaria or wings at his heels. In his hand he bears his *caducéus*
or staff, with two serpents twined about it, and which sometimes
has wings at its extremity. The ancient statues of Hermés were
nothing more than wooden posts with a rude head and a pointed
beard carved on them. They were what is termed *ithyphallic*, and
were set up on the roads and footpaths, and in the fields and
gardens. The Hermæ were also pillars of stone, and the head o:
some other deity at times took the place of that of Hermés; such
were the Hermérakles, Hermathénæ and others. One of these
compounds may have given origin to the tale of Hermaphrodítos
    By Homer and Hésiod Hermés is called,[2] 1. *Argos-Slayer*
2. *Beneficent*;[3] 3. *Kind*; 4. *Strong* or *powerful*;[4] 5. *Performer o:
Messenger*;[5] 6. *Well-spying*; 7. *Gold-rodded*; 8. *Glorious.*

Mythologists are pretty generally agreed in recognising in the
Hermés of the original Pelasgian system a chthonic power. The
simplest derivation of his name is from ἔρα, *the earth*; and he is
we may observe, the son of Zeus and Maia, who is probably
Mother Earth.[6] He seems to have been a deity of productive
ness in general, but he came gradually to be regarded as presiding

---

[1] *Caduceus -um* is a Latin corruption of κηρύκειον (καρύκειον, Dor.), th
herald's staff. This was an olive-staff twined with fillets (στέμματα), whic
were gradually converted to wings and serpents.
    [2] 1. ἀργειφόντης : 2. ἐριούνιος : 3. ἀκακήτα : 4, σῶκος : 5. διάκτορος : 6. ἐΰ
σκοπος : 7. χρυσόρραπις : 8. κύδιμος.
    [3]   Ἑρμείαν δὲ πατὴρ Ἐριούνιον ὠνόμασ᾽ αὐτόν·
         πάντας γὰρ μάκαράς τε θεοὺς θνητοὺς τ᾽ ἀνθρώπους
         κέρδεσι κλεπτοσύναις τ᾽ ἐξαίνυτο τεχνήεσσαις.
                    The Phorónis in *Etym. Mag. v.* ἐριούνιος.
    [4] " As guardian of the herds, as the Dioscuri, Σωκοί, guardians of shipmen.
Welcker, *Tril.* 217.
    [5] Buttmann (*Lexil, s. v.*) makes διάκτορος to be from the same root wit
διάκονος, and identical in signification, i. e. *messenger.* Müller (*Proleg.* 355
considers it too dubious a term to admit of any positive conclusion being draw
from it.
    [6]   Τῷ Μαίας ἀγροτῆρι κούρῳ.—Eurip. *Elec.* 462.
It seems to be the same as the Latin Maia, who was the earth. Hence perhap
it is that the Romans wrote the name of Hermés' mother (Μαῖα) Maia, not Mæ

more particularly over flocks and herds.[1] From this last view some of his Hellénic attributes may be simply deduced. Thus the god of shepherds was naturally regarded as the inventor of music; the lyre is ascribed to Hermés as the pipes are to his son Pan, music having been always a recreation of the shepherds in the warm regions of the south. In like manner as the shepherd-lads amuse themselves with wrestling and other feats of strength and activity, their tutelar god easily became the president of the *palæstra*. So also, trade having of old consisted chiefly in the exchange of cattle, Hermés, the herdsman's god, was held to be the god of commerce;[2] and the skill and eloquence employed in commercial dealings made him to be the god of eloquence, artifice, and ingenuity, and even of cheating.[3] As herdsmen are the best guides in the country, it may be thence that Hermés was thought to protect wayfarers,[4] and thence to be a protector in general.[5] For this cause, among others, it may have been that godsends or treasure-trove were ascribed to him.[6]

The rural deity, when thus become active, sly, and eloquent, was well adapted for the office which was assigned him of agent and messenger of the king of the gods, to whom we also find him officiating as cup-bearer.[7] We may however best perhaps seek the origin of Hermés as herald and envoy in the principle of secondary derivation. As a being whose operations extended into the interior of the earth, Hermés would seem to have been in some points of view identified with Hadés. In Pindar[8] we may observe this latter deity himself performs the office generally assigned to Hermés, that of conducting the departed to Erebos. It may have been on this account that Solón directed the Athenians to swear by Zeus, Poseidón, and Hermés, but it is more probable that this last is Butés, the Attic tutelar deity.[9]

---

[1] Hence he was called νόμιος, Aristoph. *Thesm.* 977 ; ἔφορος γὰρ τῶν θρεμμάτων δ θεὸς says the Scholiast; and he was worshipped at Koróneia under the title of ἐπιμήλιος, Paus. ix. 34, 3.

[2] This is the only point of similarity between the Grecian Hermés and the Italian Mercurius.

[3] Hence probably his epithet δόλιος. Aristoph. *Plut.* 1157. *Thesm.* 1202. Paus. vii. 27, 1. As the giver of gain he was called κερδῷος. Luc. *Tim.* 41. Eudocia, p. 256.

[4] Ἑρμῆς πομπαῖος.

Πομπαῖος ἴσθε τόνδε ποιμαίνων ἐμὸν
ἱκέτην.—Æsch. *Eum.* 91.

where we may observe the allusion to the rural character of the god.

[5] He is said to have been called στροφαῖος (Et. Mag. *s. v.*), from the turning (στροφή) of the door on its hinges, as his statue was placed at the door.

[6] What was thus found was called ἕρμαιον. When Lucian's Timón comes on the treasure he cries out Ἑρμῆ κερδῷε. [7] See above, p. 100.

[8] *Ol.* ix. 33 (50) *seq.*: see above, p. 84. [9] See Part II. ch. v. *ad fin.*

On looking over the adventures of Hermés above related, it will appear that most of them refer to his character as a rural deity.[1] Such are his patronage of Phorbas, and his being the sire of Eudóros in Homer; the hymn in his honour, which plainly represents him as a rural deity;[2] his being the sire of the cattle-stealer Autolykos (*Very-Wolf*);[3] of the two heroes 'rich in corn-fields;' and of the shepherd Daphnis, and the gods Pan and Priápos. The rural character of Hersé and Aglauros will be shown in the sequel. We shall also find that it was Hermés who gave to Nephelé the gold-fleeced ram to save her children from their malignant step-mother.[4] In Theokritos[5] Hermés is one of the gods who comes to console the dying shepherd Daphnis; and in the poems of the Greek Anthology he is usually represented as a rural deity. In one place[6] the offering to him is milk and honey; in other parts of it[7] fishermen when grown old dedicate their implements to Hermés, either as the god of arts and trade, or as the deity presiding over increase in general.

We will now consider the well-known epithet Argeiphontés, or *Argos-slayer*, given to this god. The general opinion derives it from the legend of Ió, but it has been doubted if that adventure was known to Homer, who calls the deity by this name in passages the genuineness of which cannot well be disputed.[8] The sense of that legend shall be discussed in its proper place; here we will only observe, that if it should appear to be as old as the age of Homer, there can be no further dispute about the origin of the epithet, though its meaning will still remain a subject of inquiry. Supposing however such not to be the case, it may be asked how the rural deity, the field-god, came by the appellation Argeiphontés? The word *Argos* bears in Greek the following senses: 1. *White* or *Shining*; 2. *Swift* (in speaking of dogs, and thence the name of a dog); 3. *Idle*; to which we may venture to add, 4. *Land*, as identical with ἄγρος. The latter half of the compound was generally derived from φένω, *to kill* or *destroy*; by some however from φαίνω, *to show* or *shine*. Hence some interpreted

---

[1] See Müller, *Proleg.* 355.   [2] See *vv.* 491, 567.

[3] This may, however, be an instance of what we term secondary derivation (see p. 9), and the original root of Autolykos have been ΛΥΚΗ, *lux*, for all the mothers given him (p. 146) denote radiance or brightness, and one of his grand-sires is Morning-star. He may therefore have been originally a light-being with a suitable sire, and Hermés not have been his father till his name was derived from λύκος: see *Augeas* and *Otos and Ephialtés*.

[4] By his touch, it was said, he turned the fleece to gold. Sch. *Apoll. Rh.* ii. 1144.

[5] *Idyll.* i. 77.   [6] Anthol. ix. 72.

[7] *Ib.* vi. 5, 23, 28, 29.   [8] *Il.* ii. 103. *Od.* i. 38.

Argeiphontés *Free-from-bloodshed,* others *White-* or *clear-showing ;*[1] and a modern mythologist[2] renders it *White-shining,* equivalent to *White* (λευκὸς), a name by which Hermés was worshipped in Bœótia.[3] We must confess that we are not satisfied with any of these explanations; and should the derivation from the story of Ió not be approved of, none appears more probable than the one we ourselves formerly suggested, that the term may signify *Field-slayer,*[4] and be applied to Hermés as the god of husbandry, under whose auspices the land was ploughed up, and the grass or corn cut down. The eyes of Argos might then have originally signified the flowers with which the meads are bespread.[5] It is to be observed that, in the version of the story of Ió followed by Ovid,[6] Hermés appears as a goatherd, and kills Argos with the *harpé,* a rural implement.

We offer this hypothesis, however, only as a conjecture, perhaps we should say as a mere sport of imagination ; for we are inclined to regard the mythe of Ió as one of the most remote antiquity.

Chapter XI.

DÉMÉTÉR,—PERSEPHONÉ.

Δημήτηρ, Δηώ, Δώς. (*Ceres.*)

Περσεφύνεια, Περσεφόνη. (*Proserpina.*)

DÉMÉTÉR and her daughter Persephoné are so closely connected, that it would be extremely difficult, or rather impossible, to treat of the one without the other : we therefore combine the two deities.

Démétér, a daughter of Kronos and Rhea, and by Zeus mother of Persephoné,[7] was evidently the goddess of the earth, *Mother-Earth* (γῆ μήτηρ), whom some ancient system married to Zeus, the

---

[1] Sch. *Il.* ii. 103. "The poet," he says, "knows nothing of the love of Ió, and all about Argos was feigned by the later writers." Id. xxiv. 24. Sch. *Od.* i. 38.   [2] Schwenk, 125.   [3] Tzetz. *Lyc.* 680.

[4] Nonnos (xxxvi. 421) calls Dionýsos θαλασσοφόνος. Græfe, however, queries if it should not be θαλασσονόμος. Could that strange poet have alluded to the practice of mixing sea-water with wine ?

[5]
> Ye valleys low, where the mild whispers use
> Of shades and wanton winds and gushing brooks,
> On whose fresh lap the swart-star sparely looks,
> Throw hither all your *quaint enamelled eyes,*
> That on the green turf suck the honey'd showers,
> And purple all the ground with vernal flowers.
>   Milton, *Lycidas,* 136 *seq.*

[6] *Met.* i. 717.   [7] Hés. *Theog.* 454, 912.   *Od.* xi. 217.

god of the heavens.[1]   In Homer she is but slightly mentioned, and she does not appear among the gods on Olympos.   She seems to have been early distinguished from the goddess called Earth,[2] and to have been regarded as the protectress of the growing corn and of agriculture in general.

The most celebrated event in the history of Démétér is the carrying-off of her daughter Persephoné by Hades, and the search of the goddess after her through the world.   It is noticed by Hésiod;[4] but the Homéridian hymn in her honour contains perhaps the earliest narrative of this event, which, though apparently unknown to Homer, became a favourite theme with succeeding poets, after whom Ovid has related it,[5] and Claudian has sung it in a peculiar poem, of which unfortunately a part is lost.

Persephoné, sang the Homérid, was in the Nysian plain with the Ocean-nymphs[6] gathering flowers.   She plucked the rose, the violet, the crocus, the hyacinth, when she beheld a Narcissus of surprising size and beauty, an object of amazement to 'all immortal gods and mortal men,' for one hundred flowers grew from one root;[7]

> And with its fragrant smell wide heaven above
> And all earth laughed, and the sea's briny flood.

Unconscious of danger the maiden stretched forth her hand to seize the wondrous flower, when suddenly the wide earth gaped, Aïdóneus in his golden chariot rose, and catching the terrified goddess carried her off in it shrieking to her father for aid, unheard and unseen by gods or mortals, save only by Hekaté the daughter of Persæos, who heard her as she sat in her cave, and by king Hélios, whose eye nothing on earth escapes.

So long as the goddess beheld the earth and starry heaven, the fishy sea and beams of the sun, so long she hoped to see her mother and the tribes of the gods; and the tops of the mountains and the depths of the sea resounded with her divine voice.   At length her mother heard; she tore her head-attire with grief, cast

---

[1] The Scythians said that Earth was the wife of their Zeus.   Hérod. iv. 59.

[2] *Il.* v. 500, "blond Démétér" is represented as presiding over the winnowing of corn.   In *Od.* v. 125 her amour with Iasión is related.

[3] Gæa is joined with Zeus and Hélios as a person.   *Il.* iii. 104, 278.

> Officium commune Ceres et Terra tuentur ;
> Hæc præbet causam frugibus, illa locum.—Ov. *Fast.* i. 673.

[4] *Theog.* 914.   [5] *Met.* v. 341 *seq.*   *Fast.* iv. 417 *seq.*

[6] According to some accounts Aphrodíté, Athéna, and Artemis were the companions of their sister Persephoné on this occasion, Hygin. 146.   Claud, *Rapt. Pros.* ii. 11 *seq.*   Stat. *Achil.* ii. 150.

[7] Her plucking the narcissus was noticed in an ancient hymn ascribed to Pamphôs.   Paus. ix. 31, 9.

...ark robe around her, and like a bird hurried 'over moist and dry.' Of all she inquired tidings of her lost daughter, but neither gods nor men nor birds could give her intelligence. Nine days she wandered over the earth, with flaming torches in her hands; she tasted not of nectar or ambrosia, and never once entered the bath. On the tenth morning Hekaté met her, but she could not tell her who it was had carried away Persephoné. Together they proceed to Hélios; they stand at the head of his horses, and Démétér entreats that he will say who the ravisher is. The god of the sun gives the required information, telling her that it was Aïdóneus, who by the permission of her sire had carried her away to be his queen; and he exhorts the goddess to patience, by dwelling on the rank and dignity of the ravisher.

Hélios urged on his steeds; the goddess, incensed at the conduct of Zeus, abandoned the society of the gods, and came down among men. But she now was heedless of her person, and no one recognised her. Under the guise of an old woman,—'such,' says the poet, 'as are the nurses of law-dispensing kings' children, and housekeepers in resounding houses,'—she came to Eleusis, and sat down by a well, beneath the shade of an olive.[1] The three beautiful daughters of Keleos, a prince of that place, coming to the well to draw water, and seeing the goddess, inquired who she was and why she did not go into the town. Démétér told them her name was Dós, and that she had been carried off by pirates from Krété, but that when they got on shore at Thorikos, she had contrived to make her escape, and had wandered thither. She entreats them to tell her where she is; and wishing them young husbands and as many children as they may desire, begs that they will endeavour to procure her a service in a respectable family.

The princess Kallidiké tells the goddess the names of the five princes, who with her father governed Eleusis, each of whose wives would, she was sure, be most happy to receive into her family a person who looked so god-like: but she prays her not to be precipitate, but to wait till she had consulted her mother Metaneira, who had a young son in the cradle, of whom, if the stranger could obtain the nursing, her fortune would be made.

The goddess bowed her thanks, and the princesses took up their pitchers and went home. As soon as they had related their adventure to their mother, she agreed to hire the nurse at large wages:

> And they, as fawns or heifers in spring-time
> Bound on the mead when satiate with food;

---

[1] The tradition was that she sat on the stone thence named Laughterless (ἀγέλαστος). Sch. on *Aristoph. Knights*, 782.

> So they, the folds fast-holding of their robes
> Lovely, along the hollow cart-way ran ;
> Their locks upon their snoulders flying wide
> Like unto yellow flowers.

The goddess rose and accompanied them home. As she entered the house a divine splendour shone all around; Metaneira filled with awe offered the goddess her own seat, which however she declined. Iambé the serving-maid then prepared one for her, where she sat in silence, thinking of her ' deep-bosomed ' daughter, till Iambé by her tricks contrived to make her smile, and even laugh. But she declined the cup of wine which Metaneira offered her, and would only drink the *kykeón*, or mixture of flour and water. She undertook the rearing of the babe, who was named Démophoón, and beneath her care ' he throve like a god.' He ate no food, but Démétér breathed on him as he lay in her bosom, and anointed him with ambrosia, and every night she hid him ' like a torch within the strength of fire,' unknown to his parents, who marvelled at his growth.[1]

It was the design of Démétér to make him immortal, but the curiosity and folly of Metaneira deprived him of the intended gift. She watched one night, and, seeing what the nurse was about, shrieked with affright and horror. The goddess threw the infant on the ground, declaring what he had lost by the inconsiderateness of his mother,[2] but announcing that he would be great and honoured, since he had ' sat in her lap and slept in her arms.' She tells who she is, and directs that the people of Eleusis should raise an altar and temple to her without the town on the hill Kallichoros.

> Thus having said, the goddess changed her size
> And form, old-age off-flinging, and around
> Beauty respired ; from her fragrant robes
> A lovely scent was scattered, and afar
> Shone light emitted from her skin divine ;
> And yellow locks upon her shoulders waved :
> While, as from lightning, all the house was filled
> With splendour.

She left the house, and the maidens awaking at the noise found their infant-brother lying on the ground. They took him up, and kindling a fire prepared to wash him ; but he cried bitterly, finding himself in the hands of such unskilful nurses.

In the morning the wonders of the night were narrated to

---

[1] The Egyptians had a similar story of their Isis, borrowed no doubt, like so many others, from the Greeks : see Plut. *De Is. et Os.* 15, 16.

[2] Metaneira is probably Μετανόειρα, i. e. the one who repented of her folly.

Keleos, who laid the matter before the people, and the temple was speedily raised. The mourning goddess took up her abode in it, but a dismal year came upon mankind; the earth yielded no produce, in vain the oxen drew the curved ploughs in the fields, in vain was the seed of barley cast into the ground; 'well-garlanded Déméter' would suffer no increase. The whole race of man ran risk of perishing, the dwellers of Olympos of losing gifts and sacrifices, had not Zeus discerned the danger and thought on a remedy.

He dispatches 'gold-winged Iris' to Eleusis to invite Déméter back to Olympos, but the disconsolate goddess will not comply with the call. All the other gods are sent on the same errand, and to as little purpose. Gifts and honours are proffered in vain; she will not ascend to Olympos, or suffer the earth to bring forth, till she shall have seen her daughter.

Finding that there was no other remedy, Zeus sends 'gold-rodded Argos-slayer' to Erebos, to endeavour to prevail on Hadés to suffer Persephoné to return to the light. Hermés did not disobey: he quickly reached the 'secret places of earth,' and found the king at home seated on a couch with his wife, who was mourning for her mother. On making known to Aïdóneus the wish of Zeus, 'the king of the Subterraneans smiled with his brows' and yielded compliance. He kindly addressed Persephoné, granting her permission to return to her mother. The goddess instantly sprang up with joy, and heedlessly swallowed a grain of pomegranate which he presented to her.

> Then many-ruling Aïdóneus yoked
> His steeds immortal to the golden car;
> She mounts the chariot, and beside her mounts
> Strong Argos-slayer, holding in his hands
> The reins and whip; forth from the house he rushed
> And not unwillingly the coursers flew.
> Quickly the long road they have gone; not sea
> Nor streams of water, nor the grassy dales,
> Nor hills retard the immortal coursers' speed,
> But o'er them going they cut the air profound.

Hermés conducted his fair charge safe to Eleusis: Déméter on seeing her 'rushed to her like a Mænas on the wood-shaded hill,' and Persephoné sprang from the car to meet and embrace her mother.

When their joy had a little subsided, Déméter anxiously inquired if her daughter had tasted anything while below; for if she had not, she would be free to spend her whole time with her father and mother; whereas if but one morsel had passed her lips, nothing could save her from spending one-third of the year with her husband; she should however pass the other two with her and the gods:

> And when in spring-time, with sweet-smelling flowers
> Of various kinds, the earth doth bloom, thou'lt come
> From gloomy darkness back,—a mighty joy
> To gods and mortal men.

Persephoné ingenuously confesses the swallowing of the grain of pomegranate, and then relates to her mother the whole story of her abduction. They pass the day in delightful converse:

> And joy they mutually received and gave.

'Bright-veiled Hekaté' arrives to congratulate Persephoné, and henceforward becomes her attendant. Zeus sends Rhea to invite them back to heaven. Démétér now complies,

> And instant from the deep-soiled cornfields fruit
> Sent up: with leaves and flowers the whole wide earth
> Was laden:

and she taught 'Triptolemos, horse-lashing Dioklés, the strength of Eumolpos, and Keleos the leader of the people,' the mode of performing her sacred rites. The goddesses then returned to Olympos. " But come," cries the Homérid,

> But come, thou goddess who dost keep the land
> Of odorous Eleusis, and round-flowed
> Paros, and rocky Anthrón, Déó queen,
> Mistress, bright-giver, season-bringer, come:
> Thyself and child, Persephoneia fair,
> Grant freely, for my song, the means of life.
> But I will think of thee and other songs.

Such is in all probability the oldest account of this celebrated event. In progress of time it underwent various alterations; the scene was as usual changed, and circumstances were added or modified. In the beautiful versions of it given by the above-mentioned Latin poets, the scene is transferred to the grove and lake in the neighbourhood of Henna in Sicily, the nymph Arethusa gives intelligence of the ravisher, and Askalaphos (who for his mischief-making is turned into an owl)[1] tells of Persephoné's having plucked a pomegranate in the garden of Hadés and put seven of the seeds into her mouth. In this, as in other legends, the fancy of poets and vanity of the inhabitants of different places have taken abundance of liberties with the ancient tale.

---

[1] Another legend says that Démétér placed a stone atop of him in Erebos, which Héraklés rolled away. Apollod. i. 5, 3 ; ii. 5, 12.

There are, as we have already observed, no traces of this mythe in Homer. Démétér is only incidentally mentioned by him; and he does not intimate any connexion between her and Persephoné, who appears merely as the daughter of Zeus [1] and queen of Hadés.

There can be little doubt we think of its being an allegory. Persephoné signifies the seed-corn, which when cast into the ground lies there concealed,—that is, she is carried off by the god of the under-world: it reappears,—that is, Persephoné is restored to her mother, and she abides with her two-thirds of the year. As however the seed-corn is not a third part of the year in the ground, it is probable that by the space of time which Persephoné was to spend with the god in the invisible state, was intended to be expressed the period between the sowing of the seed and the appearance of the ear, during which the corn is away ; and which space of time in some species of grain, barley for instance, is usually about a third of the year.[2]

The vanity of the people of the hungry soil of Attica made them pretend that corn was first known and agriculture first practised in their country. They fabled that the goddess gave to Triptolemos (*Thrice-plough*), who occupies the place of Démophóon[3] in the foregoing legend, her chariot drawn by dragons, in which he flew through the air, distributing corn to the different regions of the earth.[4] This last circumstance betrays the late age of the fiction; for, as we have already observed, in the time of Homer celestial horses were the only draught-cattle of the gods.

Démétér, though of a gentle character in general, partook of the usual revengeful disposition of the gods. The origin of the Stellio, or spotted lizard, is referred to her having thrown in the face of a boy, who mocked at her as she was drinking some gruel, what was remaining of it in the vessel.[5] She more justly punished with ever-craving hunger Erysichthón, who impiously cut down her sacred grove. This infliction gave occasion for the exercise of the filial piety and power of self-transformation of the daughter

---

[1] *Od.* xi. 217.

[2] The festival of the Thesmophoria was celebrated in Attica in the *fourth* month, Pyanepsión (Oct.–Nov.), which was the time of sowing the corn, and that of the Anthestéria or great spring-feast in the *eighth* month, Anthestérión (Feb.–Mar.). So in Judæa the corn, namely the barley, was sown in the month Marchesvan (Oct.–Nov.), and it was reaped in the month Abib or April. See Lightfoot, *Hor. Heb.* 340, 1004. Winer, *Realwörterbuch, vv.* Gerste, Saat.

[3] Though it is not noticed in the Hymn to Démétér, it is plain from his name (δῆμος and φάω) that this was the original teacher of agriculture.

[4] Kallim. *Hymn* vi. 22. Paus. i. 14, 2. Ov. *Met.* v. 645. Hygin. 147 Poet. Astr. ii. 14. Serv. *on Geor.* i. 19.

[5] Nicander *ap. Anton. Lib.* 24. Ov. *Met.* v. 451.

of Erysichthón, who by her assuming various forms enabled her
father to sell her over and over again, and thus obtain the means
of living after all his property was gone.[1]

The former of these legends is evidently one of those sports of
fancy in which the Greeks loved to indulge; the latter may admit
of a simple explication. Erysichthón's name may be akin to
ἐρυσίβη, *mildew*; and Hellaníkos[2] said that he was also called
Æthón (Αἴθων, *burning*), from his insatiate hunger. Now the
destructive devouring mildew is plainly the enemy of Démétér, to
whom, under the title of Erysibia, the Rhodians prayed to avert
it;[3] and who accordingly is represented as punishing it as it were
for its transgression. Müller, therefore, is content with this
explanation of the legend. To us, however, the following seems
to be a more probable solution. Erysichthón is the *ploughman*,[4]
the agriculturist whose greed and desire for more and more
produce is well-known to be in some cases almost insatiable.[5]
This the legend ascribes to the wrath of the deity presiding over
agriculture in punishment of an act of impiety. The moral then is
apparent, and the mythe, of the same class with those of Tantalos
and Ixíon, inculcates moderation and piety toward the gods.

Homer says[6] that Démétér lay with Iasíon in a 'thrice-
ploughed' field, and that Zeus, offended at the deed, struck the
mortal lover with his thunder. Hesiod[7] makes Krété the scene of
this event, and adds that Plutos (*Wealth*) was their offspring.
Authorities differ as to the parentage of Iasíon; some make him
a son of Zeus and Elektra, and brother of Dardanos;[8] others a
son of Minós or Kratés, and the nymph Phronia.[9] The meaning
of the mythe is apparent.

At Onkeion near Thelpusa, on the banks of the Ladón in
Arcadia, stood a temple of Démétér-Erinnys. The legend connected with it was as follows.[10] When the goddess was in search
of her lost daughter, Poseidón, filled with desire, continually
followed her. To elude him she changed herself into a mare, and
mingled with the mares of Onkos; but the sea-god assumed the
form of a horse, and thus accomplished his wishes. The produce
of their union was the celebrated steed Areíon; and from the
anger of the goddess at being thus abused she was named

---

[1] Nicander *ap. Anton. Lib.* 17. Ov. *Met.* viii. 738 *seq.* Tzetz. *Lyc.* 1393.
It is related somewhat differently by Kallimachos, Hymn vi.
[2] Athen. x. 416.   [3] Müller, *Proleg.* 162.
[4] From ἐρύω, *to draw, drag, tear up,* and χθών.
[5] *Avari agricolœ,* Verg. *Geor.* i. 47.   [6] *Od.* v. 125.
[7] *Theog.* 969.   [8] Hellaníkos *ap. Sch. Od.* v. 125.
[9] *Sch. Od. ut sup.* Sch. *Theocr.* iii. 50.   [10] Paus. viii. 25, 4.

Erinnys.[1] It was also a part of the tradition that beside Areión she bore a daughter to the god, who, the Phigalians said, was the Despœna (Persephoné). They also showed a cavern on Mount Elæon, to which Démétér retired when her daughter had been carried off, clothing herself in deep black. The absence of the goddess, said the tradition, caused a general failure of the crops, and mankind were in danger of famine; but no one knew the place of her retreat till Pan in his huntings chanced to see her. He gave information to Zeus, who sent the Fates to her, at whose persuasion she remitted her anger, and ceased from mourning. She was worshipped at this cave under the name of *Black* (μέλαινα), and her statue in it was clad in black, with the head and mane of a horse.[2]

This last mythe has nothing perhaps very peculiar in it; the former is regarded as one of the many forms in which the physical fact of earth and water being the causes of growth and increase in the natural world has been enveloped.[3] Perhaps the Démétér-Erinnys was viewed as the 'grim' earth [4] of winter when torrents spring forth from its womb. These might very aptly be represented by the steed *Flowing* (ῥείων or ῥέων);[5] and this view of nature was peculiarly appropriate in Arcadia.

The chief seats of the worship of these deities were Corinth, Thébes, Attica; Arcadia, where they were called the *Great Goddesses*,[6] and Persephoné in particular *Mistress* (δέσποινα);[7] and the fertile isle of Sicily, which was given by Zeus to his daughter on her day of unveiling (ἀνακαλυπτήρια), that is, at her marriage;[8] as also was Thébes according to the poet Euphorión.[9]

The form of Démétér is copied from that of Héra, with whom she is in reality identical. She has the same majestic stature and matronly air, but of a milder character. Her usual symbols

---

[1] Ὅτι τὸ θυμῷ χρῆσθαι καλοῦσιν ἐρινύειν οἱ Ἀρκάδες. Paus. *ut supra*.

[2] Paus. viii. 42, 1.   [3] Völcker, *Myth. der Jap.* 165 *seq.*

[4] Grim Nature's visage hoar.—Burns's *Vision.*

[5] Like κρείων, κρέων, the α is merely euphonic. The cyclic Thébaïs named Areión κυανοχαίτης, and Antimachos said of him,

Αὐτὴ γαῖ' ἀνέδωκε, σέβας θνητοῖσιν ἰδέσθαι.

The place of his birth is Onkeion (*tumid*, ὄγκος); he is the steed of Adrastos (*fruitful*, ἁδρὸς, ἁδροσύνη), son of Talaos (*flourishing*, θάλλω). Paus. *ut supra.* He is similar to Pégasos.

[6] Paus. viii. 31, 1; iv. 26, 8. Soph. *Œd. Col.* 682.

[7] Paus. viii. 10, 10; 27, 6; 35, 2; 36, 9; 37, 1–10; 42, 1.

[8] Plut. *Timol.* 8. Among the Arabs, when a bridegroom is left for the first time alone with his bride he gives her a present of money, *the price of unveiling the face*, and then removing the shawl with which she is covered, beholds her face, probably for the first time. Lane, *Thousand*, etc., i. 323.

[9] Sch. *Eur. Phœn.* 684. See Müller, *Orchom.* 217; *Dor.* i. 415.

are poppies, which sometimes compose a garland for her head, sometimes are held in her hand. She is frequently represented with a torch in her hand,—significant of her search after Persephoné. At times she appears in her chariot drawn by dragons. Persephoné is represented seated on a throne with Hadés.

The only epithets given to Démétér by Homer are,[1] 1. *Blond* or *Yellow-haired*; and 2. *Fair-tressed*, the appropriateness of which terms to the goddess of the corn is apparent.[2] Beside these epithets Hésiod gives her two others; 3. *Well-garlanded*; and 4. *Food-full*. She was termed by other poets, 5. *Youth-rearing*; 6. *Bright-fruited*; 7. *Bright-gifted*; 8. *Season-bringer*; 9. *Gold-sickled*, or perhaps *Gilder*; 10. *Green*; all epithets well suited to the goddess of agriculture. Démétér was also named, 11. *Law-giver*, as agriculture was regarded as the source of civil regulations. Under this title she was honoured in a festival named Thesmophoria at Athens and Ephesos. She had a temple at Megara under the title of, 12. *Sheep-bringer*.[3] In Bœótia she was worshipped as Démétér-Achæa.[4]

The Homeric epithets of Persephoné are,[5] 1. *Illustrious*; 2. *Terrible*; and 3. *Holy*. Hesiod gives her one of the usual epithets of beauty, 4. *White-armed*. She was also named, 5. *Sable-vested*; 6. *White-horsed*, &c.

The name of Démétér offers, as we have seen, no difficulty whatever; but that of her daughter is by no means so easy of explanation; and here, as in similar cases, the question is, what was the original conception of this goddess? Was she simply regarded as the queen of the monarch of Erebos, or as the daughter of Mother Earth, and a personification of the corn? In the latter case critics consider her name to signify *Food-shower*;[6]

---

[1] 1. ξανθή: 2. καλλιπλόκαμος: 3. εὐστέφανος: 4. πολυφόρβη: 5. κουροτρόφος: 6. ἀγλαόκαρπος: 7. ἀγλαόδωρος: 8. ὡρηφόρος: 9. χρυσάορος: 10. χλόη: 11. θεσμοφόρος: 12. μαλοφόρος.

[2] In the Northern mythology, Sif, the goddess of the summer-earth, is termed Hárfagra, i. e. Fair-haired.   [3] Paus. i. 44, 3.

[4] Plut. *De Is. et Os.* 69. Hesych. and Et. Mag. *s. v.* It was said to be derived from the grief (ἄχος) of the goddess. Welcker, however (*Schwenk*, p. 293), says it is the same as γαία; and Müller (*Proleg.* 291) renders it *good*, from the Laconic χάος, χαίος, ἀχαῖος, which have that signification in Aristoph. *Lys.* 91, 1157, and Hesychius n ἀχαία.

[5] 1. ἀγαυή: 2. ἐπαινή: 3. ἀγνή: 4. λευκώλενος: 5. μελάμπεπλος: 6. λεύκιππος. By the Latin poets Proserpina was termed *pulchra, furva, severa*, and *Juno inferna*.

[6] Völcker, *Myth. der Jap.* p. 201, 202. Welcker *in Schwenk*, 299. These critics derive the name from φέρω, φέρβω, *to feed*, and φάω, φαίνω, *to show*. Schwenk (247) renders it *Lighting*, regarding, as we think justly, the first part of the name as akin to πῦρ, and to the *Per* in *Perse*, *Perseus*: see below *Perseus.*

in the former it might mean *Light-destroyer,* a name corresponding well with Aïdés and Erebos.[1]

We have ventured to offer this conjecture concerning the origin of the name Persephoné, because we think critics have gone into an extreme respecting the religious opinions of the ancient Pelasgians. For as there appears reason to suppose their religion to have been of a very rural character, the view generally taken is that they were, like our modern political economists, a race who thought only of production and consumption, and regarded no deities but such as were promoters of increase. We however deem that, like every other people, the Pelasgians believed in a future state, and that they worshipped a deity presiding over that unseen world. It may be doubted whether they gave him a consort (for in the Italian system such was not the case), but the probability is that the Achæans derived that principle of their religion from their Pelasgian forefathers. In such case the spouse of the invisible god might very naturally be termed the *Light-destroyer.* The epithets of Persephoné certainly accord far better with an original queen of Erebos than with the gentle innocent daughter of Démétér.[2] As, however, the Koré went underground, and so became invisible, it was easy by the ordinary process to identify her with the invisible spouse of Hadés.

We cannot take our leave of Démétér and the Koré,[3] without saying a few words on the subject of the celebrated *mysteries* of Eleusis, in which they were the great objects of adoration. But instead of going into all the mysticism which has been written respecting them, both in ancient and modern times, we will content ourselves with giving some of the results of the inquiries of the learned and judicious Lobeck, referring those anxious for fuller information to his valuable work entitled *Aglaophamus.*

In the very early ages of Greece and Italy, and probably of most countries, the inhabitants of the various independent districts into which they were divided had very little communication with each other, and a stranger was regarded as little better than an enemy. Each state had its own favourite deities, under whose especial protection it was held to be, and these deities were propitiated by sacrifices and ceremonies, which were different in different places. It is further to be recollected, that the Greeks believed their gods

---

[1] It is commonly rendered *Death-bearer,* from φέρω φόνον. The Persephatta of the dramatists seems to be only a corruption of Persephoné.

[2] Voss and Nitzsch (*on Od.* x. 491) agree with us respecting the original character of Persephoné. The former renders her name *Hinwegtödtende.*

[3] Κόρη, *maiden,* the Attic name of the daughter of Démétér.

M

to be very little superior in moral qualities to themselves, and they
feared that if promises of more splendid and abundant sacrifices
and offerings were made to them, their virtue might not be
adequate to resisting the temptation. As the best mode of escaping the calamity of being deserted by their patrons, they
adopted the expedient of concealing their names, and of excluding
strangers from their worship. Private families in like manner
excluded their fellow-citizens from their family-sacrifices; and in
those states where ancient statues, aërolites, and such like were
preserved as national palladia, the sight of them was restricted to
the magistrates and principal persons in the state.[1]

We are to recollect that Eleusis and Athens were long independent of each other.[2] The worship of Démétér and the Koré
was the national and secret religion of the Eleusinians, from which
the Athenians were of course excluded as well as all other Greeks.
But when Eleusis was conquered, and the two states coalesced, the
Athenians became participators in the worship of these deities;
which however remained so long confined to them as to have given
origin to a proverb (Ἀττικοὶ τὰ Ἐλευσίνια) applied to those who met
together in secret for the performance of any matter.[3] Gradually,
with the advance of knowledge and the decline of superstition and
national illiberality, admission to witness the solemn rites celebrated each year at Eleusis was extended to all Greeks of either
sex and of every rank, provided they came at the proper time, had
committed no inexpiable offence, had performed the requisite
previous ceremonies, and were introduced by an Athenian citizen.[4]

These mysteries, as they were termed, were performed with a
considerable degree of splendour, at the charge of the state and
under the superintendence of the magistrates; whence it follows
as a necessary consequence, that the rites could have contained
nothing that was grossly immoral or indecent.[5] There does not
appear to be any valid reason for supposing, as many do, that a
public discourse on the origin of things and that of the gods, and
other high and important matters, was delivered by the Hierophant, or person who bore the highest office in the mysteries
whose name would rather seem to be derived from his *exhibiting
the sacred things*,—ancient statues, probably of the goddesses,—
which were kept carefully covered up, and only shown on these
solemn occasions. The delivering of a public discourse would in
fact have been quite repugnant to the usages of the Greeks in
their worship of the gods, and the evidence offered in support of
this supposition is extremely feeble. But the singing of sacred

[1] *Aglaoph.* 65, 273, 274.   [2] *Ib.* 214, 1351. Müller, *Dor.* i. 201.
[3] *Aglaoph.* 271.   [4] *Ib.* 14, 28, 31.   [5] *Ib.* 116.

hymns in honour of the goddess always formed a part of the service.[1]

The ancient writers are full of the praises of the Eleusinian mysteries, of the advantage of being *initiated*, i.e. admitted to participate in them, and of the favour of the gods in life, and the cheerful hopes in death, which were the consequence of it. Hence occasion has been taken to assert, that a system of religion little inferior to pure Christianity was taught in them. But these hopes, and this tranquillity of mind and favour of Heaven, are easy to be accounted for without having recourse to so absurd a supposition. Every act performed in obedience to the will of Heaven is believed to draw down its favour on the performer. The Mussulman makes his pilgrimage to the Kaaba at Mecca, the Catholic to Loretto, Compostella, or elsewhere; and each is persuaded that by having done so he has secured the divine favour.[2] So the Greek who was initiated at Eleusis,—whose mysteries, owing to the fame in which Athens stood, the able writers who so loudly extolled her and everything belonging to her, the splendour and magnificence with which they were performed, eclipsed all others,—retained ever after a lively sense of the happiness which he had enjoyed when admitted to view the interior of the illuminated temple, and the sacred things which it contained, when to his excited imagination the very gods themselves had seemed visibly to descend from their Olympian abodes, amidst the solemn hymns of the officiating priests.[3] Hence there naturally arose a persuasion, that the benign regards of the gods were bent upon him through after-life; and, as man can never divest himself of the belief of his continued existence after death, a vivid hope of enjoying bliss in the next world.

It was evidently the principle already stated, of seeking to discover the causes of remarkable appearances, which gave origin to most of the ideas respecting the recondite sense of the actions and ceremonies which took place in the Eleusinian mysteries. The stranger, dazzled and awed by his own conception of the sacredness and importance of all that he beheld, conceived that nothing there could be without some mysterious meaning. What this might be, he inquired of the officiating ministers, who as various passages in Hérodotos and Pausanias show, were seldom without a legend or *Sacred Account* (ἱερὸς λόγος), as it was called, to explain the dress or ceremony, which owed perhaps its true origin to the caprice or sportive humour of a ruder period. Or if the

---

[1] *Aglaoph.* 63, 193. Müller, *Proleg.* 250, 251.   [2] *Aglaoph.* 70, 71.
[3] *Ib.* 44 *seq.* 63. See Mortimer's description of the effect of the solemn vice in St. Peter's at Rome on his mind, in Schiller's *Maria Stuart*, act i. 6. See also Shakespeare's *Winter's Tale*, act iii. sc. 1.

initiated person was himself endowed with inventive power, he explained the appearances according in general to the system of philosophy which he had embraced.[1] It was thus that Porphyrius conceived the Hierophant to represent the Platonic Démiurgos or creator of the world; the Torch-bearer (*Daduchos*), the sun; the Altar-man (*Epibómios*), the moon; the Herald (*Hierokéryx*), Hermés; and the other ministers, the lesser stars. These fancies of priests and philosophers have been by modern writers formed into a complete system, and Ste Croix in particular describes the Eleusinian mysteries with as much minuteness as if he had been actually himself initiated.[2]

It is to be observed, in conclusion, with respect to the charges of impiety and immorality brought against the Eleusinian mysteries by some Fathers of the Church, that this arose entirely from their confounding them with the Bakchic, Isiac, Mithraic, and other *private* mysteries, mostly imported from Asia, which were undoubtedly liable to that imputation. It must always be remembered, that those of Eleusis were *public*, and celebrated by the state.[3]

CHAPTER XII.

SISTER-GODDESSES,—MUSES, HORÆ, CHARITES, EILEITHYIÆ, MŒRÆ, KERES, ERINNYES.

Μοῦσαι.[4] (*Camenæ.* 𝕸𝖚𝖘𝖊𝖘.)

In the early ages of the world, when the principle of assigning a celestial cause to every extraordinary effect was in full operation, the powers of song and memory were supposed to be excited by certain goddesses who were denominated Muses. In Homer they are called the daughters of Zeus,[5] and described as exhilarating the banquets of the gods by their lovely voices, attuned to the lyre of Apolló.[6] When about to give the catalogue of the ships of the Achæans, the poet invokes the Muses, the daughters of Zeus, to prompt his memory.[7]

No definite number of the Muses is given by Homer, for we cannot regard as his the verse[8] in which they are said to be *nine* Perhaps originally, as in the case of the Erinnyes and so many

---

[1] *Aglaoph.* 180, 181.
[2] See Warburton, *Divine Legation.* Ste Croix, *Recherches sur les Mystères* &c. Creuzer, *Symbolik.*
[3] *Aglaoph.* 116, 197, 202, 1263. Müller, *Proleg.* 248 *seq.*
[4] *Dor.* Μώσαι, Æol. Μοῖσαι. [5] *Il.* ii. 490. *Od.* i. 10.
[6] *Il.* i. 604. [7] *Il.* ii. 484 *seq.* [8] *Od.* xxiv. 60.

other deities, there was no precise number. Pausanias[1] gives
an old tradition, according to which they were three,—Meleté
(*Practice*), Mnémé (*Memory*), and Aœdé (*Song*). Aratos[2] said they
were four, the daughters of Zeus and the nymph Plusia (*Wealthy*),
and that their names were, Thelxinoé (*Mind-soother*), Aœdé,
Meleté, and Arché (*Beginning*). Alkman and some other poets
made the Muses the daughters of Heaven and Earth;[3] Euripidés[4]
says they were the daughters of Harmonia and born in Attica.
The more received opinion makes them, as in the proœmium to
the Theogony,[5] nine, the daughters of Zeus and Mnémosyné
(*Memory*).

The names of the Muses were,[6] Kalliopé, Kleió, Melpomené,
Euterpé, Erató, Terpsichoré, Urania, Thaleia, and Polymnia.

Later ages assigned a particular department to each of the
Muses, and represented them in various postures and with various
attributes.[7]

Kalliopé presided over Epic Poetry; she was represented
holding a close-rolled parchment, and sometimes a trumpet.

Kleió presided over History; and appeared holding a half-
opened roll. The invention of the lute or guitar (κιθάρα) was
ascribed to her.

Melpomené, over Tragedy; she was veiled, and was leaning
on a club, and holding a tragic mask in her left hand. Her
instrument was the lyre named Barbiton.[8]

Euterpé, over Music; she held two flutes, and the invention of
the tragic chorus was ascribed to her.

Erató, the muse of Marriage-feasts and pantomimic dancing
(ὄρχησις), played on the stringed instrument named *phorminx*.
She is said to have invented hymns to the gods.

Terpsichoré, the muse of the choric Dance (χορεία), appeared in
a dancing posture. The pipe (αὐλός) was indebted to her for its
origin.

Urania, the muse of Astronomy, held in one hand a globe, in
the other a rod with which she was employed in tracing out some
figure.

Thaleia, the patroness of Comedy, held a comic mask in one

---

[1] Paus. ix. 29, 2.   [2] Cic. *De Nat. Deor.* iii. 21.   Eudocia, 294.
[3] Diod. iv. 7.   Paus. *ut sup.* 4.   [4] *Med.* 830.
[5] *Theog.* 53 *seq.* 76, comp. *v.* 917.
[6] Καλλιόπη (*Fair-Voice*), Κλειώ (*Proclaimer*), Μελπομένη (*Songstress*), Εὐ-
τέρπη (*Delighter*), Ἐρατώ (*Love-inspirer*), Τερψιχόρη (*Dance-lover*), Οὐρανία
(*Celestial*), Θάλεια (*Blooming*), Πολυμνία (*Hymnful*).
[7] Diodór. iv. 7.   Sch. *Apoll. Rh.* iii. 1.   Eudocia, 293.   Anthologia, ix. 504,
505.
[8] Horace (*Carm.* i. 1, 34) gives this instrument to Polymnia.

hand, and in the other a crooked staff. She was also regarded as the patroness of husbandry and planting.

Polymnia, the muse of Eloquence and the Mimic art, had the fore-finger of her right hand on her mouth, or carried a roll.

Pieria in Macedonia is said by Hesiod[1] to have been the birth-place of the Muses; and everything relating to them proves the antiquity of the tradition of the knowledge and worship of these goddesses having come from the North into Hellas.[2] Almost all the mountains, grots, and springs from which they have derived their appellations, or which were sacred to them, are, we may observe, in Macedonia, Thessaly, or Bœótia (*Aonia*). Such are the mountains Pimpla, Pindos, Parnassos, Helikón, the founts Hippo-kréné, Aganippé, Leibéthron, Kastalia, and the Korykian cave.

The Muses, says Homer,[3] met the Thracian Thamyris in Dórion (in the Peloponnése), as he was returning from Œchalia. He had boasted that he could excel them in singing; and enraged at his presumption, they struck him blind, and deprived him of his knowledge of music.

Shortly after the birth of the Muses, the nine daughters, it is said, of Pierios, king of Æmathia, challenged them to a contest of singing. The place of trial was Mount Helikón. At the song of the latter the sky became dark and all nature was put out of harmony, but at that of the Muses the heaven itself, the stars, the sea, and rivers stood motionless, and Helikón swelled up with delight, so that his summit would have reached the sky had not Poseidón directed Pégasos to strike it with his hoof. The Muses then turned the presumptuous maids into nine different kinds of birds.[4]

The Muses did not escape the darts of Love. Kalliopé bore to Œagros a son named Línos,[5] who was killed by his pupil Héraklés. She also had by the same sire Orpheus, whose skill on the lyre was such as to move the very trees and rocks, and the beasts of the forest assembled round him as he struck its chords. He was married to Eurydiké,[6] whom he tenderly loved; but a snake

---

[1] *Theog.* 53.

[2] See Buttmann, *Mythol.* i. 293. Voss, *Myth. Br.* iv. 3. Müller, *Orchom.* 381. *Proleg.* 219. Comp. above, p. 17. [3] *Il.* ii. 594.

[4] Nikander *ap. Anton. Lib.* 9, where the names of the birds are given · these of course were the names of the nine maids in Nikander. Ovid, who also relates the legend (*Met.* v. 300 *seq.*), says they were turned into magpies, and he is followed by Statius, *Silv.* ii. 4, 19. The tale seems indebted for its origin to the Muses' name, Pierides, from Pieria.

[5] Apollod. i. 3, 2. Others made Apolló the sire of Linos and Orpheus. Hésiod (*Fr.* 97) said that Urania was the mother of Linos : see Conon, 19.

[6] Argiopé according to Hermésianax.

having bitten her as she ran through the grass, she died. Her disconsolate husband determined to descend to the under-world, to endeavour to mollify its rulers, and obtain permission for her to return to the realms of light. Hadés and Persephoné listened to his prayer; and she was allowed to return, on condition of his not looking on her till they were arrived in the upper-world. Fearing that she might not be following him, the anxious husband looked back, and thereby lost her. He now avoided human society; and despising the rites of Dionýsos, was torn to pieces by the Mænades. The Muses collected the fragments of his body, and buried them, and at their prayer Zeus placed his lyre in the skies.[1]

Kleió, having drawn on herself the anger of Aphrodíté by taunting her with her passion for Adónis, was inspired by her with love for Pieros the son of Magnés. She bore him a son named Hyakinthos.[2] Euterpé, or according to some, Kalliopé, or Terpsichoré, bore Rhésos to the god of the river Strymón;[3] Melpomené was by Acheló os the mother of the Sirens. Hymenæos, the god of marriage, was said to be the offspring of the divine Urania, but the name of his sire is unknown.[4] Those who took a less sublime view of the sanctity of marriage gave him Dionýsos and Aphrodíté for parents.[5] He was invoked at marriage festivals.[6] By the Latin poets he is presented to us arrayed in a yellow robe, his temples wreathed with the fragrant plant *amaracus*, his locks dropping odour, and the nuptial torch in his hand.[7]

Beside the usual epithets common to all goddesses, and derived from beauty and dress, the Muses were styled,[8] 1. *Sweet-speaking;* 2. *Perfect-speaking;* 3. *Loud-voiced;* 4. *Honey-breathing.*

[1] Apollod. *ut sup.* Apoll. Rh. i. 23. Hermésianax *ap. Athén.* xiii. 597. Ov. *Met.* x. xi. Verg. *Geor.* iv. 454 *seq.* Conon, 455. Eudocia, 318. Diod. iv. 25. No mention of Orpheus occurs in Homer or Hésiod. Pindar (*Pyth.* iv. 176 (313) *seq.*) reckons him among the Argonauts. It were idle to notice the fancies of Creuzer and others respecting the mysteries introduced by him into Greece long before the time of Homer. According to these mystics (*Symb.* iii. 148 *seq.*) he was a priest of the Light-religion,—that of Apolló or Vishnú,—and vainly resisted the raving orgies of the Dionýsos or Seeva worship when it reached Greece. See Lobeck's *Aglaophamus* for all that the most extensive learning, joined with sense and sane philosophy, has been able to do toward ꞓ_acidating the real nature and character of the poems and institutions ascribed to Orpheus: see also Müller, *Proleg.* 379 *seq.* The name Orpheus is perhaps connected with ὄρφνος, ὄρφανος, *orbus, furvus.*
[2] Apollod. *ut sup.* [3] Id. *ib.* Eur. *Rhés. passim.* Sch. *Il.* x. 435.
[4] Catull. lxi. 2. Nonn. xxxiii. 67. [5] Serv. *Æn.* iv. 127.
[6] ᾿Ω ῾Υμὴν, ῾Υμέναι᾿ ἄναξ. Eur. *Tróad.* 311. *Hymen o Hymenœe!* Catull. *ut sup.*
[7] Catull. *ut sup.* Ovid. *Hér.* xxi. 157 *seq.* *Met.* x. 1 *seq.*
[8] 1. ἡδυεπεῖς: 2. ἀρτιέπειαι: 3. λιγίφθογγοι: 4. μελίπνοοι.

The most probable derivation of the name Muse (Μοῦσα), seems to be that which deduces it from the obsolete verb ΜΑΩ *to inquire* or *invent*. The Lydians, who spoke a language akin to the Greek, called, we are told, the Muses Nymphs, or the Nymphs Muses, apparently using the terms as synonymous.[1] We everywhere find the Muses connected with founts; Eumélos of Corinth said they were three in number, the daughters of Apolló, and he called them Képhisó, Apollónis, and Borysthenis,[2] two of which names are evidently derived from those of rivers; and the comic poet Epicharmos in his drama named Hébé's Wedding, where the gods appeared as thorough *bons-vivants*, made the *seven* Muses the daughters of Pieros and Pimpleia (*Fattener* and *Filler*), and named them after seven rivers.[3] They probably figured in this comedy as the presidents of the fish-market. If, however, the Muses were not generally regarded as connected in some way with the water the poet would hardly have thus represented them, as the humour would not have been fully appreciated by the audience. We may further observe that the musical Sirens were placed by the poets at the edge of the water, possibly from a feeling of a connection between that element and music, and that water-deities were held to be prophetic.

The Latins, it would also appear, connected their Camenæ with the fountains; for Egeria was one of them, and her fount long continued to be an object of veneration. The Gotho-German race (whose language and religion bear so great an affinity to those of Greece) seem also to have connected music with the water in their ancient religious system; and this notion still remains part of the popular creed in northern Europe, as is proved by the many legends of the songs of Mermaids, Nixes, Necks, and similar beings of the waters current among the people in Germany and Scandinavia.[4] In the Edda the abode of Saga the goddess of narration, is by Söquabæk, i.e. the rushing stream or waterfall. In fact, this, like almost every other article of popular belief, has its origin in nature. There is music in the sound of water as it purls or murmurs along in the rivulet, (the very terms *prattling, babbling, tinkling, warbling,* applied to brooks and streams by our poets prove it,) and even the waterfall espe-

---

[1] Steph. Byz. *v.* Τύῤῥηβος. Sch. *Theocr.* vii. 92. Suidas, Photius, Hesych. *v.* νύμφη. Serv. *Buc.* vii. 21.

[2] Eudocia, 294. Tzetz. *on Hés.* Ἔργ. *init.*

[3] Eudocia and Tzetzés, *ut sup.* The names as amended by Hermann are Neiló, Tritóné, Asópó, Achelóis, Heptapora, and Rhodia, (the two last from rivers named by Homer, *Il.* xii. 20, and Hésiod, *Theog.* 341) the seventh, Tiripló, is evidently corrupt; Hermann proposes Pactóló.

[4] The reader will find several of these legends in my *Fairy Mythology.*

cially when heard in the distance, makes melody to the attentive ear. The rivulet is also the favourite haunt of the poet; its quiet murmur induces calmness over the spirit, and puts the mind into a frame adapted for the reception of poetic images.[1] Hence it has been said, by him who, like the early bards of Greece, was one of Nature's own poets, that

> The Muse nae poet ever fand her
> Till by himsel he learned to wandér,
> Adoun some trotting burn's meander,
> And think na lang.

We are therefore inclined to regard as correct the theory which sees in the Muses original nymphs of the springs, to whom the poets ascribed their inspiration.[2]

῟Ωραι. *Horæ.* (**Seasons** or **Hours.**)

When in the Ilias[3] Héra and Athéna drive out of Olympos in the chariot of the former goddess, to share in the conflict of the Achæans and the Trojans, the gates of heaven, which the Horæ keep, whose charge is to open and close the dense cloud, creak spontaneously to let them pass. On the return of these goddesses, at the mandate of Zeus, the Horæ unyoke their steeds, fasten them in their stalls, and lay up the chariot. They are also mentioned by Poseidón[4] as bringing round the period at which he and Apolló were to be paid their wages by Laomedón.

Hésiod says[5] that the Horæ were the daughters of Zeus and Themis, and he names them Eunomié (*Order*), Diké (*Justice*), and Eiréné (*Peace*), who, he adds, *watch over* (ὡρεύουσι) the works of mortal men. In another place[6] he says, that Diké is a virgin revered by the gods of Olympos; and that when any one acts unjustly, she sits by her father Zeus, and complains of the iniquity of man's mind, " that the people may suffer for the transgressions of their kings."

By an unknown poet[7] the Horæ are called the daughters of Kronos (Time ?), and by late poets they were named the children of the year, and their number was increased to twelve.[8] Some made them seven or ten in number.[9]

The Horæ seem to have been originally regarded as the presidents of the three seasons into which the ancient Greeks divided

---

[1]   Such sights as youthful poets dream
           On summer-eves by haunted stream.—Milton.

[2] See Hermann, *De Musis fluvialibus Epicharmi et Eumeli* (*Opusc.* ii. 288) and Buttmann, *Mytholog.* i. 273 *seq.* Creuzer first advanced this theory.

[3] *Il.* v. 749 ; viii. 393.   [4] *Il.* xxi. 450.   [5] *Theog.* 903.

[6] Ἔργ. 256.   [7] *Ap.* Stobæum : see the lines in Lobeck, p. 60f.

[8] Nonn. xi. 486 ; xii. 17.   [9] Hygin. 183.

the year.[1]   As the day was similarly divided,[2] they came to bo regarded as presiding over its parts also; and when it was further subdivided into *hours*, these minor parts were placed under their charge and named from them.[3]

Order and regularity being their prevailing attributes, the transition was easy from the natural to the moral world; and the guardian goddesses of the seasons were regarded as presiding over law, justice, and peace, the great producers of order and harmony among men.

It is possible however, but not agreeable to analogy, that the reverse was the case, and that the transition was from moral to physical ideas.

By Pindar[4] the Horæ are named, in their moral capacity, the bestowers of wealth,—a poetic clothing, one might say, of the homely maxim 'honesty is the best policy,'—for peace, order, and honesty are what most surely contribute to its acquisition. The Athenians worshipped two Horæ, named Thalló (*Bloom-giver*) and Karpó (*Fructifier*), viewing them as physical beings.[5] By the poets they were frequently confounded with the Charites, and regarded as the bestowers of beauty.[6]

Homer calls the Horæ,[7] 1. *Gold-filleted*. The epithets in the Orphic hymns are chiefly derived from the flowers which they produce; such as, 2. *Flower-full*; 3. *Odour-full*;[8] etc.

Χάριτες. (*Gratiæ.* 𝔊𝔯𝔞𝔠𝔢𝔰.)

The Charites or Graces, like the Muses and other sister-goddesses, are spoken of by Homer in the plural, and their number is indefinite. They are graceful and beautiful themselves, and the bestowers of all grace and beauty both on persons and things.   They wove the robe of Aphrodíté;[9] the beauty of the two attendants of Nausikaa[10] was given them by the Charites; and the ringlets of the beautiful Euphorbos are compared[11] to those of these lovely goddesses.   Aphrodíté[12] joins in their dance; and in the song of Démodokos, they wash and

---

[1] See Welcker, *Tril.* 500 *note*.   [2] *Il.* xxi. 111.

[3] Quint. Smyr. ii. 595.   Nonn. *ut sup.*   [4] *Ol.* xiii. 6 (9) *seq.*

[5] Paus. ix. 35, 2.   One of the Horæ was said to have borne to Zephyros a son named Karpos.   Serv. *Buc.* v. 48.

[6] Theocr. i. 150.   Mosch. ii. 160.   Apoll. Rh. *ap. Athen.* vii. 283.

[7] 1. χρυσάμπυκες : 2. πολυάνθεμοι : 3. πολυόδμοι.

[8] The Greek πολὺς and the Germanic *voll*, *full*, are plainly the same word, and used alike in composition.   The former is placed at the beginning, the latter at the end of the compound.

[9] *Il.* v. 338, and that of Dionýsos, Apoll. Rh. iv. 425.

[10] *Od.* vi. 18.   [11] *Il.* xvii. 51.   [12] *Od.* xviii. 194.

anoint her, when filled with shame she flies to Paphós.[1] Yet though they seem to have been particularly attached to the goddess of love, the queen of heaven had authority over them;[2] and she promises Pasithea, one of the youngest of the Graces, for a wife to Sleep, in return for his aid in deceiving Zeus. By later writers she is even said to be their mother.[3]

The Homéridian hymn to Artemis describes that goddess as going to the 'great house' of her brother at Delphi, and regulating the dance of the Muses and the Graces.

Zeus, says Hésiod,[4] was by Eurynomé, the daughter of Ocean, the father of the 'three fair-cheeked Charites' Aglaïé (*Splendour*), Euphrosyné (*Joy*), and lovely Thalié (*Pleasure*). 'From their eyes,' continues the poet, 'as they gazed, distilled care-dispelling love; and they looked lovely from beneath their brows.' According to Antimachos,[5] the Charites were the daughters of Helios and Ægle (*Splendour*); while according to others[6] their parents were Dionýsos and Aphrodíté. Hermésianax[7] made Peithó (*Persuasion*) one of their number; in Nonnos their names are Pasithea, Peithó and Aglaïé.[8]

Orchomenos in Bœótia was the chief seat of the worship of these goddesses. Its introduction was ascribed to Eteoklés, the son of the river Képhissos. They were three in number, but it was not known what names he had given them.[9] The Lacedæmonians worshipped but two, whom they named Kléta (*Renowned*) and Phaënna (*Bright*).[10] The Athenians originally adored the same number, under the names of Hégemoné (*Leader*) and Auxo (*Increaser*).[11]

The Charites were at all times in the creed of Greece the goddesses presiding over social enjoyments, the banquet, the dance, and all that tended to inspire gaiety and cheerfulness.[12] They are represented as three beautiful sisters, dancing together: sometimes they are naked, sometimes clad.

The Charites had the epithets common to goddesses.

Εἰλείθυιαι. *Ilithyiæ.*

The Eileithyiæ, whose office it was to preside over the births of mankind, are in the Ilias[13] called the daughters of Héra. In

---

[1] *Od.* viii. 364. See also the beautiful fragment of the Kypria. Athén. xv. 682.   [2] *Il.* xiv. 267.   [3] Nonn. xxxi. 184. Eudocia, 430.
[4] *Theog.* 907.   [5] Paus. ix. 35, 5.   [6] Serv. *Æn.* i. 720.
[7] Paus. *ut supra.*   [8] Dionys. xxiv. 263.
[9] Paus. *ut sup.* Hésiod, *ap. Sch. Pind. Ol.* xiv. 1. Pind. *Ol.* xiv. 1 *seq.* Theocr. xvi. 104.
[10] Paus. *ut sup.* and iii. 18, 6.   [11] Paus. *ut sup.*   [12] Pind. *Ol.* xiv. 5 (7).
[13] *Il.* xi. 270. Paus. i. 44, 3. In *Il.* xvi. 187, and x.x 103, Eileithyia occurs in the singular.

the Odyssey[1] and in Hesiod[2] their number is reduced to one. We also meet with but one Eileithyia in Pindar,[3] and the subsequent poets in general.

There was a cave at the river Amnisos, near Gortýna in Krété, sacred to Eileithyia, who according to the tradition of the country was born there.[4] Eileithyia was worshipped at Délos, where a hymn, ascribed to the ancient Lykian poet O'lén, was sung in her honour, in which she was said to be the mother of Love.[5] She had also a temple at Athens.[6]

Eileithyia was called,[7] 1. *Labour-aiding*; 2. *Gentle-minded*,[8] etc.

It is not by any means an improbable supposition, that Eileithyia was originally a moon goddess.[9] Hence, if this was also the original character of Artemis, the identification of them was easy. The moon was believed by the ancients to have great influence over growth in general;[10] and as moreover a woman's time was reckoned by moons, it was natural to conceive that the moon-goddess presided over the birth of children.

Μοῖραι. (*Parcæ, Fata.* **Fates.**)

In the Ilias, with the exception of one passage,[11] the Mœra is spoken of in the singular number and as a person, almost exactly as we use the word *Fate*. But in the Odyssey this word is used as a common substantive, followed by a genitive of the person, and signifying *Decree*.

The Theogony of Hesiod limits the Mœræ, like so many other goddesses, to three, and gives them Zeus and Themis for their parents.[12] In an interpolated passage of that poem they are

---

[1] *Od.* xix. 188. [2] *Theog.* 922. [3] *Ol.* vi. 42 (72), *Nem.* vii. 1.
[4] *Od. ut supra.* [5] Paus. i. 18, 5; viii. 21, 3; ix. 27, 2.
[6] Isæos, Περὶ τοῦ Δικαιογ. Κλήρ. 8. [7] 1. μογοστόκος: 2. πραΰμητις.
[8]   Mild as any maid
      Full of sweet hope her [Lucina's] brow seemed, and her eyes
      Darting fresh comfort like the morning skies.—Drayton, *Mooncalf*
[9] Welcker (*Kret. Kol.* pp. 11, 19) derives her name from ἔλη, *light*, and θύω, *to move rapidly :* but see above, p. 121.
[10] "Crescente luna frumenta grandescunt." Plin. *Nat. Hist.* xviii. 30; see also ii. 99, x. 54, and elsewhere. Varro *de R. R.* i. 7. Plut. *de Is. et Os.* 41. *Qu. Rom.* 77. Eudocia, 11. Lucil. *ap. Gell.* xx. 8. Hor. *Sat.* ii. 4, 30. Fulgent. ii. 19. "The moon is believed by the Hindú naturalists to have a powerful effect on vegetation, especially on certain plants." Wilford in *Asiat. Res.* iii. 385, 4to edit. [11] *Il.* xx. 49.
[12] *Theog.* 904. Some critics regard this passage as an interpolation; probably because the Horæ have just been given as childen of Zeus by Themis, and analogy would seem to assign only one set of children to one mother. If they are right the Fates are unnoticed in the Theogony.

classed among the children of Night.[1] Empedokles[2] said that they were the offspring of Kronos and Eurynomé, and Plato terms them the daughters of Necessity.[3] Their names in Hésiod are Klóthó (*Spinster*), Lachesis (*Allotter*), and Atropos (*Unchangeable*); but he does not speak of their spinning the destinies of men. This office of theirs is however noticed both in the Ilias and the Odyssey. In the former it is said[4] by Héra of Achilleus, that the gods will protect him that day, but that hereafter he will suffer 'what Æsa [a name synonymous with Mœra] span with her thread for him when his mother brought him forth;' and in the latter,[5] Alkinoös says of Odysseus, that he will hereafter suffer ' what Æsa and the heavy Kataklóthes span with the thread for him when his mother brought him forth.'

It is probable that Homer, in accordance with the sublime fiction in the Theogony, regarded the Mœræ as the offspring of Zeus and Law, for in him they are but the ministers of Zeus, in whose hands are the issues of all things.[6] Æschylos[7] makes even Zeus himself subject to the Mœræ, whose decrees none could escape.

The poets styled the Mœræ,[8] 1. *Unerring*; 2. *Severe-minded*, etc.

Mœra probably comes from μείρω, and Æsa from δαίω, both signifying to *divide*. It is a very remarkable coincidence, that the Norns, the Destinies of Scandinavian theology, should also be spinsters, and three in number.[9] Perhaps however a reference of both to time, with its three portions, may explain this coincidence.

Κῆρες. (*Mortes.*)

The Kéres are personifications of violent deaths.[10] The word *Kér* is used by Homer in the singular and in the plural number, and both as a proper and as a common noun, but much more frequently as the former. When a common noun, it seems to be equivalent to *fate*. Achilleus says, that his mother gave him the

---

[1] *Theog.* 217.   [2] See above, p. 62.
[3] *Rep.* x, 617.   [4] *Il.* xx. 127.
[5] *Od.* vii. 197. Buttmann, following the Scholia, Eustath. and Hesychius, would read κατὰ κλῶθες, instead of κατακλῶθες. Nitzsch defends the common reading.
[6] See Nitzsch *on Od.* iii. 236.   [7] *Prom.* 515. See also Hérod. i. 91.
[8] 1. ἀπλανέες : 2. βαρύφρονες.
[9] The Norns are named Urdur, Verdandi, and Skuld (*Past*, *Present*, *Future*). Plato (*l.c.*) introduces the Mœræ singing τὰ γεγενότα, τὰ ὄντα, τὰ μέλλοντα, " quo nullus mihi succurrit auctor," says Lobeck, *Aglaoph.* 970.
[10] *Il.* xi. 332 ; xii. 326. See Wolf *on Il.* i. 97 ; ii. 302. Nitzsch *on Od.* iii. 236. Paus. v. 19, 6.

choice of two *kéres* ;—one to die early at Troy; the other, to die after a long life at home.[1]

On the shield of Achilleus[2] Kér appears in a blood-stained robe, with Strife and Tumult, engaged in the field of battle; and on that of Héraklés[3] the Kéres are described as raging in the fight, and glutting themselves with the blood of the wounded. By Apollónios[4] they are named ' the swift dogs of Hadés,' a character under which they are also represented by Sophokles.[5]

In the Theogony these goddesses are the daughters of Night and sisters of the Mœræ,[6] who also appear on the shield of Héraklés, and with whom they are sometimes confounded,[7] as they also are with the Erinnyes.[8] They bear a strong resemblance to the Valkyries (*Choosers of the Slain*) of Northern mythology.[9]

The Kéres were styled,[10] 1. *Implacable*; 2. *Stern-looking*, etc.

'Ερινννύες. (*Furiœ. Diræ.* 𝔉𝔲𝔯𝔦𝔢𝔰.)

These goddesses are frequently named by Homer, but he says nothing of their origin or number. In the Theogony they spring from the blood of Uranos when mutilated by his son Kronos, whose own children they are according to Empedoklés,[11] while Æschylos and Sophoklés call them the children of Night,[12] and the Orphic Hymns assign them the rulers of Erebos for parents.[13] Like the sister-goddesses of the Athenian creed in general they seem to have been, at least in Attica, only two in number originally.[14] But we afterwards find them, like the Fates and others, increased to three, named Aléktó (*Unceasing*), Megæra (*Envier or Denier*) and Tisiphoné (*Blood-avenger*).[15]

The Erinnyes were worshipped at Athens as the *Venerable* (σεμναὶ) *Goddesses*, and at Sikyón as the *Gracious* (Εὐμενίδες)[16] both of which were apparently placatory appellations. They had a temple in Achaia, which if any one polluted with crime dared to enter he lost his reason.[17]

---

[1] *Il.* ix. 410.   [2] *Il.* xviii. 535.   Comp. Hés. 'Ασπίς, 156.
[3] Hés. 'Ασπίς, 249. (See above, p. 36.) Paus. *ut sup.* Welcker, *Nach. zur Tril.* 346.   [4] *Argon.* iv. 1666.   [5] *Elec.* 1387.
[6] Theog. 217.   The passage, however, is interpolated : see above, p. 173.
[7] Quint. Sm. ii. 510 ; x. 286 ; xiii. 235.
[8] Æschyl. *Seven ag. Thebes,* 1058. *Eum.* 959. Soph. *Œd. Tyr.* 472. Eur. *Hér. Fur.* 870.   *Elec.* 1252.   Verg. *Æn.* viii. 701.
[9] The Anglo-Saxons used their term Wælcyrge to express Bellona, Erinnyes, etc. Grimm, *Deut. Mythol.* p. 389.
[10] 1. ἀμείλιχοι : 2. δεινωποί.   [11] See above, p. 62.
[12] Æsch. *Eumen.* 317, 413. Soph. *Œd. Col.* 40, 106. Comp. Verg. *Æn.* vi 250; vii. 331 ; xii. 845. Ov. *Met.* iv. 451.   [13] Hymn lxx.
[14] See Sch. *Soph. Œd. Col.* 42.   [15] See Eur. *Or.* 408, 1650. *Tr.* 457
[16] Paus. ii. 11, 4.   [17] Id. vii. 25, 7.

In the poets we find the Erinnyes styled,[1] 1. *Hateful*; 2. *Gloom-roaming*; 3. *Dark-skinned*; 4. *Swift-footed*.

The Greek term ἐρινὺς has, we think, been justly defined[2] as a "feeling of deep offence, of bitter displeasure, at the impious violation of our sacred rights by those most bound to respect them." This perfectly accords with the origin of the Erinnyes in the Theogony, and with those passages of the Homéric poems in which they are mentioned; for they are there invoked to avenge the breach of filial duty,[3] and are named as the punishers of perjury:[4] even beggars have their Erinnyes, that they may not be insulted with impunity;[5] and when a horse has spoken in violation of the order of nature, the Erinnyes deprive him of the power of repeating the act.[6] The Erinnyes, these personified feelings, may therefore be regarded as the maintainers of order both in the moral and the natural world. There is however another view taken of these goddesses, in which they are only a form of Démétér and the Koré, the great goddesses of the earth. For everything in nature having injurious as well as beneficial effects, the bounteous earth itself becomes at times grim, as it were, and displeased with mankind, and this is Démétér-Erinnys. In the Arcadian legends of this goddess, and in the concluding choruses of the Eumenides of Æschylos, may be discerned ideas of this nature.[7] The epithet given to the Erinnyes by Empedoklés[8] would seem to confirm a view of them already noticed.[9]

CHAPTER XIII.

THEMIS, IRIS, PÆEON, HYPNOS, THANATOS, MOMOS, NEMESIS, TYCHE, PERSONIFICATIONS.

Θέμις. (*Themis.* 𝕷𝖆𝖜.)

THIS goddess appears in the Ilias[10] among the inhabitants of Olympos, and in the Odyssey[11] she is named as presiding over the assemblies of men, but nothing is said respecting her rank or her origin. By Hésiod[12] she is said to be a Titaness, one of the

---

[1] 1. στυγεραί: 2. ἠεροφοίτιες: 3. κυανόχρωτοι: 4. τανύποδες.
[2] Müller, *Eumen.* 186.
[3] *Il.* ix. 454, 568 *seq.*; comp. *Il.* xxi. 412. *Od.* ii. 135.
[4] *Il.* xix. 258; comp. *Il.* iii. 278.   [5] *Od.* xvii. 475.   [6] *Il.* xix. 418.
[7] See above, p. 159. Müller, *Eumen.* 191 *seq.*   [8] See above, p. 62
[9] See above, p. 40.   [10] *Il.* xv. 87; xx. 4   [11] *Od.* ii. 68.
[12] *Theog.* 135, 901 *seq.* Pind. *Ol.* xiii. 6 *seq.*

daughters of Heaven and Earth, and to have borne to Zeus, the Mœræ and the Horæ, Peace, Order, Justice,—the natural progeny of Law (Θέμις),[1] and deities beneficial to mankind. Æschylos[2] makes her the mother of Prometheus and (if the verse be genuine) the same as Earth. In Pindar and the Homéridian Hymns Themis sits by Zeus on his throne to give him counsel.[3]

Themis is said[4] to have succeeded her mother Earth in the possession of the Pythian oracle,[5] and to have voluntarily resigned it to her sister Phœbe, who gave it as a christening gift[6] to Phœbos-Apolló.

Ἶρις. (Iris.)

The office of this goddess, in the Ilias, is to act as the messenger of the king and queen of Olympos, a duty which is performed by Hermés in the Odyssey, in which poem there is not any mention made of Iris. Homer gives not the slightest hint of who her parents were; but analogy might lead to the supposition of Zeus being her sire, by some mother who is unknown. Hésiod[7] says that swift Iris and the Harpies, who fly 'like the blasts of the winds or the birds,' were the children of Thaumas (Wonder) by E'lektra (Brightness) the daughter of O'keanos. It is evidently the Rainbow (ἶρις) that is here meant, which is thus personified in the usual theogonic manner. There is little mention of Iris in the subsequent Greek poets; but, whenever she is spoken of, she appears quite distinct from the celestial phænomenon of the same name. In Kallimachos[8] and the Latin poets[9] she is appropriated to the service of Héra; and is by these last invariably, and even we may say clumsily, confounded with the rainbow. According to the lyric poet Alkæos, who is followed by Nonnos, Iris was by Zephyros the mother of Love.[10]

---

[1] Perhaps it is in this sense that Shakespeare (Meas. for Meas. ii. 4) terms law all-bui ding, i.e. which raises the whole social edifice.

[2] Prom. 18, 209, 874. The dubious verse is v. 210, but comp. v. 1091.

[3] Pind. Ol. viii. 22 (28). Hom. Hymn xxiii.

[4] Æsch. Eum. 1 seq. Eur. Iph. Taur. 1260. Ov. Met. i. 321.

[5] Welcker (Tril. 39) says that Themis is merely an epithet of Earth; Hermann also makes her a physical being, rendering her name Statina; while Böttiger (Kunst-Myth. ii. 110) says, "she is the oldest purely allegoric personification of a virtue." In fact her name (from θέω, to set) may be taken in either a physical or a moral sense.

[6] γενέθλιον δόσιν. We know not how else to express it. It was the gift bestowed on the child the day it was named, which was usually the eighth day after the birth. See Terence, Phormio, i. 1, 12.

[7] Theog. 265.   [8] Hymn to Délos, 216 seq.

[9] Verg. Æn. iv. 693 seq.; v. 606 seq.; ix. 2. Ovid, Met. i. 270; xi. 585. seq. Stat. Theb. x. 81, 118. Val. Flac. vii. 186.

[10] See above, p. 131.

Homer styles Iris *Gold-winged*,[1] and, according to Aristophanés,[2] ne likens her to a timid trembling pigeon :

> *Epops.* But how shall mankind take us gods to be and not jackdaws, when we fly and have wings on ?
>
> *Peisth.* Tut, you fool ; why, by Jove, there is Hermés himself who's a god, yet he flies and wears wings too ;
> And many other gods do the very same thing. There is Victory flies with her gold-wings,
> And, by Jove, so does Love ; and then Iris, said Homer, was just like a tremulous pigeon.

Iris is called,[3] 1. *Storm-footed* ; 2. *Wind-footed* ; 3. *Swift-footed* ; 4. *Swift* ; 5. *Gold-winged*, etc.

The name Iris is usually derived from ἐρῶ, εἴρω, *to say*, which suits the office of the goddess, and will accord with the rainbow in a view of it similar to that given in the Book of Genesis.[4] Hermann renders Iris *Sertia*, from εἴρω, to *knit* or *unite*, as the rainbow seems composed (*conserta*) of seven colours. Should this be the true etymon, the former and the office of the goddess may be indebted for their origin to the principle of secondary derivation.

Παιήων, Παιών, Παιάν. *Pæeon, Pæon.*

Pæéon is in Homer the family surgeon of Olympos. Nothing is said about his origin. All we are told is, that he cured Arés when wounded by Diomédés,[5] and Hadés of the wound in his shoulder given him by Héraklés,[6] and that the Egyptian physicians were of his race.[7] His attributes were afterwards transferred to Apolló, with whom he was perhaps originally identical.[8]

Ὕπνος καὶ Θάνατος. (*Somnus et Mors.* Sleep and Death.)

These two deities are called by Hésiod[9] the children of Night. By Homer they are, for a very natural and obvious reason, said to be twins. When, in the Ilias,[10] Sarpédon, the heroic and

---

[1] *Il.* viii. 398; xi. 185. This is the only line in Homer which makes against Voss's theory, of none of Homer's gods being winged. It is remarkable that Payne Knight, who seems to have known nothing of that theory, rejects the episodes viii. 350–484 ; xi. 179–217.

[2] *Birds*, 574. He probably had in view Hom. *Hymn* i. 114.

[3] 1. ἀελλόπους: 2. ποδήνεμος: 3. πόδας ὠκέα: 4. ταχεῖα: 5. χρυσόπτερος.

[4] See *Il.* xi. 27 ; xvii. 527.   [5] *Il.* v. 899.   [6] *Il.* v. 401.

[7] *Od.* iv. 232, " Merum scholion,"—P. Knight.

[8] See above, p. 110. Müller, *Dor.* i. 319. Nitzsch, *on Od.* iv. 232. Hésiod (*Sch. Od.* iv. 231) as well as Homer made Pæón distinct from Apolló. Solon would appear to have done the same, *v.* 57 compared with *v.* 53.

[9] *Theog.* 212, 758.   [10] *Il.* xvi. 676 *seq.*

noble-minded son of Zeus, falls by the hands of Patroklos, Apolló
at the command of his father washes his body in the waters of the
stream, anoints it with ambrosia, and, clothing it in ambrosial
garments, commits it to the twin brothers Sleep and Death to
convey to Lykia, there to be interred by his relatives and friends.

In the same poem, when Héra[1] resolves by her arts and beauty
to melt the soul of Zeus in love, and lay him asleep on Mount
Gargaros, that Poseidón may meanwhile give victory to the
Achæans, she takes her way thither from Olympos over Lémnos,
where she meets Sleep. She accosts him as the king of all gods
and men, and prays him to aid in her project, promising as his
reward a seat and footstool, the workmanship of Héphæstos.
Sleep reminds the goddess of the imminent danger which he
formerly ran, for having at her desire sealed the eyes of Zeus in
slumber when Héraklés was on his return from Troy, during
which she raised a storm that drove the hero to Kós; and Zeus,
awaking in a rage, knocked the gods about the house, searching
for Sleep, who only escaped by seeking the protection of Night,
whom Zeus revered too much to offend. Héra, by urging that the
affection of Zeus for the Trojans could not be supposed equal to
that for his own son, and finally by offering and swearing to give
him one of the younger Charites for his spouse, overcomes the
fears of Sleep, who accompanies her to Ida, where taking the
shape of a bird he sits in a tree till she has beguiled her lord.
Sleep, having accomplished his task, speeds to the battle-field to
inform Poseidón of what he had done.

The Latin poet Ovid,[2] after some Grecian predecessor, or, as is
far more probable, from the stores of his own luxuriant imagination, gives a beautiful description of the cave of Sleep near the
land of the Kimmerians, and of the *cortége* which there attended
on him, as Morpheus, Ikelos or Phobétér, and Phantasos; the
first of whom takes the form of man to appear in dreams, the
second of animals, the third of inanimate objects.

Death was brought on the stage by Euripidés in his beautiful
drama of Alkéstis. He is deaf to the entreaties of Apolló to spare
the Thessalian queen, but, vanquished by Héraklés, is forced
to resign his victim.

Μῶμος. Momus.

This god of raillery and ridicule does not appear to have been
known to Homer. By Hésiod[3] he is classed among the children of

---

[1] *Il.* xiv. 230 *seq.* imitated by Nonnos, xxxi. 103 *seq.*
[2] *Met.* xi. 592 *seq.*: comp. Stat. *Theb.* x. 84 *seq.*; and Ariosto, *Orl. Fur*
c. xiv. st. 92 *seq.*   [3] *Theog.* 214. See above, p. 44.

Night. He is alluded to by Plató and Aristotle; and Lukian,[1] as might be expected, makes some use of him.

Νέμεσις. *Nemesis.*

This goddess is in the Theogony a daughter of Night.[2] The tradition at Rhamnus in Attica, where she had a temple (whence she was named Rhamnusia), was that O'keanos was her father.[3] Helené, the cause of the war of Troy, was figuratively styled the offspring of Zeus and Nemesis.[4]

The name of this goddess comes most simply from νέμω, *to distribute;* and she was originally regarded as a personification of the power which regulates and orders the natural and the moral worlds. As the castigation of infractions of order was a part of her office, she was chiefly viewed as the punisher of pride, insolence, and arrogance. This is her usual character in the dramatists.

At Smyrna two Nemeses were worshipped.[5] The goddess adored at Kyzikos under the name of Adrésteia, said by the poet of the Phorónis to be the same with Kybelé,[6] is named Nemesis by Antimachos.[7] This Asiatic Nemesis is probably the goddess of nature.[8]

Τύχη. (*Fortuna.* Fortune.)

Fortune, that unseen power which exercises such arbitrary dominion over human affairs, was also deified, and had her temples and altars in Greece. By Hésiod and by one of the Homérids[9] she is classed among the Ocean-nymphs. Pindar in one place[10] calls her 'the child of Zeus Eleutherios;' elsewhere[11] he says that she is one of the Destinies. Alkman called her the sister of Law and Persuasion, and daughter of Forethought (Προμηθεία).[12] In her temple at Thébes[13] Fortune held Wealth (Πλοῦτος) in her arms. whether as mother or nurse was uncertain. The image of this goddess made by Bupalos for the Smyrnæans had a hemisphere (πόλος) on its head, and a horn of Amaltheia in its hand.[14]

---

[1] *Hermot.* 20. *True Hist.* ii. 3. Nigr. 32: see also Babrius 59. ed. Lach.
[2] *Theog.* 223: above, p. 44. [3] Paus. i. 33, 4. [4] See Part II. chap. ix.
[5] Paus. vii. 5, 3. [6] Sch. *Apoll. Rh.* i. 1129.

[7] Ἔστι δέ τις Νέμεσις μεγάλη θεὸς, ἣ τάδε πάντα
πρὸς μακάρων ἔλαχεν· βωμὸν δέ οἱ εἷσατο πρῶτος
Ἄδρηστος, ποταμοῖο παρὰ ῥόον Αἰσήποιο,
ἔνθα τετίμηταί τε καὶ Ἀδρήστεια καλεῖται.—*Ap.* Strab. xiii. 1, 13, p. 588.

[8] See Welcker *in Schwenk,* 261, 304.
[9] *Theog.* 360. Hom. *Hymn to Dém.* 420. [10] *Ol.* xiii. 1 *seq.*
[11] *Ap. Paus.* vii. 26, 8. [12] *Ap.* Plut. *de Fort. Rom.* 4.
[13] Paus ix. 16, 2. [14] Paus. iv. 30, 6.

Personifications.

The practice of personifying natural and moral qualities (of which the preceding articles are instances) seems to have been coeval with Grecian poetry and religion. It was not however by any means peculiar to Greece; it will probably be found wherever poetry exists.[1] But it was only in ancient Greece and Italy that these personifications were objects of worship, and seemed to be regarded as having a real personal existence.

In Homer, to whom as the original fountain we continually revert, we meet with several of these moral qualities appearing as persons. Terror and Fear, the children of Arés and Strife his sister, rouse with him the Trojans to battle.[2] Strife is said to be small at first, but at last to raise her head to the heaven. She is sent forth[3] amidst the Achæans by Zeus, bearing the signal of war; and, standing on the ship of Odysseus in the centre of the fleet, shouts so as to be heard at either extremity. When Arés[4] hears of the death of his son Askalaphos, Terror and Fear are commanded to yoke the steeds to his car for the war.

Prayers (Λιταί), says the poet,[5] are the daughters of great Zeus, lame and wrinkled, with squinting eyes. They follow Mischief ("Ατη), and tend those whom she has injured: but Até is strong and firm-footed, and gets far before them, afflicting men whom they afterwards heal. Elsewhere[6] he relates that Até is the daughter of Zeus, who *injures* (ἀᾶται) all; that her feet are tender, and that she therefore does not walk on the ground, but on the heads of men. Having conspired with Héra to deceive her father, he took her by the hair and flung her to earth, with an oath that she should never return to Olympos.

The Theogony of Hésiod contains a number of these personified qualities; they also occur in the subsequent poets. Thus Æschylos[7] introduced on the stage Strength (Κράτος) and Force (Βία), and Euripidés[8] Madness (Λύσση). Sophoklés,[9] by a very beautiful and correct figure, terms Fame 'the child of golden Hope'; and the Athenians erected an altar to this personification,[10] as they also did to Shame and Impetuosity, and above all to Mercy;[11] for with all their faults, and though from the defects of

---

[1] See the fine personification of Wisdom in the Proverbs of Solomon, ch. viii.
[2] *Il.* iv. 440.   [3] *Il.* xi. 3 *seq.*   [4] *Il.* xv. 119.
[5] *Il.* ix. 502 *seq.*   [6] *Il.* xix. 91 *seq.*   [7] *Prom. init.*
[8] *Her. Fur.* 822.   [9] *Œd. Tyr.* 157.
[10] Paus. i. 17, 1. See Hés. Ἔργ. 760. Æschinés *ag. Timarch.* 18. *False Embassy,* 47. Verg. *Æn.* iv. 173 *seq.* Stat. *Theb.* iii. 426. Val. Flac. ii. 116 *seq.* For the House of Fame see Ov. *Met.* xii. 39 *seq.* and Chaucer and Pope.   [11] Paus. *ut sup.*

their political constitution they were occasionally stimulated to deeds of cruelty by their unprincipled demagogues, the Athenians were by nature one of the most humane peoples of the ancient world.

The more stern Spartans, we may observe, erected temples to Fear, to Death, and to Laughter.[1]

Wealth (Πλοῦτος) was also deified. The Theogony makes him very appropriately the offspring of Démétér by Iasios.[2] He appears as an actor in the comedy of Aristophanés named from him, and in the Timón of Lukian.

CHAPTER XIV.

DIONYSOS.

Διώνυσος, Διόνυσος, Βάκχος, Βακχεύς. (*Liber.*)

No deity of Grecian mythology has given occasion to greater mysticism than Dionýsos, the god of wine. Creuzer,[3] for example, the prince of mystics, deduces his worship from India, and makes him identical with the Seeva of that country. According to him, the Vishnú-religion had, at a period far beyond that of history, spread itself over the West, and in Greece was known as that of Apolló, the god of the sun and light. The wild religion of Seeva, which had overcome the milder one of Vishnú on its natal soil, followed it in its progress to the West, proceeded as the religion of Dionýsos through Egypt and anterior Asia, mingling itself with the systems of these countries, and entered Greece, where, after a long struggle with the Apolló system, the two religions finally coalesced, the Dionýsiac casting away some of its wildest and most extravagant practices.

This hypothesis rests on no stable evidence; and it has been, as appears to us, fully refuted and exposed by the sober and sagacious Voss,[4] who, rejecting all air-built theory, bases his system on fact and testimony alone. We will here attempt, chiefly under his guidance, to illustrate the changes which it is probable the mythology of this god gradually underwent after the time of Homer.

It has been very justly observed by Lobeck,[5] that almost all the passages in Homer in which there is any mention of or allusion to this god have been suspected by the ancient critics, either on

[1] Plut. *Cleom.* 9. [2] *Theog.* 969; see above, p. 158. [3] *Symbolik.*
[4] *Anti-Symbolik.* [5] *Aglaophamus,* p. 285.

account of some circumstances in themselves, or because they
occur in places justly liable to suspicion.   The first of these
passages is that in the sixth book of the Ilias,[1] where Diomédés
and Glaukos encounter in the field of battle.   Here the former hero,
who had just wounded no less than two deities, asks the latter if
he is a god, adding, that he would not fight with the celestial
gods ;

> For not long-lived was Dryas' son the stout
> Lykoörgos who with the Celestials strove ;
> Who whilom o'er the holy Nyseïon chased
> The raging Dionýsos' nurses and they all
> Flung to the ground their sacred things when stricken
> By the man-slaying Lykoörgos' goad ;
> While Dionýsos terrified dived down
> Into the sea, where Thetis in her lap
> Received him trembling, for great fear had seized
> Upon him at the shouting of the man.
> Him thence the gods who live at ease abhorred,
> And Kronos' son with blindness struck him, nor
> Was he long-lived when hated of the gods.

Language more unsuitable surely could not be put into the mouth
of Diomédés ; and we may observe that there is a kind of instinct
of propriety, as we may term it, which always guides those poets
who sing from inspiration and not from art, leading them to
ascribe to the personages whom they introduce no ideas and no
language but what accurately correspond to their situation and
character.   This consideration alone, when well weighed, may
suffice to render the above passage extremely suspicious.

The passage in the fourteenth book,[2] in which Zeus, so inde-
corously recounts his various amours to Héra is liable to the same
objection, and was rejected by Aristarchos and several of the best
critics of antiquity.   In this the god says that ' Semelé bore him
Dionýsos, *a joy to mortals.*'   The place in which Andromaché is
compared to a Mænas,[3] besides that it occurs in one of the latter
books, is regarded as an interpolation.

These are the only passages in the Ilias in which there is any
allusion to Dionýsos.   In the Odyssey[4] it is said that Artemis
slew Ariadné in the isle of Dia, ' on the testimony (μαρτυρίησιν) of
Dionýsos ; ' but the circumstance of the *o* in the second syllable of
his name being short in this place satisfied the grammarian
Héródian, and ought to satisfy any one, that the line in question
is spurious.   In the last book of this poem[5] Thetis is said to have
brought an urn (ἀμφιφορῆα), the gift of Dionýsos, to receive the

[1] *Il.* vi. 130.   [2] *Il.* xiv. 325.   [3] *Il.* xxii. 460.
[4] *Od.* xi. 325.   [5] *Od.* xxiv. 74.

ashes of Achilleus; but the spuriousness of that part of the poem is well known. It was further observed by the ancient critics, that Marón, who gave the wine to Odysseus, was the priest of Apolló, not of Dionýsos.

Hésiod, when enumerating the children of Zeus, says,[1]

> To him also bare Kadmeian Semelé,
> Mingling in love's delight, a famous son ;
> The joy-inspiring Dionýsos, she
> A mortal; him immortal, but now both
> Are deities.

And again he says,[2]

> The gold-haired Dionýsos made the blond
> Ariadné, Minós' maid, his blooming spouse,
> And Kronos' son gave her immortal life.

Far perhaps inferior in point of antiquity to Hésiod is the Homéridian hymn to Dionýsos, which contains the following adventure of the god,—a tale which Ovid[3] has narrated somewhat differently.

Dionýsos once let himself be seen in the form of a handsome youth on the shore of a desert island. Some Tyrsénian pirates were sailing by, who when they espied him jumped on shore and made him captive, thinking him to be of royal birth. They bound him with cords; but these instantly fell off him, and the god sat smiling in silence. The pilot perceiving these apparent signs of divinity, called to the crew that he was a god, and exhorted them to set him on shore, lest he should cause a tempest to come on. But the captain rebuked him sharply, desired him to mind his own business, and declared that they would take their captive to Egypt or elsewhere and sell him for a slave. They then set sail, the wind blew fresh, and they were proceeding merrily along; when, behold! streams of fragrant wine began to flow along the ship; vines with clustering grapes spread over the sail; and ivy, laden with berries, ran up the mast and sides of the vessel. His shipmates in affright now called aloud to the pilot to make for the land; but the god assuming the form of a grim lion seized the captain, and the terrified crew to escape him leaped into the sea and became dolphins. The pilot alone remained on board; the god then declared to him who he was, and took him under his protection.

Another of these hymns relates, that the Nymphs received Dionýsos from his father, and reared him in a fragrant cavern of the valleys of Nysa. He was counted among the Immortals; and

[1] *Theog.* 940.   [2] *Theog.* 947.   [3] *Met.* iii. 532 *seq.* Hygin 1**

when he grew up, he went through the woody vales crowned with bay and ivy : the Nymphs followed him, and the wood was filled with their joyous clamour.

In these poems the mention of the ivy, and the epithet *noisy* (ἐρίβρομος), testify, as we shall see, their late age. Pindar also calls Dionýsos *Ivy-bearing* (κισσοφόρος) and *noisy* (βρόμιος). Héro- dotos and the tragedians describe what we consider to be the mixed religion of Dionýsos.

The idea of mere mortals, or the offspring of gods and mortals, being raised to divine rank and power, does not occur in the Ilias. Ganymédés and, we may add, Tithónos, who were mortal by both father and mother, were carried off, the former by the gods to be the cup-bearer of Zeus,[1] the latter by Ḗós ;[2] and it is to be presumed, though Homer does not expressly say so, that they were endowed with immortality. But all the *half-caste*, as we may call them, Héraklés, Achilleus, Sarpédón, Æneias, have no advantage over their fellow-mortals, except greater strength and more frequent aid from the gods.

But in the Odyssey we find the system of deification commenced. The sea-goddess Inó-Leukothea, who gives Odysseus her veil to save him from being drowned, was, we are told, a daughter of Kạdmos (a name which does not occur in the Ilias), ' who had be- fore been a speaking mortal, but was now allotted the honour of the gods in the depths of the sea.' And again ; Odysseus beholds in the realms of Hadés the *image* (εἴδωλον) of Héraklés, pursuing his usual occupations when on earth ; but *himself* we are told ' enjoys banquets among the immortal gods, and possesses fair-ankled Hébé.' It is not however said that he had obtained the power of a god.[3]

Supposing therefore Dionýsos to have been, as his name might appear to indicate, one of the original Grecian deities, he may have been regarded as a son of Zeus by a goddess named Semelé,[4] who in after-times, in pursuance of a practice hereafter to be ex- plained, may have been degraded to the rank of a heroine, and Dionýsos have consequently become the son of Zeus by a mortal mother. The vintage is in wine-countries at the present day, like hay-making and harvest-home in England, a time of merry-making and festivity ; and the festival of the deity presiding over it may have been a very joyous one, and celebrated with abundance of noise and mirth. Such, we say, *may* have been (for we venture not to assert it) the original Dionýsiac religion of Greece ; and

---

[1] *Il.* xx. 234.   [2] See *Il.* x. 1.   *Od.* v. 1.

[3] *Od.* v. 333 ; xi. 601. The last of these passages is undoubtedly spurious, and the first is perhaps not altogether free from suspicion.

[4] Hésiod (*Theog.* 940 *seq.*) places Semelé, Alkméné and Ariadné with the *goddesses* who bore children to gods.

when we recollect the very incidental manner in which Démétér, undoubtedly one of the most ancient deities, is noticed in the Ilias, it should not excite any great surprise to find the poet totally omitting all mention of the wine-god.[1]

To pass from conjecture to certainty, it appears quite clear that the part of Thrace lying along the northern coast of the Ægæan was in the earliest times a chief seat of the Dionýsiac religion, where the worship of the god of wine was celebrated with great noise and tumult by the people of that country; and, supposing the passage in the sixth book of the Ilias to be genuine, some account of it had possibly reached the ears of Homer. The Thracian worship of Dionýsos, it is not improbable, was not introduced into Greece till after the time when the Æolians colonised the coast of Asia about the Hellespont.[2] Here they became acquainted with the enthusiastic orgies of the Great Mother, and of the god Sabazios;[3] who, as it would appear, was similar to Dionýsos, and an object of veneration both to Phrygians and Thracians, and who was worshiped under the form of an ox, as being the patron of agriculture. As polytheism is not jealous, and readily permits the introduction of new deities into the system, particularly if their attributes or festivals have a resemblance to any of the old ones,[4] the worship of this new god was adopted by the Grecian colonists, and diffused over the isles and continent of Greece: not, however, without considerable opposition from the sober common-sense of several individuals of eminence, as appears by the mythic tales of Labdakos, Pentheus and Perseus, which are apparently real occurrences thrown back into the mythic age.[5] The original Grecian festivals, though of a joyous cheerful character, were so widely different from the raving orgies and wild licentiousness of this Dionýsiac religion, that it is quite evident the latter could not have been known in Greece during the Achæan period.[6]

[1] See end of this chapter.

[2] Not till a century or two after the time of Homer, in the opinion o: Lobeck, *Aglaoph.* p. 672.

[3] Sch. *Aristoph. Birds*, 873. *Lys.* 388. *Wasps*, 9.

[4] See above, p. 17. It was thus that there was a great resemblance observed between the Dionýsia of Athens and the Saturnalia of Rome.

[5] Had the consul Postumius (Livy, xxxix. 8) lived before history was written at Rome, and had the Bakchic orgies obtained a footing in that city, he would probably have figured as a Pentheus in the mythic annals of Rome. "Mythology," says Müller (*Dor.* i. 293), "often first clothes the events of history in a fabulous garb, and then refers them to an early and unknown time."

[6] Müller, *Dor.* i. 10. "Ægyptia numina gaudent plangoribus, Græca choreis, Barbara strepitu cymbalistarum et tympanistarum et ceraularum."— Apul. *de Gent.* p. 49.

There can be no doubt of the Dionýsiac religion, with its nocturnal orgies and indecent extravagance, having been very prevalent among the Greeks at the time when the Iónians were permitted to settle in Egypt. It is in no small degree surprising with what facility the Grecian and Egyptian systems coalesced, with what open-mouthed credulity the Grecian settlers and travellers swallowed all the fictions of the cunning priesthood of that country, and with what barefaced assurance the latter palmed on their unsuspecting auditors the most incredible lies. In reading the Euterpé of Hérodotos, one might fancy one's self beholding Captain Wilford listening with devout belief to his artful Pundit;[1] so little suspicion does the Father of History betray of his having oeen played upon by the grave linen-clad personages who did him the honour to initiate him in their mysteries.

The theory boldly advanced by the Egyptian priesthood was, that all the religion of Greece had been imported into that country by colonies of Egyptians—a people, by the way, without ships or materials for building them, who had no ports, and who held the sea in abhorrence[2]—who civilised the mast-eating savages that roamed its uncultivated wilds, and instructed them in the nature and worship of the gods. The deities of Greece were therefore to find their prototypes in Egypt; and Dionýsos was honoured by being identified with Osíris, the great god of the land of Nile.[3] Hérodotos informs us how Melampus, who introduced his worship into Greece, had learned it from Kadmos the Phœnician, who had derived his knowledge of course from Egypt,[4] As the realm of Osíris did not abound in vines,[5] the ivy with its clustering berries which grew there was appropriated to the god;[6] and it now became one of the favourite plants of Dionýsos, as appears by the Homéridian hymn above cited.

The Egyptians had fabled that their god Osíris had made a progress through the world, to instruct mankind in agriculture and planting.[7] The Greeks caught up the idea, and represented the son of Semelé—for the popular faith did not give up the old legend of his Thébau birth—as roaming through the greater part

---

[1] See the Asiatic Pesearches.
[2] See Ukert, l. i. 41. Heeren, *Ideen* II. ii. 225, 288, 377.
[3] Hérod. ii. 144.   [4] Id. ii. 49.
[5] Hérodotos (ii. 77) says positively that there were no vines in Egypt. Egyptian vines are mentioned in *Genesis*, xl. 9. *Num.* xx. 5; and see Wilkinson, *Manners and Customs of the ancient Egyptians*, ii. 142 *seq.*
[6] Plutarch (*De Is. et Os.* 37) says that the Egyptians called it Chenosíris, *i. e. Plant of Osíris.*
[7] Kodór. i. 17. Plut. *de Is. et Os.* 13. Eudocia, 110: ccmp. Tibull. i. 7, N *seq*

of the earth. In the Bakchæ of Euripidés the god describes himself as having gone through Lydia, Phrygia, Persia, Baktria,
Média, Arabia, and the coast of Asia, inhabited by mingled Greeks
and barbarians, throughout all which he had established his
dances and his religious rites.

When Alexander and his army had penetrated to the modern
Cábul, they found ivy and wild vines on the sides of Mount Méros
and on the banks of the rivers : they also met processions, accompanied by the sound of drums, and party-coloured dresses, like
those worn in the Bakchic orgies of Greece and Lesser Asia.
The flatterers of the conqueror thence took occasion to fable that
Dionýsos had, like Héraklés and their own great king, marched as
a conqueror throughout the East; had planted there the ivy and
the vine; had built the city Nysa; and named the mountain
Méros, from the circumstance of his birth from the *thigh* (μηρὸς) of
Zeus.[1] At length, during the time of the Græco-Baktric kingdom,
some Greek writers, on whom it is not impossible that the Brahmins imposed, as they have since done on the English, gave out
that Dionýsos was a native Indian, who, having taught the art
of wine-making in that country, made a conquering expedition
through the world, to instruct mankind in the culture of the vine
and other useful arts. And thus the knowledge of the vine came
to Greece, from a land which does not produce that plant.[2]

This last is the absurd hypothesis which we have seen renewed
in our own days, and supported by all the efforts of ingenious
etymology.

The story of the Grecian Dionýsos is as follows :[3] Zeus, enamoured of the beauty of Semelé the daughter of Kadmos, visited
her in secret. Héra's jealousy took alarm, and under the form of
an old woman she came to Semelé, and, by exciting doubts of the
real character of her lover, induced her when next he came to
exact a promise that he would visit her as he was wont to visit
Héra. An unwary promise was thus drawn from the god before
he knew what he was required to perform; and he therefore
entered the bower of Semelé in his chariot, the lightning and
thunder flaming, flashing and roaring around him. Overcome

---

[1] Diodór. ii. 38. Arrian, *Hist. Indic. sub init.*

[2] Plut. *Aq. et Ig. Comp.* 7. Diodór. iii. 63. A. W. Schlegel, though in
general inclined to what we call the mystic theory, expressly denies in his
Indian Library that the Greeks had, previous to the conquests of Alexander,
any idea of an expedition of Bakchos to or from India. We ask the advocates
of the Indian origin of the Bakchic religion for their proofs, and get nothing
in reply but confident assertion or slight resemblances of names and ceremonies.

[3] Apollod. iii. 4–5. Ov. *Met.* iii. 253 *seq.* Hygin. 167, 179. Eudoc. 118,
373.

with terror, Semelé, who was now six months gone with child, expired in the flames, and Zeus took the babe, which was prematurely expelled from her womb, and sewed it up in his thigh.[1] In due time it came to the birth, and Zeus then naming it Dionýsos gave it to Hermés to convey to Inó, the sister of Semelé, with directions to rear it as a girl.

Héra, whose revenge was not yet satiated, caused Athamas, the husband of Inó, to go mad; and Zeus, to save Dionýsos from the machinations of Héra, changed him into a kid, under which form Hermés conveyed him to the nymphs of Nysa, who were afterwards made the Hyades, and by whom he was reared.[2] When he grew up he discovered the culture of the vine, and the mode of extracting its precious liquor; but Héra struck him with madness, and he roamed through great part of Asia. In Phrygia Rhea cured him, and taught him her religious rites, which he now resolved to introduce into Hellas. When passing through Thrace he was so furiously assailed by Lykurgos, a prince of the country, that he was obliged to take refuge with Thetis in the sea; but he avenged himself by driving Lykurgos mad, who killed his own son Dryas with a blow of an axe, taking him for a vine-branch; and his subjects afterwards bound him and left him on Mount Pangæon, where he was destroyed by wild horses, for such was the will of Dionýsos.

When Dionýsos reached his native city, the women readily received the new rites, and ran wildly through the woods of Kithærón. Pentheus, the ruler of Thébes, however, set himself against them; but Dionýsos caused him to be torn to pieces by his mother and his aunts. The daughters of Minyas, Leukippé, Aristippé and Alkathoé, also despised his rites, and continued plying their looms, while the other women ran through the mountains. He came as a maiden, and remonstrated, but in vain; he then assumed the form of various wild beasts; serpents filled their baskets; vines and ivy twined round their looms, while wine and milk distilled from the roof; but their obstinacy was unsubdued. He finally drove them mad; they tore to pieces the son of Leukippé, and then went roaming through the mountains, till Hermés touched them with his wand, and turned them into a bat, an owl, and a crow.[3]

---

[1] See Hérod. ii. 146.

[2] It was also said that Makris (above, p. 91), the daughter of Aristæos received from Hermés, in Eubœa, ' the Nyseian son ' of Zeus and reared him there on honey. Apoll. Rh. iv. 1134 *seq.*

[3] Corinna and Nicander *ap. Anton. Lib.* 10. Ælian, *Var. Hist.* iii. 42. Plut. *Quæst. Gr.* 38. Ov. *Met.* iv. 1 *seq.* The pleasing tale of Pyramus and Thisbé

Dionýsos next proceeded to Attica, where he taught a man named Ikarios the culture of the vine. Ikarios having made wine, gave of it to some shepherds, who thinking themselves poisoned killed him. When they came to their senses they buried him; and his daughter Erigoné, being shown the spot by his faithful dog Mæra, hung herself through grief.[1] At Argœ the rites of Dionýsos were received, as at Thébes, by the women, and opposed by Perseus, the son of Zeus and Danaé; Zeus however reduced his two sons to amity,[2] and Dionýsos thence passed over to Naxos. where he met Ariadné. It was on his way thither that his adventure with the Tyrrhénians occured. Dionýsos afterwards descended to Erebos, whence he fetched his mother, whom he now named Thyóné, and ascended with her to the abode of the gods.[3]

Like every other portion of the Grecian mythology, the history of the vine-god was pragmatised when infidelity became prevalent. That most tasteless of historians Diodóros gives us, probably from the cyclograph Dionysios, the following narrative.[4]

Ammón, a monarch of Libya, was married to Rhea, a daughter of Uranos; but meeting near the Keraunian mountains a beautiful maiden named Amaltheia, he became enamoured of her. He made her mistress of the adjacent fruitful country, which from its resembling a bull's horn in form was named the Western Horn, and then Amaltheia's Horn, which last name was afterwards given to places similar to it in fertility. Amaltheia here bore him a son, whom, fearing the jealousy of Rhea, he conveyed to a town named Nysa, situated not far from the Horn, in an island formed by the river Tritón. He committed the care of him to Nysa, one of the daughters of Aristæos: while Athéna, who had lately sprung from the earth on the banks of the Tritón, was appointed to keep guard against the assaults of Rhea. This delicious isle, which was precipitous on all sides, with a single entrance through a narrow glen thickly shaded by trees, is described in a similar manner with Panchaia, and other happy retreats of the same nature. It therefore had verdant meads, abundant springs, trees of every kind, flowers of all hues, and evermore resounded with the melody of

---

introduced by this poet (perhaps a Milesian one) is nowhere else to be found. Nonnos (vi. 339 seq.) tells a strange legend of the love of Pyramos (so he names the Nile) for Thisbé. Are these Pyramid and Thébes?

[1] Apollod. iii. 14, 7. Hygin. 130.
[2] See Part II. ch. vii. *Perseus.*
[3] Apollod. iii. 5, 3. Paus. ii. 31, 2; 37, 5. Diodór. iii. 62; iv. 25. H.r Carm. ii. 19, 29 seq.
[4] Diodór. iii. 68 seq.

birds.[1] Dionýsos, after he grew up, became a mighty conqueror and a benefactor of mankind, by whom he was finally deified.

Though the adventures of Dionýsos were occasionally the theme of poets, especially of the dramatists, they do not appear to have been narrated in continuity, like those of Héraklés, until long after the decline of Grecian poetry. It was in the fifth century of the Christian æra, that Nonnos, a native of Panopolis in Egypt, made the history of Dionýsos the subject of a poem, containing forty-eight books, the wildest and strangest that can well be conceived, more resembling the Ramayana of India than anything to be found in ancient or modern occidental literature. Its chief subject is the war of Dionýsos against Dériadés king of the Indians, the details of which are probably the inventions of the poet;[2] in other parts he seems to have adhered with tolerable fidelity to his authorities, and the Dionýsiaka may be regarded as a vast repertory of Bakchic fable, deserving of far more attention than has hitherto been bestowed on it.[3]

The worship of this god prevailed in almost all parts of Greece. Men and women joined in his festivals, dressed in Asiatic robes and bonnets; their heads wreathed with vine- and ivy-leaves, with fawn-skins (νεβρίδες) flung over their shoulders, and *thyrses* or blunt spears twined with vine-leaves in their hands, they ran bellowing through the country *Io Bacche! Euoi! Iacche!* &c., swinging their thyrses, beating on drums, and sounding various instruments. Indecent emblems were carried in processions, at which modest virgins assisted; and altogether few ceremonies more lax or indecent are celebrated in India at the present day, than polished Athens performed in the Phrygio-Grecian Dionysia,[4] though ancient and modern mystics endeavour to extract profound and solemn mysteries from them.

[1]
.... that Nyseian isle
Girt with the river Triton, where old Cham,
Whom Gentiles Ammon call and Libyan Jove,
Hid Amalthea and her florid son,
Young Bacchus, from his step-dame Rhea's eye.
Milton, *Par. Lost*, iv. 275.

The poet makes here one of his usual slips of memory (*Tales and Popular Fictions*, p. 22), for Amalthea was *not* hid in the isle.

[2] Stephanus Byzantinus (*v.* Γάζα) quotes the Bassarika, a poem by one Dionysios, which treated of this war.

[3] Of Nonnos Hermann (*Doct. Met.* p. 211) says, *Vir fervidioris ingenii et in primis ad poësim factus.* He appears to have been well versed in the various poems ascribed to Orpheus, in which Dionýsos was the subject of strange mystery. As our object is alone the genuine mythology of Hellas, we do not enter on those matters. See Lobeck's *Aglaophamus.*

[4] See Démosth. *Neæra*, 1371. Aristoph. *Acharn.* 259 *seq*

The women, who bore a chief part in these frantic revels, were called *Mænades, Bakchœ, Thyiades, Euades,* names of which the origin is apparent.

Dionýsos was represented in a variety of modes and characters by the ancient artists. The Theban Dionýsos appears with the delicate lineaments of a maiden, rather than those of a young man; his whole air and gait are effeminate; his long flowing hair is, like that of Apolló,[1] collected behind his head, wreathed with ivy or a fillet; he is either naked, or wrapped in a large cloak, and the *nebris* is sometimes flung over his shoulders; he carries a crook or a thyrse, and a panther generally lies at his feet. In some monuments Dionýsos appears *bearded*, in others *horned* (the Bakchos-Sabazios), whence in the mysteries he was identified with Osíris, and regarded as the Sun. He is sometimes alone, at other times in company with Ariadné or the youth Ampelos.

His *triumph* over the Indians is represented in great pomp. The captives are chained and placed on waggons or elephants, and among them is carried a large *cratér* full of wine; Dionýsos is in a chariot drawn by elephants or panthers, leaning on Ampelos, preceded by Pan, and followed by Silénos, the Satyrs, and the Mænades, on foot or on horseback, who make the air resound with their cries and the clash of their instruments. The *Indian* Bakchos is always bearded.

It is with reason that Sophoklés[2] styles Dionýsos *many-named* (πολυώνυμος), for in the Orphic hymns alone we meet with upwards of forty of his appellations. Some of the principal of them are, *Bakchos*[3] and *Bromios,* from the noise with which his festivals were celebrated; *Bassareus,* from the fox-skin dresses named *bassarœ* worn by the Thracians; *Dithyrambos,* from the odes of that name, or from his double birth (δίς θύρα); *Eleleus* and *Euios,* from the shouting: *Lyœos,* as *loosing* from care; *Lenœos,* from the *wine-press.*

Dionýsos was also called,[4] 1. *Muse-leader;* 2. *Bull-headed;* 3. *Fire-born;* 4. *Dance-rouser;* 5. *Mountain-rover;* 6. *Sleep-giver,* &c.

It seems probable that in the original (i.e. Pelasgic) conception

---

[1]   Solis æterna est Phœbo Bacchoque juventas;
        Nam decet intonsus crinis utrumque deum.—Tibull. i. 4, 37.

[2] *Antigone,* 1115.

[3] The maintainers of the Indian hypothesis observe that Bagis is one of the names of Seeva. According to Müller (*Orchom.* p. 384), Bakchos (the same perhaps with Iakchos (was the πάρεδρος of Démétér of Thébes, and was totally distinct from the Thracian Dionýsos.

[4] 1. μουσαγέτης: 2. ταυροκέφαλος: 3. πυριγενής: 4. ἐγερσίχορος: 5. ὀρει-μανής: 6. ὑπνοδότης.

of Dionýsos he was not merely the wine-god; for such restricted
notions are contrary to the genius of the ancient Grecian religion,
in which each people assigned its peculiar deities a very extensive
sphere of action, as gods of the sun, the moon, the heaven, the
earth, and other parts of nature. Dionýsos was therefore, it is
likely, regarded as a deity presiding over growth and increase in
general;[1] and as Hermés, who seems to have been originally of
coextensive power with him, was gradually restricted and made a
god of cattle alone, so Dionýsos may have been limited to the care
of plants, particularly the vine.[2]

Water and heat being the great causes of growth, we find this
deity closely connected with both these elements. Thus the infant
Dionýsos is committed to the water-goddess Inó, and to the Hyades
and to Silénos. His temples at Athens[3] and Sparta[4] were in
places named *marshes* (ἐν λίμναις), and he was styled *Of-the-Marsh*
(λιμναῖος), and *Marsh-sprung* (λιμνηγενής). In some places he was
called the *Rainer* (ὕης);[5] his festival, the Anthestéria, was celebrated in the spring, the season of showers, and it was so named
from the flowers and blossoms, of which he was the author; whence
he was styled the *Flowery* and the *Lover-of-flowers*.[6]

The relation of Dionýsos to the celestial heat seems to be expressed in the story of his birth, and also in the dog Mæra (Μαῖρα),
another name for Sirius the dog-star;[7] the name of his companion
Marón[8] also seems to refer to heat; and perhaps the true origin
of the god's own epithet, μηρογενής, usually rendered *Thigh-born*,
lies in this word. It is moreover not impossible that the real
root of his mother's name may be σέλας.[9]

In favour of this god's presiding over cattle is alleged the well-

---

[1] Ὅτι δ᾽ οὐ μόνον τοῦ οἴνου Διόνυσον ἀλλ᾽ καὶ πάσης ὑγρᾶς φύσεως
Ἕλληνες ἡγοῦνται κύριον καὶ ἀρχηγὸν ἀρκεῖ Πίνδαρος μάρτυς εἶναι λέγων·
Δενδρέων δὲ νομὸν Διόνυσος πολυγηθὴς αὐξάνοι, Ἁγνὸν φέγγος ὀπώρης.—
Plut. *de Is. et Os.* 35.

[2] Among the epithets of Dionýsos we meet with Συκίτης (from σῦκος, *fig*,
Athén. iii. 78) and Δενδρίτης (Creuz. *Sym.* ii. 360).

[3] Sch. *Aristoph. Frogs*, 216.   [4] Strab. viii. 5, 1, p. 363.

[5] See Passow, *s. v.*

[6] Ἄνθιος (Paus. i. 31, 4): Ἀνθεύς (Id. vii. 21, 6): Εὐανθής (Athén.
viii. 563): Φιλανθής (Eurip. *Fr. Incert.* 169). A name of Dionýsos was
Εἰραφιώτης, which Schwenk (p. 150) very ingeniously supposes to be equivalent to εἰαροφυώτης, *Spring-born*: comp. Welcker, *Nach. zur Tril.* 187, 188.
See above, p. 130.

[7] See above, p. 189. Ikarios would seem to be connected with ἰκμάς, ἰχώρ,
and therefore to denote *moisture*. His daughter is Erigoné (*Spring-born*).

[8] Μάρων Εὐάνθεος υἱός. *Od.* ix. 196.

[9] See Schwenk, 147. Σεμέλη may have been originally Σελέμη, and have
denoted the *bright* season which brings the grape to maturity. There was, we
may observe, a river of Achaia named Σέλεμνος, *i. e.* Bright-stream.

known circumstance of the goat being the victim offered to him; his being in his infancy conveyed to Nysa in the form of a kid, and his being worshipped under that name. He also wore the goatskin dress of the goatherds; and in Attica and Hermioné he was named μελάναιγις, a name which in the former place was connected with the fabulous origin of the festival of the Apaturia. Welcker[1] is of opinion that Dionýsos was originally the object of worship to the lower classes, the goatherds, and such like (in Attica the tribe of the Ægikoreis); and that as they gradually rose in consideration, their god was associated with those of the nobles; and that thence he always appeared of an inferior rank to those with whom he was joined. This critic accounts on the same principle for the very slight mention of Dionýsos in the Homeric poems, namely, that he was of too low a rank to be an actor of importance in those aristocratic verses, which only told of kings and nobles, and the gods whom *they* adored.

The name Dionýsos is one of the most difficult to explain in Grecian mythology. After Voss's able exposure we may venture to reject the notion of its being the same with Devanisi,[2] a title of the Hindú god Seeva, and view in Dionýsos a Grecian god with a Grecian name. The most probable (though by no means quite satisfactory) interpretation of it is *God-of-Nysa*, which last place occurs frequently in his legend.[3] Like Tritón, however, it has been multiplied, for we find a Nysa on Helikón in Bœótia,[4] in Thrace, in Naxos, at the foot of Mount Tmólos in Lydia, in Arabia, in India, in Africa, and elsewhere;[5] beside that indefinite one whence Persephoné was carried away by Hadés. It therefore is a matter of uncertainty which was the original Nysa.

We do not recollect having anywhere met with an explanation of the singular circumstance of the double birth of Dionýsos. Yet when we call to mind that he is the wine-god, and may therefore be regarded as the wine itself, the mystery may seem to admit of a very simple solution. The future wine, we are to recollect,

[1] See Welcker, *Ueber das Satyrspiel* (*Nach. zur Tril.* 186–211), where much valuable matter on the subject of Dionýsos will be found.

[2] "The merest tyro in Sanscrit may, with a single dash of his pen, dispel all the magic of Devanisi, a name unknown in Indian literature. The compound is contrary to the rules of the language, for it should be Nisideva, like Divaspati, *Lord-of-heaven*, and others." Bohlen, *Das Alte Indien*, i. 142.

[3] If the original signification of δῖος be *bright* (above, p. 47), there might have been a verb ΔΙΩΝΥΩ, ΔΙΩΝΥΜΙ (like δεικνύω, δείκνυμι), from which might be derived Διώνυσος, i. e. *Bright-god*.

[4] Strab. ix. 2, 14, p. 405. See Müller, *Orchom.* 89, 383: he decides in favour of this Nysa.

[5] Sch. *Il.* vi. 123. Voss, *Myth. Br.* iv. 190 *seq.*

O

lies concealed within the grapes all through the bright season denoted by Semelé, and perhaps the thunder and lightning which accompany the first immature birth of the infant wine-god may denote the aërial phænomena of that time of the year; for in the South of Europe the spring and the autumn are the seasons in which they most prevail: or possibly they indicate the joyous, riotous hilarity of the vintage. From the grapes the wine comes forth in an imperfect immature condition, and to attain its proper state of perfection it must undergo a further period of concealment in *amphoræ*, etc.; receptacles of a widely different nature from the soft tender grapes in which it had taken its origin. This fact then may have been given a mythic form by the fiction of the immature deity being sewed up in the thigh of Zeus, his sire, a fiction which may have derived its origin from an apparent derivation of his name.

CHAPTER XV.

FOREIGN DEITIES:—KYBELE, KOTYTTO AND BENDIS, ARTEMIS OF EPHESOS, ISIS.

OUR object in introducing the present chapter is to give a slight view of the manner in which the intercourse with Asia and Egypt, which had such an injurious effect on the religion of Greece, commenced. We know not how we can better open the subject, than by quoting the following just and philosophic observations of a writer [1] for whom we entertain the highest respect and esteem:—

"After that most happy age, whose image we behold expressed in the poems of Homer, had passed away, a great change took place in civil affairs, but a still greater in religions, in pursuits, and inclinations; and the whole of Greece was so much altered, that if any one passes from the perusal of Homer to that of those writers who lived in the time of the Persian war, he will feel as if removed to another region, and seem hardly to recognise those old Achæans, who happy with the present, careless of the future, prompt to act, mindless of what they had done, were aloof from all the causes of anxiety and superstition. But when, as reason gradually ripened, the Greeks began to examine the involved conceptions of the mind, and to know themselves, there succeeded that more mature and solicitous age, at which when men arrive they feel more strongly and acutely the incentives of pleasure

---

[1] Lobeck, *Aglaophamus*, 312 *seq.*

and of virtue, fluctuating alternately, with great commotion of mind, and often with extreme *ennui*, between what they condemn and what they desire. Hence that anxiety about hidden matter, and those presages of the future, and the various superstitions which consciousness of guilt and despair of salvation are wont to produce. The entrance and traces of this new age of Greece we are prevented from clearly discerning by the obscurity of those times, which, being illumed by hardly any literary monuments, may be said to resemble a region covered with dark clouds, through which the tops of the towers and castles elevate themselves, while the ground and foundation lie concealed. But that there was a great agitation of the human mind, and some new efforts, is proved by the perfection of lyric poetry, which commenced a little after the time of Hésiod, and by the origin of philosophy and the advance of the elegant arts. We presently see magnificent temples raised to the gods and heroes, solemn games instituted throughout the towns, the number and the insignia of the priests, especially when the regal power had been abolished, increased. But that at the same time the mystic ceremonies, whose first traces appear in the Hésiodic and Kyklic poems, were diffused far and wide, and occupied the whole of life with new superstitions, is manifest from the number of jugglers who then roved through Greece, expiating by certain secret rites not only blood and manslaughter, but also prodigies, sacrileges, and whatever piacular offences either individuals or states had committed."

Having enumerated the principal of these men, such as Abaris, Aristeas, Onomakritos of Lokris, and Epimenidés, our author thus proceeds :—

" Meantime Egypt, the parent of superstition and sacerdotal falsehood, was laid open ; and who that reflects on the long and frequent intercourse of the two nations, and the vaniloquence of the one and the credulity of the other,[1] will hesitate to concede that the contagion had secretly insinuated itself into Greece before the time of Pythagoras ? But it is not without reason believed, that during the same period the mystic poems of Musæos, Eumolpos, Orpheus, and that which was called the Minyas, were made public ; in all of which were scattered new fables about the lower-world, and hopes of a more happy life and Elysian abodes promised to those who received the sacred decrees of the gods, and equal punishments threatened to the despisers of them. What ! is not the religion of the subterrane deities sanctioned by those Athenian laws, which direct that those who have committed manslaughter

[1] Comp. Paus. ix. 36, 5.   Ukert, I. i. 51, *note*.

o 2

should be brought before the King of the Sacred Affairs, and being absolved by the judgment should be solemnly purified,—of which laws Drakón is said to have been the author? This religion was also confirmed by Solón; who, in cases of manslaughter, directed to swear by three deities, Hikesios, Katharsios, and Exakesterios. Nor were the psychomanty and evocations of the dead, which we read of in the stories of Archilochos, Periander, and Pausanias, built on any other foundation: and these were posterior to Homer; for if his contemporaries had known anything of that art, he needed not to have sent Odysseus to the nether-world. After a little interval succeeded Pythagoras, the author of a portentous wisdom, and that twilight-season in which poets began to philosophise and philosophers to poetise.

"In these four centuries, therefore, which elapsed between Homer and the Persian wars, the greatest change was made in all matters pertaining to the worship of the gods. They contain the origin and growth of solemn lustrations, mysteries, hieratic medicine, and fanatic poetry: in these too the most ancient poems of Bakis, Pamphós, Olén, and the Sibyls, appear to have been patched up, and all the avenues of pious frauds to have been thrown open. Whence the conclusion is easy, that the web of the Orphic fable, which is all composed of the same kind of threads with those, was not woven by Pro-selénian philosophers, but was commenced perhaps a century or two after Homer, and completed a little before the time of Onomakritos."[1]

It is needless to remind our readers, that we have no account on which we can place reliance of any intercourse between the Greeks and foreign nations previous to the Trojan war, save the commercial one with the Phœnician merchants who visited their harbours. The revolution named the Return of the Hérakleids, which is said to have occurred somewhat less than a century after that event, caused portions of the Achæan race to abandon their country and seek new settlements. They are supposed to have turned their eyes to the former realms of the Trojan monarchs, whose power had been broken; and the first colonies were planted by the Æolians along the coast, from the island of Kyzikos in the Propontis to the mouth of the Hermos. The Iónians and the Dórians afterwards came and settled to the south of that river; and thus the coast of Asia was occupied to a considerable extent by the Grecian colonies.

We cannot trace in Homer any difference beween the religion of the Achæans and that of the Asiatics. In the case of the

---

[1] Comp. Müller, *Proleg.* 387.

Trojans, who are regarded (and we think justly) as a portion of the Pelasgic race, this need not surprise us; but the poet is equally silent with respect to anything of the kind between them and the Phrygians, wnose religion we know to have been different.[1] It does not however seem to have been the practice of the *Aœdi* to attend to distinctions of this kind; for Odysseus, we may observe, in all his wanderings never found any want of an interpreter, as good Greek was spoken wherever he came, and he everywhere met with Grecian manners and customs. The silence therefore of the poet throws no impediment in the way of our assuming that, when the Grecian colonies settled on the Hellespont, they found there a religion very different from their own; the one being calm and cheerful, the other wild and orgiastic. This religion was that of

Κυβέλη. Κυβήβη. ⌣*hea. Ops.*)

Kybelé, also called the Great Mother, was regarded by the Phrygians and Lydians[2] as the goddess of nature or of the earth. Her temples stood on the summits of hills; such as that of Dindymos in the isle of Kyzikos, of Berekynthos, Sipylos, Kybelos; from which last she is said to have derived her name, though the reverse is more likely to be the truth. At Pessínus was preserved the aërolite[3] which was held to be her heaven-sent image.

The following pragmatised account of Kybelé is given by Diodóros.

Kybelé was daughter to king Mæón and his queen Dindymé. She was exposed by her father on Mount Kybelos, where she was suckled by panthers and lionesses, and was afterwards reared by shepherdesses, who named her Kybelé. When she grew up she displayed great skill in the healing art, and cured all the diseases of the children and cattle. They thence called her the *Mountain-Mother.* While dwelling in the woods she formed a strict friendship with Marsyas, and had a love-affair with a youth named Attis. She was afterwards acknowledged by her parents; but her father, on discovering her intimacy with Attis, seized that unhappy youth and put him to death. Grief deprived Kybelé of her reason: with dishevelled locks she roamed, to the sound of the drums and pipes which she had invented, over various regions of the earth, even as far as the country of the Hyperboreans, teaching mankind agriculture: her companion was still the faithful Marsyas. Meantime a dreadful famine ravaged Phrygia: the oracle, on being consulted, directed that the body of Attis should be buried, and

---

[1] See Müller, *Dor.* i. 10. [2] Hérod. v. 102.
[3] See our note on Ovid's *Fasti,* iv. 276.

divine honours be paid to Kybelé. A stately temple was accordingly erected to her at Pessínus by king Midas.[1]

It is apparent from this account that Kybelé, Marsyas, and Attis were all ancient Phrygian deities. Marsyas, as we have seen, was a river-god; and Attis, whose name occurs frequently in the dynasties of the Lydian kings (who according to the usual practice were named after their god), was probably, like Adónis, a personification of the Sun, of whose union with Earth we have apparently another instance in Amphíón and Niobé. The Lydian legend of the birth of Attis is curious and significant.[2]

Like Asiatic worship in general, that of Kybelé was *enthusiastic*. Her priests, named Galli and Korybantes, ran about with dreadful cries and howlings, beating on timbrels, clashing cymbals, sounding pipes, and cutting their flesh with knives.[3] The box-tree and the cypress were considered sacred to her; as from the former she made the pipes, and Attis was said to have been changed into the latter.

We find from Pindar and the dramatists[4] that the worship and the mysteries of the Great mother were common in Greece, particularly at Athens, in their time.

The worship of Kybelé was introduced into Rome A.U.C. 547, when a solemn embassy was sent to Attalus king of Pergamos, to request the image at Pessínus which had fallen from heaven. The monarch readily yielded compliance, and the goddess was conveyed to Rome; where a stately temple was built to receive her, and a solemn festival named the Megalesia was celebrated every year in her honour.[5] As the Greeks had confounded her with Rhea, so the Latins made her one with their Ops, the goddess of the earth.[6]

In works of art Kybelé exhibits the matronly air and composed dignity which distinguish Héra and Démétér. Sometimes she is veiled, and seated on a throne with lions at her side; at other times riding in a chariot drawn by lions. Her head is always crowned with towers. She frequently beats on a drum, and bears a sceptre in her hand.

---

[1] Diodór. iii. 58, 59. He probably took his account of Kybelé from Dionýsios of Samos, not from Xanthos the Lydian, as Creuzer (*Symb*. ii. 46) supposes: see Lobeck, 640, *note*.   [2] Paus. vii. 17, 10.

[3] Lauer observes that there is always something gloomy and stern in those religions of which Earth is the chief object. This however is only very partially true of the Grecian worship of Démétér, and does not at all apply to the religion of ancient Italy.

[4] Pind. *Pyth*. iii. 78 (137) *cum Schol*. Eur. *Hip*. 144. *Bac*. 78. *Fr. Crétens*.

[5] Liv. xxix. 14. Ov. *Fast*. iv. 179 *seq*. with our notes.

[6] Lucret. ii. 598 *seq*. Verg. *Æn*. iii. 111; vi. 785; x. 252. Ov. *ut supra*. Id. *Trist*. ii. 24. Tibull. i. 4 68.

The name Kybelé is probably derived from the *cymbals* (κύμ-βος, κύμβαλα) used in her worship.

Κότυς ἠ Κοτυττὼ καὶ Βενδίς. (*Kotyttó et Bendis.*)

Kotys or Kotyttó was a goddess worshipped by the Thracians, whose kings were frequently named from her. She was apparently identical with the Phrygian Kybelé.[1] Her worship was introduced at Athens and at Corinth, where it was celebrated *in private* with great indecency and licentiousness.[2]

Bendis, another Thracian goddess, had some analogy with Artemis and Hekaté,[3] and she also was probably the same with Kybelé. Her worship was adopted at Athens; her temple named the Bendideion was in the Peiræeus,[4] and a festival named the Bendideia was celebrated in her honour.[5]

Ἄρτεμις ἐν Ἐφέσῳ. (*Diana Ephesia.*)

The Ephesian Artemis was another Asiatic goddess whose worship was adopted by the Greeks. From their confounding her with their own Artemis, it would seem that they regarded her as the Moon-goddess; though her attributes might lead to an identification of her with Kybelé.[6]

The most ancient statue of the Artemis of Ephesos was a black stone which had fallen from heaven,—an aërolite of course. Her subsequent ones were a sort of Pantheón, a compound of various attributes. She is covered with breasts and with the heads of animals, and stands an image either of the natural fecundity of the earth, or of that supposed to be induced by the influence of the moon.

Nothing can be clearer than that this goddess was originally distinct from the Artemis of the Greeks. Yet in after times we find them so completely identified, that the Ephesians in the reign of Tiberius maintained,[7] " that Apolló and Diana were not born in Délos, as was commonly supposed; but that the river Kenchrios and the grove Ortygia, where the travailing Latona, resting against an olive-tree which still existed, brought forth these deities, were with them." In like manner the people of Tegyra in Bœótia appropriated to themselves the birth of Apolló, calling a hill near his temple Délos, and two springs Palm and

---

[1] Strabo, x. 3, 16, p. 470.
[2] See Buttmann, *Mythol.* ii. 159 *seq.* Lobeck, 1007 *seq.* These writers have collected all the passages in the ancients relating to this subject.
[3] Palæph t. 32. Eudocia, 418. Hesych. *v.* δίλογος.
[4] Xen. *Hell.* ii. 4. [5] Plat. *Rep.* i. 354. [6] See Müller, *Dor.* i. 403.
[7] Tac. *Ann.* iii. 61: see also Strab. xiv. 1, 20, p. 639.

Olive; they also took to themselves the Delphian legends of Tityos and Pythón.[1] We even find the whole mythic cycle of Létó, Apolló, and Artemis, transferred to Egypt,—Létó becoming Butó, Apolló O'ros, and Artemis Bubastés, and an island in the Nile, said (for Hérodotos could not perceive it to move) to be a floating one, Délos.[2]

Ἶσις. Isis.

Isis was one of the chief deities of Egypt and spouse of Osíris. Her worship was introduced during the Alexandrian period into Greece, and afterwards into Rome. The Isiac mysteries were among the *secret* ones, and abounded in gross superstition, vile juggling, and scandalous indecency. As the goddess herself is by Hérodotos[3] identified with the Grecian Démétér, we are to suppose that she was one of those personifications of nature, or of the productive power of the earth, which we find among most ancient nations.

Egypt is once mentioned in the Ilias.[4] In the Odyssey,[5] Egypt, the Egyptians, and the river Ægyptos are spoken of; and from these passages we may perhaps collect, that the Greeks, particularly the Krétans, used in those times to make piratical incursions on that country. Hésiod[6] names the Nile.

"Homer's Egypt," says Zoega,[7] "seems to me to be altogether fabulous; it presents nothing local, nothing characteristic. His Egyptians are Greeks; the presents which they give to Menelaos are such as a Greek would have given; Egyptian antiquity knows nothing of tripods. The poet had merely picked up some obscure reports of a rich city, Thébes, an island, Pharos, and that the Egyptians were good physicians, and used a kind of opium. The historic circumstances of the voyage of Menelaos, his adventures there, etc., are fictions. Regarded from this point of view many difficulties vanish, and many fine systems fall to pieces. The land of Egypt no longer increases in extent a whole day's journey toward the north, Memphis is no longer founded after the destruction of Troy. The more ancient Greeks named the Delta Egypt, the rest Thébes, for which reason Memphis might very

---

[1] Plut. *Pelop.* 16.   [2] Hérod. ii. 155, 156.

[3] Hérod. ii. 156. Diodór. ι. 13, 14. Elsewhere Diodóros says (i. 11) that Osíris and Isis were Sun and Moon. Isis was also as the goddess of Saïs identified with Athéna, Plut. *de Is. et Os.* 9. Osíris was by some regarded as the Nile which fructified the land of Egypt, but we incline to think he was a being of a far higher order.   [4] *Il.* ix. 381.

[5] *Od.* iv. 351, 355, 477, 483 ; xiv. 246. 257 *seq.* ; xvii. 426 *seq.*

[6] *Theog.* 338. The passage, however, is probably an interpolation. See above, p. 46.   [7] Ap. Völck. *Hom. Geog.* 129.

well be the Thébes of Homer. This poet had no knowledge of the true site of Thébes."

From Hérodotos[1] we learn, that when (Ol. 27) the Egyptian prince Psammitichos was driven by his competitors for the throne to seek shelter in the marshes of the Delta, he was told by the oracle of Butó that brazen men from the sea would be his avengers. Shortly afterwards some Karians and Iónians, who were out a-pirating, were driven by stress of weather to Egypt, where they landed and began to plunder the country. As, after the Grecian fashion, they wore brass armour (a sight unusual to the Egyptians),[2] word was broight to Psammitichos that brazen men had landed and were plundering. Calling to mind the oracle, he sent to invite them to enter his service: they consented, and with their aid he made himself master of Egypt. He assigned them a settlement near the Pélusiac mouth of the Nile, whence their descendants were about eighty years afterwards removed to Memphis by Amasis to serve as his guards.[3] This monarch appointed the town named Naukratis, which he allowed the Greeks to build on the Kanóbic arm of the Nile, to be the emporium of the trade of Greece and Egypt, just as Canton used to be that of the trade between China and Europe. Vessels were allowed to enter that port alone; and if driven into any other by stress of weather, they were obliged to sail for it, or their cargoes, if the wind was still rough, were conveyed thither in barges round the Delta. Amasis, who was a great favourer of the Greeks, permitted them to erect altars and consecrate pieces of land (τεμένεα) to their national deities. These religious colonies extended far up the country, and we even find the Samians in one of the Oases.[4]

When the Iónians and Karians settled in Egypt, Psammitichos put some Egyptian children under their care, to be instructed in the Greek language; and, as everything in that country was regarded on the principle of castes, these and their descendants formed the caste of Interpreters, whom Hérodotos found there *two centuries* afterwards.[5] We may thus see at once how in a space of two hundred years, by means of these interpreters, and of the introduction of the worship of the Grecian deities, the artful priesthood of Egypt may have contrived to frame the system above noticed, of the derivation of the religion and civilisation of Greece from the land of the Nile.

From this digression we return to the gods of Greece.

[1] Hérod. ii. 152, 153. The historian asserts positively, that previous to this time the Greeks knew nothing certain about Egypt.
[2] Yet in the *Odyssey* (xiv. 268; xvii. 437 the Egyptians are armed in brass
[3] Hérod. ii. 154. [4] Id. iii. 26. [5] Id. ii. 154.

CHAPTER XVI.

RURAL DEITIES:—PAN, SATYRS, SILENOS, PRIAPOS, NYMPHS.

Πάν.   Pan.

THIS god is unnoticed by Homer and Hésiod, but according to one of the Homérids he was the son of Hermés by an Arkadian nymph.[1] Hermés, he says, smitten with love for the daughter of Dryops (*Woody*), abandoned Olympos and took service as a shepherd in Arkadia. He succeeded in gaining the heart of the 'well-tressed nymph,' and a child was the result of their secret interviews. But so monstrous was his appearance, that the nurse on beholding him fled away in affright. Hermés immediately caught him up, wrapped him carefully in a hare-skin, and carried him away to Olympos: then taking his seat with Zeus and the other gods, he produced his babe. All the gods, especially Dionýsos, were delighted with the little stranger; and they named him Pan (i.e. *All*), because he had charmed them *all*.

Others fabled that Pan was the son of Hermés by Pénelopé, whose love he gained under the form of a goat, as she was tending in her youth the flocks of her father on Mount Taÿgeton.[2] Some even went so far as to say that he was the offspring of the amours of Pénelopé with *all* her suitors.[3] According to Epimenidés,[4] Pan and Arkas were the children of Zeus and Kallistó. Aristippos made Pan the offspring of Zeus and the nymph Œnéis,[5] others again said he was a child of Heaven and Earth.[6] There was also a Pan said to be the son of Zeus and the nymph Thymbris or Hybris, the instructor of Apolló in divination.[7]

The worship of Pan seems to have been confined to Arkadia till the time of the battle of Marathón, when Pheidippidés, the courier who was sent from Athens to Sparta to call on the Spartans for aid against the Persians, declared that, as he was passing by Mount Parthenion near Tegea in Arkadia, he heard the voice of Pan calling to him, and desiring him to ask the Athenians why they paid no regard to him, who was always, and still would be, friendly and assisting to them. After the battle the Athenians consecrated a cave to Pan under the Akropolis, and offered him annual sacrifices.[8]

---

[1] Hom. *Hymn* xviii.
[2] Hérod. ii. 145.   Sch. *Theocr.* vii. 109.   Eudocia, 323.   Tzetz. *Lyc.* 772.
[3] Sch. *Theocr.* i. 3.   Eudocia, *l. c.*   Serv. *Æn.* ii. 44.
[4] Sch. *Theocr.* i. 3.   Eudocia, *l. c.*   [5] Id. *ib.*   [6] Sch. *Theocr.* vii. 123.
[7] Above, p. 110.   [8] Id. ibid. vi. 105.   Plut. *Arist.* 11.

Long before this time the Grecian and Egyptian systems of religion had begun to mingle and combine. The goat-formed Mendés of Egypt was now regarded as identical with the horned and goat-footed god of the Arkadian herdsmen;[1] and Pan was elevated to great dignity by priests and philosophers, becoming a symbol of the *universe*, for his name signified *all*. Further, as he dwelt in the woods, he was called *Lord of the Hyle* (ὁ τῆς ὕλης κύριος);[2] and as the word *hyle* (ὕλη) by a lucky ambiguity signified either *wood* or *primitive matter*, this was another ground for exalting him. It is amusing to read how all the attributes of the Arkadian god were made to accord with this notion. "Pan," says Servius,[3] "is a rustic god, formed in similitude of nature; whence he is called Pan, i.e. *All:* for he has horns in similitude of the rays of the sun and the horns of the moon: his face is ruddy, in imitation of the æther: he has a spotted fawn-skin on his breast, in likeness of the stars: his lower parts are shaggy, on account of the trees, shrubs, and wild beasts: he has goat's feet, to denote the stability of the earth: he has a pipe of seven reeds, on account of the harmony of the heaven, in which there are seven sounds: he has a crook, that is a curved staff, on account of the year, which runs back on itself, because he is the god of all nature. It is feigned by the poets, that he struggled with Love and was conquered by him, because, as we read, Love conquers all, *omnia vincit amor*."

In Arkadia, his native country, Pan appears never to have attained to such distinction. So late as the days of the Ptolemies, Theokritos[4] could thus allude to the treatment which he sometimes there experienced from his worshippers:

> And if thou do so, Pan beloved, may ne'er
> The Arkadian boys thy shoulders and thy sides
> Pelt with their squills when little meat is had;
> But if thou otherwise incline, may pain
> Seize thee when all thy skin is torn with nails,
> And in hot nettles may thou lie to rest:

which the scholiast tells us was the Arkadians' mode of treating the god when they were unsuccessful in hunting.[5]

---

[1] Hérod. ii. 46. [2] Macrob. *Sat.* i. 22.

[3] On *Verg. Buc.* ii. 31. See also Sch. *Theocr.* i. 3. Eudocia, 323.

[4] *Idyll.* vii. 106.

[5] The Samoyedes, when successful in hunting, smear their gods with fat; if unsuccessful, they beat them and throw them in the dung. Voss, *Myth. Br.* i. 84. Comp. Suet. *Calig.* 5, and Blunt's *Vestiges of Ancient Manners and Customs in Italy and Sicily*, pp. 125, 126. Sailors in the Mediterranean, during a storm, maltreat the image of St. James; and the Franconians, when the vintage failed, used to fling that of St. Urban into the brook or the mire. Grimm, *Deut. Mythol.* p. 443.

The Homérid already quoted, who is older than Pindar,[1] describes in a very pleasing manner the occupations of Pan. He is lord of all the hills and dales : sometimes he ranges along the tops of the mountains, sometimes pursues the game in the valleys, roams through the woods, floats along the streams, or drives his sheep into a cave, and there plays on his reeds music not to be excelled by that of the bird "who among the leaves of flower-full spring laments, pouring forth her moan, a sweet-sounding lay."

> And with him the clear-singing mountain-nymphs
> Move quick their feet, by the dark-watered spring
> In the soft mead, where crocus, hyacinths,
> Fragrant and blooming, mingle with the grass
> Confused, and sing, while echo peals around
> The mountain's top.

The god meanwhile moves his feet rapidly as he joins in the dance, with the skin of a lynx on his back, and delighted with the sweet song.

In after times the care of Pan was held to extend beyond the herds. We find him regarded as the guardian of the bees,[2] and, as the giver of success in fishing and fowling.[3] He is also represented as haunting the sea-shore.[4]

The god of herdsmen was not without his amours ; he is said to have captivated the goddess of the night, Seléné, under the form of a white ram.[5] He was fortunate in an amour with the nymph E'chó, by whom he had a daughter named Iambé ;[6] but he could not gain the love of Syrinx, another of the nymphs. Syrinx was a Naïs of Nonakris in Arkadia, and devoted to the service of Artemis. As she was returning one day from the chase, and passed by Mount Lykæon, Pan beheld her and loved ; but when he would address her, she fled. The god pursued : she reached the river Ladón, and unable to cross it implored the aid of her sister-nymphs ; and when Pan thought to grasp the object of his pursuit, he found his arms filled with reeds. While he stood sighing at his disappointment, the wind began to agitate the reeds, and produced a low musical sound. The god took the hint, cut seven of the reeds, and formed from them his *syrinx* (σύριγξ) or pastoral pipe.[7] Another of his loves was the nymph Pitys, who was also

---

[1] Voss. *ut sup.*

[2] Μελισσοσόος, Anthol. ix. 226.

[3] *Ib.* vii. 11–14, 179–187.

[4] Æsch. *Pers.* 449. Theocr. v. 14.

[5] See above, p. 55. There was a cave in Arkadia sacred to the Moon and Pan Lykæos. Phorphyr. *de Antr. Nymph.*

[6] Luc. *Dial. Deor.* 22. Et. Mag. *v.* 'Ιάμβη.

[7] Ov. *Met.* i. 690 *seq.* This legend does not occur elsewhere. In the very ancient song of Deborah (*Judges* v. 16) we meet with the word *Sheriqoth* (שְׁרִקוֹת) used of pastoral music. It is therefore not unlikely that the *syrinx* and its name came to Greece from the East.

loved by Boreas. The nymph favoured more the god of Arkadia, and the wind-god in a fit of jealousy blew her down from the summit of a lofty rock. A tree of her own name ($\pi i \tau v s$, *pine*) sprang up where she died, and it became the favourite plant of Pan.[1]

What are called *Panic terrors* were ascribed to Pan; for loud noises, whose cause could not easily be traced, were not unfrequently heard in mountainous regions; and the gloom and loneliness of forests and mountains fill the mind with a secret horror, and dispose it to superstitious apprehensions; hence perhaps it is, that madness was believed to be the consequence of encountering the rural deities.

The ancients had two modes of representing Pan. The first, according to the description already given, as horned and goat-footed, with a wrinkled face and a flat nose.[2] But the artists sought to soften the idea of the god of shepherds, and they portrayed him as a young man hardened by the toils of a country life. Short horns sprout on his forehead, to characterize him; he bears his crook and his syrinx; and he is either naked, or clad in the light cloak called *chlamys*.[3]

Like many other gods who were originally single, Pan was multiplied in course of time, and we meet with Pans in the plural.[4]

Pan was called,[5] 1. *Goat-footed*; 2. *Noise-loving*; 3. *Dance-loving*; 4. *Bright-locked*; 5. *Cave-dwelling*; 6. *Sea-roaming*.

The name Pan ($\Pi \grave{a} v$) is probably nothing more than the contraction of $\pi \acute{a} \omega v$, *feeder* or *owner*,[6] and may have been in its origin only an epithet of Hermés. Buttmann connects Pan with Apolló-Nomios, deeming his name to be the contraction of Pæan;[7] while Welcker says it was the Arkadian form of $\Phi \acute{a} \omega v$, $\Phi \grave{a} v$, apparently regarding him as the sun.[8]

---

[1] Nonn. xlii. 259 *seq.* Luc. *ut sup.* Geopon. xi. 4 : see Brouk. *on Propert.* i. 18, 20.　　[2] See Luc. *Bakchos*, 2.　　[3] See Sil. Ital. xiii. 326 *seq.*

[4] Plató, *Laws*, vii. 815. Aristoph. *Eccles.* 1089. Moschos, iii. 22. Anthol. i. 108.

[5] 1. $a i \gamma \iota \pi \acute{o} \delta \eta s$: 2. $\phi \iota \lambda \acute{o} \kappa \rho o \tau o s$: 3. $\phi \iota \lambda \acute{o} \chi o \rho o s$: 4. $\grave{a} \gamma \lambda a \acute{\epsilon} \theta \epsilon \iota \rho o s$: 5. $\grave{a} \nu \tau \rho o$-$\delta a \iota \tau o s$: 6. $\grave{a} \lambda \acute{\iota} \pi \lambda a \gamma \kappa \tau o s$.

[6] " $T \grave{a} \nu$ for $\tau \acute{a} \omega \nu$, from $\tau \acute{a} \omega$, whence imper. $\tau \hat{\eta}$: so $\Pi \grave{a} \nu$, $\Pi a \iota \grave{a} \nu$, $\Ersigma \rho \mu \grave{a} \nu$, $\nu \epsilon \grave{a} \nu$, $\xi \nu \nu \grave{a} \nu$, $\mu \epsilon \gamma \iota \sigma \tau \acute{a} \nu$." Schneider on Soph. *Œd. Tyr.* p. 138.

[7] Mythol. i. 169. He refers to Alkmáón, Alkmán; Amytháón, Amyth'n.

[8] *Kret. Kol.* 45, *note:* see also Schwenk, 213. Pan was among the light-deities of Athens (above, p. 141), but, as it was late when his worship came thither, the later derivations of his name may have been regarded as the true ones.

Σάτυροι. *Satyri.* 𝕾𝖆𝖙𝖞𝖗𝖘.

Hésiod[1] is the first who mentions the Satyrs; he says that they, the Kurétes and the mountain-nymphs, were the offspring of the five daughters whom the daughter of Phoróneus bore to Hekatæos, i.e. probably Apolló.

The Lakonian term for a Satyr was Tityros,[2] which also signified the buck-goat or the ram[3] that led the flock; Æschylos calls a Satyr *Buck-goat* (τράγος).[4] In all views of the Satyrs they appear to be a rough, shaggy kind of beings.

The Satyrs were associated with Dionýsos, and they formed the chorus of the species of drama named from them. It is not unlikely then that they are indebted for their deification to the festivals of that god, and that they were originally nothing more than the rustics who formed the chorus, and danced at them in their goat-skin dresses.[5] Their name may be merely the reduplication of θήρ.[6]

Σειληνύς, Σιληνός. *Silenus.*

Hermés and the Silens 'mingle in love' with the nymphs in pleasing caverns, according to a Homérid,[7] and Pindar[8] calls Silénos the Naïs' husband; the Kentaur Pholos was the son of Silénos by the nymph Melia.[9] Sókratés used to compare himself, on account of his wisdom, his baldness, and his fiat nose, to the Silens born of the divine Naïdes.[10] Others said that Silénos was a son of Earth, and sprung from the blood-drops of Uranos.[11] Marsyas is called a Silén.[12] Like the sea-gods, Silénos was noted for wisdom.

It would therefore appear that a Silén was simply a river-god;[13] and the name probably comes from ἴλλω, εἴλω, to *roll,* expressive of the motion of the streams.[14] The connection between Silénos

[1] Fr. 94.
[2] Sch. *Theocr.* iii. 2; vii. 72. Eustath. *Il.* xviii. p. 1214. Ælian, *Var. Hist.* iii. 40. Τίτυρος is apparently the Doric form of Σάτυρος. The Satyrs and Tityrs, however, are spoken of as distinct classes. Strab. x. 3, 7, 10, p. 466.
[3] Sch. *Theocr.* iii. 2. Serv. *Buc.* i. 1.   [4] Fr. *ap.* Plut. *De Cap.* etc. 2.
[5] Welcker, *Nach. zur Tril.* 211 *seq.* See above, p. 70, *note* 8.
[6] Euripidés (*Kyk.* 624) calls them θῆρες; the Ionians named them φῆρες: see Voss, *Myth. Br.* ii. 291.
[7] *Hymn* iv. 262.   [8] *Fr. Dith.* 15.   [9] Apollod. ii. 5, 4.
[10] Xen. *Symp.* v. 7 : see also Ælian, *Var. Hist.* iii. 18.
[11] Serv. *Buc.* vi. 13. Nonn. xiv. 97; xxix. 262.   [12] Above, p. 110.
[13] See Nonn. xix. 285 *seq.* 343; xxiii. 160 *seq.* Diodór. iii. 72. The blood-drops of Uranos would then be the rains.
[14] In Latin *silanus* is a stream or spout of water. Festus *v.* Tullios. Thus "Corpora *silanos* ad aquarum strata jacebant," Lucret. vi. 1263. "Cum eduxisset fuscinam, tres *silani* sunt secuti," Hygin. 169. "Confert aliquid ad somnum *silanus* juxta cadens" Ceisus, ii. 19.

and Dionýsos and the Naïdes thus becomes easy of explanation, all being deities relating to moisture.

Midas, king of the Brygians in Macedonia, had at the foot of Mount Bermion a garden, in which grew spontaneously roses with sixty petals, and of extraordinary fragrance.[1] To this garden Silénos was in the habit of repairing; and Midas,[2] or his people, by pouring wine into the fount from which he was wont to drink, intoxicated him, and he was thus captured.[3] Midas put various questions to him respecting the origin of things, and the events of past times.[4] One was, What is best for men? Silénos was long silent; at length, when he was constrained to answer, he said, "Ephemeral seed of a toilsome fate and hard fortune, why do ye oblige me to tell what it were better for you not to know? Life is most free from pain when one is ignorant of future evils. It is best of all for man not to be born . . . . . . the second is, for those who are born to die as soon as possible.[5]" He also, it is said,[6] gave the king a long account of an immense country which lay without the Ocean-stream, the people of which once invaded the land of the Hyperboreans.

According to another version of this legend,[7] as Dionýsos was in Lydia on his return from the conquest of the East, some of the country people met Silénos staggering about, and binding him with his own garlands, led him to their king. Midas entertained him for ten days, and then conducted him to his foster-son, who, in his gratitude, desired the king to ask what gift he would. Midas craved that all he touched might turn to gold. His wish was granted; but when he found his very food converted to precious metal, and himself on the point of starving in the midst of wealth, he prayed the god to resume his fatal gift. Dionýsos directed him to bathe in the Paktólos, and hence that river became auriferous.[8]

Silénos was represented as old, bald, and flat-nosed, riding on a hollow-backed ass, usually intoxicated, and carrying his can (*cantharus*), or tottering along supported by his staff of fennel (*ferula*).[9]

Πρίαπος. *Priapus.*

This god was introduced late into Grecian mythology.[10] He was a rural deity, worshipped by the people of Lampsakos, a city on the

---

[1] Hérod. viii. 138.
[2] Paus. 1. 4, 5.
[3] Hérod. *ut supra.* Xen. *Anab.* i. 2. Conon, 1.
[4] Serv. *Buc.* vi. 13.
[5] Aristot. *De Anima.* Plut. *Consol. ad Apoll.* Op. vii. p. 352, edit. Hutten.
[6] Theopomp. *ap.* Ælian. *Var. Hist.* iii. 18.
[7] Ov. *Met.* xi. 85 *seq.* Hygin. 191. Serv. *Æn.* x. 142. Max. Tyr. 30.
[8] Compare the story of Pythés and his wife in Plut. *De. Mul. Virt. ad fin.*
[9] On the subject of Silénos see Welcker, *Nach. zur Tril.* 214 *seq.*
[10] S rat. xiii 1, 12, p. 587.

Hellespont famous for its vineyards. Priápos was not—as is supposed, from the employment usually assigned him by the Romans after they had adopted his worship—merely the god of gardens, but of fruitfulness in general. "This god," says Pausanias,[1] "is honoured elsewhere by those who keep sheep and goats, or stocks of bees; but the Lampsakenes regard him more than any of the gods, calling him the son of Dionýsos and Aphrodíté." In Theokritos,[2] the shepherds set his statue with those of the Nymphs at a shady fountain, and a shepherd prays to him, promising sacrifices if he will free him from love; and by Vergil[3] bees are placed under his care. Fishermen also made offerings to him as the deity presiding over the fisheries;[4] and in the Anthology[5] Priápos (*Of-the-Haven*) (λιμενίτας) is introduced, giving a pleasing description of the spring, and inviting the mariners to put to sea. The Priaps (for Priápos also was multiplied) are enumerated by Moschos[6] among the rural deities:

> And Satyrs wailed and sable-cloaked Priaps;
> And Pans sighed after thy sweet melody.

It was fabled[7] that Priápos was the son of Aphrodíté by Dionýsos, whom she met on his return from his Indian expedition at the Lampsakene town Aparnis. Owing to the malignity of Héra, he was born so deformed that his mother was horrified, and *renounced* (ἀπαρνεῖτο) him, whence the place derived its name. Others said[8] that he was the son of Dionýsos by Chioné, or a Naïs; others,[9] that he had a *long-eared father,*—Pan or a Satyr perhaps, or it may be his own sacred beast the ass;[10] finally there were those who gave him Hermés[11] or Adónis,[12] or even Zeus himself for a sire.[13] In reality he is only an epithet of Dionýsos, expressive of the noise and riot of the orgies of that god in Thrace and Phrygia.[14]

Priápos, like the other rural gods, is of a ruddy complexion. His cloak is filled with all kinds of fruits; he has a sithe in his hand, and usually a horn of plenty. He is rarely without his indecent symbol of productiveness.

[1] Paus. ix. 31.
[2] Theocr. *Idyll.* i. 21. *Epigr.* iv.
[3] *Geor.* iv. 110.
[4] Anthol. vi. 33, 190, 192.
[5] *Ib.* x. 1–9.
[6] *Idyll.* iii. 27.
[7] Sch. *Apoll. Rh.* i. 932.
[8] Sch. *Theocr.* i. 21.
[9] Afranius *ap. Macrob. Sat.* vi. 5.
[10] Ov. *Fast.* i. 391; vi. 345.
[11] Hygin. 160.
[12] Eudocia, 24. Sch. *Apoll. Rh. ut sup.* Tzetz. *Lyc.* 831.
[13] Eudocia, 345.
[14] See Athén. i. p. 30. Priápos is i. q. Briápos, from βρι ἀπύω, *to shout aloud.* Homer (*Il.* xiii. 251) terms Ares βριήπυος.

Νύμφαι. *Nymphæ.* Nymphs.

The imagination of the Greeks peopled all the regions of earth and water with beautiful female forms called Nymphs, divided into various orders, according to the place of their abode. Thus[1] 1. the Mountain-nymphs (*Oreiades*) haunted the mountains; 2. the Dale-nymphs (*Napœœ*), the valleys; 3. the Mead-nymphs (*Leimoniades*), the meadows; 4. the Water-nymphs (*Naïdes, Naïades*), the rivers, brooks, and springs; 5. the Lake-nymphs (*Limniades*), the lakes and pools. There were also, 6. the Tree-nymphs (*Hamadryades*), who were born and died with the trees; 7. the Wood-nymphs in general (*Dryades*);[2] and 8. the Fruit-tree-nymphs or Flock-nymphs (*Méliades*),[3] who watched over gardens or flocks of sheep.

The Nymphs occur in various relations to gods and men. Their amours, of which we have seen some instances, were numerous. The charge of rearing various gods and heroes was committed to them: they were, for instance, the nurses of Dionýsos, Pan, and even Zeus himself; and they also brought up Aristæos and Æneias. They were moreover the attendants of the goddesses; they waited on Héra and Aphrodíté, and in huntress-attire pursued the deer over the mountains in the company of Artemis.

In the Fairy Mythology,[4] a work, for which, as our first effort in this department of literature, and which recalls the memory of many agreeable hours, we certainly feel a partiality, we thus expressed ourselves on the subject of the Nymphs:

"In the Homéric poems, the most ancient portion of Grecian literature, we meet the various classes of Nymphs. In the Odyssey, they are the attendants of Kalypsó, herself a goddess and a nymph. Of the female attendants of Kirké, the potent daughter of Hélios, also designated as a goddess and a nymph, it is said,

> They spring from fountains and from sacred groves,
> And holy streams that flow into the sea.[5]

Yet these Nymphs are of divine nature; and when Zeus, the father of the gods, calls together his council,

---

[1] 1. ὀρειάδες: 2. ναπαῖαι: 3. λειμωνιάδες: 4. ναῖδες, ναϊάδες: 5. λιμνιάδες: 6. ἁμαδρυάδες: 7. δρυάδες: 8. μηλιάδες.

[2] It is plain that δρῦς and the Germanic *tree* are the same word. Οἱ γὰρ ἀρχαῖοι πᾶν δένδρον δρῦν ἐκάλουν. Sch. *Aristoph. Knights*, 672. Δρῦς has apparently this signification *Il.* xxii. 126; xxiii. 118. *Od.* xix. 163. Hérod. vii. 218. Soph. *Trach.* 768. In Nonnos δρῦς is constantly *tree*, and δρυόεις, *wooden.* See *Tales and Popular Fictions*, p. 70.

[3] Μῆλον is *an apple* or *a sheep.*   [4] ii. 224 *seq.*; p. 444, new edit.

[5] *Od.* x. 350.

P

> None of the streams, save Ocean, stayed away,
> Nor of the Nymphs, who dwell in beauteous groves,
> And springs of streams, and verdant grassy slades.[1]

The good Eumæos prays to the Nymphs to speed the return of his master, reminding them of the numerous sacrifices which Odysseus had offered to them. In another part of the poem[2] their sacred cave is thus described :

> But at the harbour's head a long-leafed olive
> Grows, and near to it lies a lovely cave,
> Dusky and sacred to the Nymphs, whom men
> Call Naiades. In it large craters lie,
> And two-eared pitchers, all of stone ; and there
> Bees build their combs. In it, too, are long looms
> Of stone, and there the Nymphs do weave their robes,
> Sea-purple, wondrous to behold. Aye-flowing
> Waters are there. Two entrances it hath ;
> That to the north is pervious unto men ;
> That to the south more sacred is, and there
> Men enter not, but 'tis the Immortals' path.

Yet though thus exalted in rank, the Homéric Nymphs frequently 'blessed the bed' of heroes; and many a warrior who fought before Troy could boast descent from a Naïs or a Néréis.

"One of the most interesting species of Nymphs are the Hamadryades, those personifications of the vegetable life of plants. In the Homéridian hymn to Aphrodíté, we find the following full and accurate description of them. Aphrodíté, when she informs Anchíses of her pregnancy, and her shame to have it known among the gods, says of the child,[4]—

> But him, when first he sees the sun's clear light,
> The Nymphs shall rear, the mountain-haunting Nymphs,
> Deep-bosomed, who on this mountain great
> And holy dwell, who neither goddesses
> Nor women are.[5] Their life is long ; they eat

---

[1] *Il.* xx. 7. We believe there is no word in the English language which so nearly expresses the Greek πίσεα as this old, now provincial, term. The Anglo-Saxon ꝼlæꝺ is certainly a valley ; all the spots denominated *slades* that we have seen were rich, grassy, irriguous, but somewhat depressed lands. Mr. Tod says that Lye gives in his Anglo-Saxon Dictionary the Icelandic *Slaed.* Certainly not in the copy which we consulted. *Slett*, by the way, is the Icelandic word and it signifies *a plain.* *Slade* is frequently employed in the Poly-Olbion of Drayton ; ex. gr. :

> Through the *slades* where beauteous Severn plays.

[2] *Od.* xiii. 102.   [3] See Kallim. *Hymn* iv. 83 *seq.*   [4] *v.* 256 *seq.*
[5] αἳ ῥ' οὔτε θνητῆς οὔτ' ἀθανάτοισιν ἕπονται. This passage is very obscure but we think the above is the sense of it. Hermann, we observe, has rendered in the same manner. Ilgen regards the whole as an interpolation, taken perhaps from some theogony.

Ambrosial food, and with the Deathless frame
The beauteous dance. With them in the recess
Of lovely caves, well-spying Argos-slayer
And the Sileni mix in love. Straight pines
Or oaks high-headed spring with them upon
The earth man-feeding, soon as they are born;
Trees fair and flourishing; on the high hills
Lofty they stand; the Deathless' sacred grove
Men call them, and with iron never cut.
But when the fate of death is drawing near,
First wither on the earth the beauteous trees,
The bark around them wastes, the branches fall,
And the Nymph's soul at the same moment leaves
The sun's fair light.

"They possessed power to reward and punish those who pro-
onged or abridged the existence of their associate-tree. In the
Argonautics of Apollonios Rhodios, Phineus thus explains to the
heroes the cause of the poverty of Peræbios: [1]

But he was paying the penalty laid on
His father's crime; for one time, cutting trees
Alone among the hills, he spurned the prayer
Of the Hamadryas Nymph, who, weeping sore,
With earnest words besought him not to cut
The trunk of an oak-tree, which, with herself
Coeval, had endured for many a year.
But, in the pride of youth, he foolishly
Cut it; and to him and his race the Nymph
Gave ever after a lot profitless.

"The scholiast gives on this passage the following tale from
Charón of Lampsakos:

"A man, named Rhœkos, happening to see an oak just ready to
fall to the ground, ordered his slaves to prop it up. The Nymph,
who had been on the point of perishing with the tree, came to him
and expressed her gratitude to him for having saved her life, and
at the same time desired him to ask what reward he would.
Rhœkos then requested her to permit him to be her lover, and the
Nymph acceded to his desire. She at the same time charged him
strictly to avoid the society of every other woman, and told him
that a bee should be her messenger. One time the bee happened
to come to Rhœkos as he was playing at draughts, and he made a
rough reply. This so incensed the Nymph that she deprived him
of sight.

"Similar was the fate of the Sicilian Daphnis. A Naïs loved
him, and forbade him to hold intercourse with any other woman
under pain of loss of sight. Long he abstained, though tempted

---

[1] *Argonautica*, ii. 475 *seq.*

by the fairest maids of Sicily. At length a princess contrived to intoxicate him: he broke his vow and the threatened penalty was inflicted.[1]"

The nymph E′chó ('Hχώ, *resounder*) had been, as we have seen, beloved by the god Pan. She was also, we are assured, of a most accommodating disposition to Zeus; and while he was engaged in his pranks with the other nymphs, E′chó, being of a very loquacious character, used to keep Héra in chat till the nymphs had time to make their escape. When Héra discovered the artifice, she declared by way of punishment, that in future she should have but little use of her tongue; and immediately she lost all power of doing any more than repeat the sounds which she heard. E′chó happening to see the beautiful youth Narkissos, the son of the river-god Képhissos by the nymph Leiriopé,[2] as he was hunting, became deeply enamoured of him. She followed his steps everywhere, but was long unable to accost him. At length

> It happed the youth was from his faithful band
> Of comrades parted, and he called aloud,
> *Is any here?* and Echo answered, *Here.*
> Amazed, on every side he turns his view,
> And in loud tones cries, *Come;* and Echo calls
> The caller. Back he looks, and no one yet
> Approaching, cries, *Why fliest thou?* and receives
> As many words in answer. By the sound
> Of the alternate voice deceived, he still
> Persists, and says, *Let us meet here;* and, ne'er
> To sound more grateful answering, Echo cried,
> *Let us meet here,* and issued from the wood.

But at the sight of her the youth fled. Vexed at the ill-success of her advances, and ashamed to appear, she henceforth lurked in solitary caverns, and her love wore her away till nothing remained but her voice and bones. The former still remains, and may be heard among the hills; the latter were turned to stone. Narkissos however, suffered the penalty of his hard-heartedness to her and other nymphs and maidens; for seeing his own figure in a clear spring, he became enamoured of it, and pined away till he was converted into the flower which bears his name.[3]

These we may see are fables invented, in the usual manner,

---

[1] Sch. *Theocr.* i. 66; viii. 93. Serv. *Buc.* v. 20. Parthen. *Erot.* 2 Ælian, *Var. Hist.* x. 18. Diodór. iv. 87. Ovid. (*Met.* iv. 276) says she turned him into a rock.

[2] i. e. *Lilyish, of lilies,* like λείρινος; see above, p. 15. It evidently refers Narkissos' name.

[3] Ov. *Met.* iii. 341 *seq.* Paus. ix. 31, 7, 8. Conón, 24. Eudocia, 3 Hygin. 271.

account for the origin of the echo and the narcissus. That of the former was everywhere regarded as being animated. Thus the Scandinavians named it Dvergamál, saying that it was the voice of the Dwarfs; the original natives of the West-Indies regarded the echoes as the voices of the departed, who still dwelt in the woods and mountains; [1] the same is the theory at the present day in China. [2] In the French province of Auvergne the echo is called La Filleta Muda, [3] and its name in Irish is Mac-alla, i. e. Son-of-the-Rock. [4] The narcissus grows abundantly about Mount Helikón, the scene of Narkissos' transformation. Its name in Arabic and Persian, *Nirkis, Nirgis*, would seem to prove the ordinary derivation from ναρκέω to be wrong. It was sacred to Déméter and the Koré. [5]

It was fabled, that in the early ages of Southern Italy, when the people there were in the pastoral state, the Epimelian- or Flock-nymphs were once seen dancing at a place called the Sacred Rocks in Messapia. The young shepherds quitted their flocks to gaze on them; and, ignorant of their quality, declared that they could dance better themselves. The nymphs were offended, and after a long dispute the shepherds began to contend with them. The motions of the rustics were of course awkward and ungraceful, those of the nymphs light and elegant, as became goddesses. The former were vanquished; and the nymphs cried out to them, " O youths, you have been contending with the Epimelian nymphs! you shall therefore be punished." The shepherds instantly became trees where they stood, at the temple of the nymphs; and to this day, says Nikander, a voice as of lamentation is heard at night to issue from the grove. The place is called that of the Nymphs and the Youths. [6]

Dryops, the son of the river Spercheios, who dwelt at Mount Œta, had a daughter named after himself, Dryopé. She fed the flocks of her father, and the Hamadryades, conceiving a strong affection for her, made her their schoolfellow and taught her to

---

[1] Peter Martyr in Irving's *Life of Columbus*.

[2] " The Chinese have strange prejudices and opinions about this place. They told me that the spirits of men after death often chose to dwell amidst this wild and beautiful scenery; and they said it was they that now repeated these sounds and echoed them from hill to hill."—Fortune, *Journey to the Tea-countries of China*, p. 65.

[3] Miss Costello, from whose Tour in Auvergne we have derived our knowledge of La Filleta Muda, renders it The Fickle or Changeable Maid. But as Muda is *mute* or *silent* in Provençal, we are inclined to think that the meaning is the Silent Maid, i. e. she who never speaks till she is spoken to.

[4] Euripidés (*Hec.* 1110) calls the echo ἥσυχος πέτρας ὀρείας παῖς.

[5] Soph. *Œd. Col.* 682.　　[6] Nikand. *ap. Ant. Lib.* 31. Ov. *Met.* xiv. 514.

dance and sing hymns to the gods. Apolló beheld her dancing with them, and fell in love with her. He changed himself into a tortoise, with which they began to play and amuse themselves. Dryopé placing it in her bosom, the god changed himself into a serpent : the nymphs fled in affright, and he gained his object. The maid returned home, and shortly afterwards married Andræmón the son of Mylos. Her son by Apolló was named Amphissos, who founded at the foot of Œta a town of the same name, and ruled over the whole of that part of the country. He built a temple to his sire; at which when Dryopé appeared one day, the Hamadryades carried her away and concealed her in the wood. In her stead they caused a poplar to grow up, and a spring of water to gush out beside it. The nymphs communicated their own nature to Dryopé ; and her son Amphissos out of gratitude raised them a temple, and instituted games, at which no woman was permitted to be present; because when Dryopé was taken away, two maidens who were present informed the people of it, and the incensed nymphs turned them both into fir-trees.[1]

Terambos, who dwelt at the foot of Mount Othrys, abounded in flocks, which he himself fed on the mountains. The nymphs assisted him, for they were charmed with his singing and his music, in which he excelled all the men of his time, being the inventor of the lyre and the shepherd's pipe, and they often danced to his melody. Pan also loved him, and one time warned him to drive his flocks down into the plain, as a most terrific winter was coming on : but Terambos, elate with youth and confidence, despised the admonition of the friendly deity, and even mocked at and ridiculed the gentle amiable nymphs, saying that they were not the children of Zeus at all, but of Deinó daughter of the Spercheios, and that Poseidón had once when in love with one of them turned the rest into poplars, and kept them in that form as long as he thought proper. Soon however the presage of Pan proved true : the winter came on ; all the streams and torrents were frozen, the snow fell in great quantities, and the flocks of Terambos vanished along with the paths and the trees. The nymphs then changed Terambos himself into the animal called by the Thessalians *kerambyx* (κεράμβυξ), or cockchafer, ' of which the boys make a plaything and cutting off the head carry it about; and the head with the horns is like the lyre made from the tortoise.[2] '

[1] Nikand. *ap. Ant. Lib.* 32.   Ov. *Met.* viii. 330.
[2] Nikander, *ap. Ant. Lib.* 22.   Ovid, *Met.* vii. 354.   We need hardly observe that the legend was invented to account for the origin of the cockchafer. Ovid (*ut sup.*) tells of Kerambus that at the time of Deukalión's flood he sustained himself in the air with wings furnished by the nymphs, and thus escaped.

The word Nymph (νύμφη) seems to have originally signified *bride*, and was probably derived from a verb ΝΥΒΩ, *to cover* or *veil*.[1] It was gradually applied to married[2] or marriageable *young* women, for the idea of youth was always included. It is in this last sense that the goddesses of whom we treat were called Nymphs.[3]

CHAPTER XVII.

WATER-DEITIES:—OKEANIDES, NEREUS, NEREÏDES, PHOR-KYS, TRITON, PROTEUS, GLAUKOS, LEUKOTHEA AND PALÆMON, RIVER-GODS.

Ὠκεανίδες, Ὠκεανῖναι. *Oceanidæ.* Ocean-nymphs.

THE Ocean-nymphs, three thousand in number, were daughters of O'keanos and Téthys, and sisters of the rivers. Their office was to rear the children of men. From their names they appear to be personifications of the various qualities and appearances of the water of the Ocean-stream.[4]

Νηρεύς. *Nereus.*

Néreus, though not mentioned by name in Homer, is frequently alluded to under the title of the *Sea-elder* (ἅλιος γέρων), and his daughters are called Néréides. According to Hesiod[5] he was the son of Pontos and Earth, and was distinguished for his knowledge and his love of truth and justice, whence he was termed an *elder*:[6] the gift of prophecy was also assigned him. When Héraklés was in quest of the apples of the Hesperides, he was directed by the nymphs to Néreus. He found the god asleep, and seized him; Néreus on awaking changed himself into a variety of forms, but in vain: he was obliged to instruct him how to proceed before the hero would release him.[7] He also, if we may credit a Latin poet,[8]

---

[1] Akin to the Latin *nubo* and *nubes.*

[2] *Il.* iii. 130. *Od.* iv. 743. In this last place it is used of Pénelopé, who was not very young; but it is the *old nurse* who speaks.

[3] For beings of other mythologies answering to the Grecian Nymphs, see *Fairy Mythology, passim.*

[4] See Hés. *Theog.* 346 *seq.* Göttling *in loc.*   [5] *Theog.* 233.

[6]
καλέουσι γέροντα
οὕνεκα νημερτής τε καὶ ἤπιος οὐδὲ θεμιστέων
λήθεται ἀλλὰ δίκαια καὶ ἤπια δήνια οἶδε.   Hés. Theog. 234.

[7] Apoilod. ii. 5. See our notes on Milton, *Par. Lost,* iii. 603.

[8] Hor. *Carm.* i. 15, imitating Bakchylidés, in whom the woes were announced by Kassandra : see Porphyr. *in loco*

foretold to Paris, when he was carrying away Helené, the evils he would bring on his country and family.

Néreus was married to Dóris, one of the Ocean-nymphs, and by her he had the nymphs named Néréides.[1]

Νηρηΐδες.   Nereides.

The Néréides, or nymphs of the sea, were fifty in number; but the mythologists do not agree exactly in the names which they put into the catalogue. The best known of them are, Amphitríté the wife of Poseidón, Thetis the mother of Achilleus, and Galateia, who was loved by the Kyklóps Polyphémos.

The sea-nymphs, like all the other female deities, were originally conceived to be of a beautiful form, with skin of a delicate whiteness and long flowing hair. A constant epithet of Thetis is silver-footed (ἀργυροπέζα); and it was for venturing to compare herself in beauty with the Néréides, that Kassiopé brought such misfortune on her daughter Andromeda. But the painters and sculptors who contributed so much to degrade the other deities, robbed the sea-nymphs also of their charms by bestowing on them green hair, and turning their lower parts into those of a fish; thus giving them a form exactly corresponding with the modern idea of a mermaid.

The individual names of the Néréides are significatory of the qualities and phænomena of the sea. According to Hermann they are personifications of the waves, and Scandinavian mythologists give the same explanation of the nine daughters of Niordr, the Eddaic god of the sea.

Φόρκυς, Φόρκος.   Phorkys.

Phorkys is called by Homer a Ruler (μέδων) of the Sea and a Sea-elder. His daughter Thoósa was by Poseidón the mother of the Kyklóps Polyphémos.[2] A harbour in Ithaka[3] is said to belong to him.

Hésiod[4] makes him a son of Pontos and Earth, and father by Kétó of the Grææ, the Gorgons, the Echidna, and the serpent which watched the golden apples.[5] The Sirens were also said to be his daughters.[6]

---

[1] Hermann (*Opusc.* ii. 178) renders Néreus *Nefluus* (νη ρεῖν), and understands by it the bottom of the sea; it rather comes from νάω, *to flow*: see above, p. 15.   [2] *Od.* i. 71.   [3] *Od.* xiii. 96.   [4] *Theog.* 270 *seq.*

[5] Hermann (*ut sup.*) renders Phorkys *Furcus*, and makes him to signify the rocks and cliffs. We feel disposed to derive his name from φέρω (see p. 15), indicative of the sway and motion of the sea. He would thus be the appropriate sire of the Grææ and Gorgons. He had, we see, a daughter named Thoósa (Θοώσα), i. e. *Impetuous*. Kétó (κεῖμαι), Hermann says, is the sunken rocks.

[6] Soph. *ap. Plut. Sympos.* ix. 14.

Τρίτων. Tritón.

According to Hésiod,[1] Tritón was a son of Poseidón and Amphitríté, who, 'keeping to the bottom of the sea, dwelt with his mother and royal father in a golden house.' Later poets made him his father's trumpeter. He was also multiplied, and we read of Tritons in the plural number.

Like the Néréides, the Tritons were degraded to the fish-form. Pausanias[2] tells us that the women of Tanagra in Bœótia, going into the sea to purify themselves for the orgies of Bakchos, were, while there, assailed by Tritón; but on praying to their god, he vanquished their persecutor. Others, he adds, said that Tritón used to carry off the cattle which were driven down to the sea, and to seize all small vessels; till the Tanagrians placing bowls of wine on the shore, he drank of them, and becoming intoxicated threw himself down on the shore to sleep; where as he lay, a Tanagrian cut off his head with an axe. He relates these legends to account for the statue of Tritón at Tanagra being headless. He then subjoins,—

"I have seen another Tritón among the curiosities of the Romans, but it is not so large as this of the Tanagrians. The form of the Tritons is this:—the hair of their head resembles the parsley that grows in marshes, both in colour and in the perfect likeness of one hair to another, so that no difference can be perceived among them: the rest of their body is rough with small scales, and is of about the same hardness as the skin of a fish: they have fish-gills under their ears: their nostrils are those of a man, but their teeth are broader, and like those of a wild beast: their eyes seem to me azure; and their hands, fingers and nails are of the form of the shells of shell-fish: they have, instead of feet, fins under their breast and belly, like those of the porpoise."

The name Tritón probably signifies Wearer-away[3] from the corrosive power of the sea, and he thus, like so many other deities, is only an epithet of his sire. It is remarkable that the name of the Hindú god Vishnú, who is regarded as air or water, signifies Penetrator.[4]

Πρωτεύς. Proteus.

In the fourth book of the Odyssey Homer introduces this sea-god. He styles him, like Néreus and Phórkys, a Sea-elder,[5] and gives him the power of foretelling the future.[6] He calls him

---

[1] Theog. 930.   [2] Paus. ix. 20, 21.
[3] From τρύω, τιτράω, tero, whence also Amphitríté: see, however, Lauer's theory above, p. 159.   [4] Bohlen, Das Alte Indien, i. 202.
[5] Od. iv. 384.   [6] Ib. v. 561 seq.

Egyptian, and the servant of Poseidón,[1] and says that his task
was keeping the seals or sea-calves.[2]   When Meneláos was wind-
bound at the island of Pharos, opposite Egypt, and he and his
crew were suffering from want of food, Eidothea the daughter of
Próteus accosted him, and bringing seal-skins directed him to
disguise himself and three of his companions in them; and when
Próteus at noon should come up out of the sea and go to sleep
amidst his herds, to seize and hold him till he disclosed some
means of relief from his present distress.

Meneláos obeys the nymph; and Próteus drives up and counts
his herds, and then lies down to rest.   The hero immediately
seizes him, and the god turns himself into a lion, a serpent, a
pard, a boar, water, and a tree.   At length, finding he cannot
escape, he resumes his own form, and reveals to Meneláos the
remedy for his distress.   He at the same time informs him of the
situation of his friends, and particularly notices his having seen
Odysseus in the island of Kalypsó,—a clear proof that his own
abode was not, as has been asserted, confined to the coast of Egypt.

This part of the Odyssey has been beautifully imitated by
Vergil in the fourth book of his Georgics, where Aristæos on the
loss of his bees seeks in a similar way a remedy from Próteus.
The scene is here transferred to the peninsula of Palléné, and the
god is described as of a blue colour, the hue which painters had
been pleased to bestow on the marine deities: he has also a
chariot drawn by the biped sea-horses.

Homer does not name the parents of this marine deity, and
there is no mention of him in the Theogony.   Apollodóros makes
him a son of Poseidón,[3] and Euripidés would seem to make
Néreus his sire.[4]

Those who embraced the theory of representing the gods as
having been originally mere men, said that Próteus was a king
of Egypt; and the Egyptian priests told how he detained Helené
when Paris was driven to Egypt, and gave him an image or
phantom in her stead, and then restored her to Meneláos.[5]

The name of this deity, signifying *First* (πρὸ, πρῶτος), was too
inviting to escape the mystics.   They regarded him as a symbol
of the original matter which developed itself into the four elements whose form he took: the lion was æther, the serpent earth,
the tree air, and the water itself.[6]   The simplest derivation, however of his name is, we think, to suppose that it was originally
Πλωτεύς, the *floater*, *swimmer*, or *sailor*.

[1] *Od.* v. 385.   [2] *Ib.* v. 411.
[3] Apollod. ii. 5, 9.   [4] *Helené*, 15.
[5] Below, Part II. chap. the ast. *The Returns.*   [6] See *Orphic Hymn.* **xxv**.

Γλαῦκος. *Glaukos.*

Glaukos, as is evident from his name, was an original god of the sea, probably only another form of Poseidón, whose son he is in some accounts.[1] Like the marine gods in general, he had the gift of prophecy; we find him appearing to the Argonauts[2] and to Menelaos,[3] and telling them what had happened, or what was to happen. In later times sailors were continually making reports of his soothsaying.[4] Some said he dwelt with the Néréides at Délos, where he gave responses to all who sought them;[5] according to others, he visited each year all the isles and coasts with a train of monsters of the deep (κήτεα), and unseen foretold in the Æolic dialect all kinds of evil. The fishermen watched for his approach, and endeavoured by fastings, prayer and fumigations to avert the ruin with which his prophecy menaced the fruits and cattle. At times he was seen among the waves, and his body appeared covered with mussels, sea-weed and stones. He was heard evermore to lament his fate in not being able to die.[6]

This last circumstance refers to the common pragmatic history of Glaukos. He was a fisherman, it was said,[7] of Anthédón in Bœótia, and observing one day the fish which he had caught and thrown on the grass to bite it, and then to jump into the sea, his curiosity excited him to taste it also; immediately on his doing so he followed their example, and thus became a sea-god. It was also said[8] that he obtained his immortality by tasting the grass which had revived a hare he had run down in Ætólia; also[9] that he built and steered the Argó, and that during the voyage Zeus made him a god of the sea.

Glaukos, we are told,[10] seeing Ariadné in Naxos, where she had been abandoned by Theseus, became enamoured of her; but Dionýsos seized him, bound him with a vine-band, and drove him from the island. His love for Skylla we shall presently relate.

Λευκοθέα καὶ Παλαίμων. *(Matuta et Portunus.)*

Inó, the daughter of Kadmos and wife of Athamas, flying from her husband, with her little son Melikertés in her arms, sprang from a cliff into the sea. The gods out of compassion made her a goddess of the sea under the name of Leukothea, and him a god

---

[1] Euanthés *ap. Athén.* vii. 296.
[2] Apoll. Rh. i. 1310 *seq.*
[3] Eur. *Orest.* 362 *seq.*
[4] Paus. ix. 22, 7.
[5] Aristot. *ap. Athén. ut supra.*
[6] Plat. *Rep.* x. 611, *cum* Schol.
[7] Paus. *ut supra.* Ov. *Met.* xiii. 904 *seq.*
[8] Nikander *ap. Athén. ut supra.*
[9] Possis *ap. eund.*
[10] Euanthés *ap. eund.* Several other opinions about Glaukos will be found in this place of Athénæos.

under that of Palæmón. Both were held powerful to save from
shipwreck, and were invoked by sailors. The fable appears to be
ancient; as Leukothea, who gives her veil to Odysseus when
tossed in a storm, is called 'fair-ankled Inó, daughter of Kadmos,'
and her transformation is mentioned.[1]

Palæmón was usually represented riding on a porpoise. The
Isthmian games were celebrated in his honour.[2]

We should suppose it hardly necessary to remind the reader,
that, according to all analogy of Grecian mythology, Palæmón
and Inó-Leukothea (a form like Phœbos-Apolló, Pallas-Athéné)
were original water-deities. Leukothea is supposed to be derived
from the *white* waves, and Inó may be merely Iló, and be connected with ἴλλω *to roll*.[3] Palæmón (*Champion*) seems to refer to
the Isthmian games.[4] Melikertés is said to be a name of Poseidón;
it may however be the Phœnician Melcart, introduced into the
Kadmeian cycle when Kadmos had become a Sidónian.

Πόταμοι.   Fluvii.   River-gods.

Each river was held to have its presiding deity, who dwelt in it
and directed its waters. These gods had their houses and children;
and the love-adventures of some of them, such as Alpheios and
Acheloós, are recorded by the poets. The rivers were all the sons
of O'keanos and Téthys.[5]

The River-gods were represented of a handsome human form,
crowned with reeds, and wearing dark-blue mantles of fine tex-
ture. They were often given the head or horns of a bull, indicative of their roaring or winding, of their strength or of their
influence on agriculture;[6] or it may have been that the earth being
regarded as a cow, the rivers which fecundate her were viewed as
bulls.[7] A bull was the sacrifice to them, as to Poseidón.[8]

The rivers of Greece, it may be here observed, derived in general
their appellations from their physical characters. Thus some were
named from their nutritive or fecundating power, as the Alpheios,
the Péneios and the Pamísos; others from their rapidity, as
the Spercheios, Ilyssos, Inachos, Inópos, Selléeis, Asópos, Æas,

---

[1] *Od.* v. 333. Nitzsch *in loc.*   [2] Paus. i. 44, 88.

[3] Or with ἰλὺς, ἕλος. Völck. *Myth. der Jap.* 125.

[4] Welcker, *Nach. zur Tril.* 134. Others make it *quasi* ἀλαίμων, from ἅλς
(Völck. *ut sup.* and Schwenck, 184); and this was probably the original form,
and the change was made after the institution of the Isthmian games. See
above, p. 118, *note*[9].   [5] Hés. *Theog.* 237.

[6] Sch. *Eur. Orest.* 1573. Ælian, *Var. Hist.* ii. 33.

[7] " Apidem in theologia et cultu Ægyptiorum habitum fuisse symbolum sa-
crosanctum Nili, aut potius fertilitatis quam fluvius hicce agris Ægyptiorum
inducebat," Jablonski, *Panth. Ægypt.* ii. 215.   [8] *Il.* xi. 728.

Apidanos, Amphrýsos, Eurótas, Keladón; others simply from the flowing of their waters, as the Neda, the Nedón, the Anápos, the Anauros, and perhaps the Enípeus.[1] The Ladón, like our Mole, was probably named from its secret course, and the Képhissos may have been the *Hollower* or *Digger-away* (σκάπτω, like κάπετος), and Achelóos, like our Exe, Esk, simply the Water (*aqua*). The rivers of our own country and of most others have obtained their names in a similar manner.

Chapter XVIII.

DEITIES OF THE ISLES AND COAST OF OCEAN:—HESPE-RIDES, GRÆÆ, GORGONS, HARPIES, WINDS.

'Εσπερίδες.   *Hesperides.*   𝔚𝔢𝔰𝔱𝔢𝔯𝔫-𝔐𝔞𝔦𝔡𝔰.

ACCORDING to Hésiod[2] the 'clear-voiced' Hesperides dwelt 'out in (πέρην) the bright Ocean' opposite where Atlas stood supporting the heaven, and they had charge of the trees that bore the golden fruit. In this task they were aided by a serpent named Ladón.[3] These apples were said to have been the gift of Earth to Héra on her wedding-day.[4] One of the tasks imposed on Héraklés was that of procuring some of them for Eurystheus.

Hésiod says that the Hesperides were the daughters of Night without a father. Others, however, to assimilate them to their neighbours, the Græœ and Gorgons, gave them Phorkys and Kétó for parents.[5] Their names are said to have been Ægló, Erytheia, Hestia, and Arethusa,[6] or rather Ægló, Hesperé, and Erythéis.[7]

The abode of these Western-Maids was evidently an island *in*

---

[1] The verbs from which these names are derived are ΠΑ'Ω, σπέρχω, ἴλλω, ΑΙΩ, ἀΐσσω, πιδύω, ῥώομαι, κελαδέω, νάω. On the principle of double termination (above, p. 15), Erasínos may come from ῥέω.

[2] *Theog.* 215, 274, 518.

[3] *Lurker,* from λήθω. Hésiod (*Theog.* 333) enumerates among the progeny of Phorkys and Kétó the 'dread serpent which in a cavern of dark earth at its great extremity watches the golden apples,' but he does not intimate any connexion between him and the Hesperides. Peisander, it would seem (Sch. *Apoll. Rh.* iv. 1396) first named him Ladón, and called him the offspring of Earth.

[4] Pherekýdés *ap. Sch. Apoll. ut sup.*

[5] Sch. *Apoll. Rh.* iv. 1399.

[6] Apollod. ii. 5, 11.

[7] Apoll. Rh. iv. 1427 *seq.* Milton, following Apollónios, has

> Hesperus and his daughters three
> That sing about the golden tree.—*Comus,* 981

the Ocean, and not the gloomy land *beyond* it;[1] for the poets, led
by the analogy of the lovely appearance of the western sky at sunset, viewed the West as a region of brightness and glory. Hence
they placed in it the Isles of the Blest, the ruddy isle Erytheia, on
which the bright oxen of Hadés and Géryoneus pastured, and the
isle of the Hesperides, in which grew the golden fruit,—all places
of light and bliss.

When Atlas had been fixed as a mountain in the extremity of
Libya, the dwelling of the Hesperides was usually placed in his
vicinity; some, however, set it on the shores of lake Tritón;[2]
others in the country of the Hyperboreans.[3]   Their apples are supposed by some to have been a fiction, indebted for its origin to the
accounts of the oranges of Africa and Spain; but this fruit was,
we believe, first brought to the West from Asia; and, as far as we
can at present discern, the Western-Maids and their trees are a
pure poetic creation belonging to the mythology of Héraklés.

Γραῖαι.   *Grææ.*   **Grey-Maids.**

The 'fair-cheeked' Græae were daughters of Phorkys and Kétó;
they were hoary-haired from their birth, whence their name.
They were two in number, 'well-robed' Pephrédó (*Horrifier*), and
'yellow-robed' Enyó (*Urger, Driver*).[4] We find them always united
with the Gorgons, whose guards they were, according to Æschylos.[5]
This poet[6] describes them as '*three* long-lived maids, swan-formed,
having one eye and one tooth in common, on whom neither the sun
with his beams nor the nightly moon ever looks.'   Perseus, he
says,[7] intercepted the eye as they were handing it from one to the
other, and having thus blinded the guards was enabled to come on
the Gorgons unperceived.   The name of the third sister given by
the later writers is Deinó (*Terrifier*).[8]

Γοργόνες.   *Gorgones.*   **Gorgons.**

Homer speaks of an object of terror which he calls Gorgó, and
the Gorgeian Head.   He places the former on the shield of Aga-

---

[1] Πέρην merely signifies *out in*, as

Νήσων αἵ ναίουσι πέρην ἁλὸς, Ἠλιδος ἄντα.

Il. ii. 626.   (Heyne, *in loc.*)

Τιτῆνες ναίουσι, πέρην Χάεος ζοφεροῖο.   Hés. *Theog.* 814.

[2] See Ap. Rh. iv. 1396. Lucan, ix. 357.   [3] Apollod. *ut. sup.*
[4] Hés. *Theog.* 270 *seq.* See above, p. 93. In Ovid also (*Met.* iv. 773
their number is only two.
[5] Eratosth. *Cat.* 22. Hygin. *Poet. Astr.* ii. 12: see Völcker, *Myth. Geog.* 41
[6] *Prom.* 800 *seq.*
[7] Eratosth. Hygin. Völcker, *ut sup.* Æschylos, as it would appear, said
that he flung the eye into Lake Tritónis.   [8] Apollod. ii. 4, 2.

memnón;[1] and when describing Hektór eager for slaughter, he says that he had 'the eyes of Gorgó and of man-destroying Arés.'[2] The Gorgeian Head was on the ægis of Zeus,[3] and the hero of the Odyssey fears to remain in Erebos lest 'Persephoneia should send out the Gorgeian head of the dire monster'[4] against him.[5] Euripidés says[6] that Earth produced the Gorgón in the Giant-war, and that Pallas-Athéné killed her and placed her head on her breast-plate. Along with the Grææ, according to the Theogony,[7] Kétó bore to Phorkys the Gorgons, 'who dwelt out in (πέρην) the bright Ocean in the extremity toward night, where the clear-voiced Hesperides abide.' It names them Stheinó, Euryalé, and Medusa, which last alone was mortal. Poseidón, it is added, lay with her in a 'soft mead amid the spring-flowers,' and when her head was cut off by Perseus, the 'great' Chrysáór[8] and the steed Pégasos[9] sprang forth. Æschylos calls the Gorgons the 'three sisters of the Grææ, winged, serpent-fleeced, hateful to man, whom no one can look on and retain his breath,' i.e. live.[10] They were also re. presented as winged on the ancient chest of Kypselos at Olympia.[11] On the shield of Héraklés the Gorgons are girt with serpents.[12] Others describe them as having their heads environed with scaly snakes, and with huge teeth like those of swine, brazen hands and golden wings. Their looks, it is added, turned all who beheld them to stone.[13]

The Gorgons and the Grææ are always mentioned together, and they seem to have been appropriated to the mythe of Perseus. We might therefore suppose them to have been a pure poetic fiction, were it not that, as we shall show, the Gorgon in that mythe, Medusa, is merely another form of Pallas-Athéné. It is therefore not improbable that the theory of some mythologists of the present day may be the true one; namely, that the *two* Gorgons and *two* Grææ are only personifications of the terrors of the sea, the former denoting the large *strong* billows of the *wide* open main, the latter the *white*-crested waves that dash against

---

[1] *Il.* xi. 36.   [2] *Il.* viii. 349.   [3] *Il.* v. 741.   [4] *Od.* xi. 633.
[5] It may be doubted if Homer was acquainted with the story of Perseus: the passage in which he is mentioned (*Il.* xiv. 519) is, we think, justly regarded as an interpolation. Völcker (*Myth. Geog.* 15) refers to *Il.* xix. 116, 123; but that passage, besides its being in one of the later books, is liable to objection: see Heyne and Payne Knight *in loc.*
[6] *Ión,* 989.   [7] *Theog.* 274 *seq.*
[8] See below, *Akrisios,* etc. *ad fin.*   [9] See below, *Bellerophontés ad fin.*
[10] *Prom.* 800 *seq.*   [11] Paus. v. 18, 5.   [12] Hés. 'Ασπίς, 233.
[13] Apollod. ii. 4, 2. Tzetz. *Lyk.* 838. Sch. *Æsch. Prom. ut sup.*

the rocks of the coast.[1] They must have originally belonged to the Sea (*Pontos*), whose grandchildren they are, and not to the calm soft-flowing Ocean, whither they were transported when they had ceased to be regarded as personifications, and had been introduced into the mythe of Perseus. As in this mythe Medusa (*Mistress*) —whose name is of a nature totally different from theirs—was added to the Gorgons, the principle of uniformity probably led to a similar increase of the Grææ.

All these beings are, we think, placed by the Theogony in Oceanic isles; they may however have dwelt on the opposite coast, though we believe few who are well versed in the cosmology of those times will assign them that gloomy region; most certainly they are not on this side of Ocean. Hither, however, they were all removed in the course of time, and even to the Syrtes and Kyréné.[2] In short, with the exception of Hésiod and Stasínos,[3] every writer of antiquity places them somewhere in Libya. This however is not to be wondered at, for it is only a part of the system of localisation, which assigned a definite abode in well-known countries to all the beings of fable, which brought for example the transoceanic Kimmerians over to the fertile plains of Campania in Italy.[4]

"Αρπυιαι. Harpyiæ. 𝕳𝖆𝖗𝖕𝖎𝖊𝖘.

The Harpies or *Snatchers*[5] of Homer[6] and Hésiod are personifications of storm-winds (θύελλαι). The former says nothing of their form or parentage; the latter terms them *well-haired* (a usual mark of beauty), and says that they were sisters of Iris, daughters of Thaumas and E'lektra, swift as birds or as the blasts of wind.[7] Their names, he says, are Aelló (*Storm*) and O'kypeté (*Swift-flyer*). Homer says that Xanthos and Balios, the steeds of Achilleus, were the offspring of Zephyros by the Harpy Podargé

---

[1] Hermann, *De Mythol.* etc. (*Opusc.* ii. 180). Völcker, *Myth. der Jap.* 212. *Myth. Geog.* 17. Hermann renders Pephrédó and Enýó, *Auferona* and *Inundona*.

[2] There seems to us to be much probability in Völcker's (*Myth. Geog.* 227 *seq.*) reading of Κυρήνης for Κισθήνης in Æschylos' *Prométheus*, 799; for this poet, as we have just seen, places the Gorgons near lake Tritónis.

[3]

Τῷ δ' ὑποκυσσαμένη τέκε Γόργονας, αἰνὰ πέλωρα,
αἳ Σαρπηδόνα ναῖον ἐπ' ὠκεανῷ βαθυδίνῃ,
νῆσον πετρήεσσαν.—*Cypr. ap. Herodian.*

[4] Serv. *Æn.* vi. 106. Strab. v. 4, 4, p. 243.

[5] From ἁρπάζω. There was a species of hawk named ἅρπη (*Il.* xix. 359). Le?'ei? derived Harpy from the Semitic *Arbeh* (אַרְבֶּה) *locust.*

[6] *Il.* xvi. 149. *Od.* i. 241; xiv. 371; xx. 61 *seq.*

[7] *Theog.* 267 *seq.*

(*Swift-foot*), whom he met grazing in a mead by the stream of Ocean.[1] Vergil names one of the Harpies Kelænó.[2]

In the Argonautic cycle the Harpies appear as the tormentors of Phineus. They are there represented as odious offensive monsters with female faces, and the bodies, wings, and claws of birds.[3]

We place the Winds here for the sake of convenience as they are connected with the Harpies, though their abode was not on the isles or shores of Ocean.

῎Ανεμοι. (*Venti.* 𝔚𝔦𝔫𝔡𝔰.)

The winds are represented in the Ilias as gods:[4] Iris goes to them as they are feasting in the dwelling of Zephyros, to inform them of the prayer of Achilleus that they would inflame the pyre of Patroklos. In the Odyssey,[5] the winds are not directed by separate deities, but all are under the charge of Æolos. We may, as a matter of course, observe that the Wind-gods of Homer are not winged.

The Winds were divided into *wholesome* and *noxious*. The former, which were Boreas (*North*), Zephyros (*West*), and Notos (*South*), were according to Hésiod[6] the children of Astræos (*Starry*) and E'ós (*Dawn*). The other winds (μαψαῦραι), he says,[7] are the race of Typhóeus, whom he describes as the last and most terrible child of Earth. In these he probably includes the East-wind, which in Greece, as over the rest of Europe, is, we may observe, pernicious.

Boreas (Βορέας) was called *Clear-weather-* or *Frost-producer* (αἰθρηγενής).[8] He loved O'reithyia, the daughter of Erechtheus king of Athens, and carried her off.[9] The Athenians ascribed the destruction of the fleet of Xerxés by a storm to the partiality of Boreas for the country of O'reithyia, and built a temple to him after that event.[10] Boreas is also said by Homer[11] to have turned

---

[1] *Il.* xvi. 149. From this and from *Od.* xx. 65, 77, it may perhaps be inferred that the shore of Ocean was the abode of the Harpies.

[2] *Æn.* iii. 211. Tzetz. *Lyc.* 166.

[3] See Part II. chap. the last. *Argonautics.* Æschyl. *Eum.* 50. Vergil, *ut supra,* 216 *seq.*   [4] *Il.* xxiii. 194 *seq.*

[5] *Od.* x. 1. Apoll. Rh. iv. 765. Verg. *Æn.* i. 52.   [6] *Theog.* 378.

[7] *Ib.* 869. There is an apparent difficulty here, for Typhóeus (see above, p. 43) is an internal volcanic power; but it was an ancient opinion that these violent agitations of the atmosphere proceeded from the interior of the earth: hence, for example, the name of the Rhipæan mountains.

[8] *Il.* xv. 171; xix. 358; also αἰθρηγενέτης, *Od.* v. 296: see Appendix E.

[9] See Part II. chap. v. *O'reithyia.*   [10] Hérod. vii. 189.   [11] *Il.* xx. 223.

himself into a horse out of love to the mares of Erichthonios, and to have begotten on them twelve foals.

Zephyros (Ζέφυρος) is described by Homer as a strong-blowing wind, but he was afterwards regarded as gentle and soft-breathing. Love was the offspring of Zephyros and Iris,[1] and one of the Seasons bore to this wind-god a son named Karpos (*Fruit*).[2] The Latin poets made him the husband of their goddess Flora.[3]

The South- (Νότος) and East-wind (Εὖρος) have been left without adventures.[4] The Winds have all wings or horses and chariots in the works of the later poets and the artists.[5]

The names Euros and Zephyros probably come from ἠώς and ζόφος, which denoted the East and West.[6] Boreas is thought to be Oreas (from ὄρος), as rushing from the mountains. Notos perhaps signifies *wet* (from νάω, *to flow*?), and is akin to the German *nass* and Dutch *nat*.

CHAPTER XIX.

INHABITANTS OF THE ISLES AND COASTS OF THE WEST-SEA.—LOTUS-EATERS, KYKLO'PES, GIANTS, ÆOLOS, LÆSTRYGONIANS, KIRKÉ, SIRENS, SKYLLA AND CHARYBDIS, PHAETHUSA AND LAMPETIE, KALYPSO', PHÆAKIANS, SYRIA, AND ORTYGIA.

THE romantic geography of the most romantic poem of Greece, the Homéric Odyssey, is now to occupy our attention. Its poet is in our eyes a Grecian Ariosto, and we should as soon hope to discover the true position of the isle of Alcina as of those of Kirké and Kalypsó.[7] The moment he conducts his hero away

---

[1] See above, p. 131.   [2] Serv. *Buc.* v. 48.

[3] See Mythology of Italy, *Flora*.

[4] In the poetry of Persia the East-wind takes the part assigned to Zephyros in that of Europe. The cause is the different geographic positions of the countries; for while in Europe the west-wind comes cooled by its passage over the waters of the Atlantic, in Persia the east-wind comes cooled by its passage over the Himalaya and the high plains of Tibet. The same will probably b the case in Australia when it comes to have poetry.

[5] The idea of giving wings to the wind is so natural a one, that we meet with it even in Hebrew poetry: see *Ps.* xviii. 11; civ. 3; *Hos.* iv. 19.

[6] See Buttmann, *Lexil. v.* ἀήρ.

[7] "People," said Eratosthenés, "w. discover whither Odysseus wandered when they find the artist who stitched the leathern bag that held the winds." Strab. i. 2, 15, p. 24: comp. Völcker *Myth. Geog.* 11, 12.

from Greece, he engages him in magic regions amidst ogres, fairies, and monsters of various kinds, as numerous as ever were encountered by the knights of Gothic romance. To form these he appears to have taken possession of the cosmogonic Kyklópes and Giants and to have transformed them; to have adopted the tales of Phœnician mariners, and to have transferred the wonders of other mythic cycles to the West-sea, which he made the scene of his hero's adventures.

It is a question among critics whether the Odyssey is or is not the work of one mind, whether the domestic scenes in Ithaka, and the wondrous adventures related to Alkinoos, are parts of one continuous preconceived narrative. Into this interesting subject we are not required at present to enter, for the geography of these parts is distinct, the one lying in the domains of romance, the other confining itself to the sober realms of the actual earth. We will first direct our attention to the latter.[1]

In the Ilias the only places noticed out of Greece to the west are the isles over which Odysseus ruled. The Odyssey would seem to intimate a knowledge of Italy and Sicily; for a place named Temesa, whither the Taphians used to sail to barter iron for copper, is mentioned;[2] and in Italy, in ancient times a most cypriferous region, there was a place named Temesa, or rather Tempsa.[3] The people of this place are said to speak a language different from Greek,[4] and this circumstance also would accord well with Italy. But on the other hand the Greeks, when they began to plant colonies in Italy and Sicily, fell into the habit of localising all the names of peoples and places in the romantic fictions of their *aœdi*; and further, Tempsa lies on the west side of Italy, and there was also a place named Tamesos in the isle. which bestowed its appellation on the metal it yielded—Kypros,[5] and the Taphians, we are told, used to sail even as far as Sidón.[6] Nothing therefore can be collected with certainty from Tamesa. But it may be said that the Sikelans, who dwelt in Italy and Sicily, are spoken of in the Odyssey;[7] this people however are

---

[1] On the Homéric geography the best work by far is that of Völcker, so frequently alluded to in these pages. The *Aelteste Weltkunde* of Voss has two great defects; he *will* localise every place and people, and he is resolute in maintaining the two poems to be the produce of one mind, and *denies* all interpolation. In fact, he was greatly wanting in imagination and in true poetic feeling, as also in delicacy of the critical sense. [2] *Od.* i. 183.

[3] Strab. vi. i, 5, p. 255. Mela, ii. 4. Ov. *Met.* xv. 52, 707.

[4] 'Αλλοθρόους ἀνθρώπους. Od. *ut supra*. This may only denote a different pronunciation: see Nitzsch *in loc.*

[5] The majority of the critics (Nitzsch, *ut supra*) are of opinion that this is the place meant. [6] *Od.* xv. 425 *seq.* *Od.* xx. 383.

also said to have inhabited E'peiros,[1] in which case nothing definite results from the mention of them. Sikania is also spoken of,[2] but it is in the part of the poem which ancient critics pronounced to be spurious.   We think ourselves therefore justified in supposing that the *Singer* of the Odyssey may have chosen to regard all westwards of Greece as one wide sea, in which he was at liberty to place what isles he pleased, and people them as his fancy prompted.   On this principle we now will trace the wanderings of Odysseus, the Sindibad of Greece.[3]

Λωτοφάγοι. *Lotophagi.* Lotos-eaters.

Odysseus, when doubling the Cape of Malea in Lakónia on his return from Troy,[4] encountered a violent north-east wind (βορέης), which drove him for nine days along the sea, till he reached the country of the Lótos-eaters.   Here, after watering, he sent three of his men to discover who the inhabitants were.   These men on coming among the Lótos-eaters were kindly entertained by them, and given some of their own food, the Lótos-plant, to eat.   The effect of this plant was such, that those who tasted it lost all thoughts of home, and wished to remain in that country.   It was by main force that Odysseus dragged these men away, and he was even obliged to tie them under the benches of his ship.

As the coast of Kyréné lies opposite the Peloponnése, and is much nearer to it than Egypt is to Krété, we must suppose the country of the Lótos-eaters to have been far more to the West. They seem in the poet's view to have been the last tribe of ordinary men in that direction, and to have dwelt on the verge of the land of fable.   The Lótos, under the name of Jujuba, is, we may observe, a part of the food of the people of the north coast of Africa at the present day.

---

[1] See Sch. *Od.* xviii. 85, and Niebuhr's Essay in the Cambridge Philolog. Museum, i. 174 *seq.*   [2] *Od.* xxiv. 307.

[3] The root of Odysseus is ὁδός (see above, p. 15), and its signification is therefore the *Traveller*.   Now as Odysseus is one of the principal heroes of the Ilias, it would seem to follow that the series of adventures which illustrate his name must have been known long before the time of that poem, and that, therefore, the poet of the Odyssey found them ready to his hand, and connected them, making, of course, additions and alterations, with the war of Troy, with which, in fact, their connection is very slight.   In the original fiction Odysseus may have been made prince of Ithaka on account of the western position of that island on the verge of the West-sea, the scene of his adventures.   His wife (see p. 15) is the industrious *Weaver* (πήνη) or *Toiler* (πένομαι) and her *web* is probably indebted to her name for its origin.   [4] *Od.* ix. 80.

Κίκλωπες. *Kyklopes.*

When Odysseus left the country of the Lótos-eaters, he sailed on further, i.e. westwards,[1] and came to that of the Kyklópes, which could not have been very far distant, or the poet would, in that case, as he always does, have specified the number of days occupied in the voyage. The Kyklópes are described as a rude, lawless race, who neither planted nor sowed, but whose land was so fertile as spontaneously to produce them wheat, barley, and vines. They had no social institutions, neither assemblies nor laws, but dwelt separately, each in his cave, on the tops of lofty mountains, and each without regard to others governed his own wife and children.

In front of a harbour of their land lay a well-wooded fertile isle, abundantly stocked with goats. But the Kyklópes, having no ships, could not derive any advantage from it. Odysseus, leaving the rest of his fleet at this island, went with one ship to the country of the Kyklópes. Here he entered the cave of the Kyklóps Polyphémos, who was a son of Poseidón by the nymph Thoósa, the daughter of Phorkys. The Kyklóps on his return in the evening with his flocks, finding strangers there, inquired who they were; and on Odysseus saying that they had been ship-wrecked, and appealing to his mercy and reverence for the gods, he declared that the Kyklópes regarded not the gods, for they were much more powerful than they: he then seized two of the Greeks, and dashing them to the ground like young whelps killed and devoured them. When he fell asleep Odysseus was going to kill him, till recollecting the huge rock,—one which the teams of two-and-twenty four-wheeled wagons could not move,—with which he had closed the door, he refrained. Against the next evening Odysseus had prepared a piece of the Kyklóps' own olive-staff, which was as large as the mast of a merchant-vessel; and when the monster had devoured two more of his victims he gave him wine to drink, and then while he was sleeping profoundly, heated the stick in the fire, and aided by four of his companions bored out his eye with it. Polyphémos roaring out with pain, the other Kyklópes came to inquire what had befallen him; but on his in-forming them that *Nobody* (Οὖτις)—the name which Odysseus had given himself—was killing him, thinking it was some disease they left him, recommending him to pray to his father. Next morning,

---

[1] Ἔνθεν δὲ προτέρω πλέομεν. *Od.* ix. 105. The wind had been north-east, and it is not said that it had changed. We apprehend that by προτέρω the poet always means *further on* in the same direction: see Thiersch, *Urgestalt der Odyssee*, pp. 110, 111. Völcker, *Hom. Geog.* 111.

when Polyphémos turned out his sheep and goats, his prisoners fastened themselves under their bellies, and so escaped. Odysseus, when a little way out at sea, called out his real name, and the Kyklóps hurled immense rocks at him, which were near sinking his ship.

Nothing is said by the poet respecting the size of the Kyklópes in general, but every effort is made to give an exaggerated idea of that of Polyphémos. When Odysseus first sees him, he compares him to 'a woody peak of lofty mountains, when it appears separate from others.' The crash of the bundle of wood which he brings home in the evening, when it is cast on the ground, terrifies the Greeks who were hiding in his cave: the teams of twenty-two wagons could not move the rock with which he closed his door: his staff was in length and thickness equal to the mast of a large ship: the first rock which he flung at the ship of Odysseus was 'the top of a great hill,' and falling before the vessel it drove her back to the shore; the second was still larger.

Yet, possibly, we are not to infer that the Kyklópes were in general of such huge dimensions or cannibal habits. Polyphémos was not of the ordinary Kyklóps-race, being the son of Poseidón and a sea-nymph: he is also said[1] to have been the strongest of the Kyklópes. It is not a little remarkable, that neither in the description of the Kyklópes in general, nor of Polyphémos in particular, is there any notice taken of their being one-eyed; yet in the account of the blinding of the latter, it seems to be assumed as a thing well known. We may hence perhaps infer that Homer followed the usual derivation of the name.[2]

Both ancients and moderns agree in regarding Sicily as the country of the Kyklópes:[3] we however cannot help thinking that it was on the coast of Libya;[4] for it lay at no great distance from that of the Lótos-eaters, which was evidently on that coast. The poet merely says, 'We then sail on further, and come to the land of the Kyklópes;' and if it had been an island, he would, as usual, have noticed the circumstance: he would also have told us with what wind they sailed to it, if it had been at anything like the distance which Sicily is from Libya: and further, though the fertility of Sicily may accord with that of the Kyklópes' land, yet it

---

[1] *Od.* i. 70.   [2] See above, p. 39.

[3] Strab. i. 2, 9, p. 20.   Völcker, *Hom. Geog.* 110 *seq.* This critic places the Kyklópes and the other fabulous tribes which we shall meet with on the west coast of Sicily.

[4] " Homerus eos continentis habitatores fecit, non insulæ Siciliæ."—Broukhus. *ad Tibull.* iv. 1, 56.

does not offer the caverns on mountain-tops in which they abode, nor can any island answering to that of the Odyssey, stretching before a harbour, be shown in it. If the little islet of Ortygia at Syracuse should be thought of, we reply, that it in no point accords with the description in the poem.

It is thus then that the Thunder, Lightning, and Flame of the Theogony appear to have become one-eyed giants in the hands of our poet. When they had been localised in the neighbourhood of volcanoes it was a simple process to convert them into smiths, the assistants of Héphæstos.[1] As they were now artists in one line, it gave no surprise to find them engaged in a task adapted to their huge strength, namely that of rearing the massive walls of Tiryns, thence named Kyklópian, for which purpose it is said they were brought, seven in number, by Prœtos from Lykia.[2]

Polyphémos' love for the Néréis Galateia is well known from the bucolic poets.[3] The river Akis in Sicily was originally a shepherd, whom in his jealous rage the monster crushed beneath a rock for being more acceptable to the nymph of the waters than himself.[4]

Γίγαντες. Gigantes. Giants.

The Giants would seem to have been placed by the poet in a region to the west of the land of the Kyklópes; for the original country of the Phæakians lay between their respective territories.[5] They are called *wild tribes* (ἄγρια φῦλα), but akin to the gods,[6] by whom it would appear they were destroyed for their impiety.[7] They were apparently of huge stature;[8] yet the daughter of Eurymedón, their last king, was by Poseidón mother of the king of the Phæakians, a people of the ordinary size.[9]

In the Theogony [10] it is merely said that the 'great' Giants were among those beings which sprang from the drops of the blood of Uranos which fell on the earth. We have shown that they most probably were productive beings; and, from the analogy of the Titans, we may infer that as soon as their object was effected they were removed from the upper regions and consigned to inactivity. This too may gradually have taken the form of a war, and hence has been derived the view of the Giants given by the singer of the Odyssey when he introduced them into his poem; there was also a poem named Gigantomachia. The first extant poet, how-

---

[1] Kallim. iii. 46. Verg. *Geor.* iv. 173. *Æn.* viii. 416 *seq.*
[2] Sch. *Eur. Orest.* 955. Strab. viii. 6, 11, p. 372.
[4] Ovid. *Met.* xiii. 750 *seq.* 'Ακὶς may be akin to *aqua*.
[6] *Od.* vii. 205, 206.
[8] *Od.* x. 120.
[10] *Theog.* 185. The following verse is an interpolation.

[3] Theocr. xi.
[5] *Od.* vi. 4 *seq.*
[7] *Od.* vii. 60.
[9] *Od.* vii. 56 *seq*

ever, who speaks of this war is Pindar,[1] who names the plain of
Phlegræ as the field of battle, and Apolló and the hero Héraklés
among the combatants on the side of the gods, which brings its
date down much lower than that of the Titan-war.   It is probable
also that Pherekýdés narrated the war in detail., and that we have
in Apollodóros an abridgment of his narrative.

According to this writer,[2] Earth, enraged at the overthrow of
the Titans, bore by Uranos the Giants, beings of huge size and
strength, of dreadful aspect, with long hair and beards, and
serpent-feet.   Their birth-place, some said, was Phlegræ, others
Palléné.   They hurled rocks and flaming trees against the skies.
Their chiefs were Porphyrión and Alkyoneus, which latter was
immortal as long as he was in the land that gave him birth.   It is
also related of him that he drove the oxen of the Sun out of the
isle of Erytheia.   An oracle had told the gods that they could not
destroy the Giants without the aid of a mortal ; and Earth, aware
of this, devised a mode to prevent their obtaining it; but Zeus,
by forbidding the Dawn, Moon, and Sun to shine, frustrated her
project, and, at the call of Athéna, Héraklés appeared on the side
of the gods.   He shot Alkyoneus with an arrow, but the ground,
when he fell on it, restored him to vigour.   The hero then, by
the advice of Athéna, carried him out of Palléné, and so he died.
Porphyrión rushed at Héraklés and Héra, but Zeus filled him with
passion for the latter, and when he tore her robe and would force
her, she cried out, and Zeus and Héraklés slew him.   Ephialtés
was shot by Apolló in the left, by Héraklés in the right eye;
Dionýsos slew Eurytos with his *thyrsos;* Hekaté, or rather
Héphæstos, who hurled red-hot lumps of metal, killed Klytios;
Athéna flung the isle of Sicily on Enkelados as he fled, and stripped
Pallas of his skin, which she afterwards wore as armour.   As
Polybótés, flying through the sea, came to Kós, Poseidón cast a
piece of it on him, and thus formed the isle of Nisyros.   Hermés,
wearing the helmet of Hadés, killed Hippolytos, Artemis Gratión,
the Mœræ Agrios and Thoón, who fought with brazen clubs.   Zeus
struck the rest with thunder, and Héraklés despatched them with
his arrows.

Earth, the same writer proceeds,[3] now more enraged than ever,
mingled with Tartaros and brought forth, in Kilikia, Typhón, half
man, half beast, far exceeding in magnitude all her former progeny.
The upper part of his form, that of a man, out-topped the moun-

---

[1] *Pyth.* viii. 12 (15).   *Nem.* i. 67 (100) ; vii. 90 (133).   See also Eur. *Ión.*
206 *seq.*
[2] Apollod. i. 6, 2.   Comp. Verg. *Æn.* iii. 578.   Hor. *Carm.* ii. 19, 21 *seq.* ;
iii. 4, 49 *seq.*   Claud. *Gigantomachia.*   [3] Apollod. i. 6, 3.

tains, and his head touched the stars; one hand reached the east, the other the west; above he had a hundred dragon-heads, beneath the huge spires of snakes. His whole body was winged; his hair and beard waved in the wind; he shot fire from his eyes. He whirled burning rocks against the skies with loud whizzing and roars, while flames burst forth from his mouth. The gods, in dismay, fled into Egypt, and there concealed themselves under the form of various animals.[1] Zeus struck him from afar with his bolts, and when he came close terrified him with his adamantine falchion, and pursued him as he fled as far as Mount Kasios, on the confines of Arabia. There, seeing him wounded, he grappled with him, but Typhón, entangling him in his spires, held him and seized the falchion, with which he cut out the sinews of his feet and hands. He then took him on his shoulders and carried him through the sea to Kilikia, and placed him in the Korykian cave. He wrapped the sinews up in the hide of a bear, and gave them in charge to the she-dragon Delphýné, a semi-ferine maid. But Hermés and Ægipan contrived to steal them from her, and fitted them again to Zeus, who, on recovering his strength, suddenly descended from the sky mounted on his car drawn by winged steeds, and striking Typhón with his bolts, chased him to the mountain named Nysa. Here the Mœræ deceived him to his ruin; for being persuaded by them that ripe fruits would renew his strength, he ate of them. Being again then put to flight, he came to Thrace, about Mount Hæmos, whose hills he flung, but when they were driven back on him by the thunder he cast up much blood (αἷμα), and hence the mountain derived its name. As he was flying through the Sicilian sea Zeus cast Ætna on him, and hence that mountain emits flames.

The Typhón here described is plainly the Typhóeus of the Theogony,[2] which, as we have seen, is the personification of volcanic action. That poem, however, speaks[3] of another being named Typháón, which it terms a ' wild wind,' who in union with Echidna (the Delphýné apparently of the preceding narrative) was the sire of Kerberos the dog of Hadés, Orthros the dog of Géryoneus, the Lernæan Hydra and the Chimæra. It may, however, be suspected that Typhóeus and Typháón are the same, for if the latter be himself called a wind, the former is said to be the sire of the violent

---

[1] This change of form of the gods was related by Pindar: see Porph. *De Abst.* iii. p. 251 : comp. Ov. *Met.* v. 325.

[2] Homer (*Il.* ii. 782) places the bed of Typhóeus in Arimi, i. e. in Kilikia, where Pindar (*Pyth.* i. 16 (32), Fr. Schol. 7) places Typhós. Ovid (*Met.* v. 346 *seq.*) says that it was Typhóeus that was placed under Ætna. The greater part of the first two books of Nonnos' poem is occupied by the conflicts of Zeus and Typhóeus.　　　　　　　　　　　[3] *Theog.* 306.

and tempestuous winds. In what precedes we may discern an attempt to connect the Grecian mythology with the animal worship of Egypt; Typhón being, it is said, the proper name of the malignant dæmon of that country, the unsated foe of Osíris.

Ovid[1] gives rather a peculiar view of the war of the Giants. He says, transferring to them the acts of the Alóeids, that they piled Pelion, Ossa and Olympos on each other, to scale the heavens, and that when they were overthrown an impious race of men sprang from their blood.

Αἴολος ἐν νήσῳ Αἰολίῃ.   Æolus in Æolia insula.

After their escape from the Kyklóps, Odysseus and his companions sailed *further on*, and came to the floating-isle (πλώτη νῆσος) of Æolos Hippotadés,[2] 'dear to the immortal gods.' This island was entirely surrounded by a wall of brass and by smooth precipitous rocks: and here Æolos dwelt in continual joy and festivity, with his wife and his six sons and as many daughters, whom, after the fashion set by Zeus, he had married to each other, The isle had no other tenants.   The office of directing and ruling the winds had been conferred on Æolos by Zeus; and when he was dismissing Odysseus, after having hospitably entertained him for an entire month, he gave him all the winds but Zephyros tied up in a bag of ox-hide.   For nine days and nights the ships ran merrily before the wind: on the tenth they were within sight of Ithaka; when Odysseus, who had hitherto held the helm himself, fell asleep; his comrades, who fancied that Æolos had given him treasure in the bag, opened it; and forthwith the winds rushed out, and hurried them back to the Æolian island.   Judging from what had befallen them that they were hated by the gods, the director of the winds drove them with reproaches from his isle.

As the Æolian was a *floating-isle*, it is evidently as needless to look for its exact position as for that of Laputa.[3]   At the time when Odysseus came to it, it must have been lying near the country of the Kyklópes; but we are not told whether it remained immovable during the month that he spent in it, or the time that elapsed between his departure and return.   We are to suppose that wherever it might be, the winds were sure to return to it. The Latin poets, following the later Greeks, have placed Æolos in Strongyla, one of the Liparæan islands.[4]

---

[1] *Met.* i. 151 *seq.*   [2] i. e. *Windman* son of *Horseman.*

[3] It seems strange that Völcker should have left this circumstance so entirely out of view, and have determined Æolia to be one of the Ægatian islands. *Hom. Geog.* 114.

[4] Strab. i. 2, 9, p. 20; vi. 2, 11, p. 276.   Verg. *Æn.* i. 52; viii. 416.

Λαιστρυγόνες. *Lœstrygones.* 𝕷𝖆𝖊𝖘𝖙𝖗𝖞𝖌𝖔𝖓𝖎𝖆𝖓𝖘.

The country of the Læstrygonians lay very far to the west. Odysseus, when driven from his isle by Æolos, sailed *on further* for six days and nights, at the end of which time he reached the land of the Læstrygonians; and the distance thence to the Ææan isle, which we shall show to be near the extremity of the Sea, could not have been considerable, as the length of time consumed in the passage thither is not specified.

The Læstrygonians are another of those huge androphagous races, whom the invention of the poet has placed on the coast of Libya. Unlike the Kyklópes, they lived in the social state; their king was named Antiphatés, their town Læstrygonia or Télépylos (it is uncertain which), and the fountain near it Artakia. There was a port at a little distance from the city, which all the ships of Odysseus, but the one he was himself on board of, entered. A herald with two others were then sent to the city: they met the daughter of Antiphatés at the fount Artakia, and were by her directed to her father's house. On entering it they were terrified at the sight of his wife, who was 'as large as the top of a mountain.' She instantly called her husband from the market-place, who seized one of them and killed and cooked him for dinner. The other two made their escape, pursued by the Læstrygonians, who with huge rocks destroyed all the ships and their crews which were within the harbour,—that of Odysseus, which had not entered, alone escaping.

When describing the country of the Læstrygonians, the poet says,[1]

> Lamos' high town,
> Far-gated Læstrygonia, where aloud
> The herdsman as he drives in calls, and he
> Who drives out hears him. There a sleepless man
> Might double wages earn; as neatherd one,
> And one as keeper of the snowy sheep;
> For near the paths are of the day and night.

The ancients explained this by the custom of pasturing the oxen at night, on account of the gad-fly (οἶστρος), whose persecution was thereby avoided: but, as Völcker justly observes, there was nothing so remarkable in this practice as to induce the poet to place it among the wonders of the West. It is much more probable that the solution of the difficulty will be found in the notion, presently to be noticed, of the abode of the Sun and Dawn being in the West, which may have engendered a belief that at the

---

[1] *Od.* x. 81.

western extremity of the earth the night was of extremely short continuance.[1]

Notwithstanding the great distance which lay between the country of the Kyklópes and that of the Læstrygonians, most of the localisers of the Homéric fables place both of them in Sicily.[2] Others regarded Formiæ on the west coast of Italy [3] as the abode of the Læstrygonians; acting in this consistently: for when the floating island of Æolos was determined to be one of the Liparæan isles, and the cape of Circæum to be that of Kirké, it followed of course that the land of the Læstrygonians which lay somewhere between them must be on the coast of Italy.

Κίρκη ἐν νήσῳ Ἀλαίῃ.   *Circe in Æœa insula.*

When Odysseus and his surviving companions had escaped from the Læstrygonians, they *sailed on,* that is still westwards, till they came to the Ææan isle,[4] the abode of Kirké.   This isle may be regarded as the most westerly of those scattered by the poet over the Mediterranean, for it appears to have lain on the very edge of the Ocean-stream; and all the other isles and coasts mentioned in the poem, except the O'gygian isle of Kalypsó, lie manifestly between it and Greece.

Kirké is one of those deities whom Homer calls *human-speaking* (αὐδήεσσαι), and who do not seem to have possessed the power of moving through the air or along the water, but dwelt continually in one place.   She is said by him [5] to be the daughter of Hélios by the O'keanis Persé, and own sister of the *grim* (ὀλοόφρων)[6] Æétés.

The island of Kirké was small: her abode was in the centre of it, deeply embosomed in wood.   She dwelt alone, attended by four nymphs; and all persons who approached her dwelling were turned by her magic art into swine.   When the comrades of Odysseus, whom he sent to explore her residence, had tasted of

[1] See *Kirké* and *Ortygia,* in this chapter : also Völcker, *Hom. Geog.* p. 116.
[2] Thuc. vi. 2.   Strab. i. 2, 9, p. 20.   Tzetz. *Lyc.* 956.   Sil. Ital. xiv. 125. Plin. *Nat. Hist.* iii. 8.   They fixed on the country about Leontíni.   Völcker prefers the north-west point of the island.
[3] Hor. *Carm.* iii. 16, 34 ; 17, 1.
[4] It is remarkable that the names of the four islands which the poet makes to be the abodes of superior beings are all formed of νῆσος and an adjective.
[5] *Od.* x. 135.
[6] *Od.* x. 137.   This term is applied in the Ilias to the serpent, the boar, and the lion ; in the Odyssey it is an epithet of Atlas, Minós, and Æétés.   Buttmann (*Mythol.* ii. 240) has shown that its proper meaning is *grim, stern :* see also Passow, *s. v.* and Nitzsch.

the drugged draught which she set before them, she struck them with her wand, and immediately they underwent the usual change. But when Odysseus himself, hearing of their misfortune, set out to release them or share their fate, he was met by Hermés, who gave him a plant named *Moly*, potent against her magic, and directed him how to act. Accordingly when she reached him the medicated bowl he drank of it freely, and Kirké thinking it had produced its usual effect, striking him with her wand bade him go join his comrades in their sty. But Odysseus drawing his sword threatened to slay her; and the terrified goddess bound herself by a solemn oath to do him no injury. She afterwards at his desire restored his companions to their pristine form, and they all abode in her dwelling for an entire year.

At the end of that period they were anxious to depart, but the goddess told the hero that he must previously cross the Ocean, and enter the abode of Aidés, to consult the blind prophet Teiresias. Accordingly they left her isle rather late in the day, as it would appear, and impelled by a favouring north-wind their ship reached by sunset the opposite Coast of Ocean, the land of perpetual gloom. Odysseus obeyed the directions of the goddess in digging a small pit, into which he poured mulse, wine, water, flour, and the blood of the victims. The dead came trooping out of the house of Aidés, and Odysseus there saw the heroines of former days, and conversed with the shades of Agamemnón and Achilleus. Terror at length came over him; he hastened back to his ship; the stream carried it along, and they reached the Ææan isle while it was yet night.

We have here a proof that the course of the Ocean was northwards; for the north-wind (βορέας) is required to carry them over (the House of Aidés lying probably south-west of the isle of Kirké), and the current and the breeze of its surface bring them back. It would also appear that, as soon as the ship left the Ocean and entered the Sea, it was at the Ææan island.

Kirké is said to have had by Odysseus a son named Télegonos (*Far-born*),[1] who, as we shall see, unwittingly slew his own father. The Theogony also gives them for offspring Argios or Agrios and Latínos, 'who afar in the recess of the holy isles ruled over all the renowned Tyrsenians.' Hésiod said elsewhere[2] that Hélios had brought Kirké in his chariot to her isle off the coast of Tyrrhenia.

It is curious to observe the liberties which the later writers allowed themselves to take with the narratives of Homer and

---

[1] *Theog.* 1014.   [2] Sch *Apoll. Rh.* 1.

Hésiod. These poets expressly say that Æétés and Kirké were brother and sister, and children of the Sun, yet Dionysius the kyklographer makes Kirké the daughter of Æétés by Hekaté, the daughter of his brother Persés. This pragmatiser goes on to say that she was married to the king of the Sarmatians, whom she poisoned, and seized his kingdom; but governing tyrannically she was expelled, and then fled to a desert isle of the Ocean, or as some said to the headland named from her in Italy;[1] for in the localisation of the imaginary isles and regions visited by Odysseus, the promontory of Circæum on the coast of Latium was fixed on for the abode of Kirké. The fact of its not being an island offered no difficulty, as it was asserted that it once had been surrounded with water to a great extent;[2] a thing in itself by no means improbable, but which must have been at a time long anterior to history, or even to mythology.

The Latin poets thence took occasion to connect Kirké with their own scanty mythology. It was fabled, for example, that she had been married to king Picus, whom by her magic art she changed into a bird.[3] Another legend made her the mother of Faunus by the god of the sea.[4]

The *Moly* (μῶλυ) is said by these late writers to have sprung from the blood of a giant slain by Hélios, in aid of his daughter in her island. Its name, we are told, comes from the fight (μῶλος); its flower is white, as the warrior was the Sun.[5]

In the Æææan isle, the poet says,[6] are 'the house and dance-place of E'os, and rising of the Sun.' By this he is usually understood to mean that this isle, in opposition to the country beyond the Ocean, from which his hero had just returned, lay within the realms of day.[7] This may very possibly be the truth; but we cannot help fancying that our poet, in the plenitude of his authority, had seized on the Argonautic cycle, and transferred Æétés and the Æææan isle to the West, from their proper place in the East;[8] and he may have retained the description of that isle, which accords perfectly with its eastern position, but which requires a sleight of ingenuity, like that just noticed, to make it suit the West.

On surveying the 'beautiful wonders' of the Odyssey, it is impossible not to be struck with the resemblance which some of them

---

[1] Diodór. iv. 45.   Eudocia, 261.   Sch. *Apoll. Rh.* iii. 200.
[2] Plin. *Nat. Hist.* iii. 5.   Serv. *Æn.* iii. 386 : comp. Apoll. Rh. iv. 659 *seq*
[3] See below, *Mythology of Italy.*   [4] Nonn. xiii. 330.
[5] Ptol. Héphæst. iv.   [6] *Od.* xii. 3.
[7] Sch. *in loc.*   Völcker, *Hom. Geog.* 131.
[8] See below, *Argonautica.*

bear to those of the Thousand and One Nights. Odysseus and Kirké remind us at once of king Bedr and queen Láb; and the Kyklópes and the Læstrygonians will find their parallel in the adventures of Sindibad. Are these, it may be asked, mere coincidences, or did the tales of the West find their way to the East? On this question we have offered some remarks elsewhere, to which we must refer the curious.[1]

Σειρῆνες. *Sirenes.* 𝕾𝖎𝖗𝖊𝖓𝖘.

Leaving the Ææan isle on their homeward voyage, Odysseus and his companions came first to the island of the Sirens. These were two maidens[2] who sat in a mead close to the sea, and with their melodious voices so charmed those who were sailing by, that they forgot home and everything relating to it, and abode there till their bones lay whitening on the strand. By the directions of Kirké, Odysseus stopped the ears of his companions with wax, and had himself tied to the mast, and thus was the only person who heard the song of the Sirens and escaped.

Hésiod[3] described the mead of the Sirens as blooming with flowers (ἀνθεμόεσσα), and their voice he said[4] stilled the winds. Their names were said to be Aglaiophémé (*Clear-speaker*) and Thelxiepeia (*Magic-speaker*); and it was feigned that they threw themselves into the sea with vexation at the escape of Odysseus.[5] But the author of the Orphic Argonautics places them on a rock near the shore of Ætna, and makes the song of Orpheus end their enchantment, and cause them to fling themselves into the sea, where they were changed into rocks.[6]

It was afterwards fabled that they were the daughters of the river-god Achelóos by the Muse Terpsichoré or Kalliopé, or by Steropé, daughter of Portháon.[7] Some said that they sprang from the blood which ran from him when his horn was torn off by Héraklés.[8] Sophoklés calls them the daughters of Phorkys;[9] and Euripidés terms them the children of Earth.[10] Their number was also increased to three, and their names are given with much variety. According to some they were called Leukosia, Ligeia

---

[1] *Tales and Popular Fictions*, p. 125. [2] *Od.* xii. 52, 167.
[3] Sch. *Apoll. Rh.* iv. 892. [4] Sch. *Od.* xii. 169.
[5] Sch. *Od.* xii. 39.
[6] Orph. *Argon.* 1284 *seq.*: comp. Nonn. xiii. 312 *seq.*
[7] Apoll. Rh. iv. 895. Apollod. i. 3, 4. Ov. *Met.* v. 552. Tzetz. *Lyc.* 712. Eudocia, 373.
[8] Theon Sophista. [9] *Ap. Plut. Sympos.* ix. 14. [10] *Hel.* 168.

and Parthenopé,[1] while others named them Thelxiopé or Thelxinoé,
Molpé, Aglaophonos;[2] and others, again, Peisinoé, Aglaopé,
Thelxiepeia.[3] One was said to play on the lyre, another on the
pipes, and the third to sing.[4] Apollónios gives them as companions
to Persephoné in her maiden-days.[5]

Contrary to the usual process, the mischievous part of the
character of the Sirens was in process of time left out, and they
were regarded as purely musical beings with entrancing voices.
Hence Plató in his Republic[6] places one of them on each of the
eight celestial spheres, where their voices form what is called the
music of the spheres; and when (Ol. 94, 1) the Lakedæmonians
had laid siege to Athens, Dionýsos, it is said, appeared in a dream
to their general, Lysander, ordering him to allow the funeral rites
of the new Siren to be celebrated, which was at once understood
to be Sophoklés, then just dead.[7]

Eventually, however, the artists laid hold on the Sirens, and
furnished them with the feathers, feet, wings, and tails of birds.[8]

The ordinary derivation of the word Siren is from σείρα, *a chain*,
to signify their attractive power. To us the Semitic *Shîr* (שִׁיר),
song, seems more likely to be the true root, and we regard them
as one of the wonders told of by the Phœnician mariners.[9]

Σκύλλη καὶ Χάρυβδις.   *Scylla et Charybdis.*

Having escaped the Sirens, and shunned the Wandering Rocks,
which Kirké had told him lay beyond the mead of these songsters,

---

[1] Eudocia, 373. Tzetz. *Lyc.* 712. The tomb of Parthenopé gave name to
the city afterwards called Neapolis (Naples). Milton thus alludes to these
names of the Sirens:

> By Thetis' tinsel-slippered feet,
> And the songs of Sirens sweet,
> By dead Parthenopé's dear tomb,
> And fair Ligea's golden comb,
> Wherewith she sits on diamond rocks,
> Sleeking her soft alluring locks.—*Comus*, 877.

We may observe how he confounds them with the Teutonic mermaids.

[2] Sch. *Apoll. Rh.* iv. 892. Eudocia, 373.   [3] Tzetz. *ut sup.*
[4] Tzetz. *ut sup.* Serv. *Æn.* v. 864.   [5] *Arg.* iv. 896.
[6] Lib. x. p. 617. Comp. Milton, *Arcades* 62 *seq.*
[7] Paus. i. 21, 1. Plut. *Numa*, 4. Σοφοκλέους βίος. Plin. *Nat. Hist.* vii. 29
[8] So they are described by Apollónios, iv. 898.
[9] Many of the names placed in the West by the poet of the Odyssey appear
to be of Semitic origin. Thus, beside the one in the text, the Elysian Plain
may be fairly derived from *'álass* (עָלַץ) *to rejoice;* Erebos from *'ereb* (עָרַב)
evening; Kimmerians from *kámar* (כָּמַר) *to be dark.* In Hindú cosmology the
south pole, the abode of Yama, the Hindú Hadés, is named Kúmerú, i. e. Lower
Merú; but this is a mere coincidence of sound.

Odysseus came to the terrific Skylla and Charybdis, between which the goddess had informed him his course lay. She said[1] he would come to two lofty cliffs opposite each other, between which he must pass. One of these cliffs towers to such a height that its summit is for ever enveloped in clouds, and no man even if he had twenty hands and as many feet could ascend it. In the middle of this cliff, she says, is a cave facing the west, but so high that a man in a ship passing under it could not shoot up to it with a bow. In this den dwells Skylla (*Bitch*), whose voice sounds like that of a young whelp: she has twelve feet, and six long necks, with a terrific head and three rows of close-set teeth on each. Evermore she stretches out these necks and catches the porpoises, sea-dogs, and other large animals of the sea which swim by, and out of every ship that passes each mouth takes a man.

The opposite rock, the goddess informs him, is much lower, for a man could shoot over it. A wild fig-tree grows on it, stretching its branches down to the water: but beneath, ' divine Charybdis ' three times each day absorbs and regorges the dark water. It is much more dangerous, she adds, to pass Charybdis than Skylla.

As Odysseus sailed by, Skylla took six of his crew; and when, after he had lost his ship and companions, he was carried by wind and wave, as he floated on a part of the wreck, between the monsters, the mast by which he supported himself was sucked in by Charybdis. He held by the fig-tree till it was thrown out again, and then resumed his voyage.

Such is the earliest account we have of these monsters, in which indeed it may be doubted if Charybdis is to be regarded as an animate being. The whole fable is evidently founded on the wonderful tales of sailors respecting the distant regions of the Mediterranean. The ancients, who were so anxious to localise all the wonders of Homer, made the straits of Messina the abode of Skylla and Charybdis; but as there is no whirlpool there at all resembling Charybdis, the most that can be said is, that that strait may have given occasion to the fable. Homer, however, would seem to place the cliffs of Skylla and Charybdis somewhere between the Wandering Rocks and the Thrinakian isle (if this last be Sicily); for it is after passing those rocks that Odysseus comes to the latter island, on which the oxen of the Sun grazed.

In Homer the mother of Skylla is named Krataeis;[2] but her sire is not mentioned; Stésichoros called her mother Lamia.[3] Hésiod said she was the daughter of Phorbas and Hekaté;

---

[1] *Od.* xii. 73.
[3] Eu locia, 377.

[2] *Od.* xii. 124.
[4] Sch. *Apoll. Rh.* iv. 828.

Arkesiláos said, of Phorkys and Hekaté;[1] while others asserted that Triton was her sire.[2]

Later poets feigned that Skylla was once a beautiful maiden, who was fond of associating with the Néréides. The sea-god Glaukos beheld and fell in love with her;[3] and being rejected, applied to Kirké to exercise her magic arts in his favour. Kirké wished him to transfer his affections to herself; and filled with rage at his refusal, she infected with noxious juices the water in which Skylla was wont to bathe, and thus transformed her into a monster.[4] According to another account the change in Skylla's form was effected by Amphitríté, in consequence of her intimacy with Poseidón.[5] Charybdis was said to have been a woman who stole the oxen of Héraklés, and was in consequence struck with thunder by Zeus, and turned into a whirlpool.[6]

Φαέθουσα καὶ Λαμπετίη ἐν νήσῳ Θρινακίῃ. *Phaethusa et Lampetie in Thrinakia insula.*

Both Teiresias and Kirké had straitly charged Odysseus to shun the Thrinakian isle, on which the flocks and herds of the Sun-god fed, under the care of his daughters Phaëthusa and Lampetié, and to which he would come immediately after escaping Skylla and Charybdis.[7] Odysseus was desirous of obeying the injunctions which he had received; but as it was evening when he came to the island, his companions forced him to consent to their landing and passing the night there. They promised to depart in the morning, and took an oath to abstain from the cattle of the Sun. During the night a violent storm came on; and for an entire month afterwards a strong south-east wind (Euros and Notos) blew, which confined them to the island. When their provisions were exhausted, they lived on such birds and fish as they could catch. At length, while Odysseus was sleeping, Eurylochos prevailed on them to slaughter some of the sacred oxen in sacrifice

---

[1] Id. *ib.* and Sch. *Od.* xii. 85. [2] Eudocia, 377.

[3] The poetess Hédyla said (Athén. vii. 297) that he used to come to Skylla's cave.

Ἢ κόγχου δώρωμα φέροντ' Ἐρυθραίας ἀπὸ πέτρης,
ἢ τοὺς ἀλκυόνων παῖδας ἐτ' ἀπτερύγους,
τῇ νύμφῃ δυσπείστῳ ἀθύρματα. Δάκρυ δ' ἐκείνου
καὶ Σειρὴν γείτων παρθένος ᾠκτίσατο.

[4] Ov. *Met.* xiv. 1 *seq.* Hygin. 199. [5] Tzetz. *Lyc.* 650.

[6] Serv. *Æn.* iii. 420. The root of Charybdis may be *khárab* (חָרֵב) 'to dry up,' used of streams and of water in general. She might be indebted for her origin to the Phœnician accounts of the floods and ebbs of the tide in the Ocean. [7] *Od.* xi. 106; xii. 127. See above, p. 50.

to the gods, and to vow by way of amends a temple to Hélios.[1] Odysseus on awaking was filled with horror and despair at what they had done; and the displeasure of the gods was manifested by prodigies; for the hides crept along the ground, and the flesh lowed on the spits. They fed for six days on the sacred cattle; on the seventh the storm fell, and they left the island, but as soon as they had lost sight of land, a terrible west-wind, accompanied by thunder, lightning, and pitch-darkness, came on. Zeus struck the ship with a thunderbolt: it went to pieces, and all the sacrilegious crew were drowned.

The resemblance between Thrinakia and Trinakria,[2] a name of Sicily, has induced both ancients and moderns to acquiesce in the opinion of the two islands being identical. Against this opinion we will observe, that the Thrinakian was a *desert isle* ($\nu\hat{\eta}\sigma o s\ \dot{\epsilon}\rho\dot{\eta}\mu\eta$),[3] that is, an uninhabited isle; and that during the whole month that Odysseus and his men were in it they did not meet with any one, and could procure no food but birds and fish; that it is called the *excellent isle of the god*,[4] whose peculiar property it therefore must have been; that according to the analogy of the Odyssey it must have been a small island, for such were the Ææan, the O'gygian, and all the other isles we meet with;—not one of which circumstances agrees with Sicily. It seems therefore the more probable supposition, that the poet regarded the Thrinakian isle as an islet of about the same size as those of Kirké and Kalypsó, belonging to the Sun-god, and tenanted only by his flocks and herds, and his two daughters their keepers. He must also have conceived it to lie much more to the west than Sicily, for it could not have been more than the third day after leaving the Ææan isle that Odysseus arrived at it.

Καλυψὼ ἐν νήσῳ Ὠγυγίῃ. *Calypso in Ogygia insula.*

Odysseus, when his ship had gone to pieces, fastened the mast and keel together, and placed himself on them. The wind changing to the south-east ($\nu\acute{o}\tau o s$) carried him back to Skylla and Charybdis. As he came by the latter, she absorbed the mast and keel, but the

---

[1] The episode (xii. 374–390) of the complaint of Hélios to Zeus was rejected by the ancient grammarians. We may observe that the cosmology in it is at variance with that of the Odyssey, for Hélios menaces a *descent* to Erebos:

Δύσομαι εἰς Ἀΐδαο, καὶ ἐν νεκύεσσι φαείνω.

[2] Thukydidés (vii. 1) is we believe the first writer who uses the name Trinakria.   [3] *Od.* xii. 351.

[4] *Od.* xii. 261. Θρινακία may possibly be connected with θέρω, θέρος, θερινός, and other terms expressive of heat, summer, etc.

hero caught hold of the fig-tree, and held by it till they were thrown out again. He then floated along for nine days; and on the tenth reached the O'gygian isle,[1] the abode of Kalypsó, by whom he was most kindly received and entertained. She detained him there for eight years, designing to make him immortal, and to keep him with her for ever : but Hermés arriving with a command from Zeus, she was obliged to consent to his departure She gave the hero tools to build a bark or light vessel, supplied him with provisions, and reluctantly took a final leave of him.

Kalypsó, that is *The Concealer* (the poet after his usual manner giving her a significant name), is called by Homer[2] the daughter of Atlas : Hésiod[3] makes her an O'keanis, and Apollodóros[4] a Néréis. Like Kirké she was a *human-speaking* goddess, and dwelt in solitary state with her attendant nymphs ; but her abode was a cavern, while the daughter of Hélios possessed a mansion of cut-stone. Her isle presented such a scene of silvan beauty as charmed even Hermés, one of the dwellers of Olympos.[5] According to Hésiod[6] she bore to Odysseus two sons named Nausithoos and Nausinoos.

The poet seems to have conceived the O'gygian isle to lie in the north-western part of the West-sea, far remote from all the other isles and coasts ; and he thus brought his hero into all parts of that sea, and informed his auditors of all its wonders. A south-east wind carried Odysseus thither on his mast in nine days and nights from Charybdis. When he left the O'gygian isle, sailing in his bark, as directed by Kalypsó, with the constellation of the Bear on his left, that is in an easterly or south-easterly direction, he came on the eighteenth day within sight of Scheria, the country of the Phæakians.

Οἱ Φαίηκες ἐν Σχερίῃ.   Phœaces in Scheria.

The Phæakians dwelt originally, we are told, in Hypereia, near the Kyklópes ;[7] but being oppressed by that savage race, they migrated to the isle of Scheria. They were led thither by their king Nausithoos, the son of Poseidón by Períboa the youngest daughter of Eurymedón king of the Giants.[8] They were, like the Kyklópes and Giants, a people akin to the gods,[9] who appeared

---

[1] See Appendix D.
[3] *Theog.* 358. Hom. *Hymn.* v. 422.
[5] *Od.* v. 72 *seq.*
[7] *Od.* vi. 4.
[9] *Od.* v. 35. Nitzsch *in loc.* vii. 205. Alkæos said that they sprang from the drops of blood which fell from Uranos when mutilated by his son. Sch. Apoll. *Rh.* iv. 992.

[2] *Od.* i. 52 ; vii. 245.
[4] Apollod. i. 2.
[6] *Theog.* 1017.
[8] *Od.* vi. 7 ; vii. 56.

manifestly, and feasted among them when they offered sacrifices,[1] and did not conceal themselves from solitary wayfarers when they met them.[2] They had abundance of wealth, and lived in the enjoyment of it undisturbed by the alarms of war; for as they 'dwelt remote from gain-seeking man,'[3] no enemy ever approached their shores; and they did not even require to make use of bows and quivers.[4] Their chief employment was navigation: their ships, which went with the velocity of the wing of birds or of thought,[5] were, like the Argó, endued with intelligence: they knew every port, and needed no pilot when impelled by the rowers.[6]

As Odysseus sailed in his bark from the O'gygian isle, the island of Scheria appeared to him on the eighteenth day, 'like a shield in the dark sea;'[7] and when the storm by which Poseidón destroyed his bark had subsided, he was carried along, as he swam, by a strong northerly wind for two days and nights, and on the third day he got on shore in that island.[8] The princess Nausikaa, when reproving the false alarm of her maids at the sight of him, says,[9]

> Stop, maidens! whither fly ye seeing a man?
> Haply ye deem it is some enemy?
> This man is not injurious, nor are there
> Any who come to the Phæakians' land
> With hostile thoughts; for dearly are they loved
> By the Immortals. Apart from all we dwell
> In the wave-full sea, the most remote, and ne'er
> Do others with us intercourse maintain.

In another place, when noticing the occasion for scandal which her appearance in company with Odysseus might give, she supposes some one to say,[10] " Is it some stranger who has strayed from his ship that she has taken under her care, since there are no people near us?" All this would seem to indicate some very remote position; and a passage in which Alkinoos says, that the Phæakians had conveyed Rhadamanthys to Euboea[11] and returned on the same day, might lead to the supposition of Scheria's being to the west of Ithaka; for the abode of Rhadamanthys was the E'lysian Plain on the shore of Ocean.[12] It was on the west side of

---

[1] *Od.* vii. 201. Nitzsch *in loc.*   [2] *Od.* vii. 204.   [3] *Od.* vi. 8.
[4] *Od.* vi. 270.   [5] *Od.* vii. 36.   [6] *Od.* viii. 556 *seq.*
[7] *Od.* v. 279 *seq.*   [8] *Od.* v. 385 *seq.*   [9] *Od.* vi. 200.
[10] *Od.* vi. 278.
[11] *Od.* vii. 321 *seq.* Payne Knight pronounces the whole passage 311–333 to be spurious, and we think his reasons satisfactory. Aristarchos suspected the first six lines.
[12] *Od.* iv. 564: see Part II. chap. iv. *Tityos.*

Ithaka, we may observe, that the Phæakians landed Odysseus; and if we are right in placing the Kyklópes on the coast of Libya, Scheria most probably lay in the sea somewhere to the north of it. The truth is, the Phæakians and their island are altogether as imaginary as any of the isles and tribes which we have already noticed,—all as ideal as those visited by Sindibad or Gulliver,— a circumstance which in reality gives additional charms to this most delightful poem.[1]

The place determined by both ancients and moderns to be Scheria is the island of Kerkýra,[2] the modern Corfu, which lies at a very short distance from the coast of E'peiros. It would not perhaps be allowable to urge, that the circumstances of the preceding paragraph do not by any means apply to Kerkýra, for we know not what the Iónian Singer's idea of it may have been. All we will say is, that his language respecting it accords much better with some imaginary western isle than with Kerkýra; and that if the Kyklópes were on the coast of Libya, Kerkýra could not have been Scheria. The firm persuasion of the identity of these two islands seems to have been produced by two passages of the poem, the one in which Eurymedusa, the attendant of Nausikaa, is said to have been brought from Apeiros, which is taken to be E'peiros;[3] the other the fictitious narrative of Odysseus to Pénelopé,[4] in which, speaking in an assumed character, he says that Odysseus, when shipwrecked after leaving the Thrinakian isle, had reached Scheria, and had gone thence to Thesprótia, which was consequently supposed to be near it; and as Kerkyra was the principal island in that direction, it was at once inferred to be that of the Phæakians. Völcker lays great stress on the circumstance of Pénelopé's seeing nothing incongruous in the narrative; but it surely does not follow that she knew anything of either the Thrinakian isle or Scheria, and Odysseus may have taken the liberty of assigning a false position to this last place. We finally think, that if Thesprótia and its oracle at Dódóna were so well known to the poet as they seem to have been, he never could have described the Phæakians, supposing Kerkyra to be their island, as dwelling so remote.

[1] This is also the opinion of Nitzsch. *Erklär. Anmerk. zur Odyssee*, ii. 72-78, 150-2. The name Phæakians signifies *the Illustrious, the Renowned*, from φάω.

[2] Thuk. i. 25; iii. 70. Apoll. Rh. iv. 982 *seq. cum Schol.* Tzetz. *Lyc.* 818.

[3] The first syllable of ἄπειρος is short, that of ἤπειρος is long. On this however we should lay no stress.

[4] *Od.* xix. 371 *seq.*

Two islands remain to be considered, in order to finish our view of the isles and coasts of the Homeric West-sea. These are

'Ορτυγία καὶ Συρία. *Ortygia et Syria.*

Kalypsó says[1] to Hermés, that ' rose-fingered' E'ós took O'ríon, and that 'gold-seated' Artemis slew him with her gentle darts in Ortygia. Eumæos,[2] describing his native isle Syria, says that it lies *beyond* (καθύπερθεν) Ortygia, where are the *turnings* (τροπαὶ) of the sun. Syria, he proceeds, is not large, but it is fruitful, abounding in sheep, in pasturage, in vines, and in corn; it is never visited by famine or by any disease; but when the people grow old, 'silver-bowed Apolló comes with Artemis and kills them with his gentle darts.' It contained two towns; between the inhabitants of which, who were governed by one king, all things in it were divided. The Phœnicians and Taphians visited it for the sake of trade.

It is almost impossible, we should think, not to recognise in Ortygia and Syria two happy isles of the West-sea, apparently sacred to Apolló and Artemis; and we must marvel at those ancients and moderns who place them in the Ægæan, making the one the same as Délos,[3] and the other identical with Syros one of the Kyklades.[4] The Phœnicians, be it observed, who stole away Eumæos, sailed with a favourable wind homewards during six days: on the seventh Eumæos' nurse died, and wind and water carried them on to Ithaka, where they sold him to Laërtés. Their course was therefore evidently from the west or north-west toward Sidón, as Ithaka lay in their way. When however the Greeks settled in Sicily, they named the islet in the port of Syracuse Ortygia; and the point of land opposite to it was probably pronounced to be Syria.

The '*turnings of the sun*' seems merely to denote a westerly position, and to be an expression of the same nature with that of the '*risings of the sun*' being in the Æœan isle. Müller[5] sees in it a reference to the sun-dial of Pherekýdés of Syros, and therefore regards the verse which mentions it as the interpolation of a rhapsodist.

The narrative of Eumæos may serve to throw some light on the

---

[1] *Od.* v. 121. [2] *Od.* xv. 403 *seq.*
[3] Apoll. Rh. i. 419. Verg. *Æn.* iii. 124, 143, 154. Servius on *v.* 73. Strab. x. 5, 5, p. 486. Müller (*Die Dorier*, i. 377) maintains that the Ortygia of this place in the Odyssey is Délos. As this passage does not appear in the English translation of his work, we may perhaps infer that his opinion changed.
[4] Strab. x. 5, 8, p. 487. Müller asserts positively in his *Orchomenos* (p. 126) that this is the island meant in the Odyssey. Perhaps (see preceding note) he changed this opinion also. [5] *Orchom.* 326

trade of the Phœnicians in those early ages. Supposing Syria to have lain to the west of Greece, it follows that this people were known to make commercial voyages in that direction; and we may also collect from it that it was chiefly ornamental articles (ἀθύρματα) which they offered for sale. The ship whose crew carried off Eumæos continued an entire year at Syria, to dispose of her cargo and lay in one in return,—a circumstance which may tend to illustrate the three years' voyages of the fleets of king Solomon.[1] It also appears that the Greeks made voyages to both the East and the West; for the nurse of Eumæos was daughter of Arybas a wealthy Sidónian, who had been carried away from her native country by Taphian pirates, and sold to the father of Eumæos.

We have now completed our survey of the magic isles and coasts, the mild and savage tribes, the gentle or pernicious goddesses, with which poetic imagination, working probably on the 'shipman's tale' of marvellous adventure of frequent peril, had filled the little-explored waters of the Mediterranean. While presenting our own hypothesis respecting them, we wish not to conceal those of others, or dogmatically demand assent to what we advance. Our object has been to endeavour by these elucidations to enhance the delight which every person of taste must feel when perusing one of the most charming monuments of human genius,—the Odyssey of Homer.

> Farewell ye continents, and of the deep
> Ye isles, and Ocean's waters, and the Sea's
> Great streams, ye springs and rivers, and ye hills
> Wood-hung; for I have now gone o'er the whole
> Flood of the sea, and all the winding track
> Of continents. But may the blissful gods
> Themselves the meed due to my song bestow.[2]

---

[1] 1 Kings x. 22: comp. Pliny, *Nat. Hist.* xii. 19.
[2] Dionysios, *Periegésis*, 1181 *seq.*

MYTHOLOGY OF GREECE.

PART II.—THE HEROES.

CHAPTER I.

INTRODUCTION.

Origin and First State of Man.

THE origin of mankind, like that of the earth their abode, is a subject which will be found to have engaged the thoughts of almost every race that occupies its surface. The mind feels itself invincibly impelled to this reflection, from observing the changes and revolutions which continually take place around it. Each revolving year brings to the vegetable world the seasons of decay and of reviviscence; mankind are born, flourish, and die; a new generation is ever filling up the vacancies caused by death; races migrate; where population once flourished, there is desolation; where once the wilderness spread, is heard the busy hum of men, and commerce and agriculture display their stores. Has it always been so? is the question man naturally asks himself. Has the world ever gone on thus decaying and renewing?—and he carries back his thoughts through ages and generations, till for very weariness he is obliged to stop somewhere and suppose a beginning.

A remnant of primæval tradition, or the natural operation of the mind itself, has led almost all races to conceive the original state of man to have been one of peace and happiness. At all periods of his life man looks back to the gay and careless days of childhood with pleasure and regret. Then, while his faculties were new and unworn, each part of nature was a source of bliss; then suns shone more brightly, plants diffused more fragrance, the melody of groves was poured forth more rapturously, the day closed in joy, the morning awoke to renewed delight. It was easy and it was natural to transfer these ideas to the race of man; to suppose them also to have commenced in blissful infancy, amid the abundant wealth and careless ease of nature, and to have passed progressively through different stages, deteriorating in each successive stage, as unhappily the greater part of mankind do, and from the innocence of childhood advancing to the selfishness and hardened vice of mature and declining age. Most mythic systems therefore have their Golden Age.[1]

Ages of the World.

Homer nowhere speaks of cosmogony or of the ages of the world. Hésiod, who is the first that treats of them, gives in his didactic poem the following venerable mythe.[2]

The gods first made the Golden race of men, who were in the time when Kronos ruled in heaven.[3] They lived like gods, free from toils and care, and death was to them a sinking into gentle slumber; and when earth had covered this race, they became good terrestrial dæmons, the guardians of mortal men, to mark their just and unjust deeds. They move along the earth shrouded in darkness, and are the bestowers of wealth. Such is their regal honour.[4]

The gods made a second far inferior race, called the Silver race, resembling the golden neither in appearance nor in disposition. A hundred years each child spent in ignorant simplicity with its mother, and when they attained to youth they lived but a short time, for they would not abstain from mutual injury, nor pay the service due to the gods. Zeus in indignation put a period to the race.

Zeus now made a third, the Brazen race of men, unlike the silver race. These were formed from ash-trees: their delight was in war and deeds of violence. They ate not corn, but they had souls of steel, and prodigious strength. Their arms were brass, their houses brass, with brass they wrought, 'for black iron was not yet.' At length, slain by each other's hands, they went down to the 'mouldy house of cold Aïdés,' and left no fame behind them.

A fourth and better race was next placed on the earth by Zeus, namely the divine race of Heroes, in former times called Semigods. These also were carried off by war and combat. They fought at Thébes, on account of the sheep of Œdipus, and sailed to Troy for 'well-haired Helené.' When they died, Zeus removed them to the ends of the earth, where they dwell, away from man, in the Islands of the Blest, and live in bliss, earth producing for them 'honey-sweet fruit' thrice in each revolving year.

The poet draws a dismal picture of the fifth or Iron race of men; a picture often since his time re-drawn by moralists and poets in every region of the earth, for this is the race who still possess it. This race, says Hésiod, will never cease day or night

---

[1] Comp. Völcker, *Myth. der Jap.* 256. [2] Ἔργ. 109 : see above, p. 62.
[3] See above, p. 43. [4] See Plató, *Laws,* iv. p. 713.

from toil and misery; the gods will give them grievous cares, yet good will still be mixed with the evil. Zeus will destroy this race also, when they become 'hoary-templed.' Fathers will not be at unity with their children, nor brethren with each other; friends and guests will be discordant, children will not honour their aged parents. Club-law will prevail, faith and justice will be in no repute, the evil-doer and the violent will be most esteemed, 'evil-loving Envy' will accompany wretched man. Shame and Aversion (*Nemesis*) will wrap themselves in their 'white mantles' and depart to the gods, leaving misery to man; and there will be no defence against evil.

Arátos[1] is the next in order of time who mentions the ages of the world. He speaks of but three races of men,—the golden, the silver, and the brazen. Justice (Δίκη), he says, dwelt familiarly among the first, teaching them what was right and good. When the silver race succeeded she retired to the mountains, whence she occasionally came down in the evening-time, and approaching their abodes upbraided them with their evil doings. Unable to endure the third race, who first forged arms and fed on the flesh of the labouring ox, she flew up to heaven and became the constellation of Astræa or the Virgin.

Ovid[2] makes the races of men four in number,—golden, silver, brazen, and iron. The first enjoyed a perpetual spring, the earth producing everything spontaneously for them: in the time of the second the division of the seasons took place: the third were martial, but not yet utterly wicked: the fourth gave way to every species of vice and crime, Astræa left the earth, and Zeus destroyed them by a deluge of water.

In all these accounts it is to be observed that it is *races* of men, not *ages* of the world, which are spoken of.[3] Hésiod makes these races separate creations: the first two, he says, were made by the gods, the last three by Zeus, who attained the supremacy of heaven in the time of the second or silver race. Earth covers each race before its successor is made. Arátos expressly says that the golden were the parents of the silver, and these of the brazen race of men. Ovid would appear to view the subject in the same light.

To dispel the gloomy prospect presented by the delineation of the vices and miseries of man in the last stage of the progression, it was asserted, that as the four seasons, commencing with a bright

---

[1] *Phænomena*, 100 *seq.*   [2] *Met.* i. 89 *seq.*

[3] So also Vergil (*Buc.* iv. *passim*, *Geor.* ii. 537) and Claudian (*Rapt. Pros.* ii. 286). The modern error has arisen from not observing that in these places of the poets *ætas* is the translation of γένος.

golden spring and ending with a gloomy iron winter, form the solar year, which is continually renewed: so the four ages of the world compose a mundane year which will also be renewed and the iron race be succeeded by a new one of gold, when Kronos will once more assume the government, and the former innocent and happy state return.[1]

A mythologist, of whom even when we dissent from his opinions we must always admire the sound learning, ingenious reasoning, and high moral feeling,[2] gives the following view of the mythe of the races of man.

This mythe is an oriental one, derived from the same source with the narrative in the first chapters of Genesis, and introduced into Grecian literature by Hésiod, who may be regarded as the Plató of his age. It contained originally, as it is given by Arátos, only the first three ages. Its object was not to give a view of the gradual deterioration of mankind, but to exhibit the relation of the deity to the wickedness of the human race, and particularly to impress the belief that when evil has attained its *maximum* the gods will destroy mankind. To this intent it was necessary to commence with a state of innocence; and the original framer of the mythe probably made the silver and brazen races, instead of successively following that of gold, exist simultaneously after it,— effeminacy and violence, the two vices into which virtue is most apt to degenerate, being their respective characters,—and feigned that the former was gradually extirpated by the latter, which was then destroyed by the gods; but this was misunderstood by Hésiod. The account of the fourth and fifth races was an application of the ancient mythe to the actual world, and from a moral it became a continuation of the narrative. As the working of iron was regarded as a later invention than that of brass or copper, and as it is a harder metal, it was naturally selected to express the last and worst race of men; but as tradition spake distinctly of the Heroic race who fought at Thébes and Troy, it was necessary to distinguish it from the iron one: hence the cycle is, as it were, repeated; but the latter one, being founded on reality, consists of only two parts. The heroes who correspond to the golden race are like them rewarded after death, but in an inferior degree: the iron are menaced with utter destruction like the brazen.

This critic is further of opinion that in the original narrative the three races were represented as becoming after death three different classes of spirits, the golden celestial, the silver terrestrial, and the brazen infernal; answering to the good and evil

[1] Verg. *Buc.* iv. 6. Voss. *in loc.* Seneca, *Octavia*, ii. 1. 16 *sq.* On the other hand see Lobeck, *Aglaoph.* 791 *s q.*   [2] Buttmann, *Mythol.* ii. 1 *sq.*

angels of the religions of the East; but that, as the Grecian religion acknowledged no evil spirits, the poet found it necessary to cut away this last part of the original mythe.

Völcker[1] on the other hand considers the Heroic race to have been an essential part of the original mythe, which he regards chiefly on that account as being a post-Homéric composition, framed with a regard to the Homéric and other contemporary poems.   He also thinks that the lines in which Hésiod describes the deification of the golden race are an interpolation, inserted at the time when the intercourse prevailed with Egypt, and Grecian philosophers visited that country.   As we do not esteem the notion of a community of mythology between Greece and Asia and Egypt in the ante-Homéric times to rest on any solid foundation, though we freely acknowledge the sublimity of that theory, we feel disposed to acquiesce to a certain extent in this last opinion, and to reject the ingenious hypothesis stated above.[2]

'Ιαπετὸς, Ἄτλας, Μενοίτιος, Προμηθεὺς καὶ Ἐπιμηθεύς.[3]
Iapetos, Atlas, Menœtios, Prometheus et Epimetheus.

According to the Theogony the Titan Iapetos espoused Klymené[4] (*Bright-one*), a daughter of O'keanos, by whom he was the father of four sons, Atlas, Menœtios, Prométheus and Epimétheus.   We find Iapetos frequently joined with Kronos, apart as it were from the other Titans; and it is worthy of notice, that in the Theogony (where there is more of order and method than is usually supposed) the account of Iapetos and his progeny immediately succeeds that of Kronos and the gods sprung from him. These circumstances, combined with the plain meaning of the names of his children, led to the conclusion of Iapetos being intended to represent the origin of the human race.

The gods, as we have seen, are the offspring of Time, and as man, according to the sacred Scriptures, is 'born unto misery,' it may not be unreasonable to find in the name of the progenitor of mankind a reference to this condition; and hence perhaps we

[1] *Myth. der Jap.* 250 seq.
[2] We however agree with Buttmann in thinking that in the original mythe there were only four ages.   The Hindús, it may be observed, have also *four* Yúgas or ages of the world, and we must recollect the analogy of the four seasons.
[3] On the subject of Iapetos and his children, see the excellent work of Völcker so frequently quoted in the preceding pages.
[4] *Theog.* 507 seq.   Some said Æthra (Timæos *ap.* Sch. *Il.* xviii. 486), others Asia, others Libya; these two last refer to the abodes of Prométheus and Atlas.

might venture to render Iapetos the *Afflicted* or the *Oppressed*.[1] The name of his wife may then refer to that faded splendour which still adheres to man, while those of his sons express the qualities of the human mind; Atlas being the patient and persevering, Menœtios the hot and impetuous, Prométheus the prudent, and Epimétheus the imprudent.[2]   These we will now proceed to illustrate.

Menœtios is called by Hésiod[3] the *insolent* and the *haughty*; and Zeus, it is added, struck him with his thunder and precipitated him into Erebos on account of his 'insolence and excessive manhood;' perhaps intimating that pride and haughtiness and extreme reliance on his powers hurry man to death. It is said by later writers that for his share in the Titan-war Menœtios was hurled into Tartaros, but this arose from the misunderstanding of that mythe.[4]

Atlas (*The Endurer*) occupies a much larger space in mythology than Menœtios.   Homer[5] calls him the *grim being* (ὀλοόφρων). 'who knows all the depths of the sea, and keeps the long pillars which hold heaven and earth asunder.'   In the Theogony[6] he is said to support the heaven on his head and hands in the extreme West, a task assigned him by Zeus, in punishment, the later writers say. for his share in the Titan-war.[7]

Atlas was the father of the fair nymph Kalypsó, who so long detained Odysseus in her umbrageous isle in the distant West.[8] Pléioné, an Ocean-nymph, bore him seven daughters, named Pléiades after their mother;[9] he was also said to be the father of the nymphs named Hyades.[10]   When, therefore, we consider the signification of his name in connection with the position assigned him by Homer and Hésiod, and the species of knowledge ascribed to him, and his being the father of two of the

---

[1] From ἵπτομαι (ἵπτω) *to oppress*, or ἰάπτω *to strike;* it thus resembles Job in signification. Its connection with the Japhet of Scripture we can neither affirm nor deny.

[2] Atlas, with *a* euphonic, from τλάω *to endure;* Menœtios, from μένος *strength, passion, rage* (see Welcker, *Tril.* 68 *note*, above, p. 15). Some derive it from μένειν τὸν οἶτον, as significatory of man's *mortality*. The derivations of Prométheus and Epimétheus are obvious.

[3] *Theog.* 510, 514.

[4] Apollod. i. 2, 3. The accuracy of the Theogony is deserving of notice; as Menœtios belonged to the human race, Erebos and not Tartaros was his proper prison.   [5] *Od.* i. 52, see above, p. 237.

[6] *Theog.* 517 *seq.*   [7] Hygin. 150.   [8] *Od.* .. 51.

[9] Sch. *Il.* xviii. 486, from the Kyklic poets. Hésiod (Ἔργ. 383) terms them Ἀτλαγενέων.   [10] Timæos, *ap.* Sch. Il. *ut sup.*

celestial constellations, it will be perhaps difficult to avoid assenting to the opinion of one of our ablest mythologists, that in Atlas we may view a personification of "navigation, the conquest of the sea by human skill, trade, and mercantile profit."[1]

It is perhaps hardly necessary now to remind the reader that the Atlas of Homer and Hésiod is not the personification of a mountain. In the days however when the true sense of the venerable mythes of the old time had been lost, Atlas, the keeper of the pillars that support the heaven, or the dæmon who discharged that office himself, became a mountain of Libya. It is however remarkable that in all the legends of this kind it is the god or man Atlas who is turned into or gives name to the mountain. Thus according to one[2] Atlas was a king of the remote West, rich in flocks and herds, and master of the trees which bore the golden apples. An ancient prophecy delivered by Themis had announced to him that his precious trees would be plundered by a son of Zeus. When therefore Perseus, on his return from slaying the Gorgón, arrived in the realms of Atlas, and seeking hospitality announced himself to be a son of the king of the gods, the western monarch, calling to mind the prophecy, attempted to repel him from his doors. Perseus, inferior in strength, displayed the head of Medusa, and the inhospitable prince was turned into the mountain which still bears his name.

Another account[3] said that Atlas was a man of Libya devoted to astronomy, and that having ascended a lofty mountain to make his observations he fell from it into the sea, and both sea and mountain were named from him. His supporting the heaven was usually explained by making him an astronomer and the inventor of the sphere.[4]

In Prométheus and Epimétheus are personified the intellectual vigour and weakness of man. In this mythe however there is great confusion, for its original sense seems to have been lost very early, and Prométheus to have been viewed as a Titan and the creator or instructor of man.[5]

In Homer there is no allusion whatever to Prométheus. Hésiod says,[6] that when the gods and men had a controversy at Mékóné, Prométheus took an ox, and dividing it put the flesh

---

[1] Völcker, *Myth. der Jap.* 51, with whose views Müller agrees.
[2] Ov. *Met.* iv. 631 *seq.* Serv. *Æn.* iv. 246. Tzetz. *Lyc.* 879. Et. Mag. υ. ἄτλας.   [3] Tzetz. *Lyc.* 879.
[4] Diodór. iii. 60; iv. 27. Verg. *Æn.* i. 741. Serv. *in loc.*
[5] Æschylos makes him a son of Themis : see above, p. 176.
[6] *Theog.* 521 *seq.* Ἔργ. 47 *seq.*

and entrails in the hide, and wrapping the bones up in the inside fat, desired Zeus to take which he would. The god, though aware of the deceit, selected the bones and fat, and in revenge he withheld fire from man; but Prométheus again deceived him, and stealing the fire in a hollow staff,[1] brought it and gave it to man. Zeus then sent Pandóra on earth to deceive man to his ruin, and he bound Prométheus with chains to a pillar, and sent an eagle to prey without ceasing on his liver, which grew every night as much as it had lost in the day. After a long interval of time, however, he consented to Héraklés' slaying the eagle and freeing the sufferer.

In this narrative there is a combination of a local mythe of Sikyón (anciently called Mékóné), with a doctrine of a much higher nature. The former legend was manifestly devised to account for the custom at Sikyón, as at Sparta, of offering to the gods in sacrifice the bones of the victim wrapt in the caul, instead of some of the choicest parts of the flesh, as elsewhere;[2] the latter mythe may be perhaps thus explained.

The first men lived in a state of bliss on the abundant productions of the earth. The spring was perpetual[3] and cold was unfelt, and they therefore needed not fire, which Zeus in kindness withheld from them. But the inquisitive, inventive genius of man (i.e. Prométheus) introduced fire, and the arts which result from it, and man henceforth became a prey to care and anxiety, the love of gain, and other evil passions which torment him,[4] and which are personified in the eagle that fed on the inconsumable liver of Prométheus.[5] In a word we have here a Grecian mythe of the fall of man, which we shall presently find carried out in that of Pandóra.[6]

---

[1] Νάρθηξ, *ferula.*   [2] See Welcker, *Tril.* 78. Voss. *Myth. Br.* ii. 353 *seq.*

[3] " Ver erat æternum," Ovid ; " Ver magnus agebat Orbis," Verg. speaking of the beginning of the world ; and Milton says,

> universal Pan,
> Knit with the Graces and the Hours in dance,
> Led on *the eternal spring.*

The human imagination feels in fact compelled, as it were, to conceive an endless spring as a condition of a place of bliss.   [4] See Müller, *Prolcg.* 122.

[5]

> Qui vultur jecur intimum pererrat,
> Et pectus trahit intimasque fibras,
> Non est quem tepidi vocant poetæ,
> Sed cordis mala, livor atque luxus.
>
> Petronius *ap. Fulgent.* ii. 9

Comp. Lucret. iii. 992 *seq.*

[6] We are fully aware of the difficulty presented by the Hésiodic narrative of the stealing of the fire, and that it would seem from it that Zeus had de-

The simple narrative of Hésiod was as usual expanded by later writers, and Mount Kaukasos was fixed on as the place of Prométheus' punishment. The pragmatisers also explained the mythe after their own fashion. Prométheus was, they say, a king of the Scythians, and his country was wasted by a river named *Eagle* ('Aετόs), whose inundations when he was unable to prevent, his subjects laid him in chains. But Héraklés coming thither opened a passage for the Eagle into the sea, and thus freed the captive monarch.[1]

The name of Prométheus led to his being viewed as the bestower of all knowledge on mankind.[2] A philosophic mythe in Plató[3] says that the gods formed man and the other animals of clay and fire within the earth, and then committed to Prométheus and his brother the task of distributing powers and qualities to them. Epimétheus prayed to be allowed to make the distribution. Prométheus assented; but when he came to survey the work, he found that the silly Epimétheus had abundantly furnished the inferior animals, while man was left naked and helpless. As the day for their emerging from the earth was at hand, Prométheus was at a loss what to do; at length as the only remedy he stole fire, and with it the artist-skill of Athéna and Héphæstos, and gave it to man. He was also regarded as the creator of the human race. Another legend[4] said that all mankind having perished in Deukalión's flood, Zeus directed Prométheus and Athéna to make images of clay, on which he caused the winds to blow, and thus gave them life. A third[5] said that Prométheus had formed a man of clay, and that Athéna on beholding it offered him her aid in procuring anything in heaven that might contribute to its perfection. Prométheus said that he could not tell what there might be in heaven to his purpose, unless he could go thither and judge for

---

prived mankind of it in consequence of the trick played him by Prométheus. Still we think with Völcker that the sense of the original mythe is the one given above. [1] Sch. *Apoll. Rh.* ii. 1248.

[2] Æsch. *Prom.* 442 seq.

Βραχεῖ δὲ μύθῳ πάντα συλλήβδην μάθε,
πᾶσαι τέχναι βροτοῖσιν ἐκ Προμηθέως.—vv. 505, 506.

[3] *Polit.* p. 274. *Protag.* p. 320. *Phileb.* p. 16.
[4] Etym. Mag. and Steph. Byz. v. 'Ἰκόνιον. It is apparently derived from the Bible ...rιʌtive.
[5] Apollod. i. 7, 1. Ov. *Met.* i. 82. Hor. *Carm.* i. 3, 29 seq. Fulgent. *Myth.* i. 9. Serv. *Buc.* vi. 42. As Servius quotes Sapphó as an authority, Welcker (*Tril.* 71 *note*) seems to have reason for thinking that this legend should be assigned to that poetess. It is remarkable that there is no mention of Pandóra in it. See in Horace (*Carm.* i. 16, 13) and Claudian (*De IV. Cons. Honor.* 228 *seq.*, and *In Eutrop.* ii. 490 *seq.*) other accounts of this creation of man.

8

himself. The goddess then bore him to heaven in her sevenfold shield, and there seeing everything animated by the celestial heat, he secretly applied his *ferula* to the wheel of the Sun's chariot and drew thence some of the fire, which he then applied to the breast of his man and thus animated him. Zeus, to punish Prométheus for his theft, bound him and appointed a vulture to prey on his liver, and the incensed gods sent fevers and other diseases among men.

As Cura (Care), says an ancient fable,[1] was crossing a river she observed the marly clay, and began to make a man out of it. Jupiter happening to come by, she asked him to animate it; he did so, but when Cura went to give it her own name, he insisted on its being named from himself. While they were disputing, Earth arose and asserted her right to it, as she had furnished the body. They took Saturn for arbitrator, and he decided that, as Jupiter had given it life, he should have the body, but that as Cura had formed it she should possess it while it lived, and that it should be called Man (*Homo*), because it was made of earth (*humus*).

On the story of Prométheus has been founded the following very pretty fable, which adds another instance to the many legends we have already given, invented to account for properties and relations of animals.

When Prométheus had stolen fire from heaven for the good of mankind, they were so ungrateful as to betray him to Zeus. For their treachery they got in reward a remedy against the evils of old age; but not duly considering the value of the gift, instead of carrying it themselves, they put it on the back of an ass, and let him trot on before them. It was summer-time, and the ass quite overcome by thirst went up to a fountain to drink; but a snake forbade all approach. The ass, ready to faint, most earnestly implored relief : the cunning snake, who knew the value of the burden which the ass bore, demanded it as the price of access to the fount. The ass was forced to comply, and the snake obtained possession of the gift of Zeus, but with it as a punishment for his art he got the thirst of the ass. Hence it is that the snake by casting his skin annually renews his youth, while man is borne down by the weight of the evils of old-age. The malignant snakes moreover, when they have an opportunity, communicate their thirst to mankind by biting them.[2]

[1] Hygin. 220. The etymology at the end proves this to be a Latin fiction. Parnell's beautiful imitation of it is well known.

[2] Ælian, *de Nat. An.* vi. 51, and Nikand. *Ther.* 340 *seq.* with tne Scholia. Nikander terms it an ὠγύγιος μῦθος. They derived it from the Κωφοί a satiric drama of Sophoklés' now lost.

The wife of Prométheus was Pandóra,[1] or Klymené,[2] or Hésioné,[3] or Asia.[4] His only child was Deukalión.

Πανδώρα. Pandora.

The celebrated mythe of the introduction of evil into the world by means of a woman is related at large by Hésiod in his didactic poem, and is touched on in the Theogony.[5] The following is the ingenious, and in general correct, view of it given by an able mythologist.[6]

According to some very ancient mythe the first of mankind were two brothers, Prométheus and Epimétheus, that is, Fore-thought and After-thought. These first men lived in intimate relation with the gods, who, as we may have already seen, were by no means beings of pure benevolence; on the contrary, they and mankind were to one another somewhat like patrons and clients, lords and vassals. The latter recognised the power of the former, who on their part could not well dispense with the gifts and respect of men; and men, like the tenants of griping landlords, were obliged to be very circumspect, that is, to use a good deal of *forethought* in their actions, to get every advantage they could in their dealings with the gods. This is intimated in the transaction respecting the fire of which Zeus is said to have deprived men, and which Prométheus stole and brought back to earth.

Zeus, then, the mythe goes on to relate, was incensed at this daring deed, and resolved to punish the men for it. He therefore directed Héphæstos to knead earth and water, to give it human voice and strength, and to make the fair form of a virgin like the immortal goddesses : he desired Athéna to endow her with artist-knowledge, Aphrodíté to give her beauty and desire, and Hermés to inspire her with an impudent and artful disposition. When formed she was attired by the Seasons and Graces; each of the deities gave the commanded gifts, and she was named Pandóra (*All-gift*). Thus furnished she was brought by Hermés to the dwelling of Epimétheus; who, though his brother had warned him to be upon his guard and to receive no gifts from Zeus, dazzled with her charms took her to his house and made her his wife. The evil effects of this imprudent act were speedily felt. In the house of these first men stood a closed jar, which they had been forbidden to open. Forethought, as may be supposed, had rigidly obeyed this direction, and had hitherto kept his brother also from transgressing it. But the case was now altered : a woman, whose

---

[1] Hésiod, *ap. Sch. Apoll. Rh.* iii. 1086.
[2] Sch. *Od.* x. 2.
[3] Æsch. *Prom.* 560.
[4] Hérod. iv. 45.
[5] Ἐργ. 47 *seq.; Theog.* 570 *seq.*
[6] Buttmann, *Mythol.* i. " Pandora."

chief attribute is *curiosity*, was come into the house: dying to know what the jar contained she raised the lid, and all the evils hitherto unknown to man poured out and spread over the earth. In terror at the sight of these monsters, she clapped down the lid just in time to prevent the escape of Hope, who thus remained with man, his chief support and comfort.

This fable of Pandóra is certainly not capable of being reconciled with other Hellénic mythes of the origin of mankind, such as the one which we have given above; but incongruities little discomposed those ancient bards, and if a mythe contained a moral that pleased them, they were indifferent about its harmonising with others. Contradictions however becoming apparent, Prométheus and his brother ceased to be looked on as the first men, but Pandóra still kept her place as the first woman. Prométheus and Epimétheus were soon regarded as the symbols of Prudence and Folly, and were held to be gods. From the remote period in which the legends placed them they could only be regarded as Titans, and accordingly by Hésiod and Æschylos they are placed among the ante-Kronid race. Prométheus was also speedily raised to the rank of creator of mankind, to whom he gave the fire which he had stolen from heaven. Yet even so late as the times of Augustus some vestige of the old sense of the mythe seems to have remained; for Horace classes Prométheus with Dædalos and Héraklés, and speaks of him as a man.[1] It is remarkable however that Æschylos represents him only as the benefactor and instructor of mankind.[2]

The next step in the corruption of the mythe, says the critic, was to change the jar ($\pi i \theta o s$)[3] in which the evils were inclosed, and which lay in the house of the men, into a *box* brought with her from heaven by Pandóra. It is rather strange how this notion could have prevailed, when the species of vessel was so expressly

[1]
> Audax omnia perpeti
> *Gens humana* ruit per vetitum nefas.
> Audax *Iapeti genus*
> Ignem fraude mala gentibus intulit:
> *   *   *   *   *   *
> Nil *mortalibus* arduum est.—*Carm.* i. 3, 25.

The Epicurean poet was however disposed to regard all the popular gods as having been originally mere men. Elsewhere (*Ib.* ii. 13, 27) he places Prométheus with Tantalos in Erebos.

[2] Among other things he makes him say (*Prom.* 252) that he had relieved mankind from anxiety about the future by giving them *hopes*,

τυφλὰς ἐν αὐτοῖς ἐλπίδας κατῴκισα,

which is rather at variance with the mythe of Pandóra.

[3] Πίθος, akin to the Latin *vas*, the German *fass*, and our words *butt* and *pot*, was a kind of large pitcher or jar with a wide mouth and a close-fitting lid. It was usually earthen, and was mostly employed for holding wine.

stated by Hésiod, who also mentions its *great lid* (μέγα πῶμα), a phrase which does not at all accord with such a box as Pandóra could have carriea with her. Further it is said that 'Hope alone remained in the *infrangible house* within the jar;'[1] where, though interpreters in general have understood the word *house* to signify the jar, an unprejudiced reader will rather conceive the passage to denote that a house was the scene of the event, and that Hope alone stayed in the dwelling of man.

When higher notions of the Deity prevailed, this mythe underwent a further change, and it was fabled that Zeus had inclosed all blessings in a jar, which he set in the abode of man. But, tormented with curiosity, man raised the lid, and all the blessings flew away to heaven, where they abide shunning the earth. Hope alone remained, as he let down the lid before she had escaped.[2]

Such is what may be regarded as the best explanation that has been given of this ancient mythe. We will now make a few observations on the subject.

In the first place, as Buttmann and many others have observed, the resemblance between this mythe and the Scripture narrative of Eve and the forbidden fruit is so very striking, that one might be induced to regard it as a rivulet derived from the original fount of tradition. It is however more probably an ebullition of that spleen against the female sex occasionally exhibited by the old Grecian bards, and of which Simónidés has left us a notable instance.[3] The points of resemblance between the Grecian mythe and the Hebrew narrative are these:[4] Pandóra and Eve; the tree of the knowledge of good and evil, and the jar of evils; and the introduction of evil into the world by the first woman. But Eve was tempted, Pandóra was not; the former was actuated by a noble instinct, the love of knowledge; the latter merely by vulgar female curiosity.

It seems very strange that the ancients should have taken so

[1] Μούνη δ' αὐτόθι 'Ελπὶς ἐν ἀρρήκτοισι δόμοισι
    ἔνδον ἔμιμνε πίθου ὑπὸ χείλεσιν, οὐδὲ θύραζε
    ἐξέπτη· πρόσθεν γὰρ ἐπέμβαλε πῶμα πίθοιο.—῎Εργ. v. 96.

[2] Babrius, 58, ed. Lachmann.

[3] *Frag.* 2. Gaisford, *Poetæ Minores*, i. 410. Phokyllides, *Fr.* 2.

[4] Milton runs the parallel pretty closely:

    What day the genial angel to our sire
  Brought her in naked beauty more adorned,
  More lovely than Pandora, whom the gods
  Endowed with all their gifts ; and oh ! too like
  In sad event, when to the unwiser son
  Of Japhet brought by Hermes, she ensnared
  Mankind with her fair looks, to be avenged
  On him who had stolen Jove's authentic fire.--*Par. Lost*, iv. 712 *seq.*

little notice of this mythe.   There is no allusion to it in Pindar or the tragedians, excepting Sophoklés, one of whose lost satiric dramas was named Pandóra or the Hammerers.   It was equally neglected by the Alexandrians ; Apollodóros merely calls Pandóra the first woman.   In fact, with the exception of a dubious passage in Theognis,[1] where Hope is said to be the only good deity that remained among men,—Temperance, Faith, and the others having left the earth and gone to Olympos,—which may be founded on this mythe, we find no allusion to it in Grecian literature, except in the fable of Babrios, who appears to have flourished a little later than Phædrus, in Nonnos,[2] who left nothing untouched, and in the epigrammatist Makedonios.[3]   It seems to have had as little charms for the Latin poets ; even Ovid (strange as it may appear) passing it over in perfect silence.   Hyginus[4] merely says that when Prométheus formed men of clay, Zeus directed Héphæstos to make a woman of clay also, whom Athéna animated and the other gods adorned with gifts ; and that she was given in marriage to Epimétheus, and became the mother of Pyrrha, the first mortal woman.

It is also deserving of notice, that Hésiod and all the others agree in naming the vessel which Pandóra opened a *jar* ($\pi i\theta os$, *dolium*),[5] and never hint at her having brought it with her to the house of Epimétheus.   Yet the idea has been universal among the moderns that she brought all the evils with her from heaven shut up in a *box* ($\pi u\xi is$).   We can only account for this by supposing that at the restoration of learning the narrative in Hésiod was misunderstood ; and of this we have a convincing proof in Natalis Comes, one of the earliest of the modern mythologists.   He says that Zeus sent Pandóra to Prométheus with all the evils inclosed in a vessel (*vasculo*), and that when Prométheus refused to receive her she went to Epimétheus, who took the lid off the vessel and let out all the evils, but that he shut up Hope, and kept the vessel with her in it.[6]   This then became the current idea, and we see how even so eminent a scholar as Buttmann was deceived by it, and led to suppose such to have been the prevalent opinion among the ancients.

[1] *Parænésis*, 1135 *seq.*: comp. Eur. *Tr.* 676.   Ov. *Ex Pont.* i. 6, 29.
[2]   Οὐράνιον γάρ
οὐκ ὄφελέν ποτε κεῖνο πίθου κρήδημνον ἀνοῖξαι
ἀνδράσι Πανδώρη, γλυκερὸν κακόν.—Dionys. vii. 56.
[3] Anthologia (Palat.), x. 71.   [4] *Fab.* 142.
[5] Porphyrion (*on Hor. Carm.* i. 3, 29) says that the evils all broke out *patefacto dolio*, and that Pandóra was the agent.
[6] *Mythol.* lib. iv. chap. vi.   Lylius Giraldus, who tells the story in the same way, puts the evils *in pyxide*.

Δευκαλίων καὶ Πύρρα. *Deucalion et Pyrrha.*

We have seen that the ancient mythology of Greece contained accounts of the two great events of the Creation and Fall of man. In like manner the important event of the Deluge has a place among the ancient Hellénic mythes; but unfortunately it has come down to us only in a late form, and apparently mixed up with circumstances borrowed from the narrative in the Mosaic history. It is to the following effect.[1]

Deukalión, the son of Prométheus, was married to Pyrrha the daughter of Epimétheus and Pandóra, and he reigned over the country about Phthia. When Zeus designed to destroy the brazen race of men, Deukalión by the advice of his father made himself an ark (λάρνακα), and putting provisions into it entered it with his wife Pyrrha. Zeus then poured rain from heaven and inundated the greater part of Greece, so that all the people, except a few who escaped to the neighbouring lofty mountains, perished in the waves. At that time the mountains of Thessaly were burst, and all Greece without the Isthmos and the Peloponnése was overflowed. Deukalión was carried along this sea in his ark for nine days and nights until he reached Mount Parnassos. By this time the rain had ceased, and he got out and sacrificed to Zeus *Flight-giving* (φύξιος), who sent Hermés desiring him to ask what he would. His request was to have the earth replenished with men. By the direction of Zeus he and his wife flung stones behind them; and those which Deukalión cast became men, those thrown by Pyrrha women; and from this circumstance came the Greek name for *people*.[2]

This narrative, it may easily be seen, is of a very narrow and even unpoetic character; it restricts the general deluge to Greece Proper, indeed perhaps originally to Thessaly;[3] and it most incongruously represents others as having escaped as well as Deukalión, yet at the same time intimates that he and his wife alone had been preserved in the catastrophe. What is said of the Brazen Age is quite at variance with the narrative in Hésiod, and is a very clumsy attempt at connecting two perfectly independent and irreconcilable mythes. The circumstance of the *ark* would seem to have been learned at Alexandria,[4] for we elsewhere find the dove noticed. "The mythologists," says Plutarch,[5] "say that

---

[1] Apollod. i. 7, 2.

[2] Ὅθεν καὶ λαοὶ μεταφορικῶς ὠνομάσθησαν ἀπὸ τοῦ λᾶας, ὁ λίθος. The escape to Parnassos, and the origin of men from stones, are noticed by Pindar, *Ol.* ix. 43 (64) *seq.*   [3] See Aristot. *Meteor.* i. 14.

[4] It may however have owed its origin to the resemblance between λάρναξ and Παρνασσός, which we are told was originally called Λαρνασσὸς from it. Sch. *Apoll. Rh.* ii. 705.   [5] *Le Sol. Animal.* 13.

a pigeon let fly out of the ark was to Deukalión a sign of bad weather if it came in again, of good weather if it flew away." The sacrifice and the appearance of Hermés also strongly remind us of Noah.

The Latin writers[1] take a much nobler view of the Deluge. According to them, it overspread the whole earth, and all anima. life perished except Deukalión and Pyrrha, whom Ovid, who gives a very poetic account of this great catastrophe, conveys in a small boat to the summit of Parnassos; while others make Ætna[2] or Athós[3] the mountain which yielded them a refuge. According to this poet, they consulted the ancient oracle of Themis respecting the restoration of mankind, and received the following response:

> From the fane depait,
> And veil your heads and loose your girded clothes,
> And cast behind you your great parent's bones.

They were at first horror-stricken at such an act of impiety being enjoined them, but at length Deukalión penetrated the sense of the oracle.[4]

Deukalión and Pyrrha are evidently pure beings of fiction, personifications, as their names would seem to suggest, of water and fire;[5] and meant, as some think,[6] to indicate, that when the passage through which the Péneios carries off the waters that run into the vale of Thessaly, which is on all sides shut in by lofty mountains, had been closed by some accident, they overflowed the whole of its surface, till the action of subterranean fire opened a way for them. We cannot by any means assert

---

[1] Ov. *Met.* i. 253 *seq.* Hygin. 153. Serv. *Buc.* vi. 41. Nonnos (vi. 206 *seq.*) gives, as usual, a most extravagant account of this deluge, which he represents as universal.

[2] Hygin. *ut sup.*   [3] Servius, *ut sup.*

[4] The Greek poets called the stones by a very natural figure γῆς ὄστεα. We know not what Greek authority Ovid followed in this narrative. It is remarkable that we find the very same notion among the native tribes of South America. "The Makusis," says Sir R. Schomburgk, "believe that the only being who survived a general deluge repeopled the earth by converting stones into human beings." Other tribes say, that one man and woman were saved by taking refuge on the summit of a lofty mountain, and that they threw over their heads the fruits of the Mauritia palm, from the kernels of which sprang men and women: see Humboldt's *Views of Nature*, p. 147, Bohn's edit.

[5] Pyrrha is evidently connected with πύρ, but is perhaps only the ordinary name denoting the colour of the hair or skin, and is joined with Deukalión as it were by way of contrast. Deukalión probably comes from δεύω (whence δεύκης) *to wet:* see Welcker, *Tril.* 549 *note.* Völcker, *ut sup.*

[6] See Völcker, *Myth. der Jap.* 342 : comp. Strab. ix. 5, 2, p. 430. We do not regard this as by any means a probable theory.

that this inundation was a real event, of which the memory had
been retained by tradition from times long anterior to Homer and
Hésiod, who make no mention of it: neither should we perhaps
be too forward to maintain that a tradition of the great deluge
was preserved by the early inhabitants of Greece. Where there
are not letters to fix it, tradition is, as abundant instances prove,
remarkably fleeting and unstable; and we should perhaps come
nearest to the truth if we were to say, that those tribes who appear
to have retained a recollection of that great event, have inferred
it from the evident tokens of inundation which are to be seen on
various parts of the earth's surface; a theory by no means at
variance with the Mosaic account of the Deluge.

Another Grecian tradition[1] made O'gygés (also a personification
of water[2]) to be the person who was saved at the time of the deluge
which overflowed Greece, but the accounts remaining about him are
very scanty. The historians made him a king of Attica or Bœótia.

Deukalión was regarded as the great patriarch of Greece, or the
progenitor of those races which derived their origin from Thessaly,
and were believed to have advanced southwards, conquering and
displacing the tribes which previously occupied the more southern
parts. This flood, we may observe, did not extend to the Peloponnése, and the traditions of that country spoke of different
progenitors of the human race.[3]

Early Inhabitants of Greece.

The Homéric poems exhibit to us the people of Greece at the
time of the Trojan war as a race very far removed from the savage
state, as being well acquainted with agriculture, commerce and
navigation, though probably ignorant of money and letters, and
exhibiting in all their institutions a considerable degree of civilisation. They had not yet any common name, and seem to have
had but little previous intercourse with foreign nations. Nothing
can be collected from these poems respecting the origin of the
people.

As some nations of Asia were under the system of castes and
the direction of the sacerdotal caste, and as some of the early
tribes of Europe seem to have been similarly situated, some
modern writers assume such to have been the early state of Greece,
and even fancy that they discern in certain places of the Ilias

---

[1] Paus. ix. 5, 1. Tzetz. *Lyc.* 1206. Eudocia, 438. Euseb. *Præp. Ev.* x.
10. Syncellus, p. 63. Nonn. iii. 204 *seq.*   [2] See Appendix D.

[3] Pelasgos in Arkadia (Asios *ap. Paus.* viii. 1, 4), Inachos or Phoróneus in
Argos (Akusiláos and Plató: see Sturz. *Pherekyd.* 233), O'ros in Trœzén (l aus.
ii. 30, 5).

(such for example as the quarrel between Agamemnón and Kalchas), traces of the conflict between the temporal and the sacerdotal power.[1] The gigantic buildings which still exist in the Peloponnése and elsewhere, and which are alluded to in the Homéric poems, also seem to them to indicate a state of society resembling that of Egypt or India, where huge pyramids and temples were raised by serfs, beneath the direction of a caste of priests, whom they were bound to obey. But unfortunately for this hypothesis, the various huge monuments of this kind which Egypt, India, and 'the Celtic' present, are works of show rather than of real utility, being almost all altars, temples, tombs, or obelisks; while those of Greece are massive walls and strong treasuries, manifestly designed to preserve the wealth of an industrious and civilised people from the rapacity of invaders by sea or by land. The evidence in effect of sacerdotal dominion having ever prevailed in Greece is so slight that it hardly needs an examination.[2]

Language, manners, religion, and monuments indicate that Greece and Italy, and a part of Lesser Asia were at an early period the abode of one race of men, who were devoted to the arts of peace and eminently skilled in agriculture. This people are generally called the Pelasgians or Pelargians, a name which may have been given to a portion of them by more warlike tribes, from their favourite occupation of cultivating the land, but which we have no reason to suppose was ever common to the whole race.[3] They are mentioned by Homer;[4] and Kaucónes,[5] Leleges,[6] and other tribes are also spoken of as dwelling in Greece in the ante-Hellénic period.

Whether the Achæans,[7] the race whose exploits the Homéric poems record, were this Pelasgian race,[6] or one which had conquered them, is what we have no means of determining. The poems give not a hint on the subject, and conjecture will yield but little that is satisfactory. They present no traces whatever of previous invasions and conquests, and it is therefore not at all

[1] See Schlegel's well-known *Review of Niebuhr's History of Rome.*

[2] See Nitzsch *on Od.* iii. 439.

[3] The Pelasgians were fond of cultivating the rich soil on the banks of streams. Strab. xiii. 3, 3, p. 621. Völcker, *Myth. der Jap.* 364. Müller, *Min. Pol.* 3. *Orchom.* 125.

[4] *Il.* ii. 681, 840; x. 429; xvii. 288. They are among the allies of the Trojans: *Od.* xix. 177.   [5] *Od.* iii. 366: comp. *Il.* x. 429.

[6] Hés. *Fr.* 25: comp. *Il.* x. 429; xxi. 86.

[7] Also called Danaans and Argeians. 'Αχαιὸς, according to Völcker (*ut sup.* 365), is of the same family with *aqua*, and relates to agriculture also. Müller (*Proleg.* 291) says it signifies *good*, and is equivalent to ἀριστεύς.

[8] Hérod. vii. 94, 95. Niebuhr, *Hist. of Rome*, i. 29.

improbable that the martial character of the race who fought at Thébes and Troy may have been developed by peculiar circumstances from the peaceful one which is usually supposed to have distinguished the Pelasgians.[1]

Previous to the Dórian migration, which is an undoubted historic event, there is supposed to have been some commotion in Thessaly, produced probably by the irruption of a Thesprótian tribe into that country,[2] which caused a portion of the former inhabitants to emigrate into Bœótia and expel some of those whom they found there.[3] But it was the Dórian migration which produced the greatest changes in Greece, and sent so many colonies to the East and the West. It was probably at this time that the word Hellénes came into use; for the Greeks, finding themselves to differ in language and manners from the tribes with which they were now in contact, adopted a common name by which to distinguish themselves.[4]

It would therefore seem to be the most probable hypothesis on this subject, to suppose the Greeks to have been always one people, under different denominations, with that diversity of character and manners among the various portions of them which will be produced by local situation and other accidental circumstances,[5] and which should cause no greater surprise than the diversity of dialects of the one language which prevailed in ancient Greece as in modern Italy.

Religion will always vary with modes of life, and there is therefore no improbability in the supposition of that of the Pelasgians, that is of the people of Greece before the Achæan period, having been chiefly of a rural character,[6] such as it continued to be in Arkadia to a late period; and that, as we have seen in the case of Hermés, when the Achæan and Hellénic characters prevailed, the deities like the people put off the rustic character, their attributes changed, and offices dissimilar to their original ones were assigned them. The original meaning also of many mythes may have gone

---

[1] See Wachsmuth, *Hellenische Alterthumskunde*, i. 44. Thus the people of Scandinavia, who afterwards became so terrible to more southern countries, are described by Tacitus (*Germ.* c. 44) as being of rather a mild and peaceful character. [2] Hérod. vii. 176. Müller, *Orchom.* 377.

[3] These are said to have been the Bœótians, who conquered and expelled the Kadmeians from Thébes. This event is a mere conjecture, and it would rather seem to have been the Epigoni who destroyed the Kadmeian power. The word Bœótian occurs in Homer in the Catalogue, and in *Il.* v. 710; xiii. 685; which last however is considered spurious. See also *Il.* xiv. 476; xvii. 597.

[4] Hésiod ('Epγ. 528, 663) first employed the term Hellénes to designate the whole people. See Welcker, Ἀret. Κόl. 49. Niebuhr, *ut sup.*

[5] Comp. Müller, *Proleg.* 336.

[6] Comp. Völcker, *Myth. der Jap.* 369 seq.

out of use; what had been symbolic and allegoric may have been understood literally and regarded as a real event; purely imaginary beings have been esteemed actual personages, and the legends relating to them have been treated as genuine history; and hence have arisen many of the mythic persons, whose names indicate them to have been personifications of natural objects, or epithets of the divinity in whose mythology they became actors. There is, further, much probability in the hypothesis that what afterwards became mysteries were ancient Pelasgian forms of worship, preserved in particular places, and jealously confined to a particular people, but which were gradually communicated to others.[1] In short, it would appear, that the religion, manners, genius, and national character of the Greeks of the historic times had their roots in those of the ante-historic and even ante-mythic inhabitants of the country, whom we denominate Pelasgians. We have already pointed out the incredibility of the hypothesis of the coming of foreign colonists to Greece. The various supposed instances will be examined as they occur.

In Grecian history we are to distinguish three periods, the Pelasgian, the Achæan, and the Hellénic. The first is as we have seen ante-historic and even ante-mythic, and its existence is only to be inferred from a few feeble traces; the second is the mythic, which is rich in events, though the far greater part, if not the entire, are but the creations of fancy; the third, commencing with the Dórian migration, and being for some space of time mytho-historic or history mingled with fable,[2] assumes toward the time of Solón the lineaments of truth, and becomes real history. It is this last period alone which presents materials for the historian.

The mythic history of Greece, to which the present portion of our work is devoted, will present numerous instances of the practice of embodying tribes, institutions, religious ceremonies, etc., in the person of some fabled individual,—the personification of their name; a practice by no means confined to Grecian mythology, as it will be found to pervade that of almost every other people. The names of rivers, mountains, and other natural objects, made persons also largely contribute to swell the amount of our mythic array; to these when we add those noticed in a preceding paragraph, few or none will remain to which we can venture to assign an actual and real existence.[3]

---

[1] See above, p. 161. Also Müller, *Orchom.* 453. *Proleg.* 250.
[2] Comp. Buttmann, *Mythol.* ii. 210, 217, 226. Müller, *Proleg.* 165.
[3] See Müller, *ut sup.* 179, 285 *seq.* Hermann, *Ueber das Wesen,* etc. 104. Welcker, *Tril.* 356, 387. The very same appearance is presented in the mythic and semi-mythic history of Scandinavia and other countries whose annals are homesprung and domestic.

These mythic personages are usually denominated Herves (ἥρωες),—a word in Homer only indicative of civil rank and pre-eminence.[1] It afterwards became significative of beings of a class superior to common men;[2] and many of those to whom Homer and Hésiod apply the term *hero*, in its primary sense, were in after-times honoured as deities, with temples, sacrifices, and prayers,—becoming in fact the *Saints* of heathen Greece.[3] In general, however, they only resumed their pristine rank; for the hero of one period was not unfrequently the god of a preceding one, and he thus became a god once more in the eyes of posterity.

The whole mythic history of Greece is genealogic; all the per-sonifications which we have just noticed are woven through one another in a most marvellous manner, and the gods also bear a conspicuous part in the history as progenitors of various Heroic families. Any attempt therefore at introducing the accuracy of chronology into such a chaos is absurd in the extreme;[4] and it is only with the glimmer of the dawn of real Grecian history,—of which the first or mytho-historic portion, as we have said, com-mences with the Dórian migration,—that the regular succession of events can be traced with any appearance of probability. The mythic portion of a nation's annals must be always regarded as a world in itself,[5] the creation of fancy, where the real assumes the garb of the imaginary, and becomes indistinguishable from it; where no event can be pronounced to be absolutely true; where fancy and ingenuity are ever at liberty to sport and to lead the inquirer an eager and a delightful chase after the forms which float before him in the distance, but fade into mist when he at-tempts to grasp them. It is a region of sunshine and fragrance in which the song of the bard evermore resounds, pleasant to view and curious to explore; where the search after truth is rewarded by insight into the powers and operations of the human mind, and the fancy is continually nourished and inspired by gay and mag-nificent imagery.

Though chronology, properly so called, cannot be introduced nto mythic history, it has however a chronology of its own, and nay be divided into distinct periods. In the mythic history of Ĭreece, for instance, we find an indefinite period, in which are to

---

[1] The Greek ἥρως is plainly the Latin *herus*, German *herr*, i. e. *master* :— ρωῖνα, and the German *herrinn*, *mistress*, are nearly the same.

[2] Pind. *Ol.* ii. 2. Hor. *Carm.* i. 12, 1. Hérodotos (iii. 122) thus distin-ζuishes between Minós and Polykrates. Ἥρως ἐστὶ ὃ μήτε ἀνθρωπός ἐστί, ιἥτε θεός, καὶ συναμφότερος ἐστί. Luc. *Dial. Mort.* 3.

[3] See Lobeck, p. 1233.

[4] Comp. Buttmann, *Mythol.* ii. 226. Müller, *Orchom.* 136; *Proleg.* 330.

[5] Comp. Müller, *Proleg.* 103.

be placed Kadmos, Kekrops, Perseus, and other heroes; then follow the times of Héraklés and Théseus and the Argonautic expedition; this period is succeeded by that of the Théban Wars, after which come the War of Troy and the Returns of the Heroes, with which the mythic portion of Grecian history terminates.

Two courses present themselves to the narrator of this mythic history. He may either take the genealogical one, and relate the history of each mythic family consecutively; or he may pursue the subject geographically, and distribute the mythes according to the regions which are assigned as the scenes of them. Without venturing to assert that it is the best, we have given the preference to the latter mode, and shall commence at Thessaly, the most northerly portion of Greece.

It must be previously stated, that the genealogists make Deukalión the father of Hellén, who was the father of Dóros, Æolos, and Xuthos, which last had two sons, Achæos and Ión.[1] Of these personified races Æolos alone occupies any space in mythology. His sons were Krétheus, Athamas, Sisyphos, Salmóneus and Periéres;[2] some of whom belong to the mythology of Thessaly, others to that of the Peloponnése, and thus seem to indicate a close connection in the mythic period between these extremes of Hellas.

CHAPTER II.

MYTHES OF THESSALY.

THE legends of which Thessaly is the scene are few in number, and are nearly all confined to the district about Pelion and the bay of Pagasæ; their subjects are chiefly the Æolids, or heroes of the race of Æolos, and the ancient Minyans.

Ἄδμητος καὶ Ἄλκηστις.   Admetus et Alcestis.

Krétheus the son of Æolos married Tyró, the daughter of his brother Salmóneus. By her he had three sons, namely Æsón, Amytháon and Pherés.[3] This last built the city of Pheræ, which was named from him: his son Admétos married Alkéstis the daughter of Pelias, a son of Tyró by Poseidón.[4]

When Apolló was banished from Olympos, the legend says, he

---

[1] Thus according to Abulgazi (*Gen. Hist. of Tatars*, ch. 2 and 3) Japhet the son of Noah had a son named Turk, who had two sons named, the one Tatar, and the other Mongol.

[2] Hés. *Fr.* 23. Eurip. *Fr. Æolos*, 23. Apollod. i. 7, 3. This last writer names several other children of Æolos.   [3] *Od.* xi. 257.   [4] *Ib.* 253.

became the servant of Admétos,[1] and it was during the period of his service that Admétos sought the hand of Alkéstis. Pelias would only give her to him who should yoke a lion and a wild boar to his chariot, and this Admétos effected by the aid of his divine herdsman. Apolló also obtained from the Fates that, when the day appointed for the life of Admétos to terminate should come, he might defer it if any one would die in his place. When the fatal day arrived Admétos implored his aged father and mother to lay down their small remnant of life for his sake, but they were deaf to his prayers. With a generous self-devotion Alkéstis then proffered herself as the substitute. She therefore died, and was laid in the tomb; but Héraklés happening to come just at this time to the house of Admétos, and hearing what had occurred, went and sat at the tomb, and when Death (or according to others Hadés himself) came, he seized him, and forced him to resign his victim, whom he then restored to her husband. It was also said that Héraklés fetched Alkéstis back out of Erebos.[2]

If, as has been hinted above, Admétos was Hadés, Alkéstis the *Strong-one* (ἀλκή) may have been Persephoné. Her name would then answer to *Strong* (ἴφθιμος), one of his epithets, and to *Awful* (ἐπαινή), one of those of his queen. On this however we would lay no stress; for we are inclined to regard the mythe just related as one devised in honour of the female sex, and without any mystic or recondite meaning.[3] Whatever the circumstance may have been that caused an epithet of Hadés to be made the hero of it— perhaps some connection with the mythology of Héraklés—it was but natural to select a corresponding term for the name of his wife.

Ἰάσων καὶ Μήδεια. *Iason et Medea.*

Krétheus was succeeded in the dominion over Iolkos, which he had founded, by his son Æsón. This prince married Alkimédé daughter of Phylakos, or, as others said, Polymédé or Polyphémé daughter of Autolykos, or Theagnoté daughter of Labdakos, by whom he had a son named Iasón.[4] By force or fraud he was deprived of his kingdom by his half-brother Pelias,[5] who sought the life of the infant Iasón; and to save him his parents gave out

---

[1] Above, p. 108.
[2] Eur. *Alkéstis.* Apollod. i. 9, 15. Hygin. 50, 51. Fulgent. i. 27.
[3] Few persons, we believe, are aware of the fact that Thomson's drama of Edward and Eleanora is an imitation, in one scene nearly a translation, of the Alkéstis of Euripi.lés.
[4] Apollod. i. 9, 16. Sch. *Apoll. Rh.* i. 46. Tzetz. *Lyc.* 175.
[5] Pind. *Pyth.* iv. 109 (193) *seq.* Others said that on the death of Æsór Pelias reigned as guardian to the infant Iasón. Sch. *Od.* xii. 69.

that he was dead, and meantime conveyed him by night to the cave of the Kentaur Cheirón, to whose care they committed him.[1]

An oracle had told Pelias to beware of the 'one-sandalled man,' but during many years none such appeared to disturb his repose. At length, when Iasón had attained the age of twenty, he proceeded unknown to Cheirón to Iolkos, to claim the rights of his family. He bore, says the Theban poet, two spears; he wore the close-fitting Magnésian dress, and a pard-skin to throw off the rain, and his long unshorn locks waved on his back. He entered the market-place, and the people, who knew him not, marvelled if he were Apolló or the 'brazen-carred spouse of Aphrodíté,' i.e. Arés. Just then Pelias came by in his mule-car; and the moment he looked on him, and perceived that he had but one sandal, he shuddered. He asked him who he was, and Iasón mildly answered his question, telling him that he was come to demand the kingdom of his fathers which Zeus had given to Æolos. He then went into the house of his father, by whom he was joyfully recognised. On the intelligence of the arrival of Iasón, his uncles Pherés and Amytháon, with their sons Admétos and Melampus, hastened to Iolkos. Five days they feasted and enjoyed themselves; on the sixth Iasón disclosed to them his wishes, and went accompanied by them to the dwelling of Pelias, who at once proposed to resign the kingdom, retaining the herds and pastures, at the same time stimulating Iasón to the expedition of the Golden Fleece.[2]

Another account is that Pelias, being about to offer a sacrifice on the shore of the sea to his sire Poseidón, invited all his subjects. Iasón, who was ploughing on the other side of the Anauros, crossed that stream to come to it, and in so doing lost one of his sandals. It is said that Héra, out of enmity to Pelias, who had neglected to sacrifice to her, took the form of an old woman, and asked Iasón to carry her over, which caused him to leave one of his sandals in the mud; her object was to give occasion for Médeia's coming to Iolkos and destroying Pelias.[3] When Pelias perceived Iasón with but one sandal, he saw the accomplishment of the oracle, and sending for him next day, asked him what *he* would do, if he had the power, had it been predicted to him that he should be slain by one of his citizens. Iasón replied, that he would order him to go and fetch the Golden Fleece. Pelias took him at his word, and imposed this task on himself.[4]

Iasón proclaimed his enterprise throughout Greece, and the

---

[1] Apollod. i. 9, 16.   Apoll. Rh. i. 10.   Hygin. 12, 13.   [2] Pind. *ut sup.*
[3] Apollónios (iii. 67 *seq.*) makes her say that her object was to make trial of the humanity of men.
[4] Pherekýdés *ap. Sch. Pind. Pyth.* iv. 75 (133).

bravest heroes hastened to share in the glory. The fleece was gained by the aid of Médeia the daughter of the king of Kolchis, and the Argó, as the vessel in which they sailed was named, returned to Iolkos in safety.[1] But during the absence of Iasón, Pelias had driven his father and mother to self-destruction, and put to death their remaining child. Desirous of revenge, Iasón, after he had delivered the fleece to Pelias, entreated Médeia to exercise her art in his behalf. He sailed with his companions to the Isthmos, and there dedicated the Argó to Poseidón; and Médeia shortly afterwards ingratiated herself with the daughters of Pelias, and by vaunting her art of restoring youth, and proving it by cutting up an old ram, and putting him into a pot whence issued a bleating lamb, she persuaded them to treat their father in the same manner.[2]

Pelias was buried with great splendour by his son Akastos, and the most renowned heroes of the time in Greece contended at the games celebrated on the occasion. Akastos drove Iasón and Médeia from Iolkos, and they retired to Corinth, where they lived happily for ten years; till Iasón, wishing to marry Glauké or Kreüsa, the daughter of Kreón king of that place, put away Médeia. The Kolchian princess, enraged at the ingratitude of her husband, called on the gods for vengeance, sent a poisoned robe as a gift to the bride, and then killing her own children mounted a chariot drawn by winged serpents, and fled to Athens, where she married king Ægeus, by whom she had a son named Médos; but being detected in an attempt to destroy Théseus, she fled with her son. Médos conquered several barbarous tribes, and the country which he named after himself, and finally fell in battle against the Indians. Médeia, returning unknown to Kolchis, found that her father Æétés had been robbed of his throne by his brother Persés: she restored him, and deprived the usurper of life.[3]

In narrating the adventures of Iasón and Médeia we have followed Apollodóros, who seems to have adhered closely to the versions of the legend given by the Attic tragedians, in whose hands the hero and heroine have undergone the same fate with those of other places whose people were politically opposed to the sovereign democracy of Athens. We will now give the more trustworthy accounts of others.

In the Theogony Médeia is classed with the goddesses[4] who honoured mortal men with their love. Iasón brought her from

---

[1] The particulars of this voyage will be related below.
[2] Apollod. i. 9, 27.   [3] Id. ib.
[4] Médeia is said to be *immortal* by Pindar (*Pyth.* iv. 18) and Musæos (*ap* Sch. *Eurip. Med.* 9).

the realm of her father Æétés, where he had achieved the many
grievous tasks which the haughty insolent king Pelias had imposed
on him. He made her his spouse, and she bore to the 'shepherd
of the people' a son named Médeios, whom Cheirón reared in the
mountains, and ' the will of great Zeus was accomplished.'[1] It is
evident therefore that this poet supposed Iasón to have reigned at
Iolkos after his return from his great adventure.

According to the poem of the Nostœ, Médeia restored Æsón to
youth,[2] while Simónidés and Pherekýdés say that she effected this
change in Iasón himself,[3] and Æschylos that she thus renewed the
Hyades, the nurses of Dionýsos, and their husbands.[4] There is also
a difference in the accounts of the manner in which she contrived
to destroy Pelias; for it is said that before the Argó came to
Iolkos Médeia landed secretly on the coast, and assuming the form
of an ancient priestess of Artemis; went to the house of Pelias, and
deceived his daughters as above related.[5] She then made the appointed signal to Iasón, who landed and took possession of the
kingdom, which however he shortly after gave up to Akastos the
son of Pelias, who had accompanied him on his voyage, and retired with Médeia to Corinth.[6]

Iasón is said to have put an end to his life after the tragic fate
of his children ; or, as another account has it, when the Argó was
falling to pieces with time Médeia persuaded him to sleep under
the prow, and it fell on him and killed him.[7] Médeia herself, we
are told, became the bride of Achilleus on the E'lysian Plain.[8]

Neither Iasón nor Médeia can well be regarded as a real historic
personage. Whether the former, whose name is nearly identical
with Iasón, Iasios, Iasos, is merely a personification of the Ioniar
race (Ἰάονες), or, in reference to a mythe to be noticed in the sequel
signifies the *healing, atoning* god or hero, may be doubted. Médeia
seems plainly to be only another form of Héra, and to have been
separated from her in the manner of which we have already given
instances. She is the *counselling* (μῆδος) goddess; and in the
history of Iasón we find Héra always acting in this capacity toward
him who, as Homer says,[9] was *very dear* to her,—an obscure hint

---

[1] *Theog.* 992 *seq.* Pelias is here to Iasón what Eurystheus is to Héraklés.
[2] Argum. *Eurip. Médeia.* Sch. *Aristoph. Knights,* 1318. Ov. *Met.* vii. 15?
seq.
[3] Arg. *Eur. Méd.*   [4] Arg. *Eur. Méd.* Ov. *ut sup.* v. 294.
[5] Hygin. 24. Diodór. iv. 51, 52. Paus. viii. 11, 2. Ov. *ut sup.* Mülle?
(*Orchom.* 268) thinks this was a mere fiction of the tragedians.
[6] Hygin. *ut sup.* Diodór. *ut sup.*   [7] Arg. *Eurip. Médeia. Ib.* 1386.
[8] Ap. Rh. iv. 811 *seq.* Ibykos and Simonidés *ap. Sch. on v.* 815.
[9] *Od.* xii. 72.

pernaps of the love of Iasón and Médeia. Médeia also always acts a friendly part; and it seems highly probable that the atrocities related in the close of her history are pure fictions of the Attic dramatists.[1] The bringing of Iasón and Médeia to Corinth seems also to indicate a connexion between the latter and Héra, who was worshipped there under the title of Akræa (*Of-the-height*), and the graves of the children of Médeia were said to be in the temple of this goddess. It was an annual custom at Corinth that seven youths, and as many maidens, children of the most distinguished citizens, clad in black, with their hair shorn, should go to this temple, and singing mournful hymns offer sacrifices to appease the deity. The cause assigned for this rite was as follows. Médeia reigned at Corinth, but the people, disdaining to be governed by an enchantress, conspired against her, and resolved to put her children (seven of each sex) to death. The children fled to the temple of Héra, but they were pursued and slain at the altar. The anger of heaven was manifested by a plague, and by the advice of the oracle the expiatory rite above mentioned was instituted.[2] There was also a tradition that Médeia resided at Corinth, and that she caused a famine to cease by sacrificing to Démétér and the Lémnian nymphs; and that Zeus made love to her, but she would not hearken to his suit, fearing the anger of Héra, who therefore rewarded her by making her children immortal,[3]—a thing which she had attempted in vain to do herself by hiding them in the temple of the goddess,[4] whose priestess, like Ió, she probably was in this mythe; and a personification therefore of one of her epithets.

It is also remarkable that the only place, beside Corinth, in which there were legends of Médeia, was Kerkýra,[5] an island which had been colonised by the Corinthians.

Homer and Hésiod say[6] that Æétés and Kirké were the children of Hélios by the Ocean-nymph Persé or Perséis,[7] and that Æétés was the father of Médeia by the O'keanis Idyia. According to Eumélos,[8] he was the son of Helios and Antiopé,[9] and born at Ephyra or Corinth, which his sire gave to him; but he committed

---

[1] Müller, *Orchom. ut supra*.

[2] Parmeniskos *ap.* Sch. *Eurip. Medeia*, 9, 275. Paus. ii. 3, 7. It was said that the Corinthians by a bribe of five talents gained Euripidés to lay the guilt of the murder of her children on Médeia herself. Schol. *ut sup.*

[3] Sch. *Pind. Ol.* xiii. 53 (74).   [4] Paus. ii. 3, 11.

[5] Apoll. Rh. iv. 1154, 1217.   [6] *Od.* x. 138. *Theog.* 956 *seq.*

[7] Æétés (connected with αἴθω) may be the *Bright-* or *Fiery-one*, an epithet of the Sun: see above, p. 18.

[8] *Ap.* Sch. *Pind. Ol.* xiii. 53 (74).

[9] Perhaps the moon: see below, *Zethos and Amphíón.*

T 2

the charge of it to Bunos, and went to Kolchis. It would thus appear that the whole mythe of Æétés and Médeia is derived from the worship of the Sun and Héra at Corinth.

Πηλεὺς καὶ ᾿Αχιλλεύς.   Peleus et Achilles.

By Ægína the daughter of the river-god Asópos Zeus was the father of Æakos, who dwelt in the island named from his mother. The children of Æakos were, Péleus, Telamón, and Phókos. The last having been slain by his brothers out of jealousy, Æakos banished them from the island. Péleus fled to Phthia, and was there purified of the murder by Eurytión the son of Aktór, whose daughter Polymélé he married. Being so unfortunate as to kill his father-in-law by accident at the Kalydonian hunt, he fled to Iolkos, where he was purified by Akastos the son of Pelias.[1] At the funeral games of Pelias he contended with the fair maid Atalanté; and Hippolyté or Astydameia the wife of Akastos beholding fell in love with him, and solicited him by letters, but in vain, to gratify her passion. Out of revenge she then sent to inform his wife that he was going to marry Steropé the daughter of Akastos; and without inquiring into the truth of the tale, the credulous Polymélé strangled herself. Hippolyté, with the usual artifice of a disappointed woman, next accused Péleus to her husband of an attempt on her honour.[2] Akastos believed the charge, but not thinking that he could lawfully put to death one whom he had purified, invited him to join in a hunt on Mount Pelion. A dispute arising there among the hunters about their respective success, Péleus cut out the tongues of all the beasts which he killed and put them into his pouch. The companions of Akastos getting all these beasts, derided Péleus for having killed no game; but pulling out the tongues, he declared that he had killed just so many.[3] He fell asleep on Mount Pelion, and Akastos taking his famous sword, which had been made by Héphæstos, and hiding it under the cowdung, went away, leaving him there, in hopes that the Kentaurs would find him and kill him.[4] When Peleus awoke he sought for his sword, but in vain; and the Kentaurs coming on him would have put him to death, but for Cheirón, who saved him, and then looked for and returned him his sword.[5]

---

[1] This Welcker (*Tril.* 546) thinks is merely a genealogical fiction.
[2] Pind. *Nem.* v. 26 (48) *seq.*
[3] In a similar manner, in the Sháh-námeh, Gúshtasp proves that he had slain the monsters, the glory of whose destruction was claimed by others.
[4] Ilés. *Fr.* 85.   Pind. *Nem.* iv. 59 (95) *seq.*
[5] Apollod. iii. 13, 1.   Sch. *Apoll. Rh.* i. 224.   Eudocia, 338.

Shortly after Péleus attacked and took Iolkos single-handed according to Pindar;[1] but aided by Iasón and the Dioskuri, according to others, who add that he put Hippolyté to death and marched his troops into the town between her severed members.[2]

To reward the virtue of Péleus the king of the gods resolved to give him a goddess in marriage. The spouse selected for him was the sea-nymph Thetis, who had been wooed by Zeus himself and his brother Poseidón, but Themis having declared that her child would be greater than his sire, the gods ceased from their suit and withdrew.[3] Others say that she was courted by Zeus alone, till he was informed by Prométheus that her son would dethrone him.[4] Others again maintain that Thetis, who was reared by Héra, would not assent to the wishes of Zeus, and that the god in his anger condemned her to espouse a mortal,[5] or that Héra herself selected Péleus for her spouse.[6]

Cheirón, being made aware of the will of the gods, advised Péleus to aspire to the bed of the nymph of the sea, and instructed him how to win her. He therefore lay in wait, and seized and held her fast, though she changed herself into every variety of form, becoming fire, water, a serpent, and a lion.[7] The wedding was solemnized on Pelion: the gods all honoured it with their presence,[8] and bestowed armour on the bridegroom;[9] Cheirón gave him an ashen spear,[10] and Poseidón the immortal Harpy-born steeds Balios and Xanthos.[11] The Muses sang, the Néréides danced, to celebrate the wedding, and Ganymédés poured forth nectar for the guests.[12]

When the celebrated son of Péleus and Thetis was born, his mother wished to make him immortal. She therefore placed him unknown to Péleus each night in the fire, to purge away what he had inherited of mortal from his father; and by day she anointed him with ambrosia. But Péleus watched, and seeing the child panting in the fire cried out. Thetis, thus frustrated in her design, left her babe, and returned to her sister-Néréides. Péleus then

---

[1] *Nem.* iii. 34 (58); iv. 54 (88).
[2] Pherekýdés *ap.* Sch. *Pind. Nem.* iii. 32 (55). Apollod. *ut sup.*
[3] Pind. *Isth.* viii. 27 (58) *seq.*
[4] Apollod. *ut sup.* Sch. *Il.* i. 519.
[5] Apollod. *ut sup.*
[6] *Il.* xxiv. 59. Apoll. Rh. iv. 805 *seq.*
[7] Pind. *Nem.* iv. 62 (101). Soph. *Fr. ap.* Sch. *Nem.* iii. 32 (60).
[8] *Il.* xxiv. 62.
[9] *Il.* xvii. 195; xviii. 84.   [10] *Il.* xvi. 143.
[11] *Il.* xvi. 867; xvii. 443; xxiii. 277.
[12] Eurip. *Iph. in Aul.* 1036 *seq.* Catull. *Nuptiæ Pel. et Thet.*

conveyed the infant to Cheirón, who reared him on the entrails of lions and on the marrow of bears and wild boars, and named him Achilleus, because he never applied his *lips* (χεῖλη) to a breast.[1]

According to the Ægimios[2] (a poem ascribed to Hésiod), Thetis cast her children as they were born into a caldron of boiling water, to try if they were mortal. Several had perished, unable to stand the test, when Péleus lost patience and refused to let the experiment be tried on Achilleus. His goddess-wife then deserted him. These fictions, we may see, are evidently posterior to Homer, who represents Péleus and Thetis as dwelling together all the lifetime of their son.[3]

Of Péleus it is further related, that he survived his son and even grandson,[4] and died in misery in the isle of Kos.[5] The history of Achilleus forms an important portion of the events of the Trojan War.

Ἰξίων. Ixion.

Ixíon was the son of Antión or Peisón; others gave him Phlegyas or the god Arés for a sire. He obtained the hand of Dia the daughter of Déioneus, having according to the usage of the heroic ages, promised his father-in-law large nuptial gifts (ἔδνα); but he did not keep his engagement, and Déioneus seized his horses and detained them as a pledge. Ixíon then sent to say that the gifts were ready if he would come to fetch them. Déioneus accordingly came, but his treacherous son-in-law had prepared in his house a pit filled with fire, and covered over with bits of wood and dust, into which the unsuspecting prince fell and perished. After this deed Ixíon's mind became deranged, and its atrocity being such, neither gods nor men would absolve him, till at length Zeus himself took pity on him and purified him, and admitted him to his house and table on Olympos. But, incapable of good, Ixíon cast an eye of desire on the wife of his benefactor, and dared to make love to her. Héra in concert with her lord formed a cloud in the likeness of herself, which Ixíon embraced. He boasted of his fortune, and Zeus precipitated him to Erebos, where Hermés fixed him with brazen bands to an ever-revolving fiery wheel.[6]

This mythe is probably of great antiquity, as the customs on

---

[1] Apollod. *ut sup.*
[2] *Ap.* Sch. *Apoll. Rh.* iv. 816.
[3] *Il.* i. 396 ; xvi. 574 ; xviii. 89, 332, 440 ; xix. 422.
[4] *Od.* xi. 494. Eurip. *Andromaché.*
[5] Kallimachos *ap.* Sch. *Pind. Pyth.* iii. 96 (167). On the subject of Péleus and Thetis see chap. xii. *Æakos.*
[6] Pind. *Pyth.* ii. 21 (39) *seq. cum Schol.* Hygin. 62. Sch. *Il.* i. 268.

which it is founded only prevailed in the heroic age. Its chief object seems to have been to inspire horror for the violation of the duties of hospitality on the part of those who, having committed homicide, were admitted to the house and table of the prince, who consented to perform the rites by which the guilt of the offender was supposed to be removed. The most extreme case is given by making Ixíon, that is the *Suppliant*,[1] and the first shedder of kindred blood as he is expressly called[2] (the Cain of Greece), act with such base ingratitude toward the king of the gods himself, who, according to the simple earnestness of early mythology, is represented like an earthly prince receiving his suppliant to his house and board. The punishment inflicted was suitable to the offence, and calculated to strike with awe the minds of the hearers; for we should always remember that these ancient mythes were articles of real and serious belief.[3]

Κένταυροι καὶ Λαπίθαι.   Centauri et Lapithæ.

The Kentaurs and Lapiths are two mythic tribes which are always mentioned together. The former are spoken of twice in the Ilias under the name of *Wild-men* (φῆρες), and once under their proper name.[4] We also find the name Kentaurs in the Odyssey.[5] They seem to have been a rude mountain-tribe, dwelling on and about Mount Pelion. There is no ground for supposing that Homer and Hésiod conceived them to be of a mingled form, as they were subsequently represented. In the fight of the Kentaurs and Lapiths on the shield of Héraklés, the latter appear in panoply fighting with spears, while the former wield pine-clubs.[6] Pindar is the earliest poet extant who describes them as semi-ferine. According to him[7] the offspring of Ixíon and the cloud was a son named Kentauros, who when grown up wandered about the foot of Pelion, where he copulated with the Magnésian mares, who brought forth the Kentaurs, a race partaking of the form of both parents, their lower parts resembling their dams, the upper their sire.

By his wife Dia, Ixíon had a son named Peirithoos, who mar-

---

[1] From ἵκω, *to come to, to supplicate*: see Welcker, *Tril.* 549 *note.* Müller, *Eumen.* 144; the father given him by Æschylos, Antíon (ἀντιάω, *to entreat*), and by Pherekýdés, Peisíon (πείθω, *to persuade*), fully answers to this character; his other sire to the other side of it.

[2] Pind. *Pyth.* ii. 31 (57). Æschyl. *Eumen.* 718.

[3] See Welcker, *Tril.* 547 *seq.* Müller, *Eumen.* 144 *seq.*

[4] *Il.* i. 268; ii. 742; xi. 832.

[5] *Od.* xxi. 303.

[6] Hés. 'Ασπίς, 178 *seq.* : see above, p. 97 note (*).

[7] *Pyth.* ii. 42 (78) *seq.*

ried Hippodameia daughter of Adrastos king of Argos. The chiefs of his own tribe, the Lapiths, were all invited to the wedding, as were also the Kentaurs, who dwelt in the neighbourhood of Pelion; Théseus, Nestór, and other strangers, were likewise present. At the feast, Eurytión, one of the Kentaurs, becoming intoxicated with wine, attempted to offer violence to the bride; the other Kentaurs followed his example, and a dreadful conflict arose, in which several of them were slain. The Kentaurs were finally driven from Pelion, and obliged to retire to other regions.[1]

According to the earliest version of this legend, Eurytión the Kentaur, being invited to the house of Peirithoos, got drunk and behaved so ill, that the heroes rose and dragging him to the door cut off his ears and nose, which was the occasion of 'strife between the Kentaurs and men.'[2] In the Catalogue it is said that Hippodameia bore Polypœtés to Peirithoos, the son of Zeus, on the day that he drove the 'shaggy Wild-men' from Pelion to the land of the Æthikans;[3] and Nestór says[4] that he came from Pylos at the invitation of the Lapith chiefs to aid them against the Wild-men, whom they routed with great slaughter. From all this we may collect the tradition of a protracted conflict between the rude Kentaurs and the more civilized Lapiths, which ended in the expulsion of the former. When Héraklés was on his way to hunt the Erymanthian boar, he was entertained by the Kentaur Pholos; and this gave rise to a conflict between him and the other Kentaurs, which terminated in the total discomfiture of the latter.[5]

One of the most celebrated of the Lapiths was Kæneus, who was said to have been originally a maiden named Kænis. Poseidón having violated her, she prayed him as a compensation to turn her into a man, and grant that she should be invulnerable.[6] The god assented, and in the fight between the Kentaurs and Lapiths, the former finding it impossible to wound Kæneus kept striking him with 'green pines,' and the earth finally opened and swallowed him.[7] It is also said that Kæneus, filled with confidence

---

[1] Ov. *Met.* xii. 210 *seq.* He seems to have followed the drama of Æschylos named the Perrhæbian Women. Diodór. iv. 70.

[2] *Od.* xxi. 295 *seq.*   [3] *Il.* ii. 742 *seq.*   [4] *Il.* i. 269 *seq.*

[5] See below, chap. iv. *Héraklés.*

[6] Ov. *Met.* xii. 18ɔ *seq.* Verg. *Æn.* vi. 448. (Serv. *in loc.*) Eudocia, 249.

'Ο δὲ χλωραῖς ἐλάταισι τυπεὶς
ᾤχεθ' ὑπὸ χθόνα Καινεὺς, σχίσας ὀρθῷ ποδὶ γᾶν.

Pind. *Fr. Incert.* 148.

Apoll. Rh. i. 59 *seq.* Orph. *Argonaut.* 168 *seq.* It was probably from this

in his strength and invulnerability, set up his spear in the market and ordered the people to worship it as a god; for which act of impiety Zeus punished him by the hands of the Kentaurs.[1]

The most renowned of the Kentaurs was Cheirón, the son of Kronos by the nymph Philyra.[2] He is called by Homer[3] 'the most upright of the Kentaurs.' He reared Iasón and his son Médeios, Aktæón, Héraklés, Asklépios, and Achilleus, and was famous for his skill in surgery,[4] which he taught the two last heroes. But having been accidentally wounded by one of Héraklés' poisoned arrows, he suffered extreme pain, till, on his prayer to Zeus for relief, he was raised to the sky and made the constellation of the Bowman.[5]

It is the opinion of Buttmann[6] that the Kentaurs and the Lapiths are two purely poetic names, used to designate two opposite races of men; — the former, the rude horse-riding tribes which tradition records to have been spread over the north of Greece; the latter, the more civilised race, which founded towns, and gradually drove their wild neighbours back into the mountains. He therefore thinks the exposition of Kentaurs as *Air-piercers* (from κεντεῖν τὴν αὕραν) not an improbable one, for that very idea is suggested by the figure of a Cossack leaning forward with his protruded lance as he gallops along. But he regards the idea of κένταυρος having been in its origin simply κέντωρ[7] as much more probable. Lapiths may, he thinks, have signified *Stone-persuaders*[8] (from λᾶας πείθειν), a poetic appellation for the builders of towns. He supposes Hippodameia, as her name seems to intimate, to have been a Kentauress, married to the prince of the Lapiths,[9] and thus accounts for the Kentaurs having been at the wedding.

Müller[10] regards the Lapiths as being the same people with the Phlegyans, shortly to be described.

---

circumstance that the father of Kæneus is named Elatos; his own name (from καινὸς, new) refers to his metamorphose.

[1] Sch. *Il.* i. 264. Eudocia, 249.   [2] Above, p. 62.   [3] *Il.* xi. 832.

[4] Χειρουργία: the name Χείρων plainly comes from χείρ.

[5] Ov. *Fast.* v. 379 *seq.* Hygin. *Poet. Astr.* ii. 38.

[6] *Mythologus*, ii. 22.

[7] Like διάκτορος, ἀλάστορος. He holds the word λάστανρος, which he regards as a corruption of λάστωρ (from λᾶν to desire), to be perfectly parallel to κένταυρος. Welcker (*Kret. Kol.* 34 *note*) approves of this etymon. See above, p. 15.

[8] The Dioskuri were for an opposite reason called Λαπέρσα (Frag. Soph. *apud Stob.*).   [9] See Sch. *Od.* xxi. 303.   [10] *Orchom.* 195.

Κήϋξ καὶ Ἀλκυόνη.   *Céÿx et Alcyone.*

Kéyx was the son of Morning-star (Ἐωσφόρος), and king of Trachis. He married Alkyoné a daughter of Æolos the son of Deukalión. Pride, it is said, caused the ruin of both. He called his wife Héra, and was by her styled Zeus in return. Zeus indignant at their impiety turned them both into birds, of their own names.[1]

Another version of this legend[2] says, that Kéyx going to Claros to consult the oracle of Apolló perished by shipwreck, and that his wife on finding his lifeless body on the strand cast herself into the sea. The gods out of compassion changed them both into the birds called Halkyóns. During seven days of winter the Halkyón sits on her eggs, and during seven more she feeds her young on the surface of the sea, which then is calm and free from storm, and these are called the Halkyón-days.[3]

In this legend and in all (except the preceding one) relating to him, Kéyx, we may observe, bears a gentle and amiable character.

Kéyx is introduced into the mythe of Héraklés, whose friend he is said to have been. The Wedding of Kéyx (Γάμος Κήϋκος) was a celebrated event in that hero's history, and the subject of a poem ascribed to Hésiod.[4] The splendid robe also, which when poisoned by Déianeira caused the death of the hero, was the gift of that prince.

It is probable that in the original conception of Kéyx in the mythology of Héraklés he was simply the Brilliant or Illustrious Prince,[5] expressive of his rank or his munificence. With this accords the name of his sire, as also that of his brother Dædalión and his niece Chioné.[6] But as there was a sea-bird whose name resembled his,[7] a later age fabled that he was converted into this

---

[1] Apollod. i. 7, 4. Sch. *Aristoph. Birds*, 251, 300.

[2] Ov. *Met.* xi. 410 *seq.* Hygin. 65.

[3] Eup. *Iph. Taur.* 1089 *seq.* Sch. *Aristoph. ut sup.* Sch. *Theocr.* vii. 57. Eudocia and Suidas, *v.* ἀλκυών. ἡμερ. Plut. *de Sol. Anim.* 35. Plin. *Nat. Hist.* ii. 47.   [4] See Müller, *Dor.* i. 542.

[5] From κάω, καίω : see below, chap. v. *Kadmos.*

[6] See above, p. 146. Dædalión may come from δαίω, *to burn*.

[7] Κήξ, *sea-gull.* The Scholiast on Aristophanés (*ut sup.*) says he was turned into the bird named κηρύλος, which, he adds, Antigonos said was the male of the Halkyón. He further informs us from him that when the males grow old the females carry them on their wings. It is very difficult to say what birds these were, most certainly not kingfishers. In all probability they were sea-gulls, whose cry is mournful. Moschos (iii. 40) makes the male Halkyón different from the κηρύλος · see Verg. *Geor.* iii. 338.

bird, and then assigned him Alkyoné, the name of another sea-bird, as his spouse, and invented the legends given above to account for their transformation.

CHAPTER III.

MYTHES OF ÆTOLIA.

THE hero princes of Kalydón in Ætólia derived their origin from Zeus by Prótogeneia the daughter of Deukalión. Her son, who was named Aëthlios,[1] had come at the head of a colony of the Æolids to E'lis; where he was the father of Endymión, who enjoyed the love of the goddess Seléné. Ætólos, one of the sons of Endymión by a Naïs, having accidentally killed Apis the son of Phoróneus or Iasón, fled to Kurétis which he named after himself Ætólia. His sons were Pleurón and Kalydón, who built towns of their own name. Agénór the son of Pleurón had by Epikasté (the daughter of Kalydón) a son and a daughter named Portháón and Démoníké; and Portháón was by Euryté (grand-daughter of the river-god Achelóos) the father of Agrios, Melas, and Œneus.[2]

From this genealogy may, we think, be collected the tradition of E'lis having in ancient times received a colony from Thessaly, and also of E'leians, or Epeians as they were named, having migrated to Ætólia.[3] This last however may be only a late fiction, to give a colour of right to the Ætólian conquest of E'lis at the time of the Dórian Migration. We may observe that the genuine mythic legends of Kalydón have been connected with the ethnographic genealogy.

Οἰνεύς. *Œneus.*

Œneus the son of Portháón married Althæa daughter of Thestios, a son of Démoníké by the god Arés. By her he had four sons, Toxeus, Thyreus, Klymenos, and Meleagros, and two daughters, Gorgé and Déianeira.

Œneus was devoted to agriculture, and it was said that the god Dionýsos gave him a vine-plant and taught him the mode of its culture;[4] in reward it was added for his allowing the god's

---

[1] Aëthlios is the personification of the Olympic games.

[2] *Il.* xiv. 115 *seq.*; for the above genealogy see Apollod. i. 7, 5 *seq.* Paus. v. 1.

[3] The relation between the Epeians and the Ætólians seems to be intimated in *Il.* xxiii. 632 *seq.*

[4] Apollod. *ut sup.* Hygin. 129. Compare Athén. ii. 35, and Servius and Probus on *Geor.* i. 9.

familiarity with Althæa, by which he became the father of Déianeira.[1] Œneus, it is also said, killed with his own hand his son Toxeus for leaping over the fence of his vineyard.[2]

When Œneus was offering sacrifices to the gods at the conclusion of his harvest, he omitted to notice Artemis. The offended goddess immediately sent a wild boar of huge size and strength to ravage the lands of Kalydón, and destroy the cattle and people. A general hunt was proclaimed, and the boar was slain; but the death of Meleagros the brave son of Œneus was the consequence. Althæa did not long survive her son, whose death she had caused. After her death Œneus married Peribœa the daughter of Hipponoos, by whom he had a son named Tydeus;[3] who, having slain either his uncle, his cousins, or his brother (for writers differ), fled to Adrastos at Argos. When Œneus was grown old and helpless, and his son Tydeus was dead, the sons of his brother Agrios dispossessed him of his kingdom, and kept him in prison.[4] But Diomédés the son of Tydeus coming secretly to Kalydón slew all the sons of Agrios but two, who escaped to the Peloponnése; and as his grandfather was now too old to reign, he gave the kingdom to Andræmon, who had married Gorgé the daughter of Œneus.[5] He took the old man with him to the Peloponnése; but the two surviving sons of Agrios, watching their opportunity, killed the aged prince at the house of Télephos in Arkadia. Diomédés brought his body to Argos, and buried it where the town called from him Œnoé was afterwards built.[6]

Μελέαγρος. *Meleager.*

The tale of the Kalydonian Hunt is probably a legend of great antiquity. In the Ilias,[7] when Phœnix joins his entreaties to those of Odysseus to prevail on Achilleus to lay aside his wrath and aid the Achæans, he quotes the case of Meleagros as an instance of the impolicy of not yielding readily and in time; " I remember this event," says he, " long ago, not lately, how it was; and I will tell it to you all, my friends."

[1] Hygin. *ut sup.*   [2] Apollod. *ut sup.*
[3] Tydeus is called an Ætólian by Homer,—*Il.* iv. 399.
[4] Sch. *Aristoph. Achar.* 393.   [5] See *Il.* xiii. 216 *seq.*
[6] Apollod. *ut sup.* Paus. ii. 25, 2.
[7] *Il.* ix. 527 *seq.* We know not what may be the feeling of others, but for our part we remember when this tale of old Phœnix and Nestór's narrative (*Il.* xi. 670 *seq.*) of the war of the Pylians and Epeians used to give us a peculiar degree of pleasure. They carried us back from the remote age of the war of Troy into a period removed still further in gray antiquity. The pleasure is, to our apprehension, something akin to that inspired by the contemplation of very ancient ruins. See, however, Appendix II.

He relates the circumstance of the neglect of Artemis by Œneus at his harvest-home feast (θαλύσια), and her vengeance. Hunters and dogs were collected from all sides, and the boar was, with the loss of several lives, at length destroyed. A quarrel arose between the Kurétes and the Ætólians about the head and hide, and a war was the consequence. As long as Meleagros fought, the Kurétes had the worst of it, and could not keep the field; but when, enraged at his mother Althæa, he remained with his wife the fair Kleopatra and abstained from the war, noise and clamour rose about the gates, and the towers of Kalydón were shaken by the victorious Kurétes: for Althæa, grieved at the fate of her brother, who had fallen in the fight, had with tears invoked Aidés and Persephoneia to send death to her son.

The elders of the Ætólians supplicated Meleagros; they sent the priests of the gods to entreat him to come forth and defend them: they offered him a piece of land (τέμενος), at his own selection, of fifty gyas,[1] half arable, half vine-land. His aged father Œneus ascended his chamber and implored him, his sisters and his mother supplicated him, but in vain. He remained inexorable, till his very chamber was shaken, when the Kurétes had mounted the towers and set fire to the town. Then his wife besought him with tears,—picturing to him the evils of a captured town, the slaughter of the men, the burning of the town, the dragging away into captivity of the women and children. Moved by these circumstances, he clad himself in arms, went forth, and repelled the enemy; but not having done it out of regard to them, the Ætólians did not give him the proffered recompense.

Such is the more ancient form of the legend, in which it would appear that the Ætólians of Kalydón and the Kurétes of Pleurón alone took part in the hunt. In aftertimes, when the vanity of the different states of Greece made them send their national heroes to every war and expedition of the mythic ages, it underwent various modifications.

Meleagros, it is said,[2] invited all the heroes of Greece to the hunt, proposing the hide of the boar as the prize of whoever should slay him.

Of the Ætólians there were Meleagros and Dryas son of Arés; of the Kurétes the sons of Thestios; Idas and Lynkeus sons of Apharcus came from Messéné; Kastór and Polydeukés, sons of Zeus and Léda, from Lakonia; Atalanté daughter of Iasos, and Ankæos and Képheus sons of Lykurgos from Arkadia;

---

[1] πεντηκοντόγυον. The size of the γύα is not known.
[2] Nikander ap. Anton. Lib. 2. Apollod. i. 8, 2. Ov. Met. viii. 270 seq. Sch. Aristoph. Frogs, 1236. Diod. iv 34. Hygin. 181–5.

Amphiaráos son of Œklés from Argos; Telamón son of Æakos from Salamis; Théseus son of Ægeus from Athens; Iphiklés son of Amphitryón from Thébes; Péleus son of Æakos, and Eurytión son of Aktór, from Phthia; Iasón son of Æsón from Iolkos: Admétos son of Pherés from Pheræ; and Peirithoos son of Ixíón from Larissa.[1]

These chiefs were entertained during nine days in the house of Œneus. On the tenth, Képheus and Ankæos and some others refused to hunt in company with a maiden; but Meleagros, who was in love with Atalanté, obliged them to give over their opposition. The hunt began; Ankæos and Képheus speedily met their fate from the tusks of the boar; Péleus accidentally killed Eurytión; Atalanté with an arrow gave the monster his first wound; Amphiaráos shot him in the eye; and Meleagros ran him through the flanks and killed him. He presented the skin and head to Atalanté; but the sons of Thestios, offended at this preference of a woman, took the skin from her, saying that it fell to them of right, on account of their family, if Meleagros resigned his claim to it. Meleagros in a rage killed them, and restored the skin to Atalanté.

When Meleagros was seven days old, the Mœræ, it was said, came, and declared that when the billet which was burning on the hearth should be consumed the babe would die.[2] Althæa on hearing this snatched the billet, and laid it up carefully in a chest. But now her love for her son giving way to resentment for the death of her brothers, she took the billet from its place of concealment, and cast it once more into the flames. As it consumed, the vigour of Meleagros wasted away; and when it was reduced to ashes, his life terminated. Repenting when too late of what she had done, Althæa put an end to her life by a cord or a sword. Kleopatra died of grief; and his sisters, who would not be comforted in their affliction, were by the compassion of the gods, all but Gorgé and Déianeira, changed into the birds called Meleagrides.[3]

There was another tradition, according to which Meleagros was slain by Apolló the protecting deity of the Kurétes.[4]

---

[1] In the Meleagros of Euripidés there was a long description given of the arms and appearance of each of the chiefs: see *Fr. Meleag.* 6.

[2] Compare the similar circumstance in the Icelandic Nornagestssaga, cap. xi.

[3] Apollod. *ut sup.* Nikander, *ut sup.* Ov. *ut sup.* 446 *seq.* Hygin. 174. Tzetz. *Lyc.* 492.

[4] Paus. x. 31, 3, 4, from the E'œæ and Minyas. He says that the earliest author extant who mentioned Meleagros' death by the billet, was the tragedian

Two distinct classes of names may be recognised in these Ætólian legends, the one relating to agriculture, the other to war. The former are Œneus (*Viny*), Melas (*Black-soil*), Agrios (*Wild* or *Rustic*), Althæa (*Grower*), Meleagros (*Land-loving*); the latter Portheus or Porthâón (*Destroyer*), Démoniké (*People-subduer*), Toxeus (*Archer*), Thyreus and Tydeus (*Impetuous*, θύω), Klymenos (*Renowned*), Déianeira (*Man's-foe*), and several others. The former would seem to belong to the peaceful rural Pelasgian times, the latter to owe their origin to the character of the Ætólians of a later period.

CHAPTER IV.

MYTHES OF BŒOTIA.

THE mythology of Bœótia consists of two cycles, answering to the natural division of the country. The former belongs to the southern part, and chiefly relates to Thébes (Θῆβαι) and the Kadmeians : the latter to the northern part and Orchomenos and the Minyans. This last cycle is closely connected with that of the Argonautics. We will commence with the cycle of Thébes.

Κάδμος. *Cadmus.*

Poseidón, says the legend, was by Libya the father of two sons, Bélos and Agénór; the former of whom reigned in Egypt. The latter having gone to Europe married Télephassa, by whom he had three sons, Kadmos, Phœnix, and Kilix, and one daughter, Európé. Zeus becoming enamoured of Európé carried her away to Kréte; and Agénór, grieving for the loss of his only daughter, ordered his sons to go in quest of her, and not to return till they had found her. They were accompanied by their mother and by Thasos a son of Poseidón. Their long search was to no purpose : they could get no intelligence of their sister; and fearing the indignation of their father, they resolved to settle in various countries. Phœnix therefore established himself in Phœnicia, Kilix in Kilikia;

Phrynichos in his play of the Pleurónian Women, from which he quotes the following lines :

κρυερὸν γάρ οὐκ
ἤλυξεν μόρον, ὠκεῖα δέ νιν φλὸξ κατεδαίσετο
δαλοῦ περθομένου ματρὸς ὑπ' αἰνᾶς κακομηχάνου.

He justly adds that it was probably no original fiction of the poet's, but a current story. Æschylos also alludes to it, *Choeph.* 605 *seq.*

Kadmos and his mother went to Thrace, where Thasos founded a town also named from himself.[1]

After the death of his mother Kadmos went to Delphi, to inquire of the oracle respecting Európé. The god desired him to cease from troubling himself about her, but to follow a cow as his guide, and to build a city where she should lie down. On leaving the temple he went through Phókis, and meeting a cow belonging to the herds of Pelagón he followed her. She went through Bœótia till she came to where Thébes now stands, and there lay down. Wishing to sacrifice her to Athéna,[2] Kadmos sent his companions to fetch water from the fount of Arés; but the fount was guarded by a serpent, who killed the greater part of them. Kadmos then engaged with and destroyed the serpent: by the direction of Athéna he sowed its teeth, and immediately a crop of armed men sprang up, who slew each other, either quarrelling or through ignorance: for it is said that when Kadmos saw them rising he flung stones at them; and thinking it was done by some of themselves, they fell upon and slew each other. Five only survived; Echíon (*Viper*), Udæos (*Groundly*), Chthonios (*Earthly*), Hyperénór (*Mighty*), and Pelór (*Huge*). These were called the Sown (σπάρτοι); and they joined with Kadmos to build the city.[3]

For killing the sacred serpent Kadmos was obliged to spend a year[4] in servitude to Arés. At the expiration of that period Athéna herself prepared for him a palace, and Zeus gave him Harmonia the daughter of Arés and Aphrodíté in marriage. All the gods, quitting Olympos, celebrated the marriage in the Kadmeia, the palace of Kadmos. The bridegroom presented his bride with a magnificent robe, and with a collar, the work of Héphæstos, given to him, it is said, by the divine artist himself. Harmonia became the mother of four daughters, Semelé, Autonoé, Inó, and Agaué; and of one son, Polydóros.

After the various misfortunes which befel their children, Kadmos and his wife quitted Thébes, now grown odious to them, and migrated to the country of the Enchelians; who, being harassed by the incursions of the Illyrians, were told by the oracle that if they made Kadmos and Harmonia their leaders they should be

---

[1] Apollod. iii. 1, 1. This genealogy is given somewhat differently by Pherekýdés (Sch. *Apoll. Rh.* iii. 1179): Sch. *Eurip. Phœn.* 5.

[2] The oracle said, to Earth : see above, p. 142.

[3] Ov. *Met.* iii. 1 *seq.* Pherekýdés *ut sup.* Apollod. iii. 4, 1. Pherekýdés says that Arés gave the teeth to Kadmos, and desired him to sow them. Hellanikos (*ap.* Sch. eund.) says that only the five Spartans were produced from the teeth

[4] ᾿Αΐδιον ἐνιαυτόν. "The year then was eight years," Apollod. : **see above,** p. 122.

successful. They obeyed the god, and his prediction was verified. Kadmos became king of the Illyrians, and had a son named Illyrios. Shortly afterwards he and Harmonia were changed into serpents, and sent by Zeus to the E'lysian Plain, or, as others said, were conveyed thither in a chariot drawn by serpents.[1]

The mythe of Kadmos is, by its relation to history, one of considerable importance. It is usually regarded as offering a convincing proof of the fact of colonies from the East having come to Greece and introduced civilisation and the arts. We will therefore here briefly examine it.

In the Ilias, though the Kadmeians are spoken of more than once,[2] the slightest allusion is not made to Kadmos; in the Odyssey [3] the sea-goddess Inó-Leukothea is said to have been a mortal, and daughter of Kadmos. Hésiod[4] says that the goddess Harmonia was married to Kadmos in Thébes. Pindar frequently speaks of Kadmos; he places him with the Grecian heroes Péleus and Achilleus in the Island of the Blest;[5] but it is very remarkable that this Théban poet never even hints at his Phœnician origin. It was however an article of general belief in Pindar's time.[6]

There is a curious coincidence between the name Kadmos and the Semitic term for the East, Qedem[7] (קֶדֶם), and this may in reality be the sole foundation for the notion of a Phœnician colony at Thébes; for none of the usual evidences of colonisation are to be found. We do not, for example, meet with the slightest trace of Phœnician influence in the language, manners, or institutions of Bœótia. It is further a thing most incredible, that a seafaring commercial people like the Phœnicians should have selected as the site of their very earliest foreign settlement a place situated in a rich fertile valley away from the sea, and only adapted for agriculture, without mines, or any of those objects of trade which might tempt a people of that character. It is also strange that the descendants of these colonists should have so entirely put off the Phœnician character as to become noted in after-ages for their dislike of trade of every kind. We may therefore, we think,

---

[1] Apollod. ut sup. Apoll. Rh. iv. 517. Ov. Met. iv. 563 seq. Nonn. xliv. 115. Ptol. Heph. 1.

[2] Il. iv. 391; v. 804; xxiii. 680.   [3] Od. v. 333.

[4] Theog. 937, 975.   [5] Ol. ii. 78 (142).

[6] It is mentioned, as we have seen, by Pherekýdés and Hellaníkos.

[7] According to this theory Kadmeians would signify Eastmen or Ostmen, he name the Scandinavians gave themselves in Ireland. But these left traces t least of their language. The Saracens also were named from the Arabic harak, east.

U

venture to dismiss this theory and seek a Grecian origin for Kadmos.[1]

Homer and Hésiod call the people of Thébes Kadmeians or Kadmeionians, and the country the Kadmeian land;[2] the citadel was at all times named the Kadmeia. Kadmos is therefore apparently (like Pelasgos, Dóros, Ión, Thessalos, and so many others) merely a personification of the name of the people. Here then we might stop, and leave the Kadmeians to rank with the Iónians, Thessalians and others, of whose name it is difficult to assign a probable origin. It is however said that Kadmos signifies *Prince* or *General*, that Kadmeia is therefore *Palace*, and that the people thence derived their name,[3]—a case we believe contrary to all analogy. Again, we are reminded that Kadmilos or Kadmos was a name of Hermés in the mysteries of Samothrake, which were instituted by the Tyrrhenian Pelasgians, who, at the time of the Dórian migration being driven from Bœótia, settled on the islands in the north of the Ægæan. We are further reminded that the name Kadmos occurs only at Thébes and Samothrake; that Harmonia was an object of worship in this last place, and that the Kabeiræan deities were also worshipped at Thébes. Hence it is inferred that Kadmos-Hermés, *i. e.* Hermés *Regulator* or *Disposer*, a cosmogonic power, gave name to a portion of the Pelasgian race, and that in the usual manner the god was made a mortal king.[4]

We must confess that this ingenious theory fails to convince us, and we are inclined to think that it was the circumstance of Kadmos (the personified Kadmeians), happening also to signify the *Regulator*, that gave rise to all this mystery in which he is enveloped. It was certainly his name that led to the idea of giving him Harmonia for his bride. The influence of names is also we think perceptible in the oracle given to the Enchelians, namely to take Kadmos and Harmonia for their leaders, that is, to adopt regular discipline, and they would be victorious in war. The name of this people (ἐγχέλεις, *eels*) may have had its effect on the legend of the change of Kadmos and Harmonia into serpents.

---

[1] See Müller, *Orchom.* 113 *seq.*

[2] Καδμηΐδι γαίῃ. Hés. Ἔργ. 162.

[3] Welcker (*Kret. Kol.* 22 *seq.*) deduces Κάδμος from ΚΑ'ΖΩ, *to adorn*, or *order*. He as usual gives a profusion of cognate terms. The word κάδμος he regards as exactly answering to κόσμος, the name of the chief magistrate in Kréte. The verb ΚΑ'ΖΩ is however only a conjecture of this critic's own, as the theme of κέκασμαι and other tenses of καίνυμαι. They are all evidently connected with καίω, κάω, *to burn*, and hence (like φλέγω) *to blaze, shine, be illustrious.* The Kadmeians may then be similar to the Phlegyans and the Phæakians, etc.

[4] Müller, *Orchom.* 461 *seq. Proleg.* 146 *seq.* See on the other side Welcker *ut sup.* 31 *seq.* Lobeck, 1253 *seq.*

By the Spartans (*Sown*) in this legend are probably meant the Eupatrids, or ancient nobility of Thébes, of which there may have been only five Houses (γένεα). As such were fond of representing themselves as autochthons, and the serpent was the symbol of constant residence,[1] and the teeth might represent military prowess, the legend of the serpent slain by Kadmos may be interpreted in a political sense, of the conquest of the country and the origin of the Théban patricians.[2]

It is rather remarkable that the names of the children of Kadmos seem all to refer to the element of water. Inó is a goddess of the sea, Agaué and Autonoé occur in the list of the Néréides, and Polydóré is the name of an Ocean-nymph.[3] Semelé herself may refer to the *brightness* (σέλας) of water,[4] and her name be like E'lektra, Galateia, Galéné, Glauké, Ianthé, and other names of water-nymphs. Still we are unable to discern any relation between the water and the Kadmic family.

Σεμέλη. *Semele.*

Semelé, the daughter of Kadmos, enjoyed the fatal honour of the love of Zeus. The jealousy of Héra suggested to the unfortunate fair-one the imprudent request which cost her her life. Her offspring was Dionýsos, who became a god presiding over the vintage.[5]

Αὐτονόη, Ἀρισταῖος, καὶ Ἀκταίων. *Autonoe, Aristœus, et Actœon.*

Autonoé was married to Aristæos, the son of Apolló by the nymph Kyréné, the daughter of Hypseus son of the river-god Péneios, and king of the Lapiths of Thessaly. Kyréné was averse from all feminine occupations, and passed her days in hunting the wild beasts, and thus protecting the cattle of her father. One day as she was engaged in combat with a lion, Apolló beheld her, and filled with admiration of her beauty and her courage, he called out to Cheirón to quit his cave and come and look at her. To the questions of the god respecting her the Kentaur replied, by informing him that he was to be her spouse, and to carry her in his golden car over the sea to the rich garden of Zeus, where Libya would joyfully receive her in a golden abode; that there she would bear a son, whom Hermés would take to the 'well-seated Seasons and Earth,' who would feed him with nectar and ambrosia, and render him immortal; and that he should be called Zeus, and holy Apolló, Agreus (*Hunter*), and Nomios

---

[1] Hérod. i. 78.
[2] See Welcker *ut sup.* 78 *seq.*
[3] Hés. *Theog.* 246, 258, 354.
[4] See above, p. 192.
[5] See above, p. 187.

(*Herdsman*), and Aristæos.   The god forthwith seized the nymph and in his car drawn by swans[1] conveyed her to the part of Libya afterwards named from her, and 'silver-footed Aphrodíté' received them on their arrival, and spread the bridal couch.[2]

The invention of the culture of the olive and of the art of managing bees was ascribed to Aristæos.[3] Tradition also said that one time when the isle of Keos was afflicted by a drought, caused by the excessive heat of the dog-days, the inhabitants invited Aristæos thither; and on his erecting an altar to Zeus Ikmæos (*Moistener*), the Etésian breezes breathed over the isle, and the evil departed.   After his death he was deified by the people of Keos.[4]   Vergil[5] has elegantly related the story of the love of Aristæos for Eurydiké the wife of Orpheus; his pursuit of her, and her unfortunate death; on which the Napæan nymphs, her companions, destroyed all his bees; and the mode adopted by him on the advice of his mother to stock once more his hives.

Aktæón was the offspring of the marriage of Aristæos with Autonoé.   He was reared by Cheirón, and becoming passionately devoted to the chase, passed his days chiefly in pursuit of the wild beasts that haunted Mount Kithærón.   One sultry day, as he rambled alone, he chanced to surprise Artemis and her nymphs as they were bathing.   The goddess, incensed at his intrusion, flung some water upon him and turned him into a stag.   She also inspired with madness the fifty dogs that were with him, and they ran down and devoured their unhappy master.   Then they went about whining in quest of him, till they came at last to the cave of Cheirón, who appeased their grief by making an image of Aktæón.[6]   Another cause assigned for the anger of the goddess was Aktæón's boasting that he was superior to her at the chase;[7] while others ascribed his transformation and death to the jealousy of Zeus, who feared that he would marry Semelé.[8]

Aristæos, as is quite evident from the names given him by Pindar, was an original deity, Zeus-Aristæos, or Aristos, or Apolló-Agreus, or Nomios.   He was a rural god, presiding over cattle and game, the culture of the vine and olive, and especially the management

[1] Pherekýdés *ap.* Sch. *Apoll. Rh.* ii. 498.   [2] Pindar, *Pyth.* ix.
[3] Apoll. Rh. iv. 1132.   Aristotle (*ap.* Sch. *Theocr.* v. 53) said he was taught them by the nymphs who had reared him.
[4] Apoll. Rh. ii. 506 *seq.* Sch. on *v.* 498. Servius and Probus on *Geor.* i, 14.
[5] *Geor.* iv. 282 *seq.* Ov. *Fast.* i. 363 *seq.*
[6] Kallim. v. 107 *seq.* Apollod. iii. 4, 4. Ov. *Met.* iii. 137 *seq.* Hygin. 180, 181. Nonn. v. 287 *seq.*
[7] Eurip. *Bakchæ,* 337 *seq.*   [8] Stésichoros *ap. Paus.* ix. 2, 3.

of bees. The chief seats of his worship were Arkadia[1] (whence it was carried over to Keos), Thessaly,[2] and as this was inhabited by the Minyans, some of whom were among tne colonists to Kyréné, it was taken thither; and finally Bœótia, whence we find him united to one of the daughters of Kadmos.[3] Apolló was also an object of especial veneration to the settlers at Kyréné; and in the oldest part of the city there was a fount named Kyré, sacred to him, whence perhaps came the name of the town itself.[4] It was moreover a habit of the early Greek colonies to fancy or feign that in the mythic ages their patron-gods or heroes had already taken possession of the place in which they were now settled under their auspices and protection.[5] In no place were there more of these traditions than in Kyréné, and hence probably arose the mythe of Apolló's carrying the nymph from the foot of Pélion, and having by her a son named Aristæos.

The mythe of Aktæón may be thus explained. On the summit of Pelion stood a temple of Zeus-Aktæos,[6] to which, when the dog-days began, a party of noble youths selected by the priest, ascended clad in fresh-stript sheep-skins to protect them from the cold and there sacrificed to the god to avert the evil influence of the dog-star.[7] Now Aktæón's father Aristæos had done just the same at Keos, and this shows a connexion between their mythes, that in fact they were two epithets of the same god. The fifty hounds of Aktæón answer to the fifty dog-days. One account[8] said that Artemis threw a stag's-hide over him, and thus caused the error of his dogs, and this might refer to the sheep-skins; the cave of Cheirón was on Mount Pelion. The tale of the image may perhaps be connected with the following legend. There was an image in a rock that caused injury to the land of Orchomenos; the oracle of Delphi, on being consulted, directed that whatever was remaining of Aktæón should be hidden in the earth, and a brazen figure of that image be made, and bound with iron to the rock, and that then the evil would cease.[9]

Ἰνὼ καὶ Ἀθάμας. Ino et Athamas.

Inó was married to Athamas, son of Æolos, and king of Orchomenos.

This prince, it is said, had been already married to Nephelé

---

[1] Verg. Geor. iv. 283. Nonn. xiii. 275 seq. [2] Apoll. Rh. ii. 514.
[3] See Müller, Orch. 348. [4] Hérod. iv. 158. [5] See Müller, Proleg. 143.
[6] So named probably from the Δημήτερος ἀκτή : see Welcker in Schwenk. 305. By the principle of secondary derivation Aktæón may have been made hunter, from ἄγω.
[7] Dikæarchos in the Geograph. Minor. ii. 29.
[8] Stésichoros, ut sup. [9] Paus. ix. 38, 5

(*Cloud*), by whom he had two children, Phrixos and Hellé. He then espoused Inó the daughter of Kadmos, who bore him two sons, Learchos and Melikertés. Inó feeling the usual jealousy of a step-mother, resolved to destroy the children of Nephelé. For this purpose she persuaded the women to parch the seed-corn unknown to their husbands. They did as she desired, and the lands consequently yielded no crop. Athamas sent to Delphi to consult the oracle how the threatening famine might be averted; and Inó persuaded the messengers to say that Apolló had directed that Phrixos should be sacrificed to Zeus. Compelled by his people Athamas reluctantly placed his son before the altar; but Nephelé snatched away both her son and her daughter, and gave them a gold-fleeced ram she had obtained from Hermés, which carried them through the air over sea and land. They proceeded safely till they came to the sea between Sigeion and the Chersonése, into which Hellé fell, and it was named from her Helléspontos (*Helle's Sea*). Phrixos went on to Kolchis, to Æétés the son of Hélios, who received him kindly, and gave him in marriage Chalkiopé his daughter. He there sacrificed his ram to Zeus Phyxios, and gave the golden fleece to Æétés, who nailed it to an oak in the grove of Arés.

Through the enmity of Héra to Inó, who had suckled the infant Dionýsos, Athamas was afterwards seized with madness. In his phrensy he shot his son Learchos with an arrow, or, as others say, dashed him to pieces against a rock. Inó fled with her other son; and being closely pursued by her furious husband, sprang with her child from the cliff of Moluris near Corinth into the sea. The gods took pity on her and made her a sea-goddess under the name of Leukothea, and Melikertés a sea-god under that of Palæmón.[1]

Athamas, being obliged to leave Bœótia, inquired of the god where he should settle. He was told to establish himself in the place where he should be entertained by the wild beasts. Having wandered over many lands, he came one day to where some wolves were devouring the thighs of sheep. At the sight of him they fled, abandoning their prey. Judging this to be the fulfilment of the oracle, he settled in that place, built a town which he named from himself Athamantia; and marrying Themistó the daughter of Hypseus, had by her four sons named Leukón, Erythrios, Schœneus, and Ptóos.[2]

It is thus that we find this important mythe related by Apollodóros. There are however many variations in the tale. Thu~

---

[1] See above, p. 220.   [2] Apollod. i. 9, 1, 2.

it is said that Inó was Athamas' first wife, and that he put her away by the direction of Héra and married Nephelé, who left him after she had borne two children, on finding that he still kept up an intercourse with Inó. When the response of the oracle came to Athamas he sent for Phrixos out of the country, desiring him to come and to bring the finest sheep in the flock for a sacrifice. The ram then spoke with a human voice to Phrixos warning him of his danger, and offering to carry him and his sister to a place of safety. The ram, it was added, died at Kolchis.[1] It was also said that the flight of Phrixos was caused by his rejection of the amorous advances of his step-mother or his aunt,[2] and again that in the time of dearth he offered himself as a voluntary victim.

It has been already observed that the tragic poets allowed themselves great liberties in their treatment of the ancient mythes. There is none which has suffered more at their hands than the present one, for it was a favourite subject with them. Thus Euripidés in his Inó said that Athamas thinking that Inó had perished in the woods married Themistó; but Inó, who was alive, came and lived as a maid-servant unknown in the house of her husband. Here Themistó made her the confidant of her design to destroy her step-children, and directed her for that purpose to dress *them* in black and her own in white, that she might be able to distinguish them. Inó however reversed the orders, and Themistó unwittingly killed her own children, and then seeing what she had done slew herself.[3]

We will now endeavour to point out the meaning of this very obscure legend. Athamas it is plain belonged to the Minyans, who dwelt in Bœótia and about the bay of Pagasæ in Thessaly. At Alos in this last region stood a temple of Laphystian[4] Zeus, about which there was the following tradition.[5] To punish the crime of Athamas the oracle directed that the eldest person of his posterity should abstain from entering the Prytaneion or senate-house, or if found there should be offered as a sacrifice. Many of those in this situation fled the country, and such as returned and were caught in the Prytaneion were led forth to sacrifice bound with woollen fillets. These persons were said to be the descendants of Kytissóros the son of Phrixos, who had come from Kolchis and

---

[1] Philostephanos, *ap.* Schol. *Il.* vii. 86.
[2] Hygin. *Poet. Astr.* ii. 20.
[3] Hygin. 4. Nonnus, ix. 247 *seq.* The last trait reminds one of Petit Poucet and the Ogre.
[4] *Flight-giving*, according to Müller, who says that λαφύσσω is the same as σπεύδω, φεύγω; but in Homer (see *Il.* xi. 176) it signifies, *to devour, swallow up greedily.*
[5] Hérod. vii. 127.

saved his grandfather Athamas, when the people were about to sacrifice him as a sin-offering by command of the oracle. By this act Kytissóros had drawn the anger of the gods on his posterity.

It is not unlikely then that this mythe of Athamas took its rise from the sin-offering (κάθαρμα), a real or symbolic human sacrifice which prevailed in various parts of Greece; and of which this was the most sublime form, as it represented not criminals, as elsewhere, but the noblest members of society, the descendants of Zeus himself, expiating by their lives for the sin not of themselves but of the people.[1] We shall find this mythe connected with the Argonautic Expedition.

'Αγαυῆ καὶ Πενθεύς.   Agave et Pentheus.

Agaué, the remaining daughter of Kadmos, was married to Echíón, one of the Spartans. Her son Pentheus succeeded his grandfather in the government over Thébes. During his reign, Dionýsos came from the East and sought to introduce his orgies into his native city. The women all gave enthusiastically in to the new religion, and Mount Kithærón rang to the frantic yells of the Bakchantes. Pentheus sought to check the phrensy; but, deceived by the god, he went secretly and ascended a tree on Kithærón to be an ocular witness of the revels. While there he was descried by his mother and aunts, to whom Dionýsos made him appear to be a wild beast, and he was torn to pieces by them.[2]

The name of Pentheus, it is plain, is derived from the *grief* (πένθος) occasioned by his fate. Agaué (*Illustrious*) is an epithet of Persephoné, who may have been made a heroine, as Thébes was a principal seat of the worship of Démétér and the Koré.

Ζῆθος καὶ 'Αμφίων.   Zethus et Amphion.

After the death of Pentheus Thébes was governed by Polydóros the son of Kadmos, who married Nyktéis the daughter of Nykteus. Their son was Labdakos, who on succeeding his father opposed himself like Pentheus to the religion of Dionýsos, and underwent a similar fate. As his son Laïos was only a year old, the throne was occupied by Lykos the brother of Nykteus.

Both Lykos and his brother, it is said, had fled from Eubœa for killing Phlegyas the son of Arés; and as they were related to Pentheus, he enrolled them among the citizens of Thébes. Lykos on the death of Labdakos was chosen polemarch by the Thébans;

---

[1] See Müller, *Orchom.* 161 *seq.* and our Ovid's *Fasti*, Excurs. vi.
[2] Eur. *Bakchæ.* Apollod. iii. 5, 2. Ov. *Met.* iii. 511 *seq.*

and he seized on the regal power, which he held 'or twenty years, till he was killed by Zéthos and Amphíon.

These were the sons of Zeus by Antiopé the daughter of Nykteus. Terrified at the threats of her father when the consequences of her frailty became apparent, Antiopé fled to Sikyón, where she married Epópeus. Nykteus out of grief put an end to himself, having previously charged his brother Lykos to punish Epópeus and Antiopé. Lykos accordingly marched an army against Sikyón, took it, slew Epópeus, and led Antiopé away captive. On the way to Thébes she brought forth twins at Eleutheræ. The unhappy babes were exposed on the mountain; but a neatherd having found them, reared them, calling the one Zéthos, the other Amphíon. The former devoted himself to the care of cattle; the latter passed his time in the practice of music, having been presented with a lyre and taught to play on it by Hermés.

Meantime Lykos had put Antiopé in bonds, and she was treated with the utmost cruelty by him and his wife Dirké. But her chains loosed of themselves, and she fled to the dwelling of her sons in search of shelter and protection. Having recognised her, they resolved to avenge her wrongs : they attacked and slew Lykos, and tying Dirké by the hair to a bull let him drag her till she was dead : they then cast her body into the fount which was named from her. They expelled Laïos, seized on the government, and walled-in the town; for which purpose the stones are said to have moved in obedience to the lyre of Amphíon.

Zéthos married Thébé, from whom he named the town. Amphíon espoused Niobé the daughter of Tantalos, who bore him an equal number of sons and daughters. Elated with her numerous progeny she set herself above Létó, who was the mother of but two children; the latter complained to Apolló and Artemis, and the sons of Niobé soon fell by the arrows of the former, while her daughters perished by those of his sister.

> Nine days they lay in blood, and there was none
> To bury them, for Kronidés had made
> The people stones; but on the tenth the gods
> Celestial buried them : she then of food
> Thought, being tired out with shedding tears.
> Now 'mid the rocks among the lonely hills
> In Sipylos, where are they say the beds
> Of the goddess-nymphs who by the Achelóos dance,
> Although a stone, she yet broods o'er the woes
> Sent by the gods.[1]

---

[1] *Il.* xxiv. 602 *seq.* It is here said that Niobé had six sons and six daughters. Hésiod (Sch. *Eur. Phœn.* 160) said ten of each sex ; the tragedians (*Id. ib.*) said seven, but this was probably on account of the chorus.

It was said that one son and a daughter named Chlóris escaped, and that Amphíon in attempting, out of vengeance, to destroy the temple of Apolló, perished by the shafts of that deity.[1]

According to another tradition[2] Zéthos was married to Aédón the daughter of Pandareos, by whom he had only a son named Itylos, and a daughter Néis. Aédón, jealous of the superior fecundity of her sister-in-law Niobé, resolved to kill her eldest son Amaleus in the night. As the two cousins slept together, she directed her own son Itylos to lie inside; but he mistook or neglected her directions, and in the dark she killed him instead of Amaleus.[3] When she discovered what she had done she prayed to the gods to take her out of the world, and she was changed into a nightingale (ἀηδών). Zéthos is also said to have fallen by the arrows of Apolló.

This legend is thus noticed in the Odyssey :[4]

> As when Pandareos' daughter, green Aédón,
> Sings lovely in the opening of the spring,
> Seated amid the dense leaves of the trees,
> She, frequent changing, poureth forth her voice
> Tone-full, lamenting her son Itylos,
> King Zéthos' child, whom erst with ruthless brass
> She in her folly slew.

We shall find another form of it among the mythes of Attica.

In this story also there are great variations, caused chiefly, it is probable, by the tragedians. By Homer[5] Antiopé is called the daughter of Asópos, and Asios made her the wife of Epópeus at the time of her conception.[6] It is indeed not improbable that this poet represented these twins, like those of Léda, as being the one immortal the other mortal, corresponding to the nature of their sires. The mythe in every view of it has, we think, a physical aspect. Lykos and Nykteus are plainly *Light* and *Night*; Antiopé the daughter of the latter is the *Beholder* (ἀντὶ ὄψ), or simply the *Opposer*,[7] and may remind us of the moon, which at the full sits so calmly looking down on the earth, or which then rises in the

---

[1] Apollod. iii. 5, 6.   Or *Met.* vi. 146 *seq.*   Hygin. 9.
[2] Sch. *Od.* xix. 518.   [3] See above, p. 295.
[4] *Od.* xix. 518.   [5] *Od.* xi. 259.

> Ἀντιόπη δ᾽ ἔτεκε Ζῆθον καὶ Ἀμφίονα δῖον,
> Ἀσωποῦ κούρη ποταμοῦ βαθυδινήεντος,
> Ζηνί τε κυσαμένη καὶ Ἐπωπέϊ ποιμένι λαῶν.
>   *Ap. Paus.* ii. 3, 4.

[7] See above, p. 15.   Apollónios (iv. 1090) terms Antiopé εὐῶπις.

evening opposite to the sun;[1] her husband's name Epópeus is apparently of similar import; her mother is Polyxó (Polylyxó), *Light-full*. Amphíon is the *Circler* (hence he walls-in Thébes), and Zéthos is perhaps the *Warmer* or *Inflamer*.[2] The Twins, the offspring of the Deity and the Moon, may then be the Sun who goes each day his round, and whose beams give warmth to the earth.

The mythe of Niobé also is capable of a physical sense. This *goddess*,[3] whose name denotes *Youth* or *Newness*,[4] is the daughter of Tantalos, the *Flourishing-one*, and the mother of Chlóris, the *Green-one*. In her then we may view the young, verdant, fruitful earth, 'the bride of the sun'[5] (Amphíon), beneath the influence of whose fecundating beams she pours forth vegetation with lavish profusion. The revolution of the year, denoted by Apolló and Artemis—other forms of the sun and moon,—withers up and destroys her progeny; she weeps and stiffens to stone—the torrents and frost of winter; Chlóris the *Green-one* remains, and spring clothes the earth anew with verdure.[6]

Some however think that in this story of the Antiopids glimpses are given of the ancient political state of Thébes. It is observed that there is no connection between them and the Kadmic line; that given above being plainly the work of late times to account for their appearance at Thébes. Müller[7] therefore sees in the former a race of priest-kings devoted to the service of Démétér and Hermés-Kadmos, while the two 'white-horsed gods'[8] were gallant warriors who walled-in and fortified the city for the defence, it is

---

[1] Καὶ Φαέθων ['Ήλιοs] ἰσόμοιρὸς ἔην ἀντώπιδι Μήνῃ.—Nonn. vi. 76.

Less bright the moon,
But *opposite* in leveled west was set.—Milt. *Par. Lost*, vii. 375.

"At that hour of the day when *face to face* the rising moon *beholds* the setting sun."—Longfellow, *Hyperion*, ii. 10.

[2] From ζέω, *ferveo*. The name of Ǽétés' mother also was Ántiopé: see above, p. 275. We have elsewhere (above, p. 54) the Sun the father of the Moon, and on the hypothesis of night preceding day, the Moon might be regarded as the mother of the Sun. Zeus-Epópeus is like Zeus-Tyndareós, Zeus-Amphitryón. Epópeus and Antiopé are related in signification like Amphitryón and Alkméné.

[3] Soph. *Antig.* 834. *Elek.* 150. Dióné, one of the Hyades, is her mother, Ov. *Met.* vi. 174. Hygin. 9. Sapphó (*Athén.* xiii. 571) says

Λατὼ καὶ Νιόβη μάλα μὲν φίλαι ἦσαν ἐταῖραι.

[4] "Νιόβη, i.e. Νεόβη (νίοψ, νέος, like θιὸs, σιὸs for θεὸs) a Νέαιρα or Καινώ." Welcker, *Kret. Kol.* 7. Völcker, *Myth. der Jap.* 356: see above, p. 51.

[5] See Appendix I.

[6] See Völcker, *ut sup.*, *Cambridge Phil. Mus.* ii. 354, and above, pp. 51 and 198.

[7] *Orchom.* 227 *seq.*   [8] Eur. *Phœn.* 606.

said,[1] of Kadmos the priest-king, against the warlike Phlegyans. In fine this writer would seem to view in ancient Thébes a political state of things somewhat similar to that in France under the last Merovingians, or still more resembling that of Japan at the present day. Welcker's[2] views are not very dissimilar. He sees in the story of the Twins a *Diarchy*, as at Sparta and at Rome in its origin, and he conceives it to have been established by one of the ancient houses, as Nykteus is called the son of Chthonios. He also discovers that the Antiopids favoured the religion of Dionýsos, to which the Kadmeians were so hostile; in Amphíon's love of music and union with Niobé he finds evidence of the early introduction of the Lydian melody into Thébes.

Λάϊος. Laïus.

Laïos, when driven from Thébes by the Antiopids, retired to the Peloponnése, where he was entertained by Pelops, whose son Chrysippos he instructed in the art of driving a chariot. On the death of Amphíon he succeeded to the throne of Thébes; and he married the daughter of Menœkeus, called by Homer Epikasté, by others Iokasté. The oracle however warned him against having children, declaring that he would meet his death by means of his offspring. He long abstained from his wife: at length, having one time drunk too much wine on a solemn occasion, his love overcame his prudence, and Iokasté gave birth to a son, whom his father delivered to his herdsman to expose on Mount Kithærón. The herdsman, moved to compassion according to one account,[3] gave the babe to a neatherd belonging to Polybos king of Corinth; or, as others say, the neatherds of Polybos found the infant after it had been exposed, and brought it to Peribœa the wife of that prince, who being childless reared it as her own, and named it Œdipus on account of its *swollen feet*;[4] for Laïos, previous to its exposure, had pierced its heels. Many years afterwards Laïos, going on his way to Delphi accompanied only by his herald Polyphontes, met in a narrow road in Phókis a young man also driving in a chariot. On his refusal to leave the way at their command, the herald killed one of his horses; and the stranger, filled with rage, slew both Laïos and his herald, and then pursued his journey. The body of Laïos was found and honourably buried by Dama-

---

[1] Pherekýdés, *ap.* Sch. *Apoll. Rh.* i. 755.
[2] *Kret. Kol.* 82 *seq.*
[3] Soph. *Œd. Tyr.* 1038 *seq.*
[4] From οἰδέω *to swell*, and πούς *a foot*. The true meaning however would seem to be *the Son of Tumour*, i.e. the *Swollen* or *Inflated-one*: see above, p 15.

sistratos king of Platææ; and Kreón the son of Menœkeus occupied the throne of Thébes.[1]

Οἰδιπόδης ἢ Οἰδίπους καὶ Ἰοκάστη.   *Œdipus et Iocasta.*

The foundling Œdipus was brought up by Polybos as his heir. Happening to be reproached by some one at a banquet with being a supposititious child, he besought Peribœa to inform him of the truth; but unable to get any satisfaction from her, he went to Delphi and consulted the oracle.   The god directed him to shun his native country, or he should be the slayer of his father and the sharer of his mother's bed.   He therefore resolved never to return to Corinth, where so much crime as he thought awaited him, and he took his road through Phókis.   He it was who encountered Laïos, and unwittingly accomplished the former part of the oracle.

Immediately after the death of Laïos, Héra, always hostile to the city of Dionýsos, sent to afflict Thébes a monster named the Sphinx,[2] sprung from Typhón and Echidna.   She had the face of a woman; the breast, feet, and tail of a lion; and the wings of a bird.   She had been taught riddles by the Muses, and she sat on the Phikean Hill and propounded one to the Thébans.   It was this: "What is that which has one voice, is four-footed, two-footed, and at last three-footed?"   The oracle told the Thébans that they would not be delivered from her until they had solved her riddle.   They often met to try their skill; and when they failed, the Sphinx carried off and devoured one of their number.   At length, his son Hæmón having become her victim, Kreón offered by public proclamation the throne and the hand of his sister Iokasté to whoever should solve the riddle of the Sphinx.   Œdipus, who was then at Thébes, hearing this, came forward and answered the Sphinx, that it was a Man; who when an infant creeps on all fours, when a man goes on two feet, and when old uses a staff, a third foot.   The Sphinx flung herself down to the earth and perished; and Œdipus now unknowingly accomplished the remainder of the oracle.   He had by

[1] Apollod. iii. 5, 7.   Diodór. iv. 64.   Eudocia, 312.
[2] The Sphinx is not mentioned by Homer; but the legend is noticed in the *Theogony* (*v.* 326), where she is called Φῖξ, and she and the Nemeæan Lion are said to be the offspring of Chimæra by the dog Orthros.   Though this legend is probably older than the time of the first intercourse with Egypt, the Theban monster bears a great resemblance to the symbolical statues placed before the temples of that land of mystery.

In the *pragmatising* days it was said (Paus. ix. 26) that the Sphinx was a female pirate, who used to land at Anthédon and advance to the Phikean Hill, whence she spread her ravages over the country.   Œdipus came from Corinth with a numerous army, and defeated and slew her.

his mother two sons, Eteoklés and Polyneikés, and two daughters, Antigoné and Isméné.

After some years Thébes was afflicted with famine and pestilence; and the oracle being consulted, desired the land to be purified of the blood which defiled it. Inquiry was set on foot after the murderer of Laïos, and a variety of concurring circumstances brought the guilt home to Œdipus. Iokasté, on the discovery being made, ended her days by a cord, and her unhappy son and husband in his grief and despair put out his eyes. He was banished from Thébes; and accompanied by his daughters, who faithfully adhered to him, after a tedious period of miserable wandering he arrived at the grove of the Erinnyes, at Kolónos, a village not far from Athens, and there found the termination of his wretched life.[1]

Such is the form in which the story of Œdipus has been transmitted to us by the Attic dramatists. We will now consider its more ancient forms.

The hero of the Odyssey, when relating what he had seen in Erebos, says,

> The mother of Œdipodés I saw,
> Fair Epikasté, who a direful deed
> In ignorance committed, with her own
> Son marrying, and he espoused her
> Having his father slain ; but soon the gods
> Made the truth known to men. He then lived on
> In pleasant Thébes, o'er the Kadmeians ruling,
> Though woes enduring through the gods' decrees
> Severe ; but she went to the house of Aidés
> The stern gate-keeper, to the lofty roof
> A strong cord tying, when oppressed with woes ;
> Leaving to him afflictions manifold,
> Such as the Erinnyes of a mother send.

In the Ilias[2] the funeral games are mentioned which were celebrated at Thébes in honour of the 'fallen Œdipodés.' Hésiod[3] speaks of the heroes who fell fighting at the seven-gated Thébes on account of the sheep of Œdipodés. It would also seem that, according to the above passage of the Odyssey, and to the epic poem the Œdipodeia,[4] Epikasté had not any offspring by her son,

---

[1] Apollod. iii. 5, 8, 9. Diodór. ut sup. Soph. Œd. Kol.
[2] Il. xxiii. 679. The word δεδουπότος is rather ambiguous, but it is probably merely dead. Il. i. 191: comp. ἐναοίζω to slay.   [3] Ἔργ. 162.
[4] Paus. ix. 5, 11. Pherekýdés (Sch. Phœn. 52) said that the sons of Iokasté were Phrastór and Laonytos, who fell in battle against the Minyans. When

Euryganeia the daughter of Hyperphas being the mother of his well-known children. According to the kyklic Thebaïs,[1] the fatal curse of Œdipus on his sons had the following origin. Polyneikés placed before his father a silver table which had belonged to Kadmos, and filled a golden cup with wine for him; but when he perceived the heir-looms of his family thus set before him, he raised his hands and prayed that his sons might never divide their inheritance peaceably, but ever be at strife. Elsewhere the Thébaïs[2] said that his sons having sent him the loin instead of the shoulder of the victim, he flung it to the ground, and prayed that they might fall by each other's hands. The motives assigned by the tragedians are certainly of a more dignified nature than these, which seem trifling and insignificant. This story affords convincing proof of the great liberties which the Attic tragedians allowed themselves to take with the ancient mythes. It was purely to gratify Athenian vanity that Sophoklés, contrary to the current tradition, made Œdipus die at Kolónos; his blindness seems also to be a tragic fiction. Euripidés makes Iokasté survive her sons, and terminate her life by the sword.[3]

Τειρεσίας. *Tiresias.*

In all the unhappy history of the Labdakids at Thebes this celebrated soothsayer occupies a distinguished place: and his fame was apparently widely extended in the most remote times. Kirké tells the hero of the Odyssey, when anxious to return to Ithaka, that he must previously 'seek the dwelling of Aïdés and awful Persephoneia, to consult the soul of the Théban Teiresias, the blind prophet, whose mental powers are perfect; to whom, though dead, Persephoneia has granted reason, that he alone should have sense while others flit about mere shades.'[4] When Odysseus afterwards goes to the abode of Aïdés, Teiresias approaches him bearing his golden staff; and he alone of the dead recognises the mortal hero before he has tasted the blood; of which, however, he drinks previous to revealing to him the future.[5]

Teiresias is said to have been the son of Euerés and the nymph Chariklό of the race of Udæos, one of the Spartans of Thébes.

---

the year (of mourning for Iokasté?) was ended, he adds, Œdipus married Euryganeia, and on her death Astymedusa the daughter of Sthenelos.
[1] Athén. xi. 465.
[2] *Ap.* Sch. *Soph. Œd. Col.* 1440.   [3] See below, *Théban Wars.*
[4] *Od.* x. 490.   [5] *Od.* xi. 90 *seq.*

Various accounts are given as to the cause of his blindness : one ascribes it to his having seen Athéna bathing;[1] another, to his having divulged to mankind the secrets of the gods.[2] The Melampodia related,[3] that Teiresias, happening to see two serpents copulating on Mount Kithærón, killed the female, and was suddenly changed into a woman. In this state he continued seven years ; at the end of which period, observing two serpents similarly engaged, he killed the male, and thus returned to his pristine state. On some occasion Zeus and Héra fell into a dispute, whether the greater portion of the pleasures of love falls to man or to woman. Unable to settle it to their satisfaction, they agreed to refer the matter to Teiresias, who had known either state. His answer was that of ten parts but one falls to man.[4] Héra incensed deprived the guiltless arbitrator of the power of vision. Zeus, as one god cannot undo the acts of another, gave him in compensation an extent of life for seven generations, and the power of foreseeing coming events.

Teiresias lived at Thébes, where he was contemporary with all the events of the times of Laïos and Œdipus, and the two Théban wars.[5] At the conclusion of the last he recommended the Thébans to abandon their city, and he was the companion of their flight. It was still night when they arrived at the fountain of Tilphussa. Teiresias, whose period of life was fated to be coextensive with that of the city of the Kadmeians, drank of its waters, and immediately died. The victorious Argives sent his daughter Mantó along with a portion of the spoil to Delphi, according to the vow which they had made. In obedience to the command of the oracle, Mantó afterwards went thence, and marrying Rhakios of Mykénæ or of Kréte, founded the town and oracle of Klaros on the coast of Asia. She bore to Rhakios (or, as others said, to Apolló) a son named Mopsos, a celebrated prophet.[6]

---

[1] Pherekýd. *ap. Apollod.* iii. 6, 7.   Kallim. Eἰs Λουτ. Παλ. 75 *seq.*
[2] Apollod. *ut sup.*
[3] Id. *ut sup.* Sch. *Od.* xii. 494.   Tzetz. *Lyc.* 682, 683.   Ov. *Met.* iii. 316 *seq.* Hygin. 75. Apollodóros and Hyginus make Kylléné the scene of Teiresias' adventure.   There are other differences also in the narrative.

[4] In the Bakchæ of Euripidés he appears as the contemporary even of Kadmos. So in the Epos of Persia, Zál, Rústem and other heroes are coeval with a long succession of monarchs.

[5]
Οἵην μὲν μοίραν δέκα μοιρῶν τέρπεται ἀνήρ,
τὰς δέκα δ' ἐμπίπλησι γυνὴ τέρπουσα νόημα.

[6] The Thébaïs *ap.* Sch. *Apoll. Rh.* i. 308.   Pausanias, vii. 3.   Tzetz *Lyc.* 980.   The legend (Verg. *Æn.* x. 199) which makes Mantó the founer of Mantua in Italy evidently owes its origin to similarity of name.

The name Teiresias is apparently derived from τέρας, *prodigy*, and that of his daughter from μάντις.

Μινύαι καὶ Φλεγύαι. *Minyæ et Phlegyæ.*

No names are more completely buried in the depths of mythology than those of the Minyans and Phlegyans. Even to Homer but a slight breath of their fame seems to have come.[1]

Pausanias[2] relates, that the country about Orchomenos in Bœótia was first possessed by Andreus, the son of the river Péneios, who named it from himself Andréis. He was succeeded by his son Eteoklés, who is said to have been the first who sacrificed to the Graces. Eteoklés gave a portion of his territory to Halmos the son of Sisyphos of Corinth, to whose posterity, on Eteoklés' dying childless, the kingdom came: for Halmos had two daughters, Chrysogeneia and Chrysé; the former of whom was by Arés mother of Phlegyas; the latter bore to Poseidón a son named Minyas.[3] Phlegyas obtained the dominion after Eteoklés, and named the country Phlegyantis. He also built a city called Phlegya, into which he collected the bravest warriors of Greece. These separated themselves from the other people of the country, and took to robbing and plundering. They even ventured to assail and burn the temple of Delphi; and Zeus, on account of their impiety, finally destroyed them with lightning and pestilence. A few only escaped to Phókis.

Minyas reigned next, and was wealthier than any of his predecessors. He built the first treasury, similar to that of Atreus at Mykénæ. Pausanias saw the ruins of it, and describes it as being of great size and strength. The son of Minyas was Orchomenos, who gave name to the town; and with him the race of Halmos ended, and the territory fell to the descendants of Athamas and Phrixos. Klymenos, one of these, having been slain in a quarrel with the Thébans at the feast of Poseidón at Onchéstos, his son Ergínos made war on them, and reduced them to an annual tribute, which they paid till relieved from it by

[1] Homer never mentions the Minyans; but he uses the adjective Minyan as an appellative of the wealthy city of Orchomenos in Bœótia to distinguish it from that in Arkadia, and he also (*Il.* xi. 722) applies it to a stream in the Peloponnése. He speaks (*Il.* xiii. 302) of the Phlegyans.

[2] Paus. ix 34 *seq.*

[3] According to Pausanias, the son of Chrysé was Chrysés the father of Minyas; but the authors followed by the scholiast on Apollonios (iii. 1094) give the more probable genealogy of the text.

X

Héraklés.   Ergínos was father of the celebrated architects Agamédés and Trophónios.   Two of this family, Askalaphos and Ialmenos, were at the siege of Troy, and with them ends the mythic history of Orchomenos.

The Argonauts were called Minyans, according to the mythologists, because the greater part of them were descended from Minyas on the female side;[1] and the daughters of Minyas are celebrated in the mythe of Dionýsos, on account of their contempt for his rites, and their consequent punishment.[2]

The subject of the Minyans has been treated at great length by Müller[3] and Buttmann.[4]   The result of their inquiries is as follows.

Minyans was the mythic name of one of the early races of Greece, probably a portion of the Æolian.   They inhabited the northern part of Bœótia and the southern of Thessaly, and practised and acquired considerable wealth by commerce and navigation; this is denoted by the names derived from *gold* which occur in their genealogy, by Poseidón's forming a part of it, and by the tradition of the great wealth of Orchomenos. Their port was Iolkos, and their dock-yard Pagasæ.   The Argonautic expedition was one undertaken by them; and the assemblage of the heroes from all parts of Greece was the addition of later times, which also assigned the wrong origin of the name Minyans given to the heroes, which we have just mentioned. It is a remarkable fact, that Orchomenos was one of the seven cities which had a share in the Amphiktyonic assembly on the Argolic island Kalaureia.   The remaining six were states in the neighbourhood; and nothing but superior wealth and naval power could have induced them to admit the distant Orchomenos into their association.   Everything conspires, they think, to prove, that the whole of the Ægæan coast of Greece, especially that possessed by the Minyans, carried on an active commerce by sea at a period long anterior to history.

The Phlegyans, whose name corresponds with their fate, are by Buttmann regarded as belonging to the universal tradition of an impious people being destroyed by fire from heaven,—the well-known history of the origin of the Dead Sea, which, as the legend of Philémón and Baukis might seem to show, early made its way into Greece.   Müller regards the Phlegyans as being the same with the Lapiths and the military class of the Minyans.

---

[1] Apoll. Rh. i. 229.
[3] *Orchom.* 133 *seq.*

[2] See above, p. 188.
[4] *Mythol.* ii. 194 *seq.*

It was probably their name which gave occasion to the legend of their destruction.[1]

Τροφώνιος καὶ ᾿Αγαμήδης. *Trophonius et Agamedes.*

When Ergínos, king of Orchomenos, had been overcome by Héraklés, his affairs fell into such a reduced state, that in order to retrieve them he abstained from matrimony. As he grew rich and old, he wished to have children; and going to Delphi, he consulted the god, who gave him in oracular phrase the prudent advice to marry a young wife.[2]

Ergínos accordingly following the counsel of the Pythia, married, and had two sons, Trophónios and Agamédés; some, however, said that Apolló was the father of the former. They became distinguished architects, and built the temple of Apolló at Delphi,[3] and a treasury for king Hyrieus. In the wall of this last they placed a stone in such a manner that it could be taken out, and by this means from time to time purloined the treasure This amazed Hyrieus; for his locks and seals were untouched, and yet his wealth continually diminished. At length he set a trap for the thief, and Agamédés was caught. Trophónios, unable to extricate him, and fearing that when found he would be compelled by torture to discover his accomplice, cut off his head.[4] Trophónios himself is said to have been shortly afterwards swallowed up by the earth.[5]

According to Pindar,[6] when they had finished the temple of Delphi they asked a reward of the god. He promised to give it on the seventh day, desiring them meanwhile to live cheerful and happy. On the seventh night they died in their sleep.

There was a celebrated oracle of Trophónios at Lebadeia in

[1] The Phlegyans were probably the *Illustrious*, from φλέγω, to make re-nowned: see Pind. *Pyth.* v. 42 (60). *Nem.* x. 2 (4). *Isth.* vii. 23 (33).
[2] Paus. ix. 37, 3.   [3] Hom. *Hymn to Apoll.* 296.
[4] The same trick is also said to have been played on Augeas, king of E'lis, by Trophónios the *step-son* of Agamédés the Arkadian architect. Charax *ap Sch. Aristoph. Clouds,* 509. It also formed an episode of the Télegonia. The reader will observe the similarity between this legend and that related by Hérodotos (ii. 121) of the Egyptian king Rhampsinitos. Buttmann and Müller think the supposition of the story being taken from Hérodotos, and told of persons and places in Greece, too absurd to deserve refutation. But these ingenious writers should have known that no practice is more common, and that abundant instances of it are to be found in all times and countries : see *Tales and Popular Fictions, passim.* We are, however, disposed to regard this as one of the tales which the Egyptians (who, by the way, seem never to have been an inventive people) borrowed from the Greeks.
[5] Paus. *ut supra.*
[6] *Ap.* Plut. *De Cons. ad Apoll.* Op. vii. p. 335 ed. Hutten. Plutarch at the same time tells the similar story of Kleobis and Bitón from Hérod. i. 31.

Bœótia. During a great drought the Bœotians were, it was said, directed by the god at Delphi to seek aid of Trophónios in Lebadeia. They came thither, but could find no oracle: one of them however happening to see a swarm of bees, they followed them to a chasm in the earth, which proved to be the place sought.[1]

Trophónios was named[2] Zeus-Trophónios, that is, the *Nourishing* or *Sustaining* Zeus (from τρέφω). He is probably therefore a deity from the Pelasgian times, a giver of food from the bosom of the earth, and hence worshipped in a cavern. Agamédés (the *Thoughtful* or *Provident*) is perhaps only another title of the same being; and as corn was preserved in under-ground treasuries or granaries, the brothers may in one sense have been the builders, in another the plunderers of these receptacles.[3]

Ὦτος καὶ Ἐφιάλτης.   Otus et Ephialtes.

O'tos and Ephialtés the sons of Alóeus, says the Ilias,[4] kept Arés confined for thirteen months in a brazen prison (κεράμῳ), and he had perished there if their stepmother Eribœa had not informed Hermés, who stole him out of it. Odysseus sees in Erebos Iphimedeia the wife of Alóeus, who said she had 'mingled' with Poseidón, and she bore two sons O'tos and Ephialtés, the tallest whom earth reared, and the handsomest next to O'ríón. At nine years of age they were nine ells in height and nine cubits in breadth. They menaced the Immortals, and prepared to pile Ossa on Olympos and Pélion on Ossa, in order to scale heaven, but Apolló killed them before the down had grown on their cheeks.[5]

Thus far Homer. Pindar[6] says that they died in Naxos; by their own hands, according to a later tradition.[7] It was also a tradition that they dwelt at Askra (of which they were the founders) at the foot of Helikón, which mountain they consecrated to the Muses.[8] Their tombs were shown at Anthédón.[9]

We know no mythe more difficult than this of the Alóeids. The names of their father and stepmother [10] relate to agriculture, and the confining of the war god and the worship of the Muses

---

[1] Paus. ix. 40. He also relates (*ib.* 39) the mode of consulting the oracle.
[2] Strab. ix. 2, 38, p. 414. Liv. xlv. 27.
[3] See Müller, *Orchom.* 198, 150 *seq.* 242.
[4] *Il.* v. 385 *seq.*
[5] *Od.* xi. 305 *seq.* Nitzsch *in loc*
[6] *Pyth.* iv. 88 (156) *seq.*
[7] Above, p. 116.
[8] Paus. ix. 29, 1.
[9] Id. *ib.* 22, 6.
[10] Ἀλωεὺς, from ἀλωὰ, *threshing-floor.* Ἐρίβοια, from ἔρι and ΒΟ'Ω, βόσκω, *to feed.*

would seem to give them a rural and pacific character; while their descent from Poseidón and Iphimedeia, and the attempt to scale heaven, indicate turbulence and impiety. Here then, as in analogous cases, we are disposed to regard the former as the more ancient form of the mythe. In such case the original conception of them may have been similar to that of the Molionids of E'lis, namely, that, as their names would seem to indicate,[1] they were merely a popular representation of the hand-mill, the brothers being in the one case the sons of the *Thresher*, in the other of the *Grinder*. It was possibly their names that led to the fiction of their piling mountains, and Poseidón was then the appropriate sire of youths of so fierce and turbulent a character.

Τιτυός. Tityus.

Among those personages of ancient times whom the hero of the Odyssey is represented[2] as beholding in Erebos was a huge being named Tityos, a son of Earth, whom he describes as lying stretched on the ground, where he covered nine *plethra*[3] of land, while a vulture seated at each side of him fed on his liver, to which he could offer no resistance. The reason assigned for his punishment is his having attempted to offer violence to Létó, the chaste spouse of Zeus, as she was passing on her way to Pytho through Panópeus in Daulis.

It was afterwards said[4] that Tityos was a son of Zeus by Elara (a person of whom we have no other notice), a daughter of Orchomenos, and that when she was pregnant, fearing the jealousy of Héra, he placed her within the bosom of the earth. According also to one account[5] Tityos was slain by Apolló and Artemis, to another by Apolló,[6] to a third[7] by Artemis alone, and as it might appear in punishment of an attempt on herself.

In another part of the Odyssey[8] we are told that the Phæakians took Rhadamanthys to the isle of Eubœa and back again in the one day, his object in going thither being to *look on* Tityos the son of Earth.

Tityos is to all appearance a being of the same class with Ixíon, Sisyphos and Tantalos, invented with a moral view, to show the divine hatred of vice and crime. His offence, as we may see, was

---

[1] Ὦτος from ᾽ΩΘΩ, ὠθέω, *to push*; ᾽Εφιάλτης, from ἐπί and ἰάλλω, *to put.*
[2] *Od.* xi. 575 *seq.*
[3] The *plethron* was the sixth part of the stade, *i. e.* 100 feet.
[4] Sch. *Od.* vii. 324. Sch. *Apoll. Rh.* i. 761.
[5] Paus. iii. 18, 15.   [6] Sch. *Od. ut supra.*
[7] Pind. *Pyth.* iv. 90 (160). Euphor. *ap. Sch. Apoll. Rh.* i. 181.
[8] *Od.* vii. 323.

nearly the same as that of Ixíon, but its origin would seem to have been mere animal lust, of which appetite he is the personification. Hence vultures prey on his liver (the supposed seat of lust), and his name (like those of Sisyphos and Tantalos) is evidently a reduplication of θύω, indicative of the violence and impetuosity of carnal appetite.

It might seem as if in some form of the legend his place of punishment was the Isle of Eubœa, whither the righteous Rhadamanthys was conveyed from his abode on the E'lysian Plain to gratify his eyes (ἐποψόμενον) by actually beholding the punishment of so great an offender against the sovereign of Olympos.

Ἡρακλῆς. (Hercules.[1])

Elektryón, the son of Perseus king of Mykénæ, had given his daughter Alkméné in marriage to his nephew Amphitryón. Having had the misfortune to kill his father-in-law, Amphitryón was forced to fly from Mykénæ. Alkméné and her brother Likymnios accompanied his flight, and he was kindly received at Thébes by Kreón, who purified him from the guilt of bloodshed.[2]

While Amphitryón was absent on an expedition against the Téleboans, Zeus, who had become enamoured of Alkméné, assumed the form of her husband, and was admitted by her without suspicion to all his privileges. He related to her all the events of the war, and by his power extended the night to three times its usual duration. Amphitryón on his return was surprised at the indifference with which he was received by his wife; but on coming to an explanation with her, and consulting Teiresias, he learned that it was no less a personage than Zeus himself who had assumed his form.[3]

Alkméné brought forth twins, Héraklés the son of Zeus, the elder by one night, and Iphiklés, the progeny of her mortal lord. The children were but eight months old, when Héra sent two huge serpents into the chamber to destroy them. Alkméné in terror called to her husband to save them, but Héraklés raised himself up on his feet, caught the two monsters by the throat and strangled them.[4]

When come to a proper age Héraklés was instructed in the management of a chariot by Amphitryón himself; he was taught wrestling by Autolykos, archery by Eurytos, the use of arms by

[1] In compliance with established usage we place this hero here, though there is little reason for regarding him as an original Théban hero. See Appendix K.   [2] See chap. vii. Amphitryón.
[3] Pherekýd. ap. Sch. Od. xi. 265.   Apollod. ii. 4.   Diodór. iv. 9.
[4] Pind. Nem. i. 33 (49) seq.   Theocr. Idyl. xxiv.

Kastór, to play on the lyre by Linos the brother of Orpheus, whose services were however but ill rewarded by the young hero, as he killed him with a blow of the lyre for having struck him. He was called to account for this deed, but he justified himself by citing a law of Rhadamanthys, which said that 'whoever defends himself against any one who makes an unjust assault on him is guiltless,' and he was acquitted.[1]

Amphitryón however, to prevent the recurrence of such an event, sent him away to where his herds were feeding, and there he grew up to great size and strength. His look was terrible, for he was the son of Zeus; his stature was four cubits; fire flashed from his eyes: his arrow and his dart never missed. In his eighteenth year, while he was still with his father's herds, he slew a huge lion which lay in Mount Kithærón, whence he used to attack the herds of Amphitryón and of Thestios king of the Thespians. Héraklés when going to engage the lion was hospitably entertained by Thestios for fifty days. Each night one of the fifty daughters of his host ascended the couch of the hero, for Thestios was desirous to propagate the race of the son of Zeus. But Héraklés, unaware of this design, fancied that but one of the maidens had enjoyed his embraces.[2] Revolving time, however, beheld fifty of his progeny. He slew the lion, whose hide he ever after wore on his shoulders, and made the skin of his head serve him as a helmet.[3]

As he was returning from this hunt, he met the heralds sent by Ergínos to receive tribute from the Thébans. The cause of the payment of this tribute was as follows: the charioteer of Menœkeus had wounded Klymenos, king of the Minyans, with a stone in Onchéstos the sacred field of Poseidón. That prince, being brought in a dying state to Orchomenos, charged his son Ergínos to avenge his death. Ergínos in consequence led an army against the Thébans, and having slain a number of them concluded peace on condition of their paying him for twenty years an annual tribute of a hundred oxen. It was for this tribute that the heralds were going to Thébes when they were met by Héraklés, who cutting off their ears and noses, and tying their hands to their necks with cords, bade them take

---

[1] The law according to Aristotle (*Eth.* v. 8) and Seneca (*de Mort. Claud.* 14) was Εἴ κε πάθοι τά κ' ἔρεξε δίκη κ' ἰθεῖα γένοιτο. We know not to what poem this verse belonged.

[2] Apollod. *ut sup.* Some said seven, others one might. See Heyne *in loc.*

[3] Homer arms Héraklés with a bow and arrows (*Il.* v. 393. *Od.* viii. 224; xi. 607): Hésiod describes him with shield and spear. Peisander and Stésichoros were the first who gave him the club and lion-skin. Athen. xii. 513.

that tribute to Ergínos and the Minyans. Incensed at this insult offered to his heralds, Ergínos made war anew on Thébes;
but Héraklés, having been furnished with arms by Athéna, and
being appointed by the Thébans their general, slew Ergínos
and routed the Minyans, on whom he imposed a tribute the
double of what the Thébans used to pay. In this battle Amphitryón fell valiantly fighting. Kreón gave his daughter Megara
in marriage to Héraklés,[1] and her younger sister to Iphiklés.
Alkméné, the mother of the hero also married Rhadamanthys
the son of Zeus, who was then living at Okaleia in Bœótia.[2]
Héraklés was presented with a sword by Hermés, a bow by
Apolló, a golden breast-plate by Héphæstos, horses by Poseidón,
a robe by Athéna. He himself cut his club in the Nemeæan
wood.[3]

Some time after this war with the Minyans he fell into madness, owing to the envy of Héra, and flung his own three children by Megara, and two of his brother Iphiklés', into the
fire. As a punishment for this deed he went into voluntary
exile, and was purified by Thestios. He then went to Delphi,
and inquired of the god where he should settle. The Pythia
then first named him Hérakles,[4] for hitherto he had been called
Alkeidés from his grandfather, and she desired him to settle at
Tiryns, and serve Eurystheus twelve years, and perform twelve
tasks to be imposed by him. She added that when these tasks
were all accomplished, he would be made immortal. The hero
obeyed, went to Tiryns, and there served Eurystheus.

The cause of Eurystheus' obtaining this power was as follows:
The day on which Alkméné was to be delivered in Thébes, Zeus,
in exultation, announced to the gods that a man of his race was
that day to see the light, who would rule over all his neighbours. Héra, pretending incredulity, exacted from him an oath
that what he had said should be accomplished. Zeus, unsuspi-
cious of guile, swore, and Héra hastened down to Argos, where

[1] *Od.* xi. 269.

[2] According to Pherekýdés (*ap. Ant. Lib.* 33), when Alkméné, who long
survived her son, died, and the Héracleids were about to bury her at Thébes,
Zeus directed Hermés to steal her away and convey her to the Isles of the
Blest, where she should espouse Rhadamanthys. Hermés obeyed, and placed a
stone instead of her in the coffin. When the Hérakleids went to carry her
forth to be buried, they were surprised at the weight, and opening the coffin
found the stone, which they took out, and set it up in the grove where her
Héróon stood at Thébes.

[3] Apollod. *ut sup.* Diodór. iv. 14.

[4]
  'Ηρακλέην δέ σε Φοῖβος ἐπώνυμον ἐξονομάζει,
  ἥρα γὰρ ἀνθρώποισι φέρων κλέος ἄφθιτον ἕξεις.
           Et. Mag. *v.* 'Ηρακλῆς.

the wife of Sthenelos the son of Perseus was seven months gone of a son. The goddess brought on a premature labour, and Eurystheus came to light that day, while she checked the parturition of Alkméné, and kept back the Eileithyiæ. The oath of Zeus was not to be recalled, and his son was fated to serve Eurystheus.[1]

The *first* task imposed by Eurystheus was to bring him the skin of the Nemeæan lion. This animal was the progeny of Typhón[2] and Echidna, and invulnerable. On his way to engage him Héraklés arrived at Kleónæ, where he was hospitably entertained by a labouring man named Molorchos. His host being desirous to offer a sacrifice, Héraklés begged of him to reserve it till the thirtieth day, saying that if he should then return victorious he might offer it to Zeus the Saviour; but if he fell in the conflict, to make it a funeral offering to himself as a hero. When he came to the Nemeæan wood and had discovered the lion, he began to ply him with his arrows, but finding soon that he was invulnerable, he grasped his club and pursued him to his den, which was pervious. He then built up one of the entrances, and going in at the other, and grasping the lion's throat in his hands, held him till he was suffocated.[3] Then taking him on his shoulders, he proceeded towards Mykénæ, and coming on the last day of the appointed period to Molorchos' abode, he found him just on the point of offering the victim for him as being dead. Having offered the sacrifice to Zeus the Saviour, he brought the lion to Mykénæ. But when Eurystheus saw this proof of the wonderful strength of Héraklés, he prohibited his entrance in future into the city, and ordered him to announce the performance of his tasks before the gates. Some even say that the terror of Eurystheus was so great, that he had a brazen jar made, in which he used to hide himself underground, and employ the herald Kopreus, the son of Pelops, to set him his tasks.[4] This Kopreus, having slain Iphitos, had fled to Mykénæ, and abode there with Eurystheus who had purified him.

The *second* task was to destroy the Lernæan hydra or watersnake, another progeny of Typhón and Echidna,[5] which abode in the marsh of Lerna, whence she used to come out on the land, and kill the cattle and ravage the country. This hydra had a huge body with nine heads, eight of them mortal, and one in the middle immortal. Héraklés mounted his chariot, which was driven by Ioláos, the son of his brother Iphiklés; and on coming to Lerna, he stopped the horses and went in

---

[1] Hom. *Il.* xix. 98 *seq.*   [2] Hésiod (*Theog.* 327) says of Orthros.
[3] See the description of the combat in Theocr. *Idyll.* xxv.
[4] *Il.* xv. 639.   [5] Hés. *Theog.* 313.

quest of the hydra, which he found on a rising ground near the springs of Amymóné, where her hole was. He shot at her with fiery darts till he made her come out; and he then grasped and held her while she twined herself about his legs. The hero crushed her heads with his club, but to no purpose, for when one was crushed two sprang up in its stead. A huge crab also aided the hydra, and bit the feet of Héraklés. He killed the crab, and then he called upon Ioláos to come to his assistance. Ioláos immediately set fire to the neighbouring wood, and with the flaming brands searing the necks of the hydra as the heads were cut off, effectually checked their growth.[1] Having thus got rid of the mortal heads, Héraklés cut off the immortal one and buried it; setting a heavy stone on the top of it, in the road leading from Lerna to Eleos. He cut the body of the hydra up into pieces, and dipped his arrows in her gall. Eurystheus however denied that this was to be reckoned among the twelve tasks, since he had not destroyed the hydra alone, but with the assistance of Ioláos.

The *third* task was to fetch the horned hind alive to Mykénæ. This hind haunted Œnoé, had golden horns, and was sacred to Artemis. Héraklés, not wishing to kill or wound her, pursued her for an entire year.[2] When the animal was tired with the chase, she took refuge in Mount Artemision, then fled to the river Ladón, and, as she was about to cross that stream, Héraklés struck her with an arrow, caught her, put her on his shoulder, and was going with his burden through Arkadia, when he met Artemis and her brother Apolló. The goddess took the hind from him, and reproached him for violating her sacred animal. But the hero excusing himself on the plea of necessity, and laying the blame on Eurystheus, Artemis was mollified, and allowed him to take the hind alive to Mykénæ.

The *fourth* task imposed by Eurystheus was to bring him the Erymanthian boar also alive. This animal frequented Mount Erymanthos, and thence laid waste the region of Psóphis. Héraklés took his road over Mount Pholoé, where he was hospitably entertained by Pholos the Kentaur, the son of Silénos and the nymph Melia.[3] The Kentaur set before his guest roast meat, though he himself fared on it raw. Héraklés asking for wine, his host said he feared to open the jar, which was the

---

[1] The hydra was a sophist, says Sókratés, with his usual irony (Plat. *Euthyd.* 297).

[2] Pindar (*Ol.* iii. 31 (55)) makes the hind lead the hero a chase to the country of the Hyperboreans.

[3] Pholoé and Pholos may come from φύω, denoting the grassy and woody mountain. The names of the parents of Pholos would accord with this signification.

common property of the Kentaurs; but when pressed by the hero he consented to unclose it for him. The fragrance of the wine spread over the mountain,[1] and soon brought all the Kentaurs armed with stones and pine-staves to the cave of Pholos. The first who ventured to enter were driven back by Héraklés with burning brands: he hunted the remainder with his arrows to Malea. They fled there to Cheirón, who having been expelled from Pélion by the Lapiths was dwelling at that place. As Héraklés was here shooting at the Kentaurs, one of his arrows went through the arm of Elatos and stuck in the knee of Cheirón. Grieved at this unhappy event, Héraklés ran up, drew out the arrow, and applied to the wound a remedy given by Cheirón himself; but in vain, the venom of the hydra was not to be overcome. Cheirón retired into his cave, longing to die, but unable on account of his immortality, till, on his expressing his willingness to die for Prométheus, he was released by death from his misery. The other Kentaurs fled to different places; some remained at Malea; Eurytión went to Pholoé, Nessos to the river Euénos; Poseidón took the rest and sheltered them in Mount Eleusin. When Héraklés returned to Pholoé, he found Pholos lying dead along with several others; for, having drawn the arrow out of the body of one of them, while he was wondering how so small a thing could destroy such large beings, it dropped out of his hand and stuck in his foot, and he died immediately.[2] Héraklés buried him, and then set out to hunt the boar, and driving him from his lair with loud cries, chased him into a snow-drift, where he caught and bound him, and then took him to Mykénæ.

To clear out in one day all the dung in the stable of Augeas (*Bright*) king of Ełis, the son of Poseidón (or rather of the Sun) was the *fifth* task imposed by the relentless Eurystheus.[3] When Héraklés came to Augeas, he said nothing to him of the commands of Eurystheus, but offered for a tenth of his herds to clean out his stables in one day. Augeas agreed, not thinking the thing possible; and Héraklés took Phyleus, that prince's own son, to witness the agreement. He then broke down a part of the wall of the court, and turning in the rivers Péncios

---

[1] Theocr. vii. 149.

[2] The proper scene of the adventure with the Kentaurs must have been Thessaly, as in Euripidés, *Her. Fur.* 359 *seq.*

[3] Theocr. *Idyll.* xxv. From his name and his flocks and herds it is evident that the Sun was the original sire of Augeas; his violent character then caused him to be regarded as the son of Poseidón: see above. 76, 309. His name, by a different derivation (see above, p. 9) may have caused the abundance of his possessions.

and Alpheios by a canal, let them run out at the other side. Augeas, on learning that this was one of the tasks imposed by Eurystheus, not only refused to stand to his agreement, but denied that he had promised anything, and offered to lay the matter before the judges. When the cause was tried, Phyleus honestly gave testimony against his father; and Augeas, in a rage, even before the votes had been given, ordered both his son and Héraklés to depart out of E'lis. The former retired to Dulichion; the latter went to Dexamenos at O'lenos, whom he found on the point of being compelled to give his daughter in marriage to the Kentaur Eurytión. Dexamenos imploring his aid, he killed the Kentaur as he was coming for his bride. Eurystheus however refused to count this also among the twelve tasks, saying that he had done it for hire.

The *sixth* task was to drive away the Stymphalid birds. These were water-fowl, which, afraid of the wolves, fled to lake Stymphális, which lay embosomed in wood near the Arkadian town Stymphálos. While Héraklés was deliberating how he should scare them, Athéna brought him from Héphæstos brazen clappers. He stood under a neighbouring hill, and rattled them : the birds terrified rose in the air, and he then shot them with his arrows.[1]

His *seventh* task was to fetch the Krétan bull.[2] This animal had been sent up by Poseidón when Minós had vowed to sacrifice whatever should appear from the sea. Struck with the beauty and size of the animal, Minós substituted another, and put him among his herds. Poseidón in anger made the bull run wild and furious. When Héraklés arrived, Minós gave him permission to take him if he could. The hero succeeded, and brought and showed him to Eurystheus. He then let him go : and the bull roved over Sparta and Arkadia, and crossing the Isthmos came to Marathón in Attica, where he did great mischief to the inhabitants.

For his *eighth* task he was enjoined to bring to Mykénæ the mares of Diomédés of Thrace. This was a son of Arés and Kyréné, and king of the Bistonians. His mares were androphagous. Héraklés sailed thither with some volunteers, and having overcome the grooms, led the mares to the sea. The Bistonians pursued with arms. Héraklés leaving the mares in charge of Abdéros, his favourite, the son of Hermés, a Lokrian of Opus, went to engage them. Meantime the mares tore their keeper to pieces; and the hero having defeated the Bistonians

---

[1] Pherekýdés, *ap. Sch. Apoll. Rh.* ii. 1054.

[2] The scene of the first six adventures was, we may observe, the Peloponnése.

and slain Diomédés, built a city by the tomb of Abdéros, and named it after him. He brought the mares to Eurystheus, who turned them loose; and they strayed on to Mount Olympos, where they were destroyed by the wild beasts.

The *ninth* task was to bring to his master the girdle of Hippolyté, queen of the Amazons,[1] who dwelt about the river Thermódón. This nation was composed of women who were renowned for their valour. When they bore children, they reared the females alone. They cut off their right breasts, that they might not impede them in drawing the bow. Hippolyté was mistress of the belt of Arés, as a token of her exceeding all the Amazons in valour. This girdle Eurystheus coveted for his daughter Admété, and he ordered Héraklés to bring it to him.

Having drawn together some volunteers, among whom were Theseus and Kastór and Polydeukés, the hero sailed to the isle of Paros, where four sons of Minós dwelt. Two of the ship's company happening to be slain by them, Héraklés killed several of the Parians, and besieged the rest, till they offered to give him any two he wished in the place of the companions he had lost. He chose Alkæos and Sthenelos, the sons of Androgeós, and then sailed on to Mysia, where he was hospitably entertained by Lykos, king of the Mariandynians, whom he aided against the Bebrykians, and slew their king Mygdón, the brother of Amykos. He took a large portion of their territory and gave it to Lykos, who named it Hérakleia. The hero reached at length the haven of Themiskýra, where Hippolyté came to inquire the cause of his arrival, and on hearing it she promised to give him her girdle. But Héra, taking the form of an Amazon, went and persuaded the rest that the strangers were carrying off their queen. They instantly armed, mounted their horses, and came down to the ship. Héraklés, thinking that Hippolyté had acted treacherously, slew her, and taking her girdle made sail homewards.

He stopped at Troy, then in great distress from the wrath of Poseidón and Apolló. These gods had contracted with Laomedón, king of Troy, to build a wall round the town; but when the wall was completed, Laomedón refused to pay the wages agreed on, and dismissed them, threatening to cut off their ears. He even menaced to tie Apolló hand and foot and transport him to the distant islands.[1] To punish him Apolló sent a

---

· See Appendix L.

[2] *Il.* xxi. 441; see above, p. 109. The poet (*Il.* xx. 145) mentions the combat of Héraklés with the sea-monster. He also tells (v. 640) of the taking of Troy by Héraklés, on account of the horses, relating to which Laomedón had broken his word.

pestilence, and Poseidón a flood bearing a huge sea-monster who carried off all the people to be found in the plain. The oracle being consulted declared that there would be no end of the evil till Laomedón had given his daughter Hésioné[1] for food to the monster. He therefore exposed her, fastened to a rock which overhung the sea. Héraklés, having seen the maiden, offered to deliver her if Laomedón would give him the mares which Zeus had presented to Trós, in exchange for his son Ganymédés. Laomedón assented, and Héraklés slew the monster and delivered Hésioné[2]: but the faithless Trojan refused to keep his word, and the hero sailed away, threatening to return and make war on Troy.

His *tenth* task was to bring the oxen of Géryoneus from the island of Erytheia (*Ruddy-isle*), which lay out in the Ocean,[3] and was inhabited by Géryoneus the son of Chrysáór,[4] and Kallirrhoé, an O'keanis.[5] He had the bodies of three men united: they cohered above, but below the loins they were divided into three. His oxen were of a purple (*i. e.* brilliant) hue, and were guarded by his herdsman, named Eurytión, and the two-headed dog Orthros, the progeny of Echidna and Typhón.

Héraklés took his road through Libya, and when he came to

---

[1] Hésioné is the same as E'ioné (name of a Néréis, Hés. *Theog.* 255) and comes from ἠϊὼν *strand*.

[2] Tzetzés (*Lyc.* 33) says, that when the monster opened his mouth the hero jumped into it, and that he remained for *three* days cutting and hacking within him. He then emerged, but with the loss of all his hair. This may have been derived from the history of the prophet Jonah.

[3] Apollodóros, following Pherekýdés, says "which is now called Gadeira," but that island has surely no river or mountain in it. Hésiod (*Theog.* 290 *seq.*) clearly places Erytheia *out in* (περήν) the Ocean, that is toward its further coast. It was probably the temple of the Phœnician Melkart (who was identified with Héraklés) at Gades, which gave occasion to this localisation of Erytheia, and also to the legend of the Pillars.

[4] See chap. vii. *Akrisios*, etc., *ad fin.*

[5] Though we could not perhaps satisfactorily prove it, we have a strong notion that Géryoneus (Géryonés or Geryón) is only another form of Hadés. They both, we may observe, had herds of oxen, and the two-headed dog of the former answers to the three-headed dog of the latter. Admétos, apparently another form of Hadés, was also famous for his herds. We find the herds of Hadés pasturing under the care of Menœtios, near those of Géryoneus in the isle of Erytheia, and we meet them again in the under-world under the care of the same herdsman. This looks very like two different forms of the same legend; the hero in the one seeking the abode of Hadés in the west, in the other in the under-world. The name Géryoneus (from γηρύω) might correspond in signification with κλυτὸς and κλύμενος, epithets of Hadés. On the other hand, Géryoneus might be a son, *i. e.* a form of the Sun-god who was the father of children by various Ocean-nymphs, and who kept flocks and herds. Chrysáór was an epithet of Apolló, *i. e* the Sun.

the verge of Europe and Libya he erected two pillars, one on each side of the strait, as monuments of his journey.[1] Being scorched with the burning rays of the sun, he had the hardihood to bend his bow against the Sun-god; who, admiring his courage, gave him his golden cup to carry him over to Erytheia. As he was crossing, O'keanos appeared to him, and by agitating his waters, and tossing the cup in which he was sailing, endeavoured to frighten him; but on the hero's bending his bow at him he ceased, and called him to hold his hand.[2] Having reached the island, he passed the night on Mount Abas. The dog Orthros discovering him flew at him, but Héraklés struck him with his club, and killed Eurytión who came up to his aid. Menœtios, who kept in the same place the oxen of Hadés, having informed Géryoneus of what had befallen, he pursued and overtook Héraklés, as he was driving the cattle along the river Anthemus. He there attacked him, but was slain by his arrows; and Héraklés, placing the oxen in the cup, brought them over to the continent, where he returned his vessel to the Sun-god. He drove his cattle through Ibéria, and came to Lygia, where Alébión and Derkinos, the sons of Poseidón, attempted to carry them off.[3] These he slew, and then went on through Tyrrhénia. At Rhégion one of his bulls broke away,[4] ran through the country, swam over to Sicily, and came to the lands of Eryx the son of Poseidón, who ruled over the Elymians. Eryx put the bull among his herds; and Héraklés, committing the care of his other cattle to Héphæstos, went in quest of the stray one. When he found him, he required Eryx to give him up; but he refused, unless he would wrestle with him. Hérakles accepted the challenge, and flinging him three times to the ground killed him. He then drove his cattle along the Iónian Sea. At the recess of the sea ' (i. e. the head of the gulf) Héra set the oxen mad, and they ran raging through the hills of Thrace. Héraklés pursued them; and having overtaken a part of them at the Hellespont, he drove them toward the Peloponnése, leaving the

[1] Pind. *Nem.* iii. 21 (35) *seq.* Völcker, *Myth. der Jap.* 61.
[2] Pherekýdés *ap. Athen.* xi. 470. Peisander said it was O'keanos, Panyasis said Néreus, that gave him the cup (Athen. *ut sup.*). See above, p. 46.
[3] According to Æschylos (*Prom. Loosed, Fr.* 128), Héraklés being hard pressed by the Lygians in the combat, and having spent his arrows, Zeus aided him with a shower of stones, with which he pelted and overcame his enemies. This was when he was on his way to the Hesperides (Strab. iv. 1, 7, p. 183). Hyginus (*l oet. Astr.* ii. 6), also quoting Æschylos, says it was on his return from Erytheia.
[4] Ἀπορρήγνυσι. This country, said Hellaníkos (Dion. Hal. i. 35), was henceforth named Italia, Italos (*Vitulus*) being an ox in the language of the country.

others to run wild. When he came to the Strymón, in anger with that river he filled its bed with stones, so that it became no longer navigable.[1] He finally brought the oxen to Eurystheus, who sacrificed them to Héra.

The preceding tasks had been performed in the space of eight years and a month; but Eurystheus refused to allow for those of killing the hydra and cleansing the stables of Augeas. He now imposed the *eleventh* task,—that of bringing him the apples of the Hesperides.[2]

On his way in quest of the apples Héraklés came to the river Echedóros, where he was challenged to a single combat by Kyknos the son of Arés and Pyréné. Arés defended his son; and Zeus ended the conflict by casting a thunderbolt between the combatants. Héraklés passed on through Illyria, thence to the E'ridanos, and came to the nymphs, the daughters of Zeus and Themis. These directed him to Néreus, whom he found asleep; and, in spite of his numerous changes of form, bound and held him fast, and never let him go till he had told him where the golden apples were. Having gotten this information, he went on to Tartéssos, and crossing over to Libya went on till he came to Irassa by lake Tritónis,[3] where Antæos the son of Poseidón reigned, who was wont to kill all strangers by forcing them to wrestle with him, and to hang their skulls on the temple of his sire. Héraklés engaged him; and, finding that every time he threw him to the ground he rose with renewed strength, he held him in his arms till he died. Antæos, on account of this property, was said to be the son of Earth.[4]

From Libya he went to Egypt, where Busíris, another son of Poseidón, reigned. This king, in consequence of an oracle, used to offer up strangers on the altar of Zeus: for Egypt having been afflicted with a dearth for nine years, a Kyprian named Phrasios (*Sayer*), a great soothsayer, came thither, and said that it would cease if they sacrificed a stranger every year to Zeus. Busíris sacrificed the prophet himself first, and then continued the practice. Héraklés on his arrival was seized and dragged to the altar; but he burst his bonds, and slew Busíris, his son Amphidamas, and his herald Chalbés.[5]

---

[1] This is a mythic origin of the shallows in the Strymón.
[2] See above, p. 221.
[3] Sch. *Pind. Pyth.* ix. 105 (183): comp. Milton, *Par. Reg.* iv. 564.
[4] 'Ανταῖος (*Opponent*, from ἀντί). This legend was perhaps invented after the Greeks had settled in Libya, and was designed to express the incessant opposition which they experienced from the original inhabitants. Müller, *Dor.* i. 458.
[5] The conjecture of Müller (*ut sup.*), that Busíris is Osíris with the Egyptian

He then roamed through Arabia, where he killed Æmathión the son of E'ós and Tithónos, and then through the mountains of Libya, whicn he cleared of the wild beasts with his arrows; and having come to the eastern course of Ocean, he was once more accommodated with the Sun-god's radiant cup, in which ne crossed to the opposite side.[1] He came to where Prométheus lay chained, and, moved by his entreaties, shot the eagle that preyed on his liver. Prométheus out of gratitude warned him not to go himself to take the golden apples, but to send Atlas for them, and in the mean time to support the heavens in his stead. The hero did as desired, and Atlas at his request went and obtained three apples from the Hesperides; but he said he would take them himself to Eurystheus, and that Héraklés might continue to support the heavens. At the suggestion of Prométheus the hero feigned consent, but begged him to hold them ill he had made a pad to put on his head. Atlas threw down the apples, and resumed his burden; and Héraklés then picked them up, and went away.[2] He brought the apples to Eurystheus, who returned them to him; and he then gave them to Athéna. The goddess carried them back to the garden of the Hesperides vhence they had been taken.[3]

The *twelfth* and last task imposed by Eurystheus was to bring Kerberos from the under-world. When preparing for this expedition, Héraklés went to Eumolpos at Eleusis, desirous to e initiated; but he could not be admitted, as he had not been urified of the blood of the Kentaurs. Eumolpos however purified him, and he then saw the mysteries, after which he proceeded to Tænaron in Lakonia, where the entrance to the under-world was, and went down it, accompanied by Hermés and Athéna.[4]

The moment the shades saw him they fled away in terror,— all but Meleagros and Medusa the Gorgón.[5] He was drawing is sword on the latter, when Hermés reminded him that she as a mere phantom. Near the gates of the palace of Hadés e found Théseus and Peirithoos, who had attempted to carry

ticle *pe* prefixed, is highly probable. The legend was framed, he thinks, hen the Greeks first began to have intercourse with Egypt, and expresses eir idea of the former inhospitable character of the people of that country.

[1] Pherekýdés *ap. Sch. Ap. Rh.* iv. 1396. Heyne and Müller, for Πέργη read *pala.* It would almost seem as if the rock of Prométheus was on the opposite coast of Ocean. It is however more consistent with analogy to conceive on the eastern extremity of the earth.

[2] Pherekýdés *ut sup.* Others said that Héraklés killed the guardian-dragon and took the apples himself. Eurip. *Her. Fur.* 395 *seq.* Apollod. *ut sup.*

[3] Apollod. *ut sup.*

[4] *Il.* viii. 367. Perseus was similarly aided by these deities.

[5] This is founded on *Od.* xi. 634.

Y

off Persephoné, and had in consequence been fixed on an enchanted rock by the offended monarch of Erebos. When they
saw Héraklés they stretched forth their hands, hoping to be
relieved by his might. He took Théseus by the hand, and
raised him up;[1] but when he would do the same for Peirithoos,
the earth quaked, and he left him. He then rolled from off
Askalaphos, the son of Acherón and Gorgyra, the rock which
Démétér had cast on his body. Wishing to give the shades
blood to drink, he took one of the oxen of Hadés, and killed it.
Menœtios, the son of Keuthonymos the herdsman, immediately
challenged him to wrestle. Héraklés laid hold on him, broke
his ribs, and but for the prayers of Persephoné would have killed
him on the spot. He then asked Plutó to give him Kerberos;
and the god consented, provided he could take him without using
his weapons. He found him at the gate of Acherón; and protected only by his corslet and lion's skin, he flung his arms about
his head, and grasping him by the neck made him submit, though
the dragon in his tail bit him severely. He brought him through
Trœzén to Eurystheus; and when he had shown him, took him
back to the under-world.

The hero, having now performed all his tasks, returned to
Thébes, where he gave Megara in marriage to his nephew Ioláos.
Wishing himself to marry again, and hearing that Eurytos
king of Œchalia,[2] had declared that he would give his daughter
Iolé to him who should overcome himself and his sons in shooting
with the bow, he went thither, and won the victory, but did
not obtain the promised prize. Iphitos, the eldest son, was for
giving his sister to Héraklés, but Eurytos and his other sons
refused, lest he should destroy her children, if she had any, as he
had done those of Megara. Shortly afterwards the oxen of Eurytos
being stolen by the noted thief Autolykos, his suspicions fell
upon Héraklés. Iphitos, who gave no credit to this charge
betook himself to that hero, and besought him to join in search
of the lost oxen. Héraklés promised to do so, and entertained

---

[1] For an effect of this on the bodily conformation of the Athenians, see Sch
Aristoph. Knights, 1365.

[2] There were three places named Œchalia in Greece; on the banks of th
Péneios in Thessaly, in Eubœa, in Messéné. Each of these claimed Eurytos
Homer (*Od.* viii. 226; xxi. 14 *seq.*) seems to be in favour of the last: he say
that Eurytos having challenged Apolló at archery was killed by the god; an
his son Iphitos, coming to Héraklés in quest of his mares and foals, was slai
by hir in violation of the rights of hospitality. In both cases the scen
is apparently in the Peloponnése. In the Catalogue (*Il.* ii. 730) the Thessalia
Œchalia is the city of Eurytos; while the Taking of Œchalia and the Ægimio
as it would seem, are in favour of that in Eubœa. They are followed b
Sophoklés, Apollodóros, and the current of writers.

him; but falling again into madness, he precipitated Iphitos from the walls of Tiryns. In order to be purified of this murder he went to Néleus, who being a friend of Eurytos refused to comply with his desire. Héraklés then went to Amyklæ, where he was purified by Déiphobos the son of Hippolytos. But he fell notwithstanding into a severe malady on account of the murder of Iphitos; and going to Delphi to seek relief, he was refused a response by the Pythia. In his rage at her denial he went to plunder the temple, and taking the tripod was about establishing an oracle for himself. Apolló came to oppose him; but Zeus hurled a thunderbolt between the combatants, and put an end to their contest. Héraklés now received a response, that his malady would be removed if he let himself be sold for three years as a slave, and gave the purchase-money to Eurytos as a compensation for the loss of his son.[1]

Accordingly, in obedience to the oracle, he was conducted by Hermés to Lydia, and there sold to Omphalé the queen of the country.[2] The purchase-money (three talents, it is said) was offered to Eurytos, but he refused to accept it.

When the term of his servitude was expired, he prepared, being now relieved of his disease, to take his long-threatened vengeance on Laomedón. He accordingly collected a fleet of eighteen[3] fifty-oared vessels, manned by a valiant band of volunteer warriors, and sailed for Ilion. Leaving the fleet under the charge of Œklés, he led his men against the town; but while he was advancing toward it, Laomedón fell on the ships, and Œklés was slain in the attack; Laomedón was however driven back and besieged in the town. Telamón son of Æakos succeeded in making a breach in the walls, and entered; but Héraklés followed close on him with his drawn sword, for he would have no one thought his superior. When Telamón saw this he began to collect the stones which were lying near him; and on his asking him what he was doing, said that he was raising an altar to Héraklés Kalliníkos (*Victor*). Héraklés slew with his arrows Laomedón and all his sons but Podarkés. He gave Hésioné to Telamón as a reward of his valour, and allowed her to choose one among the captives to be set at liberty. When she had fixed on her brother Podarkés, Héraklés replied that he must first be made a slave, and that then she might give something for him and redeem him. She took her golden veil off her

---

[1] Pherekýdes *ap. Sch. Od.* xxi. 23. Æsch. *Agam.* 1048. Soph. *Trach.* 252 *seq.*

[2] The Lydians had a hero named Sandón similar to Héraklés, Lyd. *de Magist.* ii. 64. Omphalé, we are told, clad him in a robe dyed with *sandyx:* see Müller, *Proleg.* 188.

[3] Homer (*Il.* v. 641) says *six* ships.

Y 2

head, and with it bought him; and hence he was afterwards
named Priamos (*Purchased*) instead of Podarkés (*Swift-foot*).

As Héraklés was sailing homewards from Troy, he was assailed
by a furious storm, sent by Héra,[1] which drove him to the isle
of Kós. The inhabitants taking the strangers for pirates assailed them with stones, and endeavoured to prevent their landing; but they were defeated, and their king Eurypylos, the son
of Poseidón and Astypalæa, was slain. Héraklés himself was
wounded in the fight by Chalkodón. Having ravaged Kós, he
went at the call of Athéna to Phlegra, where he fought with the
Gods against the Giants.

Not long afterwards he collected an army of Arkadians and
volunteers from most of the towns of Greece, and marched
against Augeas; who put his E'leians under the command of
his nephews Eurytos and Kteátos, the sons of Molioné and
Aktór, who excelled all men of that time in strength.[2] Héraklés happening to fall sick, made a truce with the Molionids;
but when they heard of his illness, they attacked his army, and
killed several of his men. He retired at that time; but in the
third Isthmiad afterwards, when the E'leians sent the Molionids
to Kleónæ to offer sacrifice, he waylaid and killed them. He
then led an army into E'lis, took the city, slew Augeas and his
sons, and set Phyleus on the throne. He also established the
Olympic games, raised an altar to Pelops, and built altars to the
twelve gods in order.

After the capture of E'lis he marched against Pylos, took the
city, and killed Néleus and all his sons, except Nestór, who was
living with the Gerénians.[3] He is also said to have wounded
Hadés and Héra as they were aiding the Pylians.[4] He then
marched to Lakedæmón, to punish the sons of Hippokoón for
having slain Œonos the son of Likymnios. For as this youth
was gazing on the palace of Hippokoón, the house-dog flew at
him: he flung a stone at the dog; which so enraged the son
of Hippokoón, that they rushed out with sticks and beat him to
death.[5] Héraklés therefore, to avenge his death, collected an
army. At Tegea in Arkadia he asked Képheus, who had twenty
sons, to join in the expedition; but Képheus, afraid lest during
his absence the Argives might make an attempt on Tegea,

---

[1] *Il.* xv. 26 *seq.*
[2] Pind. *Ol.* xi. 26 (31) *seq.*: see chap. x. *Eurytos* and *Kteatos.*
[3] *Il.* xi. 690 *seq.*: see chap. x. *Néleus.*
[4] The line, *Il.* v. 397,

  Ἐν Πύλῳ ἐν νεκύεσσι βαλὼν ὀδύνῃσιν ἔδωκε,

alludes perhaps to this event: see Pind. *Ol.* ix. 30 (45) *seq.*; above, p. 80.
[5] Paus. iii. 15, 4.

declined the proposal. Héraklés then, who had in a water-urn a brazen ringlet of the Gorgón, which Athéna had given him, presented it to Aëropé the daughter of Képheus, and told her, that if when a hostile army should approach she would show it three times from the walls without looking at it herself, they would take to flight. Képheus and his sons then joined Héraklés; but they all fell in battle, and with them Iphiklés the brother of the hero. Hippokoón himself was slain in the engagement, his sons were taken prisoners, and his kingdom was given to Tyndareós.

Returning through Tegea, Héraklés violated, without knowing her, Augé the daughter of Aleos. She secretly brought forth a son, whom she laid in the sacred inclosure ($\tau\epsilon\mu\epsilon\nu\sigma$) of Athéna. A famine coming on the land, Aleos went into the *temenos* of the goddess; and searching about, found his daughter's infant, which he exposed on Mount Parthenion. But the babe was protected by the care of the gods; for a hind, which had just calved, came and suckled him; and the shepherds finding him named him Télephos from that circumstance.[1] Aleos gave his daughter Augé to Nauplios the son of Poseidón, to sell her out of the country; and he disposed of her to Teuthras king of Teuthrania on the Kaÿster in Mysia, who made her his wife.[2] Télephos having, when grown up, consulted the oracle respecting his parents, came to Mysia, where he was kindly received by Teuthras, whom he succeeded in his kingdom.

Héraklés went afterwards to Kalydón, where he sought the hand of Déianeira the daughter of Œneus.[3] He had to contend for her with the river-god Achelóos, who turned himself into a bull; in which form one of his horns was broken off by the victorious hero. The vanquished river-god gave him in exchange for it the horn of Amaltheia.[4] Héraklés afterwards assisted the

---

[1] Τήλεφος, from ἔλαφος *a hind.* Its true signification is *Far-shining* (τηλέφαος); Augé (Αὐγή) is *Bright.* The legend is connected with the worship of Athéna Alea (above, p. 141): see Paus. viii. 47. Welcker, *Kret. Kol.* 12.

[2] Euripidés (*ap. Strab.* xiii. 1, 69, p. 915) says that Aleos put his daughter and her babe in a coffer and cast them into the sea, and that Athéna guided it to the mouth of the Kaïkos, where it was found by Teuthras, who married Augé and adopted her child.

[3] When he met Meleagros in Erebos the latter besought him to marry his sister, Sch. *Il.* xxi. 194.

[4] Amaltheia (above, p. 70) was the goat that suckled the infant Zeus; the same is probably derived from ἀμαλός, *tender,* or from ἀμέλγω, *to milk.* It was a pleasing fiction to make her horn pour forth ambrosia and nectar. According to later writers Amaltheia was a nymph, the possessor of the horn, the daughter of O'keanos (Sch. *Il.* xxi. 194), or Hæmonios (Pher *ap. Apollod.* 7, 5), or O'lenos. Theón. *ad Arat.* 64

Kalydónians against the Thesprótians, and took the city of
Ephyra, over which Phylas reigned, by whose daughter Astoyché
he became the father of Tlépolemos.

One day at the table of Œneus, as Eunomos the son of Archi-
telés was, according to custom, pouring water on the hands of
the guests, Héraklés happening unawares to swing his hand
suddenly struck the boy and killed him.[1] As it was evidently
an accident, the father forgave the death of his son; but Héraklés resolved to banish himself, agreeably to the law in such
cases, and he set out with his wife for Trachis, the realm of his
friend Kéyx. On their way they came to the river Euénos,
where Nessos[2] the Kentaur had taken his abode, and carried
over travellers, saying he had received this office from the gods
as a reward for his uprightness. Héraklés went across through
the water himself, having agreed on the price for the convey-
ance of Déianeira. Nessos attempted to offer violence to his
fair freight. She resisted, and cried out loudly; and Héraklés,
hearing her screams, shot Nessos through the heart as he came
on shore. The dying Kentaur thought on revenge: he called
Déianeira to him, and told her if she would possess a philtre, or
means of securing the love of Héraklés, to keep carefully the
blood which flowed from his wound—an advice with which she
incautiously complied.

As they were going through the country of the Dryopians
Héraklés became extremely hungry, and meeting a man named
Theiodamas driving a wain with two oxen, he unyoked one of
them, and killed, dressed, and ate it. He took with him Hylas
the son of Theiodamas, who became his especial favourite. While
residing with Kéyx he aided Ægimios, king of the Dórians,
against whom the Lapiths under the command of Korónos had
made war, on account of a dispute respecting their boundaries,
and had besieged him in his town. Héraklés slew Korónos,
and put Ægimios in possession of the whole country that had
been in dispute. He afterwards killed Laogoras king of the
Dryopians and his children, as he was feasting in the sacred
ground of Apolló, on account of his violence and his aiding the
Lapiths.

As he was passing by the temple of Apolló at Pagasæ he was
opposed by Kyknos the son of Arés, who was in the habit of
plundering those who brought the sacrifices to Pythó. Kyknos
fell in the combat; and when Arés, who had witnessed the fate

---

[1] See *Fairy Mythology*, vol. i. p. 206 ; p. 129 new edit. *note*, for a somewhat
similar proof of the strength of Holger Dansk.

[2] Probably from νάω to *flow*.

of his son, would avenge him, he received a wound in the thigh from the spear of the hero.[1]

Returning to Trachis, Héraklés collected an army, and made war on Eurytos king of Œchalia (in Eubœa), whom he killed, together with his sons; and having buried those of his own men who had fallen, among whom were Hippasos the son of Kéyx, and Argeios and Melas the sons of his uncle Likymnios, he plundered the town and led Iolé away captive. At the Eubœan promontory Kénæos he raised an altar to Zeus; and wishing to offer a sacrifice, sent to Kéyx for a splendid robe to wear. Déianeira hearing about Iolé from the messenger, and fearing the effect of her charms on the heart of her husband, resolved to try the efficacy of the philtre of Nessos, and tinged with it the tunic which was sent. Héraklés, suspecting nothing, put on the fatal garment and prepared to offer sacrifice. At first he felt no effect from it, but when it warmed the venom of Nessos began to consume his flesh. In his fury he caught Lichas, the ill-fated bearer of the poisoned tunic, by the foot, and hurled him into the sea.[2] He attempted to tear off the tunic, but it adhered closely to his skin, and the flesh came away with it. In this wretched state he got on shipboard and returned to Trachis; where Déianeira, on learning the consequence of what she had done, hanged herself; and Héraklés, charging Hyllos his eldest son by her to marry Iolé when he was of sufficient age, had himself carried to the summit of Mount Œté, and there causing a pyre to be constructed, ascended it, and directed his followers to set it on fire.[3] But no one would venture to obey; till Pœas, happening to arrive there in search of his stray cattle, complied with the desire of the hero, and received his bow and arrows as his reward. While the pyre was flaming a thunder-cloud conveyed the sufferer to heaven, where he was endowed with immortality; and being reconciled to Héra he espoused her daughter Hébé, by whom he had two children named Alexiarés (*Aider-in-war*) and Anikétos (*Invincible*).

Before we enter on the consideration of the mythology of Héraklés, we will give the beautiful and ingenious, but, as appears to us, fanciful view of it taken by a modern critic.[4].

This mythe is, according to him, one of extreme antiquity and great beauty, setting forth the ideal of human perfection.

---

[1] Hésiod, 'Aσπίς. The poet here (*v.* 120) names the hero's steed Areión: see above, p. 158.

[2] From Œta says Ovid (*Met.* ix. 165, 217), who is followed by Milton (*Par Lost*, ii. 545).

[3] See Sophoklés' *Trachiniæ.*   [4] Buttmann, *Mythol.* . 246 *seq.*

consecrated to the weal of mankind, or rather in its original form
to that of the hero's own nation. This perfection, according
to the ideas of the heroic age, consists in the greatest bodily
strength united with the advantages of mind and soul recognised by that age. Such a hero is, therefore, a man: but these
noble qualities in him are of divine origin; and he is made to
be the son of the king of the gods, by a mortal mother. To
render his perfection the more manifest, the poet gives him a
twin-brother, the child of a mortal sire. As virtue is not to be
learned, Héraklés exhibits his strength and courage in infancy;
he strangles the snakes, which fill his brother with terror. The
character of the hero throughout life, as that of the avenger of
injustice and punisher of evil, must exhibit itself in the boy as
the wild instinct of nature; and the mythe makes him kill his
tutor Linos with a blow of the lyre. When sent away by Amphitryón, he prepares himself, in the stillness and solitude of
the shepherd's life, by feats of strength and courage, for his
future task of purifying the earth of violence.

The beautiful tale of Prodikos, on the choice of Héraklés
between virtue and effeminacy, is a component part of the original mythe, to which it suits so accurately. For if the virtue of
Héraklés was to be of any value, it must be the result of choice,
and he must be tempted and resist the temptation. It was also
necessary for the perfection of virtue that it should encounter
continued opposition; and Grecian mythology, which contained
no being of pure and unmixed evil, but gods of mingled character
like men, furnished in the jealous Héra a deity to oppose and
afflict the son of Zeus. But if the object of the persecution of
one power, he must be—in conformity to all analogy—under the
protection of another; and Pallas-Athéné, the goddess of wisdom
and mental energy, appears throughout the ancient form of the
mythe as the constant guardian of the hero.

The number of tasks may not have been originally twelve
though most accounts agree in that number; but they were all of
a nature agreeable to the ideas of an heroic age,—the destruction
of monsters, and bringing home to his own country the valuable
productions of other regions. These labours are chiefly allegori-
cal. The Hydra, for instance, was meant to represent the evils o.
democratic anarchy, with its numerous heads, against which
though one may not be able to effect anything, yet the union o.
even two may suffice to overcome it.

The toils of the hero conclude with the greatest and most rar
of all in the heroic age,—the conquest over death. This is repre
sented by his descent into the under-world, and dragging Kerbero

to light, as a proof of his victory. In the old mythe he was made to engage with and wound Aïdès; and the Alkéstis of Euripidés exhibits him in conflict with Death.

But virtue, to be a useful example, must occasionally succumb to human weakness and the power of the evil principle. Hence Héraklés falls into fits of madness, sent on him by Héra; and hence, like the Rinaldo and Ruggiero of romance, he becomes the willing slave of Omphalé, the fair queen of Lydia, and changes his club and lion's skin for the distaff and the female robe. The mythe at length concludes most nobly with the assumption of the hero into Olympos. His protecting deity abandons him to the power of his persevering enemy;[1] his mortal part is consumed by fire, the purest of elements; his *shade* or *image* (εἴδωλον),[2] like those of other men, descends to the realms of Hadés, while the divine portion, *himself* (αὐτὸς), ascends from the pyre in a thunder-cloud, and the object of Héra's persecution being now effected, espouses Youth the daughter of his reconciled foe.

Our chief objection to this beautiful theory is its making the mythe of Héraklés, from the very commencement, one entire and consistent fiction, framed with a moral view. This we regard as contrary to the mythic analogy, which, though it might devise single mythes, like that of Ixíon, in order to illustrate some ethic principle, never conducted the heroes through a long series of adventures like those of Héraklés.

The mythology of this hero is of a very mixed character in the form in which it has come down to us. There is apparently in it the identification of one or more Grecian heroes with Melkart,[3] a god of the Phœnicians, and perhaps with one of the deities of Egypt. Hence we find Héraklés so frequently represented as the sun-god, and his twelve labours regarded as the passage of the sun through the twelve signs of the zodiac.

The Grecian adventures of Héraklés are placed in Thessaly (chiefly about Mount Œté), Ætólia and the Peloponnése: and as the Dórians, whose princes wer supposed to be descended from Héraklés, had relations with all these countries, Müller[4]

---

[1] 'Αλλά ἐ Μοῖρ' ἐδάμασσε καὶ ἀργαλέος χ·λος "Ηρης.—*Il.* xviii. 119.

[2] *Od.* xi. 602. It is not unworthy of notic·, that in the Ilias (i. 3) it is said that the *souls* (ψυχὰς) of the heroes were sen to Aïs, *themselves* (αὐτοὺς) were made a prey for dogs and birds; while, in thi place of the Odyssey, the *image* (εἴδωλον) of Héraklés was in the house of Aïs, *himself* (αὐτὸς) was on Olympos. Two diametrically opposed species of psycholoɤ y !

[3] Malqereth (מלקרת) 'King of the City,' a ame of the Sun or of the planet Jupiter.   [4] *Dórians*, book ii. chap. 11, 12.

views in him the national hero of the Dórian race. He regards as the original exploits of the Dórian Héraklés the conquest of Œchalia, the marriage with Déianeira (that is the league between the Dórians and Ætólians for the invasion of the Peloponnése), the taking of Ephyra, with which he connects the wounding of Hadés, and the whole of the Héraklean Nekyia, and even the carrying away of the cattle of Géryoneus, whom with Hekatæos he places in E'peiros, and finally the death on the summit of Œté. He thinks that the Peloponnésian adventures were mostly invented after the time of the Dórian invasion, which they were intended to justify; there may, he allows, have been an Argive hero of perhaps the same name, who was the destroyer of the Nemeæan lion; but the enmity of Héra, the delay at his birth, the servitude to Eurystheus, etc., are Dórian legends, and meant to represent the political and religious contests between the ancient inhabitants and the invaders. The mythology of Héraklés at Thébes was, he thinks, introduced from Delphi, or by the Dóric Hérakleids. That he did not belong to the Kadmeian mythology is proved by the legend of the coming of Alkméné to Thébes, and by the fact of his temples there being without the walls,—a fact which is quite conclusive, as the ancient deities of a city always had their temples on or near the citadel. Returning to the Peloponnése; the adventures there, he says, may be divided into two classes, the combats with men and those with beasts. Of the former are the conquest of Pylos, Lakónia and E'lis, and the establishment of the Olympic games, in all of which there is a historic reference. The latter are perhaps of a symbolic nature. Many of the adventures out of Greece are to be referred to the Grecian colonists of the places which are made the scene of them.

We have thus given a sketch of the theory of this most able mythologist, and there is much in it to which it is difficult to refuse assent. But we think that, like his theory of Apolló, it is too much affected by what appears to us his exaggerated conception of the influence of Dóric ideas and institutions in Greece. There are, in fact, parts of the Héraclean mythology to our apprehension almost inexplicable on this hypothesis: his name, too, *Héra-renowned*, seems quite unsuitable to a hero of the Dórians anterior to the Migration. This however may be obviated by supposing the name of the Dórian hero to have been different, and that of the Argive to have been adopted in its stead. But again, it does not seem likely that an Argive hero should be the object of persecution to the Argive goddess; on the contrary, all analogy would lead us to suppose him, from his name, to have been her favourite.[1] We would therefore hint as a possibility, that the original Héraklés was the conception of a Peloponnésian hero,[2] who, in obedience to the great goddess of the country (the goddess of the earth), cleared it of the noxious animals that infested it, and, it may be, went on toilsome journeys to distant regions to bring home cattle and plants to adorn and improve it; but that when he had been identified with the Dóric hero a new series of adventures was devised for him, and he was made the object of the persecution instead of the favour of the Argive goddess. We do not think that the identification with Melkart had much influence beyond that of localising some of the legends, such as that of Géryoneus.

In the Homéric poems there is, as we have seen, frequent mention of Héraklés; and in the Theogony his birth at Thébes, his combats with the Nemeæan lion, the Hydra and Géryoneus, his release of Prométheus and marriage with Hébé, are noticed. In the E'œæ the conquest of Pylos and other events were recorded; the Shield relates the combat with Kyknos; and the Ægimios and Wedding of Kéyx, ascribed to Hésiod, contained adventures of this hero. Of the age of these poems however we can only make a conjecture; for it is well known that some of the Hésiodic poems, as they are called, come down even below the thirtieth Olympiad. Kinæthos of Lakedæmón, who flourished about the fifth Olympiad, composed a Hérakleia, and Peisander of Kameiros (about Ol. 33) another very celebrated one; Stésichoros of Himera (Ol. 48) also composed a lyric poem named the Géryonéis, on the expedition to Erytheia: Panyasis of Samos (Ol. 72) wrote a Hérakleia in fourteen books, containing nearly as many verses as the Odyssey.

Pherekýdés, Hellaníkos and Hekatæos all gave the adventures of Héraklés a place in their works: and Hérodóros of Hérakleia on the Pontos, a contemporary of Sókratés, composed a long Hérakleia in prose. The Attic tragedians also introduced Héraklés into their dramas; and as they viewed him as a Bœótian, his character was treated with but little ceremony on some occasions. Apollodóros and Diodóros relate the adventures of this hero; they were also the subjects of the verses of the Alexandrian and the Latin poets.

[1] All the compounds of this form seem to be in a good sense. Such are Sophoklés, Agathoklés, Calliklés, Hieroklés, Themistoklés, Euklés. Dioklés, Hermoklés, Theoklés, seem to intimate the divine favour.

[2] Héraklés, son of the *Strong-one* (Alkméne) by Zeus-Amphitryón (*Wearen out* or *Vanquisher*); also named Alkeides (*Son-of-strength*) from his grandsia Alkæos.

CHAPTER V.

MYTHES OF ATTICA.

Κέκροψ. *Cecrops.*

O'GYGES, in whose time the Bœótic flood is placed, is said by some to have been the first who reigned over Attica and Bœótia: his son Eleusínos was the founder of Eleusis.

But in general Kekrops is held to have been the first who ruled over the country called Kekropia from him, and Attica from its peninsular form. He is said by mythologists to have been an autochthón, *i.e.* one who came from no foreign country, but was born in, and as it were from, the land ; and, like autochthones in general, to have had a body composed of those of a man and a snake. In his time the gods began to choose cities for themselves; and Poseidón and Athéna both fixed on Athens. The former came and struck the middle of the future Akropolis with his trident, and formed the well of salt water in the Erechtheion ; Athéna then came, and making Kekrops witness of her taking possession, planted the olive which stood in the Pandrosion. Twelve gods sat to decide the cause; and on the testimony of Kekrops, they adjudged the place to Athéna. She named the city from herself, and Poseidón testified his anger by laying the Thriasian plain under water.[1]

Kekrops married Agraulos the daughter of Aktæos, who bore him a son Erysichthón, and three daughters, Aglauros or Agraulos, Pandrosos, and Hersé. Erysichthón died without children; Agraulos had by Arés a daughter named Alkippé,[2] and Hersé by Hermés a son named Kephalos.[3]

One of the earliest events recorded in modern histories of Greece is the coming of Kekrops at the head of a colony, from Saïs in Lower Egypt to Attica, where he civilised the rude aborigines, gave them religion, marriage, and other social institutions, and taught them to cultivate corn for their subsistence This remarkable event is placed, on the authority of the Parian Chronicle, B.C. 1582.

It may therefore seem strange that Kekrops should apparently have been utterly unknown to Homer and Hésiod; that the

[1] Apollod. iii. 14, 1. For other marks of the vengeance of this god, see Sch. *Aristoph. Eccles.* 471.   Varro, *Fr.* p. 360 (Bip.)
[2] See above, p. 95.   [3] See above p. 146.

kyklic and the lyric poets do not speak of him; that the logographers, and their follower Apollodóros, seem ignorant of his
Egyptian birth; that the same should be the case with the dramatists; and that Hérodotos should speak of the Athéna of Saïs
and of the Attic Kekrops without giving the slightest hint of any
connexion between them. Plató is, in fact, the first who intimates it; the priests of Saïs, he says, informed Solón out of
their temple-archives that the goddess Néith or Athéna was the
founder of both their cities, but that Athens was the elder by one
thousand years. When in those remote ages the people of the isle
Atlantis invaded the countries within the Pillars of Héraklés, the
Athenians bravely repelled them; and in the war Kekrops, Erechtheus, Erichthonios, and Erysichthón distinguished themselves.[1]

We should think it hardly necessary to inform the reader
that the whole story of the Atlantis, and everything relating to
it, is as pure a fiction as the Utopia or any other political romance, and that Plató makes in it the same use of Solón that he
does of Sókratés on other occasions. At all events he gives not
the slightest hint of Kekrops being an Egyptian, but rather the
very reverse. Elsewhere he states the genuine Athenian creed
of his day. 'Neither a Pelops, nor a Danaos, nor a Kadmos,
nor an Ægyptos, nor any other, who, being originally a Barba-
rian, has been naturalised among the Hellénes, has settled
among us. We are of pure Hellénic blood, no mixed people,
and hence the hatred of foreign manners and customs is especially implanted in our city.'[2]

The first notice of the Egyptian origin of the Athenians appeared in a work which went under the name of Theopompos,
but which was a forgery intended to injure him. It was named
Τρικάρανος and it attacked the traditions and history of Athens,
Sparta, and Thébes. On the other hand Kallistratos and Pha-
nodémos maintained that Saïs was colonised from Athens. In the
time of the Ptolemies it became the fashion to regard the Egyptians as the colonisers of half the world. Still it is only in an
imperfect fragment of Diodóros and in Scholia that the Egyptian
Kekrops occurs. Few then, we think, will now dissent from the
following judgment: 'The derivation of Kekrops from Saïs is
a historic *sophism* and no mythe.'[3]

---

[1] *Timœos*, 21 *seq.*   *Critias*, 108 *seq.*
[2] *Menexenos*, 245. Isocratés (*Enc. Hel.* 20 ; *Panath.* 19) omits Kekrops in
h's list of Athenian kings; and he speaks (*Panég.* 41 ; *Panath.* 258) of the
Athenian autochthony in the same manner as Plató: see also Euripidés, *Ión*
590, *Fr. Erechtheus*, i. 7 *seq.*
[3] See Müller, *Orchom.* 106 *seq.* *Proleg.* 175. Voss, *Myth. Br.* iii. 180 *seq.*

Kekrops is then, in fact, purely an ideal being, and the names of his family all relate to agriculture and to the worship of the tutelar deity of Athens. Thus he is married to *Field-dwelling* (Agraulos), the daughter of the land (Aktæos). He has one son, *Mildew*, or rather *ploughman* (Erysichthón),[1] who dies without leaving any offspring; and three daughters, *Bright-one* (Aglauros)[2] or *Field-dwelling* (Agraulos), *All-dew* (Pandrosos) and *Dew* (Hersé), of whom the first bears a daughter, *Strong-mare* (Alkippé), to the god of war; and the third a son *Shady* (Kephalos), to the rural deity Hermés. There were temples of both Agraulos and Pandrosos at Athens; and, as Athéna herself was called by these names,[3] they are in all likelihood nothing more than personifications of her epithets. As Pandrosos and Hersé are the same in signification, and the name of the latter occurs only in late writers, it is probable that, like the Athenian Graces, Seasons and others, the Kekropides were only two originally.[4] The childlessness of Erysichthón merely perhaps indicates that he had been assigned no mythic progeny.

There only remains then to be explained the name Kekrops or Kerkops; and when we recollect that the ancient Athenians wore golden *tettiges* or tree-crickets in their hair to signify their autochthony, as it was said, and that a species of this insect was named κερκώπη, we have perhaps the simple origin of Kekrops.[5]

Κραναός. Ἀμφικτύων.   *Cranaüs. Amphictyón.*

Kekrops was succeeded by Kranaos, another autochthon, in whose time the flood of Deukalión is said to have happened. He married Pedias, the daughter of Ménytés; and from his daughter Atthis, who died a maid, he named the country Atthis. Kranaos was expelled by Amphiktyón, also an autochthon, or as others said the son of Deukalión, who after a reign of twelve years was in his turn expelled by

Ἐριχθόνιος.   *Erichthonius.*

Erichthonios was by some said to be the son of Héphæstos by Atthis the daughter of Kranaos. Others relate, that Athéna

---

[1] See above, p. 158.

[2] This is the name which prevails in inscriptions, and it is probably the elder form. It is connected with αἴγλη and with γλαῦξ, and γλαυκός, and is in every way suited to the moon.

[3] Sch. *Aristoph. Lys.* 440.   Harpocrat. *v.* Ἄγραυλος.

[4] Κατὰ τῆς Ἀγραύλου ὤμνυον, κατὰ δὲ τῆς Πανδρόσου σπανιώτερον· κατὰ δὲ τῆς Ἔρσης οὐκ εὑρήκαμεν.   Sch. *Aristoph. Thes.* 540.

[5] Mr. Kenrick, in his ingenious Essay on the Mythic Kings of Attica, in the Philological Museum (ii. 357), thinks that the original form was Κρέκοψ from κρέκω. Like our own *cricket*, these terms and *tettix* are onomatopœic.

coming one day to the workshop of Héphæstos to get some arms, the artist was filled by Aphrodíté with desire, and attempted to offer violence to the maiden-goddess. She fled; he pursued, and though lame overtook her, but was unable to overcome her resistance. The legend proceeds to relate the birth of Erichthonios after a manner which gives no very high idea of Athenian delicacy. The goddess resolved to bestow immortality on the babe. She laid him therefore in a coffer, which she gave in charge to Pandrosos, the daughter of Kekrops, with an injunction not to open it. Pandrosos was obedient; but the curiosity of her sisters made them unclóse the coffer, in which they beheld the babe, who terminated in a snake. As a punishment Athéna struck them with madness, and they precipitated themselves from the Akropolis. Erichthonios was reared by Athéna in her *temenos*; and when he was grown up he expelled Amphiktyón, and reigned over Athens. He set up the statue of Athéna on the Akropolis, and instituted the festival of the Panathensæa. He is said to have been the first who used the four-horse chariot. He had by the Naïs Pasithea a son named Pandíon, who succeeded him. Erichthonios when he died was buried in the *temenos* of Athéna by his son; or, according to others, by the goddess herself, whose favourite he had been, and whom in life she had often visited.[1]

Another account of the birth of Erichthonios says, that Héphæstos having made golden seats for Zeus and the other gods, Héra when she sat in hers was unable to rise. Héphæstos was called to set his mother free; but he, who had done it through malice for her having flung him out of heaven, replied that he had no mother. Dionýsos, however, contrived to make him drunk, and while in that state he released the goddess. Zeus then desired him to demand a reward; and Poseidón, who bore a grudge to Athéna, persuaded him to ask her in marriage. Zeus granted his desire, but recommended his daughter to stand on her defence.[2]—The remainder of the legend is nearly the same as the former one.

In every representation of this mythe Erichthonios is an autochthon, or *child of the soil*, as Homer terms Erechtheus.[3]

Πανδίων. *Pandion.*

Pandíon succeeded his father in the kingdom. In his reign Démétér and Dionýsos came to Attica. The former was entertained by Keleos, the latter by Ikarios. Pandíon married

---

[1] Apollod. iii. 14, 5, 6.　　　　　　[2] Hygin. 166.
[3] Τέκε δὲ ζείδωρος Ἄρουρα. *I.* ii. 584: comp. Eur. *Ión.* 28.

Zeuxippé, the sister of his mother, by whom he had two sons, Erechtheus and Butés, and two daughters, Prokné and Philoméla.[1]

Πρόκνη, Φιλομήλα, καὶ Τηρεύς.   Procne, Philomela, et Tereus.

Pandíon being at war about boundaries with Labdakos king of Thébes, called to his aid Téreus the son of Arés out of Thraké.[2] Having with his assistance come off victorious in the contest, he gave him his daughter Prokné in marriage, by whom Téreus had a son named Itys. After some time Prokné became desirous of seeing her sister, and at her request Téreus went to Athens and prevailed on Pandíon to let Philoméla accompany him back to Thraké. On the way he violated her; and fearing that the truth might be discovered, he cut out her tongue and confined her: she contrived however to communicate her story to her sister by means of characters woven in a peplos. Prokné then sought out and released her sister; and killing her own son Itys, served his flesh up to his father. The two sisters fled away; and Téreus, discovering the truth, pursued them with an axe as some, with a sword as others more justly tell. Finding themselves nearly overtaken by him, they prayed to the gods to change them into birds; Prokné immediately became a *Nightingale* (ἀηδών), and Philoméla a *Swallow* (χελιδών); Téreus was also changed, and became a *Hoopoe* (ἔποψ, upupa).[3]

Like so many others, this story also is told with considerable variations. According to some, Téreus had early conceived a passion for Philoméla, and he obtained her in marriage by pretending that Prokné was dead.[4] Again there is great discrepancy respecting the transformations, some saying that Prokné, others that Philoméla was the nightingale.[5] This last, which has the signification of the name in its favour, was not however the prevalent opinion; it is in fact almost peculiar to the Latin writers. It was also said that Téreus was changed into a hawk,[6] and that Itys became a wood-pigeon.[7]

---

[1] Apollod. ut sup.

[2] He was said to be the prince of the Thrakians, who were supposed to have dwelt in the old times in Daulis. Thuk. ii. 29. Apollod. iii. 14, 8. Conon, 31. Paus. i. 41. 8; x. 4, 8. Daulias was an epithet of the nightingale.

[3] Apollod. iii. 13. Ovid, *Met.* vi. 424 *seq.* Hygin. 45. Conon, 31. Sch. *Aristoph. Birds*, 212. Eudocia, 327. Serv. *Buc.* vi. 79.

[4] Apollod. ut sup. Hygin. ut sup.

[5] Prokné is the nightingale in Æsch. *Sup.* 60 *seq.* Apollod. ut sup. Sch. *Aristoph.* ut sup. Conon ut sup. Paus. x. 4, 9. Varro, *L. L.* v. 76. Plut. *Symp.* viii. 7, 2. Nonn. ii. 131; xii. 75.—Philomela, in Ovid, ut sup. *Art. Amat.* ii. 383. Hygin. ut sup. Eudocia, ut sup. Hor. *Carm.* iv. 12, 5. Vergil. *Geor.* iv. 15, 513. Statius, *Silv.* v. 3, 84.

[6] Hygin. ut sup.   [7] Serv. *Buc.* vi. 79.

The fable seems to be one of considerable antiquity. We have already seen it under another form in the Odyssey.[1] Hésiod in one place[2] calls the swallow Pandíonis, evidently alluding to it; and elsewhere he is said[3] to have related that the nightingale had been deprived of all her sleep, the swallow of one ualf of hers, in consequence of that unhallowed meal in Thrake. The legend is one of those invented to account mythically for the habits and properties of animals. Every spring the south of Europe is visited by various birds which have wintered in the warmer regions of Africa. Among these are the swallow, the 'herald of the spring,' the pensive nightingale and the hoopoe. This last is of the tenuirostral tribe of birds, which includes the humming-birds and birds of Paradise; it is about twelve inches long, with a slender *falcate* or sword-shaped bill of two and a half inches in length, and a crest on its head. Its habits are solitary and it feeds on insects. The note of the nightingale, which was strangely regarded as lugubrious,[4] the red spots on the breast of the swallow,[5] and the long bill and hunting habits of the hoopoe, may have led Grecian imagination to combine them in fiction, and hence the origin of the present mythe. The Scholiast on Aristophanés[6] tells us that Téreus when pursuing the fugitives kept crying ποῦ ποῦ (*where, where?*), while Philoméla in terror cried Τηρεύς, and Prokné mournfully uttered Ἴτυ Ἴτυ, and that each, since their transformation, continues to utter these notes.

With respect to the names in this legend Philoméla is apparently *Song-loving*,[7] and would therefore seem most appropriate to the nightingale, while Prokné, which is evidently connected with πρὸ, πρωΐ, is well suited to the swallow;[8] so that in fact

---

[1] See above, p. 298.   [2] Ἔργ. 568.   [3] Ælian, *Var. Hist.* xii. 20.
[4] On this subject see *Tales and Popular Fictions*, p. 17.
[5] See Verg. *Georg.* iv. 15.   [6] *Birds*, 212.
[7] See Welcker, *Der. Ep. Cyc.* p. 274 *note*.
[8] The κνη may be merely a termination, see p. 15, or it may be connected with κινέω (see Soph. *Elek.* 18), or with *cano*. In either case it would denote the swallow as the announcer of the spring :

Ἄγγελε κλυτὰ ἔαρος ἀδυόδμου, κυανέα χελιδοῖ.
Simónid. *ap. Sch. Aristoph. Birds*, 1410.

or of the dawn : see Verg. *Æn.* viii. 456.   Gray's *Elegy*, st. 5.
It might also denote the nightingale as herald of spring :—

Ἦρος δ᾽ ἄγγελος, ἱμερόφωνος ἀηδῶν.
Sapphó, *ap. Sch. Soph. Elek.* 148.

Still my nightingale
That with sweet accents doth assure me that
My spring of happiness comes fast upon me.
Massinger, *Great Duke of Florence*, i. 2.

Z

the names may have changed places. Téreus is probably *Θή-ρευς*, i.e. the *Hunter*,[1] and its similarity to Térés, a name of the kings of Thrake, may have caused him to be represented as a native of that country; while if it be true[2] that the swallows do not build in Daulis, the reason is plain why it should have found a place in the legend. Itys of course derived his name from the note of the nightingale.

'Ερεχθεύς. *Erechtheus.*

On the death of Pandíon his sons Erechtheus and Butés divided his offices between them, the former taking the kingdom, the latter the priesthood of Athéna and Poseidón-Erichthonios. Butés married Chthonia the daughter of his brother, and the sacerdotal family of the Butads deduced their lineage from him.

Erechtheus married Praxithea, a grand-daughter of the river-god Képhisos, and had by her five sons, Kekrops, Pandóros, Métión, Orneus, and Thespios; and four daughters, Prokris, Kreüsa, O'reithyia, and Chthonia. Being engaged in a war with the Eleusinians, he consulted the god about the event; and received for answer, that victory would fall to him who should sacrifice one of his daughters. He forthwith offered up his youngest daughter Chthonia; and her sisters, as they had entered into a resolution that when one lost her life the others would end theirs, all voluntarily put an end to themselves. Erechtheus was victorious, and slew Eumolpos the son of Poseidón, an ally of the Eleusinians, but was himself destroyed afterwards by that god.[3]

The four daughters of Erechtheus, here named, were, as we shall find, all married, and their several histories are incompatible with this tale of their sacrifice. It is probable therefore that the mythologists have confounded them with the subjects of another mythe, according to which Protogeneia and Pandóra, the *two virgin*-daughters of Erechtheus, were offered up as voluntary victims, in a war against the Bœótians.[4]

Πρόκρις καὶ Κέφαλος. *Procris et Cephalus.*

Prokris, the eldest daughter of Erechtheus, was married to Kephalos the son of Déión the son of Æolos. They dwelt at Thorikos in Attica, and were happy, till curiosity to try the fidelity of his wife entered the mind of Kephalos. Feigning a journey of eight years he disguised himself, and came to Prokris with a splendid jewel, which he offered to her as the price of her

---

[1] Epops may be the same from *ἔπω*.   [2] Paus. x. 4, 9.   [3] Apollod. *ut sup.*
[4] See Eur. *Ión*, 281. Demosth. *Epitaph.* 8. Cic. *Pro Sext.* 21. *Tusc. Disp.* i. 48. Hesych. *v.* Παρθέρος.

favours. After much hesitation her virtue yielded; her husband then discovered himself and reproached her. She fled from him in shame, but soon after they were reconciled. Kephalos went constantly to the chase; and Prokris, suspicious, as she had failed herself, fancied that he was attracted by the charms of some other fair one. She questioned the slave who used to accompany him; and he told her that his master frequently ascended the summit of a hill, and cried "Come, Nephelé, come!" Prokris went to the designated hill, and concealed herself in a thicket; and on Kephalos' crying "Come, Nephelé, come!" she rushed forwards to her husband, who in his astonishment and confusion threw his dart and killed her.[1]

This legend also is told with great variations. It was said that Kephalos refused to comply with the wishes of E'ós, pleading his fidelity to his wife, and that the goddess changed his form to put the faith of Prokris to the test. Prokris on finding how she had been deceived fled to Kréte, where Minós gave her an inevitable dart, and a dog named Lælaps (*Whirlwind*), which no beast could escape. She then cut her hair short, and attiring herself as a man came to Thorikos and challenged Kephalos to a match at hunting. He was easily overcome, and seeing the wonderful virtues of the dog and dart he sought to obtain them. The terms were those he had himself proposed to Prokris. He yielded; Prokris then discovered herself and reproached him, but they were soon reconciled and she gave him the dog and dart. The story then concludes as above related.[2]

According to another account the virtue of Prokris had not been proof against the offer of a golden coronet from a suitor named Pteleón. Her infidelity being discovered by her husband, she fled to Minós king of Kréte, whom she enabled to have children, and received the dog and dart in return.[3]

Kephalos for his involuntary crime was sentenced by the court of Areiopagos to perpetual banishment. He went to Thébes, which was at that time ravaged by a fox which nothing could overtake, and joined Amphitryón in the chase of it: his dog Lælaps ran it down; but just as he was catching it, Zeus turned them both to stone.[4] Kephalos then aided Amphitryón against

[1] Pherekýdés, *ap. Sch. Od.* xi. 321. For Nephelé Ovid has Aura.
[2] Hygin. 189. Ov. *Met.* vii. 661 *seq.* Ariosto has founded on this his tale of Adonio. *Or. Fur.* xliii. 72 *seq.*
[3] Apollod. iii. 15, 1. Anton. Lib. 41. Kallimachus (iii. 209) places Prokris with Kyréné and Atalanté among the companions of Artemis; from whom it s also said (Paus. ix. 19, 1) she received the dog.
[4] Apollod. ii. 4, 7. Paus. *ut sup.* From Photius (*Lex* p. 428) it would appear that this event was celebrated in the Thébais of the *Epic Cycle.*

the Teleboans, and on their conquest he settled in an island named from him Kephalonia.[1]

Prokris is noticed in the Odyssey,[2] and the story is probably one of some antiquity. Though, as we have seen, an attempt was made to convert Kephalos into an historic personage, he is probably the son of Hermés and Hersé,[3] perhaps in the original form of the mythe Pandrosos, and his name appears to signify the twilight (*diluculum*), which is taken away by the Dawn.[4] The name of Prokris seems also to refer to the early day ($\pi\rho\omega\hat{\iota}$), and it may have been an epithet of E'ós or only another form of Prokné.

'Ωρείθυϊα.   Orithyia.

As O'reithyia, the daughter of Erechtheus, was playing or gathering flowers on the banks of the Ilyssos, she was beheld by the wind-god Boreas. Enamoured of her beauty, he seized and carried her away to Thraké, where she bore him the winged youths Zétés and Kalaïs; and two daughters, Chioné and Kleopatra.[5]

Chioné was loved by Poseidón, to whom she bore a son named Eumolpos; to conceal her weakness she threw the babe into the sea to the protection of his father. Poseidón took him to Æthiopia, and gave him to his daughter Benthesikýmé to rear. When Eumolpos was grown up, the husband of Benthesikýmé gave him one of his two daughters in marriage; but Eumolpos, attempting to offer violence to the sister of his wife, was forced to fly. He came with his son Ismaros to Tegyrios, a king of Thraké, who gave his daughter in marriage to Ismaros. But Eumolpos, being detected plotting against Tegyrios, was once more forced to fly, and he came to Eleusis. Ismaros dying, Tegyrios became reconciled to Eumolpos, who returned to Thraké, and succeeded him in his kingdom. War breaking out between the Athenians and the Eleusinians, the latter invoked the aid of their former guest, and Eumolpos fell in battle against Erechtheus.[6]

The two sons of Boreas were among the Argonauts, and they delivered Phineus, who had been married to their sister Kleopatra, from the Harpies. They were afterwards slain by Héraklés in the isle of Tenos.[7]

---

[1] This is a mere coincidence of name.   [2] *Od.* xi. 321.   [3] See above, p. 147.

[4] See above, pp. 57, 146. Κέφαλος quasi κνέφαλος, from κνέφας: see Buttmann, *Lexil. v. κελαινός.* Κνέφας τὸ λευκόφως, Sch. *Aristoph. Frogs,* 1385.

[5] Plató, *Phædr.* 229. Apollod. iii. 15, 2. Apoll. Rh. i. 211 *seq. cum Sch.* Hellaníkos (*ap. Sch. Od.* xiv. 533) said that O'reithyia was on the Akropolis as a basket-bearer (κανηφόρος) in the worship of Athéna-Polias when she was carried off.

[6] Apollod. *ut supra.*   [7] Apoll. Rh. i. 1300 *seq.*

Here we find a physical mythe in union with an historic legend. It was a tradition in Attica that the sacred family of the Eumolpids belonged to the mythic Thrakians, whom we find sometimes on Hélikón, sometimes in Thraké. The present legend, by making Eumolpos a son of the sea-god and grandson of the north wind, and giving him a son named Ismaros, plainly intended to deduce the Eumolpids from Thraké, while the name Tegyrios would seem to point to Bœótia, where there was a town named Tegyra.

The spouse of the north wind was very appropriately named *Mountain-rusher* (ὄρος θύω), their children are *Blower* (Ζήτης), *Inflamer* or *Drier-up* (Κάλαϊς)[1], and *Snowy* (Χιόνη), to whom for the sake of uniformity another daughter was added, whose name however shows that she could not have belonged to the original mythe.[2] It is, we should think, quite evident that O'reithyia was not the daughter of a king of Attica; yet the real Erechtheus may have been her mythic sire.

Κρέουσα, Ξοῦθος καὶ Ἴων.　Creusa, Xuthus et Ion.

Kreüsa, the third daughter of Erechtheus, married Xuthos the son of Hellén, to whom his father had assigned the Peloponnése. Her sons by him were Ión and Achæos.

According to Euripidés, in the drama named from him, Ión was the fruit of the secret love of Kreüsa with Apolló. When she had given birth to him she laid him in the cave where she had met the god; and Hermés, at Apolló's desire, conveyed him to Delphi. He was there reared and dedicated to the service of the temple; and when some years after Xuthos and Kreüsa came to consult the oracle on the subject of progeny, Ión was recognised by his mother, and as the true representative of the Erechtheids he occupied the throne, and from his four sons Teleón, Hoplés, Ergadés and Ægikoreus the four tribes of Attica were named.

Κέκροψ, Πανδίων.　Cecrops II., Pandion II.

On the death of Erechtheus the sceptre passed to his son Kekrops II. The successor of Kekrops was his son Pandíon II.,

---

[1] Zétés is easily deduced from ζάω *to blow*. Kalaïs is probably derived from καίω *to burn*, *dry up* (αὖρα βόρειος ὑπέκαε πάντα, Longus, p. 3, ed. Vill.; comp. *uro*, Verg. *Georg.* i. 77), like κᾶλον *firewood*, κήλεος *burning*, κηλὰς *windy*, as κηλὰς νεφέλη *cloud-portending wind*, κηλὰς ἡμέρα *a windy day* : see Welcker, *Tril.* 565 *note*.

ψυχρὸς ἄνεμος Βορέης πνεύσει . . . . ἔοημον ἐκκαύσει καὶ ἀποσβέσει χλόην ὡς πῦρ.—Σοφία Σειράχ, xliii. 20.

[2] We shall find that Perseus, Lykáón and others had only *one* daughter.

who was expelled by his cousins the Métionids. He retired to Megara, where he married Pylia the daughter of king Pylos; who, being obliged to fly for the murder of his brother Bias, resigned Megara to his son-in-law, and retiring to the Peloponnése built Pylos. Pandíon had four sons, Ægeus, Pallas, Nisos, and Lykos, who conquered and divided among them the Attic territory, Ægeus, as the eldest, having the supremacy.[1]

Νῖσος καὶ Σκύλλα. *Nisus et Scylla.*

In the war waged by Minós king of Kréte against the Athenians, on account of the death of his son Androgeós, Megara was besieged, and it was taken by the treachery of Skylla the daughter of Nisos. This prince had a golden or purple lock of hair growing on his head; and as long as it remained uncut, so long was his life to last. Skylla, having seen Minós, fell in love with him, and resolved to give him the victory. She cut off her father's precious lock as he slept, and he immediately died: and the town was then taken by the Krétans. But Minós, instead of rewarding the maiden, disgusted with her unnatural treachery, tied her by the feet to the stern of his vessel, and thus dragged her along till she was drowned.[2] Another legend[3] adds, that Nisos was changed into the bird called the *Sea-eagle* (ἀλιάετος), and Skylla into that named *Kiris* (κεῖρις[4]); and that the father continually pursues the daughter to punish her for her crime. According to Æschylos[5] Minós bribed Skylla with a golden collar.

Αἰγεύς. *Ægeus.*

Ægeus the son of Pandíon, being childless went to Delphi to consult the oracle. The meaning of the response which he received being dubious,[6] he took his way homewards through Trœzén, in order to consult Pittheus the wise son of Pelops. Pittheus, divining the sense of the oracle, made his guest drunk, and put him to sleep with his own daughter Æthra; and Poseidón, it was also said, took advantage of the same night. Ægeus when departing charged Æthra if she bore a son to rear him,

---

[1] Apollod. *ut sup.* Soph. *Fr. Ægeus.* Sch. *Aristoph. Wasps*, 1218.
[2] Apollod. *ut sup.* Sch. *Eurip. Hyp.* 1195.
[3] Ov. *Met.* viii. 145. Verg. *Ciris*, and *Georg.* i. 404; in *Buc.* vi. 74 the poet confounds this with a totally different Scylla.
[4] From κείρω, *to cut* or *devour*,—from her *cutting off* her father's lock, says the legend,—from the rapacity of the bird more probably.
[5] *Choëph.* 616 *seq.*
[6] The god said,

ἀσκοῦ τὸν προὔχοντα ποδάονα, φέρτατε λαῶν,
μὴ λύσῃς, πρὶν ἐς ἄκρον Ἀθηναίων ἀφίκῃαι.

and to tell no one whose he was. He moreover placed his sword and shoes under a large stone, and directed her to send his son to him when he was able to roll away the stone and take them from under it.

Ægeus returned to Athens; and when Médeia came thither from Corinth, he married her. He also celebrated Panathé-næan games; in which Androgeós the son of Minós overcame all his opponents. Ægeus, envious of his worth, engaged him to go and fight with the Marathónian bull, and the valiant youth fell in the attempt. According to other accounts, Ægeus laid an ambush for him as he was going to Thébes, where games were to be celebrated by Laïos.

Minós made war on Athens to avenge the death of his son. Megara fell as above related. Athens held out; but being closely pressed with hunger, the Athenians, according to an ancient oracle, sacrificed on the grave of the Kyklóps Geræstos the four daughters of Hyakinthos, who had settled there.[1] This bloody deed was of no avail; and the oracle declared, that the naming of the satisfaction he required must be left to Minós himself. He demanded seven youths and seven maids to be sent every ninth year to be devoured by the Minótaur. This hard condition was for some time complied with. At length Théseus, the son of the king, voluntarily proposed to attempt their deliverance. He went, and succeeded; but he forgot to change his black sails to white, as agreed on in case of success; and Ægeus, thinking that his son was lost, cast himself from the Akropolis and perished.[2]

Θησεύς. *Theseus.*

The son of Ægeus by Æthra was named Théseus. When grown to the proper age, his mother led him to the stone under which his father had deposited his sword and shoes, and he removed it with ease and took them out. He was now to proceed to Athens and present himself to his father. As the roads were infested by robbers, his grandfather Pittheus pressed him earnestly to take the shorter and safer way over the Sarónic gulf; but the youth, feeling in himself the spirit and the soul of a hero, resolved to signalise himself like Héraklés, with whose fame all Greece now rang, by destroying the evil-doers and the monsters

---

[1] See above, p. 338. There was a similar tradition about the daughters of León, whence the Leókorion derived its name; see Cic. *de Nat. Deor.* iii. 19.

[2] Plut. *Thes.* 22. Diodór. iv. 61. Paus. i. 22, 4. Catull. lxiv. 242. Others said that he flung himself from a rock into the sea, which was named from him. Nikokratés (*ap. Sch. Apoll. Rh.* i. 831), Hygin. 43. Serv. *Æn.* iii. 74. Statius (*Theb.* xii. 625) says it was from Sunie i.

that oppressed the country; and he determined on the more perilous and adventurous journey by land.

His first day's journey brought him to Epidauros, where dwelt a man named Periphatés, a son of Héphæstos. This ferocious savage always went armed with an iron club, whence he was called *Club-bearer* (κορυνήτης); and all travellers stood in terror of his cruelty. When he saw Théseus approach, he immediately assailed him; but he speedily fell beneath the blows of the young hero, who took possession of his club, and bore it ever afterwards as a memorial of his first victory.[1]

Théseus now pursued his journey, and met with no interruption till he came to the Isthmos of Corinth. Here he found another 'faitour,' who, from the great mischief that he did to all the surrounding country, was called by no other name than that of Sinis,[2] i. e. *Evil-doer*. His strength was so great, that he was able to take by their tops the pine-trees with which the Isthmos was at that time overgrown, and bend them to the ground; and hence he was called *Pine-bender* (πιτυοκάμπτης). He posted himself on the road, and obliged all passengers to take hold of a pine with him and bend it, and when it was bent he would let it go, and the tree flying up the unhappy stranger was dashed to the ground and killed. Théseus, on being challenged, though he had never before attempted such a feat, held down the tree with ease; and then, to punish Sinis for his previous cruelty, killed him, and hung him out of one of the pines.[3]

Before he left the neighbourhood of the Isthmos, Théseus delivered the people of Krommyon, a village near Corinth, from a huge sow which ravaged their lands. He hunted and killed this monster.

As he approached the borders of Megara, he came to the narrow path overhanging the sea, where the robber Skirón—from whom the pass derived its name—had fixed his abode. The practice of Skirón was, when any stranger came to him, to invert the duties of hospitality; and instead of giving water to wash the feet of his guest, to insist on the guest's washing the feet of the host. This ceremony was performed on the pass; and while the guest was engaged in the operation, Skirón would give him a kick, which tumbled him down into the sea, where a huge tortoise always lay ready to devour the bodies of those who were thrown down. Théseus killed Skirón himself, and flung his body down to the tortoise.[5]

---

[1] Apollod. iii. 16, 1. Plut. *Thés.* 8. Diodór. iv. 59.   [2] From σίνω, *to injure.*
[3] Plut. and Diodór. *ut sup.* Hygin. 38.
[4] Plut. *Thés.* 9. Strab. viii. 6, 22, p. 380. Paus. ii. 1, 3. Diodór. *ut sup.*
[5] Plut. Diodór. and Hygin. *ut sup.* Sch. *Eurip. Hip.* 979.

Théseus came now to Eleusis, where Kerkyón, said to be a son of Héphæstos, reigned. Like many of those whom Héraklés encountered, Kerkyón forced all comers to wrestle with him, and killed the vanquished. Théseus accepting the challenge overcame him, and paid him in his own coin.[1]

Not far from thence, on the banks of the Képhissos, Théseus met with Damastés, named the *Beater-out* or *Stretcher* (προκρούστης), and the *Hurtful* (πολυπήμων). This Damastés had two iron bedsteads, one long, the other short. When a stranger came, he took him, if short of stature, to the long bedstead, and stretched and pulled him, as he said, to make him fit it, till the life left him. But if the stranger should be tall, he assigned him the short bedstead, and then cut as much off him as made him of the same length as his bed. But Théseus meted to him with his own measure.[2]

Having overcome all the perils of the road, Théseus at length reached Athens, where new danger awaited him. He found his father's court all in confusion. The Pallantids, or sons and grandsons of Pallas the brother of Ægeus, had long seen with jealousy the sceptre in the hands of an old man, and meditated wresting it from his feeble grasp. Thinking however that his death could not be very remote, they resolved to wait for that event, but they made no secret of their intentions. The arrival of Théseus threatened to disconcert their plan. They feared that if this young stranger should be received as a son by the old king, he might find in him a protector and avenger; and they resolved to poison his mind against him. Their plot so far succeeded, that Ægeus was on the point of sacrificing his son, when he recognised him, and then acknowledged him in the presence of all the people. The Pallantids had recourse to arms, but Théseus defeated and slew them.[3]

Médeia it is also said, who was married to Ægeus, fearing the loss of her influence when Théseus should have been acknowledged by his father, resolved to anticipate that event; and moved by her calumnies, Ægeus was presenting a cup of poison to his son, when the sight of the sword left with Æthra discovered to him who he was.[4]

The bull which Héraklés had brought from Kréte was now at Marathón, and the country was in terror of his ravages. Théseus, probably deeming this a good opportunity of recommending himself to the people over whom he was likely to reign, resolved to deliver them from the ferocious animal. He went in quest of him, overcame and exhibited him in chains to the astonished

[1] Plut. Diodór. and Hygin. *ut sup.* Sch. *Eurip. Hip.* 979.
[2] Id. *ib.*   [3] Plut. 13   [4] Plut. 12.

eyes of the Athenians, who did not know which was the greater, their admiration of the victory or their terror of the combat. Théseus then sacrificed the bull to Apolló Delphinios.[1]

The Athenians were at this period in deep affliction, on account of the tribute which they were forced to pay to Minós king of Kréte. Théseus resolved to deliver them from this calamity, or to die in the attempt. Accordingly when the third time of sending off the tribute came, and the youths and maidens were according to custom drawn by lot to be sent, in spite of the entreaties of his father to the contrary, he voluntarily offered himself as one of the victims. The ship departed as usual under black sails, which Théseus promised his father to change for white in case of his returning victorious. When they arrived in Kréte, the youths and maidens were exhibited before Minós; and Ariadné the daughter of the king, who was present, became deeply enamoured of Théseus, by whom her love was speedily returned. She furnished him with a clue of thread, which enabled him to penetrate in safety the windings of the labyrinth, till he came to where the Minótaur lay, whom he caught by the hair and slew. He then got on board with his companions, and sailed for Athens. Ariadné accompanied his flight, but was abandoned by him on the isle of Dia or Naxos.[2]

Before he returned to Athens, Théseus sailed to Délos to pay his vow; for ere setting out on his perilous expedition, he had made a vow to send annually, if successful, to the temple of the god, a ship with gifts and sacrifices.[3] He also consecrated in that island to Aphrodíté a statue made by Dædalos, on account of the aid she had given him. He moreover, to commemorate his victory, established there a dance, the evolutions of which imitated the windings of the labyrinth.[4]

On approaching the coast of Attica Théseus forgot the signal appointed by his father, and returned under the same sails with which he had departed; and the old king, thinking he was bereaved of his newly-found son, ended his life. Théseus, with the general approbation, mounted the vacant throne.

---

[1] Plut. 14. Diodór. *ut sup.* Hygin. *ut sup.*

[2] Plut. 15–19. See below, chap. xii. *Ariadné.*

[3] Plut. 21. The practice of sending a ship annually to Délos—whatever may have given occasion to it—long continued. While it was absent no sentence of death could be executed in Athens; because, as it was said, it commemorated the deliverance of the youths and maidens. The ship sent, called the Paralian Galley, was maintained to be the very same one in which Théseus had sailed; though it had been so often repaired, as to give occasion to a celebrated question among the sophists respecting its identity. Plut. *Thés.* 23.

[4] This is evidently founded on the lines of Homer, *Il.* xviii. 590 *seq.*

The hero now turned his thoughts to legislation. The Attic territory had been divided by Kekrops into twelve Démes or villages, each of which had its own government and chief magistrate, and was almost wholly independent. The consequence was, frequent and sanguinary wars among them. Nothing but pressing external danger forced them to union, which was again dissolved as soon as the storm was over.

Théseus therefore invited not merely the people of Attica, but even strangers and foreigners, to settle at Athens, then nothing but a castle on a rock. By his prudence and his authority he induced the heads of the villages to resign their independent sovereignty, and entrust the administration of justice to a court, which should sit constantly at Athens, and exercise jurisdiction over all the inhabitants of Attica. He abolished the former division of the people into four tribes, and substituted that of a distribution into three classes, of the Nobles, the Agriculturists, and the Manufacturers. The nobles were put in possession of all offices and dignities; but the choice of the persons from the body of the nobles to fill them was left to the people.

The result of these judicious regulations was the increase of the city of Athens, and of the population in general: the establishment of just liberty, and at the same time the augmentation of the royal power, and the reduction of that of the nobles, heretofore the source of such continual broils and dissensions. As a further means of uniting the people, Théseus established numerous festivals, particularly the Panathenæa, solemnised with great splendour every fifth year, in commemoration of this union of the inhabitants of Attica.

Théseus firmly established the boundaries of the Attic territory, in which he included Megaris, and set up a pillar on the Isthmos of Corinth to mark the limits of Attica and the Peloponnése. Near this pillar he renewed the Isthmian games, in imitation of the Olympic lately established by Héraklés.

These civic cares did not prevent Théseus from taking part in military enterprises: he accompanied Héraklés in his expedition against the Amázons, who dwelt on the banks of the Thermódón; and distinguished himself so much in the conflict, that Héraklés after the victory bestowed on him, as the reward of his valour, the hand of the vanquished queen Antiopé. When the Amázons afterwards in revenge invaded the Attic territory, they met with a signal defeat from the Athenian prince.

Théseus was also a sharer in the dangers of the Kalydonian hunt; he was one of the adventurous band who sailed in the Argó to Kolchis; and he aided his friend Peirithoos and the

Lapiths in their conflict with the Kentaurs. The friendship between him and Peirithoos was of a most intimate nature; yet it had originated in the midst of arms. Peirithoos had one time made an irruption into the plain of Marathón, and carried off the herds of the king of Athens. Théseus, on receiving information, went to repel the plunderers. The moment Peirithoos beheld him, he was seized with secret admiration; he stretched out his hand as a token of peace, and cried, " Be judge thyself ! What satisfaction dost thou require ? "—" Thy friendship," replied the Athenian; and they swore inviolable fidelity.

Like faithful comrades, they aided each other in every project. Each was ambitious in love, and would possess a daughter of the king of the gods. Théseus fixed his thoughts on Helené the daughter of Léda, then a child of but nine rears. Placing her under the care of his mother Æthra at Aphidnæ, Théseus prepared to assist his friend in a bolder and more perilous attempt; for Peirithoos, after the death of Hippodameia, resolved to venture on the daring deed of carrying away from the palace of the monarch of the under-world his queen Persephoné. Théseus, though aware of the risk, would not abandon his friend. They descended together to the region of shadows ; but Aïdés, knowing their design, seized them, and placed them on an enchanted rock at the gate of his realms; where they sat unable to move, till Héraklés passing by in his descent for Kerberos free'd Théseus, but was by a divine intimation prevented from aiding his friend, who remained there everlastingly in punishment of his audacious attempt.[1]

After the death of Antiopé, who had borne him a son named Hippolytos, Théseus married Phædra the daughter of Minós and sister of Ariadné. This princess was seized with a violent affection for the son of the Amázon,—an affection produced by the wrath of Aphrodité against Hippolytos for neglecting her deity, and devoting himself solely to the service of Artemis, or against Phædra as the daughter of Pasiphaé. During the absence of Théseus the queen made advances of love to her step-son, which were indignantly repelled by the virtuous youth. Filled with fear and hate, on the return of her husband she accused to him his innocent son of an attempt on her honour. Without giving the youth an opportunity of clearing himself, the blinded prince, calling to mind that Poseidón had promised him the accomplish-

---

[1] Those who would assign a historic foundation to the wild and fanciful fictions of ancient poets, tell us that Persephoné was wife to Aïdóneus king of the Molossians that his dog was called Kerberos, who tore Peirithoos to pieces, etc. We have already expressed our dissent from this tasteless mode of procedure.

ment of whatever wish he should first form, cursed and implored destruction on his son from the god. As Hippolytos, on leaving Trœzén, where Théseus and his family then resided, was driving his chariot along the sea-shore, a monster sent by Poseidón from the deep terrified his horses; they burst away in fury, heedless of their driver, dashed the chariot to pieces, and dragged along Hippolytos entangled in the reins, till life abandoned him. Phædra ended her days by her own hand; and Théseus, when too late, learned the innocence of his son.[1]

The invasion of Attica by Kastór and Polydeukés, to avenge the carrying off of their sister, and an insurrection of the Pallantids, brought on Théseus the usual fate of all great Athenians,—exile. He voluntarily retired to Lykomédés, king of the island of Skyros, and there he met with his death, either by accident or by the treachery of his host: for ascending with Lykomédés a lofty rock, to take a view of the island, he fell or was pushed off by his companion, and lost his life by the fall. The Athenians honoured his memory by feasts and temples, placed him among the gods, and called their city the town of Théseus.

We will now pursue the explanation of the legendary history of Attica from the time of Kekrops.

It is not necessary for us, we presume, to set about proving that king *Rocky* or *Hilly* (Kranaos), his wife *Plain* (Pedias) and his daughter *Attica* (Atthis) are not historic personages. It is equally needless to show that Amphiktyón, or rather Amphiktión,—the personification of the people who dwelt about (*ἀμφικτίονες*) Thermopylæ, and were united for a common political and religious object,—could not have been a real person, much

---

[1] See the *Hippolytos* of Euripidés and also the noble *Phèdre* of Racine. The circumstance of women accusing those who have refused their favours is common to the history and the fable of most countries. The earliest instance on record is that of Joseph and Potiphar's wife; and, under the names of Yúsuf and Zúleikha, their adventure is the theme of romance over the Mohammedan East. The stories of Péleus, Bellerophontés, Hippolytos, Tennes and Muenos (Plut. *de Fluv.* 8), occurs as we may perceive in Grecian mythology, and those of Sir Lanval (*Fairy Mythology,* i. p. 54, p. 35 new edit.) and of Tristan and Belinda (Tristan de Leonnois) are to be found in the romance of the middle ages. The case most similar to the present occurs in the Persian Sháh-Námeh, where Siyawush the son of Ky Káús, king of Persia, is, on rejecting the amorous advances of his stepmother Súdabeh, accused by her to his father; but the gallant youth clears himself by going through the ordeal of fire, riding in golden helm and snowy raiment between the flaming piles, kindled by two hundred men. Another case is that of the sons of Camar-er-remán, in the *Thousand and One Nights.*

less a king of Attica. We will therefore commence with Erich-thonios or Erechtheus, whom the more ancient tradition viewed as the first Attic king.

We have seen how entirely Kekrops and his family belong to the worship of Pallas-Athéné. Beside this goddess, the symbol of the mild celestial heat, the ancient people of Attica adored Héphæstos, the terrestrial fire or heat which was the origin of metallurgy; Hermés, the deity who wrought within the earth, giving increase to fruits and cattle; and Poseidón, the great nourishing principle of water. These are the only deities whom we find noticed in the early Attic mythes.

The two kings Erechtheus and Erichthonios are, as we shall now endeavour to show, the same person, and in reality nothing more than the name by which Poseidón was worshipped on the Akropolis. It is well known that none but the ancient deities of the nation ever had temples or altars on the Akropolis; but we find that a part of the temple of Athéna-Polias was named the Erechtheion, and was sacred to Erechtheus, and that in it there were altars of Héphæstos, Butés and Poseidón, on which last sacrifices were made to Erechtheus.[1] In this temple also was the well of salt water which Poseidón was said to have produced with his trident; and it was called the Erechthean Sea.[2] That Erichthonios and Erechtheus were the same, appears from this, that Homer and Hésiod tell of the latter what others relate of the former. In fact Erechtheus is only the abbreviated form of the name, which signifies *Earth-shaker*.[3] It need not surprise us to find this deity, when made a hero, assigned the origins above related. It is probable also that in the ancient legend there was a *Holy Marriage* (ἱερὸς γάμος) of Héphæstos and Athéna,[4] the terrestrial and celestial heat, of which the off-spring may have been represented as a serpent-formed son (Eri-chthonios), that is, the tender twining-plant[5] which proceeds from the seed, and of which the care was committed to the sisters *Dew* and *Field-dwelling*, or *Bright-one*, i.e. which was nourished by dew and by the mild influence of the bright moon. The other circumstances of the legend may be referred to the imagin-

---

[1] Paus. i. 26, 5.

[2] Θάλασσα ᾽Ερεχθηῖς. Apollod. iii. 14, 1: comp. Herod. viii. 55. Paus. *ut sup.* Another name of this well was ἡ κλεψύδρα, Sch. *Aristoph. Birds*, 1693.

[3] ᾽Ερεχθοχθόνιος, from ἐρέχθω to shake, and χθὼν earth, softened on account of the aspirates to ᾽Εριχθόνιος, and then reduced to ᾽Ερεχθεύς, Kenrick, *ut sup.* Tzetzés (*Lyc.* 156, 158) calls Poseidón Erechtheus, παρὰ τὸ ἐρέχθω, τὸ κινῶ.— Athénagoras says (*Leg.* 1), ῾Ο δὲ ᾽Αθηναῖος ᾽Ερεχθεῖ Ποσειδῶνι θύει: and Phavorinus, ᾽Ερεχθεύς, Ποσειδῶν ἐν ᾽Αθήναις.   [4] Cic. *De Nat. Deor.* iii. 22.

[5] By a derivation of Erichthonios from ερι or ἔρα, and χθών: see above, p. 9.

ation of those who took on them to embellish and extend it, and to the freaks of etymology in which the ancients found such pleasure in indulging. The ascribing to Erichthonios the invention of the four-horse chariot, is a confirmation of his identity with Poseidón; and it may be observed, that his Trojan namesake was renowned for his stud.[1]

But, as we may see, there was another hero who had an altar in the temple of Athéna Polias, namely Butés, the brother of Erechtheus and *eponymus* of the sacerdotal Butads,[2] and according to the preceding analogy he also must have been a deity. In him then we view the Attic god answering to the Arkadian Hermés. His own name plainly signifies the *feeder*;[3] that of his wife is Chthonia. Hermés has in the usual way taken his place in the legends.

It may be that Pandíon is indebted for his Attic royalty to his part in the mythe of the nightingale and the swallow,[4] which was perhaps only appropriated by the Athenians, like that of Oreithyia, and possibly that of Kephalos and Prokris, though this last (and indeed the former also) seems to be a genuine Attic mythe. As for Kekrops II. and Pandíon II., they are manifestly employed merely to establish a connexion between the Erechtheids and Théseus; and Pylos would probably never have been king of Megara, if the Néleids of Pylos had not come to Attica at the time of the Dórian Migration.

We are now to consider Ión, the personification of the Iónians. The mythe above noticed was evidently devised to account for the abode of this tribe in Attica, where their settlement was probably effected by conquest. Whence they came is uncertain; but the name of the Iónian sea would seem to place their original abode on the north coast of the Peloponnése.[5] As Ión is the son of Apóllo (for Xuthos is apparently nothing more than an epithet of that god),[6] they are to be regarded as the introducers of the worship of Apólló into Attica, where it seems to have been originally confined to the military class. The name Kreúsa (*Princess*) in this legend (like it and Kréon (*Prince*) in so many others), shows that it was a mere fiction and did not speak of real persons.

Lykos, Pallas and Nisos, the sons of Pandíon, have as little claim to reality as any of the others. As the Lykeion at Athens

---

[1] *Il.* xx. 221.   [2] See above, p. 338.   [3] From ΒΟ'Ω, βόσκω.
[4] Pandíon, i. e. *All-divine* or *All-bright*, or rather *All-illumining* (see above, pp. 15, 47), may be the sun of spring, or that season itself, when these birds appear.
[5] Mr. Kenrick's derivation of this name is very plausible;—'Ηιονία, 'Ιηονία, 'Ιαονία, the *sea-coast*.   [6] Ξούθος, *yellow-haired*, is the same as ξανθός.

was said to have been named from Lykos, and there was on it a
temple of Apolló Lykios,[1] it is not unlikely that the god and the
prince were the same person. Pallas may in like manner have
been connected with the patron-goddess of the city.[2] The port of
Megara (or perhaps the peninsula which formed it) was named
Nisæa,[3] and thence probably was derived the name of the king
Nisos. The story of him and his daughter Skylla is one of the
many tales of maidens betraying their parents and country for
love of lucre. We shall find the tale repeated in Pteriláos and
Komæthó, and every one has heard of the Roman Tarpeia.[4]

Ægeus is plainly only another name for Poseidón, who was
also named Ægæos[5] and Ægæón.[6] In fact it was also said that
Poseidón was the father of Théseus,[7] who comes from Trœzén
(where Poseidón was the guardian-god—πολιοῦχος), and clears
the Isthmos (which was sacred to that god) of monsters and
evil-doers. We also find that Théseus was worshiped on the
eighth day of the month, which was the sacred day of Poseidón.[8]
There seems to have been a distinction between the ancient
Poseidón-Erechtheus of the agricultural Pelasgic people of Attica
and the Poseidón-Ægeus of the Iónians, to whom Théseus evidently belongs, the latter being regarded more as the god of the
sea and of navigation, corresponding with the more active military character of the Iónian race. In proof of Théseus being
of this race, we may observe that he seems to be rather in opposition with the ancient deities of the place. Some of the evil-doers
whom he slays are sons of Héphæstos; and though the veneration
of the Athenians for their guardian-goddess, and that analogy
which did not admit of enmity between the ruling deity and the
hero of the place, prevented Athéna's being viewed as hostile to

---

[1] Paus. i. 19, 3.

[2] We are also told of a giant Pallas, from whom the goddess derived her
name; and in the Ægeus of Sophoklés,

.... τῆς δὲ γῆς τὸ πρὸς νότον
ὁ σκληρὸς οὗτος καὶ γίγαντας ἐκτρέφων
εἴληχε Πάλλας,

is said of this son of Pandíon.

[3] Νισαία is plainly the same as νησαία.

[4] The daughter of the governor of the castle of Abydos thus betrayed it to
the Turks. In the Sháh-Námeh, Meliketh (*Princess*), daughter of an Arab
chief, delivers up himself and his castle to Sháh-púr, with whom she had
fallen in love. Eutychius (p. 368) tells the same of another Arab princess
who delivered up her father's castle to Ardshír the first of the Sassanians.

[5] Pherekýdés, *ap. Sch. Apoll. Rh.* i. 831.

[6] Kallim. *Fr.* (Bentl.) 103. Lyc. *Cass* 135. Hesychius and Phavorinu
s. v. See Appendix D.   [7] Eur. *Hip.* 887, 1169.

[8] Plut. *Thēs.* 36. See Müller, *Proleg.* 271, 272.

him, we may perceive that he is almost the only hero whom she does not assist. In the mythology of Théseus we only meet with the Iónian deities Poseidón and Apolló.

Théseus, whose name signifies the *Orderer* or *Regulator*, can only then be regarded as an imaginary person. Being however the patron-hero of the people among whom literature flourished most, he is presented to us under a more historic aspect than the other heroes.[1] Though his adventures are manifestly formed on those of Héraklés, whom he is said to have emulated, we are struck by the absence of the marvellous in them; for if we except the descent to Erebos, they are hardly more wonderful than those of the Messénian Aristomenés. The poem which recorded them was apparently of no great merit, and the history of Théseus yielded few subjects to the Attic dramatists. When they brought him on the stage it was scarcely ever as the principal character of the piece. He always however appears as the model of a just and moderate ruler, the example of a strict obedience to the dictates of law and equity, the protector of the suppliant, the scourge of the evil-doer, and the author of wise and good regulations. In the spirit of casting splendour on actual political relations by throwing them back to the mythic ages, the dramatists and orators of Athens did not hesitate to make Théseus the founder of the democracy!

Δαίδαλος καὶ Ἴκαρος. *Dœdalus et Icarus.*

Dædalos was the son of Eupalamos, son of Métión, son of Erechtheus: he was celebrated for his skill in architecture and statuary, of which latter art he was regarded as the inventor. His nephew, named Talós, showed a great genius for mechanics; having, from the contemplation of a serpent's teeth, invented a saw, and applied it to the cutting up of timber. He is also said to have invented the compass. Dædalos, jealous of the skill, and apprehensive of the rivalry of the young man, cast him down from the Akropolis and killed him.[2] For this murder he was banished by the court of Areiopagos, and he betook himself to Minós king of Kréte, for whom he built the Labyrinth. He also devised an ingenious species of dance for Ariadné the daughter of that monarch;[3] but having formed the wooden cow

---

[1] Homer never mentions him, for *Il.* i. 265 and *Od.* xi. 630 are Attic interpolations.

[2] Apollod. iii. 15. Ov. *Met.* 236 *seq.* This last writer says that the nephew of Dædalos was changed into a bird of his own name, Perdix; while the former names him Talós, and says that Perdix was the name of his mother.

[3] *Il.* xviii. 590.

2 A

for Pasiphaé, he incurred the displeasure of the king, and was thrown into prison. Having by means of Pasiphaé escaped from confinement, he determined to fly from Kréte; but being unable to get away by sea, he resolved to attempt flight through the air. He made wings of feathers united by wax for himself and his son Ikaros. With these they mounted into the air; but Ikaros ascending too high, and approaching too near the sun, its heat melted the wax, and the youth fell into the sea and was drowned. Dædalos arrived in safety in Sicily, where he was kindly received by Kókalos king of that island, who took up arms in his defence against Minós when he pursued him thither.[1]

Dædalos, as his own name (which perhaps was merely an epithet of Héphæstos)[2] and those of his progenitors show, was a personification of manual art.[3] He was the Eponymos of the class of Dædalids or statuaries at Athens, and there were various wooden statues ·preserved till late times, and said to be the work of his hands. Ikaros[4] was a suitable name for his son, and the resemblance between it and the name of the Ikarian sea probably gave occasion to the legend of the flight through the air.

CHAPTER VI.

MYTHES OF CORINTH.

THE ancient name of Corinth was said to have been Ephyra, so called from one of the Ocean-nymphs.[5] Its situation rendered it in the earliest times a place of great commerce, for it was the thoroughfare between Hellas and the Peloponnése; and as it had a port on each sea, the wares of the East and the West usually passed through it, the voyage round cape Malea being considered so very dangerous. As might be expected, the principal object of worship at Corinth was the god of the sea. Poseidón and Hélios, said the legend, once contended for the

---

[1] Apollod. ut sup. Ov. Met. viii. 183 seq. Diodór. iv. 76, 77. Hygin. 39, 40.

[2] The root δαίω is to kindle, burn, also to cut, distribute ; while ΔΑ'Ω is to teach or learn.

[3] The resemblance between Dædalos and Völlundr the artist of Scandinavian mythology is very striking : see Tales and Popular Fictions, p. 270 seq. Völlundr's name also signifies, ingenious, crafty.

[4] From εἴκω, like εἰκών, ἴκελος.   [5] Eumélos ap. Paus. ii. 1, 1.

possession of the land; Briareós was chosen arbitrator, and he assigned the Isthmos to the former, the Akrocorinth or Akropolis to the latter.[1] We shall therefore find the Corinthian legends relating chiefly to trade and navigation.

Σίσυφος. Sisyphus.

Sisyphos, the son of Æolos, was said to be the founder of Ephyra. He married Merope the daughter of Atlas, by whom he had four sons, Glaukos, Ornytión, Thersandros and Halmos.[2]

When Zeus carried off Ægína the daughter of Asópos, the river-god in his search after her came to Corinth. Sisyphos, on his giving him a spring for the Akrocorinth, informed him who the ravisher was. The king of the gods sent Death to punish the informer; but Sisyphos contrived to outwit Death, and even to put fetters on him; and there was great joy among mortals, for no one died. Hadés however set Death at liberty, and Sisyphos was given up to him. When dying he charged his wife to leave his body unburied; and then complaining to Hadés of her unkindness, he obtained permission to return to the light to upbraid her with her conduct. But when he found himself again in his own house, he refused to leave it. Hermés however reduced him to obedience; and when he came down, Hadés set him to roll a huge stone up a hill, a never ending still beginning toil, for as soon as it reached the summit it rolled back again down to the plain.[3]

The craft of Sisyphos, of which the following is an instance, was proverbial. Autolykos the son of Hermés, the celebrated cattle-stealer, who dwelt on Parnassos, used to deface the marks of the cattle which he carried off in such a manner as to render it nearly impossible to identify them. Among others he drove off those of Sisyphos, and he defaced the marks as usual; but when Sisyphos came in quest of them, he, to the great surprise of the thief, selected his own beasts out of the herd; for he had marked the initial of his name under their hoofs.[4] Autolykos forthwith cultivated the acquaintance of one who had thus proved himself too able for him; and Sisyphos, it is said, seduced or

---

[1] Paus. ii. 1, 6. As Briareós was also called Ægæón (*Il.* i. 403), he is here probably Poseidón himself.

[2] Paus. ii. 4, 3.

[3] Pherekýdés (*ap. Sch. Il.* vi. 153; *Sch. Soph. Aj.* 625). Sch. *Pind. Ol.* i. 60 (97). Theognis, 702 *seq.*

[4] The ancient form of the Σ was C, which is of the shape of a horse's hoof, a form which it still retains in the Coptic and Russian alphabets.

violated his daughter Antikleia (who afterwards married Laertés), and thus was the real father of Odysseus.[1]

Homer calls Sisyphos 'the most crafty of men;'[2] Hésiod speaks of him in a similar manner;[3] Odysseus sees him rolling his stone in Erebos.[4] Of the antiquity of his legend there can therefore be little doubt.

Sisyphos, that is the *Very-wise*, or perhaps the *Over-wise*,[5] seems to have originally belonged to that exalted class of mythes in which we find the Iapetids, Ixíon, Tantalos and Tityos, where, under the character of persons with significant names, lessons of wisdom, morality and religion were sensibly impressed on the minds of men. Sisyphos is then the representative of the restless desire of knowledge, which aspires to attain a height it is denied to man to reach, and exhausted in the effort falls suddenly back into the depths of earthly weakness. This is expressed in the fine picture of the Odyssey, where every word is significant, and where we may observe Sisyphos is spoken of in indefinite terms, and not assigned any earthly locality or parentage.[6]

In the legendary history however we find him placed at Corinth, and apparently the representative of the trading spirit of that city. He is a son of Æolos, probably on account of his name[7] (in conformity with a very usual practice in antiquity); or it may be that the crafty trader is the son of the *Windman*,[8] as the wind enables him to import and export his merchandise. He is married to a daughter of the symbol of navigation, Atlas, and her name would seem to indicate that he is engaged with men in the active business of life.[9] His children are Glaukos, a name of the sea-god, Ornytión (*Quick-mover*), Thersandros (*Warm-man*) and Halmos (*Seaman*), who apparently denote the fervour and bustle of commerce.[10]

The legends above narrated probably have their sole origin in the name of Sisyphos.

---

[1] Pherekýdés *ap. Sch. Od.* xix. 432. Sch. *Il.* x. 267. Tzetz. *Lyc.* 344. Eudocia, 375. Æsch. *Fr.* 162. Soph. *Aj.* 190. Sch. *in loc. Philokt.* 625.

[2] *Il.* vi. 153.   [3] *Fr.* 23.   [4] *Od.* xi. 593.

[5] Σίσυφος *quasi* Σι-σοφος, by a common reduplication.

[6] See Welcker, *Tril.* 550.

[7] Αἴόλος, *cunning.* Hésiod calls Sisyphos αἰολόμητις.

[8] See *Od.* x. 1 *seq.* The primary meaning of αἴόλος is *swift*; probably from ἄω, *to blow.*

[9] Μέροπες, *mortals*, from μόρος *death*; οψ is a mere adjectival ending: see above, p. 15.

[10] For all the subjects here touched on see Welcker *in Schwenk*, 320 *seq. Tril.* 550 *seq.* Völcker, *Myth. der Jap.* 118 *seq.*

Βελλεροφόντης. *Bellerophon.*

The adventures of this hero, the son of Glaukos the son of Sisyphos, form a pleasing episode of the Ilias,[1] where they are related to Diomédes by Glaukos the grandson of Bellerophontés.

The gods had endowed Bellerophontés with manly vigour and beauty. Anteia, the wife of Prœtos king of Argos, fixed her love upon him, and sought a corresponding return. But the virtuous youth rejecting all her amorous advances, hate occupied the place of love in the bosom of the disappointed queen. She accused him to Prœtos of an attempt on her honour. The credulous king gave ear to her falsehood, but would not incur the reproach of putting him to death, as she desired. He therefore sent Bellerophontés to Lykia, to his father-in-law the king of that country, giving him 'deadly characters' written in a sealed tablet,[2] which he was to present to the king of Lykia, and which were to cause his death.

Under the potent guidance of the gods Bellerophontés came to Lykia and the flowing Xanthos. Nine days the king entertained him, and slew nine oxen; 'but when the tenth rose-fingered Dawn appeared,' he asked to see the *token* (σῆμα) which he had brought from his son-in-law. When he had received it, he resolved to comply with the desire of Prœtos; and he first sent his guest to slay the Chimæra, a monster with the upper part a lion, the lower a serpent, the middle a goat (χίμαιρα), and which breathed forth flaming fire. Depending on the signs of the gods, Bellerophontés slew this monster, and then was ordered to go and fight the Solymians; and this he said was the severest combat he ever fought. He lastly slew the 'man-like Amázons'; and as he was returning the king laid an ambush for him, composed of the bravest men of Lykia; of whom not one returned home, for Bellerophontés slew them all. The king now perceiving him to be of the race of the gods, kept him in Lykia, giving him his daughter and half the royal dignity, and the people bestowed on him an ample *temenos* of arable and plantation land. By this princess Bellerophontés had three children, Isandros, Hippolochos, and Laodameia; which last was by Zeus the mother of Sarpédón. Falling at length under the displeasure of all the gods, 'he wandered alone in the Plain

---

[1] *Il.* vi. 144 *seq.* The genuineness of this episode is doubted of by Böttiger: see Völcker, *Myth. der Jap.* 118 *note*, and Appendix H.

[2] It is a disputed point whether these characters were letters, or of the same kind with the Mexican picture-writing: see Wolf's *Prolegomena to Homer*, p. lxxxi. *seq.*

of Wandering (πεδίον ἀλήϊον), consuming his soul, shunning the path of men.

Later authorities tell us[1] that Bellerophontés was at first named Hipponoos: but having accidentally killed one of his relatives named Belleros, he thence derived his second name. He was purified of the bloodshed by Prœtos, whose wife is also called Sthenobœa, and the king of Lykia is named Ióbatés. By the aid of the winged steed Pégasos Bellerophontés gained the victory over all whom Ióbatés sent him to encounter, and Sthenobœa, on hearing of his success, hung herself. Bellerophontés at last attempted by means of Pégasos to ascend to heaven: Zeus, incensed at his boldness, sent an insect to sting the steed; and he flung his rider to the earth, where he wandered in solitude and melancholy till his death.

Though Homer makes no mention of Pégasos, this steed forms an essential part of the mythe of Bellerophontés. In the Theogony it is said of the Chimæra that she was killed by Pégasos and the 'good (ἐσθλὸς) Bellerophontés.'[2] But though all seem agreed in giving the winged steed to the hero, no one tells us how he obtained him. Here however Pindar comes to our aid with a very remarkable legend, which connects Bellerophontés with Corinth—and it is the only account that really does so— and furnishes us with a key to this mythe.

According to this poet,[3] Bellerophontés, who reigned at Corinth, being about to undertake the three adventures above mentioned, wished to possess the winged steed Pégasos, who was wont to come to drink at the fount of Peiréné on the Akrocorinth. After many fruitless efforts to catch him he applied for advice to the soothsayer Polyeidos, and was directed by him to go and sleep at the altar of Athéna. He obeyed the prophet, and in the dead of the night the goddess appeared in a dream to him, and giving him a bridle bade him sacrifice a bull to his sire Poseidón-Damæos (Tamer), and present the bridle to the steed. On awaking, Bellerophontés found the bridle lying beside him. He obeyed the injunctions of the goddess, and raised an altar to her as Hippia (Of-the-Horse). Pégasos at once yielded his mouth to the magic bit, and the hero mounting him achieved his adventures.

---

[1] Pind. Isth. vii. 44 (63) seq.   Apollod. ii. 3.   Hygin. ·57.   Id. Poet. Astr. ii. 18.   Sch. Il. vi. 155.   Tzetz. Lyc. 17.

[2] Theog. 325. Ἐσθλὸς and ἀγαθὸς in the old Greek poets answer exactly to the good of the romances of chivalry, where the good knight is the brave knight. Κράτιστος and ἄριστος are among the superlatives of ἀγαθός.

[3] Ol. xiii. 60 (85) seq.

We do not well see how this narrative can be made to accord with the Homéric tale, which was however known to Pindar; for there is not the slightest allusion in it to Prœtos and Anteia, or to Lykia, and the hero apparently sets out on his adventures from Corinth. It would not therefore surprise us if the ancient form of the legend has been that a prince of Corinth had, by the aid of a winged horse, ridden through the air, and achieved adventures in various parts of the world.

But in reality the foundation of this mythe lies still deeper. In Bellerophontés we have only one of the forms of Poseidón, namely as Hippios. This god we have seen is his father;[1] and he is also the sire of Pégasos;[2] and in the two combined we have a Poseidón-Hippios, the rider of the waves,—a symbol of the navigation of the ancient Éphyra. The adventures of the hero may have signified the real or imaginary perils to be encountered in voyages to distant countries; and when the original sense of the mythe was lost, the *King* (Prœtos, πρῶτος), and his wife *Foe* (Anteia, from ἄντα),[3] and the common love-tale were introduced to assign a cause for the adventures.

In this mythe too we find that mysterious connexion between Poseidón and Pallas-Athéné and the horse more fully revealed than elsewhere. These deities are the parents of Pégasos (for Athéna and Medusa are the same), that is, probably of the ship;[4] and *he* is worshipped as the *Tamer* (δαμαῖος), *she* as the *Bridler* (χαλινῖτις).[5] The goddess was evidently viewed here in her moral capacity as the patroness of the arts, just as she was represented as superintending the building of the Argó.

Bellerophontés is a name, if possible, more enigmatic than Argeiphontés and Persephoné. It is probably derived from some word of which no traces are now to be found.[6]

---

[1] Pind. *ut sup.* 69 (99). Sch. *Il.* vi. 155. Glaukos is, like Ægeus, an epithet of the sea-god. [2] See above, p. 223.

[3] Like Antæos, above, p. 320. Or, more probably, *Entreater, Solicitor*, from ἀντιάω.

[4] In the *Theogony*, v. 282, it is said,

Τῷ μὲν ἐπώνυμον ἦν ὅτ' ἄρ' Ὠκεανοῦ περὶ π η γ ὰ ς γενθ'.

t may however be derived as well from ΠΗ ΓΩ, πηγνῦμι, to *construct* or *uild*: see above, p. 9. So in the Hebrew *ssce* (צִי), a ship, is derived from *sáwá* (צָוָה), to set up, to build.

[5] There was a temple of Athéna under this name at Corinth, Paus. ii. 4, 1, ; and Poseidón was there named Damæos. Sch. *Pind. Ol.* xiii. 68 (98). It s rather remarkable that a *ship* on which the *peplos* was hung formed a part f the Panathénaïc procession at Athens: see Philostr. *De Vit. Phil.* ii. 1 ch. *Aristoph. Equit.* 563.

[6] According to Eustathius and others τὰ ἔλλερα are τὰ κικα.

CHAPTER VII.

MYTHES OF ARGOLIS.

THE chief seat of the legendary lore of the Peloponnése was the Argolic peninsula; and here we meet with a mythic cycle totally distinct from those of Hellas Proper. The great patriarch of the latter was Deukalión, whose posterity were brought into connexion with the Kadmeians of Thébes and the Erechtheids of Attica, and to whom the principal legends of the north and west of the Peloponnése also refer. The Argive mythic history commences with the river Inachos and his son Phoróneus. It is, moreover, in this cycle alone that we find an attempt at connecting Greece and Egypt in the mythic period; for, as we have shown above, the Egyptian origin of the Attic Kekrops is an historic *sophism*, and not a mythic tradition.

Ἴναχος καὶ Φορωνεύς.   Inachus et Phoroneus.

Inachos, a son of O'keanos and Téthys, married his sister the O'keanis Melia, by whom he had a son named Phoróneus,[1] the first man according to one tradition, while another makes him collect the rude inhabitants into society and give them fire and social institutions.[2]   He also decided a dispute for the land between Héra and Poseidón in favour of the former, who thence became the tutelar deity of Argos.[3]   By the nymph Laodiké Phoróneus had a son named Apis, from whom the peninsula was named Apia; and a daughter Niobé, the first mortal woman who enjoyed the love of Zeus. Her offspring by the god were Argos and Pelasgos, and the country was named from the former, the people from the latter.

Nothing can be more simple than this genealogy. The principal river of the place is the parent or origin of the first man Phoróneus, that is, the *Rearer* or *Feeder*,[4] the introducer of the worship of the productive earth [Héra], and of agriculture and social institutions.   One of his children is an ancient or poetic name of the peninsula; the other is the *young* land blooming with verdure,[5] to whom the people and country or town are

---

[1] Apollod. ii. 1, 1.

[2] Paus. ii. 15, 5.   Like Húsheng in the romantic annals of Persia.

[3] Id. *ib.*   The river-gods Inachos, Képhisos, and Asterión were his assessors and Poseidón in revenge caused them all to fail in dry weather.

[4] From φέρω, φέρβω, *to feed.*   Welcker *in Schwenk*, 299.   It is similar in form and in signification to Trophónios.   [5] See above, p. 199.

given for offspring. We conceive it hardly possible for any one versed in mythology to see real persons here.

Ἄργος. *Argus.*

Among the descendants of Phoróneus we meet with another Argos named *All-seeing* (πανόπτης), as having eyes all over his body. His strength was prodigious: and Arkadia being at that time infested by a wild bull, he attacked and slew him, and afterwards wore his hide. He moreover killed a satyr, who carried off the cattle of the Arkadians; and watching an opportunity, when he found the Echidna (the daughter of Tartaros and Earth, who seized all passers-by) asleep, he deprived her of life: he also took vengeance on the murderers for the death of Apis. When Ió had been changed into a cow, Héra gave the charge of watching her to Argos.[1]

Ἰώ. *Io.*

Ió, the daughter of Iasos,[2] was priestess of Héra,[3] and unhappily for her she was loved by Zeus. When he found his amour suspected by Héra, he changed Ió into a white cow, and swore to his spouse that he had been guilty of no infidelity. The goddess, affecting to believe him, asked the cow of him as a present; and on obtaining her, set all-seeing Argos[4] to watch her. He bound her to an olive-tree in the grove of Mykénæ,[5] and there kept guard over her. Zeus, pitying her, directed Hermés to steal her away. The god of ingenious devices made the attempt; but as a vulture always gave Argos warning of his projects, he found it impossible to succeed. Nothing then remaining but open force, he killed Argos with a stone, and hence obtained the name of *Argos-slayer* (Ἀργειφόντης). The vengeance of Héra was however not yet satiated; and she sent a gad-fly to torment Ió, who fled over the whole world from its pursuits. She swam through the Iónian Sea, which derived its name from her; then roamed over the plains of Illyricum, ascended Mount Hæmos, crossed the Thrakian strait, thence named the Bosporos, rambled on through Skythia and the country of the Kimmerians; and, after wandering over various regions of Europe, and Asia, arrived at last on the banks of the Nile, where,

---

[1] Apollod. *ut sup.*   [2] Or, as the dramatists said, of Inachos.
[3] Æsch. *Sup.* 291.
[4] Akusiláos and Æschylos (*Sup.* 305) call him *Earth born.*
[5] The name resembling μυκάω, *to low.* Another legend derived it from the bellowing of the Gorgons when in pursuit of Perseus: see Sch. *Il.* xv. 302. Sch. *Od.* ii. 120. Paus. ii. 16, 3.

touched by Zeus, she resumed her original form and bore a **son** named Epaphos.[1]

The legend of Ió would not appear to have attracted so much of the attention of the older poets as might have been expected. Homer never alludes to it, unless his employment of the term Argeiphontés is to be regarded as intimating a knowledge of Ió. It is also doubtful if she was one of the heroines of the E'œæ. Her story however was noticed in the Ægimios, where it was said that her father's name was Peirén, that her keeper Argos had four eyes, and that the isle of Eubœa derived its name from her.[2] Pherekýdés[3] said that Héra placed an eye in the back of Argos' neck and deprived him of sleep, and then set him as a guard over Ió. Æschylos introduces Ió in his *Prométheus Bound*, and he also relates her story in his *Suppliants*.

The general opinion respecting Ió seems to be that she is the moon, and Argos the starry heaven, which, as it were, keeps ceaseless watch over her; her wanderings are thought to denote the continual revolutions of this planet.[4] In confirmation of this theory, we are assured that in the dialect of Argos Ió signified *moon*;[5] and in proof of the Egyptian theory, presently to be noticed, it is added, that Ió has the same signification in Koptic.[6]

This hypothesis appears to us to be more ingenious than true. Analogy would lead us to view in Ió a form of the Argive goddess Héra, with whom she is so closely connected; in which case as Héra is the earth, Ió cannot well be the moon.[7] Ió and Héra in this legend seem to stand to each other in the same relation as Kallistó and Artemis in one hereafter to be related: in both the nymph is an epithet of the goddess,[8] in both the

---

[1] Æsch. *Prom.* 640 *seq.* *Sup.* 291 *seq.* Apollod. *ut sup.* Ov. *Met.* i. 583 *seq.* Val. Flac. iv. 351 *seq.*

[2] See Apollod. ii. 1, 3. Sch. *Eurip. Phœn.* 1115. Steph. Byz. *v.* 'Αβαντίς.

[3] *Ap.* Sch. *Eurip. ut sup.*

[4] See Welcker, *Tril.* 127 *seq.* *Errantem lunam*, Verg. *Æn.* i. 742 ; *vaga luna*, Hor. *Sat.* i. 8, 21.

> To behold the *wandering* moon
> Riding near her highest noon,
> Like one that had been *led astray*
> Through the heaven's wide pathless way.—*Milton.*

[5] Hesych. and Suidas, *v.* 'Ιώ.   [6] Jablonski, *Panth. Ægypt.* ii. 4 *seq.*

[7] Neither is Isis the moon. See above, p. 200.

[8] Ió is perhaps derived from 'ΙΕ'Ω, ἵημι, *to send*, an epithet of Héra the earth-goddess, as the *sender-up* of vegetation : see above, p. 15. Those who make Ió the moon deduce it from ἴω, εἶμι, *to go*. Buttmann (*Mythol.* ii. 178 *seq.*) makes it the feminine of Ión, and the personification of the Iónian race.

love of Zeus is the cause of offence, in both the nymph is changed by the goddess into her sacred animal.[1] Argos is probably merely the *dog*[2] set to watch the cow; and Hermés the rural god kills him, as dogs are driven off or killed by the country-people. A gad-fly then persecutes the cow, and she runs wild all through the country. Such was perhaps the original simple legend, and it may have had its source in the notions of the loves, the marriages, the jealousies related of Héra.

The wanderings of Ió were gradually extended. The name of the Iónian sea caused her to be made to ramble along its shore; when Byzantion was founded, there were Argives among the colonists, who carried with them their domestic legends, and in honour of Ió they named the adjacent strait Bosporos (*Cowford*), feigning that she had swum across it.[3] A similar strait into the Mæótis received the same name, and Ió of course had wandered thither. Finally, when the Greeks first settled in Egypt and saw the statues of Isis with cow's horns, they in their usual manner inferred that she was their own Ió, with whose name hers had a slight similarity. At Memphis they afterwards beheld the worship of the holy calf Apis, and naturally supposing the calf-god to be the son of the cow-goddess, they formed from him a son for their Ió, whose name was the occasion of a new legend of the mode of her being restored to her pristine form.[4] And now the wanderings of Ió were extended to Egypt as their ultimate limit.

Δάναος καὶ Αἴγυπτος. *Danaus et Ægyptus.*

Epaphos, the son of Ió, is the instrument by which Grecian vanity derived the rulers of more ancient countries from its own gods and princes. He married, we are told, Memphis the daughter of the Nile, by whom he had a daughter named Libya, who bore to Poseidón Agénór the father of Kadmos and Európé,

---

[1] Ió was transformed by Héra. Æsch. *Sup.* 299. Zeus, it is added, then assumed the form of a bull. If Ió be the earth this legend has a resemblance to that of Danaé.

[2] Argos is the name of Odysseus' dog (*Od.* xvii. 292), and of one of Actæón's hounds (Apollod. iii. 4, 4. Hygin. 181). [3] Müller, *Proleg.* 131.

[4] See Müller, *Proleg.* 183, 184. Apis, he observes, with the Koptic article *Pe* prefixed (that is, Pe-Apis), was easily changed into Epaphos, which signified the *Touched.* It is well known how fond people are of turning foreign words into such as have a signification in their own language. Thus the Italians named Sir John Hawkwood the *condottiere Aguto,* and the Frank king Pharamond (Wahrmund) *Fieramonte;* our own ancestors made from Livorno *Leghorn,* and from La Coruña *The Groine;* we have heard the island of Sainte-Croix called *Sandy Crocks.* To these we may add *Beefeater* and *Sparrowgrass, Fir thingale* (Vertugalle, Fr.) and *Causeway* (Chaussée).

and Bélos, who had by another daughter of the Nile named Anchinoé two sons, Danaos and Ægyptos.[1]

Bélos assigned the country of Libya to his son Danaos; to Ægyptos he gave Arabia. The latter conquered the country of the Melampodes, and named it from himself. By many wives he was the father of fifty sons.

Danaos had by several wives an equal number of daughters. Dissension arising between him and the sons of Ægyptos, they aimed at depriving him of his dominions; and fearing their violence, he built with the aid of Athéna a fifty-oared vessel— the first that was ever made—in which he embarked with his daughters and fled over the sea. He first landed on the isle of Rhodes, where he set up a statue of the Lindian Athéna; but not willing to abide in that island, he proceeded to Argos, where Gelanór, who at that time ruled over the country, cheerfully resigned the government to the stranger who brought thither civilisation and the arts. The people took the name of their new monarch, and were called Danaans.[2]

The country of Argos being at that time extremely deficient in pure and wholesome water (Poseidón having dried up the springs),[3] Danaos sent forth his daughters in quest of some. As Amymóné, one of them, was engaged in the search, she saw a deer, at which she flung her dart; but, missing the game, the dart wounded a satyr who was sleeping in the neighbouring thicket.[4] Starting from his sleep, he beheld the beauty of the maid, and rushed toward her filled with desire. She prayed to Poseidón for aid; the god appeared, and flung his trident at the satyr, who fled; Amymóné submitted to the embraces of her deliverer, and he revealed to her the springs of Lerna.[5]

The sons of Ægyptos now came to Argos, and entreated their uncle to agree to bury in oblivion all enmity, and to give them their cousins in marriage. Danaos, retaining a perfect recollection of their injuries to him, and distrustful of their promises, consented to bestow on them his daughters, whom he divided

---

[1] The legend of Danaos and his family will be found in Apollod. ii. 1, 4. Hygin. 168–170. Sch. *Il.* i. 42; iv. 171. Sch. *Eurip. Orest.* 872.

[2] The Scholiast on Euripidés says nothing of the flight of Danaos; he seems to make Argos the original abode of the brothers.   [3] See above, p. 360, *note*[3].

[4] Æschylos wrote a satyric drama named Amymóné, hence probably the satyr in the legend. Welcker, *Nach. zur Tril.* 309.

[5] Apollod. *ut sup.* Hygin. 169. This last writer also says that Amymóné fell asleep, and while she was in that state the satyr attempted to violate her. He adds, that when Poseidón flung his trident at the satyr it stuck in a rock, and on the maiden's drawing it forth at the command of the god three streams (*silani*) of water followed it

among them by lot. But on the wedding-day he armed the hands of the brides with daggers, and enjoined them to slay in the night their unsuspecting bridegrooms. All but Hypermnéstra obeyed the cruel orders of their father; and cutting off the heads of their husbands, they flung them into Lerna, and buried their bodies with all due rites outside of the town. At the command of Zeus, Hermés and Athéna purified them from the guilt of their deed.

But Hypermnéstra had spared Lynkeus, for the delicate regard which he had shown to her modesty. Her father, at first, in his anger at her disobedience, put her into close confinement. Relenting however after some time, he gave his consent to her union with Lynkeus, and proclaimed gymnic games, in which the victors were to receive his other daughters as the prizes. It was said, however, that the crime of the Danaïdes did not pass without due punishment in the under-world, where they were condemned to draw everlastingly water in perforated vessels.[1]

The son of Amymóné by Poseidón was called Nauplios. He attained to a great age, and passed his time on the sea lamenting the fate of those who were lost in it. At length he himself met with the fate which he deplored in others.[2] He had three sons, Palamédés, Œax, and Nausimedón.

In this celebrated legend we have a very heterogeneous mixture of peoples and countries. The city of Memphis is very naturally called the daughter of the Nile, on whose banks it stood; but Libya is preposterously made the daughter and Egypt the grandson of that city, and the Phœnician god Bélos or Baal the father of Danaos and Ægyptos, *i. e.* the Argives and the Egyptians. The whole only serves to show the careless manner in which these national genealogies were fabricated.

From what has been said above respecting Kadmos, the reader, we should hope, will be prepared to regard the tale of an Egyptian colony at Argos as somewhat suspicious. In fact there was no part of Greece more thoroughly Hellénic, none which had less similarity in religion or institutions with Egypt. Moreover the origin of Danaos and his family may be easily traced to the physical character of the land.

In Homer and Hésiod Danaans is a common name of the Greeks, who are also called Argeians and Achæans. The names of nations have never, except among nomadic tribes, been derived from persons; they always come from the character of the people

---

[1] Sch. *Eurip. ut sup.* Hygin. 168. Serv. *Æn.* x 497.
[2] Apollod. *ut sup.* This is a very obscure legend.

or that of the soil.[1]　Now Argos was greatly deficieut in water (whence Homer calls it *thirsty*, πολυδίψιον), and the word δανὸs signifies *dry*. We have here then a simple derivation for the name Danaans, namely the people of the thirsty land of Argos; and in the usual manner the personification of their name is a hero, Danaos.[2]　Again, springs are *daughters of the earth*, as they are called by the Arabs; the nymphs of the springs are therefore daughters of Danaos, that is of the thirsty land.[3]　Further, a *head* (κρήνη) is a usual name for a spring in many languages, and a legendary mode of accounting for the origin of founts is to ascribe them to the *welling* forth of the blood of some person who was slain on the spot where the spring emitted its waters.[4] The number fifty is probably an arbitrary one, for we cannot discern in it a relation to the weeks of the year.[5]　It is moreover to be observed that the founts of the Inachos were in Mount Lyrkeion or Lynkeion,[6] and here perhaps lies the origin of Lynkeus, who in one form of the legend fights with and vanquishes Danaos;[7] that is, the stream from Mount Lynkeion overcomes the dry nature of the soil. We see therefore that the physical legend may have existed long before there was any intercourse with the great land of mystery, and like that of Ió have been subsequently modified so as to suit the new theory of an Egyptian colony at Argos.[8]

Προῖτος καὶ αἱ Προιτίδες.　*Prœtus et Prœtides.*

Lynkeus succeeded his father-in-law on the throne. He had by Hypermnéstra a son named Abas, to whom he left his kingdom.

[1] In Plató's *Laws* (iv. 704) it is said, respecting the name of the city to be founded, τοῦτο μὲν τάχ' ἂν ἴσως καὶ ὁ κατοικισμὸς αὐτῆς, ἤ τις τόπος, ἤ ποταμοῦ τινὸς ἤ κρήνης ἤ θεῶν ἐπωνυμία τῶν ἐν τῷ τόπῳ, προσθείη τὴν αὐτῶν φήμην καινῇ γενομένῃ τῇ πόλει. It is, we may see, not supposed that it would be named from the κατοικιστὴς or founder. Comp. Aristoph. *Birds*, 809 *seq.*

[2] Hésiod, it is said, named Danaos. Eustathius (*on Il.* iv. 171), gives as his this verse:

Ἄργος ἄνυδρον ἐὸν Δαναὸς ποίησεν ἔνυδρον.

Strabo (viii. 6, 8, p. 371) quotes the verse thus:

Ἄργος ἄνυδρον ἐὸν Δανααὶ θέσαν Ἄργος ἔνυδρον.

They discovered, he says, the four wells of the town. He does not name the poet.

[3] Four of the daughters of Danaos, namely Amymóné, Peiréné, Physadeia and Asteria were names of springs.

[4] The blood of Pentheus and Aktæón gave origin to springs on Kithærón (Philostr. *Im.* i. 14): see also Paus. ix. 33, 4, and the legend of St. Winifred's well in *Drayton's Polyolbion*, Song x. "A fountain is said to have broke out in the place where St. Osithe was beheaded, which is seen to this day near the town of Chich." *Britannia Sacra*, p. 154: see Welcker, *Tril.* 400.

[5] See Völcker, *Myth. der Jap.* 192 *seq.*

[6] Sch. *Apoll. Rh.* i. 125.　Strab. viii. 6, 7. p. 370.　　[7] Sch. *Eurip. ut sup.*

[8] Hérod. ii. 91, 171, 182: see Müller, *Orchom.* 109 *seq. Proleg.* 184 *seq.*

Abas had twin children, Prœtos and Akrisios, who struggled—ominous of their future discord—in their mother's womb. When they grew to be youths, they contended for the kingdom; and on this occasion are said to have been the inventors of shields. Prœtos was worsted, and driven out of Argos. He fled to Lykia, where the king Iobatés gave him his daughter Anteia or Stheno-bœa in marriage, and, bringing him back with an army of Lykians to the Peloponnése, made him master of Tiryns, which the Kyklópes walled for him. Akrisios was now obliged to divide their paternal territory with Prœtos: he reigned himself at Argos, and his brother dwelt at Tiryns. Prœtos had three daughters, Iphinoé, Lysippé, and Iphianassa.[1]

When these maidens grew up they were seized with insanity, and roamed in madness over the plains, the woods, the wastes of Argos and Arkadia—fancying themselves changed into cows.[2] Prœtos was greatly afflicted at the condition of his daughters. Melampus, the son of Amytháón a soothsayer, and the first who exercised the art of medicine, promised to restore them to their senses, if Prœtos would agree to give him a third of his kingdom. The demanded fee appeared out of all reason, and the father declined accepting the recovery of his daughters on such high terms. But speedily the madness of the maidens increased, and even extended to the other women, who killed their children, abandoned their houses, and fled to the wilds. The reluctance of Prœtos was now overcome: he offered to comply with the terms of Melampus; but the *mantis* would not employ his art without another third of the realm being given to his brother Bias. Prœtos now, fearing that delay would only make him advance further in his demands, consented; and the prophet set about the cure. He took a number of the ablest young men of the place, and made them with shouts and a certain inspired kind of dance chase the maidens from the mountains to Sikyón. In the chase Iphinoé, the eldest of the Prœtides, died; but the others were restored to sanity; and Prœtos gave them in marriage to Melampus and his brother Bias. He had afterwards a son named Megapenthés.[3]

The madness of the Prœtides was sung in the E'œæ, where it was ascribed to the vengeance of Dionýsos for their contempt of his rites, and he would appear to have struck them with leprosy and with inordinate lust.[4] Pherekýdés[5] and Akusiláos[6] however

[1] Apollod. *ut sup.* Sch. *Eurip. Orest.* 965.
[2] Verg. *Buc.* vi. 48. Serv. *in loco.*   [3] Apollod. *ut sup.*
[4] Apollod. *ut sup.* Eustath. *on Od.* xv. p. 1746. Suidas, *v.* μαχλοσύνη.
[5] Ap. *Sch. Od.* xv. 225.   [6] Apollod. *ut sup.*

ascribe their madness to the anger of Héra; the latter says that they made light of the statue of the goddess,—the former, that they ridiculed her temple, saying that their father's house was much finer. It was also said that they were the priestesses of the goddess and were punished by her for taking the gold off her robe and converting it to their own use.[1]

It is remarkable that the characteristic trait of their fancying themselves changed into cows is only to be found in the Latin poet Vergil. Nothing however can be more certain than that he did not invent it, and it has every appearance of being a part of the original mythe. In such case the legend of the Proetides would have a considerable analogy with that of Ió.

'Ακρίσιος, Δαναὴ, καὶ Περσεύς.   Acrisius, Danae, et Perseus.

Akrisios married Euridiké the daughter of Lakedæmón, by whom he had a daughter, whom he named Danaé. He inquired of the oracle about a son; and the god replied, that he would himself have no male issue, but that his daughter would bear a son whose hand would deprive him of life. Fearing the accomplishment of this prediction, he framed a brazen subterranean chamber,[2] in which he shut up his daughter and her nurse, in order that she might never become a mother. But Zeus had seen and loved the maiden; and under the form of a golden shower he poured through the roof down into her bosom. Danaé became the mother of a son, whom she and her nurse reared in secrecy until he had attained his fourth year. Akrisios then chanced to hear the voice of the child at his play. He brought forth his daughter and her nurse; and putting the latter instantly to death, drew Danaé in private with her son to the altar of Herkeian Zeus, where he made her answer on oath whose was her son. She replied that he was the offspring of Zeus; but her father gave no credit to her protestations. He inclosed herself and her child in a coffer and cast them into the sea to the mercy of the winds and waves.[3] The coffer floated to the little isle of Seríphos, where a man named Diktys drew it out in his nets (δίκτυα); and delivering Danaé and Perseus, treated them with the kindest attention.[4]

---

[1] Serv. ut sup.

[2] The Latin poets call it a brazen tower (turris aënea): see Hor. Carm. iii. 16, 1. Ov. Amor. ii. 19, 27. De Art. Amat. iii. 416. Claudian, In Eutrop. i. 82.

[3] See the beautiful fragment of Simónidés on the subject of Danaé.

[4] There was a legend in Italy that Ardea, the capital of the Rutulians, had been founded by Danaé. (Verg. Æn. vii. 379, 410. Serv. in locis.) It was probably caused by the resemblance between Danaé and Daunia. Daunus is the father of Turnus.

Polydektés the brother of Dik-ys, who reigned over Seríphos, fell in love with Danaé: but her son Perseus, who was now grown up, was an invincible obstacle to the accomplishment of his wishes. He had therefore recourse to artifice to deliver himself of his presence; and feigning that he was about to become a suitor to Hippodameia, the daughter of Œnomaos, he called together his vassals, and among them Perseus, to a banquet, and requested of them to contribute toward his bride-gift. Perseus inquiring what was the object of the banquet, Polydektés replied horses, and Perseus made answer that he would bring him even the head of the Gorgon. The king said nothing at the time; but next day, when the rest brought each his horse, he desired Perseus to keep his word and fetch him the Gorgon's head.

Perseus full of grief retired to the extremity of the isle, where Hermés came to him, promising that he and Athéna would be his guides. Hermés brought him first to the fair-cheeked Grææ, whose eye and tooth he stole, and would not restore until they had furnished him with directions to the abode of the Nymphs who were possessed of the winged shoes, the magic wallet, and the helmet of Hadés which made the wearer invisible. The Grææ complied with his desire, and he came unto the Nymphs, who gave him their precious possessions: he then flung the wallet over his shoulder, placed the helmet on his head, and fitted the shoes to his feet. Thus equipped, and grasping the adamantine scimitar (*harpé*) which Hermés gave him, he mounted into the air, accompanied by the gods, and flew to the Ocean, where he found the three Gorgons fast asleep.[1] Fearing to gaze on their faces, which changed the beholder to stone, he looked on the head of Medusa as it was reflected on his shield, and Athéna guiding his hand he severed it from her body. The blood gushed forth, and with it the winged steed Pégasos and Chrysáór the father of Géryoneus, for Medusa was at the time pregnant by Poseidón. Perseus took up the head, put it into his wallet, and set out on his return. The two sisters awoke, and pursued the fugitive; but protected by the helmet of Hadés he eluded their vision, and they were obliged to give over the bootless chase.[2]

Perseus pursued his aërial journey till he came to the country of the Æthiopians,[3] where he beheld Andromeda, the daughter of Képheus king of the country, fastened to a rock, a prey for a

---

[1] See p. 224.　　　　　　　　[2] Hésiod 'Aσπίς, 230 *seq.*
[3] This is probably the Æthiopia mentioned by Meneláos (*Od.* iv. 84) in the Mediterranean, to which sea the Néréides were confined.

huge sea-monster.[1] For Kassiepeia (Kassiopé), the wife of Képheus, having offended the Néréides by her presumption in setting
herself before them in point of beauty, Poseidón sympathised
with the anger of the sea-maidens, and laid waste the realms of
Képheus by an inundation and a sea-monster. The oracle of
Ammón, on being consulted, declared that only by the exposure
of Andromeda, the daughter of Kassiepeia, to the monster,
could the evil be averted. The reluctance of Képheus was forced
to give way to the determination of his subjects, and the unhappy
princess was bound to a rock. Perseus beholding her there, was
seized with love, and he forthwith promised Képheus to deliver
his daughter from the monster if he would give her to him in
marriage when saved. Képheus joyfully consented, and each
party swore to the agreement. Perseus then attacked and killed
the monster, and delivered Andromeda; but Phineus the brother
of Képheus, to whom the princess had been betrothed, plotted
to destroy the hero; who, coming to the knowledge of his designs,
displayed the Gorgon's head, and turned him and his partisans
to stone.

Perseus now proceeded to Seríphos, where he found that his
mother and Diktys had been obliged to fly to the protection of
the altar from the violence of Polydektés. He immediately went
to the royal residence; and when at his desire Polydektés had
summoned thither all the people to see the formidable head of
the Gorgon, it was displayed, and each became a stone of the
form and position which he exhibited at the moment of the transformation.[2] Having established Diktys as king over the island,
Perseus returned the shoes, the wallet, and the helmet to
Hermés, by whom they were brought back to the Nymphs. He
gave the Gorgon's head to Athéna, who set it in the middle of her
shield.

Accompanied by his mother and his wife Andromeda, Perseus
now set out for Argos; but Akrisios, fearing the fulfilment of
the oracle, left his kingdom, and retired to Larissa in Thessaly.
Perseus went thither to persuade him to return to Argos. Akrisios consented; but Teutamias, the king of Larissa, happening
at that time to celebrate funeral games in honour of his father
lately dead, Perseus engaged in them. As he was throwing the

---

[1] The scene was localised at Joppa, where the marks of the chains were to
be seen on a rock, as also the bones of the monster which M. Scaurus brought
to Rome and exhibited in his ædileship: see Strab. i. 2, 35, p. 43. Mela, i.
11. Plin. *Nat. Hist.* ix. 5. Josephus, *Bell. Jud.* iii. 9, 3.

[2] Οὕτω δ' ἐστὶ πετρώδης ἡ νῆσος ὥστε ὑπὸ τῆς Γοργόνος τοῦτο παθεῖν
αὐτήν φασιν οἱ κωμῳδοῦντες.—Strab. x. 5, 10, p. 487. This may account for
the scene being laid in this island.

discus it fell on the foot of Akrisios, who died of the wound
After this unlooked-for fulfilment of the oracle, Perseus buried
his grandfather before the city, and returned to the Peloponnése. But feeling ashamed to take the inheritance of one who
had died by his means, he proposed an exchange of dominions
with Megapenthés the son of Prœtos, and thenceforward reigned
at Tiryns. He afterwards built and fortified Mykénæ and
Mideia.[1]

According to Pindar,[2] Athéna conducted Perseus, when on
his way to the Gorgons, to the country of the Hyperboreans,
where he was hospitably entertained by that happy people. He
is also said to have turned Atlas into a mountain on his return,[3]
and the drops of the Gorgon's blood which fell on the sand-
wastes of Libya, as he flew over them, gave origin to the numerous broods of serpents by which they have ever been infested.[4]
The origin of the coral is also deduced from the sea-weed which
Perseus placed under the Gorgon's head.[5] When Dionýsos
came to introduce his orgies into Argos he was vigorously opposed by Perseus; but by the intervention of Hermés amity
was effected between the two sons of Zeus.[6] Others say that it
was Akrisios who opposed the introduction of the Bakchic orgies
into his dominions.[7]

Andromeda bore to Perseus six sons and one daughter. The
sons were Persés (who was born in Æthiopia, and being left
with his grandfather became the ancestor of the kings of Persia),[8] Alkæos, Méstór, E'lektryón, Sthenelos and E'leios. The
daughter was named Gorgophoné; and she married Periérés the
Lakonian. From Perseus the royal line at Argos were named
the Perseids.

The mythe of Perseus is probably one of great antiquity. It
is alluded to in the Ilias,[9] and in the Theogony[10] the cutting off
of Medusa's head is spoken of as a well-known event. There
does not however appear to have ever been a poem solely dedicated to the adventures of Perseus, but it is likely that they
were related at length in the E'œæ.

A mythe so very ancient as this appears to be was probably a

---

[1] The whole preceding narrative, except 'ing the deliverance of Andromeda, is
contained in the Fragments of Pherekýdé ap. Sch. Apoll. Rh. iv. 1091, 1515.
[2] Pyth. x. 31 (49) seq. 45 (70) seq.   [3] See above, p. 255.
[4] Apoll. Rh. iv. 1513. Ov. Met. iv. 6' '.
[5] Orph. Λιθικά, 552 seq. Ov. Met. iv. 740 seq.
[6] Paus. ii. 20, 4. Nonn. xlvii. 475 seq.   [7] Ov. Met. iii. 559 ; iv. 606
[8] Hérod. vii. 61, 150.   [9] Il. xiv. 319   [10] Theog. 280.

physical one in its origin, and this supposition is confirmed by many circumstances in the beautiful fairy-tale under whose form it has been transmitted to us. But still it is extremely obscure, and we can only arrive at glimpses of the signification. The following conjectures may perhaps approach to probability.

The cutting off the Gorgon's head is the main action of the mythe, and Pallas-Athéné aids the hero and enables him to achieve the adventure. This goddess was one of the most ancient deities of Argos, for she had a temple on the Larissa or citadel,[1] whence she was named, like Héra, *Of-the-Height* ('Ακρία or 'Ακρίς).[2] Hence it is probable that, as at Athens, she was regarded as a physical power. Further, we invariably find the Gorgon (not the Gorgons) connected with this goddess, and moreover Gorgó is one of her own appellations.[3] The Grecian deities, as the authors of evil as well as good, were usually viewed under two different aspects, and hence Gorgó was probably the injurious, inimical Pallas. With respect to the other names in the mythe, Akrisios is apparently connected with the Larissa, the height (ἄκρον) where tradition said he lay buried;[4] Danaé seems to refer to the *dry* land, and Perseus to belong with Persephoné and others to a family of words denoting *light* or *feeding*.[5] Further, Polydektés is an epithet of Hadés,[6] of which Diktys (*Netter*) may be a kindred term. At Athens there was an altar of Diktys and Klymené at the *temenos* of Perseus, as being his deliverers;[7] which seems to identify Dictys with Hadés, and that apparently under a beneficent point of view.

Müller therefore thus explains the mythe.[8] The parched land of Argos (Δανάη 'Ακρισιώνη), over which Pallas presides, longs for rain;[9] Zeus (*i. e.* the sky) descends in a *golden* fructifying shower, and Perseus is born. But the god of the underworld will take Danaé, that is cover the land with gloom. This is prevented by Perseus' freeing the goddess from her opposite the Gorgó, which makes the moonbeams poisonous and petrifies the land. The efficacy of her look is then directed against the under-world itself, and retains its power in the depths of the earth. The beneficent deity, the rearer of trees and corn, recovers her full influence, and the clear fructifying springs represented by Pégasos gush forth.

[1] Paus. ii. 24, 3.   [2] Hesychius, *s. v.* See above, p. 275.
[3] See the proofs, Appendix M.   [4] Clem. Alex. *Protrep.* p. 29.
[5] See above, p. 160.   [6] Hom. *Hymn to Déméter*, 9.   [7] Paus. ii. 18, 1.
[8] *Proleg.* 307 *seq.* See also Völcker, *Myth. der Jap.* 200 *seq.*
[9] The chamber of Danaé may have been called *brazen* to denote the hardness of the ground (see above, p. 34), but the ancient Kyklópian treasuries appear to have been lined with brass. See Leake, *Travels in the Morea.*

This explanation is ingenious, but deficient in simplicity. There seems to us to be an error in supposing Athéna to be *always* the Athenian Maid, and therefore the moon. The mythe of Danaé and Perseus being manifestly one of great antiquity and peculiar to Argos, we should feel rather disposed to see the Argive goddess in the Athéna who appears in it. As this goddess was the earth, the mythe in this view would form a parallel to that of Démétér-Erinnys,[1] Pégasos corresponding with Areión, while the opposite characters of the soil of Argos and Arkadia would account for the different forms of the mythic narratives. Chrysáór,[2] the brother of Pégasos, may then denote the fertility resulting from the union of earth and water, and his name may have led to his being made the father of Géryoneus, whose abode was in the Ruddy Isle in the golden fertile West.

We have already hinted that mythes were generally very simple in their origin, and gained, like streams, in their progress. It is probable then that this of Perseus at first consisted of no more than the account of his birth and the killing of the Gorgon Medusa,[3] and that the exposure in the sea, the two immortal Gorgons, Andromeda, and so forth, were posterior additions.[4] Pallas-Athéné having become the guide of heroes at the time when the mythe was extended, she may have been substituted for the original goddess.[5] We cannot believe that Hadés ever belonged to the mythe; for the names Diktys and Polydektés are sufficiently explained by the story.

Ἀμφιτρύων καὶ Ἀλκμήνη. Amphitryon et Alcumena.

Perseus was succeeded by his son Alkæos, who had a son named Amphitryón. Alkæos left the throne to his brother E'lektryón, who had married his daughter Anaxó, by whom he had several children.

Méstór, the third son of Perseus, married Lysidiké the daughter of Pelops, by whom he had a daughter named Hippo-

---

[1] See above, p. 159.

[2] Chrysáór (Χρυσάωρ) would seem here to signify *Gilder*, one who bestows radiance and lustre (see p. 18); the same is probably its meaning as an epithet of Démétér (p. 160). As an epithet of Apolló or the sun-god (p. 122) its meaning is more dubious. In favour of *Gold-sworded* we may add the following passage of the Sháh-námeh:

> The darkness, said Rústem, of night is come on,
> But soon as the Morning his *gold-sword* has drawn, etc.

[3] Medusa, *i. e. Mistress*, answers to the Arkadian Despœna: see above, p. 159.

[4] Képheus (from καίω, κάω) and Kassiepeia (from ΚΑ'ΖΩ, i. q. καίω) are probably original names of constellations see below, *O'rión*.

[5] See above, p. 288 *note* [2].

thoé, whom Poseidón carried off to the Echinadian isles. Sh
there bore him a son named Taphios, who settled at Taphos, an
called his people Téleboans, because he had gone *far* from hi
native land.[1] He had a son named Pteroláos, whom Poseidó
made immortal by setting a golden lock of hair on his head
Pteroláos had several sons, and one daughter who was name
Komæthó (*Hair-burner*).

When E'lektryón succeeded to the throne of Mykénæ, th
sons of Pteroláos came with an army of Taphians, and claime
it in right of their great-grandfather Méstór, who was elde
brother to E'lektryón; and on his refusal to comply with thei
demands, they drove off his kine. The sons of E'lektryón cam
to the rescue of their cattle. A fight ensued, in which all th
sons of E'lektryón met their death except Likymnios, who wa
still a child, and all the sons of Pteroláos fell but Euérés, wh
was in charge of their ships. The Taphians fled in their vessel
leaving the cattle, which they had driven away, in the charge o
Polyxenés king of the E'leians. Amphitryón pursued them t
E'lis, and redeemed them; for E'lektryón, desirous to avenge th
death of his sons, had given to Amphitryón the kingdom an
his daughter Alkméné, binding him by oath not to claim a hus
band's rights until he had returned from his expedition agains
the Téleboans. But as Amphitryón was driving home the cattl
which he had recovered, one of the cows chancing to run asid
he flung the stick he had in his hand after her, which happen
ing to strike E'lektryón on the head killed him. Sthenelos, th
fifth son of Perseus, taking advantage of this unlucky deed, drov
Amphitryón from Mykénæ and Tiryns; and sending for his nephew
Atreus and Thyestés, the sons of Pelops, settled them at Mideia.

Amphitryón, accompanied by his wife Alkméné and her hal
brother Likymnios,[2] retired to Thébes, where he was purified b
Kreón, who gave his daughter Perimédé in marriage to Likym
nios. Alkméné still refusing to admit the embraces of Amph
tryón till he had avenged her brothers, he applied to Kreón t
assist him in the war. To this Kreón assented, on condition c
his guest's first freeing Kadmeia from the fox which ravaged i
and which was fated never to be caught. To this animal th
Thébans were obliged to give a child every month, to save th
rest. Amphitryón undertook the task, and with the aid c
Kephalos and his dog succeeded.[3]

Strengthened by a number of auxiliaries, Amphitryón no

---

[1] ὅτι τηλοῦ ἔβη.
[2] Evidently i. q. Ligymnios (Λιγύμνιος, *Sweet-singer*), and there was prob
bly a mythe, now lost, connected with his name.   [3] See above, p 339.

went against the Téleboans. He landed, and ravaged their islands; but so long as Pteroláos lived, he could accomplish n)thing. At length Komæthó, the daughter of that prince, falling in love with Amphitryón, pulled out the fatal golden lock, and he died, and the islands were conquered.[1] Amphitryón put Komæthó to death, and then sailed with his booty to Thébes, having given the islands to his ally Kephalos and his uncle E'leios. The remainder of his history has been already related.[2]

'Ασκληπιός. *Æsculapius.*

Asklépios is called by Homer an excellent physician (*ἀμύμων ἰητῆρ*), who had been instructed by Cheirón. His sons Podaleirios and Macháón, who were also renowned for their skill in treating wounds, led to Troy the men of Trikka, Ithómé and Œchalia in northern Thessaly.[3]

As has been already related,[4] Asklépios was the son of Apolló by Korónis the daughter of Phlegyas. The care of his education was committed to Cheirón, who taught him the healing art,[5] in which he arrived at such perfection as to be able to restore life to the dead. He is said to have thus recalled from the nether-world Kapaneus and Lykurgos,[6] Tyndareós,[7] Glaukos the son of Minós, and Hippolytos.[8] Zeus on the complaint of Hadés struck him with thunder, and Apolló in revenge killed the Kyklópes, for which deed he was banished from Olympos.

The tradition at Epidauros (the great seat of the worship of Asklépios) was that Phlegyas, having come to explore the strength of the Peloponnése, was accompanied by his daughter, who was at the time pregnant by Apolló, but unknown to her father. Her labour came on in the country of Epidauros, and she exposed the babe on Mount Myrtion, afterwards named Titthion (*τίτθη nurse*). Here one of the goats that fed on the mountain gave it suck, and the goatherd's dog kept guard over it. The herdsman, missing his dog and goat, went in search of them. He thus discovered the babe, and on approaching to take it up he perceived that its body emitted a brilliant light, at which proof of divinity he drew back. The fame of the healing powers of the wonderful child was quickly spread over sea and land.[9]

---

[1] See above, p. 342. We may here observe that the Grecian mythes frequently borrowed from each other. Compare those of Kadmos and Iasón, of Andromeda and Hésioné, of Téreus and Thyestés, of Kadmos and Ilos, of Péleus, Héraklés, and Meneláos with the sea-deities, etc. The same appearance is presen·ed in the chivalric romances of the middle ages. [2] See above, p. 310.
[3] *Il.* ii. 731; iv. 194, 219; xi. 518. [4] See above, p. 106.
[5] Pind. *Pyth.* iii. 43 (75) *seq.* [6] Stésichoros, *ap. Apollod.* iii. 10, 3.
[7] Panyasis, *ap. eund.* [8] The Naupaktics, *ap. eund.* [9] Paus. ii. 26, 3-5

The Messénians asserted that Asklépios first saw the light in *their* country. His mother they said was Arsinoé the daughter of Leukippos, and the places from which his sons led the troops to Troy were in Messéné, and not in Thessaly. They showed at Gerénia the tomb of Macháon, and at Pharæ the temple of his children.[1]

Asklépios was one of those who sailed in the Argó. He had by Lampetié (*Bright-one*) the daughter of the Sun two sons, Macháon and Podaleirios, and three daughters, Panakeia (*All-heal*), Iasó (*Healer*), and Ægle (*Brightness*);[2] or rather, according to the Athenian view,[3] only the two first-named.

At Epidauros Asklépios was represented under the form of an old man with a venerable beard, wrapt in a mantle and leaning on a staff round which a serpent was twined. It was said that when he was about to raise Glaukos a serpent came and crept to his staff; he struck and killed it. Soon after another serpent came, bearing a herb in its mouth, which it laid on the head of the dead one, who instantly recovered. Asklépios took the herb and by means of it restored Glaukos.[4] Others said that Athéna had given him the blood of the Gorgon, and with what flowed from the veins of the left side he injured men, while with that of the right side he cured them.[5]

From all that is related of Asklépios it is plain that he was an original deity, probably of the Phlegyans or Lapiths. Müller,[6] who sees a great resemblance between him and Trophónios, says that his union with Apolló is merely mythologic, as they were never worshipped together, and that it was probably founded on the epithet Pæan of this god. We however feel inclined to see in Asklépios a form of the sun-god, to whose daughter he is married. Of his name no satisfactory derivation has as yet been offered.[7]

---

[1] Paus. iv. 3, 2.   Asklépiadés, *ap. Sch. Pind. Pyth.* iii. 8 (14).

[2] Hermippos, *ap. Sch. Aristoph. Plut.* 701.

[3] See Aristoph. *Plut.* 701 *seq.* Ægle then corresponds to Hersé in the mythe of Kekrops.   [4] Hygin. *Poet. Astr.* ii. 14.   [5] Apollod. iii. 10, 3.

[6] See Müller, *Orchom.* 199 *seq. Dor.* i. 307.

[7] Perhaps the root may be σκάλλω, whose original sense may have been *to cut* (σκαλμὴ *knife*, comp. *scalpo*), and thus the name, like that of Cheirón, have denoted the *surgeon*. With this the names of his daughters are in harmony. Those of his sons seem of a different nature: for Macháon is plainly the *Pugnacious*, while Podaleirios may be the *Light-* or *Swift-footed*; for λεῖος may originally have ans·ered to *lēvis* as well as *lēvis*, and λειρὸς is a leveret.

CHAPTER VIII.

MYTHES OF ARKADIA.

ARKADIA, fenced in by its mountains, never suffered from the revolutionary movements of the rest of the peninsula. Its population may therefore be regarded as unmixed Pelasgian; and its principal deities are those which seem to have been worshipped by that people, namely, Zeus, Hermés, Démétér, Artemis, and Poseidón. The Arkadian legends, which are very scanty and of a peculiar character, all refer to the worship of these deities.

Λυκάων. *Lycaon.*

Pelasgos[1] was by the O'keanis Melibœa or the nymph Kylléné the father of Lykáón king of Arkadia.

Lykáón had many wives by whom he became the father of fifty sons, who were like himself impious and cruel. Zeus, to satisfy himself of the truth of the reports that reached him, disguised himself as a poor man and sought their hospitality. To entertain the stranger, they slaughtered a boy, and mingling his flesh with that of the victims, set it before their guest. The god, in indignation and horror at the barbarous act, overturned the *table* (whence the place derived its future name of Trapezós), and struck with lightning the godless father and sons, with the exception of Nyktimos, whom Earth, raising her hands and grasping the right-hand of Zeus, saved from the wrath of the avenging deity. According to another account, Zeus destroyed the dwelling of Lykáón with lightning, and turned its master into a wolf. The deluge of Deukalión which shortly afterwards occurred is ascribed to the impiety of the sons of Lykáón.[2]

In Arkadia Zeus was worshipped under the title of Lykæos on the summit of Mount Lykæon, at the foot of which stood the town of Lykosura, said to have been built by Lykáón, who established there games called Lykæa.[3] At Mount Lykæon there

---

[1] Hésiod (*ap. Apollod.* iii. 8, 1) calls him an autochthon, and Asios said (Paus. viii. 1, 4).

Ἀντίθεον δὲ Πέλασγον ἐν ὑψικόμοισιν ὄρεσσι
Γαῖα μέλαιν' ἀνέδωκεν, ἵνα θνητῶν γένος εἴη.

[2] Apollod. iii. 8. Ov. *Met.* i. 216 *seq.* Hygin. 176. *Poet. Astr.* ii. 4. Tzetz. *Lyc.* 481.

[3] Paus. viii. 2, 1. Human victims appear to have been offered. Any one who tasted of the flesh became a wolf. Plat. *Rep.* viii. § 15

was a sacred inclosure or *temenos* of Zeus, within which neither
man nor beast cast a shadow, and any one who entered it de-
signedly was put to death.[1] These names and circumstances
might lead to the supposition that Zeus Lykæos was in Arkadia
what Apollo Lykios was elsewhere; and that the true root in
this case also was ΛΥ´ΚΗ, *lux, light;* while similarity of sound
gave occasion to the legends of wolves, of which there were many
in Arkadia. In this case Lykáón would be only another name
for Zeus, to whom he raised an altar, and he could not therefore
have been described as impious in the primitive legend. The
opposition between his name and that of Nyktimos strongly
confirms this hypothesis. It may indeed be said that Zeus derived
his appellation from the mountain; but against this is to be
observed, that there was an eminence in the territory of Kyréné
or Barké in Libya dedicated to Zeus Lykæos.[2]

Καλλιστώ καὶ ″Αρκας.   Callisto et Arcas.

Besides his other sons, and Nyktimos who reigned over Arkadia
at the time of Deukalión's flood, Lykáón had a daughter named
Kallistó,[3] who dedicated herself to the service of Artemis, and
vowed to the goddess the maintenance of perpetual virginity. But
Zeus saw and loved Kallistó; and changing himself into the form
of the huntress goddess, accompanied the maiden to the chase,
and surprised her virtue. She long concealed her shame; but at
length, as she was one day bathing with her divine mistress, the
alteration in her person was observed; and Artemis, in her anger,
turned her into a bear. While in this form she brought forth
her son Arkas, who lived with her in the woods, till the herdsmen caught both her and him, and brought them to Lykáón.
Some time afterwards she went into the *temenos* of Zeus Lykæos,
which it was unlawful to enter. A number of Arkadians, among
whom was her own son, followed to kill her; but Zeus, in memory of his love, snatched her out of their hands, and placed her
as a constellation in the sky.[4]

This fable is narrated with great difference in the circumstances. Some say it was the form of Apolló that Zeus took.
In some versions it is Zeus who turns Kallistó into a bear to
conceal her from Héra; and this goddess persuades Artemis to

---

[1] Paus. viii. 38, 6.   Plut. *Quæst. Gr.* 39.   [2] Hérod. iv. 205.
[3] Eumélos *ap. Apollod.* iii. 8, 2. Asios said that Nykteus, *i.e.* Nyktimos, was ner
father; Pherekýdes said Kéteus.   Apollod. *ut sup.*   Sch. *Eurip. Orest.* 1645.
[4] Apollod. iii. 8, 2.   Ov. *Met.* ii. 401 *seq.   Fast.* ii. 155 *seq.*   Hygin. 177.
Poet. Astr. i.   It was also fabled that, at the request of Héra, Téthys forbade
the constellation of the Bear to descend into her waves.

kill her with her arrows as a noxious beast; Zeus then, it is said, took the unborn infant and gave it to Maia to rear. It is also said that Arkas, having been separated from his mother and reared among men, meeting her one day in the woods, was on the point of slaying her, when Zeus transferred the mother and son to the skies. Finally it was, according to others, Héra herself who transformed Kallistó.[1]

Arkas succeeded Nyktimos in the government. He was the friend of Triptolemos, who taught him agriculture, which he introduced into his country, now called from himself Arkadia, and instructed its inhabitants in the mode of making bread. He also showed them how to manufacture wool,—an art which he had learned from Aristæos.[2]

In Kallistó we have another instance of the practice of converting an epithet into an attendant. On the way from the town to the Akadémy at Athens there was an inclosure sacred to Artemis, in which were wooden statues of Aristé and Kallisté. These Pausanias (who says he is borne out by some verses of Sapphó) regarded merely as epithets of the goddess.[3] He further tells us,[4] that in Arkadia, on a large mound planted with various kinds of trees, and named the tomb of Kallistó, stood a temple of Artemis-Kallisté; and he adds that it was the ancient poet Pamphós who first gave Artemis this epithet in his verses, having learned it from the Arkadians. When we add that the *Fair-one* (ἁ καλὰ) is a frequent epithet of Artemis in the Attic drama, little doubt, we should think, will remain of the identity of Artemis and Kallistó.[5]

From the analogy between Ió and Kallistó, it seems to follow that the bear was sacred to Artemis. This is strongly confirmed by the fact that at Braurón in Attica young girls between the age of five and ten years, and called *Bears* (ἄρκτοι), used to perform the sacred rites of this goddess, on which occasion they went round the temple clad in yellow, imitating the gait of these animals. One of the reasons assigned for the origin of this custom was, that Braurón, not Aulis, was the scene of the sacrifice of Iphigeneia, and that it was a bear, not a hind, that had been substituted.[6]

---

[1] Apollod. *ut sup.* Hygin. *ut sup.* See above, p. 362.
[2] Paus. viii. 4, 1.   [3] Id. i. 29, 2.   [4] Id. viii. 35, 3.
[5] See Müller, *Proleg.* 73 *seq.* Kallistó is *The Beautifier:* see above, p. 15.
[   ] may belong to Artemis as the moon-goddess:
            .... who with more pleasing light
         Shadowy *sets off* the face of things.—Milt. *Par. Lost,* v. 42.
[6] Sch. *Aristoph. Lys.* 645. Suidas, *v.* ἄρκτος. Harpocr. r. ἀρκτεύω. Müller, *ut sup.*

The resemblance between Arkas and ἄρκτος may also have had some effect on the formation of this legend.[1]

Ἀταλάντη.   Atalanta.

Iasos or Iasión, a descendant of Arkas, was married to Klymené the daughter of Minyas. He was anxious for male offspring; and on his wife's bringing forth a female, he exposed the babe in the mountains, where she was suckled by a bear, and at last found by some hunters, who named her Atalanté and reared her. She followed the chase, and was alike distinguished for beauty and courage. The Kentaurs Rhœkos and Hylæos attempting her honour perished by her arrows. She took a part in the Argonautic expedition, was at the Kalydonian hunt; and at the funeral games of Pelias she won the prize in wrestling from Péleus.[2]

Atalanté was afterwards recognised by her parents. Her father wishing her to marry, she consented, but only on condition that her suitors should run a race with her in the following manner. She was to be armed, and the suitor to have the odds; if she overtook him, she was to kill him, if not he was to win her hand. Many had thus run and perished, and their heads were fixed round the place of contest, when her cousin Meilanión offered himself to contend. He had three golden apples, which Aphrodíte had given him; these he threw as he ran; Atalanté went out of the course to pick them up, and Meilanión won the race. She then became his wife, and they had a son named Parthenopæos. It is added that they afterwards profaned the *temenos* of Zeus with their love, for which offence they were turned into lions.[3] Other authorities make the name of the victor Hippomenés, and say that on his neglecting to give thanks to Aphrodíte for her aid, she inspired him with a sudden passion, which led to the profanation of the temple of Zeus and the transformation of himself and his bride.[4]

According to other accounts[5] Atalanté was the daughter of Schœneus the son of Athamas, and was therefore a Bœótian. There is no necessity for supposing two of the same name, as has usually been done. They are both, as we see, connected with the Minyans, and are only examples of different appropriations

[1] See Welcker, *Kret. Kol.* 75. It is not improbable that, as Lauer thinks (p. 295), the assigning the bear to Artemis may have arisen from the relation between the Moon and the Bear in the skies.

[2] Apollod. iii. 9, 2. Kallim. iii. 215 *seq.* Ælian, *Var. Hist.* xiii. 1.

[3] Theognis, 1279 *seq.* Apollod. *ut sup.* Hygin. 185. Ov. *Met.* x. 560 *seq.*
Sch. *Theocr.* iii. 40. Musæos. 153.   [4] Ovid, *ut sup.* Sch. *Theocr. ut sup.*
Hésiod *ap. Apollod. ut sup.* Ovid, *ut sup.* Hygin. *ut sup.*

of the same legend. Schœneus perhaps der'ved his name from the *measured* race-ground in which Atalanté ran.

Atalanté is apparently Artemis again as a nymph. She is reared by a bear, she is devoted to a single life and the chase, and she kills the two Kentaurs as Artemis killed O'tos and Ephialtés. Her name was probably an epithet of the goddess signifying the *Joyful*,[1] or perhaps the *Patient-one*, the *Endurer* in her character of the huntress.[2]

CHAPTER IX.

MYTHES OF LAKONIA.

Τυνδάρεως καὶ Λήδα. *Tyndareus et Leda.*

LAKEDÆMÓN, the son of Zeus and Taygeté the daughter of Atlas, married Sparta the daughter of Eurótas, the grandson of the autochthon Lelex, by whom he had two children named Amyklas and Eurydiké, which last was married to Akrisios king of Argos. Amyklas had, by Diomédé the daughter of Lapithas, two sons, Kynortés and Hyakinthos, the former of whom left a son named Periérés, who was, by Gorgophoné the daughter of Perseus, father of Tyndareós, Ikarios, Aphareus, and Leukippos. According to others, the two last and Œbalos were the sons of Periérés, and Œbalos was the father of Tyndareós, Ikarios, and Hippokoón.[3]

Hippokoón had twelve sons, who drove their uncles Ikarios and Tyndareós out of Lakonia. They sought refuge with Thestios king of Ætólia, whose daughter Léda Tyndareós married. Héraklés afterwards vanquished the sons of Hippokoón, and restored Tyndareós to his country; whither he led with him his Ætólian spouse, who bore him Timandra, who was married to Echemos, Klytæmnéstra the wife of Agamemnón, and Philonoé whom Artemis made immortal.[4] Zeus, taking the form of a swan, sought the embraces of Léda; and in the same night her husband Tyndareós caressed her. By the deity she conceived Polydeukés and Helené; by the mortal, Kastór.[5]

---

[1] From α and τάλας, ταλάντερος. Hilaeira (*joyous*) is the epithet of the moon: see p. 384. [2] From τλάω, with the euphonic α like Atlas.
[3] Apollod. iii. 10, 4. Paus. iii. 1. Sch. *Eurip. Orest.* 26.
[4] Euripidés (*Iph. Aul.* 49 *seq.*) names the three daughters of Léda, Phœbé, Klytæmnéstra, and Helené—all significant, we may observe, of *brightness*. He also says (*ib.* 1150) that Agamemnón slew Klytæmnestra's first husband, named Tantalos, and barbarously killed her child by him. [5] Apollod. *ut sup.*

Ἑλένη. Helena.

There are different accounts of the birth and parentage of the celebrated Helené. The common and probably the most ancient one is that given above, that she was the daughter of Léda by Zeus, who took the form of a white swan. According to the Kypria she was the offspring of Zeus and Nemesis, who had long fled the pursuit of the god, and to elude him had taken the form of all kinds of animals.[1] At length, while she was under that of a goose, the god became a swan, and she laid an egg, which was found by a shepherd in the woods. He brought it to Léda, who laid it up in a coffer, and in due time Helené was produced from it.[2] Hésiod, on the other hand, called Helené the daughter of O'keanos and Téthys.[3]

In the Ilias Helené is termed 'begotten of Zeus,'[4] and she calls Kastór and Polydeukés her 'own-brothers whom one mother bore with her.'[5] In the Odyssey[6] these are expressly called the sons of Tyndareós. This however does not prove that Helené was held to be his daughter; and we shall see reason for supposing that she was always viewed as the child of Zeus.

The beauty of Helené is proverbial. Théseus carried her off while yet a child, and, as we shall see, her frailty caused the war of Troy. It was fabled that after death she was united in marriage with Achilleus in the White Island (Λευκή) in the Euxine, where she bore him a son named Euphorión.[7]

Πολυδεύκης καὶ Κάστωρ. Pollux et Castor.

The earliest exploit of these twin heroes, who were born at Amyklæ, was the recovery of their sister Helené from the power of Théseus, whose mother Æthra they dragged in return into captivity. They took part in all the great undertakings of their time, were at the Kalydónian hunt, accompanied Héraklés against the Amázons, sailed in the Argó, and aided Péleus to storm Iolkos. Polydeukés was the most distinguished pugilist, Kastór

---

[1] *Ap. Athén.* viii. 334.

[2] Apollod. *ut sup.* These circumstances are not in the fragment of the Kypria, but they were probably contained in the poem. Sapphó said (*ap. Athen.* ii. 57),

φασὶ δή ποτε Λήδαν
ὤϊον εὑρεῖν.

It was probably the war of Troy that made Nemesis the mother of Helené.

[3] Sch. *Pind. Nem.* x. 80 (150).   [4] *Il.* iii. 418.

[5] *Il.* iii. 238.   [6] *Od.* xi. 298 *seq.*

[7] Paus. iii. 19, 13. Conon, 18. Ptol. Héph. iv.: see above, p. 275. Euripidés (*Androm.* 1236) and Quintus Smyrnæus (iii. 775) place Achilleus in the White Island, but say nothing of a bride.

the most expert charioteer, of his day. Hermés bestowed on them the fleet steeds Phlogios and Harpagos, the children of the Harpy Podargé : Héra gave them the swift Xanthos and Kyllaros. The brothers themselves fell into the very same offence which they had punished in Théseus. Being invited to the wedding-feast by their cousins Idas and Lynkeus the sons of Aphareus, who had married their cousins Phœbé and Hilaeira the daughters of Leukippos, they became enamoured of the brides, and carried them off. Idas and his brother pursued the ravishers. In the conflict Kastór fell by the spear of Idas ; and Polydeukés, aided by the thunder of Zeus, slew the two sons of Aphareus.[1]

Another account says that the four heroes joined to drive off the herds of the Arkadians. Idas was appointed to divide the booty. He killed an ox ; and dividing it into four parts, said that one half of the prey should fall to him who had first eaten his share, and the remainder to him who next finished. He then quickly devoured his own and his brother's part, and drove the whole herd to Messéné. The Dioskuri (*Zeus-sons*), as Kastór and his brother were called, made war on Messéné. Driving off all the cattle which they met, they laid themselves in ambush in a hollow tree ; but Lynkeus, whose vision could penetrate the trees and the rocks, ascended the top of Taÿgeton, and looking over all the Peloponnése saw them there ; and he and his brother hastened to attack them.[2] Kastór fell by the spear of Idas ; Polydeukés pursued the slayers, and coming up with them at the tomb of their father Aphareus, was struck by them in the breast with the pillar belonging to it. Unretarded by the blow, he rushed on, and killed Lynkeus with his spear ; and Zeus, at the same moment, struck Idas with a thunderbolt. Polydeukés was inconsolable for the loss of his brother; and Zeus, on his prayer, gave him his choice of being taken up himself to Olympos, and sharing the honours of Arés and Athéna, or of dividing them with his brother, and for them to live day and day about in heaven and under the earth. Polydeukés chose the latter, and divided his immortality with Kastór.[3]

[1] Sch. *Il.* iii. 243. Sch. *Pind. Nem.* x. 60 (112). Hygin. 80.

[2]

Αἶψα δὲ Λυγκεὺς
Τηΰγετον προσέβαινε ποσὶν ταχέεσσι πεποιθώς·
ἀκρότατον δ' ἀναβὰς διεδέρκετο νῆσον ἅπασαν
Τανταλίδου Πέλοπος, τάχα δ' εἴσιδε κύδιμος ἥρως
δεινοῖς ὀφθαλμοῖσιν ἔσω κοίλης δρυὸς ἄμφω,
Κάστορά θ' ἱππόδαμον καὶ ἀεθλοφόρον Πολυδεύκεα.

The Kypria *ap. Sch. Pind. Nem.* x. 60 (114) and Tzetz. *Lyc.* 511.

[3] Pind. *Nem.* x. 55 (103) *seq. cum* Sch. *Theocr.* xxii. 137 *seq.* Apollod. iii. 11, 2. Tzetz. *Lyc.* 511. Ov. *Fast.* v. 699 *seq.*

The remarkable circumstance of the two brothers living and dying alternately leads at once to a suspicion of their being personifications of natural powers or objects. This is confirmed by the names in the mythe, all of which seem to refer to light, or its opposite. Thus Léda differs little from Létó, and may therefore be regarded as *darkness;* she is married to Tyndareós, a name which seems to be of a family of words relating to *light,* *flame* or *heat*;[1] her children by him or Zeus, that is by Zeus-Tyndareós, the bright-god, are Helené, *Brightness* (ἔλα, *light*), Kastór, *Adorner* (ΚΑ'ΖΩ), and Polydeukés, *Dewful* (δεύω, δευκής). In Helené therefore we have only another form of Selené;[2] the *Adorner* is a very appropriate term for the day, whose light adorns all nature; and nothing can be more apparent than the suitableness of *Dewful* to the night. It is somewhat remarkable that in the legend Helené is connected by birth with Polydeukés rather than with Kastór. The brothers may, however, be also regarded as sun and moon, to which their names and the form of the mythe are equally well adapted,[3] Kastór being the *Illumer* (from κάω, καίω), and the moon being regarded in her character of mother of dew.

To proceed to the other names of the legend, Idas and Lynkeus, that is, *Sight* and *Light,* are the children of Aphareus or Phareus, that is *Shiner* (φάω); and the two daughters of Leukippos, or *White-horsed* (an epithet of the Dioskuri),[4] are Phœbé, *Brightness,* and Hilaeira, *Joyful* (ἱλαρὸς), which last is an epithet given to the moon by Empedoklés.[5] In the Kypria they were called the daughters of Apolló.[6]

That these were original divinities is demonstrated by their being objects of worship. The Tyndarids, Dioskuri, or *Kings* ("Ἀνακες), as they were named, had their temples and statues;[7] as also had the Leukippides,[8] who, in perhaps the more correct

---

[1] It is apparently connected with δαίω and *tæda,* ν being inserted as in Lynkeus from ΛΥ'ΚΗ (see Schwenk, 193). Possibly there may have been a Pelasgian word akin to the German *zünden* and A.-Sax. τενϱan, whence *tinder.*

[2] As the moon, from her supposed watery nature, may have been held to have sprung from the ocean, Helené is made a child of O'keanos and Téthys. In Scandinavian mythology Freya (moon) is one of the children of Niordr, the god of the waters.

[3] Welcker (*Tril.* 130, 226) makes Kastór the same as Astór (*Starry*), and Polydeukés the same as Polyleukés (*Lightful*), and views them as sun and moon. *Ib.* 271.

[4] Eurip. *Hel.* 639.

[5]   "Ἥλιος ὀξυβελὴς, ἡ δ' αὖ ἱ λ ά ε ι ρ α σελήνη.
                    Ap. Plut. de Fac. in Orb. Lunæ, 2.

[6] Paus. iii. 16, 1. The moon was the daughter of the sun : see above, p. 55.

[7] Id. i. 18, 1; ii. 22, 5; iii. 14, 6. 20, 2.

[8] Id. iii. 16, 1. Léda's egg hung in their temple.

form of the legend, are their wives.[1] Helené, in like manner had her temples;[2] and there is some reason to suppose that she was identified with Eileithyia;[3] Euripidés unites her with Héra and Hébé in Olympos.[4] The Apharids were not objects of worship; perhaps because they had merely been devised as opponents to the Tyndarids, to give a mythic ground for the alternate life and death of these last, or possibly because in the legend they are Messénians.

The Dioskuri were afterwards confounded with the Kabeirean deities, and were with Helené regarded as the protectors of ships in tempests;[5] and the St. Elmo's fire was ascribed to them. They were also said to be the constellation of the Twins.

CHAPTER X.

MYTHES OF ELIS.

THE mythic tales of which E'lis is the scene are confined to the district between the Alpheios and the Neda, formerly called Pylos, where the Néleids reigned; and to Pisátis, the ancient realm of the Pelopids. Between the former and the part of Thessaly about the Pagasaïc bay there appears to have been a very early connexion, as its mythic heroes are all Æolids. It was probably colonised by the Minyans.

Σαλμωνεύς. Salmoneus.

Salmóneus, one of the sons of Æolos, settled in E'lis, where he built a city. He was a bold impious man, who asserted himself to be Zeus, and claimed all the honours due to that god. He fastened dried hides and brazen kettles to his chariot, and their clatter, he said, was thunder; and flinging lighted torches against the sky, he called them his lightnings. Zeus, incensed

---

[1] Apollod. iii. 11, 2. Paus. ii. 22, 5. Apollodóros unites Hilaeira with Kastór, but Propertius (i. 2, 15) says,

> Non sic Leucippis succendit Castora Phœbe,
> Pollucem cultu non Hilaïra soror.

[2] Eur. *Hel.* 1666. Paus. iii. 15, 3.   [3] See Welcker, *Tril.* 227.

[4]
> Ἔνθα παρ' ῞Ηρᾳ τῇ θ' ῾Ηρακλέος
> ῞Ηβη πάρεδρος θεὸς ἀνθρώποις
> ἔσται σπονδαῖς ἔντιμες ἀεί.— *Orest.* 1686.

[5] Eur. *Orest.* 1636 1689. *Hel.* 1664.

2 c

at his impiety, struck him with thunder, and consumed his city and all its inhabitants.[1]

Τυρώ.   *Tyro.*

Tyró, the daughter of Salmóneus was, after the death of her father, brought up in Thessaly by his brother Déïon. She was in love with the river Enípeus, to whose waves she often made her moan. Poseidón saw and loved her; and assuming the form of the river-god, embraced her at the mouth of the stream, whose bright waves arched over them, concealing the god and the mortal maid. The god declared then who he was, and enjoining secrecy dived into the sea. Tyró conceived from the divine embrace two sons, whom when born she exposed. A troop of mares, followed by the herdsmen, passing by where they lay; one of the mares touched the face of one of the infants with her hoof, and made it *livid* (πέλιον). The herdsmen took and reared the babes, naming the one with the mark Pelias, the other Néleus. When they grew up they discovered their mother, and resolved to kill her step-mother Sideró (*Iron*, i. e. *Iron-hearted*), by whom she was cruelly treated. They pursued her to the altar of Héra; and Pelias, who never showed any regard for that goddess, slew her before it. The brothers afterwards fell into discord, and Pelias abode at Iolkos, while Néleus settled in E'lis, where he built a town named Pylos. Tyró afterwards married her uncle Krétheus, to whom she bore three sons, Æson, Pherés, and Amytháon.[2]

Νηλεὺς καὶ Περικλύμενος.   *Neleus et Periclymenus.*

Néleus married Chlóris the daughter of Amphíon, the son of Iasos of the Minyan Orchomenos.[3] By her he had several sons of whom the principal were Periklymenos and Nestór, and one daughter named Péró. When Héraklés attacked Pylos,[4] he killed Néleus and all his sons but Nestór, who was a child, and reared among the Gerenians. Periklymenos had been endowed by Poseidón with the power of changing himself into various forms; and he took successively those of an eagle, a lion, a serpent, an ant, and other animals. He was detected by Athéna as he was sitting in the form of a bee or a fly on the pole of Héraklés' chariot, and he was killed by the hero.[5]

---

[1] Apollod. i. 9, 7. Eudocia, 372. Diodor. iv. 68. Verg. *Æn.* vi. 585. Hésiod (*Fr.* 23) calls him ἄδικος, while Homer (*Od.* xi. 235) styles him ἀμύμων.
[2] *Od.* xi. 235 *seq.* Apollod. *ut supra.*   [3] *Od.* xi. 281 *seq.*
[4] See above, p. 324.
[5] *Il.* xi. 690. Hesiod, *Fr.* 30. Apollod. i. 9, 8. Ov. *Met.* xii. 556 *seq.*

The mythic family of the Néleids seem al. to relate to the sea and water. At the head of the genealogy is Æolos (*Wind-man*), whose son is Salmóneus, *i. e.* Halmóneus (*Sea-man*), by whose daughter Poseidón is the father of Néleus, *i. e.* Néreus,[1] whose sons are Nestór (*Flower*)[2] and Periklymenos, a name answering to an epithet of Poseidón, κλυτός. The wisdom of Nestór, and his brother's power of changing his form, remind us also of the sea-deities. Péró may be of common origin with the fount Peiréné;[3] Tyró may be Tryó (*Wearer-away*), and connected with Tritón and Amphitríté.[4]

Μελάμπους καὶ Βίας.   *Melampus et Bias.*

Amytháón the son of Krétheus and Tyró settled at Pylos. He married Eidomené the daughter of his brother Pherés, by whom he had two sons, Bias and Melampus. This last lived in the country. Before his house stood an oak-tree, in a hole of which abode some serpents. His servants finding these animals, killed the old ones, whose bodies Melampus burned; but he saved and reared the young ones. As he was sleeping one day, these serpents, which were now grown to full size, came, and getting each on one of his shoulders, licked his ears with their tongues. He awoke in some terror; and to his astonishment, found that he understood the voices of the birds which were flying around; and learning from their tongues the future, he was able to declare it to mankind. Happening to meet with Apolló on the banks of the Alpheios, he was taught by him the art of reading futurity in the entrails of victims, and he thus became an excellent soothsayer.[5]

Meanwhile his brother Bias fell in love with Péró the daughter of Néleus. As the hand of this beautiful maiden was sought by most of the neighbouring princes, her father declared that he would give her only to him who should bring him from Thessaly the cows of his mother Tyró, which Iphiklos of Phylaké detained, and had them guarded by a dog whom neither man nor beast could venture to approach. Bias, relying on the aid of his brother, undertook the adventure. Melampus, previously declaring that he knew he should be caught and confined for a year but then get the cattle, set out for Phylaké. Everything

---

[1] Hence his union with Chlóris, the *Green-earth* (above, p. 299) is of the same kind as that of Poseidón with Démétér.

[2] As μήστωρ comes from ΜΑ'Ω, so Νήστωρ, Νέστωρ, may come from νάω *flow* : see above, p. 15.

[3] From περάω, πείρω, *to penetrate.*

[4] See above, p. 217.

[5] Apollod. i. 9, 11.   Sch. *Apoll. Rh.* i. 118.

fell out as he had said. The herdsmen of Iphiklos took him,
and he was thrown into prison, where he was attended by a man
and a woman. The man served him well, the woman badly.
Toward the end of the year he heard the worms in the timber
conversing with each other. One asked how much of the beam
was now gnawed through; the others replied that there was
little remaining. Melampus immediately desired to be removed
to some other place; the man took up the bed at the head, the
woman at the foot, Melampus himself at the middle. They had
not gotten quite out of the house, when the roof fell in and
killed the woman. This coming to the ears of Iphiklos, he inquired, and learned that Melampus was a *mantis*. He therefore, as he was childless, consulted him about having offspring.
Melampus agreed to tell him, on condition of his giving him the
cows. The seer then sacrificing an ox to Zeus, divided it, and
called all the birds to the feast. All came but the vulture; but
none was able to tell how Iphiklos might have children. They
therefore brought the vulture, who said that Phylakos the father
of Iphiklos had pursued him with a knife when he was a child,
for having done something unseemly; but not being able to
catch him, had stuck the knife in a wild pear-tree, where the
bark grew over it. The terror, he said, had deprived Iphiklos
of his generative power; but if this knife were gotten, and Iphiklos, scraping off the rust, drank it for ten mornings, he would
have a child. All was done as the prophet desired, and Iphiklos
had a son named Podarkés. Melampus drove the kine to Pylos
and Péró was given to his brother.[1]

The cure of the Prœtids by Melampus has been already related.

The Melampods, of whose Eponymos the history is here related, were a soothsaying family of the mythic ages belonging to
the Peloponnése. Amytháón or Mytháón (*Speaker*, μῦθος) and
Eidomené (*Seer*) are appropriate names for the parents of a
soothsayer. Melampus is (like Œdipus) an ambiguous name,
and *Black-foot* is as dubious an interpretation as *Swollen-foo*
Its true meaning seems to be *the Son of Darkness*, i. e. the *Dark*
or *Obscure-one*,[3] in allusion to the nature of prophecy.

Ἴαμος. Iamus.

The nymph Pitané, the daughter of the river-god Euróta
conceived by Poseidón the ' violet-tressed ' Euadné. She co

---

[1] *Od.* xi. 287 *seq.* Sch. *on Od.* xv. 225. Apollod. *ut supra*. Sch. *Theocr.* i
43. There was a poem named Melampodia ascribed to Hésiod. Heyne thinks
was only a part of the E'œæ.   [2] See above, p. 367.   [3] See above, p. 1.

cealed her state; and when the babe was born sent it to Æpytos, the son of Elatos, the son of Arkas, who dwelt at Phæsané on the banks of the Alpheios in Arkadia. When Euadné grew up, her charms attracted the love of Apolló. The consequence of her intercourse with the god did not escape the observation of Æpytos; who, filled with anger and concern, journeyed to Pythó, to consult the oracle about this unhappy affair. While he was absent, Euadné, who had gone to the fount, felt her pains come on. She laid down her silver pitcher and loosed her 'purple-yellow' girdle, and beneath the dark foliage brought forth her 'divine-minded' son. The 'gold-haired' god had sent the mild Eleuthó and the Mœræ to ease her labour, and bring his offspring to the light. The mourning mother left her new-born babe on the ground, and two 'green-eyed' serpents came by the direction of the gods, and fed him on 'the innocuous venom (ἰόν) of bees.'

When Æpytos returned from rocky Pythó, he inquired after the child which Euadné had borne; for Phœbos, he said, had told him that he would be a renowned prophet, and that his race would never fail. All declared that they had seen or heard nothing of the babe, who was now five days old, but lay concealed in the rushes and extensive thicket, 'his tender body bedewed with the yellow and purple rays' i.e. of the violets (ἴων) which surrounded him; and hence his mother called him Iamos—Violety.

On attaining 'the fruit of pleasing gold-crowned youth,' Iamos went into the stream of the Alpheios; and by night in the open air called on Poseidón his 'wide-powerful' ancestor, and on 'the bow-bearing guardian of god-built Délos,' to grant him public honour. The voice of his father replied, directing him to follow; and unseen he brought him to the hill of Kronos at Olympia, where he gave him the double treasure of prophecy by augury and by entrail-inspection. When Héraklés came to Olympia, and established the festival of Zeus, Iamos by his direction founded a temple, at which he and his posterity the Iamids continued to officiate.[1]

In the ode here analysed the Théban bard sings the mythic origin which had been assigned to the soothsaying Iamids of Olympia. The tradition appears to have been that they came from Arkadia. Poseidón, we may observe, is placed at the head of the genealogies of both them and the Melampods; and we

[1] Pind. Ol. vi.

are to recollect the soothsaying properties of the water-deities, and the inspiring influence of streams and founts.[1] Pindar here plays very agreeably on the relation of the name Iamos to the *violet*.

Ἐνδυμίων. Endymion.

In the legendary annals of E'lis, Endymión was the son of Aethlios, the son of Zeus by Protogeneia (*First-born*), the daughter of Deukalión; and he was the father of Pæón, Epeios, and Ætólos. He proposed the succession to the kingdom as the prize of a race to his sons; Epeios won, and the people were named from him; Pæón retired in resentment to the banks of the Axios, far away in the north, and the country there derived from him its name, Pæónia.[2]

Endymión, it is also said, gained the love of the goddess Seléné, and she bore him fifty daughters.[3] Zeus as a favour allowed him to live as long as he pleased,[4] or as others said, bestowed on him the gift of perpetual sleep. The place of his repose was a cavern of Mount Latmos in Karia, and thither Seléné used to repair to visit him. Some said he was made immortal for his righteousness; others that, like Ixíón, when raised to heaven he made love to Héra, was deceived by a cloud, and was hurled to Erebos.[5]

There can be very little doubt that this mysterious being was originally an object of worship, and that he was converted into a hero in the usual manner. As the ancient Epeians are said to have been Lelegians, and this people also dwelt in the neighbourhood of Latmos, it has been thought,[6] with much probability, that Endymión was a deity whom they worshipped. The sire assigned him is nothing more than a personification of the Olympic games (ἄεθλα); his sons express the kindred between the Epeians and Ætólians. His union with the moon, and their fifty daughters, will perhaps furnish a key to his true nature. In these daughters Böckh[7] sees the fifty lunar months which formed the Olympic cycle of four years. In such case Endymión would probably be the sun, who with the moon is the author of the months; or supposing this to have been a Lelegian mythe, and therefore long anterior to the institution of the Olympic

---

[1] See above, p. 168.   [2] Paus. v. 1.   [3] Paus. *ut supra*.

[4] Ταμίαν εἶναι θανάτου, ὅτε θέλοι ὀλέσθαι. Sch. *Apoll. Rh.* i[?]. 57, from Hésiod.

[5] Sch. *Apoll. Rh. ut sup.* from Hésiod, Peisander, Akusiláos, Pherekýdes, Epimenidés, Nikander, and others.

[6] Müller, *Proleg.* 223.   [7] *On Pind. Ol.* iii. 11 (18).

games, the daughters may have been the weeks of the year (the round number being employed as usual), of which the sun and moon are the parents. The conjunction of these bodies at the time of new moon is a matter of common observation, and Milton uses a very remarkable expression when he speaks of the moon as being at that time 'hid in her vacant interlunar *cave.*'. Endymión is perhaps the setting sun who *goes into* (ἐνδύει) the sea, or possibly in the Lelegian mythe the cavern where he meets the moon.[1]

The rationalisers said that Endymión was a hunter who used to go to the chase at night when the beasts came out to feed, and to sleep in a cavern during the day; and hence he was supposed to be always asleep.[2]

Κτέατος καὶ Εὔρυτος.   Cteatus et Eurytus.

In the Ilias[3] Nestór mentions two Epeian youths, the sons of Poseidón, whom he calls the Aktorions (Ἀκτορίωνε) and Molíons (Μολίονε). The poet elsewhere[4] names them Kteatos and Eurytos. Hésiod[5] said that their bodies grew together, and Ibykos[6] that they sprang from a silver egg. They married Théroníké and Thérophoné, the daughters of Dexamenos :[7] they fell, as we have seen, by the arm of Héraklés : their sons Amphimachos and Thalpios led the Epeians to Ilion.[8]

That this mythe is not without a meaning is a point of which few will doubt; but it is one not very easy to discover. A modern mythologist[9] regards these twins as the symbols of foreign trade, they being the children of the sea, or of *Bringer* (Ἀκτωρ

---

[1] 'As the deer of the forest of the seven azure plains (*i. e.* the sun) had retired to the *cave of the West.*' Bahar Danush. ch. vi. 'Rest in thy *shadowy cave*, O sun, let thy return be in joy.' Ossian, *Carric-thura.* In the Theogony (746 *seq.*) Night and Day have a dwelling in which they alternately abide.

[2] Sch. *Apoll. Rh. ut sup.* Our own Fletcher (*Faithful Shepherdess*, Act i.) tells

    How the pale Phœbe, hunting in a grove,
    First saw the boy Endymión, from whose eyes
    She took eternal fire that never dies ;
    How she conveyed him softly in a sleep,
    His temples bound with poppy, to the steep
    Head of old Latmus, where she stoops each night,
    Gilding the mountain with her brother's light,
    To kiss her sweetest.

[3] *Il.* xi. 709, 750; xxiii. 638.   [4] *Il.* ii. 621.   [5] *Ap. Sch. Il.* xxiii. 638.

    Τούς τε λευκίππους κούρους
    τέκνα Μολιόνας κτάνον
    ἅλικας, ἰσοκεφάλους, ἐνιγυίους,
    ἀμφοτέρους γεγαῶτας ἐν ὠέῳ ἀργυρέῳ.—Ap. *Athén.* ii. 58.

[7] **Paus.** v. 3, 3.   [8] *Il.* ii. 621.   [9] Hermann, *Ueber das Wesen*, &c. 55.

from ἄγω) and *Comer* (Μολιόνη from μολέω), and named *Acquirer* (Κτέατος) and *Wealthy*, or one to whom wealth *flows* (εὖ ῥυτός). Another critic[1] takes a widely different view of the mythe, seeing in it only an E'leian popular fable of the two millstones. Hence, he says, they are joined in the body; their mother's name is *Mill* (μύλη, mola), their father is the *Breaker* (ἄγω, ἄγνυμι), the son of *Feeder* (Phorbas),[2] their own names are *Possessor* and *Hold-fast*,[3] and they are married to *Corn-subduer* and *Corn-maker* (Θηρονίκη and Θηροφόνη),[4] the daughters of *Trough* (Δεξάμενος). This last theory, trifling as may appear to be the sense which it gives the mythe, seems to us to approximate to the truth. We have already pointed out the resemblance between the Molionids and the Alóeids. Poseidón became the father of both in the usual manner.

Τάνταλος.　Tantalus.

Odysseus, when relating to the Phæakians what he had beheld in Erebos, says,[5]

> And Tantalos I saw great woe enduring,
> Placed in a lake that reached up to his chin.
> Like one athirst he seemed, but could not drink;
> For when the old man stooped to drink intent
> The water shrank absorbed, and round his feet
> The sable earth appeared; God dried it up.
> Above his head tall leafy trees displayed
> Their fruit, pomegranates, pears and apples bright,
> And luscious figs and olives green and ripe;
> But when the old man would grasp them in his hands,
> The winds straight tossed them to the shady clouds.

Pindar says[6] that if ever mortal man was honoured by the dwellers of Olympos it was Tantalos; but that he could not digest his happiness. They admitted him, he adds, to feast at their table on nectar and ambrosia, which made him immortal; but he stole some of the divine food and gave it to his friends on earth. For this Zeus hung a stone over his head, which always menacing to descend and crush him deprives him of all joy. This poet does not mention the place of his punishment, but Euripidés, who also informs us that he was a son of Zeus, says[7] that it was the air between heaven and earth, and that the rock was suspended over him by golden chains. The offence of

---

[1] Welcker *in Schwenk.* 306 *seq.* See above, p. 309.
[2] Paus. v. 1, 11 : see above, p. 324.　　[3] See Buttmann, *Lexil. v.* ἐρύεσθαι.
[4] Welcker regards the θηρ in these names as ἀθήρ; and as ἀθήρα is *frumenty* according to Hesychius, he thinks that it signified corn in general, from θέρω, φέρω.　　[5] *Od.* xi. 582 *seq.*　　[6] Pind. *Ol.* i. 54 (85) *seq.*
[7] *Orest.* 5 *seq.*; 982 *seq.*

Tantalos, according to him, was his not restraining his tongue, that is, probably his divulging the secrets of the gods.

Tantalos was said[1] to be the son of Zeus by the nymph Plutó (*Enricher*), and he was the father of Pelops and of Niobé the wife of Amphíon. His residence was placed at the foot of Mount Sipylos in Lydia. Zeus, said another legend, cast this mountain atop of him; for Pandareos having stolen the golden dog which had guarded the goat that reared the god, gave it to Tantalos to keep; and when Hermés was sent to reclaim the dog, Tantalos denied all knowledge of it, and for his falsehood the mountain was thrown on him.

This last trifling legend is, as we may easily see, one of the many attempts at localising the ancient mythes, for Sipylos it is plain was designed to take the place of the mythic rock.

The name Tantalos is, like Sisyphos, a reduplication,[2] and his mythe is evidently one of those handed down from the ancient serious Pelasgic times. The root of Tantalos is probably θάλλω, and he represents the man who is *flourishing* and abounding in wealth, but whose desires are insatiable. The Homéric picture exhibits in a lively manner the misery of such a state, and this is probably the more ancient form of the legend. The other form[3] perhaps represents the cares and fears attendant on riches; or it may be, as has been ingeniously conjectured,[4] an image of the evils of ambition and the inordinate pursuit of honours; for when Tantalos, it was said, had attained his ultimate desire, and was admitted to the table of the gods, his joy was converted into terror by his fancying a rock suspended over his head and ready to crush him, and he sought permission to resign his place at the celestial table.

It was probably the idea of the great wealth of Lydia that caused the mythe of Tantalos to be localised at Sipylos.

Πέλοψ. Pelops.

At an entertainment given to the gods by Tantalos, he is said to have killed and dressed his son Pelops, and to have set him

---

[1] Sch. *Pind. Ol.* i. 60 (97). Anton. Lib. 36.

[2] Θάλθαλος, for euphony made Τάνταλος: θ and τ, λ and ν are frequently commuted: see Welcker *in Schwenk.* 265, and Völcker, *Myth. der Jap.* 355. We have put our account of him and his family in this place, because they first appear in E'lis, and Apollodóros (ii. 5, 1) calls Pelops an E'leian.

[3] Archilochos was the earliest writer who to Pausanias' knowledge (x. 31, 12) had mentioned the stone.

[4] Alkman *ap. Sch. Pind. ut sup.* Nikolaüs Damasc. Περὶ Παρασίτων *ap. Stob.* xiv. 7. Welcker, *Der Epische Cyclus,* 280 *seq.* Tantalos would th.n be a mythic Damoklés.

for food before them. Démétér had eaten one of the shoulders before the gods were aware of the horrid banquet of which they were about to partake. At the desire of Zeus, Hermés put all the parts back into the pot, and drew forth from it the boy perfect in all but the shoulder, which was replaced by an ivory one.[1] Poseidón, smitten with the beauty of Pelops, carried him off in his golden car to Olympos. But when his father had drawn on himself the indignation of the gods, they set Pelops once more among the ' swift-fated race of men.'[2]

When Pelops had attained to manhood he resolved to seek in marriage Hippodameia, the daughter of Œnomaos, son of Arés, king of Pisa. An oracle having told this prince that he would lose his life through his son-in-law, or, as others say, being unwilling on account of her surpassing beauty to part with her, he proclaimed that he would give his daughter only to him who should conquer him in the chariot-race. The race was from the banks of the Kladaos in E'lis to the altar of Poseidón at the Isthmos, and it was run in this manner : Œnomaos placing his daughter in the chariot with the suitor, gave him the start; he followed himself with a spear in his hand, and if he overtook the unhappy lover ran him through. Thirteen had already lost their lives when Pelops came.[3]

In the dead of the night, says Pindar, Pelops went down to the margin of the sea, and invoked the god who rules it. Suddenly Poseidón stood at his feet, and he conjured him by the memory of his affection to grant him the means of obtaining the lovely daughter of Œnomaos, declaring that even should he fail in the attempt, he regarded fame beyond inglorious old-age. Poseidón assented to his prayer, and bestowed on him a golden chariot, and horses of winged speed.[4]

Pelops then went to Pisa to contend for the fair prize. He bribed Myrtilos, the son of Hermés, the charioteer of Œnomaos, to leave out the linch-pins of the wheels of his chariot, or as others said to put in waxen ones instead of iron. In the race, therefore, the chariot of Œnomaos broke down, and falling out he was killed,[5] and Hippodameia became the bride of Pelops. To celebrate the wedding Poseidón assembled the Néréides, and raised on the strand of the sea a bridal-chamber of the waves, which arched in bright curves over the marriage-bed.[6]

[1] Sch. *Pind. Ol.* i. 25 (38).   [2] Pind. *Ol.* i 37 (60) *seq.*
[3] Sch. *Pind. Ol.* i. 70 (114).   Hygin. 84.   Diodór. iv. 73.
[4] Pind. *Ol.* i. 70 (114) *seq.*
[5] Apoll. Rh. i. 752 *seq. cum Sch.* where Pherekýdés is quoted. Tzetz. *Lyc.* 156. Hygir. 84.   [6] Himerius, *Or.* i. 6.

Pelops is said[1] to have promised Myrtilós for his aid one half of the kingdom, or as other accounts have it, to give him a share in the favours of Hippodameia. Unwilling, however, to keep his promise, he took an opportunity as they were driving along a cliff to throw him into the sea, where he was drowned. Others say, that Hippodameia being thirsty, Pelops went in search of water for her; during his absence Myrtilos attempted to offer her violence,[2] and Pelops on her complaint flung him into the sea.[3] To the vengeance of Hermés for the death of his son were ascribed all the future woes of the line of Pelops.[4]

Hippodameia bore to Pelops five sons, Atreus, Thyestés, Kopreus, Alkathoos and Pittheus; and two daughters, Nikippé and Lysidiké, who married Sthenelos and Méstór, the sons of Perseus.

In this mythe also there is much obscurity. We will commence our examination of it by inquiring into the Lydian origin of Pelops, a thing taken for granted by all historians from Hérodotos and Thukydidés[5] down to our own days.

Homer, when giving an account of Agamemnón's sceptre, says[6] that Zeus gave it to Hermés, by whom it was given to 'horse-lashing' Pelops, which signifies that Pelops was a prince rich in flocks and herds who ruled by a legitimate title. This certainly does not contradict the notion of his being a foreigner, but it does not confirm it; and it seems very strange that Homer should never have alluded to the Asiatic origin of the Atreids if it was a matter of belief in his days. Hésiod[7] probably related the winning of Hippodameia. In the Kypria it was said, that from the summit of Taygetos Lynkeus looked over the 'whole isle of Pelops Tantalidés';[8] which passage is the earliest intimation that we have of any connexion between Pelops and Tantalos, as it is the first mention of the Peloponnése. Pindar[9] calls Pelops a Lydian; and this is the earliest notice of his Asiatic descent.

The name Pelops'-isle or Peloponnése is, we think, decisive of the whole question. There was no such practice known among the Greeks in remote antiquity as that of calling a country or even a town after a person; Pelops must be therefore either the personification of a people, the Pelopians, or of some natural

---

[1] Hygin. ut supra.
[2] Tzetz. ut supra.
[3] The Myrtóan sea was said to derive its name from this event. Euripidés (Orest. 992 seq.) makes the deed to take place at Cape Geræstos in Eubœa.
[4] Soph. Elec. 504 seq. Eurip. ut sup. and 1548 seq.
[5] Hérod. vii. 8, 11. Thuk. i. 9.
[6] Il. ii. 103, 104.
[7] Sch. Pind. Ol. i. 79 (127).
[8] See above, p. 383, note.
[9] Ol. i. 24 (37).

quality or property of the land. Some therefore derive his name from ἔλα, *splendour*, and render it the *Illustrious*, an honorific appellation of prince or people.[1] Others connect it with πηλὸς, ἕλος, and the family of words relating to *water* and the land by marshes and streams.[2] This last theory is supported by the horsemanship of Pelops and the connexion between him and Poseidón; and possibly Pelops might be only another appellation of the water-god whom we find with so many names at the Isthmus. The origin of the name Peloponnése, which is certainly post-Homéric, is still however even on this hypothesis enveloped in obscurity; for in those times lands were not called after gods any more than after men.

The physical theory, supposing it to be correct, appears to be further confirmed by many circumstances of the mythe. Thus Pelops, the water-land, or perhaps the *Feeder*,[3] is the son of Tantalos the *flourishing*, and the brother of Niobé, the *young* green earth; and the legend of his being cut up and eaten *raw* by Démétér[4] may denote the breaking up of the ground in order to renew it. The name of his father-in-law may denote the vines that spread over the land, and that of his wife the numerous steeds that fed on his pastures. Hermés the rural god restores Pelops to life, and the same deity, under the name of Myrtilos, that is Myrtos, or the protector of the myrtles that love the sea-shore, enables him to win the prize. The connexion between this god and Pelops is also intimated in the tradition that the first temple of Hermés in the Peloponnése was built by Pelops.

Still, if the principle which we have advanced, of different kinds of mythes arising from different derivations of the name being related of the same object, be correct, Pelops, *i.e.* the Pelopians, might also have been regarded as a physical being, and the mythes above related owe their origin to this view of his character.

Ἀτρεὺς καὶ Θυέστης. *Atreus et Thyestes.*

Atreus and Thyestés, the sons of Pelops and Hippodameia, having out of jealousy killed their half-brother Chrysippos, were

---

[1] Welcker *in Schwenk.* 336.   The Pelopians, i. e. *Illustrious*, would be then like the Phlegyans (see p. 307), the Achæans (p. 266 *note*[7]), to which perhaps we may add the Kadmeians (p. 290), the Phæakians (p. 246), and even the Hellénes (from ἕλη); just as the Goths were the *Good*, i. e. *Brave*, the Franks the *Free*, the Slaves the *Famous* (from *slava* fame), etc.   It must not however be concealed that there is no tradition whatever of a people named Pelopians.

[2] Völcker, *Myth. der Jap.* 351 *seq.*   [3] From πάω: see above, p. 18.

[4] As ὠμὸς *raw*, and ὦμος *shoulder*, only differ in accent, ὠμοφαγία *raw-eating*, easily became *shoulder-eating* when the original sense of the mythe was lost.   The ivory shoulder was a poetic adjunct.

banished by their father, and at the same time, it is added, he pronounced a curse on them that they and their posterity should perish by means of one another. They retired to Mideia, whence on the death of Pelops Atreus came with an army to E'lis and took possession of the throne.[1]

Thyestés, it is said, afterwards seduced Aëropé the wife of Atreus, who for this offence drove him from his kingdom; and Thyestés, out of revenge, sent Atreus' son Pleisthenés, whom he had brought up as his own, to murder his father. Atreus taking the youth to be the son of Thyestés put him to death, and the curse of Pelops thus began to be accomplished.[2]

Another legend thus accounts for the enmity between the brothers. Hermés, in order to avenge his son Myrtilos whom Pelops had murdered, put a gold-fleeced lamb into the flocks of Atreus, between whom and Thyestés, according to this legend, the kingdom was disputed. Atreus, in order to prove that the kingdom by right was his, said he would produce a gold-fleeced lamb: Thyestés, however, having corrupted Atreus' wife Aëropé, had gotten the lamb; and when Atreus could not exhibit it as he promised, the people thinking he had deceived them deprived him of the kingdom. Some time after however Atreus returned and said that to prove his right he would let them see the Sun and the Pleiades moving from west to east. This miracle Zeus performed in his favour, and he thus obtained the kingdom and drove Thyestés into exile.[3]

Another legend continues the tale in a more tragic and horrible form. Atreus, it is said, invited his brother to return, promising to bury all enmity in oblivion. Thyestés accepted the proffered reconciliation; a feast was made to celebrate it: but the revengeful Atreus killed the two sons of Thyestés and served their flesh up to their father; and while Thyestés was eating he caused the heads and hands of his children to be brought in and shown to him. The Sun, it is said, at the sight of this horrible deed checked his chariot in the midst of his course.[4]

Thyestés fled to Thesprótia, whence he went to Sikyón, where his daughter Pelopia dwelt. He arrived on the very night in which she was to offer a sacrifice to Athéna, and not wishing to disturb the ceremony, he hid himself in the grove. As Pelopia was joining in the sacred dance, she slipped in the blood of the victims and defiled her clothes. Quitting the dance, she went

---

[1] Hellaníkos *ap. Sch. Il.* ii. 105. [2] Hygin. 86.
[3] Sch. *Eurip. Orest.* 811, 995. Eudocia (77) relates the story of the lamb somewhat differently.
[4] Sch. *Eurip. Orest.* 811. Hygin. 88, 258. Seneca, *Thyestés.*

down to the river to wash the dirt from her garment. When she had taken it off, Thyestés, covering his head that he might not be known, sprang from his lurking place, and forcibly embraced her. In the struggle she drew his sword from the sheath, and taking it back with her, concealed it in the temple of Athéna.

The next day Thyestés presented himself to the king of Si-kyón, and besought him to restore him to his native country. Meantime famine and plague had come to punish the crime of Atreus; and the oracle had responded, that to remove it Atreus should bring back his brother. He went to Thesprótia in search of him, where he beheld Pelopia the daughter of Thyestés; and supposing her to be the daughter of the king, demanded her in marriage. Thesprótos gave her to him. She was already pregnant by her father, and shortly after her marriage brought forth a son, whom Atreus caused to be exposed; but the herdsman, taking pity on him, reared him on the dugs of a she-goat (αἰγὸς)—whence he derived his name, Ægisthos. Atreus, hearing he was alive, had him sought for, and brought him up as his own son.

Atreus afterwards sent his sons Agamemnón and Menelάos in search of Thyestés. They went to Delphi, where they met him, who was also come to consult the god on the nature of the vengeance which he should seek to take on his brother. They seized and brought him to Atreus, who cast him into prison. Atreus then called Ægisthos, and directed him to put the captive to death. Ægisthos went to the prison bearing the sword which his mother had given him: and the moment Thyestés beheld it, he knew it to be that which he had lost, and asked the youth how he had come by it. He replied that it was the gift of his mother. At the desire of Thyestés, Pelopia came, and the whole deed of darkness was brought to light. The unfortunate daughter of Thyestés, under pretence of examining the sword, plunged it into her bosom. Ægisthos drew it forth reeking with blood, and brought it to Atreus as a proof of having obeyed his commands. Rejoiced at the death, as he thought, of his brother, Atreus offered a sacrifice of thanksgiving on the shore of the sea; but while he was engaged in it, he was fallen on and slain by Thyestés and Ægisthos.[1]

This is the most horrible legend in the Grecian mythology. It is evidently post-Homéric, for exclusive of the fact that such atrocities are quite repugnant to the spirit of the heroic ages as

[1] Hyginus, *ut supra.*

portrayed in the Homéric poems, it is utterly irreconcilable with the account of the Pelopids given in them. Of Agamemnón's sceptre it is said [1] that Héphæstos made it and gave it to Zeus, who gave it to Hermés, by whom it was presented to 'horse-lashing' Pelops, who gave it to Atreus the shepherd of the people, who when dying left it to 'lamb-abounding' Thyestés, who left it to Agamemnón. Here we have a family of princes rich in cattle legitimately transmitting the sceptre from one to the other, a state of things totally at variance with the atrocities above related. It was probably at the time when the Greeks had become familiar with Asia and the barbarous regions round the Euxine that the nameless deeds of 'Pelops' line' were invented. The author of the Alkmæonis, whoever he was, is said to have related the story of the gold-fleeced lamb.[2] We know not who first told of the horrid banquet, but we find it frequently alluded to by Æschylos,[3] though he does not appear to have made the deeds of Atreus and Thyestés the subject of a drama. Sophoklés wrote two Thyestés, and Euripidés one; and we have probably their contents in the legends transmitted to us by Hyginus.

There is a difficulty in the Homéric account of Agamemnón's being the successor of Thyestés, for he calls him more than once the son of Atreus,[4] and in the Odyssey he is murdered by Ægisthos the son of Thyestés.[5] The common solution of Atreus having left his kingdom to his brother in charge for his son, who was not of age, is not, we believe, agreeable to the Homéric usage.

With respect to the names in this mythe, when we consider the derivations given above of Tantalos and Pelops, and the rural character apparently belonging originally to the family, we might be tempted to seek for indications of the same character in the names of the other members.[6] Atreus might then, like Adrastos, find its root in ἀδρὸς or in ᾿ΑΔΕ΄Ω *to satiate*, while Thyestés might be the *Sacrificer* (θύω), on account of his numerous flocks and herds. Ægisthos plainly comes from αἴξ. But on the other hand Atreus might come from ἄτη or from a and τρέω, and Thyestés from θύω *to rage*, and thus by the

---

[1] *Il.* ii. 101 *seq.*   [2] Sch. *Eurip. Orest.* 995.
[3] *Agam.* 1096, 1217 *seq.*; 1590 *seq.*   *Choëph.* 1068.   [4] *Il.* ii. 23; xi. 131.
[5] *Od.* iv. 517 *seq.*; xi. 408 *seq.* If Nitzsch's suspicion of iv. 514–520 being an interpolation be correct, Homer may not have made Ægisthos the son of Thyestés. Atreides then, as used of Agamemnón and Meneláos, may be like Alkeides: see above, p. 331.
[6] The same peaceful character appears in the names of two of the other sons of Pelops, Kopreus (*Manurer ?*) and Pittheus (*Persuader ?*).

principle of secondary derivation, give origin to the mythes above related in accordance with the darker ones of Tantalos and Pelops.

CHAPTER XI.

MYTHES OF ACHAIA.

Μελάνιππος καὶ Κομαιθώ.   *Melanippus et Comœtho.*

ARTEMIS was worshipped at Patræ under the name of Triklaria. Her priestess was always a virgin, who held her office till she married. This priesthood was once filled by a beautiful virgin named Komæthó. A youth named Melanippos, also distinguished for his beauty, conceived a violent passion for the fair priestess, which was participated in by its object, but the parents of both the lovers refused their consent to the union. Thus thwarted in their lawful wishes, the youth and maiden lost sight of prudence, and they polluted the sanctity of the temple by the unhallowed gratification of their passion. The goddess was offended; disease and pestilence testified to the people her displeasure.

Envoys were sent to consult the Pythian oracle, and the voice of the god fixed the guilt on Komæthó and Melanippos, whom he ordered to be sacrificed to Artemis, and a youth and maiden of superior beauty to be offered annually as victims to the goddess. For many years this cruel rite remained in use, and the stream which flowed by the temple derived from it the name of *Implacable* (ἀμείλιχος). An oracle, however, held out hopes of its ceasing, when a stranger should arrive in the country bearing with him an unknown deity.

On the division of the spoils at Troy, Eurypylos the son of Euæmón had gotten a coffer containing a statue of Dionýsos, the work of Héphæstos, as was said, and given to Dardanos by Zeus. Kassandra, it was also said, had thrown this coffer in the way of the Greeks, knowing that it would prove injurious to whoever should find it. Eurypylos opening it saw the statue, and immediately lost his senses: his reason however did not entirely depart, and he had lucid intervals. In consequence of this calamity, instead of going home to Thessaly, he sailed to Kirrha, and consulted the oracle at Delphi for relief of his disorder. He was directed to take up his abode, and dedicate the coffer, where he should find people sacrificing after a strange fashion. He re-embarked, and the wind carried him to Aroé on the coast of Achaia, where he saw a procession moving along the shore, leading a youth and maiden to be sacrificed on the altar of the Triklarian Artemis. He at once perceived the accomplishment of the oracle given to him; the Achæans saw that theirs also was fulfilled, the human sacrifices ceased, the stranger was restored to his reason, the coffer of Dionýsos was dedicated, and the river changed its appellation to that of *Mild* (μείλιχος).[1]

Κόρεσος καὶ Καλλιρρόη. *Coresus et Callirrhoe.*

In Patræ stood a temple of the Kalydonian Dionýsos, whose statue had been brought thither from Kalydón. The following legend was related respecting it. While Kalydón flourished, a man named Koresos was priest of Dionýsos in that country. A maiden named Kallirrhoé became the object of his love, but unhappily the fervour of his attachment only augmented the hatred and aversion of the maiden to her lover. When neither gifts nor entreaties could avail to win her love, the priest in despair turned to his god, and besought him to avenge his sufferings. The god heard the prayer of the suppliant, and an insanity similar to intoxication fell on the Kalydonians, of which many of them perished.

In their distress, they had recourse to the oracle of Dódóna, and they learned that their calamity was the infliction of Dionýsos, and would not cease till Koresos had sacrificed Kallirrhoé, or some one who was willing to die in her stead. It was resolved to obey the oracle. Kallirrhoé could find no one possessed of sufficient affection for her to pay so high a penalty; friends, kindred, parents, all shrunk back, and the unhappy maiden was forced to submit to her cruel fate. As a victim, she was crowned and led to the altar, where Koresos stood to perform the appointed sacrifice; but at the sight of her, love overcame every other sentiment in the bosom of the priest, and he slew himself instead of the beautiful victim. This last and decisive proof of true affection quite vanquished the hitherto relentless maiden; her violent hate was converted into ardent love; and filled with pity for her lover, and shame at her own ungrateful insensibility, she retired to a fountain near the port of Kalydon, and there cut her own throat and died. The spring derived from her its name,—Kallirrhoé, *i.e.* *Fair-flowing.*[2]

[1] Paus. vii. 19.
[2] Paus. vii. 21. The legend was evidently invented to account for the name the spring. As the reader may perceive, it is the foundation of Guarini's pastoral drama, *Il Pastor Fido.*

Σέλεμνος καὶ ᾿Αργυρᾶ.   *Selemnus et Argyra.*

Selemnus was a beautiful youth, who pastured his flocks near the shore of the sea. Argyra, one of the sea-nymphs, beheld and loved him, and frequently emerging from the waters, came to enjoy his society on the banks of a river. But the beauty of the youth departing, the fickle sea-maiden ceased to regard him, and no longer sought his company. Grief at her loss killed the deserted shepherd, and Aphrodíté in compassion changed him into a river of his own name. But his love still continuing, Aphrodíté again moved with pity exerted her divine power, and caused him to forget Argyra. The waters of the Selemnos became in consequence a remedy for love, inducing oblivion on those who bathed in them.[1]

CHAPTER XII.

MYTHES OF THE ISLES.

THE principal mythic cycle which the isles present is that of Kréte (Κρήτη), an island remarkable for its estrangement from the rest of Greece during the historic period; for though Krétan archers served all parties as mercenaries, the people of Kréte took no share in the Persian, Peloponnésian, or other wars. The political insignificance of Kréte in this period might lead one to doubt of the power and dominion of the Krétan monarch Minós in the mythic period; and perhaps the truth of that dominion was too readily adopted from the Athenian legends by Thukydidés, the introduction to whose admirable work has had too much influence on the minds of some modern inquirers, who seem to forget that he had only the same sources of information respecting the mythic ages as we ourselves possess, and that the art of historic criticism was unknown in his time. The Krétan cycle is confined to the Minóic family, at the head of which are placed Zeus and Európé.

[1] Paus. vii. 23. Near the river Selemnos was the fount Argyra; hence the origin of the legend. Selemnos is probably the *Bright-stream* (from σέλας) and is thus akin to Argyra. We may recollect ἀργυροδίνης, an epithet of streams. In the south of Ireland there is a river called the Arigodheen, i. e. *The Little-silver-stream.*

Εὐρώπη. *Europa.*

Zeus, says the legend,[1] having become enamoured of the beauty of Európé the daughter of Phœnix or of Agénór and Télephassa, changed himself into a beautiful white bull, and approached her ' breathing saffron from his mouth' as she was gathering flowers with her companions in a mead near the sea-shore.   Európé, delighted with the tameness and beauty of the animal, caressed him, crowned him with flowers, and at length ventured to mount on his back.   The disguised god immediately made off with his lovely burden, ran along the waves of the sea, and stopped not till he arrived at Kréte, not far from Gortýna.   Here he resumed his own form, and beneath a plane-tree embraced the trembling maid.[2]   The fruits of his caresses were three sons, Minós, Rha-damanthys, and Sarpédón.   Asterión king of Kréte espoused Európé, and reared her sons.[3]   He was succeeded in his kingdom by Minós.

In the Ilias[4] Zeus says that the daughter of 'far-famed' Phœ-nix bore to him Minós and 'godlike' Rhadamanthys.   Hésiod probably related the story at length; but he does not appear to have made Európé a Sidónian, as was afterwards the practice. We know not when this commenced[5] or how she became the sister of Kadmos.   It probably originated in the name of her father; and as the legend very appropriately made Agénór the sire of Kadmos, Európé was also said to be his daughter, while her mother Télephassa became the inappropriate mother of Kadmos.   We shall presently see the real nature of Európé.

Μινώς, 'Ραδάμανθυς, καὶ Σαρπηδών. *Minos, Rhadamanthys, et Sarpedon.*

These three brothers fell into discord for the sake of a beauti-ful youth named Milétos, the son of Apolló, or of Zeus.   The youth testifying most esteem for Sarpédón, Minós chased them out of Kréte.   Milétos going to Karia, built a town there, which he named from himself.   Sarpédón went to Lykia, where he aided Kilix against the people of that country, and obtained the

---

[1] Hésiod and Bakchylidés *ap. Sch. Il.* xii. 292.   See also Apollod. iii. 1. Moschus, *Idyll.* ii.   Ov. *Met.* ii. 833 *seq.*   *Fast.* v. 605 *seq.*   Nonn. i. 45 *seq.*
[2] See Theophrast. *Hist. Pl.* i. 13.   Pliny, *Nat. Hist.* i. 1.   It was asserted that this tree never shed its leaves: see Pashley, *Travels in Crete,* i. 95.
[3] Zeus-Asterión is like Zeus-Tyndareós and others: see above, p. 299.
[4] *Il.* xiv. 321.
[5] Hérodotos (i. 2) is the earliest extant author who calls Európé a Sidónian

sovereignty of a part of it.   Zeus is said to have bestowed on
him a life of treble duration.[1]

Rhadamanthys ruled with justice and equity over the islands.
Having committed an accidental homicide, he retired to Bœótia,
where he married Alkméné, the mother of Héraklés.   According
to Homer,[2] Rhadamanthys was placed on the E'lysian Plain
among the heroes to whom Zeus allotted that blissful abode.
Pindar[3] seems to make him a sovereign or judge in the Island
of the Blest.   Later poets place him with Minós and Æakos in
the under-world, where their office is to judge the dead.

Minós married Pasiphaé, the daughter of the Sun and Perséis, by whom he had several children, the most celebrated of
whom were Androgeós, Glaukos, Deukalión, Ariadné, and Phædra.   The Krétans hesitating to give him the royal dignity after
the death of Asterión, to prove his claim to it he asserted that
he could obtain whatever he prayed for.   Then sacrificing to
Poseidón, he besought him to send him a bull from the bottom
of the sea, promising to sacrifice whatever should appear.   Poseidón sent the bull, and Minós received the kingdom.   He
ruled, according to Homer,[4] for nine years at Knóssos, and was
the *intimate friend* (ὁαριστής) of Zeus, who gave him wise laws
and regulations for his people.   Minós was victorious in war,
and extended his dominion over the isles of the Ægæan.

Minós had a brazen man, named Talós, given to him by Héphæstos or to Európé by Zeus, who compassed the isle thrice in each
day to prevent the landing of enemies.   His mode of destroying
them was to make himself red-hot in the fire and then embrace
them.   When the Argó approached Kréte, Médeia persuaded
Talós that she could make him immortal: he therefore suffered
her to pull out the pin in his heel, and let the *ichór* run out from
his only vein, and he thus died.[5]

The bull which Poseidón had sent out of the sea being of
large size and of a brilliant white hue, appeared to Minós too
beautiful an animal to be slain, and he put him in his herd, and
substituted an ordinary bull.   Poseidón offended at this act
made the bull run wild, and inspired Pasiphaé with a strange
passion for him, but which she had no means of gratifying

---

[1] Apollod. *ut sup.*   Sarpédón, *i. e.* Harpédón, is evidently derived from th
carrying-off (ἁρπάγη) of Európé: see Welcker, *Kret. Kol.* 9, for examples of thi
process.   Homer does not name him among the children of Európé.   It is no
unlikely that it was the resemblance of sound in Lykia and Lyktos that gav
occasion to the legend in the text.   Another account said that Lykia wa
named from Lykos the brother of Ægeus king of Attica.   Hérod. i. 173.

[2] *Od.* iv. 563 *seq.*   [3] *Ol.* ii. 75 (137).   [4] *Od.* xix. 178.

[5] Apollod. i. 9, 26. Apoll. Rh. iv. 1638 *seq.* Sch. *Od.* xx. 302. Plat. *Min.* 320

Dædalos, the celebrated Athenian artist, being at that time in Kréte, having fled from home for homicide, undertook to accomplish the wishes of the queen. He accordingly formed a hollow cow of wood, covered with the hide of a real cow, in which he inclosed Pasiphaé, and placed it in the mead where the bull used to feed. All succeeded as was desired, and Pasiphaé became the mother of Asterios, called the Minótaur (Μινώταυρος), from his having the head of a bull joined to the body of a man. Minós, in compliance with an oracle, made Dædalos build for him the Labyrinth, an edifice with numberless winding passages and turnings, from which egress was almost impossible for those who entered it. In this he placed the Minótaur, where he preyed on the victims given to him.[1] The principal actions of Minós have been already related.[2] He is said to have fallen in a war against Kókalos king of Sicily, who protected Dædalos. He was succeeded in his kingdom by his son Deukalión, whose son Idomeneus led the troops of Kréte to the war of Troy.[3]

'Αριάδνη καὶ Φαίδρα. Ariadne et Phædra.

Ariadné the daughter of Minós, as has been related above, fell in love with Théseus when he came to Kréte, and furnished him with the clew which enabled him to thread the mazes of the Labyrinth. She fled with him from her father; but Théseus, says Homer,[4] did not reap the fruits of her love; for when they arrived at the isle of Dia or Naxos, Artemis slew her on the testimony of Dionýsos. Another legend[5] says that she was deserted by Théseus, to whom Athéna appeared as he slept, and desired him to leave her and make sail for Athens; and that as Ariadné was weeping, Aphrodíté came and consoled her by an assurance that she should be the bride of Dionýsos. The god appeared, enjoyed her love, and gave her a golden crown, which was afterwards placed among the stars; she bore him a son named Œnopión.

Phædra was married to Théseus. The tale of her love for her step-son Hippolytos has been already related.

In the Theogony[6] it is said that

> The gold-haired Dionysos made the blond
> Ariadné Minós' maid his blooming spouse,
> And Kronos' son gave her immortal life.

---

[1] The Labyrinth is a pure poetic fiction; no such edifice ever did exist in Kréte. The real Labyrinth of Egypt gave occasion to it: see Höck's *Kréta*, i. p. 56 *seq.*
[2] See above, p. 342 *seq.*   [3] *Il.* xiii. 451 *seq.*   [4] *Od.* xi. 325.
[5] Pherekýdes, *ap. Sch. Od.* xi. 321. Ov. *Art. Amat.* i. 527 *seq.* Catull. xiv 76 *seq.*   [6] *Theog.* 947.

Ariadné (*Much-pleasing*) then apparently belongs to the mythology of Dionýsos, with whom she was associated in the Naxian worship, and she probably denotes the joy inspired by wine: or she may be the original name of the brilliant constellation with which she is associated, and have been made a heroine in the usual manner, and then, on account of her name, united with the wine-god. The Athenians, always anxious to enlarge their own narrow cycle at the expense of others, seem to have joined her with their Théseus, and it was thus perhaps that she became the daughter of Minós. The passage in the Odyssey would be decisive on this point, were it not that the Athenians were such tamperers with the works of the old poets that one cannot help being suspicious of all passages relating to them. The passage of the Ilias in which Ariadné is mentioned is, we think, justly regarded as a late addition.[1]

Γλαῦκος. Glaucus.

Glaukos the son of Minós pursuing, when a child, a mouse, fell into a jar of honey, and was smothered. When he could not be found, his father sent to inquire of the oracle about him. The answer he got was, that there was a three-coloured cow in his herd, and that he who could best tell what she was like could restore his son to life. The soothsayers were all assembled; and Polyeidos the son of Kœranos said, her colour was that of the berry of the briar,—green, red, and lastly black. Minós desired him to find his son; and Polyeidos, by his skill in divination, discovered where he was. Minós then ordered him to restore him to life; and on his declaring his incapacity so to do, shut him up in a chamber with the body of the child. While here, the soothsayer saw a serpent approach the body, and he struck and killed it. Another immediately appeared with a plant in its mouth, and laid it on the dead one, who instantly came to life. Polyeidos, by employing the same herb, recovered the child.[2]

Minós, before he let him depart, insisted on his communicating his art to Glaukos. He did so; but as he was taking leave, he desired his pupil to spit into his mouth. Glaukos obeyed, and lost the memory of all he had learned.[3]

On taking a survey of the circumstances of these Krétan legends, and the names of the persons who occur in them, it is difficult to avoid recognising a worship of the celestial bodies,

---

[1] *Il.* xviii. 591. Payne Knight *in loco.* It perplexed the ancient critics: see the Scholia.　　　[2] See above, p. 376.

[3] Apollod. iii. 3.1,2. Hygin. 136. Tzetz. *Lyc.* 811. It is evidently a late fiction.

more particularly of the Moon, of which last the names of the Minóic family would appear to have been appellations. Thus Európé (*Broad-face* or *Broad-one*) is the daughter of Phœnix (*Ruddy*) and Télephassa (*Far-shining*), and mother of Minós, a name not unlike *Mén*[1] (Μήν, *Moon*); and she marries Asterión (*Starry*). The wife of Minós is Pasiphaé (*All-bright*), the daughter of the Sun and Perséis; and their daughter is Phædra (*Bright*). Though we do not believe that the mystic mode of viewing the sun as a bull and the moon as a cow prevailed in early Greece, the horns of the latter gave occasion to the idea of her riding or driving steers; and perhaps the legend of Európé passing over the sea on a bull is an ancient expression of this idea. The same may have been the origin of the tale of Pasiphaé's love for the bull, and of her offspring by him, the Moon-bull, as Minótaur may best perhaps be rendered. The circumstances of the legends are mostly the inventions of the Athenians, at the hands of whose dramatists the characters of the Minóic family suffered severely.

Though we thus see in the Krétan cycle only personifications of the moon, Minós and his family may have been real persons named after their favourite deity. We regard this hypothesis however as being by no means probable. The connexion of Minós with Poseidón, the naval power ascribed to him, and the names Glaukos and Deukalión among his children, might seem to indicate a Krétan worship of the god of the sea.

There is one name however in the Krétan cycle which does not seem to have any reference to either the moon or the sea, namely Rhadamanthys. As we have seen, he is connected with Kréte, and by Homer and Pindar he is placed in the blissful abode of departed heroes in the West. He is no doubt also placed in Bœótia, but this is manifestly a late fiction, founded perhaps on his visit to Eubœa in the Odyssey.

An able mythologist,[2] observing that Hesychius has a verb ραδαμέω which he explains by βλαστάνω, *to make grow*,[3] conjectures that Rhadamanthys may be a compound of this verb and ἄνθος, *flower*, and that therefore he may have been a power of the earth

---

[1] Manú is the name of the Hindú legislator : Mén was the first mortal king of Egypt; Manés was the first king of Lydia: Minyas one of the earliest kings of Greece: Minós the first king and lawgiver of Krete. To these Buttmann (*Mythol.* ii. 232 *seq.*) joins the German Mannus, *Man*; and supposing this last to be the true meaning of all these names, infers, in his usual manner, the original unity of all these peoples and their traditions.

[2] Mr. Kenrick, in a letter to the author.

[3] Ῥαδαμεῖ, βλαστάνει; Ῥάδαμνος, βλαττός, απαλός, κλάδος, ἄνθος, καυλὸν βλαστόν.

who sent up vegetation, a Florus or masculine of Flora; and he thinks that the Isles of the Blest which Pindar describes as being profuse of flowers were therefore his appropriate abode. We cannot however yield our assent to this ingenious theory, and little given as we are to Egyptising, we feel inclined rather to seek for Rhadamanthys on the banks of the Nile. We are informed by Plutarch[1] that the Egyptian name of the abode of the dead was Amenthés ('Aμένθης), and in the Koptic version of the Scriptures Amenti is the term equivalent to our Hell ("Aιδης), while in that language Ra or Ro is *king*.[2] By inserting then a *d* in order to avoid the *hiatus* we get Rad-Amenthés, *i.e.* King of Erebos. We cannot take on us to assert whether Amenti occurs or not in the hieroglyphics, but Ement (*West*) is a word of frequent occurrence in them, and President of Ement is a constant title of Osíris, who is the lord and judge of the departed. It seems therefore to be highly probable that Ement and Amenti may be only different forms of the same word, and that the Egyptians, like so many other peoples, placed the abode of the dead in the West. It is a very remarkable circumstance, that in the Sanscrit also Rhat should be *king* and A'menthas *west*;[3] and as this coincidence could hardly be fortuitous, it affords one among the many presumptions of Egypt's having derived several of her civil and religious institutes from India. Rhat-A'menthas may in fact have been the Indian name of the ruler of Egypt, which the Egyptians adopted and gave to the ruler of the dead in the land of the West.

We have already[4] observed that Erebos may be derived from the Semitic 'Ereb *west*. It therefore seems not improbable that the Greeks obtained the name Rhadamanthys and the idea of the abode of the dead in the West mediately from Egypt. The Phœnicians of course will appear to have been the agents, but when we find Rhadamanthys so closely connected with Kréte we are tempted to look elsewhere. Now on the confines of Egypt dwelt a little people named the Philistines, whom there is no slight reason for supposing to have been a Pelasgic colony from Kréte,[5] and who always carried on an active commerce with

---

[1] *De Is. et Os.* p. 362. Τὸν ὑποχθόνιον τόπον, εἰς ὃν οἴονται ‑ὰς ψιχὰς ἀπέρχεσθαι μετὰ ‑ὴν τελευτήν, 'Αμένθην καλοῦσι, σημαίνοντος τοῦ ὀνόματος τὸν λαμβάνοντα καὶ διδόντα. The latter part is a description of the nature of the place and not the proper interpretation of the name; for it is hardly possible that so short a word could express so much. In ὑποχθόνιον here, as in καταβῆναι in Hérodotos (ii. 122), may be merely expressed Greek ideas.

[2] See Jablonski, *Opusc.* i. p. 25.

[3] See Bohlen, *Das Alte Indien*, ii. p. 459.   [4] See above, p. 240.

[5] See Hitzig, *Die Philistäer.* Pelasgi and Pelishtim may be only different forms of the same name.

Greece. It is therefore not unlikely that it was chiefly through these that Egyptian and Semitic terms and ideas reached Hellas, and thus became incorporated in its mythology.

Αἰακὸς καὶ Τελαμών. *Æacus et Telamon.*

The river-god Asópos married Metópé the daughter of the river-god Ladón, and by her had several children. His daughter Ægína attracting the love of Zeus, the amorous monarch of the gods carried her off, and struck with a thunderbolt Asópos when he pursued them, and forced him to go home again; and hence it was said, that the waters of the Asópos carried coals along them.[1]

Zeus carried his fair prize into the desert isle of Œnóné, afterwards named from her Ægína, where she brought forth a son named Æakos, who being weary of solitude, when he grew up, his father to relieve him turned all the ants in the island into men and women.[2] Æakos married Endéis the daughter of Cheirón, who bore him two sons, Telamón and Péleus. By the Néréis Psamathé, who changed herself into a fount to escape his embraces, he had another son named Phókos,[3] whom his brothers, envying his superior skill in the gymnic exercises, killed with a blow of a discus, and concealed his body in a wood : but the murder coming to light, Æakos drove them both from the island.[4]

Æakos was distinguished for his piety and his favour with the gods. When Poseidón and Apolló were set to build the walls of Troy, they made him the associate of their toil.[5] It is said that Greece being afflicted with sterility and dearth, on account of the crime of Pelops, who had cut into pieces Stymphálos king of Arkadia, and scattered the pieces about;[6] and application having been made to the oracle, the response given was, that it would only be removed on the prayer of Æakos. The righteous son of Zeus preferred his petition, copious rains descended, and the land once more flourished. When Æakos died the keys of the nether-world were by Pluto committed to his custody.[7]

---

[1] Apollod. iii. 12, 6.

[2] Hés. *Fr.* 48. This legend is very pleasingly told by Ovid (*Met.* vii. 517 *seq.*), who says that the isle was thus replenished after a pestilence. It is indebted for its origin to the resemblance in sound between μύρμηξ, ant, and Myrmidons, the tribe who are said to have dwelt in Ægina : comp. Strab. viii. 6, 16, p. 375.

[3] *Theog.* 1004.   [4] Alkmæonis *ap. Sch. Eur. Andr.* Apollod. *ut sup.*

[5] Pind. *Ol.* viii. 31 (41) *seq.*

[6] Others ascribed it to the prayers of Minós to Zeus to avenge his son Andrógeos. Diodór. iv. 61.   [7] Apollod. *ut sup.* Isocr *Evag.* 5.

Telamón, when banished by his father, fled to the neighbouring isle of Salamis, where Kychrés the son of Poseidón by Salamis the daughter of Asópos then reigned, having slain a serpent which ravaged the island. He gave his daughter in marriage to Telamón, and left him the kingdom. Telamón accompanied Héraklés to Troy: and the hero gave him Hésioné the daughter of Laomedón, by whom he had a son named Teukros. By Peridæa the grand-daughter of Pelops he had already a son called Æas; for Héraklés having prayed for male issue for his friend, an eagle (ἀετός) appeared in answer to his prayer, and the child was named from it.[1]

In the cycle of the Tyndarids we observed an apparent reference to light and fire, so in that of the Æakids, as in those of the Kadmeians and Néleids, there may be one to water. Thus we have in it Asópos, Ægína, Psamathé, Phókos, Thetis, Péleus, Achilleus, like Acheloós (aqua), Teukros (δευκρός?), Telamón (ἕλος?), Hésioné, Æas (the name of a river[2]), and Æakos, which is perhaps of the same origin.[3]

The following are astronomic mythes, which we place here for the sake of convenience.

Ὠρίων.   Orion.

The hero O'ríón is not mentioned in the Ilias; but in the Odyssey[4] we are told by Kalypsó, that ' rose-fingered ' E'ós took him, and that ' holy, gold-seated ' Artemis slew him with her ' gentle darts ' in Ortygia. In another place his size and beauty are praised.[5] Odysseus,[6] when relating what he saw in Erebos, says,

> Then next the huge O'ríón I beheld,
> Chasing the beasts o'er the asphodelian mead,
> Which in the lonely mountains he had slain,
> Bearing his brazen aye-enduring club.

O'ríón was said to be the son of Poseidón by Euryalé the daughter of Minyas; and his father gave him the power of wading through the depths of the sea, or, as others say, of walking on its surface.[7] He married Sidé, whom Héra cast into Erebos for

---

[1] Pind. *Isth.* vi. 41 (60) *seq.*   Apollod. iii. 12.   For everything relating to Ægína, see Müller's *Æginetica.*

[2] Hekatæos thus named the Aoös in Illyricum.   Strabó, vii. 5, 8, p. 316. Id. vi. 2, 4, p. 270.   Ov. *Met.* i. 580.

[3] See Appendix G.

[4] *Od.* v. 121.   [5] *Od.* xi. 310.   [6] *Od.* xi. 572.

[7] Hésiod. *ap. Sch. Nikandr. Ther.* 15.

contending with her in beauty.[1] It is also said that this hero was
earth-born.[2]

Hyria, a town of the Tanagraïc or Théban territory in Bœótia,
is said to have been the birth-place of O'ríon. As Zeus, Poseidón, and Hermés were one time, says the legend, taking a ramble
on earth, they came late in the evening to the house of a small
farmer[3] named Hyrieus. Seeing the wayfarers, Hyrieus, who
was standing at his door, invited them to enter and pass the
night in his humble abode. The gods accepted the kind invitation, and were hospitably entertained. Pleased with their host,
they inquired if he had any wish which he desired to have gratified. Hyrieus replied, that he once had a wife whom he tenderly
loved, and that he had sworn never to marry another. She was
dead: he was childless: his vow was binding: and yet he was
desirous of being a father. The gods took the hide of his only
ox, which he had sacrificed in their honour; they buried it in
the earth; and ten months afterwards a boy came to light, whom
Hyrieus named Uríon or O'ríon.[4]

When O'ríon grew up he went to the isle of Chios, where he
became enamoured of Merope the daughter of Œnopión the son
of Dionýsos and Ariadné. He sought her in marriage; but
while wooing, seized a favourable opportunity, and offered her
violence. Her father, incensed at this conduct, having made
O'ríon drunk, blinded him when asleep, and cast him on the sea-
shore. The blinded hero contrived to reach Lémnos, and came
to the forge of Héphæstos, who taking pity on him, gave him
Kédalión (*Guardian*), one of his men, to be his guide to the abode
of the Sun. Placing Kédalión on his shoulder, O'ríon proceeded
to the East; and there meeting the Sun-god, was restored to
vision by his beam. Anxious for vengeance on Œnopión, he
returned to Chios; but the Chians, aware of his intention, concealed the object of his search under the ground, and O'ríon
unable to find him retired to Kréte.[5]

[1] Apollod. i. 4, 3. Σίδη is perhaps connected with σείω, and thus corresponds with O'ríon.
[2] Id. *ib.* Nonn. xlviii. 400, 419.
[3] So Ovid calls him; he is usually styled a *prince*. As we shall presently
see he was the son of Poseidón and the Pleias Alkyoné. His name is i. q.
Hysieus, from ὕω, *to rain*.
[4] 'Απὸ τοῦ οὐρεῖν. Euphorión *ap. Sch. Il.* xviii. 1, 86. Ov. *Fast.* v. 495 *seq.*
Hygin. 195. *Poet. Astr.* ii. 34. Eudocia, 441. Pindar also would seem to have
related it (Strab. ix. 2, 12, p. 404). The unseemly legend owes its origin to
the name O'ríon, and is said to have been the invention of the Athenians: see
Müller, *Orchom.* 99. In Hyginus Hyrieus is named Byrseus, from the *hide,*
βύρσα, of course.
[5] Hés. *ut sup.*   Apollod. *ut sup.*   Hygin. *ut sup.*

The death of O'ríon is differently related. As all the legends respecting him are evidently later than the time of Homer, none ventures to assign any other cause to it than the goddess Artemis, whose wrath (though Homer rather says the contrary) he drew on himself. Some said that he attempted to offer violence to the goddess herself; others, to O'pis, one of her Hyperborean maidens, and that Artemis slew him with her arrows; others again, that it was for presuming to challenge the goddess at the discus. It was also said, that when he came to Kréte, he boasted to Létó and Artemis that he was able to kill anything that would come from the earth. Indignant at his presumption they sent a huge scorpion, which stung him, and he died. It was said, finally, that Artemis loved O'ríon, and was even about to marry him. Her brother was highly displeased, and often chid her, but to no purpose. At length, observing one day O'ríon wading through the sea with his head just above the waters, he pointed it out to his sister, and maintained that she could not hit that black thing on the sea. The archer-goddess discharged a shaft: the waves rolled the dead body of O'ríon to the land; and bewailing her fatal error with many tears, Artemis placed him among the stars.[1]

Πληϊάδες ἢ Πλεϊάδες καὶ Ὑάδες. *Pleiades et Hyades.*

The Pléiades were said to be seven in number, the daughters of Atlas and the O'keanis Pléióné. Their names were Maia, E'lektra, Taÿgeté (the mothers by Zeus of Hermés, Dardanos and Lakedæmón), Alkyoné and Kelæno (who bore to Poseidón Hyrieus the father of O'ríon and Lykos), Steropé the mother of Œnomaos by Arés), and Meropé, who married Sisyphos.[2]

These nymphs led a single life, and hunted with Artemis. O'ríon happening to see them became enamoured, and pursued them; in their distress they prayed to the gods to change their form, and Zeus in pity turned them to pigeons, and then made them a constellation in the sky.[3] Though their number was seven, only six stars are visible, for E'lektra, it is said, left her place that she might not behold the ruin of Troy; or Meropé concealed her face out of shame for having alone espoused a mortal.[4] According to Pindar, the Pléiades were passing through Bœótia with their mother when they were met by O'ríon, and his chase of them lasted for five years.[5]

---

[1] Hés., Euphoríón and others, *ut sup.* Nonn. xlviii. 398 *seq.*
[2] Sch. *Il.* xviii. 486. Apollod. iii. 10, 1. Hygin. *Poet. Astr.* ii. 21.
[3] Sch. *Il. ut sup.* from the Kyklic poets. [4] Sch. *Il. ut sup.* Hygin. *ut sup.*
[5] Et. Mag. v. Πλειάς. Hyginus (*ut supra*) says seven years.

The Hyades are by some[1] also called daughters of Atlas, but according to the best accounts they were nymphs of Dódóna, to whom Zeus committed the nurture of Dionýsos. Their names, Pherekýdés says,[2] were Ambrosia, Korónis, Eudóra, Dióné Æsula, and Polyxó, by Hésiod[3] they are named Phæsula, Korónis, Kléeia, Phæó and Eudóra. They went about with their divine charge communicating his discovery to mankind, till being chased with him into the sea by Lykurgos, Zeus in compassion raised them to the skies.[4]

The Hyades are in the head, the Pléiades in the hinder part of the sign of the Bull.

The well-known line of Homer and Hésiod,

> The Pleiads, Hyads and O'ríón's strength,

exhibits these constellations as they appear in the sky, and beyond all doubt they were thus named long before they were converted into a hunter and nymphs on the earth. It has been clearly shown that it was the union of astronomy with mythology in the Alexandrian period that gave occasion to the *catasterism* of many heroes and heroines;[5] but with O'ríón and these nymphs, and perhaps with some others, the case seems to have been reversed, the constellations having been brought down from the sky, and not the mortals raised to it.

Man loves to trace in natural objects resemblances to other objects with which he is familiar. Hence many legends of rocks, mountains, and such like. The sky too offers its similitudes; there is, for example, the Crown, with its legend of Ariadné; there is the Man in the Moon, which some said was Cain, others the man who was stoned for gathering sticks on the Sabbath; while the Greeks saw in it the Sibyl[6] and the Hindús and Æthiopians a hare or antelope.[7] The resemblance of the Wain (ἄμαξα) to a rude carriage is obvious enough, and the similitude seems to have struck both Greeks and Scandinavians;[8] it still more resembles a Plough, its name in Ireland. Its likeness to an animal is not so obvious, yet the Greeks and the North American Indians agree in naming it the Bear, and the Fúllahs of Africa

---

[1] Sch. *Il. ut sup.*   [2] *Ap. Sch. Il. ut sup.*

[3] *Ap. Sch. Arat.* 172.   [4] Pherekýdés *ut sup.*

[5] Müller, *Proleg.* 191 *seq.*, where the subject of astronomic mythes is treated with this writer's usual ability.

[6] Plut. *De Pyth. Or.* 9.   *De Ser. Num. Vind.* 22.

[7] Bohlen, *Alte Indien*, i. 243. Grimm, *Deut. Mythol.* p. 679.

[8] Its ancient name in the North is *Karlsvagn*, the Carle's or Oldman's Wain the Carle, Magnusen says, is Odin or Thor. Hence our Charles' Wain. The Icelanders call the Bears, Stori (*great*) Vagn and Litli Vagn. *Edda Sæmundar*, iii. 304.

call it the Elephant,[1] while the husbandmen in ancient Italy named it the Seven Oxen (*Triones*).[2] The Spaniards call the Pléiades the Seven Kids ;[3] to the view of the rest of Europe, except the east, they present the appearance of a hen with her brood of chickens.[4]

These last similitudes lead us to think that the original conception of the Pléiades was the Pigeons (πελειάδες),[5] as they are sometimes named, and with which supposition the legends told of them will accord. Their clustering together (whence they were also named the Bunch)[6] might easily have suggested the idea. In like manner we think it probable that the true signification of the Hyades lies in their Latin name *Suculœ*, or Little Pigs, given them for a similar reason.[7] The Latin name of the Pléiades was *Vergiliœ*, or rather perhaps *Virgiliœ*, i. e. the Bunch-stars, like the Greek name.[8] O'ríón was named by the Latins *Jugula*,[9] the *Yoked* or *Yoker*, and his Greek name probably signifies the *Rouser* or *Exciter* (˝ΟΡΩ, ὀρίνω), in allusion to his hunting, or to the storms which he raised.[10]

To the Grecian herdsman or hunter therefore at particular seasons of the year the nocturnal sky would have presented the following appearance. The broad brilliant constellation O'ríón with Sirius behind him would be a hunter and his dog, before whom the Pigeons were flying, while the Bear, the object of his pursuit, kept watching him. Thus there would be a chase in the sky similar to those on earth, and legends would naturally arise which would be localised and expanded in the usual manner.

For, as the stars rise out of the sea, as it were, nothing was more obvious than to make O'ríón the son of Poseidón and Euryalé (*Wide-sea*) ; then again, as the dawn, as it were, takes away the stars, O'ríón is carried off by E'ós ; and as the mild effulgence of the moon dims and effaces the light of the stars, so

---

[1] Mollien, *Travels in Africa*, p. 297.   [2] Varro, *De L. L.* vii. 74.

[3] *Las siete cabrillas :* see *Don Quix.* Part 2. ch. xli.

[4] In Italy they are called *Le Gallinelle ;* in France *La Poussinière ;* in Greece πούλια : in Germany *Klucke, Kluckhenne ;* in Denmark *Aftenhöne* (i. e. *Eve-hen*); in England *Hen-and-chickens.* The Slavonians name them *Oldwives*, and the Finns regard the constellation as a *sieve* with holes in it.

[5] See Appendix N. The prevalent derivation of their name from πλέω to sail, though apparently so obvious, does not seem to have occurred to the ancients. The Et. Mag. derives it from τὸ πλεῖον, i. q. τὸ πλῆρες, the year being *full* with them ; or from τὸ πολεῖν, as they *turn* in the same place or go through the appointed times.   [6] Βότρυς, Sch. *Il. ut supra.*

[7] See Nitzsch *on Od.* v. 269-275.   [8] Nitzsch *ut supra.*

[9] Varro, *De L. L.* vii. 50. Probably on account of his Belt.

[10] The Latins termed O'ríón *nimbosus, procellosus, aquosus, turbidus, niger, vehemens.*

O'ríón is slain by the gentle darts of 'holy' Artemis. The beauty and size of the constellation caused the hero to be represented as the largest and handsomest of mortals.[1] Their relati've positions in the sky gave occasion to the mythe of his love and pursuit of the Pléiades; and the proximity between the signs O'ríón and the Scorpion led to the Alexandrian fiction of the mode of the hero's death.

The story of O'ríón and Œnopión is perhaps explicable on the same principle. The constellation which rises in July loves with an ardent passion the daughter of the vine. When the grapes are gathered and pressed, they are, as it were, taken out of his sight, or he is made drunk with new wine and blinded. His journey to the East denotes the heliacal rising of the star; and when he comes back the vine is hidden from his power within the ground.[2]

It is probable that many of the individual names of the Pléiades and Hyades are those of nymphs who were previously placed in other relations. Thus Maia is in the Hymn to Hermés merely an Arkadian nymph. Taÿgeté refers to Mount Taÿgeton, and Meropé (*Mortal*) is simply the nymph united to the *mortal*. E'lektra and Steropé refer to *brightness*; and Alkyoné and Kelænó, whom the legend unites with Poseidón, are plainly related to the sea. Among the Hyades we find Dióné, the ancient goddess of Dódóna; Ambrosia, Korónis, Eudóra are names evidently given from their nourishing nature as nymphs,[3] while Phæó, Phæsula, Kléeia, and Polyxó, denote the bright stars.[4]

The poet of the Odyssey, when describing the Wandering Rocks, says,[5]

> There pass no birds along that way, not even
> The fluttering pigeons which the ambrosia bear
> To father Zeus, but always the smooth rock
> Takes one away, then to keep up the number
> The Father adds another.

Many of the ancients[6] supposed that the Pléiades were here meant; and when we consider the sportive tone of the poet, this idea will not appear entirely devoid of credibility.

[1] The Persians regarded O'ríón as Nimrod 'the mighty hunter.' Chron. Pas. and Cedrenus *ap. Tuch, Gen.* p. 232. The ancient Hebrews seem also to have regarded their *Keseel* (כְּסִיל), or O'ríón, as a huge giant bound with chains in the sky: see Job xxxviii. 31; Is. 9, 9; and the Arabs call it El-Jabbár, *the Giant.* [2] See Völcker, *Myth. der Jap.* 112 *seq.*
[3] Korónis, from KOPE'Ω, κορέννυμι, to satiate.
[4] Phæó and Phæsula, from φάω; for Kléeia see Appendix G.; for Polyxó, above, p. 299. It is contracted after the analogy of μῶνυξ, i. e. μόνος ὄνυξ.
[5] *Od.* xii. 62 *seq.* [6] Athen. xi. 490. Eustath. and Sch. *on Od.* xi. 62

CHAPTER XIII.

MYTHIC WARS AND EXPEDITIONS.

Tὰ 'Αργοναυτικά.   **Ꭲhe Argonautic Expedition.**

IASON having undertaken to sail to Kolchis for the Go-den Fleece, applied to Argos the son of Phrixos; who, with the aid of Athéna, built for him a fifty-oared galley, called from himself the Argó.[1] In her keel Athéna set a piece of timber, cut from the speaking-oak of Dódóna. When the ship was completed Iasón consulted the oracle, and was directed to invite the greatest heroes of the day to share in the dangers and glories of the voyage.

The call was readily responded to, and numerous sons of gods hastened to embark in the Argó. From the Peloponnése came Héraklés, Kastór, and Polydeukés, sons of Zeus. Péleus and Telamón, grandsons of that god, also came with Théseus, Ergínos and Ankæos, sons of Poseidón, Augeias son of Hélios, Zétés and Kalaïs sons of Boreas. There were likewise the Apharids, Lynkeus and Idas, and Meleagros, Laertés, Periklymenos, Nauplios, Iphiklos, Iphitos, Admétos, Akastos, Butés, Polyphémos, Atalanté, and many others. Idmón the seer, the son of Apolló, came from Argos; Mopsos, also a prophet, from Thessaly, and Orpheus, the son of the Muse Kalliopé, from Thrace. The steersman was Tiphys son of Agnios, from Siphæ in Bœótia. The entire number of those who embarked was fifty.[2]

When the heroes were all assembled, Mopsos took auguries, and the signs being favourable, they got on board; Iasón standing at the poop poured a libation from a golden cup, and called on Zeus, the Winds, the Sea, the Days, the Nights, and the Fate presiding over their return. Thunder then rolled in the clouds, propitious lightnings flashed through the sky; the joyful heroes grasped each his oar at the words of the soothsayer: and while Orpheus struck his lyre in concert with his voice, their oars kept time to the harmony. The gods looked down from the sky, the nymphs of Pélion gazed in wonder at this first of ships, and Cheirón leaving his mountain-cave cheered them, and prayed for their happy return.[3]

At the close of day they had reached the mouth of the bay of Pagasæ. Here they remained for two days, and then rowed along

---

[1] 'Η 'Αργώ, i. e. *The Swift*: see above, pp. 15, 150.
[2] Burmann, in his edition of Valerius Flaccus, gives the different lists of the Argonauts.   [3] Pind. *Pyth.* iv.

the coast of Magnésia, and, passing the peninsula of Palléné, at length reached the isle of Lémnos, in which there were at that time no men, and Hypsipylé, the daughter of Thoas governed it as queen. For the Lémnian women having, it is said, offended Aphrodíté, she caused them to have an ill smell; so that their husbands, unable to endure them, took to their beds the captives whom they had brought from Thrace. The Lémnian wives, incensed at this neglect, murdered their husbands. Hypsipylé alone saved her father, whom she kept concealed. This event had occurred about a twelvemonth before. The women seeing the Argonauts took them for their enemies the Thrakians, and came down in arms to oppose their landing; but on ascertaining who they were they retired and held a council, in which, on the advice of Hypsipylé's nurse, it was decided that they should invite them to land, and take this occasion of having children. The Argonauts readily accepted the invitation, Héraklés alone refusing to quit the vessel. They gave themselves up to joy and festivity, till on the remonstrances of that hero they tore themselves from the Lémnian fair ones, and once more handled their oars.

They then came to Samothraké, and thence pursued their voyage through the Hellespont into the Propontis, where they came to an island with a lofty hill in it named the Bears' Hill, inhabited by giants with six arms. The adjacent country was possessed by the Dolionians, whose king was named Kyzikos. Having been hospitably entertained by this prince, and having slain the giants who opposed their departure, they set sail, but were driven back by adverse winds. It was in the night that they returned, and the Dolionians taking them to be their enemies, the Pelasgians, attacked them ; and several of the Dolionians, and among them Kyzikos, lost their lives. With daylight discerning the error, the Argonauts shore their hair, and shedding many tears buried Kyzikos with solemn magnificence.

They then sailed to Mysia, where they left behind them Héraklés and Polyphémos; for Hylas, a youth beloved by the former, having gone for water, was laid hold on and kept by the nymphs of the spring into which he dipped his urn. Polyphémos, hearing him call, went with his drawn sword to aid him, supposing him to have fallen into the hands of robbers. Meeting Héraklés, he told him what had happened; and both proceeded in quest of the youth. Meantime the Argó put to sea, and left them behind. Polyphémos settled in Mysia, and built the town of Kios: Héraklés returned to Argos.[1]

---

[1] According to Tneokritos (*Idyll.* xiii.), the hero proceeded on foot to Kolchis. In the poem named The Wedding of Kéyx, Héraklés is said to have been left behind at Aphetæ, where he went for water, Sch. *Apoll. Rh.* i. 1290. It was

The Argó next touched at Bebrykia, where Amykos the son of Poseidón and Bithynis reigned. Every stranger who arrived in this country was forced by Amykos to engage him at the cæstus. He therefore challenged the Argonauts; and Polydeukés engaged and killed him. The Bebrykians, seeing the fate of their prince, fell on the victor; but, his companions coming to his aid, they were repelled with great loss.[1]

Leaving Bebrykia, they sailed to Salmydéssos on the Thrakian coast, where Phineus, the prophet-prince, dwelt in blindness and misery.[2] He was the son of Agénór (or of Poseidón), and was married to Kleopatra the daughter of Boreas and Oreithyia. She died, leaving him two sons; and he then married Idæa the daughter of Dardanos. Jealous of her step-children, Idæa maligned them to their father, who, believing the slander, deprived them of sight. The gods, to punish him, struck him blind, and sent the Harpies to torment him. These fell monsters came flying the instant food was set before him, carried off the greater portion of it, and so defiled what they left that no mortal could endure to eat it.[3] The Argonauts coming to consult Phineus about their future course, he promised to direct them on condition of their delivering him from the Harpies. This they undertook to do. The table was spread: the Harpies instantly descended screaming, and seized the victuals. Zétés and Kalaïs the winged sons of Boreas then drew their swords and pursued them through the air.[4] The Harpies flew along the Propontis, over the Ægæan and Greece to some islets beyond the Peloponnése, where their pursuers came up with them, and were about to slay them, when Iris appearing forbade the deed, and the Harpies were dismissed on their oath never more to molest Phineus. The isles were thenceforth named the Strophades, because the Boreiads there *turned* back.[5]

---

an ancient custom of the Bithynians, we may observe, to lament in the burning days of midsummer, and call out of the well, into which they fabled he had fallen, a god named Hylas. The Mariandynians lamented and sought Bormos the Phrygians Lityorsés, with dirges, in a similar manner. This usage of the Bithynians was adopted into their mythology by the Greek inhabitants of Kios and connected in the manner above narrated with the Argonautic Expedition and the history of Héraklés: see Müller, *Orchom.* 293. *Dor.* i. 367, 457 *Proleg.* 108.   [1] The combat is described at length by Theokritos, *Idyll.* xxii

[2] Phineus is probably connected with φθίνω.

[3] Others said he was thus punished for having revealed the will of Zeus to men (Apoll. Rh. ii. 180) or for having shown Phrixos the way to Skythia Hésiod *ap. Sch. on v.* 181.

[4] It is plain that the Harpies in this legend, as in the Theogony, are but two in number. Vergil seems to make a flock of them.

[5] Apoll. Rh. ii. 282 *seq.* Apollodóros relates the conclusion of the chase somewhat differently.

Freed from his tormentors, Phineus now instructs his deliverers in the nature of their future voyage. The Symplegades were the first danger which they had to encounter. These were huge floating rocks, which were at times driven together by the winds, and crushed whatever came between them. Mist enveloped them, and loud was the crash when they met. Even to the birds the passage was then impossible. Phineus directed the heroes to let fly a pigeon, saying if she came safely through, the Argó might venture to follow her. They obeyed the directions of the prophet, and the pigeon passed through safely with the loss of her tail; watching then the recession of the rocks, and aided by Héra and Athéna, they rowed the Argó vigorously on, and escaped so narrowly, that the rocks as they rushed together carried off some of her stern-works. The Symplegades now became fixed; for so it was in the fates, since a ship had passed through them uninjured.

Having escaped the Symplegades, they came to the country of the Mariandynians, whose king Lykos received them kindly. Here died Idmón the seer, wounded by the tusks of a wild boar. Tiphys also dying here, Ankæos undertook the steerage of the vessel.

They now kept along the southern coast of the Pontos till they came to the isle of Aretias, which was haunted by birds that shot feathers sharp as arrows from their wings. These they drove off by clattering on their shields; and while they remained in the isle, the sons of Phrixos, who were on their way to Greece, were cast on it by a storm, and they became their guides to Kolchis, where they shortly after entered the Phasis. Iasón lost no time in informing king Æétés of the cause of his coming, and in requesting him to give him the Golden Fleece. The king assented, provided he could yoke the brass-footed bulls. These were the gifts of Héphæstos to Æétés, in number two, and breathing flame from their throats. When he had yoked these, he was to plough with them a piece of land, and sow the serpent's teeth which Æétés possessed, for Athéna had given him one half of those which Kadmos sowed at Thebes.

Iasón was in perplexity about the accomplishment of these hard tasks, when Médeia, the daughter of the king, who had conceived a sudden affection for him, proffered her aid, if he would swear to marry her, and take her with him to Greece. Such aid was not to be rejected: the hero swore; and Médeia, who was an enchantress, gave him a salve to rub his body, shield, and spear. The virtue of this salve would last an entire day, and protect alike against fire and steel. She further told him, that when he had sown the teeth, a crop of armed men would

spring up and prepare to attack him. Among these she desired
him to fling stones, and while they were fighting with one another
about them, to fall on and slay them. The hero followed the advice
of the princess: he entered the sacred grove of Arés, yoked the
bulls, ploughed the land, and slaughtered the armed crop which it
produced.

But Æétés refused to give the Fleece, and meditated to burn
the Argó and slay her crew. Médeia, anticipating him, led Iasón
by night to the Golden Fleece: with her drugs she cast to sleep
the serpent which guarded it; and then taking her little brother
Apsyrtos out of his bed she embarked with him in the Argó, and
the vessel set sail while it was yet night.[1]

Æétés, on discovering the treachery and flight of his daughter,
got on shipboard and pursued the fugitives. Médeia seeing him
gaining on them *cut* her brother to pieces and scattered his limbs
on the stream;[2] and while Æétés was engaged in collecting them
the Argó escaped.[3] He then returned home, having despatched a
number of his subjects in pursuit of the Argó, threatening if they
did not bring back his daughter to inflict on them the punishment
designed for her.

At length, by a route which we shall presently trace, the Argó
entered the West Sea and came to Ææa, the isle of Kirké. The
goddess performed the usual rites of purification to remove the
blood-guilt of the death of Apsyrtos. The heroes then departed.
Ere long they came to the isle of the Sirens, charmed by whose
entrancing strains they were about to land on that fatal shore,
when Orpheus struck his lyre, and with its tones overpowered
their voices. Wind and wave urged on the Argó, and all escaped
but Butés, who flung himself into the sea to swim to the Flowery
Isle. Aphrodíté to save him took him and set him to dwell at
Lilybæon. The Argonauts now passed Skylla and Charybdis,
and also the Wandering Rocks; over these they beheld flame
and smoke ascending, but Thetis and her sister Néréides guided
them through by the command of Héra. Passing Thrinakia, the
isle of the Sun, they came to the island of the Phæakians. Some
of the Kolchians who were in pursuit of the Argonauts arriving
there, seized on the Argó, and requested Alkinoos to give Médeia
up to them. He assented, provided she was yet a maid. His
wife Areté hearing this, lost no time in joining the lovers in
wedlock; and the Kolchians then fearing to return, settled in

---

[1] Pherekýdés *ap. Sch. Apoll. Rh.* iv. 223.   [2] Id. *ib.*
[3] This event was afterwards transferred to the north side of the Euxine
where the town of Tomi (τόμοι, *cuttings*) was said to have derived its name
from it. Apollod. i. 9, 24. Ov. *Trist.* iii. 9.

the island. Sailing thence, the Argó was assailed by a tremendous storm which drove it to the Syrtes on the coast of Libya. After being detained there for some time they proceeded on their homeward voyage and came to Kréte, where the brazen man, Talós, prohibited their landing; but Médeia by her art deprived him of life. On leaving Kréte the night came on so black and dark that they knew not where they were; but Apolló, taking his stand on the rocks called the Melantian Necks, shot an arrow into the sea; the arrow flashed a vivid light, and they beheld an island, on which they landed. As this isle had *appeared* (*ἀνεφήνατο*) so unexpectedly, they named it Anaphé.[1] Here they erected an altar to Apolló Æglétés (*Lightner*), and offered sacrifices; they thence proceeded to Ægína, where they watered; and they finally arrived at Iolkos after an absence of four months.

When Pelias in Pindar[2] is urging Iasón to this celebrated adventure, he says that a dream and the response of the Delphic oracle had directed him to go to Æææa and fetch back the soul of Phrixos and the 'thick-wooled' skin of the ram which had saved him. From various circumstances it seems clear that the Argonautics were mysteriously connected with the worship of the Laphystian Zeus;[3] that they belonged to the Minyans and to them alone; and that Héraklés, Théseus, and the other heroes who did not belong to this people were added to the cycle in the progress of time by the poets and by the vanity of those whose patron-heroes they were. It may also have been that the commercial voyages of the Minyans were united with the mythic expedition. If the gold-mines of Thasos or Pangæos were wrought so early, their produce may have given its *golden* hue o the fleece. This however is no essential part of the mythe, as it is also said to be *white* or *purple*.[4]

There can be little doubt that the direction of this mythic voyage was north-east, for Lémnos and Samothraké occur in all accounts of it. Where it originally terminated cannot be said with certainty: for its limit advanced with the progress of nautical enterprise and colonisation. At Lampsakos, Kyzikos, Kios, Byzantion, and other places along the Hellespont, Propontis and Bosporos, we meet with Argonautic traditions. When it entered he Pontos the mythe took two different directions, just as the colonies themselves did, the one northwards to the Tauric Cheronése or Skythia, and this was probably the earlier one, as this

---

[1] Anaphé was one of the Sporades; both it and the Melantian Necks were ear Théra.   [2] *Pyth.* iv. 156 (283) *seq.*   [3] See above, p. 296.
[4] Simónidés and Akusiláos *ap. Sch. Apoll. Rh.* iv. 177, 1147. Sch. *Eur Med.* 5. *Purple* (*πορφύριος*) is simply *bright* (from *πῦο*)—like the Latin *candidus.*

was the first direction of the Grecian colonies; the other along
the southern coast, and finally reached the Phasis and Kolchis
which last place is first named by the Corinthian poet Eumélos
who did not flourish till after Ol. 20. This became the prevalen
opinion, and the establishment of Hérakleia and other Greciar
colonies on this coast enlarged the cycle with traditions of the
country, or with fictions of the inhabitants of the colonies.[1]

In the ancient ante-Homéric Argonautics it is probable tha
the adventurers returned by the road they went; but the poe
of the Odyssey (if our hypothesis respecting him be correct), ir
order to augment the marvels of the sea which he makes the scene o:
his hero's wanderings, transferred thither the abode of Æétés and
the Wandering Rocks through which he makes the Argó pass or
her return with the same danger as she encounters in the Argo
nautics on her outward voyage. The fame of the Odyssey soor
made it an established article of belief that the Argonauts re
turned home through the Mediterranean, and, as we have seen
they were made to pursue the same route in it with Odysseus
The only question was how to bring them thither from Kolchis.

The first course was that taken by Hésiod, who was followed
by Pindar, Hekatæos and Antimachos.[2] This was to make then
go up the Phasis, which in accordance with the early geographic
ideas was held to flow out of the Ocean, which they then entered
and proceeded along it southwards.[3] Hekatæos made them ther
sail down the Nile and so home, but according to the others they
landed on the south coast of Libya, and carrying the Argó or
their shoulders across it (for twelve days, says Pindar), launched
it on lake Tritónis and thus entered the Mediterranean. It
being afterwards proved by Artemidóros and Eratosthenés that
the Phasis had its source in the mountains, this course had to
be given up; a geographer named Timagetas then fixed on the
Istér, for he supposed this river to flow out of a great lake in the
Keltic mountains, from the opposite end of which another stream
flowed into the Tyrrhenian sea; he was followed by Apollónios
and by another poet named Peisander.[4] The geographer Skym-
nos however showed that this could not be, as the Istér flowed
directly from the Alps, and he maintained that they must have
gone up the Tanaïs; in this however he had been preceded by
the historian Timæos.[5] According to their view, the Argonauts

---

[1] There is nowhere so much information on the Argonautics to be found as
in Müller's *Orchomenos*, to which we refer our readers.
[2] Sch. *Apoll. Rh.* iv. 259, 284.   Pind. *Pyth.* iv. 25 (44) *seq.*
[3] This was the direction of its current: see above, p. 33.
[4] Sch. *Apoll. Rh. ut sup.*   [5] Id. d.

went up the Tanaïs to its head, they then carried their vessel overland to the northern ocean, where they launched it, and so sailed down the west side of Europe to the Mediterranean; the only poet who adopted this view is the pseudo-Orpheus, who assigns them the following course.

They sailed up the Phasis, to the point where it divided, and then went down the other branch named the Sarangés into the Mæótis, whence another stream ran northwards with great velocity. They entered this and were whirled along for nine days, on the tenth they were carried through the gorges of the Rhipæan mountains, and the Argó rushed through the narrow stream and came into the Ocean, called in that part by the Hyperboreans the Kronian Main and Dead Sea. Having rowed for some time through its sluggish waters, they debarked, and dragging their vessel along came on the sixth day to the country of the Long-lived (*Macrobii*), to whom the poet gives all the qualities and all the felicity of Hésiod's Golden Men. They then reached the land of the Kimmerians, which lay on the same coast; and having passed by the isle Iernis (*Ireland ?*), on the twelfth morn the sharp-sighted Lynkeus descried on the verge of Ocean 'the piny isle, in which is the extensive abode of queen Démétér,' as it lay enveloped in mist. Orpheus having warned him of the danger of approaching it, Ankæus steered for the isle of Kirké, which they reached on the third day. Leaving it, they entered the strait of Tartéssos, and passing the Pillars of Héraklés arrived in the Mediterranean.

The literature of this cycle is as follows. Iasón and the Argó are noticed by Homer;[1] Hésiod briefly narrates the principal events;[2] it is the subject of one of Pindar's finest odes,[3] and of the epic of Apollónios named from it; it is narrated in detail by Apollodóros and by Diodóros. Ovid also relates a good part of it, and there is an unfinished poem on it by the Latin poet Valerius Flaccus, which displays both genius and originality.[4] There is also the Argonautics of the pseudo-Orpheus, a poem to which the ablest critics on different grounds assign a date long posterior to the commencement of the Christian æra. To these are to be added the detached notices in other writers and in the various Scholia. Of the dramas on this subject not a single one has been preserved.[5]

[1] *Il.* vii. 469; xxi. 41.   *Od.* xii. 69 *seq.*   [2] *Theog.* 992 *seq.*
[3] The fourth Pythian.
[4] 'Valerius Flaccus amœni ingenii cultique oris poeta, nec sane temporis suorum.' Broukhus. *Propert.* ii. 20, 2.
[5] Unless we except the Médeia of Euripidés

Τὰ Θηβαϊκά. The Theban Wars.

When Œdipus, on the discovery of his involuntary crime, had either died or abandoned his throne, his sons Eteoklés and Polyneikés agreed to reign in alternate years. According to some, Polyneikés governed for the first year, and then resigned his throne to his brother; others say that Eteoklés was the first occupant of the royal seat: all are agreed that when his year expired he refused to make way for his brother. Polyneikés taking with him the collar and robe of Harmonia, fled to Argos, where Adrastos, the son of Talaos son of Bias, then reigned. It was night when the Théban exile arrived at the house of the king: before the door he met another stranger, Tydeus the son of Œneus, also a fugitive: a quarrel arose between them: at the clamour Adrastos came forth and put an end to the conflict. An oracle had told this prince that he should marry his two daughters to a lion and a bear, and he now saw its accomplishment, for such were the ornaments on the shields of the strangers. He gave Déipyla to Tydeus, and Argeia to the Théban prince, engaging to restore each to his country. The expedition against Thébes was the first resolved on, and every valiant warrior was invited to share in it.

Amphiaráos the son of Œklés was a soothsayer, and he knew by his art that it was fated that Adrastos alone should survive the war: he therefore declined taking part in the expedition, and warned the others against it. Polyneikés was advised to endeavour to gain Eriphýle (*Strife-producer*), the sister of Adrastos and wife of Amphiaráos, to his interest; for on his marriage Amphiaráos had agreed, that whenever he and Adrastos should differ in opinion, the decision should be left to Eriphýle. Polyneikés therefore gave her the collar of Harmonia, and the prophet was reluctantly forced to share in the war. He departed with evil forebodings, charging his sons to avenge his fate on their mother.[1]

The leaders were seven: Adrastos, Amphiaráos, Kapaneus, Hippomedón, — Argives; Parthenopæos, an Arkadian; Polyneikés, a Theban; Tydeus, an Ætolian.[2]

The host marched to Neméa, where a prince named Lykurgos then reigned. Being in want of water, Hypsipýlé, the Lémniar princess, whom her country-women had sold when they found that she had saved her father, and who was now nurse to the infant child of Lykurgos, undertook to guide them to a spring

---

[1] See *Od.* xi. 326 ; xv. 244 *seq.*

[2] For the two last some gave Mékisteus and Eteoklés son of Iphis.

She left the child, named Opheltés, lying on the grass, where a serpent found and killed him. The leaders on their return slew the serpent, and buried the child; and Amphiaráos, who augured ill-luck from this event, gave him the name of Archemoros.[1] They then celebrated funeral games in his honour. Adrastos gained the prize in the horse-race, Eteoklés in the foot-race, Tydeus in the cæstus, Amphiaráos in jumping and throwing the discus, Laodokos in casting the javelin, Polyneikés in wrestling, Parthenopæos in archery.

When they came to the banks of the Asópos near Kithærón, they despatched Tydeus to Thébes, to claim a restitution of the rights of Polyneikés. He arrived as the Kadmeians were feasting in the halls of Eteoklés; and, after delivering his message, challenged them to a trial of skill and strength, and easily vanquished every one who contended with him. They laid an ambush of fifty men for him on his return, all of whom except Mæón, one of their leaders, he slew.[2]

The Argive host appeared before the walls of Thébes. Each chief chose one of its seven gates to attack; Adrastos, the Homolöian; Kapaneus, the O'gygian; Amphiaráos, the Prœtian; Hippomedón, the Onkaïan; Polyneikés, the Hypsistian; Parthenopæos, the E'lektrian: Tydeus, the Krenian. Eteoklés set chiefs equal in number over the Thébans, and prepared vigorously for defence. He consulted Teiresias, who declared that victory would fall to Thébes, if Menœkeus the son of Kreón gave himself a voluntary victim; and that heroic youth, on learning the response, slew himself at the gates of the city.

The fight began: the Kadmeians were driven into the city: Kapaneus set a ladder against the wall, and was ascending, when Zeus offended at his impious language struck him with a thunderbolt.[3] The Argives fell back, and many were slain. Both hosts now resolved that the brothers should decide their quarrel in single combat. They fought, and fell by each other's hands. The battle was then rekindled with fury, and the four sons of Astakos the Théban greatly distinguished themselves, Ismaros killing Hippomedón, Leadés Eteoklés, Amphidikos Parthenopæos, and Melanippos wounding Tydeus mortally. As he lay expiring, Athéna hastened to him with a medicine which she had obtained from Zeus, and which would make him immortal;[4] but Amphiaráos, who hated him as a chief cause of the war,

[1] Opheltes (from ὄφις) as he died by the bite of the serpent. Archemor(s (*Fate-beginner*) as indicative of the evils which were to befall the chiefs.
[2] *Il.* iv. 383 *seq.*; v. 802 *seq.*; x. 285 *seq.*
[3] Kapaneus, probably from κάω, and connected with καπνός, *smoke*.
[4] Bakchvlidés *ap. Sch. Aristoph. Birds*, 1535.

perceiving what the goddess was about, cut off the head of Melanippos, whom Tydeus though wounded had slain, and brought
it to him.   The savage warrior opened it, and devoured the
brain, and Athéna in disgust withheld her aid.[1]   Amphiaráos
himself fled from the spear of Periklymenos, along the Isménos.
A thunderbolt launched by Zeus opened the ground, and himself, his chariot, and his charioteer Bató, were swallowed up.[2]
Adrastos alone, owing to the fleetness of his steed Areión, escaped.[3]

Kreón, now king of Thébes, forbade the bodies of the Argives
to be buried.   Regardless of the menaced penalties, Antigoné
gave sepulture to the body of her brother Polyneikés, and was
by Kreón remorselessly entombed alive.   Adrastos flying to
Athens took refuge at the altar of Mercy; and Théseus leading
an Athenian army against the Thébans, forced them to give the
dead bodies to their friends.   As Kapaneus lay on his burning
pyre, his wife Euadné flung herself amidst the flames, and expired.

Ten years afterwards the children ('Επίγονοι, descendants) of
the chiefs who had fallen resolved to avenge the fate of their
sires.[4]   The god when consulted promised them victory if led
by Alkmæón the son of Amphiaráos.   Alkmæón would however
first punish his mother; but Eriphýlé, who had received the robe
of Harmonia from Thersandros the son of Polyneikés, persuaded
both him and his brother Amphilochos to join in the expedition.
Ægialeus son of Adrastos, Diomédés of Tydeus, Promachos of
Parthenopæos, Sthenelos of Kapaneus, Eurypylos of Mékisteus,
were the other leaders.   Alkmæón had the chief command.[5]

They ravaged the villages about Thébes.   A battle ensued, in
which Laodamas the son of Eteoklés slew Ægialeus, and fell
himself by the spear of Alkmæón.   The Thébans then fled;
and by the advice of Teiresias, they secretly left their city, which
was entered and plundered by the Argives, and Thersandros
placed on the throne.

Alkmæón, on learning that his mother had taken a bribe
against himself, as well as his father, consulted Apolló, and by
his advice put her to death.   He was immediately assailed by
her Erinnys.   In phrensy he roamed through Arkadia, came
first to his grandfather Œklés, and from him went to Phégeus at
Psóphis, who purified him, and gave him his daughter Arsinoé
in marriage.   He presented his bride with the fatal collar and

---

[1] Eur. *Fr. Meleag.* 18.   [2] Pind. *Nem.* ix. 24 (57) *seq.*

[3] We have already (above, p. 159 *note*) given what is perhaps the original signification of the name Adrastos; but it may also be rendered *Do-nought* (*a* and
δράω) adapted to this mythe: see above, p. 9.   [4] *Il.* iv. 405.

[5] Pindar (*Pyth.* viii. 48 (68) *seq.*) makes Adrastos command in this war also.

robe; his disorder however still continued, and the Pythia said that the Erinnys would never quit him except in a place which the sea had disclosed posterior to his parricide.[1] He went to Kalydón, thence to Thesprótia, whence he was expelled, and coming to the springs of Acheloos was purified by the river-god himself, who gave him to wife his daughter Kallirrhoé. On the soil just deposited by the stream at its mouth he fixed his dwelling.[2]

Kallirrhoé now longed for the collar and robe of Harmonia, and refused to admit the embraces of her husband until she had obtained them. Alkmæón therefore returned to Psóphis, and telling Phégeus that his madness would never end till he had deposited the collar and robe at Delphi,[3] obtained them from him; but his servant having betrayed his secret, the sons of Phégeus by order of their father lay in wait for and slew him. Arsinoé on upbraiding them with the murder was put by them into a chest and brought to Agapénór the son of Ankæos, at Tegea, and accused of the crime which they had committed.

When Kallirrhoé heard of the fate of her husband, she prayed to Zeus, who had loved her, that her sons by Alkmæón might at once attain to manly age, to avenge their father. Her prayer was granted, and they hastened to vengeance. The sons of Phégeus on their way to Delphi to consecrate the collar and robe, stopped at the house of Agapénór: here they met the sons of Alkmæón, who slew them, and then went to Psóphis and killed Phégeus and his wife. The Psóphites pursued them to Tegea; but the Tegeans and some Argives aided them, and the Psóphites were forced to retire. The youths returned to their mother with the collar and robe, which by the direction of Acheloos they consecrated at Delphi, and then went to E'peiros, and founded Akarnania.

In the preceding narrative we have probably the contents of three of the poems of the Epic Cycle, namely the Thébaïs, the Epigoni and the Alkmæonis, but intermixed as usual with the arbitrary fictions of the tragedians. The wars of Thébes shared in antiquity the popular interest with that of Troy; and their claims to credibility as historic facts are perhaps equally well founded. For our own part, as we doubt of the proper historic

---

[1] Paus. viii. 24, 8.   [2] The Echinades: see Thuk. ii. 102.

[3] Ephoros (*Athén.* vi. 232) says that when Alkmæón consulted the god about the removal of his insanity, he got the following reply:

> Τιμῆεν μ' αἰτεῖς δῶρον μανίαν ἀποπαῦσαι·
> καὶ σὺ φέρειν τιμῆεν ἐμοὶ γέρας ᾧ ποτε μήτηρ
> 'Αμφιάραον ἔκρυψ' ὑπὸ γῆν αὐτοῖσι σὺν ὅπλοις.

Probably from the Alkmæonis: see above, p. 409.

character of every part of the mythic story of Hellas, we feel
disposed to view in the destiny of the Labdakids a fine fiction, or
series of fictions, constructed on perhaps a slight foundation of
reality, with a moral or religious object; to show how in the
order of nature punishment is provided for the most secret and
even unconscious violation of its laws, and how the sins of the
parents are visited on the children, which we must recognise to
be a law of nature. As usual, the names of the chief persons
are significant; Laïos is the *Unlucky*, Œdipodés the *Swollen* or
Inflated, Eteoklés *True-glorious*, Polyneikés *Strife-full*, Antigoné
Contrary-birth,[1] and so forth. There is also a moral intended
to be conveyed in the failure of the first expedition, led by arrogant boastful chiefs, who despised the signs sent by the gods,
and the success of that conducted by their more pious sons,
who acted in obedience to the will of heaven. The story of
Alkmæón is a parallel to that of Orestés, perhaps framed in
imitation of it; and, as we may see, it is connected with the
topography of western Greece.

The cyclic poems have perished, as also has the Thébaïs of
Antimachos; but the Thebaïs of the Latin poet Statius remains,
and the prose narratives of Apollodóros, Diodóros and Hyginus,
beside the scattered notices in the Scholiasts, Pausanias, and other
authors. Of the dramas on this subject there have come down to
us the noble Seven against Thébes of Æschylos, the Œdipus
King, Œdipus at Kolónos, and Antigoné of Sophoklés; and the
Phœnissæ and Suppliants of Euripidés.

Τὰ Τρώϊκα.   𝕮𝖍𝖊 𝕮𝖗𝖔𝖏𝖆𝖓 𝖂𝖆𝖗.

Zeus was, by E'lectra the daughter of Atlas, the father of
two sons, Iasión and Dardanos. The former was loved by Démétér; but Zeus on coming to the knowledge of this attachment
struck him with lightning.[2] Dardanos afflicted at the death of
his brother left Samothraké, where they had dwelt, and passed
over to the main-land, where Teukros the son of the river Skamandros and the nymph Idæa then reigned, from whom the
people were called Teukrians.[3] He was well received by this
prince, who gave him his daughter Bateia[4] in marriage, and a
part of his territory, on which he built a town called after himself
Dardanos. On the death of Teukros, he named the whole country

---

[1] Isméné, the other sister, was probably invented for the sake of uniformity:
see above, p. 341. We may observe, that the name of their mother was changed
from Epikasté to Iokasté (*Woe-adorned*) to express her fate.
[2] See above, p. 158.   [3] This name does not occur in Homer.
[4] See *Il.* ii. 813.

Dardania. He had two sons, Ilos and Erichthonios, the former of whom died childless; the latter, who succeeded to the kingdom, was the most wealthy of men. His three thousand mares and their foals fed in the marsh; and Boreas falling in love with them, changed himself into a horse, and by them had twelve foals, which like the celestial steeds could run on the ears of corn or the waves of the sea.[1] By Astyoché, daughter of the Simoïs, Erichthonios had a son named Trós, who succeeded him on the throne.

Trós married Kallirrhoé, daughter of the Skamandros, who bore him a daughter Kleopatra, and three sons Ilos, Assarakos, and Ganymédés. This last was for his beauty carried off to Olympos by the gods, to be the cup-bearer of Zeus, who gave Trós in compensation some horses of the Olympian breed.[2]

Assarakos married a daughter of the river Simoïs, by whom he had a son named Kapys, who was by Themis, the daughter of his brother Ilos, father of Anchísés, to whom Aphrodíté bore a son, named Æneias. By secretly giving mortal mares to the celestial steeds of Trós, Anchísés obtained six foals of surpassing fleetness, four of which he kept, and two he gave to draw the war-car of his son.[3]

Ilos went to Phrygia, and won at wrestling, in games given by the king, fifty youths and as many maids. The king also, in obedience to an oracle, gave him a spotted cow, and told him to build a city where she should lie down. Ilos followed the cow till she came to the hill of Até (*Mischief*), where he built the town of Ilion, named from himself. He prayed to Zeus to give him a sign, and the following day he found the Zeus-fallen Palladion lying before his tent.[4] This image of Pallas-Athéné, we are told, was three ells long, with its legs joined, holding in one hand an elevated spear, in the other a distaff and spindle.

Laomedón, the son of Ilos, married Strymó the daughter of the Skamandros, by whom he had Tithónos (who was carried off by E'ós), Lampós, Klytios, Hiketáon, Priamos[5] and Hésioné, and two

---

[1] *Il.* xx. 220 *seq.*

[2] Comp. *Il.* v. 265, 266, with xx. 234, 235, and these last with iv. 2, 3: see Hom. *Hymn* iv. 202 *seq.* One of the Kyklic poets (*ap. Sch. Eur. Orest.* 1392) said that Zeus gave Laomedón a golden vine for Ganymédés.

"Αμπελον ἣν Κρονίδης ἔπορεν οὗ παιδὸς ἄποινα
χρυσείην ἀγανοῖσιν φύλλοισιν κομόωσαν
βότρυσι τοὺς "Ηφαιστος ἐπασκήσας πατρὶ δῶκεν,
αὐτὰρ ὁ Λαομέδοντι πόρεν Γανυμήδιος ἄντι.

[3] *Il.* v. 268.

[4] Apollod. iii. 12, 3. Paus. 1. 28, 9. Arktínos (*ap. Dion. Hal. Ant. Rom.* i. 69) said it was given to Dardanos.

[5] *Il.* xx. 237; the genealogy from Dardanos to this point is given *Il.* xx 215–239.

other daughters; by the nymph Kalybé he had a son named Bukolión.[1]

Priamos reigned over Ilion after his father. He married Hekabé (Hecuba), the daughter of Dymas the Phrygian,[2] who bore him nineteen[3] children, of whom the chief were Hektór, Paris or Alexandros, Déiphobos, Helenos, Tróilos, Polités, Polydóros, Kassandra,[4] Kreüsa and Polyxené.

When Hekabé was about to lie-in of Paris, she dreamed that she brought forth a burning torch, which set all Ilion in flames. On her telling this dream to Priamos, he sent for his son Æsakos, by a former wife Arisbé, the daughter of Merops, who had been reared and taught to interpret dreams by his grandfather. Æsakos declared that the child would be the destruction of his country, and recommended to expose it. As soon therefore as the babe was born it was given to a servant to be left on Ida to perish. The servant obeyed, but on returning at the end of five days, he found that a bear had been nursing the infant. Struck with this strange event, he took home the babe, reared him as his own son, and named him Paris. When Paris grew up he distinguished himself by his strength and courage in repelling robbers from the flocks, and the shepherds named him Alexandros.[5] He was recognised by his parents in the course of time, and he verified his mother's dream.[6]

Beside his children by Hekabé Priamos had several by other women. The whole number of his offspring was fifty.[7]

The preceding Trojan history has been formed, as we may see, by Apollodóros and others from various hints in the Ilias, especially the narrative of Æneias in the twentieth book. We will now proceed to relate the war of Troy, following the Epic Cycle, of which the first portion was the Kypria of Stasínos.

Zeus seeing the earth overstocked with people, consulted with Themis how to remedy the evil.[8] The best course seeming to be a war between Hellas and Troy, Discord, by his direction, came to the banquet of the gods at the nuptials of Péleus and Thetis, and flung down a golden apple, inscribed 'The apple for the Fair' (Τῇ καλῇ τὸ μῆλον).[9] Héra, Athéna and Aphrodíté claiming it, Zeus directed Hermés to conduct them to Mount Ida to be judged by Alexandros the son of Priamos. The prize was awarded to

---

[1] *Il.* vi. 23.   [2] *Il.* xvi. 718.   Others said of Kisseus: see Eurip. *Hec.* 3.
[3] *Il.* xxiv. 496.
[4] See above, p. 107.   The story of Kassandra is unnoticed by Homer, to whom it was probably unknown.   [5] Ἀπὸ τοῦ ἀλέξειν τοὺς ἄνδρας.
[6] Apollod. iii. 12, 5.   This history of Paris is unknown to Homer. It is the legend of Œdipus, of Télephos, of Zál, of Kyros, of Romulus and Remus, etc.
[7] See *Il.* xxiv. 495.   [8] Comp. Eur. *Orest.* 1641.   [9] See Tzetz. *Lyc.* 93.

Aphrodíté, who had promised the judge the beautiful Helené in marriage.[1] Aphrodíté then directs him to build a ship, and she desires her son Æneias to be the companion of his adventure. The soothsaying Helenos and Kassandra announce in vain the woes that are to follow; the vessel puts to sea, and Alexandros arrives at Lakedæmón, where he is entertained by the Tyndarids. At Sparta he shares the hospitality of Meneláos the husband of Helené. The Trojan at the banquet bestows gifts on his fair hostess, and shortly after Meneláos sails to Kréte, directing his wife to entertain the guests while they stayed. But Aphrodíté joins Helené and Alexandros in love, and filling the ship with the property of Meneláos they embark and depart. A tempest sent by Héra drives them to Sidón, which city Alexandros takes and plunders, and sailing thence to Ilion he there celebrates his marriage with Helené.[2]

Meneláos being informed by Iris of what had occurred, returns home and consults with his brother Agamemnón about an expedition against Ilion; he then repairs to Nestór at Pylos,[3] and going through Hellas they assemble chiefs for the war. Odysseus, loath to leave home, feigned madness, but Palamédés[4] discovered his artifice by placing his young son Télemachos before his plough. The chiefs at length[5] all assembled at Aulis in Bœótia: and as they were sacrificing to the gods at a fount beneath a plane-tree, a serpent came out of the altar, and ascending the tree, where was a sparrow's nest with eight young ones, devoured them all, and then the mother herself; after which Zeus turned him into stone, whence Kalchas the soothsayer announced that they would war against Troy for nine years, and take it in the tenth.[6] They then set sail,[7] and reached

---

[1] See *Il.* xxiv. 28 *seq.*

[2] According to Hérodotos (ii. 117) the Kypria made Alexandros reach Troy on the third day.

$$\ldots\ldots\ldots\ldots\ldots\ldots\ldots\ldots \text{εὐαεΐ τε}$$
πνεύματι χρησάμενος λείῃ τε θαλάσσῃ.

See Müller, *de Cyclo*, p. 87.

[3] On this occasion Nestór relates to him the story of Epópeus and Antiopé, that of Œdipus, the madness of Héraklés, and the tale of Théseus and Ariadné. The poet had a little before introduced an account of the combat of the Tyndarids and Apharids, of which we have quoted a fragment p. 383.

[4] This name does not occur in Homer.

[5] In the Ilias (xxiv. 765) Helené says that she had been twenty years at Troy. According to Tzetzés (*Antehom.* 168) the Greeks were ten years preparing for the war.   [6] See *Il.* ii. 305 *seq.*

[7] According to Tzetzés (*Lyc.* 570) the poet of the Kypria made the Greeks stop at Délos, where Anios the son of Apolló urged them to remain for the nine years, assuring them that his three daughters would support them. These maidens were named Œnó (*Wine-giver*), Spermó (*Seed-giver*), and Eláis (*Oilgiver*).

Teuthrania in Mysia on the coast of Asia, and taking it for Troy they landed and ravaged it. Télephos[1] the king of the country came to oppose them; he killed Thersandros the son of Polyneikés, but was himself wounded by Achilleus. As they were sailing thence their fleet was dispersed by a storm, and Achilleus being driven to the isle of Skyros, espoused Déidameia the daughter of Lykomédés king of that island.[2] Télephos having by direction of an oracle come to Argos in search of a cure for his wound, he is healed by Achilleus, and undertakes to conduct the Greeks to Troy.

The fleet again assembled at Aulis, but Agamemnón having killed a deer at the chase, boasted that he was superior in skill to Artemis, and the offended goddess sent adverse winds to detain the fleet. Kalchas having announced that her wrath could only be appeased by the sacrifice of Iphigeneia, the daughter of the offender, that maiden was brought to the camp under the pretence of being married to Achilleus. As they were in the act of sacrificing her, the goddess moved with pity snatched her away, leaving a hind in her place, and carried her to Tauris, where she made her immortal.[3]

The wind now proving fair the fleet made sail, and reached the isle of Tenedos; and here Philoktétés being bitten by a water-snake, the smell from his wound proved so offensive, that they carried him to the isle of Lémnos and left him there.[4] Achilleus having joined them at Tenedos, a quarrel took place between him and Agamemnón; but it was made up, and the Achæan host passed over to the coast of Troy. The Trojans came to oppose their landing, and Protesiláos fell by the hand of Hektor; but Achilleus having slain Kyknos the son of Poseidón, put the enemy to flight.[5] An embassy was then sent, requiring the Trojans to give back Helené and the property taken with her,

---

[1] See above, p. 325.

[2] The common account is that Thetis had concealed him as a maiden among the daughters of Lykomédés, and that Odysseus discovered him by going as a pedlar with some arms among his women's wares, which at once attracted the attention of Achilleus. This narrative, which is directly contrary to that of the Ilias and the Kypria, occurred in the Epic Cycle according to the scholiast on *Il.* xix. 332.

[3] The name and story of Iphigeneia (*Strong-born*) are unnoticed by Homer. Iphigeneia is probably an epithet of Artemis. She is the same with the Artemis-Orthia of Sparta, at whose altar the boys were scourged. It was probably this rite that caused Iphigeneia to be identified with the Virgin, to whom human victims were offered by the Taurians, Hérod. iv. 103. The story of Iphigeneia was then invented to account for the similarity. There may however have been an ancient Grecian legend of Iphigeneia: see Müller, *Dor.* i. 397 *seq.* This writer thinks that Lémnos was the original mythic Tauris, whence the name was transferred to the Euxine.   [4] See *Il.* ii. 721.

[5] See Ov. *Met.* xii. 64 *seq.*

but a refusal was returned. An assault on the town having failed, the Achæans turned to ravaging the surrounding country, and took several towns. Soon after Achilleus being desirous of seeing Helené, he had an interview with her by means of Thetis and Aphrodíté; and when the Achæans had thoughts of giving over the enterprise he prevented their departure. He then took some other towns, killed Tróilos, and captured and sold for a slave Lykáón, another of the sons of Priamos. In the division of the spoil a maiden named Briséis fell to the share of Achilleus, and Chryséis the daughter of Chrysés,[1] the priest of Apolló, to that of Agamemnón. Odysseus, who had long meditated vengeance on Palamédés, now carried it into effect; a forged letter, as from king Priamos, was placed in his bed, and he was stoned by the troops as a traitor.[2]

Chrysés came to the camp to ransom his daughter, but he was driven away with insult by Agamemnón. At his prayer Apolló sent a pestilence among the Achæans. Achilleus having called an assembly to inquire into the cause of it, Kalchas declared the truth, adding that it would not cease till the maiden was restored to her father. Agamemnón expressed his willingness to give her up, but said that some maiden must be given to him in her place. A violent dispute between him and Achilleus arises; the assembly breaks up; Chryséis is sent back to her father, and the heralds of the king take Briséis away from Achilleus. The injured prince complains to his mother, at whose entreaty Zeus promises to punish the Achæans, by giving victory to the Trojans. Accordingly Achilleus abstains from war; and though the Achæans build a wall to defend their tents and ships, they are unable to resist Hektór and the Trojans favoured by Zeus. The ships are on the point of being burnt, when Achilleus allows his friend Patroklos to lead forth his troops. The Trojans are driven back to their town, but Patroklos at last falls by the hand of Hektór. Rage and grief at the death of his friend overcome the wrath of Achilleus. He is reconciled to Agamemnón; his mother brings him armour made by Hephæstos; he goes forth to battle, routs the Trojans, and slays Hektór, whose corpse he binds to his chariot, and drags round the walls of Troy. He then gives a magnificent funeral to Patroklos, and on the supplication of the aged Priamos, who comes to his tent by night with a ransom he restores the body of Hektór, which the Trojans burn with due solemnity.[3]

[1] He is probably merely a personification of an epithet of the god: see above 18.   [2] Thus far the narrative of the Kypria; that of the Ilias succeeds.
[3] The Æthiopis of Arktínos follows.

2 F

Penthesileia, daughter of Arés, queén of the Amazons, now leads her female warriors to the aid of Troy. But in the first engagement she falls by the hand of Achilleus, who struck with her beauty gives her body back to the Trojans that they may perform her obsequies. Thersítes railing at the hero, as if he had been in love with the slain, is killed by him; this causes a dissension, and Achilleus sails to Lesbos, where having sacrificed to Létó, Apolló and Artemis, he is purified of the bloodshed by Odysseus.

Memnón the Æthiopian, the son of E'ós, next appears as an ally of the Trojans.[1] He was arrayed in Héphæstean armour, and Antilochos the son of Nestór falls by his hand; he is himself slain by Achilleus, but his mother obtains immortality for him from Zeus. Achilleus chases the Trojans to the city, and as he is forcing his way in he is slain by Paris and Apolló. A furious fight arises over his body, which Aias at length takes up and carries to the ships, while Odysseus keeps off the Trojans. Thetis comes with her sisters and the Muses and mourns over her son, whose body she snatches from the pyre and conveys to the White Isle. The Achæans heap up his mound, games are celebrated, and Thetis proposing his armour as the prize of him who had done most to save his corse, Aias and Odysseus contend for it.[2]

The judges, who were Trojan captives, having awarded the arms to Odysseus, Aias loses his senses and falls on and slaughters the cattle in the camp, and then slays himself. Odysseus soon after takes Helenos by stratagem, and having learned from him how Troy might be captured, Diomédés is sent to Lémnos to fetch Philoktétés, who being cured by Macháón kills Alexandros. Meneláos mutilates the corse, which the Trojans then receive and give to the pyre.[3] Déiphobos marries Helené, and Odysseus fetches from Skyros Neoptolemos, the son of Achilleus and gives him his father's armour. The shade of Achilleus appears to the young warrior, who slays Eurypylos tho son of Telephos, an ally of the Trojans, whose town is now closely

[1] See *Od.* iv. 188.

[2] The Æthiopis ends here, and the Little Ilias of Leschés commences.

[3] Paris when a shepherd had married the nymph Œnóné, who warned him against the consequences of his voyage to Greece. She at the same time told him to come to her if ever he was wounded, as she alone could cure him. H did so now, but offended at his desertion of her, she refused her aid, and h died on his return to Ilion. Repenting of her cruelty Œnóné hastened to hi relief, but coming too late she threw herself on his pyre and died. Apollod iii. 12, 6. Quint. Smyr. x. 259 *seq.* Conón, 22. Parthen. 4. It must hav been in the Epic Cycle.

beleaguered. By the directions of Athéna Epeios constructs a huge horse of wood. Odysseus meantime disfiguring himself enters Troy as a spy; where he is recognised by Helené, and he concerts with her the mode of taking the city. He kills some of the Trojans and escapes to the ships. Diomédés then steals the Palladion out of Ilion, and the horse being completed the bravest warriors conceal themselves in it, and the rest set fire to their tents and sail away to Tenedos. The Trojans, thinking their toils and dangers all over, break down a part of their walls, and drawing the horse into the city indulge in festivity.[1]

There was a debate what to do with the horse; some were for flinging it down from the rock, others for burning it, others for consecrating it to Pallas-Athéné.[2] This last opinion prevailed, and the banquets of peace were spread. Two huge serpents now appeared and destroyed Laokoón and one of his sons, dismayed by which prodigy Æneias forthwith retired to Mount Ida. Sinón then, who had gotten into the town by means of a forged tale, raised torches as a signal to those at Tenedos. They return, the warriors descend from the horse, and the town is taken. Neoptolemos slays Priamos at the altar of the Herkeian Zeus. Meneláos kills Déiphobos and leads Helené to the ships. Aias son of Oïleus seizing Kassandra, she grasped the statue of Athéna, which he dragged with her; the Achæans were about to stone him, but he fled to the altar of the goddess. Odysseus killed Astyanax the young son of Hektór, whose widow Andromaché became the prize of Neoptolemos. Polyxené was sacrificed on the tomb of Achilleus.

Such is the narrative of the Trojan war as it appeared in the Epic Cycle. It was a subject however above all others liable to variation and addition, and were we to give all these details we should extend our narrative to a disproportionate length. We will therefore content ourselves with enumerating the names of the principal heroes mentioned by Homer. These were Agamemnón and Meneláos, sons of Atreus (the former of whom had the chief command); Nestór the son of Néleus, and his sons Antilochos and Thrasymédés; Odysseus, son of Laertés; Diomédés and Sthenelos, sons of Tydeus and Kapaneus; Aias (Ajax) and Teukros, sons of Telamón; Aias, son of Oïleus; the Krétan princes Idomeneus and Mérionés; Thoas the Ætólian, and Tlépolemos

---

[1] Here ends the Little Ilias; the remaining narrative is from the Destruction of Ilion of Arktínos.

[2] See *Od.* viii. 505 *seq.*, where it is said that it was proposed to break it up, to fling it down the rocks, or to let it remain as an offering to the gods: comp. Verg. *Æn.* ii. 32 *seq.*

son of Héraklés. The warriors from the different parts of Thessaly were led by Achilleus son of Péleus and Thetis and his friend Patroklos, Eumélos son of Admétos, Philoktétés son of Pœas, Podaleirios and Macháon sons of Asklépios, Protesiláos and other chiefs. The number of ships was one thousand one hundred and eighty-six, and they carried upwards of one hundred thousand men.[1] The Trojans were led by Hektór son of Priamos and his brothers, by Æneias son of Anchísés, and by the sons of Anténór, and they were aided by the warriors of all the adjoining countries, led by Sarpédón the son of Zeus, by Glaukos, Pandaros, Asios, and other princes.

Οἱ Νόστοι. The Returns.

After the destruction of Troy, the Achæan chiefs held a council to deliberate on their return home. Agamemnón advised to stay some days, and offer sacrifices to conciliate the gods: Meneláos urged an immediate departure: the chiefs and the people were divided. Next morning Meneláos, Nestór, Diomédés, Odysseus, and one half of the army passed over to the isle of Tenedos. Odysseus however quitted them there, and returned to Agamemnón; and the others, with the exception of Meneláos, sailed away and reached their homes in safety.[2]

Kassandra the daughter of Priamos had fallen to the share of the king of Mykénæ in the division of the spoil, and she was the companion of his return. A storm arising, he was driven to that part of the coast where Ægisthos the son of Thyestés resided. During his absence Ægisthos had carried on an adulterous intercourse with Klytæmnéstra, the queen of Agamemnón and he had set a watchman, with a promise of a large reward to give him tidings of the return of the king. As soon as he learned that he was on the coast, he went out to welcome him and invited him to his house. At the banquet in the evening with the participation of Klytæmnéstra, he placed twenty men in concealment, who fell on and slaughtered the king, with Kassandra and all his companions; who, however, died not un revenged, for Ægisthos alone was left alive.[3]

Ægisthos now occupied the throne; but Orestés the son c Agamemnón was still alive. He had been saved by his siste E'lektra, and sent to Phókis to Strophios, the prince of tha country, with whose son Pyladés he formed a strict friendshi When he grew up he and Pyladés secretly returned to Mykénæ

---

[1] See the Catalogue. The Bœótian vessels carried one hundred and twent men (*Il.* ii. 510), the Thessalian only fifty (*Il.* ii. 719; xvi. 170). A mea gives the above result.   [2] *Od.* iii. 135 *seq.*   [3] *Od.* iv. 512 *seq.*; xi. 405 se
[4] Homer (*Od.* iii. 306) says he came in the *eighth* year from *Athens.*

where he killed his mother and Ægisthos. The Erinnyes of his mother persecuting him, he fled to Delphi, whose god had urged him to commit the deed, and thence went to Athens, where he was acquitted by the court of Areiopagos. He took possession of the throne of his father, and married Hermioné the daughter of Meneláos, by whom he had two sons, Tisamenos and Penthilos, the former of whom was slain and the latter driven from his country by the Hérakleids.[1] Some say that Orestés killed at Delphi Neoptolemos the son of Achilleus, to whom Meneláos had given Hermioné in marriage.[2]

The daughters of Agamemnón were Laodiké or E'lektra, Chrysothemis, and Iphianassa or Iphigeneia.[3] The tale of the sacrifice of this last at Aulis to obtain a favourable wind has been already related.[4]

Meneláos stayed at Tenedos after his companions, whom he overtook at Lesbos. He and Nestór kept company until they reached Cape Sunion in Attica. Apolló here slew with his 'gentle darts' Phrontis, the pilot of Meneláos' ship, who was obliged to stay to bury him. Having performed the due rites, he again put to sea; but as he approached Cape Maleia, Zeus sent forth a storm which drove some of his vessels to Kréte, where they went to pieces against the rocks. Five, on board of one of which was Meneláos himself, were carried by the wind and waves to Egypt.[5]

During the eight years of his absence Meneláos visited all the adjacent coasts, Kypros, Phœnikia and Egypt, the Æthiopians, Sidónians and Erembians, and Libya,[6] where the lambs are born horned, and the sheep yean three times a year, and milk, cheese, and flesh are in the utmost abundance, for king and shepherd alike. In these various countries he collected much wealth. When leaving Egypt on his voyage homewards, he neglected offering sacrifices to the gods, and was in consequence detained by want of wind at the isle of Pharos, which was distant from that country a day's sail of a ship with a favouring breeze. They were here twenty days: their stock of provisions was nearly run out, and they were obliged to pass the day in endeavouring to catch fish to support them; when the sea-nymph Eidothea the daughter of Próteus met Meneláos wandering

---

[1] Apollod. ii. 8, 2.   [2] See Eur. *Androm.* Verg. *Æn.* iii. 330 *seq.*
[3] *Il.* ix. 145.   [4] See above, p. 432.   [5] *Od.* iii. 276 *seq.*
[6] *Od.* iv. 81 *seq.* We thus see that Meneláos visited all the eastern, as Odysseus did all the western part of the Mediterranean. Libya must have bordered on the Lotos-eaters.

alone, and informed him how to catch her father, and learn from him what he was to do. Meneláos followed her directions; and by the advice of the old sea-god[1] he returned to the river Ægyptos, and there offered due sacrifices to the immortal gods. A favourable wind was then sent by them, which speedily carried him homewards; and he arrived in his native country on the very day that Orestés was giving the funeral feast for his mother and Ægisthos, whom he had slain.[2]

Helené was, according to Homer, the companion of all the wanderings of Meneláos; but the Egyptian priests pretended that Paris was driven by adverse winds to Egypt, where Próteus, who was then king, learning the truth, kept Helené and dismissed Paris; that the Greeks would not believe the Trojans, that she was not in their city, till they had taken it; and that then Meneláos sailed to Egypt, where his wife was restored to him.[3]

Odysseus sailed with the part of the army which left Agamemnón as far as Tenedos; but he there quitted them and returned to the king.[4] On again setting out homewards[5] he landed in the country of the Kikonians in Thraké, where his men took and burned the town of Ismaros; but delaying on the coast and feasting, they were attacked by the Kikonians and driven to their ships, with the loss of six men out of each. Sailing thence they were assailed by a storm, from which they were obliged to seek refuge on shore. On the third day, the weather clearing, they put again to sea, and had a prosperous voyage till they were doubling Cape Maleia, when a violent north-east wind arose, and carried them to the country of the Lotoseaters.

The wanderings of Odysseus until his arrival in the island of the Phæakians have been already related.[6] He was most hospitably received by Alkinoos the king of that people, and one of their magic vessels conveyed him and the gifts which they had given him to his native isle; the sailors departed, leaving him, who was asleep, with his wealth on the shore. On awaking he was informed by Athéna where he was; and going to the house of his swineherd Eumæos, there met and revealed himself to his son Télemachos. After a variety of adventures, he succeeded in

---

[1] See above, p. 218.
[2] *Od.* iv. 351 *seq.*
[3] Hérod. ii. 113–121. The fiction was as old as the time of Stésichoros, who said that Próteus gave Paris a phantom (εἴδωλον) of Helené, which he took to Troy: see Plató, *Rep.* ix. 586. *Phædr.* 243. Eudocia, 35, 329. Euripidés in nis *Helené* follows this account.
[4] *Od.* iii. 162.
[5] *Od.* ix. 39 *seq.*
[6] See above, Part I. c. xix.

killing the princes who wooed his chaste spouse Pénelopé and wasted his substance.[1]

After the death of the suitors Odysseus having offered a sacrifice to the nymphs sailed over to E'lis to look after his cattle, and on his return he went as directed by Teiresias to Thesprótia, where he married the queen Kallidiké. Heading her subjects in a war against the Brygians, he was opposed by Arés and aided by Athéna, and Apolló interfered to terminate the contest. After the death of Kallidiké Odysseus gave the kingdom to his son by her, named Polypœtés, and returned to Ithaka. Soon after, Télegonos, his son by Kirké, coming in quest of him, landed and began to plunder the isle, and Odysseus going to oppose him fell by his hand.[2] Télegonos, on learning whom he had unwittingly slain, took Pénelopé and Télemachos and the body of his father with him to his mother's isle. Kirké there made them immortal, and she herself married Télemachos, while Pénelopé became the bride of Télegonos.

The literature of the Trojan war was very copious. Of the original poems the Ilias and Odyssey alone have come down to us; fragments only exist of the remaining parts of the Cycle; to judge by those of the Kypria it must have been a very beautiful poem; those of the others are too scanty to enable us to form an opinion of their merit. The brief abstract of their contents given above is derived from two fragments of the Chréstomathy of Proklos, of which the one, containing the epitome of the Kypria, was discovered by Tychsen in a manuscript of the Ilias in the library of the Escurial, the other, containing the remainder, by Siebenkees in a manuscript Homer at Venice. It is by these fragments that critics have been able to ascertain what the Epic Cycle really was.

The Cycle, as we have observed, existed long after the commencement of the Christian æra, and various poems appear to have been made from it. That of Quintus Smyrnæus, in fourteen books, contains the narrative from the end of the Ilias to the taking of Troy, which last event is the subject of the poem of Tryphiodóros, while Koluthos sang the abduction of Helené, and

---

[1] The Odyssey ends here; in the Cycle the narrative was continued by the Telegonia of Eugammón.

[2] In our remarks on the story of Soohráb in the *Tales and Popular Fictions* (p. 164) we should have said, "The circumstance of a son *thus* slain by his father, etc.," for the subject of the *Euryalos* of Sophoklés was the death of a son of Odysseus, whose birth was somewhat like that of Soohráb, and who was sent in quest of him by his mother, and through the artifice of Pénelopé fell by his hands. Parthén. *Erót.* 3.

Tzetzés in three books put into verse the events before, in, and after the Ilias. To these later times also belong the tasteless pragmatised narratives in prose ascribed to Diktys of Kréte, and Darés the Phrygian, two notorious forgeries. Much matter relating to the war of Troy will be found in Eudocia and the scholiasts, and in the Latin Hyginus.

Æschylos' magnificent trilogy, the Oresteia, consisting of the Agamemnón, the Choéphoræ, and the Eumenides, is the only portion of his works on this subject which has reached us; of Sophoklés we have the Philoktétés, Ajax and E'lektra, and of Euripidés the Hekabé, Tróades, Andromaché, Helené, E'lektra and Orestés; we have also the Rhésos of another poet. The Kassandra of Lykophrón with the notes of Tzetzes contains much Tróic matter. Ovid gives the war a place in his Metamorphoses, and Statius has left an imperfect poem on the subject of Achilleus.

––––––––––

Having arrived at the closing event of the Grecian mythology, we will now briefly consider the question of its reality. Of the number of ships and warriors before Troy we shall say nothing, it being the palpable exaggeration of national and local vanity. Who could believe, for example, that Athens, in a quarrel not her own, sent to the coast of Asia, there to remain for ten years, a force nearly equal to that which she opposed to the Barbarians when fighting for her existence at Marathón?[1] The real and only question is, did a confederate Hellénic army actually invade and conquer a powerful realm on the coast of Asia?

To this we are inclined to answer in the negative. We have seen the personages and events of Grecian mythology gradually dissolve into air as we approached them, at times however showing a slight substratum of reality which gave them support. Such was the voyage of the Argonauts; such too we think was the war of 'Troy divine.' As the former rested on the voyages of the Minyans, so the latter had its origin in the early settlements of the Greeks on the coast of Asia and the contests they had to sustain with the original owners of the soil. These settlements were probably long before the time of the Dórian Migration; for we must not give implicit credit to what is called the early Grecian history, which is nothing but a scientific product

––––––––––

[1] The Catalogue gives the Athenians fifty ships. But what is this to the ninety of Pylos? Reckoning the crews of the Athenian ships at the same rate as those of the ships of Bœótia, i. e. 150 to each, we get a total of 7500 men.

from epic poems and local traditions.[1] We have before noticed the Grecian habit of supposing that their gods or heroes had already visited or conquered the country which they themselves had acquired, and supposing therefore Achæans from the Peloponnése to have conquered a tract about the Hellespont, they may easily have conceived that the great hero of Argos, Héraklés, had done the same, or that a monarch of Argos had led a host thither and taken and plundered a large city. This may have been at first a simple tradition; it may have been then expanded in ballads; the number of warriors have been increased as colonists from other parts of Hellas came to partake in them; the artificial mounds which lie scattered over the plain, the tombs probably of princes and warriors of an extinct race, have been regarded as those of Trojan and Achæan chiefs;[2] and thus the war may have finally acquired the magnitude and importance which it displays in the Ilias.

A cause for this war was to be assigned, and the manners of the age may have suggested that of the abduction of a Grecian princess.[3] But we have shown that the person selected is a purely imaginary being, a mere personification of the moon. Other names indicate ideal personages also: those of Agamemnón and Meneláos appear to denote the *long stay* of the army before Troy; Odysseus is apparently the *Traveller*; while Achilleus, Nestór, and others are merely the heroes of different parts of Hellas introduced into the cycle of the Trojan war. Again, when we find the Greeks at war with any real people, we may observe that the names of the adverse leaders have no similarity to Grecian ones; but all those of the Trojans and their allies are if possible more Greek than those of some of the Achæan chiefs. Such are Déiphobos, Anténór, Alexandros, Andromaché; Hektór plainly signifies the *defender* (ἔχω), a name equivalent to that of his son Astyanax;[4] the leaders of the people of the *far-off* Alybé are named Odios and Epistrophos. It is thus that significant

[1] See Buttmann, *Mythol.* ii. 184, 210. If the theory respecting the Philistines (p. 408) be correct, colonies began to leave the future Hellas at a very early period.

[2] See Ritter, *Vorhalle*, &c. p. 248 *seq.* There are six of them marked on Gell's map of the Troas.

[3] Payne Knight (*Proleg.* § 54) finds the cause in the great magnitudes of the empires of Agamemnón and Priamos, and thence their mutual jealousy. He also supposes the Pelopids to have meditated the recovery of the dominion of which the Dardanids had deprived Tantalos.

[4] Οἶος γὰρ ἐρύετο Ἴλιον Ἕκτωρ. *Il.* vi. 403: see Plato, *Cratyl.* 394. Welcker, *Tril.* 288. The circumstance of most of the names of the Trojan chiefs being compounds would seem to indicate the late age of the fiction of the Trojan war.

names are given to the Kentaurs, the Amazons, and above all to that beautiful poetic creation, the Phæakians.

The union for a common object ascribed to the Greeks in this mythe is totally repugnant to their natural character; even the invasion of Xerxés failed to unite them. The length of the war too is incredible; no volunteer army would ever have remained so long absent from their homes and families. We very much doubt if the war-car ever was used in Greece. No vestige of such a custom is to be found in the historic times, and it is therefore not unlikely that this Asiatic usage was transferred by the poets to the mythic ages of Hellas. We could make many more objections than these, but we will abstain, as it is possible that our scepticism may only serve to alienate some of our readers. Our firm conviction however is, that the siege of Troy is little more real than that of Albracca, of which 'romances tell.'[1]

It is a very remarkable circumstance, and one which has been hitherto, we believe, unobserved, that the two great Epics of India, whose antiquity ascends so high, should be on subjects precisely similar to the mythic wars of Hellas. That of the Ramayana is the expedition of Rama at the head of a large army, from the north of India to the isle of Lanka or Ceylon, to recover his wife Sita, who had been carried off by Ravana, the monarch of that island. The Mahábhárata relates the civil war of the Pandús and Kúrús, kindred families, for the succession to the throne which Dhritarashtra, the father of the latter, had abandoned in consequence of his blindness, and of which his brother Pandú had then taken possession. Like Polyneikés, the five sons of Pandú are driven into exile, and like the same prince in the tragedy of Greece, they are represented as objects of righteous commiseration. Sanscrit scholars in general regard these wars as real events, but in our eyes they stand on precisely the same ground as the corresponding mythes of Hellas, Rama's expedition, for example, presenting the very same difficulties as the War of Troy.[2]

The War of Troy and the Returns terminate the mythic history of Greece. The Dórian Migration, or Return of the Hérakleids, though greatly mingled with fable, is a real event. For some centuries the history of Greece is semi-mythic and traditional; such is the form of even the Persian war. After that it is related

---

[1] Most of the objections here urged will be found in Bryant's *Dissertation on the War of Troy*, an essay which we had not read when the above was written.

[2] It may also be observed that, like the Ilias, these poems are largely interpolated the same is the case with the Sháh-nameh.

by contemporary writers, and becomes as true as that of any other people.

We have thus seen, assuming our theory to be correct, that the heroes, like the gods of Greece, were the pure creations of imagination. At the waving of the mythologic wand they have all melted into air, and Grecian history appears to us emerging from a kind of fairy-land. This is in our eyes a beautiful prospect. No one can believe the mythes in their present form: and nothing can be more dry and insipid than the manner in which the pragmatisers seek to convert them into real history. Yet in the earlier and better days of Hellas they were undoubted articles of actual belief; and Hésiod, for example, probably gave no more than the popular creed when he said of the heroes,

> And now with minds free from all care they dwell
> In the Islands of the Blest, by Ocean's deep-
> Eddying stream, the heroes fortunate,
> For whom the bounteous earth thrice every year
> Yieldeth fair blooming fruit as honey sweet.[1]

---

[1] Ἔργ. 170 seq. The inventors of the mythic legends however could hardly have believed them to be true, except in a subjective sense: see above, p. 18. Anaxagoras and other early philosophers regarded even the Ilias as an ethic allegory; but this was a mistaken view. Single mythes, however, such as those of Ixíon and Tantalos, certainly were such. It is possible that the Isles of the Blest, exclusively reserved for the Heroes, was a fiction similar to the Isle of Venus of Camões (one of the most beautiful creations of modern genius), which he assures us was an allegory. The original lines are so fine, that we cannot refrain from quoting some of them.

> Porque dos feitos grandes, da ousadia
> Forte e famosa, o mundo está guardando
> O premio lá no fim bem merecido,
> Com fama grande, e nome alto e subido.

> Que as nymphas do Oceano tão formosas,
> Tethys, e a ilha angelica pintada,
> Outra cousa não he que as deleitosas
> Honras que a vida fazem sublimada:
> Aquellas preeminencias gloriosas,
> Os triumphos, a fronte coroada
> De palma e louro, a gloria e maravilha,
> Estes são os deleites desta ilha.—*Os Lusiadas*, C. ix. st. 88.

Comp. Hor. *Carm.* iv. 25 seq. Ov. *ex Pont.* iv. 8, 55 seq. It might seem that the Chinese also have an Isle of the Blest: see the verses at the head of chap. xv. of the Chinese novel *Iu-Kiao-Li*.

MYTHOLOGY OF ITALY.

CHAPTER I.

INTRODUCTION.

Early State of Italy and Rome.

No fact of the times anterior to history seems to be more satisfactorily ascertained, than that of Italy having been long before the foundation of Rome a highly populous and industriously cultivated region. But all records of those times, if such did ever exist, are lost never to be recovered; and it is only from the remains of their operations on the solid surface of the earth —their gigantic buildings, lakes and canals—that we are left to conjecture the state of the ancient inhabitants of Italy.[1]

In the times of the early history of Rome, three principal nations possessed the central part of the Peninsula. These were the Etruscans, the Latins, and the Sabellians. The city of Rome, whose origin is involved in such obscurity, rose on the confines of these three nations: her population was formed out of them: she derived from them all her institutions; and among others her religious doctrines and rites, which she moulded and mingled in such a manner as to make it now nearly impossible to assign with certainty to each its part in the combined whole which Roman story displays.

Popular poetry is, as the example of ancient Greece shows, the great preserver of the popular religion in a society where it is of a complex and varied nature. That of Greece teemed with legends of the adventures of its gods; each of which became the theme of popular verse, passed from mouth to mouth, was sung at the festivals of the deity whose acts it recorded, was varied, changed, and modified by the narrators; and when at length, by opening an intercourse with Egypt, Greece obtained, in the papyrus, the means of preserving her literature, numbers of these legends were secured from the weakness and defects of the memory. Thousands of others still floated about, and were gradually sunk in the stream of oblivion.

But in Italy the case was different: the people of this country seem not to have possessed the lively fancy and ready invention

---

[1] See Niebuhr's *Hist. of Rome,* i. 170 *seq.*

of the natives of Hellas. Their religion was, as far as we can discern, of a more serious character; no wars or crimes polluted the beings whom they adored; and the virtue of the Italian maids and matrons was safe from the lust of the gods who ruled over mankind.[1] Hence the most fruitful source of Grecian legend was wanting in Italy; and the poet, when he would raise a hymn to accompany the sacrifice to a god, could only, like a Christian bard, extol his goodness and implore his favour. When, therefore, the papyrus made its way to Italy, though it might have found numerous ballads in praise of illustrious men, and hymns in honour of the gods to record, it met with no love-adventures of the latter to impress on its pages. The cause of this character of the Italian religion it is scarcely possible to discover; it may be that Italian genius is not inventive of circumstances and details of events. Even at the present day Italy yields to Spain in the number, variety and poetic character of the legends of the lives and miracles of the Saints, as she did to Hellas in the mythes of gods and heroes; in narrative poetry also she yields to her in quantity if not in quality, and she is infinitely less rich in romances of chivalry, while her scanty drama will bear no comparison with that of the profusely wealthy theatre of her Iberian sister.

Beside the religious systems and deities of the three nations above enumerated which Rome adopted, she early,—even in the regal period,—began, with that facility which always distinguished her, to appropriate the gods of Greece. Her knowledge of them was, it is probable, chiefly derived from the Grecian colonies in Italy; from whom she also obtained those oracles called the Sibylline Books, which are known to have been Greek, and which always enjoined the adoption of Grecian rites and Grecian deities.

When her arms had penetrated to the south of the Peninsula, and the cities of Magna Græcia acknowledged her dominion, poets of this country sought the favour of the Mistress of Italy, by celebrating her origin and her deeds in her own language. Nævius the Campanian sang, in Saturnian verse (the ancient measure of Italian poetry), the chief events from the voyage of Æneas to the end of the first Punic war. The Calabrian Ennius boldly and contemptuously sought to banish the rude free form

---

[1] See the praises which Dionysius (*Antiq. Rom.* i. 18, 19) bestows on this account on the religion of the Romans, which we may observe had no deity answering to the Erós of the Greeks. In our observations above we include all the religions of Italy; and we allude to the Hellénic, not the Pelasgian form, of the Grecian mythes. In their original and true sense they were, as we have seen, perfectly pure and moral.

of measure in which the Romans at their banquets sang the deeds of their fathers, and digested in Grecian hexameters the events which it recorded into his Annals. Grecian forms now supplanted all the old Italian ones: Grecian mythology, with all its legends, was rapidly poured in upon Rome. Each succeeding age saw the Græcomania increase: the people of education looked with contempt on the rude lays of their forefathers and their simpler religion; the homely old ballads of the Cossi and Cethegi fell into oblivion; the entire literature of Rome became Grecian; and the extant Roman poetry is little more than a transcript of that of Greece.

Italian mythes, as has been observed, do not exist. In Vergil and Ovid we meet with a few adventures of the old Italian deities framed in imitation of those of Greece, but totally repugnant to the religious ideas of Italy. For our knowledge of the objects of Italian worship we are chiefly indebted to these poets, and to Varro, Gellius, Macrobius, and the Latin Fathers of the Church. In all of them we discern the influence of the principles of Euhemerus introduced into Rome by Ennius.

The Etruscan Religion.

The disposition of the Etruscans was melancholy and serious; their form of government a rigid aristocracy, administered by an hereditary race or caste of priestly nobility. Their religion was founded on peculiar views of the world and its periods, and on the art of learning the will of the supernal powers by the thunder, the lightning, and other aërial phenomena. The rules and principles of this science were contained in books ascribed to a subterranean dæmon named Tages, who, the Tuscan legend said, had risen up, a babe in form, an aged man in wisdom, from under the soil before the plough of a peasant of Tarquinii as he was at his work, and who instructed the people in divination.[1]

According to the doctrine of the Etruscans there were two orders of gods, the one superior, *veiled* and nameless, with whom the supreme god took counsel when about to announce by lightning any change in the present order of things.[2] The other consisted of twelve gods, six male and as many female, his ordinary council. These were called by the common name of *Consentes* or *Complices* (the Latin of the Etruscan word); according to Varro[3] because they are born and die together. The general Etruscan term for a god was Æsar.[4]

[1] Cic. *De Div.* ii. 23. Ov. *Met.* xv. 558. Joh. Lydus, *De Ostentis,* iii.
[2] Sen. *Qu. Nat.* ii. 41. Festus *v.* Manubiæ. [3] *Ap Arnob.* iii. 123
[4] Suet. *Oct.* 97. Dio Cass. lvi. 29.

The supreme god of the Tuscans, answering to the Zeus of the Greeks, the Jupiter of the Romans, was named Tina.[1] A goddess named Kupra was called by the Romans Juno :[2] and another, named Menerfa or Menrfa, was the original of the Minerva of Rome. These three deities had always contiguous temples on the citadel of every Etruscan city.[3] Hence the united temples of Jupiter, Juno, and Minerva, which crowned the Capitol at Rome.

A goddess named Nortia, answering to the Roman Fortuna, was worshipped at the Tuscan cities of Sutri and Volsinii.[4] Vertumnus also was one of the principal deities of Etruria.[5] The Tuscan god of the under-world, or rather the ruler of the dead, it is said,[6] was named Mantus, and there was a goddess called Mania of a similar nature. The Lares, which form so conspicuous a portion of the Roman religion, it is probable, belonged originally to the Etruscan system.

The Etruscans had also deities answering to the Neptunus, Mars, Saturnus, Janus, Volcanus, Summanus, Vejovis and others of the Romans. Nine were held to have the power of casting the lightning, namely, Jupiter, Juno, Minerva, Vejovis, Summanus, Volcanus, Saturnus, Mars. It is uncertain who was the ninth.

As soon as an intercourse was opened between Etruria and Greece or her colonies, the Grecian mythology made most rapid progress in that country; and the deities and legends of Greece became so closely interwoven in the system of Etruria, that it is with difficulty any vestiges of the original domestic system can be traced.[7]

The Romans, previous to their acquaintance with Greece, always looked up to Etruria as their instructress. The patrician children were sent thither for education; all the royal and consular ornaments were borrowed from that country; and the science and the religious ceremonies of Rome were almost entirely derived from Etruria.

The Latin Religion.

Late writers have made it extremely probable that the Latins were a mixed people, formed out of the original inhabitants of

---

[1] Said to be a corruption of Ζῆνα.　　　　[2] Strab. v. 4, 2, p. 241.
[3] Serv. Æn. i. 422.　　　　[4] Livy, vii. 3.　Juv. x. 74.　Tertull. Apol. 24.
[5] Varr. De L. L. v. 46, ed. Müll.
[6] Serv. Æn. x. 199. He was probably the same as Orcus. On the vases he is represented as leading a horse on which the departing spirit is mounted see above, p. 84. Perhaps this idea may lurk in the epithet κλυτόπωλος, peculiar to Hadés. The Turkish proverb says that "Death is a black camel that kneels down at every door," sc. for the dead to mount.
[7] On the Tuscan religion and deities see Müller's Etrusker, Buch iii.

the country, and the Pelasgians, that extensive race which originally possessed Greece and a portion of Lesser Asia. This is
perhaps the best principle on which the great similarity of the
Latin and Greek languages can be accounted for; and it will
also in a great measure, taken however in combination with the
general one, explain the agreement of their religious systems,
and the facility with which the religion and mythology of Greece
were adopted at Rome.

It cannot be determined which of the Roman gods are to be
regarded as those of their Latin forefathers; but it is probable
that Saturnus, Ops, Janus, Jana, Pales, Pomona, and those deities
relating to agriculture (to which the Latins were greatly devoted),
were derived by the Romans from their Latin ancestors. We
shall not perhaps much err if we regard as Latin all those deities
whose Sabine or Etruscan origin does not appear.[1]

The Sabellian Religion.

Under the name of Sabellians may be comprised all the tribes
of the Apennines east of Latium. It is therefore inclusive of the
Sabines, Samnites, Marsians, and their kindred clans; and it is
by no means improbable, that the Umbrians to the north and
the Oscans to the south of them were of the same race with the
Sabellians.

The rigid virtues of a portion of the Sabellian race, particularly
the Sabines, were always the theme of praise at Rome. Grazing
and agriculture were the chief employments of these hardy tribes,
and their religion was intimately connected with these arts; and
consequently, we may suppose, bore much resemblance to that of
the Latins. It has always been asserted that a great portion of
the Roman religion was of Sabine origin.

The Sabines adored Sancus and Sabus, or Sabinus, as the
founders of their nation.[2] Mamers or Mars was also one of their
deities; an erect lance was the symbol before which he was
worshipped. According to the ancient annals of Rome[3] Tatius
the Sabine king raised altars to Ops and Flora, Diovis and
Saturnus, Sol and Luna, Volcanus and Summanus, and to
Larunda, Terminus, Quirinus, Vortumnus, the Lares, Diana and
Cloacina.

The Marsian portion of this race were as celebrated for their
skill in detecting the will of the gods by the flight and voice of

---

[1] The names of the Latin deities, which are mostly inexplicable, probably
belong to the non-Pelasgic portion of the language.
[2] Sil. Ital. viii. 422 seq.　Verg. Æn. vii. 178.　　Varro, De L. L. v. 74.

the birds, as the Etruscans for discerning it in the electric phænomena of the sky.

It is a very remarkable feature in the ancient religion of Italy, that though it admitted not of the births, marriages and generations of its deities, like that of Greece, it usually represented them in pairs, each consisting of a male and a female divinity.[1] Thus we meet with Saturnus and Ops, Saturnus and Lua, Mars and Neriene, Quirinus and Hora. In some cases the name of the goddess is only the feminine form of that of the god, as Janus Jana, Tellumo Tellus, Lupercus, Luperca, Volumnus, Volumna, Vitellius Vitellia. This principle probably ran through the whole of the ancient language, for we find *animus* and *anima* used of the vital powers, and Rome and other Italian towns politically divided into a *Populus* and a *Plebs*.[2] It may further be observed that the deities of the Italian creed have far less the air of personification than those of Hellas. They more resemble the presiding angels of the Jews and Mohammedans.

Another peculiar feature of the old Italian religion, and which testifies to its purity, warmth and simplicity, is that of calling the gods Fathers (*Patres*), and the goddesses Mothers (*Matres*), —titles of veneration or affection given by the Greeks to none but Zeus and Déméter or Earth. As this is a circumstance that seems to have almost totally escaped the notice of modern inquirers, we will here give some proofs of such being the usage among the Romans.

In the Council of the Gods of the old satirist Lucilius the following lines occurred:[3]—

> Ut nemo sit nostrum quin pater optimus Divum,—
> Ut Neptunus pater, Liber, Saturnus pater, Mars,
> Janus, Quirinus pater—nomen dicatur ad unum;

on which Lactantius observes, that "every god who is worshipped by man must in solemn rites and prayers be called Father, not only for the sake of honour but from reason, both because he was before man, and because like a father he gives life, health

---

[1] "Duplicis sexus numina esse dicuntur, ut cum in actu sunt mares sint, feminæ cum patiendi habent naturam."—Serv. *Æn.* iv. 638: comp. Sen. *Nat. Quæst.* iii. 14. "Each (Hindú) god has his lawful spouse or Sakti (*power*), endowed with the same attributes and powers as her husband, from whom she usually is sprung, and whose name she bears, as Indrani, Varuni," etc. Bohlen *Das Alt. Ind.* i. 247.   [2] See Niebuhr, *Hist. of Rome*, i. 417.

[3] *Ap.* Lactant. *Div. Inst.* iv. 3. For the union of *pater* with the name of the gods, see also Gell. v. 12.

and food." To this we may add the testimony of Servius, who says[1] that "the ancients called all the gods fathers." We have not the same direct evidence of the goddesses being called mothers,[2] but we will show by induction that such was the case. As Lactantius observes, it was chiefly in prayer that the terms Father and Mother were used; but they adhered to some of the gods, such as Jupiter. Liber does not often occur without a *pater*; neither does Dis; and we usually meet with Mater Matuta.

The Romans were fond of using their political vocabulary, even when speaking of their gods. Thus we read of gods of the Greater Houses,[3] the Ramnes and Tities, as it were, of heaven; and of the Select Gods,[4] like the Select Judges; and we also meet with a Plebs among the divinities.[5] It cannot perhaps be asserted that these divisions were made seriously, or were used by the hierarchy; but Varro[6] gives the names of twenty Select Gods; and there stood in the Forum twelve gilded statues of Consentian deities,[7] which were probably those enumerated in the following lines of Ennius, and which, by the way, are exactly the same with the twelve gods of the Greeks,

> Juno, Vesta, Minerva, Ceres, Diana, Venus, Mars,
> Mercurius, Jovis, Neptunus, Volcanus, Apollo.

These twelve deities were thus paired in the *lectisternium*, A.U. 535,[8] Jupiter Juno, Neptunus Minerva, Mars Venus, Apollo Diana, Volcanus Vesta, Mercurius Ceres. This classification is evidently Grecian; for it is only in the mythology of Greece that Neptunus and Minerva (Poseidón and Athéna) and Mercurius and Ceres (Hermés and Démétér) are connected.

---

[1] *Æn.* i. 155: comp. Propert. iv. 11, 18. Stat. *Theb.* iii. 146. Val. Flac. i. 193.
[2] Varro however says (*Fr.* p. 222 Bip.), "Diis quibusdam patribus et deabus matribus, sicut hominibus, ignobilitatem accidisse."
[3] Cic. *Tusc.* i. 13.   [4] Varro, *Fr.* p. 223 (Bip.)
[5] Ov. *Met.* i. 173.   *Ibis* 81. ·   [6] *Ut supra.*
[7] Id. *De R. R.* i. 1. He in this place names the following twelve, which he calls Consentian gods of the country: Jovis and Tellus, Sol and Luna, Ceres and Libera, Robigus and Flora, Minerva and Venus, Bonus Eventus and Lympha.   [8] Liv. xxii. 10.

Chapter II.

THE SELECT GODS.

VARRO enumerates twenty deities, whom he terms select, namely Janus, Jovis, Saturnus, Genius, Mercurius, Apollo, Mars, Volcanus, Neptunus, Sol, Orcus, Liber Pater, Tellus, Ceres, Juno, Luna, Diana, Minerva, Venus and Vesta. We shall here treat of them, but in a different order.

Jovis, Juppiter, Jupiter.

Like the Greek Zeus, the Latin Jovis, which is evidently a kindred term,[2] signified originally *God*. Hence we find it used in the plural, Joves. Divus, Dius, or Deus Jovis, was contracted to Dijovis and Diovis,[3] and Jovis Pater or Diespiter became Jupiter, answering to the Ζεὺς πατήρ of the Greeks. In the more ancient monuments of the Roman religion Jovis or Jupiter does not occur unaccompanied by an epithet.

The principal Jupiter was the Capitoline, or the Jupiter Optimus Maximus, whose temple containing the images of Juno and Minerva adorned the Capitol in Rome, and who was regarded as the great guardian of the fortunes of the city.

Jupiter Elicius was so named, as we are told, from the following circumstance.[4] In the time of Numa there occurred great thunder-storms and rain. The people and their king were terrified, and the latter had recourse to the counsel of the nymph Egeria. She informed him that Faunus and Picus could instruct him in the mode of appeasing Jupiter, but that he must employ both art and violence to extract the knowledge from them. Accordingly by her advice he placed bowls of wine at a fountain on Mount Aventine, whither they were wont to come to drink, and concealed himself in a neighbouring cavern. The rural gods came to the fount, and finding the wine drank copiously of it: they immediately afterwards fell asleep, and Numa quitting his retreat came and bound them. On awaking, they struggled, but in vain, to get free; and the pious prince, apologising for what necessity had obliged him to do, entreated that they would inform him how Jupiter was to be appeased. They yielded to his prayer, and on his loosing them drew down (" *eliciunt* ") Jupiter by their charms. He descended on the Aventine hill, which trembled beneath the weight of the deity. Numa was terrified,

---

[1] *Fr.* p. 223 (Bip.).　　　　　　　　[2] Like ζυγὸν and *jugum*.
[3] Varro, *L. L.* v. 66. Gellius, v. 12.
[4] Ov. *Fast.* iii. 285 *seq.* with our notes. Plut. *Numa*, 15.

but recovering he implored the god to give a remedy against the lightning. The ruler of the thunder assented, and in ambiguous terms conveyed the relief : " Cut a head "—" of an onion from my garden " subjoined the king,—" of a man "—" the topmost hairs" quickly replied Numa ;—" I demand a life"—" of a fish." The deity smiled, and said that his weapons might thus be averted, and promised a sign at sun-rise the following morning.

At dawn the people assembled before the doors of the king : Numa came forth, and seated on his maple throne looked for the rising of the sun. The orb of day was just wholly emerged above the horizon, when a loud crash was heard in the sky : thrice the god thundered without a cloud; thrice he sent forth his lightnings. The heavens opened, and a light buckler came gently wafted on the air and fell to the ground. Numa having first slain a heifer, took it up and named it *Ancile.* He regarded it as the pledge of empire; and having had eleven others made exactly like it by the artist Mamurius, to deceive those who might attempt to steal it, committed them to the care of the priests named Salii.

As Latiaris, that is, *Of-the-Latins,* Jupiter was annually worshipped by the Latins on the Alban Mount. The festival was named the Latin Holidays (*Feriæ Latinæ*) ; its institution was ascribed to Tarquinius Superbus. Jupiter Anxur was the chief deity of Anxur or Tarracina. Jupiter Indiges was worshipped on the banks of the Numicius, and was said to be the deified Æneas.

Jupiter was named Feretrius or *Bearer,* as the spoils of the enemy's general if slain by a Roman commander were *borne* to him. He was also called Victor and Stator, as the giver of victory and stayer of flight We also meet with Jupiter Pistor, whose altar was on the Capitol.[1] In the usual Roman manner an historical origin was given to all these names.

Jupiter was called Lucetius[2] as the author of light (*lucis*); for a similar reason he was named Diespiter, *i.e.* Dies Pater or Father of Day or of Light.[3] When the Greek philosophy was introduced into Rome Jupiter was regarded as the material heaven, as in the well-known line of the Thyestes of Ennius,

Aspice hoc sublime candens quem invocant omnes Jovem.

---

[1] Ov. *Fast.* vi. 349 *seq.*

[2] Nævius *ap. Gell.* v. 12. Festus, *s. v.* Servius (*Æn.* ix. 570) says this was his name in Oscan. It had gone so completely out of use that Vergil (*ut supra*) makes it the name of an Italian warrior.

[3] Plaut. *Capt.* iv. 4, 1. *Pœnul.* iv. 2, 48. Hor. *Carm.* i. 34, 5 ; iii. 2, 29. Diespiter is not *Pater diei,* for that is contrary to analogy : see Varro, *De L. L.* v. 66.

Juno.

The feminine to Jovis was Jovino, which was contracted by use to Juno.[1] This name therefore must have originally signified simply *goddess*, and we find it used in the plural—Junones.[2] Female slaves used to swear by the Juno of their mistress, that is, her protecting deity; for Juno was to the woman what the Genius was to the man.[3] It would even appear that women were in the habit of swearing by their own Juno.[4] Frequent mention of this Juno occurs in Inscriptions.[5]

Juno Romana or Capitolina, as one of the great tutelar deities of Rome, had her share in the stately temple on the Capitol. On the adjacent Arx, on the site of the house of the unfortunate M. Manlius, stood the temple of Juno Moneta.[6] As this temple was made the mint, the word *money* oddly enough comes from her name, the origin of which is quite uncertain.[7]

Juno Regina, the Kupra of Etruria, had a temple on the Aventine. During the siege of Veii she had been evoked in the usual manner and promised a stately temple at Rome; and after the capture of that city, says the legend, when the Roman youths appointed for the purpose approached the statue, it gave an audible reply to their demand if it was willing to be removed to Rome.[8]

As the patroness of married women Juno was named Matrona. She was called Jugalis as presiding over marriage,[9] Cinxia from the loosing of the bride's girdle,[10] and Fluonia as restraining the menstrual discharges during conception.[11] Juno Lucina, identified by the Greeks with their Eileithyia,[12] was probably so

[1] Like *providens prudens, bovicula bucula.*
[2] See Marini, *Atti de' Fratelli Arvali,* 368, 414.
[3] See below, *Genius.* Juv. ii. 98.   [4] See Tibull. iii. 6, 48.
[5] The following are in the Vat. and Cap. collections:—
" JUNONI JULIÆ AUFIDENÆ CAPITOLINÆ SACRUM D.M."
" PHŒBADI ET JUNONI HEIUS."
" JUNONI DORCADIS JULIÆ AUGUSTÆ L. VERNÆ CAPRENSIS ORNATRICIS LYCASTUS CONLIBERTUS ROGATOR CONJUGI CARISSIMÆ SIBI."
" JUNONI JUNIÆ C. SILANI F. TORQUATÆ SACERDOTI VESTALI ANNIS LXIIII. CŒLESTI PATRONÆ ACTIUS L."
[6] Liv. vii. 28. Ov. *Fast.* vi. 183 *seq.*
[7] Cic. *De Div.* i. 45; ii. 32. Suidas, *s. v.* Moneta was the ancient Latin translation of Mnemosyne, " Nam diva Monetas filia docuit." Livius, *Odyssea.*
[8] Liv. v. 21, 22. Plut. *Camill.* 6.
[9] Serv. *Æn.* iv. 16. It does not appear that *Pronuba* was a title of Juno.
[10] Festus, *s. v.*   [11] Id. *s. v.* Arnob. iii. 30. August. *de Civ. Dei,* vii. 2, 3.
[12] Dion. Hal. iv. 15. In the South of Europe the place of Juno Lucina is occupied by the Virgin: see Dante, *Purg.* xx. terz. 7; Par. xv. terz. 45. Venturi, *in loc.*: comp. Hay, *Western Barbary*, p. 26.

named as bringing children to the *light*. She was invoked by women in labour,[1] and into the treasury of her temple, which stood on the Esquiline, a piece of money was paid for the registry of every birth.[2]

Juno Caprotina was honoured by an annual sacrifice on the nones of July. At this sacrifice, which was offered under a wild fig-tree (*caprificus*), of which tree the milk or juice and twigs were used on the occasion, both free women and slaves assisted. On this occasion they wore the *toga prætexta*. Of this festival, which was common to all Latium, and which probably had a rural origin, the Roman annals told a legend connected with the political history of the state.[3]

Juno Sospita, or Sispita, that is, the *Protectress*, was worshipped from the earliest times at Lanuvium. She was represented with a goatskin about her, a spear in her hand, a small shield on her arm, and with shoes turned up at the points.[4] Another, probably Sabine, title of this goddess was Curis or Curitis.[5] Juno was generally represented armed, and it was the custom of the Romans to divide the hair of a virgin-bride with the point of a small spear.[6]

Minerva.

Minerva, or Menerva, corresponded in some measure with the Pallas-Athéné of the Greeks. She was the patroness of arts and industry, and all the mental powers were under her care.[7] She was the deity of schools: her statue was always placed in them, and school-boys got as holydays the five days of her festival called the Quinquatrus, celebrated in the month of March: at the expiration of them they presented their master with a gift called Minerval.[8] According to Varro,[9] Minerva was the protecting goddess of olive grounds; but it may be doubted whether this was not a transference to her of one of the attributes of the Grecian goddess Pallas-Athéné.

The chapel of Minerva on the Capitol was under the same roof with those of Jupiter and Juno, to the right of that of the former deity, for in the Roman religion she seems to have ranked before Juno. On the side of the Cælian hill

---

[1] Terence, *passim*.   [2] Dion. Hal. *ut sup.*

[3] Varr. *De L. L.* vi. 18. Macrob. *Sat.* i. 11. For the legend see our *History of Rome*, 119.   [4] Cic. *De Nat. Deor.* i. 29. Liv. viii. 14; xxix. 14.

[5] Plut. *Romul.* 29. Festus, *v.* Curitim.   [6] Ov. *Fast.* ii. 559.

[7] Ov. *Fast.* iii. 815 *seq.* Hence various expressions, such as *crassa* or *pingui Minerva, invita Minerva, mea Minerva,* used when speaking of the mind.

[8] Varr. *De R. R.* iii. 2.   [9] Id. *ib* i. 1.

stood a temple of Minerva Capta, the origin of which name is uncertain.[1]

The festivals of Minerva were named Minervalia or Quinquatrus. They were two in number. The former, called the Greater, was celebrated in March, the time when, according to the Tuscan discipline, Minerva cast her lightnings.[2] It was named Quinquatrus as being on the fifth day after the Ides:[3] but the ignorance of the Romans made them extend the festival to five days; it was concluded by the Tubilustrium.[4] The Lesser was on the Ides of June, and the flute-players celebrated it.[5] As both the trumpet and flute came to the Romans from Etruria, this tends to prove that the worship of Minerva was introduced from that country. No derivation of her name can therefore be given, for it does not seem to be a translation. It is very remarkable that the title Mater is never given to this goddess or to Juno—possibly on account of their Etruscan origin.

Vesta.

The same obscurity involves this goddess as the corresponding Hestia of the Greeks, with whom she is identical in name and office. There is every reason to believe her worship to have been unborrowed by the Romans, and a part of the religion of the ancient Pelasgic population of Latium,[6] as it is by all testimony carried back to the earliest days of the state, and its introduction ascribed to Numa.[7] Like Hestia she was a deity presiding over the public and private hearth: a sacred fire, tended by six virgin-priestesses called Vestals, flamed in her temple at Rome. As the safety of the city was held to be connected with its conservation, the neglect of the virgins, if they let it go out, was severely punished, and the fire was rekindled from the rays of the sun.

The temple of Vesta was round: it contained no statue of the goddess.[8] Her festival celebrated in June was called Vestalia: plates of meat were sent to the Vestals to be offered up; the millstones were wreathed with garlands of flowers, and the millasses (also crowned with violets) went about with cakes strung round their necks.[9]

---

[1] Ov. (Fast. i. 835 seq.) offers several derivations. Müller (Etrusk. ii. 49) seems to prefer the one from the taking of Fa erii.

[2] Serv. Æn. xi. 259. [3] Varr. De L. L. vi. 14.

[4] Ov. Fast. iii. 849. Varr. ut sup. Laur. Lyd. de Mens. p. 85.

[5] Ov. Fast. vi. 651 seq. Varr. De L. L. vi. 17. Festus, v. Minusc. Quinquat. [6] Dion. Hal. ii. 66.

[7] Id. ib. Liv. i. 20. Plut. Num. 9–11. Camill. 20. On the subject of Vesta and the Vestals see our Ovid, Excurs. vii. [8] Ov. Fast. vi. 295 seq.

[9] Ov. Fast. vi. 311, 347. Propert. iv. 1, 23.

In the Forum at Rome there was a statue of the Stata Mater, placed there that she might protect the flagging from the effect of the fires which used to be made on it in the night time. The people followed the example, and set up similar statues in several of the streets.[1] Stata Mater is generally supposed to have been Vesta. We find this last goddess also called *Mater*.[2]

Ceres.

Ceres was the goddess who presided over corn and tillage, thus corresponding with the Grecian Démétér. Her temple at Rome was under the care of the ædiles, as she was the goddess of the agricultural plebeians.[3] Festivals called Cerealia were celebrated in her honour at Rome, in the month of April, with *a pomp*, and horse-races.[4] The country-people previous to beginning the harvest kept the Ambarvalia to Ceres, in which they offered her honey-combs covered with wine and milk, and a victim which they led three times round the corn-field; the swains all followed, crowned with oak, and dancing and singing.[5] A similar festival named the Sementina was celebrated when the sowing of the seed was over.[6]

The name Ceres may come from *creo* or from *gero*.[7] Servius[8] says that in the Sabine language Ceres signified *bread*; but it may have done so only figuratively.

Venus.

Venus is a deity about whom it is difficult to learn anything satisfactorily. She has been so thoroughly confounded with the Grecian Aphrodíté, that almost everything peculiar to her has disappeared. She cannot however have been one of the original deities of Rome, as her name did not occur in the Salian hymns, and we are assured that she was unknown in the time of the kings.[9] She seems to have been a deity presiding over birth and growth in general, for as Venus Hortensis she was the goddess of gardens.[10] She was held to be the same as Libitina the

---

[1] Festus, *s. v.*   [2] Cic. *pro Fonteio*, 17. Verg. *Geor.* i. 498.
[3] See Niebuhr, *Hist. of Rome*, i. 610.   [4] Ov. *Fast.* iv. 393 *seq*.
[5] Verg. *Geor.* i. 345 *seq*.   [6] Ov. *Fast.* i. 661 *seq*.

   Some derive Ceres from the Hindú Srees (*Blessing*); but it was pronounced *Keres*, and the gen., i. e. the original form, is *Cerer-is*, which has only one letter in common with Srees.   [8] *Geor.* i. 7.

[9] Cincius and Varro *ap. Macrob. Sat.* i. 12.

[10] "Coquus edit Neptunum, Venerem, Cererem:" i. e. fish, vegetables, bread. —Nævius *ap.* Festum s. v. *Coquus.* "Adveneror Minervam et Venerem, quarum unius procuratio oliveti, alterius hortorum."—Varro, *De R. R.* i. 1. In Plautus (*Rud.* ii. 1, 16) the fishermen pray to Venus to give them success,—a curious coincidence with the similar invocation of the rural god Priapos: see above, p. 208.

goddess of funerals, because, says Plutarch,[1] the one and the same goddess superintends birth and death. A temple of Venus at Rome was built with the fines imposed on matrons convicted of adultery;[2] but as this was long after the introduction of the Grecian deities, nothing can be collected from it respecting the original office and character of the goddess.

Venus Cloacina or Cluacina, was so called, says Pliny,[3] from *cluere*, to purify; because when the Sabines and Romans of Tatius and Romulus were reconciled, they purified themselves on the spot with myrtle-vervain, and a statue to Venus Cluacina was afterwards erected there.[4] Another account[5] says, that a statue of an unknown deity being found in the Cloaca, it was consecrated to Venus, under the name of Cloacina.

There was at Rome a temple of Venus Frutis,[6] which last term seems to be merely a corruption of Aphrodíte. It may however be derived from *fruor* and be connected with *fructus*, and refer to her rural character. In the Circus stood a chapel of Venus Murtia, so named, it is said, from the myrtles which had grown there.[7]

At Lavinium there was a temple of Venus common to the Latin nation, and there was another similar temple at Ardea.[8]

There were two festivals at Rome named Vinalia, in each of which there appears to have been a reference to this goddess. The first was on the 23rd of April, the second day from the Palilia. The offering was made to Jupiter, but the day was also sacred to Venus.[9] Ovid directs the *meretrices* to go and worship on this day at the temple of Venus Erycina near the Colline gate, whence we may collect that such was their practice; and we have here a proof of the identification of the Roman deity with those of other religions, for that Venus was the Greek Aphrodíte worshipped on Mount Eryx, in Sicily. The second Vinalia, called the Rustica, was on the 19th of August; and here we find Jupiter and Venus again united, for on this day the Flamen Dialis, having first sacrificed a ewe-lamb, himself commenced gathering the grapes; and the gardeners kept it as a holiday,

---

[1] *Quæst. Rom.* 23.   Cic. *De Nat. Deor.* ii. 23.   Dion. Hal. **iv. 15.**
[2] Liv. x. 31.   [3] *Nat. Hist.* **xv. 29.**
[4] In the Forum, Liv. iii. 48.   [5] Lactant. i. 20.
[6] Festus *v.* Frutinal.   Cassius Hemina (*ap. Solin.* ii. 14) said that Æneas brought her image from Sicily, *i. e.* that she was the goddess of Mount Eryx.
[7] Varr. *De L. L.* v. 154. It was afterwards corrupted to Murcia (Plin. *ut supra*) and derived from *murcidum,* " quia facit hominem murcidum, id est nimis desidiosum." Aug. *De Civ. Dei,* iv. 16. Servius (*Æn.* viii. 536) says that this goddess was Venus Verticordia: see *on* Ov. *Fast.* iv. 157.   [8] Strab. v. 3, 5, p. 232.
[9] Plin. *Nat. Hist.* xviii 29.   Ov. *Fast.* iv. 863, with our notes.

for we are told that "a temple was dedicated to Venus on this day, and gardens are placed under her protection."[1]

Perhaps it may form a presumption in favour of the original rural character of Venus, that, like Pales, her name is of both genders. Thus we meet with *Deus* and *Dea* Venus, and with Venus *almus*, and Venus *alma*.[2] The name Venus, or rather Veneris, may, as was supposed, come from *venio*, but its origin is very doubtful. Venus also had the title of Mater.[3]

Liber.

The name of the ancient Italian god identified with the Grecian Diony̆sos was Liber, and Pater was so generally joined with it that we do not often meet Liber alone. It is to be observed that Liber had no share in the Vinalia; his festival, named the Liberalia, was celebrated on the 17th of March, on which day his priestesses, mean old women crowned with ivy, sat in the streets "with cakes (*libeis*), and a portable fire-place (*foculo*), sacrificing for the purchaser;" on the Liberalia also the young men assumed the *toga virilis*, or *libera*.[4] We have here instances of the effect of names in the ceremonies of the ancient religions. On the Liberalia the people bought *liba*, and youths assumed the *toga libera*; and there could hardly be any other reason for these practices. We also see the introduction of the ivy of Diony̆sos.

According to Varro,[5] on the festival-days of this god the Phallus was carried in procession on a carriage through the fields and lanes about Rome, and then into the city. He adds, that in Lavinium, where the festival lasted a month, the most indecent language was used while the Phallus was carried through the market, and that one of the most respectable matrons was obliged to place a garland on it in public. This was probably a practice derived from the early times, and the emblem of fructification was thus supposed to exert a beneficial influence on the fields, and promote the production of the fruits of the earth.

Liber was united at Rome with Ceres and a goddess named Libera, but it appears to us to be quite erroneous to suppose

---

[1] Varr. *De L. L.* vi. 20. Festus *v.* Rustica Vinalia.

[2] Macrobius (*Sat.* iii. 8) gives the following passages, "Pollentemque deum Venerem."—Calvus. "Venerem igitur almum adorans, sive femina sive mas est."—Lævinus. He also quotes "Descendo ac ducente deo," Verg. *Æn.* ii. 632, on which see Servius. [3] Solinus, ii. 14.

[4] Varr. *De L. L.* vi. 14. Ov. *Fast.* iii. 713 *seq.* [5] *Fr.* p. 225 (Bip.).

that they were the Démétér, Dionýsos and Koré of the Greeks, by whom Dionýsos does not seem to have been united with the two goddesses, as Liber was at Rome. We would propose the following hypothesis on the subject.

The temple usually called that of Ceres at Rome was in reality one of the three conjoined deities.[1] It stood at the foot of the Aventine and belonged to the plebeians, to whom it seems to have been what the Capitoline temple was to the patricians. In this latter was worshipped a Triad,—Minerva, Jovis, Jovino (Juno), *i. e.* Wisdom, and the god and goddess κατ’ ἐξοχήν; in the latter there was also adored a Triad,—Ceres, Liber, Libera. May we not then suppose, that as the priestly nobles, the patricians, adored a triad of celestials or mental deities, so the agricultural plebeians worshipped a triad of deities presiding over the fruits and products of the earth? From the employment of the plural (ναῶν, ναοὺς) by Dionysius we may further infer that the temple at the Aventine contained three *cellæ* like that on the Capitoline.

The name Liber or Liberus signifies perhaps the *Pourer* (from *libo*), and he was probably a god of productiveness by moisture. In the usual manner he appears to have had his female power conjoined with him; for previous to the vintage sacrifices were offered to Liber and Libera.[2]

There was near Rome a grove, which was the scene of the Bacchanalian revels, when they were introduced into that city; it was sacred to a goddess named Stimula or Simila, which name is most probably only a Latin corruption of Semelé.[3]

Neptunus.

Neptunus was the god of the sea, like the Greek Poseidón, whose attributes and actions were afterwards bestowed on him. The honours of the Ludi Circenses or Consualia were shared by this deity, as horse-races formed a part of them. It may however be very much doubted whether the original Italian Neptunus was held to be the patron of the horse.

The origin of the name Neptunus cannot be discovered; that given by the Latin writers is absurd. We find him called *Pater*,[4] and a goddess named Salacia is joined with him.

---

[1] Liv. iii. 55. Dionys. vi. 17, 44. Tac. *Ann.* ii. 49.
[2] Colum. xii. 18.
[3] Ov. *Fast.* vi. 503.
[4] Verg. *Æn.* v. 14. Sil. Ital. xv. 161.

Mercurius.

This god, whose name is so evidently derived from *Merx*, presided over the business of the market, and trade, commerce and profit in general.[1] He does not appear to have exercised any other office of the Grecian Hermés.

Volcanus or Mulciber.

Volcanus was the god of fire, the Héphæstos of the Greeks; but he is not represented as an artist. He was said in a not very delicate legend to be the father of Servius Tullius, whose wooden statue was in consequence spared by the flames, when they consumed the temple of Fortune in which it stood.[2] He was also the reputed sire of Cæculus, the founder of Præneste, the legend of whose birth is nearly similar to that of Servius.[3] His first name is of uncertain origin; the last very probably comes from *mulceo*, to soften.[4]

Volcanus was united with a female power named Maia, which was probably the earth. By Vergil[5] he is termed Pater.

Apollo.

This deity with an ancient Grecian name can hardly have belonged to the original system of Italy : his worship was probably adopted in the time of the Tarquins from the Italiote Greeks. By the poets he is made to possess all the attributes of the Grecian god : he was also, chiefly under his name Phœbus, identified by them with the Sun.[6] A legend of wolves caused the god, who was worshipped on Mount Soracte, to be regarded as Apollo.[7] This deity is addressed as Pater under both his names.[8]

Mamers, Mavors, Mars.

Mars is usually regarded as a god of war, yet it is doubtful if such was his original character. In Cato[9] we meet with Mars Silvanus; and ne also seems to have been one of the twelve rural Lares invoked in the hymn of the Arval Brethren.[10] At

[1] Festus *v.* Mercurius.   Plaut. *Amphit. Prol.*   Ov. *Fast.* v. 671 *seq.*   Hor. *Sat.* ii. 3, 68; 6, 5.   [2] Ov. *Fast.* vi. 627.   Dion. Hal. iv. 40.
[3] Verg. *Æn.* vii. 678 *seq.*   Serv. *in loco.*
[4] Gell. xiii. 22.   Macrob. *Sat.* i. 12.   [5] *Æn.* viii. 394, 454.
[6] Horace, *Carmen Seculare.*   [7] See below, *Soranus.*
[8] Verg. *Æn.* xi. 789.   Stat. *Silv.* i. 6, 1.   [9] *De R. R.* 134.
[10] See Müller. *Etrusk.* ii. 91, 105.

the Suovetaurilia the swains prayed to Father Mars to avert disease, blight, storm and other evils, and to prosper the corn, vines, cattle, servants and family.[1] On the Ides of October there was a chariot-race at Rome, at the end of which the right-hand winning horse was sacrificed to Mars as an offering for the happy termination of the harvest.[2]

Marspiter, *i.e.* Mars Pater, was a usual appellation of this god, both from the general principle, and because the late legend made him the father of the founder of Rome. A legend of his own birth, framed also in imitation of those of Greece, is related by Ovid, and is alluded to in one of the etymons given of his title Gradivus.[3] Juno, it said, jealous of the birth of Minerva, was on her way to make her complaint to Oceanus and Tethys, when coming to the abode of Flora a flower was shown her by that goddess, on touching which flower she conceived and gave birth to Mars.

There was a female deity associated with Mars in the usual manner. She was named Neria or Neriene, i.e. *Strong-one*;[4] and some of the *Hellenisers* said she was Minerva, that is Pallas-Athéné. On the day of the Tubilustrium at Rome there was a sacrifice to Mars and Neriene.[5]

Diana.

An ancient Latin name of the moon was Jana.[6] In the Salian hymns she was invoked as Deiva Jana, which became Deivjana,

---

[1] Cato, *De R. R.* 141. Kartekeya, the Hindú war-god, was in like manner a god of the year and the seasons. Bohlen, *Alte Ind.* i. 244.

[2] Festus *v.* October equus. Plut. *Qu. Rom.* 97.

[3] Ov. *Fast.* v. 229 *seq.* Festus *v.* Gradivus, "quia *gramine* sit natus."

[4] The feminine of Nero, which in the Sabine language signified *Strong* (Sueton. *Tib.* i.). Gellius (xiii. 22) has the following passages relating to this goddess. "Nerienen Mavortis."—Ennius. "Nerienen Martis."—Pontifical Books. "Neria Martis te obsecro pacem dare, uti liceat nuptiis propriis et prosperis uti, quod de tui conjugis consilio," &c.—Speech of Hersilia to her father T. Tatius in the annalist Cn. Gellius.

> Nolo ego Neæram te vocent, sed Nerienem,
> Cum quidem Marti es in connubium data.
>   Licinius Imbres, *Neæra.*

> Mars peregre advenieus salutat uxorem suam Nerienen.
>   Plaut. *Trinum.* ii. 6, 34.

> Te, Anna Perenna, panda καὶ λατὰ, Pales,
> Neriones et Minerva, Fortuna ac Ceres.—Varro, Σκιομαχία.

[5] See our note on Ovid's *Fasti*, iii. 849.

[6] Nigidius *ap.* Macrob. *Sat.* i. 9. "Nunquam rure audistis, Octavo Janam crescentem et contra senescentem?" Varro, *De R. R.* i. 37. See our Ovid's *Fast.* Introd. p. xiii.

and ultimately Diana,[1] who was therefore the same with the Seléné and Artemis of the Greeks. By the poets all the attributes of this last goddess were given to Diana, who was one of the Matres of Roman religion.[2]

Diana was an especial object of veneration to the agricultural Latins. Accordingly when Servius Tullius concluded a league with the Latin federation, a temple was built to Diana on the Aventine, which was common property, and in which the record of the league was preserved on a tablet.[3]

This goddess was worshipped under the name of Nemorensis, in a grove (*nemus*) at the lake near Aricia. The priest of this temple, named Rex Nemorensis, was a runaway slave, who had obtained his office by killing his predecessor ; and he always went armed with a sword to preserve himself from the attempts of other aspirants.[4] A festival of the goddess, named the Nemoralia, was celebrated here on the ides of August.[5]

Diana Nemorensis was regarded as a beneficent being, the averter of disease. A subordinate deity named Virbius, whose statue no one was permitted to touch, was worshipped along with her ; his form was that of an old man ; and it was perhaps this similarity in appearance and office with the Asklépios of Epidauros, together with an etymological sleight with his name (*Vir bis*),[6] that gave occasion to the legend of his being Hippolytos, whom at the prayer of Diana Æsculapius had restored to life. It was probably after the invention of this legend that horses were prohibited from entering the sacred grove, as they had caused the death of Hippolytos.[7]

Janus.

The masculine of Jana is Janus, the Deivos Janos of the Salian hymns, by the usual contraction Dianus. This god must therefore have been the Sun, and all that we can learn respecting him agrees with this hypothesis.

Janus was usually represented with two faces, whence he was named *Bifrons* and *Biceps*. It is said that at the taking of Falerii a statue of Janus was found with four faces; and at Rome there was a temple of Janus Quadrifrons, which was square, with a

---

[1] Varro, *Fr.* p. 323 (Bip.).   [2] Diana Mater, *Gruter, Inscr.* xli. 5.
[3] Liv. i. 45. Nieb. *Hist. of Rome*, i. 361.
[4] Strab. v. 3, 12, p. 239. Ov. *Fast.* iii. 271, 272. *Art. Amat.* i. 260. Serv. *Æn.* vi. 136.   [5] Stat *Silv.* iii. 1, 55 *seq.*
[6] The derivation, given by Buttmann, from a common root with *verbena*, seems to be the true one.
[7] Verg. *Æn.* vii. 761 *seq.* Serv. *in loc.* Ov. *Met.* xv. 492 *seq.* See Buttmann's ingenious essay on Virbius and Hippolytos, *Mythol.* ii. 145 *seq.*

door and three windows on each side.[1] There was also an ancient statue of this god in the Forum, said to be as old as the time of Numa, of which the fingers were so formed, that those of one hand represented three hundred (CCC), those of the other fifty-five (LV), the number of days in the ancient lunar year.[2] All this is explicable on the supposition of Janus being the sun, the author of the year, with its seasons, months, and days. There were some however who regarded Janus as the heaven (mundus),[3] or even as the world itself;[4] but this seems to have been founded on an absurd etymology.

Like the Hindú Ganesa, with whose name his has a curious, but incidental resemblance, Janus was invoked at the commencement of most actions;[5] even in the worship of the other gods the votary began by offering wine and incense to Janus.[6] The first month in the year was named from him; and under the title Matutinus he was regarded as the opener of the day.[7]

It was probably the similarity of sound in their names that led to the placing of gates (jani) and doors (januæ) under the care of this god.[8] Hence perhaps it was that he was represented with a staff and a key, and that he was named the Opener (Patulcius) and the Shutter (Clusius).

Under the Capitol, close by the Forum, in Rome, stood the celebrated Janus Quirinus, Janus Geminus or Porta Janualis,[9] which it was the custom to close in time of peace, leave open in time of war. Its original form is not known, but it would appear to have been a δίπυλον or sort of short archway, with a gate at either end. Ovid, but we believe he is singular in it, names it a temple, a thing it could never have been in the original sense of

---

[1] Servius, Æn. vii. 607. Macrob. i. 9.

[2] Plin. Nat. Hist. xxxiv. 7. Macrobius (i. 9) and Lydus (De Mens. iv. 1) say that it held 300 counters in one hand and 65 in the other. The former asserts this to have been the case with his statues in general.

[3] Varro, Fr. p. 224 (Bip.)

[4] Festus v. Chaos. Ov. Fast. i. 103 seq.

[5] Hor. Sat. ii. 6, 20 seq. The country people previous to reaping the corn invoked Janus and Jovis with a strues, a ferctum and wine. Cato, De R. R. 134.

[6] Ov. ut supra, 171 seq.

[7] Hor. ut supra: see below, Matuta.

[8] Buttmann (Mythol. ii. 10) gives as an example the making St. Valentine (in Germany pronounced Falentin) the protector against the falling sickness. To this we may add that Sta. Lucia is the preserver of the eyesight. Another instance perhaps is St. Vitus's dance (vite). The water-sprite is in German and the Northern languages Nixe, Nökke, Neck, and hence St. Nicholas became the patron of seamen.

[9] Varr. De L. L. v. 165. Suet. Oct. 22. Macrob. Sat. i. 2. The Janus Quir'ni of Horace (Carm. iv. 15, 9, Fea in loc.) is an error similar to the Socii nominis Latini of Livy: see Hist. of Rome, p 468,

the word. From very early times there was in it a statue of the god.[1]

The origin of this Janus and its use is involved in the deepest obscurity. It has been ingeniously conjectured[2] that it was one of the original gates of Rome, and was named Quirinus because the road to the Sabine town of Cures ran from it. But though some of the gates in the wall of Aurelian were named from the places to which the roads from them led, this was not the case with any of those in the wall of Servius, much less in that of Romulus. It has also been conjectured[3] that when the Romans and Sabines concluded a peace and alliance they built this double gate with a front to each town, which was to be open in time of war for mutual aid, closed in time of peace to prevent feuds. But this must suppose a wall of separation, which most certainly did not exist, and moreover the gates should have faced north and south if on the road from the Quirinal to the Palatine, while they really looked east and west.[4] The origin of the Janus Geminus must therefore still remain in obscurity. Both it however and the double face of the god were probably connected with the double form in which all the relations in early Rome developed themselves. This Janus was closed, we are told, in the days of the mythic king Numa. It then stood open, except for a brief interval after the first Punic war, till the time of Augustus, by whom it was thrice closed.[5]

It was a tradition at Rome that when Tatius and his Sabines had reached this gate, the god by causing a stream of boiling water to gush forth from the earth forced them to retire, and that the Romans, out of gratitude, raised an altar and chapel to him on the spot.[6]

The root of the names Janus and Jana is probably *eo*, and Janus would thus correspond with the Greek Hyperión. As Janus was so much the object of worship, the *Pater* is frequently joined to his name.

After Ennius had introduced Euhemerism into Rome Janus shared the fate of the other deities, and he became an upright mortal king, who received Saturnus when he fled to Italy. He is also said to have married his sister Camesa, or Camesena;[7] and an amour quite in the Grecian style was invented for him with

---

[1] Varro, *ut sup.* Ov. *Fast.* 1. 257. Plin. *ut sup.*
[2] Buttmann, *ut sup.*   [3] See Nieb. *Hist. of Rome*, i. 287.
[4] Ov. *Fast.* i. 139.   [5] Suet. *ut sup.*
[6] Ov. *Met.* xiv. 836 *seq.* *Fast.* i. 257 *seq.* with the Excursus.
[7] Macrob. *Sat.* i. 7. Lydus *de Mens.* iv. 1. Draco of Corcyra *ap. Athen.* xv. 692. It was a fiction of the Greeks. The Janiculan hill was in the *regio Camisene.*

the nymph Carna, or Carda, to whom as a compensation for the loss of her honour he gave the office of presiding over door-hinges.[1]

Saturnus.

This ancient Italian deity was probably regarded as the male power of the earth, the god of production; for we find him united with Ops,[2] the female power, and his statues bore the sickle, the emblem of agriculture.[3] At Rome the treasury was in his temple, intimating, it is said, that agriculture is the source of wealth.[4] The Nundines or market-days were also sacred to this god,[5] who was one of the Di Patres of Roman religion.

We find another female deity besides Ops united with Saturnus. She was named Lua Mater; and all we know of her is that she was one of those to whom the spoils of conquered enemies used to be dedicated.[6]

The Saturnalia were celebrated in December. This festival, instituted A.U. 253, lasted at first only one day (the 19th); it was then extended to three, and in the time of the emperors to seven.[7] The utmost liberty prevailed at that time: all was mirth and festivity; friends made presents to each other; schools were closed; the senate did not sit; no war was proclaimed, no criminal executed; slaves were permitted to jest with their masters, and were even waited on at table by them. This last circumstance probably was founded on the original equality of master and slave,—the latter having been in the early times of Rome usually a captive taken in war, or an insolvent debtor, and consequently originally the equal of his master.[8]

As the Golden Race of Greek tradition had been under Kronos, this festival offered another means of identifying him with Saturnus. He was said to have fled from before the arms of Jupiter, and to have concealed himself in Latium, where he civilised the rude inhabitants.

> First from Olympus' height ethereal came
> Saturnus, flying from the arms of Jove,
> An exile, of his realms despoiled. The race
> Untaught and scattered on the lofty hills
> He drew together, and unto them gave
> Laws, and the Latin race would have them called,

---

[1] Ov. *Fast.* vi. 101 *seq.*　　　　　　[2] Macrob. *Sat.* i. 10.
[3] Varro, *Fr.* p. 224.　Festus *v.* Opima Spolia.
[4] Plut. *Qu. Rom.* 42.　　　　　　[5] Id. *ħ.*
[6] Gell. xiii. 22.　Liv. viii. 1 ; xlv. 33.
[7] Liv. ii. 21.　Catull. xiv. 15.　Var. *De L. L.* vi. 22.　Macrob. *Sat.* i. 10.
[8] Dion. Hal. iv. 24.　Nieb. *Hist. of Rome*, i. 319.

Because he in this country lay concealed (*latuisset*).
The Golden Age of which they tell was then,
Beneath this king,—he in such placid peace
Ruled o'er the peoples ;[1]

and the Saturnalia were regarded as commemorative of those happy days of primeval innocence and equality.

The name Saturnus is usually derived *a satu* ;[2] but perhaps a derivation from *saturo* is to be preferred.[3] Its original form was probably Saturinus, the *Satisfier*.[4]

Ops. Tellus.

These were two names of the earth (*Terra*), under which she had temples at Rome. She was also named Bona Dea, or *Good Goddess*, Maia, Fauna and Fatua.[5] Viewed masculinely, in the usual Italian manner, the earth was named Tellumo, Tellurus, Altor and Rusor.[6]

The name Ops or Opis is plainly connected with *opes, wealth*, of which the earth is the bestower. Under this name she was united with Saturnus; and her festival, the Opalia, was on the same day with the original Saturnalia.[7]

The first of May was the festival of the Bona Dea, and the anniversary of the dedication of her temple on the Aventine.[8] She was worshipped by the Roman matrons in the house of the prætor or consul; on which occasions everything relating to the other sex was carefully excluded. As the most probable derivation of the name of this month is that from Maia, we have here a proof of this goddess and the Bona Dea being the same. Maia is apparently the female of Maius, which is said to have been a name of Jupiter at Tusculum;[9] and most probably the Tusculan Jovis-Maius was only a male Earth.[10] Fauna is the feminine of Faunus; and these two might also have been names of the earth. Of Fatua it is difficult to trace the origin; Altor is Alitor, the *Nourisher*; Rusor is perhaps connected with *rus* or *ruris*.[11] We meet with Mater Tellus, Mater Terra,[12] and Ops Mater.[13]

[1] Verg. *Æn.* viii. 318 *seq.*   [2] Cic. *De Nat. Deor.* ii. 25.   Varr. *De L.L.* v. 64.
[3] *Stercutius* was an epithet of Saturnus.   Macrob. i. 7.
[4] See our Vergil, Excursus ix.
[5] Macrob. *Sat.* i. 12.   [6] Varr. *Fr.* p. 226.   Mart. Capel. i. 30.
[7] Macrob. *Sat.* i. 10.   Varr. *De L. L.* vi. 22.
[8] Ovid. *Fast.* v. 148 *seq.*   [9] Macrob. i. 12.
[10] Μαῖα· ἡ τὰ ἀφανεῖ κεκρυμμένα εἰς τὸ ἐμφανὲς προάγουσα.   Joan. Lydus, *De Mens.* p. 264.   Hence some identify her with the Hindú Maya or Illusion, but the reference is evidently to the Earth's power of producing plants from seeds.
[11] In Latin *r* and *s* are commutable.   [12] Macrob. iii. 9.   Liv. viii. 6.
[13] Varr. *De L. L.* v. 64.

In their usual tasteless manner the Romans said that the **Bona Dea** was Fauna or Fatua, the daughter of Faunus, who out of modesty never left her bower, or let herself be seen of men; for which she was deified, and no man entered her temple.[1]

Genius.

The Genius was a very remarkable part of the religion of the Romans. They derived it from the Tuscans, in whose system it formed a prominent feature. The word Genius is evidently a Latin translation of a Tuscan term signifying *Generator*, and the Genius was therefore viewed as a deity who had the power of producing.[2] In the Tuscan system he was the son of the gods and the parent of men; and as, according to the ancient Italian doctrine, all souls proceeded from Jupiter, and returned to him after death, the Genius Jovialis was viewed as the great agent in giving life to the human embryo.[3]

It was the belief of the Romans that every man had his Genius,[4] and every woman her Juno;[5] that is, a spirit who had given them being, and was regarded as their protector through life,[6] answering in some measure to the Ferwer of Zoroastric theology; whence the Jews, and from them the Christians, derived their idea of Guardian Angels. On their birthdays men made offerings to their Genius, women to their Juno.[7] The offerings to the Genius were wine, flowers and incense.[8] It was customary to implore persons by their Genius[9] (as the Orientals

[1] Macrob. i. 12.

[2] Varro, *Fr.* p. 225.

[3] Festus *v.* Genium. Macrob. *Sat.* i. 10.

[4] Hor. *Ep.* ii. 2, 187 *seq.* Varro *ut sup.* Pers. vi. 48: comp. Plaut. *Curc.* ii. 3, 22. Martial, vi. 60, 10.

[5] Sen. *Ep.* 110, 1. Hence the *Lectus Genialis* was laid out to Genius and Juno; see Appendix O; hence also, in the case of Horatius, expiatory sacrifices were made to the Juno of his sister and the Genius of the Curiatii, or perhaps only to that of her lover: see Dion. Hal. iii. 22, with Reiske's note. In this passage of Dionysius, and in Festus (*v.* sororium tigillum), the word is Janus, not Genius; but we adopt Reiske's emendation, or rather think that the change, like that of Jana to Juno (see our Ovid's *Fasti*, Introd. p. xiii.), may have been made before the time of Dionysius.

[6] Plaut. *Capt.* iv. 2, 100. *Menœch.* i. 2, 29. Hor. *ut sup.* "Genius est deus cujus in tutela ut quisque natus est vivit." Cens. *de Die Nat.* 3: comp. Am. Marc. xxi. 14.

[7] Plaut. *Capt.* ii. 2, 40. Tibull. ii. 2, 1 *seq.* iv. 5. Varro, *Fr.* p. 323. Persius ii. 1 *seq.* "Natalibus Augusti et Tiberii Cæss...thure et vino Genii eorum invitentur." Gruter, p. 228, 8. For the worship of Juno on birthdays, Tibull iv. 6. On this occasion both Genius and Juno were sometimes named *Natalis*, sc. *deus* or *dea*: Id. ii. 2. iv. 5, 19.

[8] Tibull. ii. 2, 3. Hor. *Epist.* ii. 1, 144. *De Art. Poet.* 209: see also *Carm.* iii. 17, 14.

[9] Hor. *Epist.* i. 7, 94. Ter. *And.* i. 5, 55. Tibull. iv. 5, 8. Propert. iv. 8, 69

do by their Soul), and also to swear by it;[1] and in the Latin writers it is sometimes not easy to distinguish a man's Genius from himself.[2] The distinct worship of the Genius continued down to the demise of paganism, for we find it noticed in the Theodosian Code.[3]

Places and peoples were also believed to have their Genii or protecting spirits.[4]

Horace, in speaking of the Genius, calls him "changeable of countenance, white and black;"[5] and in the well-known appearance of his evil Genius to Brutus, the spirit was black.[6] This would seem to intimate that a man had two Genii, a good and an evil one;[7] but this does not appear to have been the Italian belief, though such a notion may perhaps have prevailed in Greece; for the philosopher Empedokles said that two Mœræ receive us at our birth, and get authority over us.[8]

Orcus, Ditis, or Dis.

If there was any deity, in the theology of the people of ancient Latium, answering to the Hadés of the Greeks, the Yama of the Hindús, it was the being named Orcus or Dis. But we have elsewhere [9] endeavoured to show that Orcus was merely Death, and that in the ancient Latin cosmology there was no place answering to the Hellénic Erebos. In confirmation of this last view it may be further observed that Varro [10] says that Dispater or Orcus was the lower part of the air, that close to the earth, in which all things arise and decay—the proper domain of Death. The former view seems to be strengthened by the fact that though Mors is feminine, Death is never represented as such

---

[1] Sen. *Ep.* 12, 2. Suet. *Cal.* 27. Plin. *Pan.* 52. Euseb. *Hist. Eccles.* iv. 15, comp. Tibull. iv. 13, 15.

[2] Hence the phrases *indulgere Genio, defraudare Genium.*

[3] "Nullus Larem igne, mero Genium, Penates nidore veneratus accendat lumina, imponat thura, serta suspendat." *De Paganis.*

[4] Verg. *Æn.* v. 95. ("Nullus locus sine Genio." Serv.) vii. 136. Liv. xxi. 62. Am. Marc. xx. 5, xxv. 2. Dio Cass. xlvii. 2.

[5] *Ep.* ii. 2, 189.   [6] Florus, iv. 7.   [7] See Serv. *Æn.* iii. 63.

[8] *Apud Plut. de Tranq. Anim.* 15. He thus names some of the pairs:—

Ἔνθ' ἦσαν Χθονίη τε καὶ Ἡλιόπη ταναῶπις,
Δῆρίς θ' αἱματόεσσα καὶ Ἁρμονίη θεμερῶπις,
Καλλιστώ τ' Αἰσχρή τε, Θόωσά τε Δηναιή τε,
Νημερτής τ' ἐρόεσσα μελάγκαρπός τ' Ἀσάφεια.

Menander (id. *ib.*) said that a dæmon, a *good* guide of life, comes to a man when he is born.

[9] See our note on Hor. *Ep.* ii. 2, 178, and Excurs. on *Ov. Fast.* ii. 533: comp. Hor. *Carm.* ii. 13, 38. Lucan. ix. 7.

[10] *De L. L.* v. 66.

in Roman works of art; and had not the Romans a male deity of this kind they would probably have made Mors masculine to represent Θάνατος, as they made Cupido masculine to take the place of Ἔρως.[1]

Verrius Flaccus[2] said that Orcus was originally pronounced Uragus (rather Urgus), which he derives from *urgeo*; but this is very uncertain, and we may have observed that the names of the Italian deities are generally of unknown origin. Dis (with which *pater* is usually joined), or Ditis, is merely a translation of the Greek Πλούτων. Its resemblance to Death is curious, but most certainly casual.

Sol et Luna.

As Hélios and Seléné were distinct from Apollo and Artemis, so Sol and Luna seem to have been very early distinguished from Dianus and Diana. Tatius, as we have seen, worshipped both Diana and Luna; we meet with Luna Mater.

Chapter III.

THE REMAINING ITALIAN DEITIES.

Quirinus.

QUIRINUS, we are told, was a war-god, answering to the Enyalios of the Greeks.[3] He is said to have been the deified founder of Rome. Like the other gods, he was addressed as *Pater*, and a goddess named Hora was associated with him.[4]

Quirinus was evidently a Sabine deity; and the derivation usually given of his name from *quiris*, a spear, would seem to make him an original war-god. It is however, not improbable that he was only the deified symbol of the town of Cures,[5] and

---

[1] Thus a celebrated Florentine usurer was nicknamed *Il* Morte: see Rosini, *La Monaca di Monza*, ch. xviii. The poets however sometimes personified *mors*: see Hor. *Carm.* i. 4, 13.

[2] Festus *v.* Orcum. In the *Fairy Mythology* (ii. 237, p. 449 new edit.) we have shown that the Italian *Orco* and the French *Ogre* were derived from Orcus. The plates in the works of Inghirami and Micali represent Mantus (the Etruscan Orcus) as a coarse large man with a wild look and pointed ears, and armed with a huge mallet. This is nearly the very form of an ogre: see Müller, *Etrusk.* i. 99 *seq.*   [3] Dion. Hal. ii. 48.

[4] "Teque Quirine pater veneror Horamque Quirini."—Ennius. Nonius (*s. v.*) says that Hora was Juventas. Ovid (*Met.* xiv. 851) makes her the deified Hersilia.   [5] See Buttmann, *Mythol.* ii. 91.

that the symbols of Rome and Cures were united in one deity. Tertullian[1] speaks of a Pater Curis of the Faliscans.

Bellona.

Bellona, anciently Duellona, the goddess of war, was so called from *bellum*, in old Latin *duellum*. She corresponds with the Enyo of the Greeks.

The temple of Bellona at Rome was without the city, near the Carmental Gate. Audience was given there by the senate to foreign ambassadors. Before it stood a pillar, over which a spear was thrown on declaration of war against any people.[2] The priests of Bellona used to gash their thighs and arms and offer to her the blood which flowed from the wounds, whence she was named Mater Sanguinis.[3]

Libitina.

Libitina was the goddess presiding over funerals: at her temple were sold all things requisite for them; and by an institution ascribed to Servius Tullius, a piece of money was paid there for every one who died, and the name of the deceased entered in a book called *Libitinæ ratio*.[4] We have seen[5] that she was held to be the same as Venus: her name, in that case, might possibly come from the old verb *libeo*.

Consus.

This deity was, as his name denotes, the god of *counsel*. His altar was in the Circus Maximus, and was always covered, except on his festival-day, the 18th of August, called the Consualia. Horse- and chariot-races were celebrated at this festival, and the working horses, mules and asses were crowned with flowers, and allowed to rest:[6] hence Consus has probably been confounded with Neptunus Equestris, as this latter god was called, to identify him with the Greek Poseidón. It was at the Consualia that the Sabine virgins were carried off by the Romans.

Laverna.

Laverna was the patron-goddess of thieves, who were anciently called Laverniones,[7] and of all in general who practised artifice

[1] *Apol.* 24.
[2] Hist. Aug. *Claud.* 4.
[3] See above, p. 458.
[4] Festus *s. v.*

[2] Ov. *Fast.* vi. 199 *seq.* with our notes.
[5] Dion. Hal. iv. 15. Suet. *Nero*, 39.
[6] Dion. Hal. i. 33. Plut. *Qu. Rom.* 48.

and fraud.[1]   At Rome she had an altar, near the gate which was called from her the gate of Laverna.[2]   There was also a temple of this goddess near Formiæ.[3]   Her name is probably derived from *lateo*, significatory of *darkness* or *obscurity*.[4]   She would seem to have been regarded as one of the Di Inferi.[5]

Sancus.

Sancus was, beyond question, an ancient Sabine deity,[6] but his exact nature is not known.   He was very early confounded with the Grecian Héraklés; but the Ara Maxima, and the priesthood of the Potitii and Pinarii, together with the gentile worship of the Fabii who were of Sabine origin, must all, as it would appear, have belonged to the old Sabine god.[7]   As a further proof, we may observe that the temple of Sancus stood on the Quirinal, the Sabine part of the city.[8]   In this temple was preserved the original treaty concluded by Tarquinius Superbus with the Gabians.[9]   There also stood in it a brazen statue of Caia Cæcilia, the thrifty spouse of Tarquinius Priscus, according to the ancient legend; and her spindle and sandals had once been preserved there.[10]

Sancus was also named Dius Fidius [11] and Semo;[12] the former, perhaps, in consequence of the resemblance of his name to the word *sanctus*; the latter is said to be *semihomo*.   Ovid, when addressing him, calls him in the usual manner, Semo Pater.[13]

The festival of Sancus was on the nones of June.   People when going on a journey used to sacrifice to him.[14]

[1]   .... Pulchra Laverna,
Da mihi fallere, da justo sanctoque videri;
Noctem peccatis et fraudibus objice nubem.
                              Hor. *Ep.* i. 16, 60.
Per deam sanctam Lavernam, quæ sit cultrix quæstuis.
                              Novius *ap. Non. v.* quæsti.

[2] Porta Lavernalis.   Varr. *De L. L.* v. 163.   [3] Cic. *ad Att.* 7, 8.

[4] It is rather curious that *t* and *v* should be commutable, yet there are many instances of it, such as τίλλω and *vello*, θέλω and *volo*, κλιτὺς and *clivus*. To these may perhaps be added *Latinus* and *Lavinum*, and certainly *vallis* and the German *thal* and English *dale*, as also *gladius* and *glaive*.

[5]   Inferis manu sinistra immolamus pocula,
Læva quæ vides Lavernæ, Palladi sunt dextera.
                    Sept. Sever. *ap. Wernsdorf. Poet. Minor.* ii. p. 288.

[6] Dion. Hal. ii. 49.   Ov. *Fast.* vi. 216, 217.   Sil. Ital. viii. 422.
[7] See Propert. iv. 9, 71 *seq.*   [8] Dion. Hal. ix. 60.   Ov. *Fast.* vi. 218.
[9] Dion. Hal. iv. 58: comp. Hor. *Epist.* ii. 1, 24, 25.   [10] Plut. *Qu. Rom.* 30.
[11] Hence the oath *Me Dius Fidius* (sc. *juvet*), answering to *Mehercle.*
[12] Livy (i. 20) calls him Sancus Semo.
[13] *Fast.* vi. 214.   [14] Festus *v.* Propter viam.

Summanus, Vejovis, Soranus.

We place these three together, as being deities of the under-world.

Summanus, or rather Submanus, was a god of Etruria, whose worship was adopted, probably very early, at Rome. A temple was erected to him close by that of Juventas at the Circus Maximus in the time of the war with Pyrrhus;[1] and his earthen statue stood on the top of the temple of Jupiter on the Capitol.[2] Nocturnal lightnings were ascribed to Summanus, as diurnal ones were to Jupiter;[3] and when trees had been struck with lightning, the Arval brethren sacrificed to him black wethers, naming him Pater.[4] He may therefore have been only a god of the night; but we are assured that he was Pluto and Dispiter.[5] Varro joins him with Volcanus, as one of the gods worshipped by the Sabine Tatius.[6] His festival, the Summanalia, was on the 20th of June. Cakes of a wheel-shape were then offered to this deity.

The most usual derivation of this name is that which makes it Summus Manium, which would then appear to be a translation from the Tuscan. But if our idea of the Di Manes and their condition be correct,[7] they could not have been under the authority of any being answering to the Hadés of Greece. A derivation therefore from *sub mane* would seem to be more probable, and the following ingenious theory[8] might be received, namely that the Roman deity named Nocturnus,[9] who ruled over the night (as the male-power of Nox), may, in the usual placatory manner, have been denominated Submanus as the forerunner and harbinger of the Dawn.

Vedjovis, Vejovis or Vedius was also an Etruscan god, for he cast lightnings. These had the property of causing previous deafness in those whom they were to strike.[10] The temple of Vejovis at Rome stood in the hollow between the Arx and the

---

[1] Ov. *Fast.* vi. 731. Plin. *Nat. Hist.* xxix. 4. The earliest notice of this deity is Plaut. *Curc.* iii. 1, 43.   [2] Cic. *Div.* i. 10.

[3] Plin. *Nat. Hist.* ii. 53. August. *De Civ. Dei*, iv. 23.

[4] Inscr. Fratr. Arv. No. 43. Gruter, *Inscrip.* p. 121.

[5] "Pluto qui etiam Summanus dicitur." Mart. Cap. ii. 40. Arnob. *adv. Gent.* v. 37.   [6] *De L. L.* v. 74.

[7] See our Ov. *Fasti*, Excurs. iv.

[8] Merkel, *Prol. in Ov. Fast.* p. ccviii.

[9] "Credo ego hac noctu Nocturnum obdormivisse ebrium." Plaut. *Amph.* i. 1, 119. "Nocturnum deum Varro in Satiris perpetuo sopore et ebrietate torpidum induxit." August. *De Civ. Dei.*

[10] Amm. Marcel. xvii. 10, 2.

Capitol (*Inter duos lucos*).[1] His statue was that of a youth with darts in his hand, a she-goat stood beside it, and a she-goat was the victim to him.[2] Hence some viewed him as Young Jupiter, while others saw in him the avenging Apollo of the Greeks.[3] He was however certainly regarded as a god of the underworld,[4] and his name was supposed to signify *Injurious God.*[5]

Soranus was a god worshipped on Mount Soracte. He was similar to the Roman Dis or Orcus.[6] His priests, named Hirpi or Hirpini, used to walk barefoot over heaps of burning coals of pine-wood, carrying the entrails of the victim.[7] There was a legend of wolves connected with this worship, which had its origin in the name of the priests (*hirpus* being the Sabine for *wolf*), and this led to an identification of the God with the Grecian Apollo.[8] Soranus was probably the Sabine name of Orcus.

Camenæ, Egeria, Carmenta.

As the Latins used the term Camena for the Greek Musa, we are to suppose that their Camenæ or Casmenæ were deities of a nature similar to the Muses.[9] We only meet with them in the legend of Numa, whom Egeria used to lead to the grove and fount which they haunted, to receive their instructions.[10] Numa is said to have enjoined the Romans to honour especially the Camena, Tacita or Silence.[11]

Egeria, the spouse and instructress of Numa, was by some regarded as one of the Camenæ; by others she is called a nymph.[12] The fount at which she used to converse with Numa was in a vale outside of the Capene gate,[13] but she had another

[1] Ov. *Fast.* iii. 430.
[2] Id. *ib.* Gellius, v. 12.
[3] Ov. *ut sup.* Gellius, *ut sup.*
[4] " Pluton quem etiam Ditem Vejovemque dixere." Mart. Cap. ii. 9. " Nec Vedium [Plutonem] cum uxore conspexerit sicut suadebat Etruria." Id. ii. 7. " Dispater, Vejovis, Manes, sive vos quo alio nomine fas est nominare." Carmen Devotionis *ap. Macrob. Sat.* iii. 3.
[5] " Deum qui non juvandi potestatem sed vim nocendi haberet....Vejovem appellaverant dempta atque detracta juvandi facultate." Gellius, *ut sup.*
[6] " Nam Dis Pater Soranus vocatur." Serv. *Æn.* xi. 785.
[7] Serv. *ut sup.* Plin. *Nat. Hist.* vii. 2. Sil. Ital. v. 176 *seq.*
[8] Same authorities.
[9] Varro's (*De L. L.* vii. 26, 27) derivation of Casmena, quasi Carmena, from *carmen*, is not improbable.
[10] Plut. *Numa,* 8, 13. Liv. i. 21. Ov. *Met.* xv. 482.
[11] Plut. *ut sup.* This was probably invented after Numa was made a Pythagorean.
[12] Plut. *ut sup.* Dion Hal. ii. 60.   [13] Juv. iii. 17.

in the grove of Diana Nemorensis, at the lake near Aricia.[1] Pregnant women used to sacrifice to her, that they might have a safe delivery.[2]

Carmenta seems to have been a deity similar to the Camenæ, for she is always represented as a prophetess. The legend makes her the mother of Evander.[3] That she was an ancient Italian deity however is clear, for she had a Flamen[4] and a festival. The Carmentalia were on the 11th and 15th of January,[5] at which time Carmenta was worshipped by the Roman matrons. They prayed on this occasion to two deities, named Porrima, Prosa, or Antivorta and Postvorta, for a safe delivery in childbirth.[6] The legend said, that one time when the senate had forbidden the Roman ladies to use carriages (carpenta), in their rage they caused abortions; the senate then rescinded their decree, and the matrons built a temple to Carmenta.[7]

Matuta, Aurora.

Mater Matuta, as she is almost always called, was, beyond question, the goddess of the dawn, the E'ós of Greece; for Lucretius says,[8]

> Tempore item certo roseam Matuta per oras
> Ætheris auroram defert et lumina pandit.

The identification of Matuta with the Greek Leukothea is a curious instance of the effect of similarity in the signification of names; for as *manum* signified *clarum*,[9] Matuta was the *Clara Dea*. The festival of Matuta, named Matralia, was on the 11th of June, and the matrons prayed at it for the prosperity of their nephews and nieces.[10]

The temple of Matuta at Rome was said to have been built by Servius Tullius.[11] This goddess had also a temple at Satricum in Latium.[12] Atilius Romulus is said to have vowed a temple to Pales Matuta.[13]

[1] Strab. v. 3, 12, p. 240. Ov. *Met.* xv. 488. Sil. Ital. iv. 365. Verg. *Æn.* vii. 762 *seq.*
[2] Festus *v.* Egeria. The name of the fount probably gave origin to the goddess, and her name then to this last notion, *alvum egerens.*
[3] Dion. Hal. i. 31. Ov. *Fast.* i. 471 *seq.*   [4] Cic. *Brut.* 14.
[5] Ov. *ut sup.* 461, 616.   [6] See our note on Ov. *Fast.* i. 633.
[7] Ov. *ut sup.* Plut. *Qu. Rom.* 56. A play of etymology in the usual Roman style.   [8] *De Rer. Nat.* v. 655, 656.
[9] Nonius, *s. v.*   [10] See our notes on Ov. *Fast.* vi. 550 *seq.*
[11] Liv. v. 19.   [12] Liv. vi. 33; vii. 27.
[13] Interp. Vet. *Verg. Geor.* iii. 1. "Nam mihi sunt totum rarissima templa per orbem," says Aurora (Ov. *Met.* xiii. 588), in allusion probably to these Italian temples, for the Greeks had erected none to E'ós.

Like so many other goddesses, Matuta appears to have had a male associate similar to herself in name. The critics certainly seem to be unanimous in regarding the Pater Matutinus of Horace[1] as Janus; for which they are no doubt not to be blamed, the poet himself having set them the example. But to us this appears to be an error, though as we see a very ancient one. The Latin language abounds above all others in adjectival terminations, many of which are perfectly equivalent. Such were those in *us* and *inus*. *Libertus* and *Libertinus* were, there is no doubt, originally the same. Valerius was Corvus or Corvinus; Postumius was Albus or Albinus; the cognomina Luscinus, Græcinus, Calvinus, Longinus, Lævinus, etc., were probably equivalent to Luscus, Græcus, Calvus, etc. In the latter centuries of the republic the preference seems to have been given to the termination in *inus*, and hence we meet with Censorinus and Marcellinus. If these observations be correct, Matutinus is the same as Matutus, and is not Janus, *i.e.*, the Sun, but a male deity answering to Matuta, the goddess of the dawn.

Fortuna.

This deity was of much greater importance in the eyes of the Italians than in those of the Greeks. Under the name of Nortia she was adored in Etruria; she was also worshipped at Antium,[2] Præneste[3] and elsewhere; and at Rome she had several fanes and altars, of which the principal were the temples of Virgo Fortuna and of Fors Fortuna,[4] both ascribed to Servius Tullius.

It is very remarkable that though the Romans were a people who more than almost any other ascribed power and influence to Fate and Chance, and though they seem to have had in their Parcæ beings analogous to the Grecian Mœræ, we never meet with the name of these beings in the Roman religion of the ancient times. In the latter days of the empire we hear of a temple of the Tria Fata near the Forum.[5]

Bonus Eventus.

Bonus Eventus is one of the gods addressed by Varro in the commencement of his work on agriculture, where he joins him with Lympha. He prays to this deity, as without his aid nothing could come to a happy termination. Bonus Eventus was re-

---

[1] Sat. ii. 6, 20.   [2] Hor. *Carm.* i. 35.
[3] Strabo, v. 3, 11, p. 238.
[4] See our notes on Ov. *Fast.* vi. 569 *seq.*, 776 *seq.*
[5] Procop. *De Bell. Goth.* i. 25.

presented with a *patera* or cup in one hand, and ears of corn in the other.[1]

Vertumnus.

Vertumnus, or Vortumnus, is a god of very dubious character. According to some he was like Mercurius, a deity presiding over merchandise.[2] Varro[3] in one place says he was a Tuscan god, and that therefore his statue was in ᛏie Tuscan street at Rome; in another,[4] he sets him among the gods worshipped by the Sabine ᛳing Tatius. Horace[5] uses Vertumni in the plural number; and the Scholiast observes, that his statues were in almost all the municipal towns of Italy.

Vertumnus (from *verto*) is probably the translation of a Tuscan name; and the most probable hypothesis respecting this god is, that he was a deity presiding over the seasons and their manifold productions in the vegetable world.[6] Ceres and Pomona were associated with him. The Vortumnalia were in October.[7]

Anna Perenna.

The ambiguity of the name of this goddess, from its resemblance to *annus, amnis, anus,* and also to the Semitic proper name *Anna,* has led to various opinions respecting her. The most probable is, that she was a deity of *the year,* as prayer was made to her for a long life.[8] She was said by some to be the Moon, or Themis, or Io, or the Atlantis Maia who reared Jupiter.[9] These latter suppositions, however, are quite improbable, as she was certainly an ancient Roman deity. Anna the sister of Dido, another account says, followed Æneas to Italy after the death of her sister; and Lavinia, jealous of the kind reception he gave her, meditated her death. Apprised by her sister in a dream, Anna fled, and coming to the banks of the Numicius, was seized by the god of the stream. When those who were in search of her came thither, her voice was heard declaring that she was a nymph of the Numicius, and was to be called Anna Perenna, because she lay in the perennial river.[10]

---

[1] Plin. *Nat. Hist.* xxxi. 8. Colum. x. 308. Am. Marc. xxix. 6.
[2] Asconius, *on Cic. in Verr.* i. 59. Scholiast *on Hor. Epist.* i. 20, 1.
[3] *De L. L.* v. 46.   [4] *Ib.* 74.   [5] *Epist.* ii. 7, 14.
[6] See Propert. iv. 2, and Müller, *Etrusk.* ii. 51. *seq.*
[7] Varro, *De L. L.* vi. 21.
[8] Ov. *Fast.* iii. 531. On Anna Perenna, see our notes on this part of the Fasti.   [9] Id. *ib.* 567 *seq.*
[10] Ov. *Fast.* iii. 545 *seq.* Sil. Ital. viii. 28 *seq.* It is a curious fact that she is still worshipped in Latium under the name of Anna Petronilla. See Blunt, *Vestiges of Ancient Manners,* &c., p. 92.

Those who derived her name from *anus* said, that at the time of the Secession there was an old woman named Anna who lived at Bovillæ, who every morning baked cakes and brought them to the people. On their return to Rome, they erected a statue to her under the name of Perenna.[1]

The festivals of Anna Perenna were celebrated on the ides of March,—a further proof of her presiding over the year, which anciently began in that month.[2] They were held near the banks of the Tiber; dancing, singing, drinking and revelling were the occupations of both sexes, and they prayed to live as many years as they drank *cyathos*.

Terminus.

This ancient deity, worshipped by Tatius and Numa, presided, as his name denotes, over boundaries. His statue was a rude stone or post, set in the ground as a mere landmark to distinguish adjacent properties. On the twenty-first of February his festival, called Terminalia, was celebrated. The owners of the adjoining lands met at his statue, on which they placed garlands, and then raising a rude altar, offered on it some corn, honeycomb, and wine, and sacrificed a lamb or a sucking-pig; they concluded by singing the praises of the god.[3]

When Tarquinius Priscus set about building the Capitoline temple, it was necessary to remove the altars of the deities who already occupied the summit of the Capitol. The assent of each deity was sought by the augurs, and all yielded it but Terminus and Juventas. The altar of Terminus therefore always stood in the temple.[4] The roof was open over the stone which represented the god, who can only be worshipped in the open air.[5]

The altar of Juventas also stood in the vestibule of the temple of Minerva.[6] There was a temple of this goddess in which a registry was kept of the names of the young men who were of the military age.[7]

---

[1] Id. *ib.* 661 *seq.*

[2]   Nec mihi parva fides annos hinc isse priores
         Anna quod hoc cœpta est mense Perenna coli.—Id. *ib.* 145, **146.**

[3] Id. *ib.* ii. 641 *seq.* The offering, Plutarch says (*Numa*, 16 ; *Qu. Rom.* **15),** was originally bloodless. We everywhere meet with proofs of the mildness and purity of the ancient religion of Latium.

[4] Dion. Hal. iii. 69.   Liv. i. 55 ; v. 54.

[5] Ov. *Fast.* ii. 672.   Serv. *Æn.* ix. 448.

[6] Dion. Hal. *ut sup.*

[7] Id. iv. 15

Silvanus.

Silvanus was a deity who had the care of fields and cattle ;[1] he also presided over boundaries.[2] Groves were consecrated to him,[3] hence perhaps his name. He was usually represented as old, and bearing a cypress plucked up by the roots;[4] and the legend of Apollo and Kyparissos was transferred to him.[5] The usual offering to Silvanus was milk,[6] or a pig, but he was an object of worship only to the male sex. He was termed *Pater* like the other gods.[7]

According to the Agrimensores every *possession* should have three Silvans, one *domestic* for the possession itself, one *agrestic* for the herdsmen, a third *oriental* for whom there should be a grove (*lucus*) on the boundary.[8] The meaning of this obscure passage probably is, that Silvanus was to be worshipped under three different titles as protector of the family, for we meet an inscription *Silvano Larum* ; of the cattle, perhaps those on the public pastures; and of the boundaries, that is, of the whole possession. The Mars Silvanus to whom Cato[9] directs prayer to be made for the health of the oxen is probably the second, the third is the *tutor finium* of Horace.

Silvanus used, we are told,[10] to molest lying-in women at night. They were therefore committed to the care of three deities, named Intercido, Pilumnus, and Deverra. Three men went by night round the house to signify that these deities were watchful : they first struck the threshold with an axe, then with a pestle (*pilum*), and finally swept (*deverrere*) with brooms ; because trees are not cut (*cæduntur*) and pruned without an axe, corn bruised without a pestle, or heaped up without brooms. Hence the names of the deities who kept the wood-god away from the lying-in woman.

Faunus. Lupercus. Inuus.

Faunus was a rural deity perhaps resembling the Grecian Pan, to whom he is so similar in name and with whom he was identified.[11] He was held to have the power of foretelling the future.[12]

---

[1] Verg. *Æn.* viii. 601.
[2] Hor. *Epod.* 2, 22.   [3] Verg. *ut sup.* Plaut. *Aul.* iv. 6, 8.
[4] Verg. *Geor.* i. 20.   [5] Serv. *Geor.* i. 20.
[6] Hor. *Epist.* ii. 1, 143. Juv. vi. 547, *cum Schol.*
[7] Id. *Epod.* 2, 21.
[8] See Scaliger's note on Festus *v.* Marspedis.
[9] *De R. R.* 80.   [10] Varro, p. 231.
[11] Ov. *Fast.* ii. 424 ; iv. 650. Hor. *Carm.* i. 17, 1.
[12] Ov. *ut sup.* Verg. *Æn.* vii. 81 *seq.*

In later times he was mortalised like all the other Italian gods, and said to have been a just and brave king, greatly devoted tc agriculture, the son of Picus and father of Latinus.[1] Like Pan, too, he was multiplied; and as there were Pans, so we also meet abundant mention of Fauns. The poets gave to Faunus and the Fauns the horns of a goat and feet of the Satyrs. Faunus Pater occurs.[2] The feminine of his name, Fauna, was a name of Earth; hence he may himself have been originally the same with Tellumo and Saturnus.[3]

Lupercus and Luperca were worshipped as the protectors of flocks from wolves (*lupos arcentes*).[4] The Lupercalia were on the 15th of February; the victims offered were goats and dogs, and the Luperci cutting the goatskin into thongs ran through the city striking all whom they met. Married women used to place themselves in their way, as the stroke of the hallowed thong was thought to cause fecundity. The god in whose honour the feast was celebrated was in the later times called Faunus or Pan.[5]

Inuus was another name of the rural deity.[6] There was a place named Castrum Inui in Latium,[7] and another near Cære in Etruria.[8]

Picus.

Picus, says the legend, was the son of Saturnus, and celebrated for his beauty and his love of horses and hunting: he was married to Canens, the daughter of Janus and Venilia, renowned for the sweetness and power of her voice. One day Picus went forth to the chase clad in a purple cloak, bound round his neck with gold. He entered the wood where Circe happened to be at that time gathering magic herbs: she was instantly struck with love, and implored the prince to correspond to her passion. Picus, faithful to his beloved Canens, indignantly spurned her advances; Circe in revenge struck him with her wand, and instantly he was changed into a bird with purple plumage and a yellow ring round its neck. This bird was called by its name *Picus*, the Wood-pecker.[9]

---

[1] Verg. *Æn.* vii. 47. Probus, *Geor.* i. 10.

[2] Calpurn, *Ec.* i. 9, 37; ii. 13.

[3] His festivals were on the Ides of February (Ov. *Fast.* ii. 193) and Nones of December (Hor. *Carm.* iii. 18, 10); each, we may observe, toward the end of the year.   [4] Arnob. iv. 3.   Serv. *Æn.* viii. 343.

[5] See Ov. *Fast.* ii. 267 *seq.* with the Excursus.   [6] Liv. i. 5.

[7] Verg. *Æn.* vi. 776.   [8] Rutil. *Itin.* 1. 232.

[9] Ov. *Met.* xiv. 320 *seq.* Plut. *Qu. Rom* 21. Servius (*Æn.* vii. 190) says that Picus was married to Pomona.

This legend seems to have been devised to give an origin for the Woodpecker in the manner of the Greeks.

Pales.

Pales was the goddess presiding over cattle and pastures. Her festival, called the Palilia, was celebrated on the twenty-first of April, and was regarded as the day on which Rome had been founded. The shepherds on the Palilia lustrated their flocks by burning sulphur, and making fires of olive, pine, and other substances. Millet, and cakes of it and milk were offered to the goddess, and prayers made to her to avert disease from the cattle, and to bless them with fecundity and abundance of food. Fires of straw were kindled in a row, and the rustics leaped thrice through them; the blood of a horse, the ashes of a calf, and bean-stalks were used for purification.[1] The statue of Pales was represented bearing a sickle.[2] Pales was also regarded as a male deity.[3]

In the Sallentine war (A.U. 485) the rural goddess Pales, as we are told,[4] demanded a temple as the price of victory.

Pomona.

Pomona (from *pomum*) was a goddess presiding over fruit-trees. Her worship was of long standing at Rome, where there was a Flamen Pomonalis, who sacrificed to her every year for the preservation of the fruit.

The story of Pomona and Vertumnus, alluded to above and probably a late fiction, is prettily told by Ovid.[5] This Hama-dryas (*i. e.* nymph) lived in the time of Procas king of Alba. She was devoted to the culture of gardens, to which she confined herself, shunning all society with the male deities. In vain Satyrs, Pans, Priapus, Silvanus, sought her love. Vertumnus too was enamoured of her, and under various shapes tried to win her favour: sometimes he came as a reaper, sometimes as a hay-maker, sometimes as a ploughman or a vine-dresser: he was a soldier and a fisherman, but to equally little purpose. At length, under the guise of an old woman, he won the confidence of the goddess, and by enlarging on the evils of a single life and the blessings of the wedded state, by launching out into the praises of Vertumnus, and relating a tale of the punishment of female cruelty to a lover, he sought to move the heart of Pomona:

---

[1] Ov. *Fast.* iv. 721 *seq.* Tibull. i. 1, 36; ii. 5, 87 *seq.* Propert. iv. 1, 19, 1, 73 *seq.* See our notes on Ovid, *ut sup.*   [2] Tibull. ii. 5, 28.
[3] Serv. *Geor.* iii. 1.   [4] Flor. i. 20.   [5] Ov. *Met.* xiv. 623 *seq.*

2 I

then resuming his real form, clasped to his bosom the no longer reluctant nymph.

Flora.

Flora was the goddess of flowers. She was a very ancient Italian deity, being one of those said to have been worshipped by Tatius. The Floralia (instituted A.U. 511[1]) were celebrated at the end of April and beginning of May.[2] They greatly degenerated in time, and became so lascivious as not to bear the presence of virtuous characters. The story of Cato the Censor, at whose appearance the feast was suspended, is well known.[3]

The Romans, who in general displayed very little elegance of imagination in the origins which they invented for their deities said that Flora had been a courtesan, who having by her trade acquired immense wealth (at Rome in the early days of the Republic!) left it to the Roman people, on condition of their always celebrating her birth-day with feasts.[4] By a far more pleasing and poetic fiction Ovid, or some earlier poet, made Flora the bride of the West-wind, whose gentle aspirations call the flowers into existence.[5]

Flora being an ancient original Latin deity, was addressed by the honorific title Mater ;[6] she had also a Flamen.[7]

Feronia.

This goddess may perhaps be placed among the rural deities. She was said to be of Sabine origin.[8] At her grove, and temple at the foot of Mount Soracte, her priests walked bare-foot over live-coals,[9] and great markets used to be held there during the time of her festival. She had also a temple, grove, and fount near Anxur.[10] Flowers and first-fruits were the offerings to her, and the interpretation of her name given in Greek was *Flower-*

[1] Vell. Pat. i. 14.
[3] Val. Max. ii. 10.
[5] Ov. *Fast.* v. 195 *seq.*
[7] Varro, *De L. L.* vii. 45.
[2] See Ov. *Fast.* v. 183 *seq.* with cr. notes.
[4] Plut. *Quæst. Rom.* 35. Lactant. 24.
[6] Cic. *Verr.* v. 14. Lucret. v. 738.
[8] Id. *ib.* v. 74.
[9] Strab. v. 2, 9, p. 226. The same was told of the priests of Soranus at the same place. Plin. *Nat. Hist.* vii. 2, 19. Verg. *Æn.* xi. 785, where Servius observes, " Varro ubique expugnator religionis ait, cum quoddam medicamentum describeret : *ut solent Hirpini qui ambula uri per ignes medicamen'o plantas tinguent.*" The experiments of some men of science in France have thrown much light on this subject. The phænomenon seems to depend on the non-conducting power of the skin and of animal matter in general. For a curious proof of the knowledge of this fact by the Caffres of South Africa, see Wood, *Hist. of Man,* i. 14.
[10] Hor. *Sat.* i. 5, 24. Verg. *Æn.* vii. 800.

bearing or *Garland-loving*, while some rendered it Persephoné.[1] She was also called Juno Virgo.[2] Feronia being regarded as the goddess of emancipated slaves, they used to receive the *pileus* in her temple.[3]

Falacer. Furina.

These two were perhaps rural deities, for Varro[4] places their Flamens with those of Volturnus or Vertumnus, Palatua (Pales?), Flora and Pomona. From their having Flamens, there being a festival named Furinalia, and Falacer being styled Divus Pater,[5] it is plain that they were ancient deities, and that they must have been of importance in the early days of Rome. Yet the most learned Romans, in the days of Augustus, did not know even who or what they were. Concerning Falacer we do not meet in their extant works with so much as a conjecture, but in an inscription[6] we find him joined with Pomona. Of Furina Varro says,[7] " her name is now hardly known to even a few persons."[8] There was a sacred grove of this goddess beyond the Tiber (in which C. Gracchus was slain), and this with the similitude of the name led Cicero and others to identify Furina with the Furies.[9] The Furinalia were on the twenty-fifth of July.

Vacuna. Marica.

The first of these was a Sabine deity: her name apparently comes from *vaco*, and she was identified with Diana, Ceres or Minerva, or Victory.[10] Marica had a grove by the Liris near Minturnæ, into which if anything was brought it was not lawful to take it out again.[11] Some said she was Circe, others Venus; Vergil makes her the mother of Latinus.[12]

Beside the above, there was a crowd of other deities held to preside over all the operations of agriculture and all parts of the country.

Rusina presided over the whole country: Collina over the hills, and Vallonia over the valleys. Epona had charge of

---

[1] Dion. Hal. iii. 32. [2] Serv. *Æn.* vii. 799.
[3] Id. *ib.* viii. 564. Compare Liv. xxii. 1. [4] *De L. L.* vi. p. 90.
[5] Id. *ib.* v. 84. vii. 45. [6] See Müller on Varro, *De L. L.* vii. 45.
[7] *De L. L.* vi. 19.
[8] Is Falacer connected with *falx* (i. e. *falcx*, *falecis*, πέλεκυς), and Furina with *far* or *furfur*?
[9] Cic. *De Nat. Deor.* iii. 18. Plut. *C. Grac.* 17. Martian. *de Nupt.* ii. 40. Ad Furinæ Satricum versus " occurs in Cicero *ad Quint. Fr.* iii. 1, 2.
[10] Sch. Hor. *Epist.* i. 10, 49. Ov. *Fast.* vi. 307. [11] Plut. *Marius*, 39.
[12] Verg. *Æn.* vii. 47. Serv. *in loco.* Lact. i. 21.

horses,[1] Bubona of oxen. Seia or Segetra looked to the seed and the springing corn. Runcina was invoked when the fields were to be weeded; Occator, when they were to be harrowed. Sator and Sarritor presided over sowing and raking. Robigus or Robigo was worshipped to avert mildew; the Robigalia were held on the twenty-fifth of April, just before the Floralia. Stercutius, or Sterculius, was the god of dunging the ground. Nodosus attended to the joints of the stalk; Volusia to the folding of the blade: Patelina had charge of the ear when it appeared: Lactens or Lactura minded it when milky; and Matura brought it to ripeness. Mellona presided over honey. Fornax was the goddess of baking: the Fornicalia were celebrated in February.[2]

The Italians had also deities of the waters. Such were the following.

Portunus vel Portumnus.

The only male deity of the sea beside Neptunus in the Italian religion is Portunus, who presided over ports and havens. His festivals, called Portunalia, were held at Rome, on the day on which a temple had been dedicated to him at the port of the Tiber.[3] The Romans, we know not for what reason, identified him with the Palæmón of the Greeks.

Portunus was perhaps only another name for Neptunus. We meet with Pater Portunus.[4]

Salacia et Venilia.

These were goddesses of the sea; the former, whose name was, not very correctly, derived from salum, was regarded as the wife or sister of Neptunus,[5] and was considered identical with Amphitríte or even Téthys.[6] The name of the latter was deduced from venio or venia, whence some viewed her as Hope.[7] Salacia was thought to preside over the retiring, Venilia over the approaching waves.[8] Vergil[9] makes Venilia the mother of Turnus; in Ovid[10] she is the wife of Janus.

Juturna.

Juturna was a water-nymph: her fountain was near the Numicius; its waters, owing to her name (from juvo), were held to

---

[1] Juv. Sat. viii. 157.
[2] For these and other similar deities see Pliny, Nat. Hist. xviii. 2. Serv. Geor. i. 21. Tertul. ad Gent. 16, 25: ad Nat. i. 11; ii. 9.
[3] Varr. De L. L. vi. 19.   [4] Verg. Æn. v. 241.
[5] Varr. De L. L. v. 72. Gell. xiii. 22.   [6] Serv. Æn. i. 144 720. Festus, s.
[7] Tert. ad Nat. ii. 11.   [8] Varro, Fr. p. 342.
[9] Æn. x. 76.   [10] Met. xiv. 334.

be very salubrious: the sick drank of them,[1] and the Romans used them in their sacrifices. There was also a fount or pool of Juturna at the Forum between the temples of Vesta and Castor. A temple was built to Juturna in the Campus Martius, and there was a festival named the Juturnalia.[2] Vergil, as usual, *Euhemerising* the old Italian deities, makes her the sister of Turnus. She was, he says,[3] violated by Jupiter, and made by him in recompense a goddess of the lakes and streams.

The rivers, such as the Tiber, the Almo, the Spino, the Numicius, were held by the Romans to be presided over by peculiar deities.[4] This was probably an original part of the old Italian religion. Like other gods they were termed Patres.[5]

The domestic gods were the Penates and Lares:—

Penates.

The Penates, so named from the *Penus* or pantry, in which they were worshipped, were the gods who were held to attend to the welfare and prosperity of the family. Cities also had their Penates, such were those of Rome and Lavinium. There were four classes of beings from which men selected their Penates, those of heaven, the sea, the under-world, and the deified souls of deceased men;[6] these last were probably the same with the Lares.

Lares et Di Manes.

In the Tuscan language the word Larth or Lars signified *lord*,[7] whence it follows that the Roman Lares were of Tuscan origin, and not Sabine. The Greeks translated the word Heroes,[8] and everything conspires to prove that the Lares were regarded as the deified spirits of men; and by a beautiful conception, the family-Lares were held to be the souls of the ancestors who watched over and protected their descendants.

The doctrine of the Lares is closely connected with that of the Genius, and the Genius and the Lar are often confounded.[9] For the Genius, as we have seen, gave being to the man, and

---

[1] Varr. *De L. L.* v. 71.   Serv. *Æn.* xii. 139.
[2] Serv. *Æn.* xii. 139.   Ov. *Fast.* i. 464.   [3] *Æn.* xii. 139.
[4] Cic. *De Nat. Deor.* iii. 20.
[5] Pater Tiberinus.   Enn. *ap. Macrob. Sat.* vi. 1.   Verg. *Æn.* viii. 72, 540; x. 421.   Liv. ii. 10.   Pater Amasenus. *Æn.* vii. 685.   [6] Arnobius, iii. 40.
[7] The resemblance between *Larth* and *lord*, though casual, is curious.
[8] Dion. Hal. iv. 2, 14.   [9] Serv. *Æn.* iii. 63.   Censor. *De Die Nat.* 3.

attended him through life; and then the soul, if virtuous, became itself a kind of Genius, that is, a protecting power. The old Latins, we are told,[1] called the soul, when it left the body, a Lemur; and if the Lemur was good, they believed that it became a family-Lar; if it was bad, it became a Larva to haunt the house: as it was not known to which class a departed soul belonged, the general term Dii Manes, that is, *Good Gods*,[2] was employed in speaking of the dead.

The term Manes seems related to Mantus and Mania, the Tuscan god and goddess of the unseen-world, and Mania is expressly called the mother or the grand-mother of the Manes,[3] and the mother of the Lares,[4] which proves the identity, as we may term it, of these classes of beings. Mania is called their mother, perhaps as giving them a new birth to perform on earth the part of protecting spirits.

Another name of the mother of the Lares was Acca Larentia, to whom the Accalia or Larentilia were celebrated on the 23rd of December, the day after the Compitalia, or feast of the Lares. This deity was afterwards converted into a prostitute (*lupa*), and the nurse of Romulus and Remus; and the rural Lares, whom the Arval brethren invoked in their songs, became her twelve stout sons in her cottage on the Aventine.

This goddess was also named Lara or Larunda. A legend, in the Greek taste, was invented of her having been a nymph, the daughter of the river-god Almo, whose tongue, for her tattling (λαλία), Jupiter cut out, and then sent her under the conduct of Mercurius to the nether-world. Her keeper violated her on the way, and she became the mother of the two Lares Præstites.[5]

Genita Mana seems also to have been a name of this goddess. It was the custom to sacrifice a dog to her, and to pray that no good house-slave (*verna*) might go away,[6] *i. e.* die.

The statues of the household Lares were set at the fire-place, arrayed in dog-skins, with the figure of a dog beside them.[7] Garlands were hung on them, and offerings of food, wine and

---

Apuleius *op. Serv. ut supra*.

[2] In old Latin *manus, manuus*, or *manis* was *good*. Festus *v.* Manuos. Serv. *ut sup*. It remains in *immanis*, and, if the reading be correct, in *Mane Geni*, Tibull. iv. 5, 9. The Arcadians called the dead χρηστοί (Plut. *Quæst. Rom.* 52; *Quæst. Gr.* 5). The term, like so many others, was placatory; the Irish and Africans call the Fairies *Good People*. *Fairy Myth.* ii. 327. p. 495, new edit.

[3] Festus *v.* Maniæ.   [4] Varr. *De L. L.* ix. 61. Marini, *Atti*, &c. ii. 373.

[5] Ovid, *Fast.* ii. 585 *seq*.

[6] Plin. *Nat. Hist.* xxix. 4. Plut. *Quæst. Rom.* 52, μηδένα χρηστὸν ἀποβῆναι τῶν οἰκογενῶν.   [7] Plut. *Quæst. Rom.* 51

incense were made to them once every month on either the Kalends, Nones or Ides.[1] In each of the streets (*compita*) of Rome there was a niche for the Lares Præstites (as at present for the Saints), in which, at the Compitalia (December 22), cakes were offered to them by the slaves who lived in the street.[2]

The Lares being presiding powers (*præstites*), there were Lares of the heaven, the sea, the roads, the villages, the streets, the towns and the country, as well as of private houses.[3]

In an Excursus, in our edition of Ovid's Fasti, on the Roman ideas on the state of the dead, we have gone into an inquiry of some length on the subject of the Lares. To this inquiry therefore, to avoid needless repetition, we refer those anxious for further information.

Among the domestic deities may be classed those presiding over marriage, — Jugatinus, Domiducus, Domitius, Manturnia, Subigus, Prema, and Partunda: and those presiding over the birth and rearing of children,—Natio, Vagitanus, Cunina, Rumina, Edusa, Potina, Statilinus, Fabulinus, Adeona, Abeona, Volumnus and Volumna, and others whose names will explain their offices. Sacrifices were made to them when the action over which they presided commenced. Thus when the child began to speak, the parents sacrificed to Fabulinus: Domiducus was worshipped when the bride was brought home to the house of her husband. Orbona took care of those who were bereft of their parents; when death came, Nenia looked to the performance of the dirges and the funeral.[4]

In the deification of moral qualities, the Italian religion far exceeded that of Greece. At Rome the altars and temples reared to them were numerous. Among those thus honoured were Hope, Fear (*Pavor* and *Metus*), Peace, Concord, Safety (*Salus*), Liberty, Virtue, Honour, Shame, and many others.

From the preceding account of the Italian religion, it will be easily seen how very much it differed from that of the Greeks, and how injudicious it is to confound them, as is so generally done. Between the Greek Hermés and the Roman Mercurius, it will be observed there is but one point of resemblance; and the

---

[1] See our note on Verg. *Buc.* i. 44. Hor. *Carm.* iii. 23. Ovid, *Fast.* ii 634. Plaut. *Aul. Prol.* 24. [2] Dion. Hal. iv. 14.

[3] *Cælopotentes, permarini, viales, vicorum, compitales, civitatum, rurales, grundul·s, domestici et familiares.* See Müller, *Etrusk.* ii. 90 *seq.*

[4] These deities are noticed by Pliny, Festus, Nonius, and the Fathers of the Church.

Roman Venus, the goddess of the gardens and of vegetable increase, is a personage very different from the Aphrodité, whose acts and attributes are so uniformly bestowed on her, that few are able to disunite them in their minds.

Such as the preceding pages represent them were the objects of Grecian and Italian worship in remote ages, and such was the mythic history which stood at the head of the annals of ancient Hellas. Greatly is it to be desired that it were possible to excite a general taste for this beautiful and attractive branch of philosophy; but too well do we know how vain would be the expectation of success. Select and few will be the audience that will listen to the strains of the ancient Aœdæ.

To one point, ere we close, we would particularly direct attention. Though some few of these ancient fictions may not fully accord with our modern notions of delicacy, yet none can be justly termed immoral; none, for example, be so prejudicial to the interests of piety and true morality as the celebrated drama *La Devocion de la Cruz* of the great Spanish dramatist Calderon; not to mention other fictions of a similar character sanctioned by the church of Rome. It is, we may observe, a remarkable fact that all the religious systems given by the Deity to man, or by His permissive will formed by man for himself, have been in their origin pure, or at least comparatively so, and have become corrupted in the lapse of time. Such it will be seen was the fate of the systems described in these pages: the mythes were misunderstood, and some of them even converted to occasions of vice. Let any one compare the Pentateuch with the Talmud, the New Testament with the practices and precepts of the Church of Rome, and he will find different and even opposite systems. So it is when the Koran is compared with the later Mohammedan writings; the Vedas with the Puranas. Nay, the horribly sanguinary system which the Spaniards found in Mexico was evidently the corruption of a far purer one which had preceded it. This is in perfect accordance with the ordinary course of nature. The moral effect on our minds should be to excite us to guard and to seek, when deteriorated, to reduce to its pristine purity the faith which Heaven has vouchsafed to bestow on us; and this effect mythology, when studied in a proper spirit, tends to produce. Surely then the study of it cannot be justly regarded as injurious or even as merely useless!

APPENDICES.

A.

The Hyperboreans.

AMONG the many errors which J. H. Voss has introduced into mythic geography, there is none which has less foundation than that of placing the Hyperboreans in the West, as not a single passage of the classics, rightly understood, favours this view.

As is observed in the text, the simple signification of the name denotes a northern site; and Hérodotos (iv. 36) says, that if there are Hyperboreans, there must be also Hypernotians. Hésiod and the author of the Epigoni, the first, he says, who mention them, cannot now be cited as witnesses to their northern position; but Aristeas the Prokonnésian (in the time of Kyros) said, that to the north of the Skythians dwelt the Issédonians, northwards of whom were the one-eyed Arimaspians, then the Griffons that watched the gold in the mountains, and finally the Hyperboreans, who dwelt thence to the sea, that is, the northern ocean (Hérod. iv. 13). Pindar no doubt places the sources of the Istér (which Hérodotos knew rose in the west) in the country of the Hyperboreans; but at that time the more general opinion was that the Istér flowed from the north; and this must have been Pindar's own opinion, for he places his Hyperboreans πνοιᾶς ὄπιθεν Βορέα ψυχροῖ. Æschylos also (Sch. Apoll. Rh. iv. 284) placed the sources of the Istér in the north. Theopompos (Æl. Var. Hist. iii. 18) told a strange tale of the people of the huge continent which lay without this world having resolved to invade it; but when they landed in the country of the Hyperboreans, and learned that *they* were the happiest of its inhabitants, they turned back in contempt. About the time of Alexander, Hekatæos of Abdéra wrote expressly on the subject of the Hyperboreans. He placed them in an island of the size of Sicily in the ocean opposite 'the Keltic'; and the fertility of the island, and the piety and happiness of the people were related in terms similar to those used of Panchaia and other happy places (Diod. ii. 27). The poet Pherenίkos said (Sch. Pind. Ol. iii. 28),

> Ἀμφί θ' Ὑπερβορέων, οἵ τ' ἔσχατα ναιετάουσι,
> νηῷ ὑπ' Ἀπόλλωνος, ἀπείρητοι πολέμοιο·
> τοὺς μὲν ἄρα προτέρων ἐξ αἵματος ὑμνείουσι
> Τιτήνων βλαστόντας, ὑπὸ δόμον αἰθρήεντα
> νάσσασθαι Βορέαο.

All subsequent authorities, down to Tzetzés, place them in the north.

At the time when the fiction of the Hyperboreans was devised, the Greeks had not yet learned by experience the fact of there being cold regions in the north, and warm in the south of the earth; they also believed in the existence of the high range of mountains which sustained the heaven; and their experience of the chill of caverns may have led them to infer that the cold blasts (ῥιπαί) of Boreas issued from caverns of this mountain-range, and thence to conceive the happiness of living *beyond* these mountains,—the only place exempt, in their apprehension, from the northern blasts.

On the subject of the Hyperboreans see Völcker's *Mythische Geographie,* i. chap. vi., and Müller's *Dorians,* i. book ii. chap. iv.

B.

The Æthiopians.

As the imagination of the Greeks produced the Hyperboreans, a people exempt from the cold which they themselves experienced, so their observation of the effect of the sun in embrowning the skin led them to conceive that the people who dwelt near his rising must be more affected than others by his beams, which were thought to have most power in that region, Herod. iii. 104. Hence they imagined the Æthiopians or *Sunburnt* men. Homer evidently places this people in the East,[a] and Mimnermos (above, p. 49) sets them in direct opposition to the Hesperides, who, as their name proves, belong to the West. There is a well-known passage of the Odyssey (i. 23, 24, Nitzsch *in loc.*) which divides the Æthiopians into two portions, the eastern and the western; but of its genuineness serious doubts are entertained, and the above-mentioned passages of Mimnermos testify strongly against such a division. Homer also (*Od.* iv. 188, xi. 521) makes Memnón, the prince of the Æthiopians, a son of E'ós. Æschylos (*Prom.* 808; *Fr.* 178) and Euripidés speak of Æthiopians only in the East. When the Greeks had become acquainted with the heat of Africa, they transferred the Æthiopians thither, and Æthiopia has continued to be the name of the country to the south of Egypt.

See Völcker's *Homerische Geographie,* page 57 *seq.,* and *Mythische Geographie,* page 114 *seq.*

C.

Κλυτός. Κλύμενος. Κλειτός. Δῖος. Γλαῦκος. Γλαυκῶπις.

It is well known that many words which denote moral qualities were, in their origin, physical terms; we are inclined to regard κλυτὸς as an instance. That in many places of Homer it signifies *renowned* or *illustrious* is not to be doubted; but it also occurs in connection with words where we think *bright* would give a better sense; such are κλυτὰ τεύχεα, δώματα, εἵματα,[b] μῆλα; κλυτὸς, the epithet of O'keanos and Poseidón, would also seem to refer to the *brightness* of the surface of the Ocean and the Sea; κλυτοτεχνής, the epithet of Héphæstos, would express the *brilliancy* of his works. This would also give a good sense to κλύμενος and κλυτόπωλος as epithets of Hadés, making them placatory, and thus calling him the *bright* instead of the *dark* god. We meet with both Klytié and Klymené among the Ocean-nymphs: and the most natural cause seems to lie in the *brightness* of the Ocean-stream. E'ós carries off Kleitos, perhaps the *Bright One.* The name of her sister would seem to indicate that the Spartan Charis Kléta was also a *Bright-one,* see p. 171.

---

[a] *Od.* v. 282. We cannot agree with Völcker, that in *Il.* xxiii. 205, Iris is going to the West. The Winds seem to be there, and she has to go *back* (αὖτις) to share the feasts of the Æthiopians.

[b] The garments which are termed in *Od.* vi. 58, κλυτὰ εἵματα are a little after (*v.* 74) called ἐσθῆτα φαεινήν.

Ἐν δ' ἑλίκεσσι βουσὶ καὶ κλυτοῖς πεσῶν αἰπολίοις. Soph. *Aj.* 375; see above, p. 50.

It is not unlikely that *brightness* was also the primary idea in the Latin verb *clueo*, as in

> Magna me facinora decet efficere,
> Quæ post mihi *clara et diu clueant.*—Plaut. *Pseud.* ii. 1, 16.
> Facito igitur ut Acherunti *clueas* gloria.—Id. *Capt.* iii. 5, 31.
> Detulit ex Helicone perenni fronde coronam,
> Per gentes Italas hominum quæ *clara clueret.*—Lucret. i. 119.

The Homéric δῖος (akin to δαίω ?), usually rendered *Divine* or *noble*, may, like κλυτός, have originally had a physical sense and have signified *bright* (see pp. 53, 61) and thence *illustrious.* We have seen (above, p. 75) that in Sanscrit Deev is b *ight-shining.*

Bright or *white* was perhaps also the original meaning of γλαῦκος ; it seems akin to γάλα, γάλακτος, to ἄγλαος, αἰγλή, γαλήνη, and to the Teutonic *grau*, *gray.* Homer (*Il.* xx. 172, Heyne) and Hésiod ('Ασπίς 430, Göttling) use the word γλαυκιόων of the fierce bright glare of the lion's eye. Empedoklés (above, p. 56) called the moon γλαυκῶπις, which could only refer to her *brightness.* Pindar (*Ol.* vi. 45 (76)) applies this term to the eyes of serpents, and Plató (*Phœdr.* 273) to those of fiery steeds, neither of which are *blue* or *green.* Theokritos (xvi. 5) has γλαυκὰν ἀῶ, the *bright-dawn*, and Tryphiodóros (*v.* 514) γλαυκὸν πῦρ. Apollonios (i. 1280) calls the Dawn χαροπή ; and the Scholiast says it is " διὰ τὸ λαμπρύνειν τὸν ἀέρα καὶ φωτίζειν. Τὸ δὲ γλαυκὸν καὶ χαροπὸν συνωνύμως λέγεται· ἀμφότερα γὰρ ἐπὶ τοῦ λαμπροῦ . . . . . Ὅθεν καὶ ἡ 'Αθηνᾶ γλαυκῶπις."

In Keltic *Geal* is *bright*, and *Gealach, the moon.*

D.

'Ωκεανός. 'Ωγύγης.

It is plain that in these words the root is ΩΚ or ΩΓ, probably signifying *water*, which in Latin is *aqua*, in Sancrit *ap* and *ogha* (*Asiat. Res.* viii. 326), in Keltic *uisge* ; the Scandinavians named the sea *Ogn*, and its god Œgir. To these perhaps may be added the Latin *æquor*, and the Anglo-Saxon *Eg, Egor*, Magnusen *Lex. Myth.* 989.

'Ωγὴν and 'Ωγῆνος were older forms of 'Ωκεανός ; *O'gygés* is the symbol of the deluge, *Gygés* is the same name, made a king like O'gygés ; Homer speaks of a Gygeian lake (*Il.* ii. 865), and a lake-nymph, Gygææ in Lydia (*Il.* xx. 390 ; Hérod. i. 93). Retaining the γ, and merely changing the vowels according to the principles of etymology, we have αἶγες, *waves*, Ægæón, Ægæos, and Ægeus, names of Poseidón, Ægæ, his abode, the Ægæan sea, the sle Ægina, and other cognate terms.

The *Ogygian Isle* is the name of Kalypsó's island. It is given this name to denote its position in the great expanse of waters, ὅθι τ' ὀμφαλός ἐστι θαλάσσης.

E.

Compounds in -γενής, -γένεια.

These compounds are generally taken in a passive sense, but some understand them actively.

---

* Suid. and Hesych. *s. v.* " Γῆν καὶ ὠγήνον καὶ τὰ ὠγήνου δώματα," Phere-yd ap. *Clem. Alex. Strom.* 6. p. 621.

We have rendered ἠριγένεια *air-born*, as we view ἦρι as the dative of ἀήρ, and hold the derivation of ἠὼς from ἄω, ἄημι to be correct. The Latin *Aurora*, same as *Aura* (Lucret. v. 656), confirms this; and it is further proved by the *act of such being the order of nature in the South.

> E quale annunziatrice degli *albori*
> L' *aura* di Maggio movesi e olezza
> Tutta impregnata dall' erba e da' fiori.
> > Dante, *Purg.* xxiv. terz. 49. comp. i. terz. 39.

> Già l' *aura* messagiera erasi desta
> Ad annunziar che sene vien *l'Aurora*.—Tasso, *Ger. Lib.* iii. st. 1.

B..ť it might also be *air-producing*, as E'ós may send the airs before her.

> L'Aurora che sorge,—Con vesti pompose,
> A sparger di rose—La strada del sol,
> Dal labbro ridente—L' aurette diffonde
> Che scherzam sull' onde—Con tremulo vol.—Rossetti, *Salterio*, i. 1.

'Ηριγένεια may even signify *Gloom-* or *Darkness*-sprung, *darkness* being the usual sense of ἀήρ in Homer, and thus denote the very brief twilight of the South. The derivation from the adverb ἦρι *early*, perhaps amounts to the same, this being in reality the dative of ἀήρ.

Αἰθρηγενής, the epithet of the north wind, is perhaps to be understood actively,[a] in accordance with what we may observe in Nature, where this wind dispels mist and vapour, and brings clear and cloudless skies, *Il.* v. 522 *seq.* (comp. Milton, *Par. Lost.* ii. 488 *seq.*). Verg. *Æn.* xii. 365 *seq.* Ov. *Met.* i. 262, v. 286. "The north-wind driveth away rain." Prov. xxv. 23.

> Come rimane splendido, e sereno
> L' hemisperio de l' aere, quando soffia
> Borea da quella guancia, ond' è più leno,
> Perchè si purga, e risolve la roffia
> Che pria turbava, sì che 'l ciel ne ride
> Con le bellezze d' ogni sua paroffia.
> > Dante, *Par.* xxviii. terz. 27, 28.

F.

Nectar and Ambrosia.

Nectar was to the Homéric gods what wine was to men. It is termed *red*, ἐρυθρόν (*Il.* xix. 38; *Od.* v. 93); it is mixed in a *crater* (*Od. ut sup.*), and handed about in cups at the celestial meals (*Il.* i. 598; iv. 3). It is not easy to decide whether the Ambrosia was a solid or a fluid. When Kalypsó is about to entertain Hermés (*Od. ut sup.*), she fills the table with ambrosia, and mixes nectar, and he *eats* and drinks. The river-god Simóeis gives the horses of Héra ambrosia to feed on (*Il.* v. 777). On the other hand, this goddess, when about to dress herself (xiv. 170), first washes her whole person with ambrosia, and then anoints herself with ambrosial oil; while the corpse of Sarpédón is washed with water, and anointed with ambrosia (xvi. 670). Thetis pours both nectar and ambrosia into the nostrils of that of Patroklos to keep it from corruption (xix. 38). Eidothea puts ambrosia under the noses of Meneláos and his comrades, to overcome the smell of their seal-skins (*Od.*

---

[a] Apollonios (iv. 765) uses it of all the winds: τοῖς αἴθραν καὶ ψύχο, ποιοῦσι, Sch. *in loc.* See also Sen. *Od.* v. 296, and Orphic Hymn lxxx

iv. 445). It is also said (xii. 63) that the ambrosia was fetched from Ocean to Zeus by pigeons.

In Hésiod and Pindar we find nectar and ambrosia spoken of together, whence it would seem to follow that they regarded the latter as meat rather than drink. Alkæos (Athén. ii. 39), however, said that the gods *ate* nectar, and Sapphó (Id. *ib.*) says

ἀμβροσίας μὲν κρατὴρ ἐκέκρατο,
Ἑρμᾶς δ᾽ ἑλὼν ἔρπιν θεοῖς ᾠνοχόησεν.

The comic poet Anaxandridés introduced Hermés (it would appear), saying

τὸ νέκταρ ἐσθίω πάνυ
μάττων διαπίνω τ᾽ ἀμβροσίαν καὶ τῷ Διὶ
διακονῶ καὶ σέμνος εἰμ᾽ ἑκάστοτε,
Ἥρᾳ λαλῶν καὶ Κύπριδι παρακαθήμενος.

Ἀμβροσίη is plainly the feminine of ἀμβρόσιος, and signifies *immortal* food (ἐδωδή), or drink (πόσις), (Butt. *Lexil. s. v.*) Νέκταρ is a substantive, probably of the same signification, from the negative νε- or νη-, and the obsolete verb ΚΤΑΩ *to kill.* It was a beautiful conception to make the gods feast on *Immortality* attended by *Youth.*

G.

Ἄιδης. Orcus. Dis.

Aïdés or Hadés is in Homer and Hésiod always the name of a person, never that of a place. We meet the phrase εἰν or εἰς Ἀΐδαο frequently; but it is manifest that δόμοις or δόμους, which is expressed on other occasions, is there to be understood.[a] There are, however, two passages of the Ilias in which Aïdes would seem to be the place; the one is *Il.* viii. 16,

Τόσσον ἔνερθ᾽ Ἀΐδεω, ὅσον οὐρανός ἐστ᾽ ἀπὸ γαίης,

but as it is a genitive, we may very well suppose δόμων to be understood. The other passage (*Il.* xxiii. 244) is more difficult,

Εἰσόκεν αὐτὸς ἐγὼν Ἄϊδι κεύθωμαι.

One MS. however (Mosc.2), reads Ἄϊδος, and the Scholiasts read κλεύθωμαι, and say it is the abbreviation of κελεύθωμαι, *i.e.* πορεύωμαι.

The *gate* or *door* of Aïdés (Ἀΐδαο πύλαι) is plainly nothing more than the entrance into the *house* of Aïdés. The χθόνιον Ἀΐδα στόμα of Pindar (*Pyth.* iv. 44 (77)) has nearly the same signification. When Hérodotos (ii. 122) says "καταβῆναι κάτω ἐς τὸν οἱ Ἕλληνες ἀΐδην νομίζουσι εἶναι καὶ κεῖθι, κ. τ. λ.," there is no necessity for our supposing ἀΐδην to be a place; for εἰς or ἐς is used of persons as well as places. The κατὰ γῆς ἔρχεται εἰς Ἀΐδην of Mimnermos (ii. 14) and the εἰς ἀναύγητον μολεῖν Ἄιδην of Æschylos (*Prom.* 1028) may be understood in the same manner. The few places of the Attic dramatists[b] in which Hades would seem to be the place, have it in the genitive; and we may perhaps venture to assert, that in *no*

---

[a] Thus the Romans said, *ad Vestæ* sc. *templum*, and *we* say at *St. Paul's* sc. *church,* at *lord B.'s* sc. *house.*
[b] Soph. *Trach.* 282. *Ajax*, 517. Eurip. *Alc.* 366. In Eur. *E'lec.* 122, we meet ἐν Ἄιδᾳ, but he probably wrote it ἐν Ἄιδα.

Attic prose writer is Hadés other than a person. Their usual phrase is ἐς, ἐξ, or ἐν Ἀιδου. It was probably the employment ἐξ Ἀιδου that led to the taking of Hadés for the place, a practice which we find fully established by the Alexandrians:[a] writers however, such as Lucian, who aimed at purity, followed the practice of the Attics.

Dis and Orcus, in like manner, always, we may venture to assert, are the person, never the place. Some passages of the poets may seem ambiguous;[b] but of the usage in the prose writers there can be no doubt. Yet modern writers of Latin almost invariably use Orcus for the place, Pluto for the person, in utter contradiction to the ancient Latin prose writers, who never, we believe, used this last term.[c] That most in use was Dis or Ditis; but Plautus, Lucretius and Horace always employed Orcus.

Both Hadés and Orcus, we may observe, occasionally signified *death*.[d]

It is remarkable that neither the Greeks (for Erebos went early out of use) nor the Latins had any name for the nether world. The former said εἰς etc. ᾅδου; the latter, *ad*, *apud*, etc. *inferos* (deos); and as this last word could not be employed in heroic poetry on account of the metre, the poets were obliged to have recourse to periphrases. The later Greeks sometimes used Acherón in this sense,[e] and they were followed by Plautus, *ex. gr.*

Nam me Acheruntem recipere Orcus noluit.—*Most.* ii. 2, 68,

and Lucretius, and occasionally by Horace, Vergil and other poets. Nepos (*Dion* 10) used it in prose. Statius (*Theb.* viii. 97) even employs Lethe for Erebos.

H.

Interpolations in Homer.

That there are many interpolations in the Ilias is a matter about which there is now little dispute; few, for example, will undertake the defence of the tenth book, the Doloneia. We are not however aware of any doubts being entertained respecting the ninth book, except as to a very few verses;[f] it

---

[a] See Theocr. i. 103; ii. 33. Mosch. i. 14. Kallim. iii. 222. They used Plutó for the person, Hadés for the place: thus "Πλούτων δὲ τὴν ἐν ᾅδη." Apollod. i. 2, 1. Hadés occurs in this sense also in the New Testament, Luke xvi. 23, Rev. xx. 13, 14. It is very remarkable that our own word *Hell* has undergone a similar change; for in the Edda Hel is the goddess of the underworld, called from her Hel, and distinguished from the place named Niflheim, as Erebos is from Tartaros.

[b] Thus in Terence (*Hec.* v. 4, 12): " Egone qui *ab* (not *ex*) Orco mortuum me reducem in lucem feceris?" and Lucan (i. 455), "Ditisque profundi Pallida regna;" and vi. 714) "primo pallentis hiatu Orci." The " janua Orci" (vi. 762), and "tenebras Orci . . . vastasque lacunas" (i. 116) of Lucretius; and the "janua, moenia, spiracula, Ditis" and "fauces Orci" of Virgil are similar to the 'Αΐδαο πύλαι of Homer: comp. *Æn.* vi. 106.

[c] " Pluton Latine est Dispiter, alii Orcum dicunt." Ennius *ap. Lact. Div. Inst.* i. 14.

[d] See above, pp. 84, 469.

[e] Bion i. 51. Mosch. i. 14. Anthol. vii. 25, 30, 181, 203, 396.

[f] Payne Knight we think justly rejects *vv.* 142-156, as repugnant to the manners of the heroic age.

may therefore appear rather hardy in *us* to say that we suspect it to be the most interpolated book in the whole poem, and all that relates to Phœnix to be a late addition. Our reasons for thinking so are as follows.

In the first place, the use of the dual number in *vv.* 182, 192 (τὼ δὲ βάτην) is altogether unexampled if there were three envoys. The explanation given by the scholiast that Aias and Odysseus were the envoys, and Phœnix only their guide, is strained, for Nestór (*v.* 168) plainly designates him as one of the envoys; it also seems strange that Achilleus (*v.* 197) should take no notice of his old tutor. Again, it is said that the dual may refer to the two parties, the envoys and the heralds; this however is refuted by *v.* 197; though in *v.* 487 it is apparently used to express Hektór and the Trojans. Finally, we are told that the dual is used for the plural *Od.* viii. 35, 48; but by comparing these passages with *Il.* iv. 393, we shall see that of the fifty-two youths spoken of two were commanders, and it is of them that the dual is used (see Eustath. and Nitzch *in loco*). In *Il.* viii. 184 *seq.* where Hektór appears to address his four horses in the dual, the line containing their names is spurious (see Scholia). Heyne (*in loc.*) has justly explained *Il.* i. 567, reading ἰόντα instead of ἰόντε. In *Il.* iii. 278 the οἱ are Hadés and Persephoné: comp. xxi. 383; in iv. 452 δύω is to be understood with χείμαρροι ποταμοί. We thus see that Homer does not use the dual for the plural, as is done in the *Hymn to Apolló*, *vv.* 487, 501.

There are other groun·ls for doubting if Phœnix formed a part of the original embassy. Why should *he* alone of all the Myrmidons quit Achilleus and adhere to Agamemnón; he who had reared him (*vv.* 485–91), and to whom Péleus had given him in charge when sending him to Ilion (*vv.* 438–43)? Surely Achilleus would have taken some notice of him when he came to his tent : we might even expect to hear a gentle reproach for having deserted him. On the whole then, we think that the introduction of Phœnix into the embassy was the work of some one who saw what a good effect it would have; and we would therefore reject *vv.* 168, 223, 426–622, 658–668, 690–692, in which are included the whole episode of Meleagros and the account of Apolló's carrying off Marpéssa (above, p. 106). We do not say that the lines, which will thus become consecutive, will exactly agree, for the interpolator here as elsewhere doubtless altered them so as to suit his purpose.

We will take this opportunity of stating the theory at which we have arrived, after much consideration, on the subject of the Homéric poems. The work of the great original bard, the true Homer, appears to us to consist of Books I.–V. VIII. IX. XI.–XVII.; we regard as additions and interpolations, made by later poets, VI. and VII., great part of VIII. and IX., the whole of X., the Catalogue, and many parts of the original poem as it now appears; finally Books XVIII.–XXIV. We cannot pretend to say where or how the poem originally terminated, bu our opinion is that the concluding part of it was removed and the present latter books substituted. The Odyssey, the work of a different original poet, appears to us to have been much less interpolated than the Ilias. The last book is manifestly, in whole or in part, an addition, and part of the Nekyia, the song of Démodokos, and some other places, and perhaps the Hunt on Parnassos are manifest interpolations. Finally our belief is that both poems were originally *written*; for the δίφθεραι used by the Iónians (Hérod. v. 58) were probably some kind of parchment, and they may have i ·wn in use from a very early period. [So we wrote some years ago, influenced chiefly by the arguments of the ingenious Spohn; reflection and reperusals of the poem have led us to think that the Hunt belongs to the origina; poet, as also the last Book, with the exception of the Nekyia, with which it commences.]

If this theory respecting the Ilias be correct, it will be seen that a hymn **to** Arés would not have been a very inappropriate title of the original poem, **as** all, or nearly all, that is soft, tender and sentimental belongs to the later poets. *Its* Hektór, for example, is brave and patriotic, but boastful and arrogant, honourable, but devoid of tenderness and mildness. The original poet had far more vigour and graphic power than his successors, while he was inferior to the least one of them in sensibility. He also appears to have been superior in judgment; *he*, we may be sure, would never have made Hektór run away from Achilleus, and none of the places which offend our taste and judgment belong, we believe, to his portion of the poem. As an instance we may observe how aptly, by the interposition of some lines describing the approach of night and the end of the battle, Books V. and VIII. would unite, while the interpolator by putting between them Books VI. and VII. to the council, the truce, the single combat and the battle, which were surely quite enough for one day, adds a needless return of Hektór to Troy, and a second single combat. In like manner Book X. extends the events of the night in a most incredible manner. Other instances might easily be given if necessary.

Exclusive of those in Book IX. and of those bracketed by Wolf, the following places of the Ilias have appeared suspicious in the eyes of various critics. They fall little short of 1000 lines, and in case of their not being genuine, not much more than half of the Ilias would belong to the original poet.

Il. i. 366–92. ii. 547–51. 553–5. iii. 3–7. 144. 396–418. iv. 55, 56. 376–98. v. 265–73. 345–6. 385–404. 410–15. 418–431. 699–702. 897–8. viii. 14–16 18–40. 92–9. 177–9. 198–212. 267–272. 350–484. xi. 17–46. 179–217. 355–68 373–5. 665–763. 766–84. 791–802. 831–2. xii. 5–34. 116, 117. 167–170. 265–77. xiii. 210–332. 352–7. 418–23. 450–4. 521–5. 623–9. 656-9. 674–700. 808–37. xix. 29–40. 114–25. 135–52. 269. 272–4. 278, 279. 317–27. 392, 393. xv. 56–77. 200–217. 530–4. 547–52. 668–73. 727–46. xvi. 55–59. 97–100. 326–329. 431–61. 505–31. 664–83. 698–711. 798–800. xvii. 187–219. 427–56. xviii. 3–16. 39–49. To these many might be added.

Il. xv. 547–52 may serve as an example of the ingenious manner in which these insertions were made. Originally it may have stood thus:—

        Ἴφθιμον Μελάνιππον, ἔπος τ' ἔφατ' ἐκ τ' ὀνόμαζε.

I.

Union of Sun and Earth.

The expression in the text (p. 299), '*bride of the Sun,*' has been taken from a very beautiful poem, named 'The Bride of Siena,' and written by a young lady, who, as we had reason to know, was guided only by her natural feeling when she took this view of the relation between the Sun and the Earth. It is, as may be seen, that by which we have endeavoured to explain the Grecian mythe of Amphíon and Niobé, and the Asiatic one of Attis and Kybelé. In fact it is so natural a view that we meet with it frequently in modern poetry, *ex. gr.*

        Rose dico e viole
        A cui madre è la Terra e paare il Sole.

                  Tasso, *Rime Amorose*, Canz. viii. 25.

In a note he says, " E detto ad imitazione di Pontano." See also his *Lo sette Giornate*, iv. 162.

Sidney thus commences his *Arcadia*:—

"It was in the time that the earth begins to put on her new apparell against the approach of her lover, and that the sunne running a most even course becomes an indifferent arbiter between the night and the day." The image was possibly suggested to him by Ps. xix. 5.

> The bridegroom sun, who late the earth espoused,
> Leaves his star-chamber early in the east;
> He shook his sparkling locks, head lively roused,
> While morn his couch with blushing roses dressed.
>
> P. Fletcher, Purple Island, ix. 1.

> The summer-sun his bride had newly gowned,
> With fiery arms clipping the wanton ground,
> And gets a heaven on earth: that primrose there,
> Which 'mongst those violets sheds his golden hair,
> Seems the sun's little son, fixed in his azure sphere.
>
> Id. Pisc. Ecl. v. 2.

> As when the cheerful sunlight spreading wide
> Glads all the world with his diffusive ray,
> And woos the widowed earth afresh to pride
> And paint her bosom with the flowery May.
>
> G. Fletcher, Christ's Victory, i. 37.

> And thou fair spouse of earth, that every year
> Gettest such a numerous issue of thy bride.—Id. ib. iv. 5.

> The sun doth his pure fire on earth bestow
> With nuptial warmth, to bring forth things below.
>
> Cowley, Answ. to Platonists.

> Mark how the lusty sun salutes the spring
>   And gently kisses everything!
> His loving beams unlock each maiden flower,
> Search all the treasures, all the sweets devour,
> Then on the earth with bridegroom heat
> He does still new flowers beget.—Id. The Gazers.

Milton (*Hymn on Nativ. v.* 36) terms the sun Nature's 'lusty paramour,, and in the fifth of his Latin elegies (*vv.* 55–94):

> Exuit invisam Tellus rediviva senectam,
>   Et cupit amplexus, Phœbe, subire tuos, &c.

he describes the bridal array of the Earth, and gives her wooing address to the Sun.

At a conference held in 1811 between the American general Harrison and some Indian chiefs, one of them named Tecumseh on finding there was no seat provided for him gave signs of great indignation. The general seeing it instantly ordered a chair for him, and one of those present bowing to him said, "Warrior, your father, general Harrison, offers you a seat." "My father!" exclaimed Tecumseh, extending his hand toward the heavens, "the sun is my father and the earth is my mother. She gives me nourishment, and I will repose on her bosom." He then threw himself upon the ground.

In the Mohammedan East "the Earth is in the spring a young bride (*braut*), and the winds and frequently also the showers and sunshine are her maids or hairdressers." Hammer, *Schirin*, i. p. 137. The Persian poets make the Spring her bridegroom.

K.

Latin forms of Greek Names.

The changes which many of the names in Grecian mythology have undergone in Latin, are a proof that the mythology of Greece was known at Rome long before the Grecian language and literature became objects of study to the Romans. The change is similar to what took place in Europe with respect to Oriental names in the middle ages, when Mohammed, for example, became Macometto, Mahomet, Mafamede, Mafoma, Macone, and Mahound. Thus the Latin form of Létó (Æolic Lató) is Latona, of Persephoné Proserpina, of Polydeukes Polluces, Pollux, of Aias Ajax, of Odysseus Ulixes or Ulisses[a] of Kyklóps Cocles, of Ganymédés Catamitus,[b] of Laomedón Alumento.[c] The Greek υ became u; for Pyrrhus, Phryges, Hyperión, Ennius has Burrus, Bruges, Huperion; and as there were no diphthongs in Latin answering to the ει and ευ of the Greeks, the vowel e was usually substituted for them, as Achilleus Achilles, Perseus Perses, Médeia Medea, Æneias Æneas; and as the Latin language was adverse to the clustering of consonants, Alkméné became Alcumena, Héraklés Hercules, Asklépios Æsculapius. The termination in ρος was changed to er, as Meleagros Meleager, Teukros Teucer, Alexandros Alexander. It is to be observed, that the only deities whose names were altered are Létó, Persephoné and Asklépios, who had no Latin parallels, the Latin practice being to employ the names of the corresponding deities of their own system.

It has often struck us that the Greek Ἑσπερία is the true origin of the Latin Hispania, and probably of Iberia also. We need not inform the reader that no letters are more commutable than n and r; at all events the change is not to be compared with that of Ganymédés. Hesperia was the Greek term for the whole of the West, including Italy, Spain, and the north-coast of Africa. The settling of the Greek colonies in Italy caused that country to get a peculiar name; and Ἑσπερία when confined to Spain, might easily have been corrupted to Ἰβηρία, and the principal river on the east coast have been thence named Ἴβηρ, which last may have been the cause of the long vowel in Iberia. We also suspect that Hesperia may be the real origin of Afer, Aferica, Africa. The wind named by the Romans Africus is, we may observe, in Spanish Abrego.

L.

The Amazons.

In the Ilias (iii. 189; vi. 186) the 'man-opposing' Amazons are mentioned as invading Phrygia, and as fought with by Bellerophontés; and in the

---

[a] In late editions of Vergil and the other Latin poets, it is spelt Ulixes in imitation of the MSS. which use x to express ss as hard. The French used to write Xaintonge and Xaintes, and still write Bruxelles and Auxerre, pronouncing the x as ss. The Latin x is usually ss in Italian, as rixa rissa, taxus tasso.

[b]   De Coclitum prosapia ted esse arbitror
    Nam ii sunt unoculi.—Plaut. Curc. iii. 23.

    Dic mihi, nunquam tu vidisti tabulam pictam in pariete
    Ubi aquila Catamitum raperet aut ubi Venus Adoneum?
                    Id. Menæch. i. 2, 34.

[c] Festus s. v. Scaliger's emendation Laumento would seem to have much in its favour, but Diodóros (xii. 24) has Λαγιδίῳ for Algido.

Æthiopis they come to the aid of the Trojans. They are represented as a nation of warlike women; their character is the same in the mythes of Héraklés and Théseus. Various legends are told of their political condition and manners, among which that of their cutting off their right breasts that they might draw the bow with the greater ease, was framed in their usual manner by the Greeks from the name, Amazons.

The actual existence of a nation of women is an impossibility. It however appears that among the Sauromatians, who dwelt on the north of the Euxine, the women dressed like the men, went to the chase and war with them (Hérod. iv. 110–117); and the sovereign power over this people is said (Plin. *Nat. Hist.* vi. 7) to have been in the hands of the women. This, then, may have been a sufficient foundation for the fables of the Greeks respecting the Amazons, whom they always place on either the north or the south coast of the Euxine, for the Libyan Amazons of Dionysios (Diod. iii. 52–55) are a pure fiction. But we also meet with Amazons in connection with the goddess of nature in Western Asia, where they are said to have founded Ephesos, Smyrna, Magnésia and other towns. They are supposed to have been the female ministers at the temples of this goddess, whom they honoured by assuming the habit and manners of men (Creuz. *Symb.* ii. 171). There is a third theory which derives them from the mythe of Athéné-Hippia, and supposes them to have been only the personification of the martial properties of that goddess (Völck. *Myth. Geog.* i. 219).

For our own part we look on the first theory as the most probable. At the time when the Ilias was composed, the Greeks were, it is likely, sufficiently acquainted with the peoples about the Euxine to know their manners, and it required but little effort of the imagination thence to form their mythic Amazons. We cannot lay any great stress on the legends of the Amazons of Ephesos, and other places on the coast, as these are all apparently late fictions. The invasion of Attica by these female warriors is merely an audacious fiction of the Athenians, without the slightest foundation in mythology; for as they framed the adventures of their Théseus on those of Héraklés, they would make *him* also a conqueror of the Amazons.

M.

Athéné-Gorgo.

The following passages prove that Gorgó was an appellation of Athéna.

Μετὰ κουρᾶν δ' ἀελλόπυδες
ἃ μὲν τόξοις Ἄρτεμις ἃ δὲ
ἐν ἔγχει Γοργὼ πάνοπλος.—Eur. *Hel.* 1315.

Οὐδ' ἂν τελείας χρυσέας τε Γόργονος
τρίαιναν ὀρθὴν στᾶσαν ἐν πόλεως βάθροις.—Eur. *Fr. Erech.* i. 51.

Οἵ τε Κελαινὰς
χρυσοχόρους ἐνέμοντο καὶ ἱλαστήρια Γοργοῦς.—Nonnos, xiii. 516.

Καλοῦσι δὲ τὴν Ἀθηνᾶν Κυρηναῖοι Γοργώ.—Palæphatus, 32.

'Teque Tritonia Armipotens, Gorgona, Pallas, Minerva."—Pseudo-Cic. *ad Pop. et Equit. Rom.*

With respect to the meaning of Gorgó, it seems to us to be, like Mormó (μορμῶ) and Brimó (βριμῶ), one of those mimetic terms to be found in all languages. Hence it may have been employed to express the terrors of the sea (p. 244), and the grim or hostile form of Athéna, or the Argive goddess (p. 372).

N.

The Pléiades.

In the following places the Pléiades are called Πελειἁδες :—

Τάσδε βροτοὶ καλέουσι Πελειάδες.

Χειμέριοι δύνουσι Πελειάδες.

Τῆμος ἀποκρύπτουσι Πελειάδες.—Hés. *Astron.*

Δίδωτι δεῦτε σ' 'Ερμᾶς ἐναγώνιος
Μαίας εὐπλοκάμοιο
παῖς, ἔτικτε δ' ''Ατλας
ἑπτὰ ἰοπλοκάμων φίλων
θυγατέρων τὰν ἔξοχον
εἶδος, αἳ καλέονται
Πελειάδες οὐράνιοι.—Simónidés.

ἔστι δ' ἐοικὸς
ὀρειᾶν γε Πελειάδων
μὴ τηλόθεν 'Ωαρίωνα νεῖσθαι.—Pind. *Nem.* ii. 10 (16).

ἔνθα νυκτέρων φαντασμάτων
ἔχουσι μορφὰς ἄπτεροι Πελειάδες.—Æschylus, *Fr.* 285.

Βᾶτε Πελειάδας ὑπὸ μέσας
'Ωρίωνά τ' ἐννύχιον.—Eur. *Hel.* 1489.

'Επταπόρου τε δράμημα Πελειάδος.—Id. *Orest.* 1005.

*Αμος δ' ἀντέλλοντι Πελείαδες.—Theocr. xiii. 25.

''Ως δ' αὔτως τρήρωσι πελείασιν ὤπασε τιμήν,
αἳ δή τοι θέρεος καὶ χείματος ἄγγελοι εἰσίν.—Mœró, above, p. 71, *note.*

Αἳ τε ποταναῖς ὁμώνυμοι πελείασιν αἰθέρι κεῖσθε.
Lamproklés.

See Athénæos, xi. 490, 491.

O.

Lectus genialis in Atrio.

Servius (on *Æn.* i. 726) tells us, on the authority of Cato,[a] that the old Romans took their meals in the Atrium of their houses. In accordance with this usage it is in the Atrium of her palace that Dido entertains Æneas and the Trojans—

Fit strepitus tectis, vocemque *per ampla* volutant
Atria.—*Æn.* i. 725.

and Cepheus the deliverer of his daughter—

Reseratis aurea valvis
Atria tota patent, pulchroque instructa paratu
Cephenum proceres, ineunt convivia regis.—Ov. *Met.* iv. 761.

---

[a] " Ut ait Cato, in atrio et duobus ferculis epulabantur antiqui : " comp.
Ov. *Fast.* vi. 305.

We need hardly observe that in these places *atria* is i. q. *atrium* the rhetorical plural.

> O noctes coenæque deum quibus ipse meique
> *Ante larem proprium* vescor!

cries Horace (*Sat.* ii. 6, 65) when describing his happiness in his Sabinum, and we know that the Lar stood by the *focus* in the Atrium. This however, it may be said, was in his *villa*, and old manners lingered in the country. But the same poet, when asking a friend to dine with him at Rome, says (*Ep.* i. 5, 7),

> Jamdudum splendet *focus* et tibi munda supellex.

And to Thaliarchus he says,

> Dissolve frigus ligna super *foco*
> Large reponens.—*Carm.* i. 9, 5.

evidently supposing him to dine in his Atrium. It would also appear from *Carm.* iii. 17, that his friend Ælius Lamia dined in his Atrium, at least when at his *villa*. On the whole we think it may be inferred that even in the Augustan age people of moderate fortune used still to dine in their Atrium. So our ancestors dined in their hall, and many of our tradespeople still dine in their kitchen.

We can now explain the *lectus genialis in aula*, also named *lectus adversus*, as being opposite the door.[*] The family, we see, dined in the Atrium, the table always faced the door, and the seat of the master and mistress was at the head of the table. This seat was originally a kind of form to hold two, afterwards a *lectus* or sofa. If the wife died or was divorced, it was removed, we are told, and one which would hold the master alone was put in its place; for the Juno being gone, there of course only remained the Genius.

Servius elsewhere (*Buc.* iv. 63) tells us of a sofa for Juno and a table for Hercules being laid in the Atrium on the birth of a male infant. This may be only an erroneous view of the *lectus genialis* at a time when it had gone totally out of use; Hercules, like Janus, taking the place of Genius.

---

[*] Materfamilias tua in lecto adverso sedet.—Labrius *ap. Gell.* xvi. 9.
> Seu tamen adversum mutarit janua lectum,
> Sederit et nostro cauta noverca toro.—Propert. iv. 2, 85

INDEX OF NAMES.

Tantalos, 392
Tartaros, 29, 37
Tavgeté, 381, 412
Tegyrios, 340
Teiresias, 303
Telamón, 276, 323, 409
Télegonos. 439
Télemachos, 431, 438
Télephos, 325, 432
Télepylos, 235
Tellúmo, ⎫
Tellúrus, ⎬ 467
Tellus, ⎭
Terambos, 214
Téreus, 336
Terminus, 478
Terpsichoré, 165, 167
Téthys, 37, 46
Teukros, 410, 435 ; (2) 428
Thaleia, 165
Thalié, 171
Thalló, 170
Thamyris, 166
Thaumas, 38
Theia, 37, 47
Theiodamas, 326
Thelxiepeia, ⎫ 240
Thelxinoé, ⎭
Themis, 175
Themistó, 295
Theophané, 76

Thersandros, 355 ; (2) 426
Théseus, 286, 343
Thespios, 338
Thestios, 283 ; (2) 311
Thetis, 277
Thoas, 417
Thoósa, 216
Thrasymédés, 435
THRINAKIAN ISLE, 242
Thyestés, 396
Thyreus, 283, 287
Timandra, 381
Tina, 448
Tiphys, 416, 419
Tisiphoné, 174
TITANS, 23, 37, 41
Tithónos, 57
Tityos, 101
Tityros, 206
Tlépolemos, 435
Toxeus, 283, 287
Triptolemos, 157
Tritogeneia, 141
Tritón, 217
Tróilos, 430, 433
Trophónios, 307
Tydeus, 284, 424, 425
Tyndareós, 381
Typhóeus, 38, 43, 233
Typhón, 233
Tyró, 386

Ulyxes, 498
Upis, 119
Uranía, 165, 167
Uranos, 23, 37

Vacúna, 483
Vagitánus, 487
Vallonia, 483
Vedius, ⎫
Vedjovis, ⎬ 473
Vejovis, ⎭
Venilia, 484
Venus, 124, 457
Vertumnus, 449, 477
Vesta, 85, 456
Vinalia, 458
Virbius, 463
Volcánus, 96, 461
Volumnus-a, 450, 487
Volusia, 484
Vulcanus, 96

Xanthos, 383
Xuthos, 270, 341, 351

Zephyros, 38, 216
Zétés, 340, 418
Zéthos, 296
Zeus, 22, 24, 38, 67, 69-75
Zeuxippé, 336

INDEX OF THINGS.

LONDON: PRINTED BY WILLIAM CLOWES AND SONS, LIMITED,
DUKE STREET, STAMFORD STREET, S.E., AND GREAT WINDMILL STREET, W.